THE HISPANIC IMAGE ON THE SILVER SCREEN

**Recent Titles in
Bibliographies and Indexes in the Performing Arts**

Memorable Film Characters: An Index to Roles and Performers, 1915-1983
Susan Lieberman and Frances Cable, compilers

Stage Lives: A Bibliography and Index to Theatrical Biographies in English
George B. Bryan, compiler

The Federal Theatre Project: A Catalog-Calendar of Productions
The Staff of the Fenwick Library, George Mason University, compilers

Victorian Plays: A Record of Significant Productions on the London Stage, 1837-1901
Donald Mullin, compiler

Costume Design on Broadway: Designers and Their Credits, 1915-1985
Bobbi Owen

Eighteenth Century British and Irish Promptbooks: A Descriptive Bibliography
Edward A. Langhans

The German Stage: A Directory of Playwrights and Plays
Veronica C. Richel, compiler

Stage Deaths: A Bibliographical Guide to International Theatrical Obituaries, 1850 to 1990
George B. Bryan, compiler

The Stratford Festival Story: A Catalogue-Index to the Stratford, Ontario, Festival, 1953-1990
J. Alan B. Somerset

Lighting Design on Broadway: Designers and Their Credits, 1915-1990
Bobbi Owen

Scenic Design on Broadway: Designers and Their Credits, 1915-1990
Bobbi Owen

THE HISPANIC IMAGE ON THE SILVER SCREEN

An Interpretive Filmography from Silents into Sound, 1898–1935

Alfred Charles Richard, Jr.

Bibliographies and Indexes in the Performing Arts,
Number 12

GREENWOOD PRESS
New York • Westport, Connecticut • London

Library of Congress Cataloging-in-Publication Data

Richard, Alfred Charles.
   The Hispanic image on the silver screen : an interpretive filmography from silents into sound, 1898-1935 / Alfred Charles Richard.
      p.   cm.—(Bibliographies and indexes in the performing arts, ISSN 0742-6933 ; no. 12)
   Includes indexes.
   ISBN 0-313-27832-6 (alk. paper)
   1. Hispanic Americans—Film catalogs. 2. Hispanic Americans in motion pictures—Film catalogs. 3. Hispanic Americans—Public opinion—Film catalogs. 4. Civilization, Hispanic—Film catalogs. 5. Motion pictures—North America—Film catalogs. I. Title. II. Series.
PN1998.R54   1992
016.79143'6520368—dc20   92-8917

British Library Cataloguing in Publication Data is available.

Copyright © 1992 by Alfred Charles Richard, Jr.

All rights reserved. No portion of this book may be reproduced, by any process or technique, without the express written consent of the publisher.

Library of Congress Catalog Card Number: 92-8917
ISBN: 0-313-27832-6
ISSN: 0742-6933

First published in 1992

Greenwood Press, 88 Post Road West, Westport, CT 06881
An imprint of Greenwood Publishing Group, Inc.

Printed in the United States of America

The paper used in this book complies with the Permanent Paper Standard issued by the National Information Standards Organization (Z39.48-1984).

10 9 8 7 6 5 4 3 2 1

Because I promised some time ago, this work is dedicated [to the memory of] Peggy Jean Richard. It is also for her family, Will, and Mammaw Lavon Swank, and Ann and Jay Steel. They were always kind and considerate.

Contents

Preface ix

Acknowledgements xv

Introduction xvii

List of Abbreviations xliii

Primitive Times 1898 - 1906 1

FEATURE FILM LISTS:

1907	3
1908	5
1909	11
1910	21
1911	33
1912	59
1913	83
1914	111
1915	139
1916	167
1917	193
1918	207
1919	221
1920	227
1921	231
1922	243
1923	267
1924	285
1925	307
1926	327
1927	343
1928	361
1929	377
1930	397
1931	425
1932	447
1933	461
1934	477
1935	497

INDEXES

Feature Film Titles Index	523
Actors and Actresses Index	549
Countries and Place Names Index	557
Subject Index	561

Preface

This work was not conceived in the dingy back rows of the now nonexistent Pastime theater in Brunswick, Maine where as a child I spent not as many Saturday afternoons as I wished I could, but nonetheless, that is where it began. I was twelve then, and recently moved from the Home of the Angel Guardian to my new home on the Maine coast. The freedom I experienced at being trusted to walk the few miles from the house to downtown allowed for an extensive exploration of a new and enjoyable environment. More significantly, it included a window to a world I had never been privileged to look through before, one filled with images of travel into a land of western adventure that seemed more real than the new found security I enjoyed.

In the early fifties, Brunswick was about as far away from the Mexican border as any place in the country could possibly be then, but I soon came to realize that that's where I'd have to head for if I did something really bad, or if my new situation did not work out. If such a circumstance arose, there would be no question of going to Canada, even if it was significantly closer. At that time "heading for the border" did not mean the Canadian border, that would have made no sense. Mexico was where anyone who had to, went to hide. If one was too young to join up with the French Foreign Legion, one still had the Mexican border as a safety valve, it was a comforting, secure and silver screen learned fantasy.

There was only one large ethnic minority in Brunswick, the French Canadians, but few of us were conscious that there was any essential difference between us French guys and the others who had no noticeable accent. Some of those who had attended the French Catholic school in town, or had been isolated within a French community elsewhere, still used words and phrases like "dat," "dis," "trow me downstairs my shoes," and "back up ahead summore." Our speech frequently provoked laughter but we just laughed along with those who might have thought what we were saying was funny. Being called a "frog" was not even necessarily a good reason to fight, we were "frogs," the other guys were "amarikcans," pronounced with a French Canadian flavor. More importantly we all went to the "show" together where in the dark we became one audience united in the belief that the good guys would always win over the bad ones. It was an easily understood and continuously reinforced message. In 1950 Hollywood's projection of good and evil was as simple and two dimensional as being able to tell the difference between black and white.

There was no "black problem" in Brunswick in 1950, there simply were no blacks living there, but as children, we knew what "they" looked like and how "they" were expected to act. There were no Mexicans either, but everyone of us at the Pastime, knew everything that could possibly be known, everything that was necessary to know about them, just in case we had to head for the border. We knew less about Blacks because the Pastime was predominantly a westerns theater, but what we knew about both groups, we learned, as many others did throughout small town North America, from the images projected on the silver screen. We were unaware of that socialization of course, and for that reason what was learned unconsciously was accepted as truth, it went unchallenged and some of it required a significant amount of re-education to remove at a later time. For many that never occurred and the collective memory they acquired in youth was transferred to their own children, long after the Pastime ceased to exist.

Most of the films which are surveyed in this first of three volumes, films that helped socialize an earlier generation, were shown at the Pastime when it was more an adult's theater. This work covers the silent era from the earliest projections and carries through the first years of the talkers. By that time, actually five years before **The Kaiser: The Beast of Berlin** [793] played at the Pastime in November of 1917, all of the Hispanic stereotypes and scenarios audiences are familiar with today had been established. According to some locals who have lived long lives and remember the old theater fondly, Broncho Billy was a particular favorite in Brunswick. Apparently the projectionist, after the second show, could be convinced to rerun Broncho's adventures another time without a great deal of coaxing and at no added charge. But where ever these films were seen in either small or big town North America, from the very first flickers in 1907, they established images and stereotypes that while experiencing some modification, have in essence continued into these more modern enlightened times. In many ways they serve those who would use them to a purpose today in the way they were utilized by a less educated public in earlier parts of this century.

It is with some hope that these scenarios will provide the readers with entertainment, a smile or two that earlier generations could see the world in such simplistic and two dimensional terms, that everything North American was good and everyplace else, especially south of the border, if not bad, was at least very different and suspect. But more importantly, this study should indicate to the reader that the continuous reestablishing and reinforcing of such stereotypes in films [working in conjunction with print media] has helped to keep a significant proportion of this country's population in comfortably acceptable projections that justify for much of the Anglo population, their felt belief that Hispanics are somehow inferior to Anglos. Some attempt has been made to indicate the nature and consequences of such damaging attitudes.

This work is not intended to be a preachment, an outlining of injustice or any other such cause oriented endeavor. It is intended to provide material heretofore not easily available to the general public and students of stereotyping and film alike, a significant body of information for their entertainment and to be used as the basis for further study.

In 1980 there were 14 million counted Hispanics in the United States. The census bureau reported that that figure had climbed to 22 million ten years later and by the end of the century, the projected number tops 30 million. Such figures do not include those who refuse to be counted and a significant number of others, the product of Anglo unions proud of their heritage, but who consider themselves to be sons and daughters of North American fathers and mothers and as such, North Americans with Hispanic ancestry. What ever the number, Hispanics makeup a significant proportion of North America's multicultural population, one that can no longer be ignored or denied and one this multiracial nation should be proud of.

Protestations by various Hispanic groups asking for fairer treatment in a variety of endeavors usually face a vocal opposition from those with other national heritage, those who try to indicate that no such preferential treatment was afforded them. Not all of these protesters have lily white skin. Bilingual education is one of the most difficult issues to deal with and is hotly debated by its opponents which also include Hispanics as well as Anglos throughout the nation. Invariably, accepted stereotypes of the Hispanic image fuel those who have the strongest negative feeling about easing their assimilation into the what they consider to be American culture.

The role film has played in helping to formulate and perpetuate that Hispanic image provides this study with its reason for being.

USING THIS WORK

In a most generalized sense, anyone curious about the movies will find something of interest in this study, more than 1800 films have been classified and described in this first volume, more than five thousand will have been when the final work is completed. Most of the scenarios listed in these pages for the first decade have never appeared in any other reference work and exist only at their original cited source.

More specifically this work has been organized for those interested in trying to assess the affects that motion pictures have had on the viewing public in establishing and continuing to perpetuate accepted stereotypes, those associated with Hispanics living anywhere, but especially in the United States, Mexico, the Caribbean, all areas south, and also in Spain and the Philippines. Others interested in censorship, its role in inhibiting certain stereotypes, the Production Code Administration, the Motion Picture Society for the Americas, the Latin American market and Hollywood's version of Hispanic history will find the raw materials with which to pursue further study.

To facilitate the use of these volumes, all of the films listed have been arranged alphabetically in the year that they were first produced. For the vast majority of the movies included, that time coincided with their release date for exhibition in theaters throughout the United States. This was not the case for some of the early Spanish language films, they have been placed in the year they were first shown in New York's Hispanic theater circuit, the year audiences were first exposed to them.

Each entry has been assigned a specific number for index reference, this is followed by the title of the film, its translated title if it appeared in Spanish and any other title it was known by. The production company and in some cases the specific producers is then indicated. Unless otherwise noted, the films were produced in Hollywood. Those made in Mexico, Argentina, Spain and Cuba are identified. All abbreviations used are found in the legend. The scenario or related material follows.

Almost all of the entries include a brief scenario which details the film's Hispanic connection: A stereotype, an historical interpretation, a specific nation, associated behavior or attitudes, a list of the Hispanic actors and actresses. Those with a special significance have been described in more detail. Many of the films have been cross-referenced with one another. The number which appears within the text in brackets and bold will refer the reader to either an earlier or later version of that film or to another which in some way is connected to that entry.

This information is followed by additional research material, in most cases at least one critical review, more often several are listed. Other entries include bibliographic citations or archival locations. Some entries make specific references to the film's script. In all cases unless otherwise indicated, the scripts for the films found in this work are located in the New York State Archives in Albany which is the repository for more than 70,000 such inclusions. They provide a photocopying service which is not available at most other script locations. A few of the films in this first volume can be obtained on video, the sources are indicated. Many of these films are still being shown currently on the various cable channels and this is also noted.

Four different indices are provided. The first index lists every film in this volume in alphabetical order with its assigned number. These numbers can be used to locate a specific entry if one does not know its production year. The second index is one of actors and actresses. Although some Anglo's have been included, the listing is made up mainly of Hispanics, as many as could be identified in each of the individual listings. The third index is place names, Mexico, the Amazon, Rio de Janeiro, and Columbus, New Mexico. The focus refers to where the action in the production is taking place, not where it was produced. The last index is topical, with everything from "greasers," the border, and cantina girls, to self-sacrificing señoritas and several hundred other themes gleaned from the various entries and listed alphabetically here.

Acknowledgements

Sincere thanks must be given publicly to Paul Lacava, Ann M. Vorisek, Andrew Cambell, and Melinda Dolbec for their capable assistance. Dennis Cronin aside from providing invaluable technical computer counseling also assisted in research. A special thanks must be given to Gary Hewitt who proved to be my most valuable right hand, when I needed more than the usual number. Bob Beveredge furnished assistance that no one else could have. Thanks Bobby.

Once more the library staff at Central Connecticut State University afforded all the assistance one could possible expect from such a capable staff. Thanks Frank, Marie and Faith.

Sam Gil at the Academy archives (the Maragret Herrick Library) and Leith Adams in charge of the Warner Brothers collection at USC, aside from being really nice people, provided me with most valuable assistance.

Hey! Frank Walsh ... Thanks for everything.

And finally, this work would not have been completed had Jennifer Davison not provided daily assistance and encouragement throughout these past ten months. There are not enough words to thank her. Thanks a lot Jennyfur!

Introduction

Popular films are an excellent reflection of a nation's collective mentality, it's national consciousness. Whether intentionally or otherwise, they reflect generally accepted, comfortable and secure perceptions of society in general and of individuals in particular. It is the overall premise of this study that Mexico in particular and Hispanics in general have, from the very first days of the motion picture industry, been subjected to the mythology of what as historians, we call the Black Legend, La Leyenda Negra. In its simplest form, that mythology emphasizes every perceived and assumed negative quality of what is thought to be the Spanish character.

The main body of this work is made up of the raw materials introduced at the turn of the century that reflected and helped formulate that part of the national consciousness which focused on Hispanics. It provides the reader with an annotated listing of almost all the motion pictures, the product of thirty-five years of film making, that helped perpetuate old and create new North American conceptions of the Hispanic image as it was and is presently perceived in the United States. This volume evaluates more than 1800 feature films and many short subjects produced as movies that made the transition from silents to sound. The completed work will provide readers with an extended survey of more than 5000 such entries and carry the study into most recent times.

It may seem to some individuals that any attempt to determine a national consciousness is at best a chancy exercise in public opinion forecasting. This is not a statistical or scientific analysis of the number of films made by the motion picture industry which relate to Hispanics in one way or another, no pretext is made about the precise nature of the scientific method employed in the evaluation of individual films. Although a significant effort was made to be objective, in the final analysis, this work is the subjective product of this individual's acculturation and conditioning by the very material subjected to classification in this study.

Arriving at a national consciousness, determining what is popularly perceived by a majority of the people living within a given community is not as difficult to do as one might think. Imprecise as they may be, comfortable and accepted attitudes about others can be arrived at by surveying and studying the media transfer of information at any given point in this nation's history. In the colonial and revolutionary war period, as print media established itself as the primary means of disseminating information over long distances, it would have been difficult to find much praise for the Indian. He was considered a savage, an enemy and a threat. Although some voices from the wilderness protested his mistreatment, the print media from earliest to most recent times helped project an image of Indian savagery that provided all the necessary justifications for the taking of the his lands. At a later time, film forcefully reaffirmed those views. Surveying that material, it would be difficult for any researcher not to conclude that the majority of the nation's white population, including law makers, considered the Indian an enemy, an uncivilized savage who inhibited progress, and a people who required the paternalistic care of a superior Anglo, Christian civilization. Behavior is easier to justify when one assumes that the divinities are with them.

Technological advances since colonial times have vastly increased the scope of mass media. When film joined the media family it significantly broadened the base of the affected public by including a non-reading audience and by providing graphic pictorializations of the events formerly described. The scenarios of Indian savagery brought to film, whether believed or not by the producers, came to be an accepted part of the public's consciousness. There were no images to the contrary until recent times. Some Anglo historians still glorify the exploits of George Armstrong Custer whose pathological hatred of Indians bordered on the psychotic. Whereas as children many of us may have innocently believed that if it was printed in the paper or a book, it had to be true, so millions of others came to accept what they could see with their own eyes as perceived reality. What was true for the Indian community was the same for Hispanics; for most Anglo audiences the two were one inferior race. The public used Indian and Mexican as interchangeable terms.

Until now the vast majority of studies dealing with Hispanic stereotyping on film have concerned themselves, somewhat understandably, with our southern neighbor, Mexico, but this narrow focus has prevented the formulation of a broader historical conception for understanding the varied consequences almost ninety years of negative Hispanic stereotyping. Mexican's enjoy a Hispanic heritage, but certainly not all Hispanics are Mexicans. The Hispanic population extends from Patagonia to the Philippines, from Central America to Spain. It is one basic premise of this work that the Hispanic image Hollywood, and the film industry as a whole, has projected since its inception, is merely the technologically advanced picturization of what is referred to as "La Leyenda Negra," the Black Legend of Hispanic historiography [303], first brought to print in the sixteenth century by Spain's enemies covetous of her vast empire and especially the gold rich lands of the Americas.

Spain was the first of the modern imperial nations. Her empire in the Americas began before 1500 and continued to exist in the Caribbean until 1898, when a more virile suzerain became overlord over the troubled lands in those beautiful blue waters. Those four hundred years of imperial rule and related circumstances provided the film industry with enough material to create scenarios that span the entire century of film making. Without that material the industry itself might not have prospered as well as it did. Certainly at its inception the movie industry would have been without the services of its most important foreign foe. To understand the development and the nature of the Hispanic image Hollywood created, the historical picture must be considered in its totality. For a population that has long de-emphasized the utility of history itself, the problem is further complicated because high school and college texts ignore or pay slight attention to the first hundred years of both hemisphere's Hispanic history. This is not a unique circumstance, not so long ago it was impossible to find mention of any positive contribution made by Blacks or women to American history. For Hispanics, the 1500's are a lost century of American history.

As film would later perpetuate and reemphasize the Black Legend, so did the history and literature of the nineteenth century. In 1847 a bastion of Boston's Anglo Saxon purity, the **North American Review** used the following words to describe their own Brahmin's [William Hickling Prescott] **History of the Conquest of Peru**: "The Spanish adventurer in America ... was a singular compound of the bigot, the pirate, and knight-errant. He was fierce, rapacious and cruel; his conduct towards the natives was restrained by no sense of honor, no touch of compassion, no regard for the laws of God or man. A demon let loose from hell to wreak his spite and vengeance upon the sons of men could hardly have matched him in savageness, perfidy and debauchery ... the religion he professed [was] a wicked perversion of the name and spirit of Christianity ... for it added the fervor of bigotry to the practice of crimes so monstrous that the natural spirit and uninstructed conscience of man would have shrunk from them with loathing and horror." Not a book review, this was much more a condemnation of a national character, commonly believed before and after the Mexican War, and one that later would be translated to film.

James Russell Lowell, renowned Bostonian, was not alone in his belief that lands acquired from Mexico would contaminate North America's white Anglo Saxon Christians. His popular **Biglow Papers**, were filled with racist misconceptions about Mexicans and Hispanic's. One of his humorous anecdotes about the war had "Mexican's pissin in the water" to prevent the thirsty American heros from quenching their thirst. According to this intellectual, Mexicans were foul, filthy with no humanity or any saving graces. Acquiring them by conquest could only mongrelize this great nation. Many of these Hispanics later found their way to the silver screen.

Protestant distaste for Mexico's religion had been acquired by Anglos long before Lowell's time. Little did the **Virgin Queen** know how far reaching the consequences of refusing Philip II's proposal would be. As the King of Spain, he was then the most powerful monarch in the world. From the discovery of the Americas and throughout sixteenth century Spanish monarchs dominated world affairs. Charles I, and later, his son Philip, controlled the destinies of much of the Christian world for almost a century. The New World itself was their personal private property. Ferdinand and Isabella had financed the venture and the Americas were the profit. The Papacy, whose authority then transcended national boundaries, confirmed in 1493 and redefined in 1497 the Spanish monarch's claim to that territory. Part of that confirmation included the accepted responsibility to teach Catholicism to the natives. Until the end of the sixteenth century no European power seriously challenged Spain's title to all of the lands in the New World. Only after the defeat of the Spanish Armada, sent to England because of Elizabeth's refusal [290], did Spain's control over all the Americas weaken. Then the English, the Dutch and French plundered Spain's imperial domain. All of these events became subjects for silent and sound film features. The enemy was always Spain, the heros, always Anglo Christians.

Philip's desire for the Virgin Queen had more to do with pride than passion. The Spanish king was the defender of the faith and had promised to prevent further division within the Roman Catholic world, a division that threatened its universal control over all Christendom. Elizabeth's father, Henry VIII had created an English Catholic church. He had sent Catherine of Aragon back to Spain. Philip might have overlooked this earlier insult had he been able to bring Elizabeth and England back into the Catholic fold, but when the lady said "no," the animosity created lasted for centuries and eventually extended itself to the Americas. History was having fun and making enemies of Spain and England. The divinities knew a good script when they saw one. With the defeat of the Armada in 1588, [1743] England was able to take advantage of Spain's diminished control over the New World's sea lanes. The **Sea Hawk**'s who destroyed the Armada moved to the Caribbean, and provided the scenarios for some of the silver screens most romantic swashbucklers.

Religious differences between Spain and England were only intensified by the manner in which the two nations ruled themselves. Spain's autocratic monarchy contrasted sharply with the slowly developing democracy in England. This significant difference was even more important to Hollywood's Hispanic imagery. Although there are numerous films which point to the inane brutality exhibited by some (Spanish) Roman Catholics zealots, (the Inquisition [303] is difficult to paint with pastel colors), there are of course, no Hollywood productions that condemn Roman Catholicism as a religion. In terms of political ideology almost all films portray Hispanic monarchy in a negative light. Invariably Spanish kings are shown to be cruel totalitarians. Conversely, as one should surely expect, Democracy has always been one of the foremost Anglo heros, featured and glorified in thousands of films.

Of all of the silver screen struggles between Spain and England, none are more fondly remembered by romantics than those which took place in the Caribbean and adjacent areas [415]. There, stalwart Englishmen, no matter their crimes or character, pirates though they be, forever kept true to the signed articles and honored England's democratic tradition. Spain was the enemy, any action against her treasure ships diminished her power and increased that of England's. For the Elizabethan sea dogs, real and fictitious, the Spanish existed only to be plundered in the sacred name of English freedom. Sir Henry Morgan was knighted for his exploits against them and became governor of Jamaica. The Black Legend of Hispanic tyranny provided the justification for this and for every single Hollywood pirate projection that glorified such British exploits. Audiences wasted no sympathy on the Spanish with Douglas Fairbanks or Errol Flynn playing the **Black Pirate** [1161], **Captain Blood** [1726] or the **Sea Hawk**, 1940. Even as children it was obvious to us who the good guys were and who we wanted to be fighting right along side of, bare chested and devoted to right, justice and dear old democratic England. Tyranny was a word that seemed naked unless used in conjunction with Spanish. Unconsciously, such films promoted the Black Legend and perpetuated the negative stereotypes that the Spanish had acquired as early as the sixteenth century.

England established her North American colonies in the seventeenth century. Independence followed in 1783. After Spain's American empire revolted in 1826 only Cuba remained under her control. In 1898 Cuba became the first imperial colony to have its independence recorded on film [71]. That conflict also provided the United States with it's silver screen debut. Political cartoons provided the most lasting imagery before film became an essential part of North American culture. Such cartoons, well before the Spanish American War most often characterized Latin America as a frail, shy Spanish señorita who required the masculine strength of an Uncle Sam to keep her secure. Acknowledging some guilt for hyperbole, the mythology has always allowed Latin America to be presented as Uncle Sam's woman, his virgin to protect. The Monroe Doctrine his patriotically colored prophylaxis employed to prevent foreign penetrations. La Leyenda Negra his justification. If any fooling around was going to take place, he would be the one to do it. Even if the simile is unrecognized by the majority of North Americans, its implications are accepted with few reservations. Cuba was our little lady to protect.

By 1895 the increased coverage of the Cuban Revolution fueled the growth of the new press, it was nurtured and fed off the public's increasing interest and demand for war news. The possibility that the United States would become involved and liberate that oppressed island from Spain's cruel tyranny was exhilarating and sold newspapers. This symbiotic feast between press, public and expansionist glory continued and in the next decade took on a new dimension, moving pictures of a developing empire. For twenty years newspaper consumption increased continuously and the youthful motion picture industry paralleled that growth. In the first decade of this century a new theater of operation was added to that taking place in the Caribbean, Mexico became one of the film industry's most important sources for feature films 19. 48].

During the first two decades of this century, as a result of all of this south of the border activity, newspapers and film confirmed what was perceived in the national consciousness to be the proper relationship between Latin and Anglo populations within the hemispheres; that perception has experienced only minor changes since the Spanish American War. Whether the product of La Leyenda Negra and the racist misconceptions it generated, or simple nationalistic pride, very recent events indicate strongly that the majority of North America's Anglo Saxon population perceives Latins, certainly those south of the Rio Grande, as inferiors, whose interests, especially in foreign policy, should be subordinate to those of this nations. Much of the responsibility for this assumption can be attributed to the expansionist press. Not a little must also be assumed by the motion picture industry which from its earliest beginnings provided intensely racist views of the entire Hispanic community. The images of Hispanic barbarity provided justification for forceful actions, but they also increased circulation and attendance to fantastic proportions. The film industry capitalized on this phenomena and together print and film media helped establish a truly national basis for these views.

The sequence of events immediately after the Spanish American War is well known: The United States acquired the Philippines and "Porto Rico," created a protectorate over Cuba, but more importantly, it's established hegemony over the Caribbean was accepted by the European powers. An American empire in the Caribbean necessitated its easy access and required its protection. The acquisition of Panama to build the canal, the protectorates established over Haiti, the Dominican Republic, Nicaragua and Panama itself were direct consequences of the war. The media, press and film glorified all of these events.

Identifying the enemy as a barbarian may not be a new idea, but it forever proves functional. With amazing rapidity hundreds of historical works on the war were published before the final peace treaty was signed. All of them praised the United States as the Anglo savior, Spain was always cast as the villain, vicious, cruel, proud and savage. **Our War With Spain For Cuba's Freedom**, provides one of the best examples: "Civilization against barbarism, freedom against oppression, education against ignorance, progress against retrogression, the West against the East, The United States against Spain," even the most inept of screen writers could find scores of silver screen scenarios in these words which characterized Spain in 1898. The title of the book is significant in itself. The paternalistic inference that it was our war, against Spain for Cuba's freedom, hid the fact that the Cubans had been fighting on their own for more than twenty bloody years. Similar views were translated to film. From earliest times Hollywood has been an ardent imperialist, especially within the hemisphere, it glorified State Department policy.

The Spanish American War also brought Pacific territories into the empire. The Philippines had been Spanish property since 1497, and remained so until the steel ships of the United States Navy blew what there was of Spain's wooden fleet right out of Manila harbor. Yet the islands proved to be a problem from the first. When the United States occupied the Philippines, armed insurrection broke out. The nationalist,

Aguinaldo [336], refused to accept United States control over his country after the defeat of Spain. With some of his men and with the assistance of what came to be called the savage Moro's [always cast as head hunters and cannibals in future films [1159], the revolutionary continued his fight for independence. That conflict took a significant number of North American and Filipino lives and resulted in some of the most savage and racist butchery United States forces ever indulged in. Both sides were guilty of atrocities and only very recently have the incidents been subjected to serious scholarly research. No one applauded the first reports of "Killing niggers in the Philippines," and most people ignored the news that this country was now employing a policy of reconcendrado camps, the same concentration camps that the expansionist press had used so well against the Spanish government in Cuba. Many early silents were set in the Philippines, but none portrayed these events. The locals were always cast as savages and continued to be as until 1941 when Pearl Harbor turned the screen Filipinos into WWII heros.

Of all of the islands acquired in the Spanish American War, Cuba has been most favored by Hollywood production. In the silent era it was the subject or location for more than sixty films. Although almost always portrayed as the sin capital of the Caribbean from the earliest talkers [1485] through the production of son of **The Godfather** and most recently, **Havana**, more feature films have focused on Cuba than any of the other islands warmed by the trade winds. Panama Canal construction after 1904 required stability within the Caribbean community. Republics in that region, whether mainland or island could not be allowed the pleasure of irresponsible behavior that might invite foreign intervention. With this justification the United States between 1901 and 1936, occupied Cuba, Panama, the Dominican Republic, Haiti and Nicaragua. None of these interventions have ever been the subject for a feature film production, but Panama and the Canal provided some of the earliest movie makers with scenes and images that were the most popular with the film going public in the first decade of flickers [20]. Back home audiences were filled with pride as they watched the project being completed. Film company's frequently traveled to the Isthmus to capture dramatic scenes many of which are preserved in the National Archives in Washington [283].

As the new century began the United States focused on Mexico. After 1910 only the successful completion of the Canal challenged events in Mexico for the attention of the North American public. No other Latin American country has occupied more North American screen time than Mexico. In silent film days more than five hundred films used it as a focal point. Another hundred plus used the Mexican border for it's action location. As a consequence of this, our southern neighbor has been subjected to more negative imagery than any of the other south of the border republics. Mexicans have been called "Convenient Villains" and so they were. Actually they were the first villains and not even challenged by the Chinese who were always lurking in the dark corners of some xenophobic scribes imagination. It is not too much to say that the convenience of an enemy so easily found just across the border aided the rapid growth and development of the film industry. In 1910 social revolution erupted in Mexico. Porfirio Diaz had controlled the nation since 1876. Supported by a well paid Army, the privileged Roman Catholic Church, a multitude of foreign investors and by the great hacendados, he was secure in his absolute power. Peons lived on estates some of which were larger than the state of Rhode Island, but were without a political voice or land of their own. Mexico was powder keg ready to explode. Diaz was respected in the United States, but he was hated and feared throughout Mexico. When Francisco Madero declared he would oppose the old dictator in the election of 1910, support for his campaign came from all who were oppressed. Secure in his position, Diaz was at first amused, but then fear made him jail Madero. Escaping in heroic fashion the latter took refuge in El Paso and issued his pronunciamiento against Diaz. Armed opposition soon broke out all over Mexico. Many hacendados were killed. The peons wanted land to provide for their families. Revolutionary leaders emerged, in the North, Pancho Villa led the way. In the state of Morelos, Emiliano Zapata carried the banner. Both pledged their allegiance to Madero and Mexico.

The local press at first supported Madero, but described the two popular revolutionaries as bandits. Villa was portrayed as a lady killer who would wed any pretty señorita willing to bed down with him. All of the stories of his brutality were later translated to film, [652] including the nonsense about his lining up Federalista soldiers one behind the other so that he could shoot them with a single bullet. It was reported that not only did Villa execute prisoners he, frequently burned their bodies or put them on the railroad tracks to be mangled. That was also recorded on film.

Most northern newspapers doubted Madero's ability, they expressed concern for North American lives and property. His desire to rule by law was ridiculed, Mexicans only understood force. Trouble soon followed. After promising to redress ancient grievances, and to provide land for the peons, Madero ordered Villa and Zapata to disband their forces. This well intentioned action proved deadly for Madero and Mexico itself. Within the year and with at least the tacit approval of the American Ambassador, Huerta, his chief general, had Madero executed and proclaimed himself President [368]. This brutal action outraged Woodrow Wilson who promptly withdrew the recognition of his government. Now began more than four and one half years of almost continuous confrontation between the two nations. Before the inevitable interventions, it was a war of words and images in which the press and motion pictures played a significant and active role.

More daily and weekly newspapers were printed in the United States between 1914 and 1916 than at any other time. Media became part of everyone's daily life. Contemporaneously the motion picture industry established itself as an essential part of American culture, its importance as a source of exciting and inexpensive entertainment grew with the issue of every new one reeler. During that time, Mexico provided both these expanding instruments of public opinion formulation with its most important nondomestic source of material. From the beginning, the escalating confrontation between Wilson and Huerta in 1912 until Pershing's punitive expedition vainly chased Villa through the mountains of northern Chihuahua, in 1916, Mexico was daily front page news. More amazing, it was the subject of more than three hundred film productions.

There can be little doubt that events in Mexico fueled the growth of the motion picture industry and conversely moving pictures helped solidify established Hispanic stereotypes. Of the total seven hundred and fifty films surveyed in these pages which were produced between 1910 and 1919 approximately fifty-five percent of them dealt specifically with Mexico. From 1911 to 1920 more than half of each years production featured either Mexico or Mexicans as the primary theme. From 1921 to 1930 the percentage dropped dramatically until it solidified to less than ten percent in each of the last three years of that decade. Of the ninety eight films with Hispanic themes, which were shown in 1930, only ten of them could be considered to have a Mexican orientation. By then other Hispanic regions occupied more screen time.

The United States intervened twice in Mexico between 1914 and 1916, newspapers and film certainly helped stir support for such action by providing the public with pictures of a land filled with lawless bandits and dirty treacherous greasers, but surprisingly, in those films produced before the Villa raid on Columbus, New Mexico, Hollywood provided significant sympathy for the forces in rebellion [339]. Only after Villa successfully "invaded" the United States did film emphasize the perceived negative side of the Mexican Revolution and Villa himself [677]. The view would change again in 1934 with the sympathetic portrayal he was given in **Viva Villa** [1712].

In between March of 1912 and April of 1914 the North American press vocally opposed Woodrow Wilson's policy of "Watchful Waiting" [154]. I have shown elsewhere that the vast majority in United States would have supported intervention during that period, but Wilson chose to wait. This policy caused him to be the object of serious criticism in the press and some humor in film [442, 724]. As much as ninety percent of the daily press then supported intervention editorially. Of three hundred newspapers surveyed in New England, only one was opposed. When the blue jackets finally took Vera Cruz in 1914 movie theaters throughout the nation interrupted the showing of their features to play the Star Spangled Banner and cheering audiences raised their voices in patriotic support. Of approximately 250 features, which focused on Mexico or Mexicans produced through 1914, only five, which involved the Mexican as an individual personality, could be considered sympathetic or favorable. From the first year in which scenarios were used in 1907, [19] the Mexican was pictured as a "greaser," cunning, sinister, lustful, lecherous, cowardly, treacherous, faithless, untrustworthy and generally no good, a man who would use his favorite weapon to stab any Anglo in the back [53, 298] at almost any time for no reason other than that it might please him. Such continuously reinforced stereotyping easily socialized early film audiences, in most cases they were simply seeing in lurid action on the screen what they read daily in the press. That such a despicable people could actually refuse to salute "Old Glory" and worse, insult the United States, stirred the patriotism of a pubescent world power. It offended individual ego's. When the navy and marines forcefully occupied Vera Cruz, the newsreel men were there to capture the action [432].

For a while World War I drove Mexico from the front pages of the daily press, but not so from motion picture screens. Almost one new two or three reeler, featuring Mexico or the border was produced for every week of 1915, forty seven in all. Sixty four had been made in 1914, sixty five would be produced in 1916, the largest number for any year in the silent era. Including some of the newsreel coverage, Mexico's Revolutionary hero, Pancho Villa was the major character [seen or unseen] in thirty-six of these productions. Villa had actually dared to invade the United States. Once called a "revolutionary," after the raid, on Columbus, New Mexico, he was typed a treacherous and bloody bandit in the daily press and in the movies [652]. Prior to the raid the Mutual Film Company [431] actually had him under contract for the exclusive rights to film his activity. Raoul Walsh had for a brief exciting time, been with Villa gathering material for a film biography. Villa loved the publicity and played to the camera, even allowing executions to be filmed. Much of the folklore pictured in later productions was generated at this time by the association of these two great showmen.

As the fall of 1917 approached, the United States prepared to enter the world conflict. The "Hun" became the new silver screen enemy. **The Kaiser, the Beast of Berlin** [793] was the feature attraction and the audience loved to hate the Germans. That passed and briefly so did interest in Mexico. In 1919-20 only thirteen films dealing with Mexico were produced. As the proud exponents of Americanism, the motion picture industry settled into making how we won the war films and Mexico had to share screen time with other Hispanic regions. Much of the action was also moved closer to the Texas/Mexico border.

Spanish or Mexican California became a popular location in the twenties for films with Hispanic themes. Although many movie goers might well have been more familiar with the "immortals" of the Alamo, in the silent era only a few films dealt with Texas independence. The Alamo was featured in an abjectly racist production as early as 1911 [155], when California achieved it's silver screen independence [132], but there were only three Alamo films before the talkers. In that time fifteen films freed California from Spanish control. In the silent era more than one hundred and twenty movies focused on Spanish/Mexican California, almost all of these included more acceptable Hispanic types as well as the negative ones.

Introduction   xxvii

Although fewer films focused directly on Mexico in the post war era, harsh characterizations continued. In 1918 **Guns and Greasers** [787] was the last movie to use that derogatory epithet in a title, but greasers still slithered through sinister scenes and some of the most pernicious señoritas yet pictured did their dirty deeds for audiences that learned new meanings for treachery and faithlessness [735]. The Mexican revolutionary also continued to be portrayed as a bloody bandit until the thirties.

Spanish California provided the location for the gradual transition of the Mexican's malevolent screen persona. In the last decade of the silent era, although negative stereotypes still persisted, the Mexican, the Spanish Californian, lost much of his negative character. Because of various external forces, Hollywood transformed his extra-legal activities into acceptable and understandable behavior which audiences could identify with. In Spanish California, the Mexican bandit became a Hispanic avenger, Zorro, not unlike a Robin Hood who had left the shady groves of Sherwood forest for the sun of southern California. By the end of the decade, the border bandit had become something of a good badman, the Cisco Kid. Zorro took care of evil deed doers in Spanish California, Cisco watched out for the same on the Texas/Arizona borders. Both became enduring hero's with North American movie goers and successfully transformed their colorful activities to television. The Family Channel on cable, once the exclusive range of fundamentalist Christian evangelists recently revived the Zorro character: **Zorro: The Legend Begins**. The masked crusader has now been introduced into millions of homes weekly to fight the forces of Spanish tyranny in 1991.

Douglas Fairbanks, played an essential role in both of the original transformations. He burst into the new decade with bull whip and black mask to thrill audiences throughout the Americas in 1920s **Mark of Zorro** [847]. In that capacity, as a Hispanic avenger and protector of the poor, he created a characterization which provided audiences with a Spanish personality they could identify with, one whose adventures they would have enjoyed sharing. He was a Spaniard on the screen, but all knew him to be the number one swashbuckling Anglo star. The tyranny he fought against was still a "greasy Spanish" captain, but Zorro, the Fox, was a good Hispanic hero who understood the meaning of democracy, justice and the North American way. **Zorro** was a huge and instant success as was the sequel **Don Q** [1108] in which Fairbanks proved to future producers that two Zorro's, father and son, could be better than one. In 1926 the plucky Ruth Roland, an "athletic but feminine" popular heroine, stared in fifteen episodes of the **Avenging Arrow**, [851] also set in the sunny south of California. There, as a female version of the Hispanic hero, she provided an even easier acceptability that there could be good Hispanics. Of course both male and female Zorro's were aristocrats, which also enhanced their attractiveness.

In 1916 Fairbanks had introduced the character of the good badman [655], an early anti-hero who lived by his western wits just in and outside of the law with some negative habits, but over all a decent sort who would help those in need. This was essentially the prototypical Cisco Kid character. But the first real Mexican good **Bad Man** [962] made his appearance on the silver screen in 1923, significantly, the year after the first attempts by the Mexican government to protest such negative characterizations.

That was also the year after the self regulatory Motion Picture Producers and Distributors of America was created by the movie moguls to quell the rapidly rising demands numerous interest groups were making that a tight censorship be employed against movies of all kinds. Those demanding such action wanted the government to exercise the censorship role. The industry realized that if it did not appear to regulate itself, there was a distinct possibility that government would do it for them. To obviate this worst case scenario, the largest of the producers created their own governing board and hired, Indiana's corn fed, pure as the driven snow, Will Hays away from the Harding Administration to head up the new censorial body. [No liquor lips had ever kissed his.] In reality Hays' main job was to promote motion pictures. He received more than six figures to do so and he did it well. The motion picture tsar's very first order of business was to deal with what had become the Mexican problem. So he went to Mexico to ensure officials that something would be done to satisfy their protests.

Mexico had achieved a degree of stability in 1922, but official United States recognition would not come until the following year. Yet the Mexican Consul General, G. S. Seguin, publicly accused Hollywood producers of using grossly exaggerated and very negative Mexican characterizations in their films. He cited four specific films [893] and singled out Famous Players and Metro as two of the chief offenders. The Consul also warned that an embargo would be instituted against the entire industry's product if significant improvement was not made quickly. There is no question that this would have hurt the industry had it been possible. Before knowing very much about the situation, Hays himself may well have worried, but in reality neither the Consul nor Hays had enough power or control in 1922 to do very much about it.

Some writers have made much of this protest, but it had very little immediate effect. Distributors and exhibiters in Mexico needed North American films to stay in business. There was no native film industry at this time and the Mexican public wanted to see Hollywood's motion pictures, which were by far the best produced anywhere. If Hollywood could picture all French women as easy, the English, foppish stuffed shirts, Canadians, dumb lumberjacks, and Germans as fat beer guzzling autocrats, then the Mexican could endure. Exhibitors in France and in Mexico protested against threatened bans claiming that such action would drive them out of business. Many of the producers did send letters to the Mexican Consul promising to change, but in reality there was little incentive to do so. The world market, the French, English and all of

Europe, cared little about Mexican bandits, some even wondered what they were complaining about, Mexico was filled with bandits. Producers may have been concerned, but soon realized that the world wanted Hollywood films. If films were banned in Mexico, the world was still a waiting market.

Although there are some brief references in the trade papers about the possibility of such bans, this researcher has found no evidence that any film Hollywood produced in the twenties was ever confiscated or experienced any more than brief delay in exhibition as a result of an official governmental action. By the end of the twenties, the United States Department of Commerce reported that Hollywood films provided between seventy-five to eighty-five percent of Latin America's total Motion picture consumption. Throughout the thirties only three North American productions were officially prevented from being exhibited and **The Gay Desperado**, 1937, [1847] had it's ban lifted after United Artists protested the action. Some Hollywood productions did experience censorial snippers, but the scenes cut usually were of a religious nature, scenes with pictures of the Virgin Mary, or individuals praying.

Yet the protest and Hays' journey did produce some results. Part of Hays' supplication to the Mexican government (as well as to other nations) was the formulation of a code of ethics relating to the nondefaming of foreign nationals and the non-distorting of any nation's history. A similar code had recently been adopted by the International Committee of the League of Nations. A cynic might consider this simply a practical measure. Throughout the twenties almost all nations developed a system of motion picture censorship which resulted in the significant cutting of some productions. But blatantly offensive films would have proved unprofitable. Hays's job was to know just what would and what would not sell in any given market, domestic or foreign. If something in a particular work was considered offensive, he would suggest it's removal. On the bottom line, it was his job to sell the Hollywood product. Anything that would inhibit sales, was targeted. As the head of the MPPDA Hays wrote to a friend that he considered the motion picture to be an "instrument of international good will," [969] that "trade followed film" and as such he wanted the industry to give the world a correct picture of North American life to promote universal international good will. That would take some time.

Although the Hays Office may have exercised no great influence in the silent era, so far as Hispanic characterizations were concerned, in the thirties and forties that would change dramatically. When the Hays Office became the Production Code Administration the newly formulated code of ethics could be enforced by refusing to grant the seal of approval. Producers were then forced accept the suggestions made that grossly negative characterizations be removed. If they refused, their films would never be exhibited. Any film could be made, but if the PCA did not grant the seal, it would never be shown.

In 1922 Hays had promised the Mexicans more than he could deliver. The **Bad Man** [962] was evidence that he possessed little power then to successfully inhibit negative characterizations. The **Bad Man** came to Hollywood directly from New York's great white way where it had been a very successful Broadway show for more than two years. When Holbrook Blinn duplicated his stage role for the screen his characterization of the genial border bandit made a fortune for First National Pictures. The film was a nation wide success and insured that the character would remain in Hollywood for a long time. Although the screen's Mexican bandit had lost some of his sinister edge, he still exhibited too many anti-social characteristics to please the Mexican government. But transformed into the Cisco Kid he became something of a tease for Anglo ladies and a romantic character many Anglo men could identify with. Almost always on the side of the oppressed, his amorous ways and dialect English allowed him to be threatening only when confronted by evil, but in his heart, he was still a Mexican bandit living within the law only when it was absolutely necessary.

Although the many Hispanics who inhabited Hollywood's Spanish California in the twenties may have presented a somewhat more positive image to North American audiences, some continued to offend the Mexican government. In 1927 Mexico was a recognized and respected member of the world community sensitive to its past portrayal as a nation devoted to revolutionary banditry. Although the total number of derogatory Mexican portrayals had diminished significantly they continued to be popular with profit minded producers. In 1927 Latin America was a major market, Mexico the largest of the Latin importers. Desirous of obviating any possible problem with its new film, **California** [1214], which featured Tim McCoy bringing that territory into the Union, MGM previewed the film for the Mexican Consul. In response the Consul wrote a long article in one of the trades protesting the continued use of negative Mexican stereotyping. He warned that if Hollywood did not stop defaming Mexico's image, the entire industry would find the border closed to its product. Of course this never happened. More than 85 percent of the films that Mexicans viewed on a daily basis were still produced in Hollywood. South of the border audiences preferred Hollywood movies. Germany, the closest rival produced one tenth as many films in a year and few of those moody motion pictures were successfully exhibited in Mexico. France provided the only other spice for local consumption. The native industry was still in its early infancy producing about thirty five films between 1921 and 1930. Mexican officials might well have faced a new revolution, had Hollywood films been banned from Mexico.

Negative stereotyping affected all the Hispanic lands. Actually, every nation in some way was subjected to the industry's conscious image making, but the images created for most of the world community were less offensive than those reserved for Hispanics in Mexico, other hemispheric nations and the Philippines. There was never a Charley Chan or Mr. Moto type hero conceived for Hispanics. It should also be noted that no such image problem existed north of the border, a border significantly longer and much more unprotected than that shared with Mexico. Canadians enjoyed positive projections in hundreds of films which glorified their struggle against the Indians, their movement west and the exploits of the Royal Canadian Mounted Police. Larger than any of the nations in either hemisphere, with more wilderness area than anywhere in the Americas including the Amazon, Hollywood sent few of it's desperate characters or innocently accused to hide in the north. Some Canadians might have had an accent, but they were portrayed as good, hard working, industrious and attractive peoples. Their silver screen stereotypes were significantly more positive than those afforded Mexicans or any other peoples of South America. A short while before the advent of sound films, Alberto Fournier, writing for **Nosotros**, then, a popular Buenos Aries monthly, "vehemently protested" the North American motion picture industry's cultural imperialism. He accused the film makers of always portraying Latins north and south of the Panama Canal as villains and scoundrels who were invariably "disloyal, cowardly, boasting ... lazy [and] grotesque mulattoes" whose only salvation could be found in the acceptance of "arbitrary intervention" by morally superior North Americans. Recently returned from abroad, he reported having attended theaters in Genoa and Damascus where some of Hollywood's "Tango" films were quite popular. The audience reaction to these productions had so depressed and infuriated him that he decided never to visit the United States. He quoted one response to Argentina's characterization: "What a land of savages! ... Certainly a most miserable country." These he claimed were typical of the audience reaction. What there was of an Argentine film industry in 1929 could not supply the world with contrary views. Film allowed the United States to become a cultural imperialist, no other nation in the world could even come close to matching it's yearly motion picture production numbers. By the end of silent days Hollywood made more than 2000 features annually. Germany, the closest rival produced 240, and France only about 74. In quality and technological expertise, there were no rivals. To maintain that supremacy the Hays office helped eliminate some negative stereotypes which might have hurt or inhibited Hollywood's ever increasing Latin market share.

More serious concern for foreign sensitivity was created by the arrival of sound. After the initial excitement generated by film's like the **Jazz Singer** passed, once the movie makers could see that merely adding sound to film would not necessarily increase profits, producers and distributors alike realized that the "talkers" posed a serious problem for overseas and South American markets. Subtitles for silent film exports had usually been provided by native distributors and exhibitors, but when actors began to talk, few could speak French, German, Latvian or Spanish. Almost immediately after the introduction of sound, shortly after movie theaters throughout the world were fitted for the new innovation, nationalists everywhere protested the use of English in their own countries. Many governments responded by increasing subsides and support to local entrepreneurs interested in beginning or expanding native companies. The introduction of sound stimulated the real development of the Mexican and Argentine film industries. Although the number of films they produced remained small until the forties, they represented a threat to Hollywood's world market and created the first real changes in their approach to projecting the Hispanic image. In 1930 the Latin American market was second only to Europe in gross receipts. Actually, it was first in the total consumption of Hollywood product if measured by linear feet consumed. South of the border admission prices were simply cheaper. As such, Latins viewed more Hollywood movies than any other peoples in the world. Desiring to maintain this supremacy the industry attempted to adjust. The experimentation produced numerous innovations not one of which was essentially satisfying to anyone but the actors and actresses involved who were happy to find themselves employed in making pictures. Most of the major production companies attempted to adapt and develop new ideas to meet the need for Spanish talkers. Some went much further than others.

Paramount established a foreign office and studio facilities just outside of Paris in Joinville where they produced, French, Italian, and more than twenty Spanish language films many of which were Spanish versions of existing productions. Fox jumped in with both feet and before 1935 completed forty-three such productions. By that time all of the studios had made some effort and approximately 113 Hollywood produced Spanish language films were shown south of the border and in domestic Hispanic theaters. Although some were profitable, by 1935 the experiment proved to be too much trouble and unnecessary. No other nation's films would replace those produced in Tinsel Town for a very long time.

Over all, these Spanish Language films exhibited a new found concern for Latin cultural sensitivities, but they were plagued with problems from the very start. Hollywood's almost complete lack of familiarity with Latin American history in general or Hispanic culture at home, south of the border or in Spain created problems. Producers had a homogeneous conception of Hispanics. Not all looked alike, but Spanish was Spanish for film makers, be it spoken by Castillianos, Mexicanos or Argentinians. Subtleties or nuances of nationalistic pride were too much for most producers and directors to understand. Hollywood sets for these new productions frequently became veritable Towers of Babel and the films often did not produce the desired result. The Anglo's stars who slaughtered what little Spanish they were required to speak often generated the most negative Hispanic reaction [1345]. One of the most positive results from the experiment was the necessity to employ a multitude of Hispanic actors and actress. A few remained in Hollywood after the Spanish language craze, but many more returned to their native Mexico, Spain and Argentina to help establish those still young film industries on firmer footing.

In the broad perspective, the films of the silent era helped solidify an already existing national consciousness formed by several hundred years of print media shaped and conditioned by the Black Legend. Film brought a new dimension to the Black Legend, it projected it upon more than ten thousand motion picture screens throughout North America and gave it an expanded base heretofore impossible. In one way or another, but essentially in an unconscious manner, the Hispanic image on the silver screen touched everyone's life. It socialized each new generation of movie goers. From the birth of the industry through the introduction of sound, it helped justify North America's adventurous interventions in the Caribbean and Mexico. It provided visual proof of the necessity for such actions, if only by projecting to ever larger audiences the overall worthlessness of the Hispanic character, almost always portrayed, as a faithless, untrustworthy, cowardly and treacherous individual that could only be trusted to plant a knife squarely in an innocent Anglo's back. As bad as the Hispanic male was, the female in affairs of the heart could be equally treacherous and always displayed an easy virtue.

From the very first flickers flashed to audiences standing in line waiting expectantly to enter makeshift nickelodeons setup in store fronts throughout working class North America, very strong images of Anglo Saxon superiority were established that even the less fortunate could take pride in believing. Of the more than 1800 films utilized in this survey more than one hundred of them featured an Anglo hero, super hero or savior. Including the Zorro character, who for many had a Spanish body, but certainly possessed an Anglo soul or disposition. Until the late twenties fewer than six such films were made which portrayed a Hispanic as a hero of any kind. It was Hollywood's camera and they could make any pictures in what ever way they wished, but the over all affect of such projections created a national consciousness that expected to win, to be in charge, to control those shown to be inferiors.

Chuck Norris, Charles Bronson and Sylvester Stylone are the most recent examples of a tradition long established in silent film days. Super hero Norris, armed only with justifications provided by the national consciousness, has been more active south of the border than any of today's film personalities. As a Texas Ranger, Aztec gold hunter, drug enforcement agent and soldier, he has terminated hundreds of malevolent Hispanics while still serving in his major theater of operation, South East Asia. If the frequently faceless nationals of foreign lands can be so easily prevented from doing their foul deeds by so forceful an Anglo, who in the audience could possibly object to the removal of a drug dealing Panamanian president, no matter what agency of this federal government had once recruited his services. Accepted justifications for dealing with such tyrants were established as early as 1909 in the **Conspirators** [42]: "Intrigue, treachery ... revolution, death and marital infidelity" surrounded the President of "Domenico" a South American republic "where a revolution takes place every minute." Such conditions required super Anglo saviors.

Richard Harding Davis allowed his **Soldier of Fortune** [509] to be brought to the screen in 1914 and for more than seventy-five years he remained an enduring character responsible for saving numerous mythical banana republics from their own internal disorder. Richard Dreyfuss performed these heroics most recently. Hollywood's south of the border nations have rarely been stable. In those troubled climes revolutions occur (if not "every minute") than daily and from the scripters analysis, only the intercession of an Anglo savior, or Uncle Sam himself can save whatever Latin land is in trouble, from itself or for itself.

Not including Mexico, the silent era screened more than thirty films which featured revolution or revolutionaries in Central and South America. All of them were blessed and benefitted by a silver screen Anglo hero, an **Americano** [632] who solved all local problems. Twenty others starred soldiers of fortune. These Anglo saviors including a **Yankee Girl** [629], **Yankee Señor** [1204], and a **Yankee Doodle Jr.** [958] who, in the finest tradition of little Chuckie Norris, singlehandedly stopped a South American revolution with only the assistance of a few firecrackers. If Mexico is included in Hollywood's silent era portrayals of Hispanicdom's violent transfers of political power, fifty five more films featured the Hemisphere's projected instability. In many of these an Anglo from across the border, not quite as droopy eyed as Robert Mitchum would be in **Bandido**, but with some of his fighting spirit, would perform the same function any time the film makers felt the revolution or that troubled nation needed a little Anglo help.

The earliest newsreels began the 'how we won the war' genre. Those taken in Cuba and in the Philippines fathered all the feature films which extol the fighting spirit and selfless dedication of North American service men. They brought home to an anxious public moving picture evidence of the heroic exploits of their citizen warriors. What the newsreels could not capture, the industry easily invented on safer battle fields which certainly conditioned the national consciousness against whoever the enemy might be. In the silent era the enemy was easily found south of the border, in the Caribbean, Central America and the Philippines. In 1909 **Up San Juan Hill**, [71] was the first non-newsreel feature which showed the folks back home how we won the war in Cuba, [the one Hispanic action which Big John Wayne never managed to fight in despite its 'ethniccentricity.']

Most of the Hispanics who found their way into silent films continued their travels into the talkers. By that time every Hispanic characterization, every scenario ever devised by scripters in and out of touch with reality, and presently familiar to today's audiences, had been employed. Time has merely adapted these stereotypical vehicles and situations to each generations needs. For example in silent days, braceros were considered to be useful cheap labor. Mexicans who crossed the Rio Bravo to find work in Texas or Arizona then worked hard. During WWII the government actually contracted to bring braceros north to help ease the manpower lost to the war

effort. A few films actually dealt with the plight of such
laborers and the abuses they suffered. More recently the
bracero has become an enemy, a real "wet back," someone who
takes jobs away from poor Anglos. Recent North American
history texts have used pictures of "Aliens sneaking across
the border" to point out the problems created by these
"illegals." The latest films while expressing some sympathy
for these people seem more concerned with the problems they
create for the Border Patrol and Anglo's in general. **El Norte**
and **Born in East LA**, are exceptions and provide a stark and
humorous contrast to the accepted stereotype.

All of the very negative Hispanic stereotypes made their way
from print media into film and were firmly established before
the end of the first decade of this century while most of the
production work was still being done in the Northeast where
Hispanics were certainly not a threatening minority. The daily
newspapers, the popular dime novels and even the Spanish
classics made their contribution. The Black Legend established
Hispanic character in print, technology transferred it to
film. In the 1880's Edward Zane C. Judson, known to millions
as Ned Buntline, fixed a wide assortment of malevolent and
sleazy Mexicans in the popular mind. The Mexican bandit,
treacherous and sinister, the faithless female, a tramp at
best often vicious, cruel and vengeful, who might take time
out to do a little cantina dancing so that she could lure the
pure hearted Anglo to her bed and his destruction, were main
characters in Buntline's imagination, maybe the monsters from
his id. But always there was the Anglo hero who somehow
managed to save the situation and preserve the North American
way.

With not too much distortion the Spanish classics and a most
popular French opera, provided their own Hispanic imagery.
Don Quixote, Don Juan and Carmen, were part of the language
and entered films in their first decade. A quixotic Don Juan
who wanted to woo a Carmen was certainly headed for trouble.
Although Bizet was French, his naughty lady was Spanish. Her
male counterpart Don Juan, may have been nicer to his ladies
than Carmen was to her men, but in the final analysis, both
used sex and their bodies in a manner that a no good Anglo
puritan would admit was acceptable, much less enjoyable.
Carmen made her first screen appearance in 1908 [31] and **Don
Juan** [43] the following year. Both made their way many times
into the talkers and were immortalized by Errol Flynn and Rita
Hayworth in 1948's **Loves of Carmen**. In time Don Juan became
the Latin lover and Carmen the Hispanic whore.

The chivalrous old romantic who travelled with his seemingly
stupid but in reality most sagacious sidekick, attacked his
first windmill in 1909 [44] and another not so long ago still
as a **Man From La Mancha**. But when Hollywood adapted the
Cervantes character to it's purpose, its influence on the
Hispanic image reinforced established stereotypes. With not
much trouble scripters transformed the old knight and his
faithful companion into a pair of good deed doing badmen who
operated just inside the law never too far from the Mexican

border. The Cisco Kid first appeared **In Old Arizona** [1338] in 1929, but still makes frequent appearances on the late show.

All three of these characters with a little embellishment and extension were transformed into frequently used silver screen personalities. There was more than a little Carmen in every Spanish or Mexican dancer that ever appeared on the silver screen. The transition from tease to tart was not a difficult one for most Anglo scripters to make. A Spanish dancer could be a not so nice lady, but a Hispanic whore could be really bad [409]. Even if no one during the silent era could say the word out loud, such a bad lady could manifest behavior that would make an Anglo gal swoon from disgust or envy.

Carmen was also responsible for characterizing most silver screen gypsies as Hispanic in origin. Hollywood's has almost always made them out to be Spanish. Even Maria Ouspenskaya, who in the **Wolf Man** might have appeared to be a Slavic refugee, had a son named Carlos who was destined to infect the offspring of the Anglo lord of Talbot manner with his own inherited curse. In most films with gypsies the Hispanic connection is more easily identified. The Carmen is invariably a dancer, the focal point of every males lascivious longings. She usually loves the King of the Gypsies son, but there is always another who wants her. Rejected, his desire for vengeance either makes him stab the vamp's true love or he demands the satisfaction of a duel which is traditionally fought either with knives or bull whips. What could be more simple. Long before Cornell Wilde was ever born that scenario had been played out many times for the continued amusement of the audience and the Carmen type who obviously enjoyed being the object of such passionate attention [28]. Before 1912 more than a dozen gypsy films had been made.

Most on screen Spanish señoritas in the silent days were not so nasty. Many exhibited self sacrificing qualities that made Anglo men want to head south. For scripters throughout film history the best of the fantasies involved having a señorita sell out her own country for the possibility of being loved by an Anglo man. That first took place in, **An Episode in the Cuban Revolution**, 1909 [46]. In the year before **A Spanish Romance** [28] had already established the fact that whenever an Anglo and a Hispanic competed for the same señorita, everyone involved and watching knew that there was no real competition. In all but two instances in silent days, the Anglo won the darkskinned señorita. As it did with gypsies, this invariably provoked the loser to seek revenge. Vengeance continued to be portrayed as a Hispanic characteristic from the first days of film making. Directed toward an Anglo hero it invariably left him unscarred but resulted in having the self sacrificing señorita trying to remove the knife from her bosom that had originally been intended for the fairskinned lad's back.

Both male and female silver screen Hispanics were hot blooded and passionate, both possessed a dual screen personality which was most often in silent days determined by social standing. If they were wealthy or possessed aristocratic blood any amorous adventures were acceptable. Shortly after Don Juan was able to speak, he was transformed into the Latin lover that made on and off screen females swoon but most Anglo men hate. Anglo men could bed down with any sweet señorita, but only married the rich ones from good families.

If he who lusted after a white woman was not a poet or some similar romantic figure like the **Sheik**, a desert Prince with a Spanish mother, if he were simply some greaser who had sneaked or slithered across the Rio Bravo looking for work on a ranch, he was "fer certin hedin fer trouble." There may have been no KKK out west to keep such horrific impulses in check, but there certainly were enough cowboys to punish any Mexican who had the presumption to even think that some virginal ranch man's daughter would consider rubbing noses with his kind [97]. That scenario remained unchanged throughout silent days and continued until the search for allies and raw materials during World War II required Uncle Sam and the film industry to allow some Hispanics "of a better class" to do "alota" kissing with Anglo women. TNT's production **Crazy From the Heart** [1991] reflects the industry's most recent liberalization of the rules. In this film the friends of the white female school principle at first object to her going out with the Mexican [called "greaser" and "beaner"] janitor, but in the final reel true love seems to have conquered some of the latent and overt Hispanic prejudice and Anglo fear about the mythology of super-sexed Hispanics, whatever class they were born into.

Even a cursory glance of this study should indicate that one of the main characters featured throughout the silent era was the Mexican or Hispanic bandit or bad man. This sinister character made his first shadowy appearance in 1906 in **The Life of an American Cowboy** [14] where he was seen "lurking" outside a saloon with evil intent in mind. In the following year he was identified as a "greaser," a epithet commonly used through out the twenties, and one that producers tried to employ long after Will Hays placed it on his banned word list in 1927. First employed to describe Mexican laborers who carried still undried bundles of cowhide on their heads as they loaded them onto ships heading north, the term was used by writers to negatively stereotype all Mexicans as a dirty unwashed peoples. Not considered to be "white man's work" on the docks of Vera Cruz, it was considered appropriate for darkskinned Mexicans who became the "greasers" who had no choice in the matter. The term itself was used in film titles as late as 1918: **Guns and Greasers** [787], but was employed to identify the Mexican in films throughout the mid twenties. In the thirties the Hays/Breen office, frequently still, had to deny Hollywood producers use of the term for proposed films including, **Bordertown**, 1935 and **Robin Hood of Eldorado**, 1936.

More than two hundred Mexican bandits, Spanish bandits, Mexican bad men and Spanish bad men are featured in this study. Some are superstitious and savage, others treacherous cowards. They are lustful, lascivious and lazy, unfaithful cruel and vengeful. They kill and torture with the knives they love as much as the Anglos they hate. Until the intercession of the Hays office, the great majority of films in which Hispanics were featured as individuals projected the worst possible image of people. Until the appearance of Spanish California's Hispanic avenger [Zorro] in 1920 [847], fewer than ten films listed in these pages portrayed Mexicans or Spaniards in a sympathetic or honorable fashion.

The affect of this continuous reinforcement helped create a negative national consciousness about Mexicans, Spaniards, and all Hispanics. If fifty percent of all the films produced with Hispanic themes between 1907 and 1920 focused on Mexico and the vast majority of those projected a highly negative image, as was the case, the North American motion picture public was subjected to a weekly barrage of negative stereotyping. Between 1911 and 1916 at least one new film was made [on the average] every week which featured Mexico. In 1916 when Villa invaded/raided the United States, at least 65 such films were produced. Although the total number of films, which focused on Mexico, diminished dramatically after 1920 and those which exhibited less harsh stereotypes, more positive Mexican images had to wait for the World War II era to be seen.

The impact of all this negative stereotyping on the national consciousness transcended personalities, it also affected the locales in which Hispanics live. Few North Americans traveling south have not been warned about the dire consequences of drinking Mexican water. That a one time president of the United States [and his writers] had the bad taste and lack of forethought to mention the alleged curse, Montezuma's revenge, while addressing an assembled group of Mexican dignitaries may defy comprehension, but in reality this should be considered merely another manifestation of the Black Legend heavily seasoned with bad taste. There is a magic about traveling to distant lands, why else would one ever leave the wonders of a St. Charles, Missouri or an Anderson, Indiana? Mexico and South America have long been considered to be lands of mystery, fraught with danger. Bandits, once thought to be everywhere, are still commonly believed to presently inhabit "the more remote areas" of Mexico. Nightly news stories of revolutionaries, terrorists and drug producers are frequently expanded into imaginative scenarios for screen productions.

Yet, there is an added dimension to Hollywood's silver screen south of the border danger. It first appeared in early silent films, but became more menacing in the twenties when the first intrepid movie travelers made their way into the far recesses of the Amazon. There were no head hunters in Akron, there may have been the parents of cannibals in Milwaukee, but head hunting in South America was a projected reality. It was the particular pleasure of certain Amazonian Indians. There, deep in the dark tropical rain forests those lurking savages [as early as 1913 [358] waited for unsuspecting Anglo travelers. Heads would be cut off, soaked in unspeakable slime and shrunk to baseball size after which lips would be stitched as neatly as those on that spherical symbol of Americanism. Somehow the motion picture crews always made it back with their heads in place, but the practice continued, at least on the screen, until most recent times when little a blond haired and blued eyed boy proved to audiences that any Anglo kid could become the leader of a tribe of Amazon Indians in **The Emerald Forest** if provided with the opportunity. True to its traditions Hollywood made him the leader of the good Indians who triumphed over the head hunting baddies.

There was still worse in Hollywood's Amazon. Long before the **Creature from the Black Lagoon** made his appearance, the animals of that tropical rain forest were scary enough. By far the most enduring, the nemesis of frequent and recent Hollywood productions was the **Piranha**, a little fish with razor sharp teeth that could clean the flesh off a cow sacrificed for that purpose in less than ten seconds. No doubt such fish could inflict painful bites, but according the **National Geographic Society**, the dangers of the little fish have been greatly exaggerated. That may be but, most North American film goers probably believe the Hollywood projection. The silver screen enlarged the size and potential danger of all the unfamiliar animals in the Amazon. When Teddy Roosevelt's exploits there were brought to the motion picture theaters [784], an adventure that almost cost the robust old gentleman his life, few remained unconvinced that the Amazon was not filled with deadly creatures and danger at every turn.

Historical truth and accuracy were never Hollywood's long suit. No producer every really thought that it should be, audiences wanted to be entertained not educated. No one ever went to the Pastime or the Rialto for a history lesson. Exciting images and fantasy were always more profitable. History was always rearranged on the big screen to suit the times and situation. Historical events were presented according to a director's own interpretation and in that context the industry was also making history by helping to create images that have endured to this day.

In a tangible sense motion pictures from the first projections opened new worlds to countless individuals who would never have had the opportunity to travel more than a few miles from their home town theaters. Until the two settled into their own individual formats, the first travelogues and newsreels were essentially the same. The first still pictures of large scale military action were taken in the Crimea. The Civil War provided that opportunity for the United States. The first such conflicts recorded on motion picture film took place in Cuba and the Philippines during the Spanish American War era. These moving images were in reality the first newsreels, a new source of mass media which along with the press helped promote the patriotism of the aspiring imperialist and the motion picture industry itself. The creators of the industry, Edison, Vitagraph, Biograph/Mutoscope and Lubin took quick advantage of the opportunity that the sinking of the **Maine** in Havana harbor provided them. As "war fever" spread like wildfire throughout the nation, these innovative producers provided the viewing public with some real, but for the most part, fabricated (in New York and New Jersey) flickering images of the ill fated and other battle ships, military camps, troop movements and related war scenes. Sigmund Lubin, who would later focus on the Mexico and its revolutionary turmoil [101], was quick to realize how well war and the flickers complemented, and promoted one another. He actually staged and reenacted Cuban battle scenes which when shown caused near delirious patriotic pandemonium among viewing audiences: **The Capture of a Spanish Fort Near Santiago**, **The Battle of Guantanamo**, **Hoisting The American Flag at Cavite**, along with Vitagraph's **The Battle of Manila Bay**, constructed with cardboard mockups and exploding gunpowder, were all fabricated recreations, but they worked. In a very real sense the Spanish American War established the embroyonic motion picture industry as a new source of media dessimination, but more importantly as affordable entertainment for the masses and the visual promoter of stereotypes.

As the excitement of defeating Spain passed, it was soon replaced by the public's exuberance over the building of the Panama Canal. Audiences everywhere were thrilled with motion pictures that proved the engineering superiority of their nation [72]. In these early films the newsreels became a mixture of documentary and travelogue, a visual record of the momentous happenings on the Isthmus. The Edison Company could be credited with having developed the travelogue more than a decade before 1910, but in that year they took their cameras and audiences for a breathtaking trip on Peru's Central Railroad from the frozen top of an Andean peak to the steaming Amazon jungle below [87], a journey few who could afford the price of admission might even dream of taking. For the great majority of the population until travel outside of the country fell to affordable prices Hollywood was a teacher providing countless individuals with moving pictures of Mexico, Central America, the Caribbean and South America that most would never have been able to see. For historians the recording of news events south of the border, selective as they might have been, was of obvious value. Many of the early documentaries captured now non-existent folk ways, practices, customs and industries that would exist today only in print [106].

All of this went into the creation of the Hispanic Image. An image that from the first has essentially remained the same, more threatening at times than at others and almost always negative. Although the harsher imagery had certainly mellowed by the end of the silents, recent decades have revived some of its more brutal images. It is difficult to discount the gratuitous savagery portrayed in film like **Scarface**. Colombian, Cuban and Jamacian drug dealers [543] are blamed for the insidious traffic that would stop immediately if the Anglo population stopped demanding drugs. It is more profitable for film makers to focus on Latin suppliers, they have become an accepted part of the national consciousness.

The requirement of finding acceptable justifications for interventions in Central American Republics, the use of United States military force against the Colombian cartels on their native soil, even the non-recognition of the present Cuban government, all promote the need for an identifiable enemy, a function which Hispanics have fulfilled since the first projections. The preoccupation with the border and illegals who supposedly steal the jobs few Anglos would want, has made an easily identifiable economic enemy of those seeking the opportunity for a better life in the land where one learns from films that such things are possible. World Communism may be disappearing, but it's presence is still vocal some ninety miles from Florida. Any positive projections of what is commonly considered to be the last bastion of Communistic totalitarianism will probably come from the Turner Broadcasting Network, not from Hollywood which has traditionally followed State Department orientations.

In conclusion, this volume has focused on the Hispanic image as it was created by film in the silent era and became an important part of the film industry's first projected stereotypes. Subsequent volumes will bring the study to the present. Although Hispanic characterizations experienced significant transformations in the silent era, losing some of the harsher imagery, most travelled into talking pictures in easily recognizable form ready to enjoy the embellishment of sound technology. In the thirties film Hispanics could still be identified by their generally minatorial appearance and conduct. When Hispanics were allowed to speak, few could do so without making North American audiences laugh or smile, secure in feeling that anyone with such an impediment had to be inferior. Few Anglo's ever empathized or, reversed the situation and pictured themselves in Latin lands trying to speak Spanish. Many travelers today are still insulted, even outraged that the Mexicans in Mexico cannot speak English.

Two factors working in conjunction would by the end of the thirties result in the first conscious effort to bring about and enforce a significant change in the silver screen's Hispanic image, the Production Code and the problems and priorities created by World War II. The newly designed Mexican Bandit made his transition into talking pictures **In Old Arizona** [1338] with Warner Baxter earning the Academy's highest honor as best actor because of his "realistic" characterization of the good badman bandit. His broken English and good heart made him less menacing to most and his amorous ways, made him much more appealing to the ladies. No matter how offensive the original might have been, the Mexican bandit was too good a character to eliminate. Providing him with a touch of Spanish California's avenging spirit and keeping him just inside the law was a creative solution that proved enormously profitable for movie makers, but essentially the stereotype remained unchanged.

From earliest times Hollywood believed its own imagery. What the producers knew they projected, what they projected, no matter how bizarre, was part of the national consciousness they helped to create and solidify in the public's mind. Trapped within their own productions, they were prisoners of their own type casting. Breaking out of that comfortable, usable and profitable mold, which had served the silver screen so well for so long, was difficult and required the services of a properly motivated Production Code Administration and an external threat, the fear of lost profits and allies.

From the first days, motion picture making was essentially a capitalist endeavor. Profit was and continues to be a powerful motive, the driving force. For more than thirty years after its creation the PCA convinced Hollywood producers that it was profitable to project more positive Hispanic images. In the thirties, Joe Breen was responsible for removing the harshest of the negative imagery from the industry's films. With the coming of the war and the creation, of the Motion Picture Society for the Americas, a new image, certainly a more positive one, was consciously produced for Hollywood's Hispanics. When the crisis passed and the PCA lost most of its censorial powers in the late fifties, the harsher images returned. Producers turned to violence to increase attendance and many remembered just how violent the Mexican image could be made to be. Films like **The Wild Bunch**, little more than a bloody slaughter of symphonic savagery, and the Spaghetti westerns gave new meaning to negative Hispanic stereotyping. The silent era set the stage but, the main characters were always waiting in the wings. With the problems created by drug traffickers, illegal aliens, Cuba and the growing Hispanic population itself, many screen Hispanics have reappeared more threatening and sinister than those of the silent era. Producers have always played on popular fears. Colombian cocaine kings and Latin terrorists of varying ideologies have become the new enemy. With the dynamic growth of the Hispanic population in the United States, soon to be the largest of all minority groups, this will change. When it becomes profitable for the industry to project a more positive Hispanic image, it will.

List of Abbreviations

afic:	American Film Institute Catalogue
COS:	Cosmopolitan [Hearst]
DEA:	Drug Enforcement Administration
EXH:	Exhibitors Herald
FBO:	Film Booking Office [of America]
FD:	Film Daily
FN:	First National
FNP:	First National Paramount
FP:	Famous Players
FP/L:	Famous Players Lasky
Indy:	Independent Production
HUAC:	House UnAmerican Activities Committee
LCFL:	Lincoln Center Film Library
MPPDA:	Motion Picture Producers and Distributors of America
MPG:	Motion Picture Guild
MPH:	Motion Picture Herald
MPW:	Moving Picture World
NYSAA:	New York State Archives, Albany
NYT:	New York Times
PDC:	Producers Distrubtors Corporation
UFA:	Deutsche Universum-Film AG, Germany
V:	Variety

THE HISPANIC IMAGE ON THE SILVER SCREEN

Primitive Times
1898–1906

The first movies were essentially a series of still pictures in motion many of which focused on the most mundane scenes, the novelty of movement was more than enough to provoke interest. Among the earliest of the brief clips made out west were two in 1898 of the Pueblo Indians when much of North America used the term "indian" and "Mexican" interchangeably: **EAGLE DANCE, PUEBLO INDIANS** [1] and **WAND DANCE, PUEBLO INDIANS** [2]. In that same year the Edison company crossed over from Arizona and shot a few hundred feet of **MEXICAN FISHING SCENE** [3] at an unidentified location. In their continued journey through the Southwest, the Edison crew also produced the **MEXICAN RURALES CHARGE** [4] **MEXICO STREET SCENE** [5], and the **TRAIN HOUR IN DURANGO MEXICO** [6]. These represent the first motion pictures produced by a North American production company of Mexico itself for exhibition. The most complete list of such films taken throughout the Southwest can be found in Howard Lamarr Wall, **Motion Pictures, 1894-1912**, [Identified from the Records of the United States Copyright Office], Library of Congress, 1953. Relying extensively on this earlier work, Kemp R. Niver, compiled, **Motion Pictures From the Library of Congress Paper Print Collection, 1894-1912**, University of California Press, 1967, which includes some descriptions.

Quick to react to world events, the Spanish American War provided the first opportunity to show this nations armed forces in their first motion picture action. The George Eastman House in Rochester, New York and the National Archives in Washington have a number of these priceless clips. As the war extended itself to the Spanish held Philippines, so did the movies. The "how we won the war" theme was one of the earliest to be employed. Two brief clips from 1899 include the **FILIPINOS RETREAT FROM TRENCHES** [7], and the **CAPTURE OF TRENCHES AT CANABA** [8]. With the fighting still raging between the Filipinos who thought that the United States would leave immediately after the defeat of the Spanish and the North American marines who could not understand why the locals were so ungrateful, there was still time shoot what remains to this day the most immediate of Hollywood identifiers telling audiences that they are viewing Hispanic Culture: In 1902 the American Mutoscope and Biograph company produced two hundred feet of **A FILIPINO COCK FIGHT** [9] and in Mexico, Edison shot the **GREAT BULL FIGHT** [10], which serves to identify to audiences that nation, more quickly than any other motif. In 1904, having convinced some of the natives that the United States was there to stay for a while, Mutoscope filmed some happy **FILIPINO SCOUTS** [11] in their **MUSICAL DRILL** [12], which became a feature attraction at the Louisiana Purchase Exposition, the world's fair held that year.

Although these certainly may be considered among the earliest of documentaries involving Hispanics, the essential characteristic of today's film, story telling, the scenario, was not yet present. **A GYPSY DUEL** [13], produced by the American Mutoscope and Biograph company in 1904, represents what might be considered the earliest shadow of a Hispanic scenario, one that remained to this day a most enduring stereotype: Hot blooded, amorous Hispanics, [Spanish gypsies] fighting to the possible death for the affection of a sweet señorita.

A significant step forward was taken with the filming in 1906 by the Edison company of **THE LIFE OF AN AMERICAN COWBOY** [14] which can be viewed at the Rochester collection. Although this film possesses no clear narrative pattern, the various tableaux-like scenes, arranged as they are, tell a story, one that could not easily be mistaken by viewers. The stereotypical characters are all there and the irony should not be lost that film was not shot anywhere in the Southwest, but in Edison's own studio in the North East: The foppish tenderfoot, the good and bad indians, the Anglo heros and the villainous Mexican were all present in this primitive production. The first scene tried to show that a not so nice Mexican, identified by sombrero and mustache and his boorish manner, was trying to force an older indian squaw to take a drink of some kind of redeye. Everyone back east knew just how crazy those indians became with a little liquor to warm their whatever, Ned Buntline had long since established the stereotypes in his dime novels. But a younger indian girl with the help of an Anglo cowboy hero, prevents the Mexican from having his way. Angered, the Mexican is then shown lurking in a menacing manner just outside the Big Horn Cafe waiting for his chance. That comes when the stagecoach takes off with the helpless heroine inside. He is then shown leading some bad indians in pursuit of the stage and actually taking the innocent little lady captive, no doubt for evil purpose. Help is sent for and comes in the form of galloping horsemen, not calvary quite yet, but the very cowboys that had saved the old squaw. They effect the rescue and in the last tableaux, the good guy and his probable reward are seen sitting beneath a tree in a secluded place. Just then the Mexican is shown emerging from behind a rock raising his gun to shoot the pair, but is prevented from doing so by the faithful indian who shoots him, much to the relief and reassurance of the viewers. All the essentials were there and for some time, would continue to be duplicated in numerous Atlantic coast studios. Although most citizens of the north east might never have seen a real Mexican, many had done a lot of reading. Having those scenarios transferred to film merely made established belief more life like.

The first real scenarios began in 1907.

Feature Film Lists

1907

[15] **DRAMA IN A SPANISH INN**, Gaumont: [A sinister looking inn keeper who has been mistreating his wife has his attention shifted to the bulging pockets of a rich guest when he openly displays his wealth. Later, as the brut is in the process of robbing the sleeping man, his wife pleads with him not to do the evil deed. But greedy desire is too strong and he strikes his victim unconscious and steals all his dineros. In the meanwhile, his wife had ridden madly for the policia who apprehend him with the money in his pockets. Rewarded by the writer for honesty and with her oppressor in jail, the abused spouse was now free to live life without fear.] **MPW**:7.20.07, p314.

[16] **THE EASTERNER**, Vitagraph: [Although much more common at a later time, the Mexican will frequently be used simply to provide local color, or to identify the region as the Southwest or near the international border. In this film which featured two timeless struggles, one between east and west and another between man's machines and the ole faithful horse, a race was planned to prove which would triumph as the competitors representing each section of the nation sped to the Atlantic coast on their prospective mounts. The film opened in a western town filled with activity, excitement and awe struck Indians and Mexicans. Although the noise of the backfiring auto scares them, the cowboys remain calm, but look on with disgust at the apparently frightened aborigines. Neither the Indians nor the Mexicans have any part in the development of the narrative, they merely establish the location and provide what will soon be referred to as comedy relief. Screen scenarios would soon establish that only the whites or Anglos could stand in very teeth and jaws of death and appear unperturbed, but dem Mexicans and dem blacks, and ingians were sure alota fun to watch git scared as rabbits over the slightest thing.] **Theatre Magazine**, April 1908. LCFL: Robinson Locke Collection of Dramatic Scrapbooks.

[17] **GYPSY'S REVENGE**, Lubin: [Although gypsy's could be found throughout the world, most of those which would make an appearance on the silver screen would be Spanish. Aside from their hot temper and their inclination to make love at almost any time, two other characteristics would be attributed to their screen persona, an inclination toward thievery, including that of children and, if wronged, an absolute necessity that vengeance be achieved no matter the cost.]

[18] **GYPSY'S REVENGE**, Vitagraph: [No information found.]

[19] **LOST MINE**, Kalem: [So far as this research is concerned, this is the first film scenario in which the term "greaser" is used in the title cards. The story begins with an opening shot identifying a bunch of "greasers" playing dice in front of a western saloon, they are easily seen to be Mexicans, with

dark complexions, sombreros, moustaches, and flashing teeth. Two of them have knives. Quickly a sheriff disperses the sleazy gamblers and the scene shifts to the saloon, where the owner and his Mexican henchman are plotting. What has apparently occurred is that the sheriff has saved from death the owner of a rich mine. Although the injured man has papers to prove it, he is hurt and cannot defend his claim. This means nothing to the greaser and the owner of the bar, they are only interested in acquiring the rights to the mine and try to steal the papers from the disabled fellow's sweetheart, first by threatened eviction and then by more forceful means. In the end the Anglo sheriff and the girl triumph over the two crooks who are driven from the town.] **MPW**:11.16.07.

[20] **PANAMA CANAL**, Edison: [The Edison company made this contribution to the nations always eager desire to watch how their "All American Canal" at Panama was progressing: The scenes of a "thoroughly up-to-date American Fire Department" in Colon were certainly fuel for the fires of nationalistic pride. Five other scenes, including the great steam shovel in operation, were visual testimony of North American engineering superiority.] **MPW**:6.1.07, p203.

[21] **THE PONY EXPRESS**, Kalem: [From these earliest times, when the "flickers" were making the transition from merely showing interesting scenes depicting far away places or some new technological marvel, as scripters developed scenarios and plots, the "Greaser" became the primary foil for the Anglo hero. The formula established during these formative years was rarely changed: As in this tale, a Mexican, a "Greaser" would make his advances to the Anglo woman, be rejected and swear revenge against her and her Anglo lover. At some point she or he or they would be captured, but not violated and in the final reel, the Greaser would be killed or punished.] **MPW**:6.8.07, p237.

1908

[22] **THE BANDIT'S WATERLOO**, Biograph: [Characterized from the start as the tale of "the Outwitting of an Andalusian Brigand by a Pretty Señora" the opening lines of this film's review read like some news articles of not so long ago warning prospective visitors heading for Hispanic lands to take the proper precautions. "The hills of Southern Spain were infested by gangs of lawless freebooters who terrorized the country and made travel in the mountains a hazardous pastime. They waylaid, robbed and often murdered the unwary tourist who chanced their way." In the late seventies, newspapers, both national and local were so filled with such stories, that tourism heading across the border seriously declined. So much so that John Gavin, actor appointed Ambassador to Mexico, was forced to make public statements emphasizing that travel to his native homeland was quite safe. Apparently it was not so in Andalusia at this point in time. There a party of "bushrangers" were shown waiting behind a big rock for an approaching "laundau" which contained an old señor, a duenna and a pretty señorita. The "inevitable" happens, the bandit chief takes all the valuables and keeps the pretty lady. She realizes that he is attracted to her and determines to use her "woman's wiles" to capture the bandit herself. Because he is a Spaniard and very susceptible to such things, her beauty easily twists the chieftain into little knots and he is about to give back the jewels when the local police sergeant shows up. From these earliest days, Hispanic police were characterized as crooked and he accepts the jewels in payment for letting the bandits go free. Undeterred, the lady still wants her jewels and when all have retired to a local hostel, she cajoles the bandit into stealing them back again. She then entices the lustful idiot up to a room where she gets him drunk and finally makes her escape with all the loot in hand. In just under nine minutes this little scenario managed to touch upon several of the stereotypes that continue to be the constantly portrayed screen persona of the Hispanic character.] **MPW**:8.8.08, p108.

[23] **COCOA INDUSTRY, TRINIDAD, BRITISH WEST INDIES**, Edison: [As the reviewer of this film explained, the motion picture now allowed almost all to travel to distant lands, that before its invention, "only the very few were privileged to visit." Included in this picturesque travelogue of the lower Caribbean islands, is a "snake charmer and his lovely daughter", and of course, the natives enjoying "carnival."] **MPW**:12.12.08, p84.

[24] **THE COWBOY'S BABY**, Selig: [This "grim reminder of pioneer days" managed to take a decent swipe at slurring three of the screens most favorite ethnic targets in just under a thousand feet of film, approximately ten minutes running time. The opening scene featured what was considered by this film's describer, to be "the most accurately staged presentation of an Indian massacre ever used in motion pictures." A hundred

"real Sioux warriors" were hired for the purpose "swooping down" "on spirited horses" to slaughter the "doomed pioneers" who fought valiantly, but being outnumbered, were all "annihilated." All but one that is. A small baby survived. He was discovered after a small band of courageous cowboys drove the filthy heathens from the remains of the wagon train they were then looting. After having given all a "Christian burial" one of the cowboys, "Joe Dayton by name" discovered the baby. His version of one helpless man and a baby made him realize that he needed the assistance of Mable Deering, who had long ago won the soft heart of the tough hero. She had refused him twice before while considering the offer made by the "prosperous Mexican cattle king," but he determined to try again. This time the baby turns the trick and the two are married, but the "greaser swears revenge" and shortly after the ceremony, while the portrayed as inept, Sing Low, Joe's Chinese servant, is watching the baby not so well, the Mexican and his mean mates, steal the child. Pursued immediately by an organized group of sincere cowboy friends of the family, "even Sing Low mounted a burro", the dirty greasers, who cannot stop the baby from crying, actually throw little Joe into a raging river and try to escape. Yet, "grace and honor" survive. The child is rescued and the Mexicans, as well as the audience, enjoyed the benefits of "swift Western justice." Sing Low was "roundly cursed for his carelessness" and vowed never to leave the cowboy's baby alone again. All the malevolent forces afflicting the Anglo west had been subdued before sundown.] **MPW**:8.8.08, p110.

[25] **THE DREYFUS AFFAIR**, [Slightly more than a decade after the tragic events which sent Dreyfus to Devil's Island, the affair became the subject for this brief one reeler. Moved, the reviewer explained that it was a "pathetic sight indeed" to see the wrongly accused soldier begin his life on what would become the silver screens most popularly projected prison. [See: 1057, 1172]] **MPW**:7.4.08, p11.

[26] **THE FIGHT FOR FREEDOM : A STORY OF THE SOUTHWEST**, Biograph: [In the years immediately preceding the Mexican Revolution, Biograph would be responsible for several one reelers which portrayed Mexicans in a sympathetic light. This story involves Pedro who shoots and kills an Anglo cowboy that had cheated him during a card game. He is also responsible for killing the sheriff who pursues him, but when the town accuses the lawman's wife of the crime, Pedro breaks her out of jail and together they make their escape. Pedro's affection for the Anglo lady are soon more than they should be, and when she is killed in an ambush designed to bring him in, his heart is broken. Remorseful he gives himself up to the authorities for sure death. Throughout the brief production, a sympathetic cast is provided to justify the Mexican's actions to the audience. This was quite uncommon in the one week productions and not the case in more than ninety-eight percent of them.] **MPW**:7.18.08, p49.

[27] **THE GREASER'S GAUNTLET**, Biograph: [Basically a moralistic play whose message was that a mother's prayer and love would

overcome all of the problems her son might face as he crossed the border to make his fortune in the land of the gringos. Jose, "the greaser," soon put mom's praying power to the test. In rapid succession he is falsely accused of a theft which a "chinaman" was really responsible for, is saved from lynching by Mildred, and in turn saves Mildred from a fate worse than death. Realizing he had no chance with the lovely lady, he finally saw the light which led him back to the Sierras where he belonged and finds the madre still on her knees praying.] **MPW**:9.19.08, p221.

[28] **A GYPSY'S REVENGE**, Pathe: [The Deity may very well claim that vengeance is its province, but Hollywood's Hispanic woman frequently had it out on loan. In the hands of a Spanish gypsy, it was usually deadly. In this story a Carmen-like gypsy girl seeks revenge against a father's son who had merely toyed with her. Dressed alluringly, her cigarette smoking by the garden gate completely captivates the young man. Now intent on keeping her, he refuses his fathers request that he should scorn the seductress which provokes a struggle and causes the parent's death. Having watched the fight with some satisfaction, the vamp informs the police of the killing. When the youth is apprehended by the authorities, he tries to choke his betrayer, but is prevented from doing so. As he is dragged away cursing her, she is seen "puffing coolly at her cigarette," her revenge complete. From earliest days, it was very dangerous to fool with a Hispanic temptress.] **MPW**: 2.1.08, pp82-3.

[29] **GYPSY'S WARNING**, Vitagraph: [No further information.]

[30] **IN GOLDEN DAYS**, Essanay: [This was the first of more than fifty features which would portray the trials and tribulations of trekking to the California gold fields in 1849. Once there the adventurers discover only that their problems have just begun.] **MPW**:12.29.08, p531.

[31] **'A LOVE TRAGEDY IN SPAIN**, Melies: ["A thrilling episode in the style of Bizet's "Carmen."" A Spanish smuggler, an old brigand, falls for a local "danseuse" who already had attracted the affection of a younger other. The two amourers struggle resulting in the death of the youth which causes the lady to reject the survivor. True to his Hispanic nature he is consumed by passion and "heroically stabs himself." Horrified, the heroine is left with blood stained hands and no one to hold them.] **MPW**:10.30.08, p345.

[32] **A MEXICAN LOVE STORY**, Vitagraph: [A married Mexican woman is aroused watching a young man making love to his sweetheart. The youth, upon seeing her immediately falls in love and invents various intrigues so that they can be together. They enjoy each others embraces for a while, but in the end, her husband throws down the gauntlet by flinging a glass full of whiskey in the younger mans face and regains his honor by killing him in a duel.] **MPW**: 4.4.08, p299.

[33] **RACE PREJUDICE**, Pathe: [The reason for the title evades this reporter. This is simply one more story of gypsy vengeance with slight variation. In this one the Spanish gypsy beauty kills her compatriot for a young peasant she has fallen in love with. There appears to be no punishment for this exercise in passion.] **MPW**:11.21.08, p409.

[34] **THE RED GIRL**, Biograph: [This little production was considered to be "Another soul stirring story of life on the frontier." The "great success" of Biograph's **Greaser's Gauntlet** [27] encouraged this firm to produce another involved tale of Mexican treachery. Showing no preference for gender and to indicate that neither male nor female from south of the border could be trusted, the producers made the primary villain in this piece a female. She is first seen smoking and playing cards with sleazy looking señors and other negative types. After she loses all of her pesos at the faro tables, she steals the Anglo heroines gold and escapes. On the run she happens to encounters a Mexican halfbreed who she successfully vamps away from his indian woman. Apparently because of their nature, it is not enough for the two to simply runaway together, they decide to torture the unfortunate indian girl before they leave. In the final reel the Anglo heroine and indian woman catch up with the despicable pair, regain the gold and arrest the Mexican Jezebel." Although the halfbreed is repentant, the red girl scorns him and sends him on his way.] **MPW**:9.19.08, p211.

[35] **A SPANISH ROMANCE**, Manhattan/Vitagraph: [In these very earliest of film scenarios, it was established from the very first that whenever an Anglo and Hispanic were rivals for the affection of the darkskinned señorita, the former would prevail. It remained a rule adhered to from 1908 to present times. Kevin Kosner had little trouble taking Anthony Quinn's woman/wife from him in the 1990 production of **Vengeance**, even if she had to die for sharing herself with him, that possibility had frequently been the writer's choice from the very first. This early film was not as harsh as many would be later and it develops a scenario not frequently deviated from. An Englishman clandestinely woos a lovely Spanish girl away from her protective father who wants to save her for one of the local rich. To insure the success of their escape, the screen writer provided a clergyman on the getaway boat to insure the conquest would not be challenged.] **V**:10.17.08, **MPW**:10.17.08, p307.

[36] **THE VAQUERO'S VOW**, Biograph: [The fickled and faithless nature of female affection knew no nationality to Hollywood scripters, but it was especially true of some Hispanic women. Selfsacrifice or selflessness, were only to be used for purpose. But from these early beginnings, the screen writers had the advantage of providing the punishment for such callousness. Here, a poor, young Mexican vaquero offered his love to the beautiful Manuella, but could provide nothing else. Though touched, she preferred a flashy musician, the idle/idol of all the local ladies. Attracted by the glamour of the adulation, she marries the musical lover only to

discover that once wed the problems were legion. Because the father had failed to provide the dowry the selfish suitor expected, he quickly became dissatisfied with her affection and turned to drink, debauchery and brutalized the hapless wife. In the end she was saved from death by the rejected Renaldo.] **MPW**: **10.17.08, p304.**

[37] **A YANKEE MAN O' WARSMAN FIGHTS FOR LOVE**, Edison: [This scenario was supposedly taken from a recent Pacific cruise of the **America** while docked in a Spanish-American port. There, a castanet clicking Spanish dancing beauty attracted the attention of our young Anglo hero. Local animosity for the "Yankees" led to an organized fight which the lad eventually won because the lady prevented his being drugged by the home boys who required other than fair play to compete with Anglo opposition.] **MPW:2.1.08, p82.**

1909

[38] **ACROSS THE ISTHMUS**, Selig: [This feature claimed to be the first moving picture of actual work on the canal shown in the public houses. Edison's work predated this by two years. Regardless, many of its clips have subsequently been used for later documentaries, including Public Television's superior, **The Panama Canal**. Nothing in the period between 1904 and 1914 so captured North America's fascination with its own coming of age than this project [225]. The North American love affair with this great engineering project is detailed in A. Richard, **Panama Canal in American National Consciousness**, Garland: 1990.] **MPW**:11.20.09, p720, **V**:11.20.09.

[39] **BEYOND THE ROCKIES**, Centaur: [Two sisters have money stolen from their home by Anglo and "Mexican renegade[s]." Later one sister is abducted by same and their gang of dirty cutthroats, and worse, she was taken across the border. But in the final reel the Anglo's triumph, Favetta and her hero, save the sister from that fate worse than you know what [1559].] **MPW**:12.18.09, pp894-5.

[40] **THE BRAZILIAN RING**, Pathe: [Spinoffs and copycat productions came early the silver screen, this film was merely a variation of the **Mexican's Gratitude** [54], set in the jungles of Brazil. A ring is used as the identifier in place of a torn card. A grateful indian saved from the noose by a sympathetic missionary, offers his savior his most prized possession, a ring in thanks for the service. Freed, he returns to his "band of cutthroats" and with their help revenges himself on his former captors by kidnapping a young town girl. Although the ransom he receives is considered to be insufficient, he discovers the that the ring he had given in gratitude was part of the package sent to retrieve the girl. Recognizing the symbol of his former salvation, the scribe provided the grateful jungle savage with the compassion to return not only the girl, but also the ransom. Script writers would rarely provide screen indians with such humanity, not until the mid 1960's would indians even cease to be savages on a regular basis.] **MPW**:2.13.09.

[41] **CONCHITA, THE SPANISH BELLE**, Urban-Eclipse: [Conchita is loved by one brother, while she herself loves the other who is an "espada" [literally, he who kills the bulls.] He refuses her but is forced by her viciousness to fight his brother in a duel. Repentant, in the last reel she tells of her treachery and the brothers reunite. Commenting on the film one of the exhibitors explained: "Such occasions were undoubtedly common enough, but are not pleasant subjects for motion pictures."] **MPW**:7.10.09, p63, 7.24.09, p125.

[42] **THE CONSPIRATORS**, Kalem: ["Intrigue, treachery", "revolution, death, and marital infidelity," surrounds the President of "Domencio", a South American republic, "where a

revolution takes place every minute." Political instability in the Latin republics was always assumed as were the other major themes of this film. For the audience in 1909, one of the reviewer felt that the "realism" portrayed in this film "was almost too strong in places." especially, because at this time such, portrayals "were reinforced by reality."] **V**:9.11.09, **MPW**: p9.11.09, p289, p346.

[43] <u>DON JUAN: OR A WAR DRAMA OF THE 18TH CENTURY</u>, Film Import and Trading Company: [The critic for this production thought it "strong of action [and] faithful in its interpretation of horrifying and thrilling episodes of an invading army." This enthusiasm speaks more for the novelty of the medium than anything else, the effort ran under nine minutes and also indicates the significant impact film productions exerted on audiences from the first. Don Juan was portrayed as the "typical Don Juan of literature" who could always find time "amidst the trials and tribulations of warfare to loosen the leashes of his heart and pay court to the lassies of the country side." All of this amorous activity seems to make him a bit crazy for the critic, but still nice: "Despite the apparent uncertainties of mind ... our hero ... proves the courage and virtue of a mind capable of love in defense of a woman in a land that lay under the siege of the enemy's guns." As time progressed, the writers would make Sevilla's warm blooded wooer much more of a lover than a warrior.] **MPW**:6.12.09, p811.

[44] <u>DON QUIXOTE</u>, Gaumont: [The search for script material was already well under way in these early days of film making. From the very start screen writers sought help from a wide array of sources, personal experience, fantasy, the daily news and even each other's films. When it finally occurred to some bright scribe that the classics might offer a little assistance, some of the others may well have changed their reading habits. Classic literature soon became a major source for screen scenarios. In the Hispanic context <u>**CARMEN**</u>, <u>**DON JUAN**</u> and <u>**DON QUIXOTE**</u> would prove to be the most frequently adapted, in one form or another, of all the classics [646, 975, 79, 337, 1277, 1343]. Individually, each will make an appearance on the silver screen in first years of primitive film making. Not a decade would pass, from then till present times, without their being used either directly or in some adaptive variation. Excluding only slightly the man from La Mancha, each new presentation would become somewhat more salacious as Hollywood scripters ever increased the hot blooded passion they ascribed their main character. In this 1909 version of the Cervantes tale, the emphasis was burlesque, which illustrated for those who wished to see them "many pictures of Spanish life" and many "promiscuous adventures."] **V**:11.6.09, **MPW**:11.06.09, p655.

[45] <u>THE EAVESDROPPER</u>, Biograph: [Sympathetic Hispanic characterizations were uncommon in this era, but not unknown, as some may claim. Although the producers of this movie had some problems with gender in naming this film's protagonist, Manuella, he was in the final scene moved, when he overhears

how selfsacrificing the two young lovers were. She was to have married him to save her padre's ranchero and was explaining this to her true love. Parental need had to be satisfied before personal desire. Moved by such feeling the older but richer suitor releases the daughter from her bond, joins the lovers hands together and leaves with them the promissory note the old Spanish Hidalgo had sought to swap his daughter for.] **MPW**:5.1.09, p562.

[46] **EPISODE OF THE CUBAN REVOLUTION**, Film Import and Trading Company: [Most of the basic scenarios and the characters that would act them out found their way into these very early projections. In the year before **A Spanish Romance** [35], established that on the screen Anglo males would almost always win over the affections of the Hispanic woman when in competition with the local Hispanic swain, this film carried the Anglo scribes fantasy one step further. Not only would the lady go willingly with the North American, she would betray her country and gladly give up her life for a touch of his approval. This little bit was described as: "A vivid drama" set in Cuba "at a time when our boys had gone forth to the defense of their country." What would remain as another continuing characteristic was identified as the reason for this humanitarian behavior on the part of the United States soldiers: The boys went to Cuba because of the "insolent conduct of Spain." For this writer, Spain had sunk the **Maine**. The price for such insolence in this case was the loss of Cuba, yet many silver screen Hispanics would learn no lessons from the incident all preferring to remain impudent and disrespectful for Anglo audiences throughout. The main character in this patriotic little piece was properly named for local approval, Col. Hansomfellow. What that may have lacked in subtlety was confirmed by the unnamed Cuban cutie who he immediately captured with his charm. At the very festive affair where all this took place, she immediately "disclaims all of the vows made to one of her own countrymen" which, one might understand, even if one were from the north, causes the rejected swain to choke the life out of the Cuban señorita, [it might have even given him a few ideas about the ship in the harbor. For the love a woman a colony was lost and reacquired.] **MPW**:6.12.09.

[47] **FIGHTING BOB**, Selig Polyscope: [Once more dad is displeased by his daughters affection for a young North American officer. He had promised her to Don Sancho de Salvatore, a wealthy Mexican. After the obvious complications the climax sees our hero and his dark eyed señorita, "who would follow him into the jaws of death," fleeing onboard his cruiser with the local policia in hot pursuit. In the final scene the lovers were saved by Bob's shipmates, who appear from all corners, throwing the locals into the sea allowing the two to make good their escape. Exhibitors claimed that their audiences were pleased to see how easily a "Yankee lieutenant [could] outwit a whole set of Spaniards." [561]] **MPW**:5.22.09, p727, 5.29.09, p755.

[48] **HIS MEXICAN BRIDE**, Centaur: [Rejected in love back east, Frank heads for Mexico to work for President Alverez of the Conchita Mining Company, who has a lovely daughter, Anita. She falls for Frank immediately, but Alverez wants her to marry Valdez, yet another wealthy Mexican. The latter, angered by her new affections attempts, as all Mexicans with knives would, to stab the Anglo in the back. Once disarmed, Frank merely chooses to "spank" the culprit which still gets him fired. Even so, Anita marries him but soon discovers that his eastern lady love wants him back. Thinking she has been deceived, and true to her Hispanic character, she plans to poison him, but love prevails and prevents him from drinking the fatal cup at the very last moment.] **MPW**:10.16.09, p547.

[49] **IN OLD ARIZONA**, Selig Polyscope: [On her way to a happy Arizona homestead a young woman rejects the advances of a Mexican suitor. Angered he frees ever horse in the Camp's remuda, leaving all present to the mercy of the dread Apache. Never fear, all ends well because of the ever ubiquitous United States Calvary.] **MPW**:1.9.09, p45, 68.

[50] **LOVE UNDER SPANISH SKIES**, Selig: [Complex and involved love and intrigue between aristocrat and peasant set in sunny Spain. Love was allowed to transcend the social barriers imposed by the strictures of social class, at least in this version of Hollywood's Spain.] **MPW**:4.10.09, p455.

[51] **MEXICAN BILL**, Lubin: [Mexican Bill, rejected in love by the Major's daughter, for apparently good reason, has no redeeming qualities. He beats up people, shoots fathers, kills loyal indian scouts, lies and implicates others for the crimes he has committed and is properly "strung up" in the last scene without benefit of trial.] **MPW**:7.17.09, p101.

[52] **A MEXICAN DRAMA**, Lux: [This film had all the "snap and dash" for which Mexicans were famous, and although he thought it entertaining, the reviewer considered it necessary to explain that it's basic theme of marital infidelity, which while it may have been common south of the border, was for the "American" the exception, not the rule." The cuckolded husband was also praised for the "vigor" with which he hunted down the seducer and killed him.] **MPW**:9.18.09, p379.

[53] **MEXICAN'S CRIME**, New York Motion Picture Co: [Alvers is scorned by a dancing señorita. He attempts to stab her suitor and then shoots her. After a fierce chase, an Anglo posse is surrounded by many Mexicans who have come to their compatriot's assistance. In the fight many of them are hurt, but the foul Mexican is brought to the justice he so deserved for his evil intention.] **MPW**:10.30.09, p624.

[54] **A MEXICAN'S GRATITUDE**, Essanay: [It would be another year or so before reviewers named and commented on the performances of the actors in the cast. G. M. Anderson, later to become the Broncho Billy of several hundred one and two reelers, was the star in this film and his performance helped establish Essanay as one of the top production companies of this time.

Essanay travelled to Mexico to make this film and would do so for many others. This production is almost unique for presenting the Mexican/Greaser in a semi sympathetic role. Having been saved from a wrongful lynching, the Mexican writes the word "Gratitude" on a card, rips it in half and gives one piece to the sheriff. In the final reel, after a vengeful cowboy has hired him to do the sheriff dirty, the greaser discovers the card, realizes who the lawman is and in turn, saves his life. [478]] **MPW**:5.1.09, p563, 5.15.09, p636. "Will Make Pictures in Mexico", 9.19.09, p381.

[55] **THE MEXICAN'S REVENGE**, Vitagraph: [Few flickers in these first days of film making could have gone much further to satisfy even the most ardent nationalist secure in the belief that his race was superior to all others. A North American cruiser puts into a liberty port just above the Mexican border where the ever present fiesta is in full swing. Quickly the captain of the cruiser falls for Rosita, "the acknowledged beauty of the town." But her immediate response to his advances fires the jealousy of Don Ramon Molina. He is further incensed when the officer obtains permission to marry the lovely. On their wedding day, the Don captures the captain with the intention to kill him. But because "there is a strain of indian blood in [his] veins, he would first torture" his captive. The spectacular climax sees Rosita on horseback leading a troop of bluejackets to save her true love. She does and all return for the wedding celebration under the protection of Old Glory waving proudly in the wind.] **MPW**:10.23.09, p583.

[56] **MEXICAN SWEETHEARTS**, Biograph: [From the earliest days of film, Latin temperament was characterized and set firmly in celluloid in an unbroken strip that stretched from that time to this: "The experience of Tantalus was never so chafing as a tantalizing sweetheart ... The strength of this phrase is better understood when one realizes the impetuous nature of the Latin type of person." To tease her sweetheart, a pretty señorita pretends to love an American soldier, which almost gets him killed because of her lover's hot blooded temper. As the smiling señorita watches the outcome of her endeavor, her enraged swain chases the boy with a knife. He manages to escape "without scars," but has learned a valuable lesson. The commentator felt that this little strip of film displayed "one of the most beautiful pieces of high class acting ever attempted by the leading character being played by a native Spaniard." It was 300 ft long, approximately three minutes of running time.] **MPW**:6.19.09, p842.

[57] **THE OCTOROON**, Kalem: [A description of life in the turpentine forests of the south, this film focuses on one of the distilling plants whose owner is of "Spanish decent". He is to all "a cruel, vindictive brute of little principle" who lusts for the beautiful octoroon. Rejected, he attempts to wreak vengeance on everyone in the cast, including her lover, until the latter kills him in a "unique duel."] **MPW**:1.23.09, p102.

[58] **ON THE BORDER**, Selig: [From the very earliest of times, the "border" came to be associated with all forms of violence. It was a zone in which anything could, and would take place, a place free from the responsibilities and restrictions of North American law, and more influenced by the lawlessness of the Mexican's love for individualized, frequently anti-social and even criminal activity, than civilized behavior. Here it was understood by actors and audiences alike that men must take the law into their own hands and adapt it to the particular situation various problems required. This early one reeler shows how the "Vigilance Committee" secures the Mexican border, and frees the town from the baddies. More significantly, it was probably the first production to present Mexico as the refuge for those hardened criminal types of any nationality or breed that required a place to hide out for a while until things cooled off. This was possible, the reviewer explained because "under the peculiar laws then existing between the United States and Mexico, our officers were not allowed to follow a culprit across the Rio Grande." So, from the very first flickers, one might read a title card which told the boys to "head for the border." [381, 597, 1430]] **V**:11.27.09, **MPW**:11.27.09, p773.

[59] **OUR BANANA SUPPLY**, Warwick: [A significant title for this educational travelogue taken in Costa Rica outlining the various aspects of the banana industry.] **MPW**:5.22.09, p688.

[60] **THE ROAD AGENTS**, Essanay: [Two road agents operating in lower California, one an Englishman, the other a Mexican, quarrel over the spoils of a successful robbery. The Mexican attempts to use his knife to settle the matter, but the Anglo disarms him and escapes with the loot. "Too cowardly to attack his late comrade openly," the Mexican assaults his former partner while he is undressing and mortally wounds him.] **MPW**:3.13.09, p312.

[61] **A ROMANCE IN OLD MADRID**, Edison: [In one simple line the reviewer for this film captured all of the most commonly accepted cliche's which Hollywood used throughout the remainder of the century to characterize Spain. The "Land of Castile has ever breathed" love, romance, music, dance, bull fighters and "dreamy eyed señoritas." In this little piece Paquita dreams, as all Spaniards especially those always taking siestas, of festival day. When it finally arrives she meets Carlos, a handsome toreador, who, without much waiting, woos her "with all the ardor of a Spaniard." After some little intrigue, the two elope and are married. It was that simple in those warm Iberian climes.] **MPW**:1.23.09, P102.

[62] **ROMANCE IN OLD MEXICO**, Vitagraph: [Love's road may never be an easy one travel, but on the early silver screens pictured version of romantic Mexico, it was from the very beginning, filled with snares and deception that more frequently than not could prove fatal to those who did not follow the straight and narrow path. As a young señorita was watering flowers outside her home, a gypsy passed and told her that she would soon quarrel with her lover, a bullfighter of

some repute. She soon does and he retreats to the cantina she
has asked him not to visit. There, the "capricious" chiquita
that provided the entertainment, dances right on his table.
Pleased, he takes her in his arms and kisses her, all of which
is observed by the gypsy who returns to tell his lady. Now
angered the girl decides to make her man jealous and chooses
his best friend to do it with. This drives the hot blooded
swain to be careless in the corrida where he is fatally gored.
The final scene sees him in the arms of the now sorrowful, but
satisfied señorita, pledging eternal fidelity, should he
recover.] **MPW**:6.5.09, p769.

[63] **ROMANCE IN THE ANDES**, Pathe: [Before the end of the first
decade of film making scripters travelled far south to broaden
the material employed in their Hispanic scenarios. In this
romance an Andean indian who had been forced to endure a
"horsewhipping administered" by a rich ranchero for stealing
a goat, retaliates by kidnapping his woman. When a posse is
formed to punish the culprit more severely, rancher and rescue
party are momentarily captured by a fierce indian tribe.
After they escape, the kidnapper is himself killed in the act
of "treacherously trying to shoot" the rancher. One reviewer
considered this a "cleverly portrayed picture representing
life in the Andes Mountains of South America."] **V**:10.30.09,
MPW:11.30.09, p621, 11.6.09, p644.

[64] **THE SEÑORITA**, Selig: [The Dime Novel heros of Ned
Buntline exhibited two characteristics which were romanticized
expressions of Anglo Saxon superiority: No dark skinned woman
could resist any Anglo's charms, which allowed him great
behavioral latitude, including the frequent discarding of such
questionable, if not inferior, affection, and it was
established from the first that any North American could
easily overwhelm an ever increasing number of Hispanic
opponents in physical combat. In such contests, the struggle
might create momentary suspense, but in matters of love, there
was never a question that the Anglo's attraction would
prevail. Frequently, as in **Flying Down to Rio**, [1607], Latin
losers were forced by the nationalistic inclinations of North
American scripters, to appear pleased, even grateful, that the
girl of their dreams had been captured by the superior Anglo.
From the industry's inception these two basic themes were
translated to film and continuously reinforced. In **The
SEÑORITA** an American is saved from the desert by a young
Mexican couple. The favor is repaid by having the Anglo steal
the girl. After being used she is gratuitously returned to
the Mexican suitor, who apparently thanks him for having
shared himself with the lucky little lady. The film ends with
the two Mexican standing in front of their humble home waving
as the gallant lad heads north, possibly pleased with himself
that he might have planted the seeds that would later grow
into a little good will. [1253]] **V**:11.27.09, **MPW**: p657.

[65] **SOUTH AMERICAN INDIANS**, Urban: [Commenting on the
possible educational value of the quickly developing new
industry, the reviewer observed: "The bringing of distant
lands and peoples to our doors is a valuable quality of the

moving-picture." This film claimed to show Argentine indians, in their "homes, at their work, at their play" and "illustrate[d] graphically" their principal characteristics. It may well have, but the Indians of the Argentine pampas were exterminated with a more deliberate efficiency than those of the North American plains, long before the moving picture films ever came into existence.] **MPW**:3.6.09, p280.

[66] **SPANISH ARMY**, Pathe: ["Interesting and educational" at close range, this documentary film purported to "give a good description of life in the Spanish Army." Recruits were shown kneeling in front of an altar in veneration after which they all kissed the Spanish flag.] **MPW**:7.3.09, p27.

[67] **THE SPANISH GIRL**, Phoenix Film: [The continuous reinforcement of vengeance as a central Hispanic characteristic made easily the most identifiable and expected stereotype of the Latin character, at times, more extreme in the female of the species. This 1909 one reeler was offered as, "A familiar tale of female vengeance, the result of faithless love." Carmecia, suffers when a bad man takes her love, steals her jewels, and runs off. Two years later the rake returns and is arrested for shooting up the town. Even back then there was no problem guessing who the sheriff's new wife happened to be. Appearing to plot with her old love, she allows he and his compatriots to leave the jail to commit a robbery, and then tricks them out of all the money. Her vengeance is complete when she warns them never to return because she has the evidence to put them away forever.] **MPW**:7.3.09, p31.

[68] **THE SPANISH GIRL**, Essanay: [Lola, the Spanish fandango dancer, entertains the vaqueros, but desires the ranch foreman who loves the Anglo belle. Enticing Jose, she intrigues with him to destroy Bad Bob's affections for his lady. Having done so, she is still scorned. Worse, Jose beats her for rejecting him. Swearing vengeance, as the scripters required all their offended Hispanics to do, she turns the vaqueros against Jose, who is saved by Bob, now the sheriff. In repayment he tells Bob that his lady had not been unfaithful. Reviewed as a "A lively bit of real life ... on the Circle A Ranch."] **MPW**:12.12.09, p889, 12.31.09, p960.

[69] **SPANISH MARRIAGE**, Pathe: [Marie, a fickled señorita, makes eyes at a handsome Frenchman, while entertaining Pepito, her fiance. This flirtation leads to matrimony, but on her wedding night, she awaits the pouting Pepito, much to her French husband's chagrin. In anger he pushes the two trysters through an open window and then leaves. The reviewer's analysis of these goingson was significant: "The picture is full of local color and gives an idea how lightly these pleasure-loving people look upon the more serious things in life."] **MPW**:12.4.09, p811, 12.11.09, p841.

[70] **A TALE OF TEXAS**, Centaur: ["A bad Mexican, Valdez" has been cheating the other cowboys at poker using six aces. Tom, a good cowboy, kicks the Mexican out of sight which of course

causes the latter to seek vengeance by wanting to "plunge his dagger" in Tom's back. Where else? Instead, he sees an opportunity to steal money and blame Tom, which he does. Pursued, he falls into a river and drowns, but the problems continue for Tom, luckily, only until the last reel, when all is resolved in the Anglo hero's favor.] **MPW:7.3.09**, p31.

[71] **UP SAN JUAN HILL**, Selig: [Two dramatic events signaled North America's coming of age at the start of this century, The Spanish American War and the building of the Panama Canal. In the first the nation used force, in the second, its incredible intellectual potential was displayed for the entire world to witness for more than a decade. Both became subjects for the earliest film features. This one reeler, while showing the heroics of the nation's armed forces, was also the first to romanticize McKinley's famed "Message to Garcia", announcing to the Cuban patriots this nation's entrance on the side of Cuba Libre.] **V**:11.27.09, **MPW**:11.27.09, p773.

[72] **WITH TAFT IN PANAMA**, Manhattan/Selig Polyscope: [The glorification of this nations engineering genius as exercised on the Isthmus became the subject for numerous documentaries. This one was advertised as showing, "Astonishing views of natives working on the Panama Canal." "It is a subject that a wise school teacher would advise her scholars to see."] **V**:3.6.09

[73] **THE YELLOW JACKET MINE**, Selig: [Very complex scenario boils down to one story of a Mexican girl who loses her Anglo lover to one of his own kind. For vengeance she helps his partner cheat the hero out of his share of the mine, recants in the final scene when and where she is made to realize that he is better off with lovely little Carrie Burke.] **MPW**:8.21.09, **p265**.

1910

[74] **AH SING AND THE GREASER** , Lubin: [This film combines the silver screen's two earliest and most enduring Anglo foils, the Mexican and the Chinaman. The ad copy speaks for itself. "A Western story, with much of the true flavor of the plains ... In some way the picture is full of the subtle charm of the elusive spirit of the West and the vigorous life it formerly sustained." "There are plenty of laughs in every scene and a scream at the finish." Enough!] **MPW**:8.6.10, p304, 8.20.10, p406.

[75] **"A BORDER TALE"**, Pathe: [The natural beauty of the yet unspoiled west was evident in this tale which involved a young woman saving a calvary troop from border brigands. Frequently, early screen writers, to prevent the complications of an inter-racial romance that might follow such self sacrificing heroism when a darkskinned lady was involved, required their heroines be repayed tragically by being killed in the action, usually by their own kind.] **V**:11.3.10.

[76] **AN OLD SILVER MINE IN PERU**, Edison: [Basically a early documentary which emphasized the primitive mining techniques still employed by the Indians as they carried heavy sacks of ore from the mine to processing vats. Those in the audience who thought the lands to the south were still in a primitive stage of development, were certainly convinced by this production. "It is like reading a page from the history of the middle ages."] **MPW**:12,31,10, p1546, 12.24.10, p1478.

[77] **BRONCHO BILLY'S REDEMPTION**, Essanay: [No one in 1910 could have thought that this less than twelve minute one realer would be readapted and remade five more times culminating in John Ford's the **Three Godfathers**, and so far as this researcher is concerned, would provide at least the germinal inspiration for the most successful, **Three Men and a Baby**. In this piece, Broncho Billy plays the prototypical good badman, he rustles cattle, is a "black night of the road", and commits countless other western crimes. But being an Anglo, he still has friends. One of these warns him that a "Vigilance Committee" is after him, so he heads out to the badlands where he discovers an abandoned "prairie schooner." Inside the covered wagon are two occupants, one a child and both very ill. Only medicine will save the day and that must be purchased in town where Billy is a wanted man. Disregarding his own safety, he resolves to get the medicine, but comes across a Mexican who offers to perform the service for him. With his eyes "gleaming" the Mex takes the money and promises that he will bring the required medicine. But Billy turns in time to see the dishonorable wretch tear up the prescription and pocket the money. Discovering this, Broncho curses the "thieving Mexican" and regains his honor by saving the two from dying himself.] **MPW**:7.30.10, p259.

[78] **A BULL FIGHT IN MEXICO**, Pathe: [A popular subject for film from the earliest days, the drama the corrida would continue through the decade of the 80's to be a central theme for scores of both tragedies and comedies. Few film images more quickly identify Mexico, Spain or the Hispanic view that man must use dynamic action in his struggle against the forces of fate. This early Pathe entry may have been filmed in Mexico, but concluded "where the real meat of the picture should commence." This seemingly cryptic criticism merely indicated that the actual killing of the bull was not shown to North American audiences.] **MPW**:3.26.10, p483, **V**:3.26.09.

The question of censorship was with the industry almost from its inception under various guises. One of the most effective organizations responsible for actually having films altered, from these earliest times, was the S.P.C.A., which was successful in having this film recalled "in toto" from the exhibitors. **MPW**:10.9.09, p487.

[79] **CARMEN**, Pathe/Film d'Art: ["A sumptuous reproduction" in which the leading actress portrays "the cold and cruel heartlessness of the beautiful cigar maker with appreciation and discretion ... this story contains so much of the weaknesses of humanity that it will always be popular." Few reviewers were ever more correct in making such a forecast. Stripped of the actual play, Carmen's character would continue to be featured as one of scripters most essentially ascribed characteristic for Hispanic females who swished and swayed their sexy frames across silver screen.] **MPW**:9.2.10, p520.

[80] **A CENTRAL AMERICAN ROMANCE**, Edison: [Another film reinforcement of what would most certainly have been the early imperialist, or even today's, favorite fantasy. A young North American "Soldier of Fortune" watches as a Hispanic officer woos a lady as she stands looking down longingly from her the traditional balcony. As the suitor sends up his love to the señorita, an old beggar accidently bumps into him. "With all the brutality of his nature" the Spaniard strikes the old man and makes him bleed. Unable to prevent himself from defending the oppressed, our young lad "knocks the officer down for his inhumanity to the helpless" viejo, only to be told by the admiring dark eyed beauty that he has struck the commander of the army and will certainly be arrested. He is and is sentenced to be shot along with the lady's brother the next day, but she manages to get a message to the ever present United States gun boat in the harbor. Blue jackets land with Old Glory leading the way. As sun rises they smash in the prison gates and demand an end to the injustice in the name their sacred nation. The commandant is punished, the brother returned and the new swain decides to stick around Central America a bit longer to see just how much more lucky he can get.] **MPW**: 6.18.10, p1113.

[81] **CHRISTOPHER COLUMBUS**, Gaumont: [Appropriately enough, the discovery of the New World provided the scripters with the theme for their first use of historical material with a Hispanic connection to make a film. Considered "Instructive

and educational," this production was said to represent "important scenes in the life of the Portuguese" navigator, alleged to have discovered the Americas. Although later Hollywood research departments would prove at least adequate and some superior, for example, Herman Lissauer's at Warners in the thirties and forties, these early scripters may have had difficulty finding even the local library: "To say whether a film of this type is accurate is impossible, since much of the information which has come down to modern times is at best fragmentary and conflicting." In any event, it is the first motion picture which touches on the life of Columbus and the discovery of the New World.] **MPW**:5.28.10, p888.

[82] **THE CHUNCHO INDIANS**, Edison: [This early documentary of Peru's Chuncho indian's at least exhibited the movie maker's faith in the superiority of North American capitalistic values. The film's producers claimed that the Chuncho were once the "most savage of all the known tribes of South America." But having recently been exposed to the benefits of white Christian civilization, "the Chucho ... have been weaned from the pursuit of war, taught the value of a peaceful life and carefully trained in the art of coffee cultivation, ... thus becoming useful members of the community."] **MPW**:10.22.10, p942, 10.27.10, p994.

[83] **A COWBOY'S GENEROSITY**, Bison: [A crafty, unprincipled and evil old Mexican roue demands the mortgage from an old couple he knows cannot pay their rent. In its place he lustfully offers to accept the daughter in payment to which the parents reluctantly agree. As was always the case in this universally adaptable scenario, she refuses and enlists the help of a North American cowboy. He comes quickly to the rescue, but is set upon by the Mexican Oil Canista's three hirelings. Ever resourceful, the Anglo manages to escape, and sets it all straight by sending the bad Mexican's away.] **MPW**:8.6.10, p317.

[84] **DON CARLOS**, Sales Company Film D'Art: [Once the scripters discovered Anglo interpretations of Hispanic history, historical epics frequently found their way to the silver screen. The "intrigues" and "treachery" which seemed to pervade at the court of Philip of Spain provided many writers with many fanciful screen scripts. In this one the Grand Inquisitor, not a likeable fellow, was responsible for provoking hate and jealousy between King and Prince which resulted in the death of the young son and banishment for the evil Inquisitor.] **MPW**:5.28.10, p908.

[85] **DOWN IN MEXICO**, Actophone: [This production provided viewers with a significant deviation from what was already accepted and expected fare. In this film the heavy was an Anglo named, Doc Bradley, who ran an El Paso dance hall filled with willing ladies and who wanted the pretty Papita to be the first choice of all his cuddling crib. Working as a flower girl, she had given all her earnings to an ungrateful and avaricious father who was willing to sell her to the bawdy house owner. But because Papita loved her vaquero, she refused to cross the border which forced the Anglo to kidnap

her. Accompanied by a band of his friends, her lover gave chase across the river and rescued her. Having captured the not so nice Anglo, the Mexican swain decided to humiliate him instead of shooting him. To do so he employed "a custom well know in Mexico" to prove him a coward. He offered the lout a box which held three pills, only one of which was considered a deadly poison, and allowed the Anglo to choose first, thereby giving him the best chance to survive the contest of nerve in which fate would decide the winner. When the frightened man refused the duel, all his patrons and the Mexicans laughed. The pills were only sugar, but they had served their purpose. There would be very few scenarios which would allow Mexicans of any social standing to best even the lowest of Anglos.] **MPW:4.23.10, p665.**

[86] **FEMALE BANDIT**, New York Motion Picture Co: [Poverty drives a peon's wife to a life of crime so that she may feed her family and sick husband. Almost caught, she manages to escape, but her horse returns home with the loot and her husband is blamed for the crimes. About to be hanged as the culprit, the wife returns in time to save the Governor's daughter from a fire and her man from the noose.] **MPW:2.5.10.**

[87] **FROM THE ARCTIC TO THE TROPICS**, Edison: [Basically a travelogue showing the breathtaking descent from the top of snow covered Andean peaks to the heat of the Amazon basin. This ride on Peru's Central Railroad has the train's occupants gradually removing numerous layers of clothing as the car approaches sea level.] **V:9.24.10**

[88] **THE HANDS OF THE UNITED STATES**, Essanay: [The film industry was quick, even in these very early days, to capitalize on current events in the Caribbean and provide scenarios that would play to nationalistic pride. Reacting to the possibility of Nicaraguan intervention in 1910 Essanay produced this justification for Marines occupying that nation. When a young North American engineer, appropriately named Smith, becomes unwittingly involved with revolutionaries, he is captured, tried and convicted of insurgency. In an obviously mock trial, he is sentenced to death by no one less than the President of that so called, "Republic." This, the United States Consul cannot allow and so cables the Secretary of War who immediately sends a destroyer to San Salvador. In the last seconds the innocent is saved by onrushing Bluejackets and Marines. As the film ends, Smith and his wife embrace while Old Glory waves proudly above them. There are very few times throughout this century that this scenario would not have played well on the nightly news, especially in most recent times.] **MPW:2.19.10, p428, 3.26.10, p481.**

[89] **HIS SPANISH WIFE**, Lubin: [Robert and Ted are partners in a plantation "in one of those South American republics where they have a revolution every three weeks or feel lonesome." Bob, who has married a local lady, is forced to go to New York, but cannot take his wife. She soon becomes "bored with ennui and piqued because of not being taken" north, and to

punish her neglectful North American esposa, she decides to "elope" with Signor Estrada.] **MPW**:3.26.10, p481, 4.9.10, p553.

[90] **INES DE CASTRO**, Pathe: [Again the scenarists reached into the back pages of Spanish history with this attempt to recreate the love intrigue between the beautiful Ines, promised to another, and Dom Pedro, son of the 14th century King Alphonso which resulted in the exile of the former and the punishment of the royal Prince.] **MPW**: 6.4.10. p954, 6.11.10, p997.

[91] **IN OLD CALIFORNIA**, Lubin: [Perdita Argenello, lived in California when it was still Mexican territory and loved Jose Manuella a wealthy young Spaniard. But as with many of Hollywood's Spanish señoritas, her big beautiful brown eyes, were always on the look out. One day she spied a handsome young troubadour, Pedro Cortes, who was "just the sort of fellow to impress a thoughtless unsophisticated girl." After they were wed, the poet proves to be a "worthless dipsomaniac and reprobate." As the years passed quickly in this one reeler, her son, with his fathers blood, proves to be a "despicable whelp," equal to his father's every indulgence. To save the boy from debauchery, she appeals to her former lover, now the Governor of Alta California fighting to keep the Baja under Mexico's control. The former swain responds by making a soldier of the boy, but not a man, his blood eternally "tainted" he dishonors his family and his patron. With love's flame still burning passionately in his broken heart, the governor keeps the truth of her son's demise from the dying mother as he kneels at her death bed 1339].] **MPW**:3.12.10, p393.

[92] **LISBON BEFORE AND AFTER THE REVOLUTION**, Gaumont: [Before and after pictures of a film crew which happened to be in Lisbon in October of 1910, when Manuel II was forced to flee to England to save his life as the insurrection against the royalist government succeed. The news footage they produced proved to be far more successful than filming the travelogue originally intended.] **MPW**:12.3.10, p.1296.

[93] **LOVE IN MEXICO**, Bison: [As early as 1910, some scenarios had already become too familiar. Exhibitors commented that there was "nothing new" no novelty in this ordinary Mexican love triangle. Dad again wanted to sell his daughter, the lovely Luzetta for gold, but she lived only for the poor peon that made her pulse palpitate more profoundly, [something like that.] To escape the father's evil design, the lovers elope, are pursued, but triumph in the end. The father even gets to keep the gold after the intended bridegroom beats him up and sends him packing.] **MPW**:7.30.10, p265, 8.6.10, p298.

[94] **LUCK OF ROARING CAMP**, Edison: [This was the first version of this Bret Harte story which described the sad adventures of an unfortunate woman and child who travel to gold rush California only to discover that the husband has been killed by claim jumpers. Mother and child are then forced to make it on their own and with much travail do so. Women were a

valuable commodity in 1849 California, certainly worth their weight in gold.] **MPH**:1.22.10, p101.

[95] **MEXICAN DOMAIN**, Urban: [This documentary was advertised as showing "views of Mexican life" presented in an "interesting and instructive" manner portraying these "pleasure loving people in their gay recreations." "One may acquire a reasonably accurate impression of Mexico by looking at this picture." From earliest times Mexico's screened imagery included two contradictory motifs, primitive Mexico, the land of the savage, bandit and barbarian and the picturesque Mexico of siestas and fiestas, the land of love and romance. Not necessarily mutually exclusive, these paradoxically opposite pictures of Mexico remained constant themes throughout the century.] **MPW**:8.6.10, p267.

[96] **A MEXICAN LEGEND**, Pathe: [At least one exhibitor was disturbed by this film featuring an indian raid on a northern Mexican monastery. "Picturesque settings do much to rescue this film from oblivion ... [but] To see a figure purporting to be Christ appear three or four times is taking liberties with the most sacred tenets .... The mixture of marauding and more or less drunken Indians is incongruous and unpleasant. Perhaps Indians did raid monasteries in Mexico, but even if they did there is no reason for reproducing one of these raids in motion pictures. Apparently some early reviewers did not have the taste for the bloody screen that some segments of the viewing public have come to enjoy.] **MPW**:11.12.10, p1127, 11.26.10, p1236.

[97] **THE MEXICAN'S FAITH**, Essanay: [Tony Perez, a Mexican, unjustly fired from one ranch, is given a chance on another where he falls for the owner's daughter, a lovely lady. Attempting to force his affections on her, she refuses what is considered an insult and is responsible for his almost being seriously horsewhipped. Saved from the beating he becomes her faithful servant and is provided with the chance to return the favor when an easterner, "black" to the core, attempts to have her abducted with the help a different "dirty greaser." Of this film an exhibitor commented: "It is illustrative of a trait in the character of a Mexican which may or may not be true, but which, nevertheless, adds interest to the picture." It was apparently difficult for some Anglo's to believe that Mexicans could display positive characteristics. What may have helped some to believe was that Tony was played by rising star, G. M. Anderson, who darken up his skin a bit to play the greaser. Soon, Anderson, as a white faced Anglo, would create film's first western hero, Broncho Billy.] **MPW**:2.12.10, p219, 2.26.10, p309, 3.12.10, p382.

[98] **THE MEXICAN'S JEALOUSY**, New York Motion Picture Co: [A scorned Mexican lover is further rebuked and insulted by the Anglo swain who humiliates him and then kicks him in the posterior. Required to plot his revenge, he and his gang of cutthroats capture Dick, the kicker, and his señorita. But Rita manages to escape and with Dick's halfbreed friend, the two Hispanics, loyal to their Anglo lord, succeed in freeing

the about to be stabbed Bob, from the vengeful Juan. Even before the flickers really became feature films, this scenario had become well established and would continue to be used throughout movie history. The dark skinned girl always betrayed her countrymen for even the possibility of receiving affection from the Anglo lover. This would hold true for female North American indians and women of all other nationalities, but it was especially the case for Hispanic women. (Of course it would have to be Ronald Reagan [well, he did have Errol Flynn with him] who would even manage to find a sympathetic German woman in the heart of Nazi Berlin willing to give up her life to insure the success of their **Desperate Journey** in 1942.}] **MPW**:5.21.10.

[99] **A MEXICAN'S WARD**, New York Motion Picture Co: [La Belle Carman, the "young and beautiful Mexican" ward of Jose Espanno was coming of age and about to receive her inheritance. To insure his continued prosperity, Jose wanted her to marry his son Pedro. It was that or enter the proverbial convent. She refuses and was forced into confinement. Luckily, Jim, a North American cowboy gets wind of this treachery and breaks her out of the convent just in time to return home to find Jose and Pedro stealing all the valuables from the hacienda safe. He of course easily dispatches the evil Mexicans and earns the unending affection of the sweet señorita.] **MPW**:3.19.10, p446.

[100] **THE MEXICAN TUMBLERS**, Pathe: [A filmed reproduction of some of the acts of a well-known group of Mexican acrobats.] **MPW**:12.17.10, p1418.

[101] **ON THE MEXICAN BORDER**, Lubin: [Phil Scott, engineer helping to extend the railroad into northern Mexico falls for Bessie who had scorned, Pedro Ramirez, a Mexican "whose reputation is decidedly evil." Tired of Pedro's "insolence", the Anglo gal rebukes him. His passion fired, Pedro revenges himself by having his sister, Manuelita, help abduct Bessie. The screen emphasized Hispanic attraction for the flamboyant proves their undoing. The culprits are uncovered, because the sisters "gaudy scarf", is left at the scene of the crime, pinpointing the kidnappers. After a hot pursuit the maiden is saved. The exhibitors praised the producers for a fine film, but also, for showing restraint in not having the villain lynched. A sincere improvement over the "bloodthirsty ruffianism" of earlier productions.] See: **Western Justice**, [112] **MPW**:12.10.10, p1367, 12.17.10, p1416.

[102] **PAPINTA**, Selig: [This very involved scenario has two Mexicans trying to wed, but finding it impossible because of the spying of an Indian who reports all to the father. Luckily there is an Anglo who interferes on their behalf allowing them to consummate their love. Displays of Anglo humanity, at times paternalistic, were infrequent, but not unknown in these early scripts.] **MPW**: 5.7.10, p751.

[103] **RAMONA**, Biograph: [This first film adaptation of Helen Hunt Jackson's very popular chronicle of the plight of the

southern California indian, proved to be quite a success and only increased the demand for the great director's services. This one reeler, directed by D. W. Griffith was less than fifteen minutes long and reinforced the director's belief that multi-reel productions were necessary if the industry was to grow and realize it's full potential. This film merely outlines the problems faced by the orphaned daughter of the great house of Moreno, a powerful Spanish family and her chosen love, Allessandro, a poor indian. With far reaching consequences, the Biograph company moved its operation from the east to, Ventura County, the actual location of Hunt's story to capture more realism. It was not long before more production companies came to realize that the sun was always shining in southern California. Then, in 1914, one of Griffith's assistance directors would redo this story using more than thirteen reels in his screen adaptation. [705, 1303]] **MPW**: 5.28.10, p897.

[104] **ROSE OF THE PHILIPPINES**, Independent M. P. CO: [This time the North American Lieutenant falls deeply in love with a "handsome Spanish-Filipino" girl. Interesting because, despite the intercession of his commanding officer and his parents, the Anglo officer chooses the native beauty over the sweetheart he left back home]. **MPW**:1.29.10.

[105] **ROSE OF THE RANCH**, Bison: [The review for this film in the **Motion Picture World** would lead the reader to believe that the action for this very typical love triangle has taken place in Italy; the characters all have names like Venneto and Giovannio, but the exhibitors comments place the action in Mexico. "A dramatic portrayal of scenes in Old Mexico." Scripters from earliest times had a conception of homogenous Hispanics, apparently they also included Italians in their composites at this time.] **MPW**:3.12.10, p401, 3.26.10, p469.

[106] **THE SISAL INDUSTRY IN THE BAHAMAS**, Lubin: [The then substitute for manila hemp, was mainly produced in the Mexican Yucatan, but also in some of the Caribbean islands. This film showed that "most of the work [was] done by negro hands, for no white person could toll under the subtropical sun and long endure." It was common in these days to make reference to hard labor as not "being white man's work." It was even more common among North Americans to consider Mexican's among the most lazy people in the world, all those siestas, but sisal work in the Bahamas or in Quintana Roo, [site of Cancun] was extremely grueling.] **MPW**:5.28.10, p900.

[107] **SPANISH FRONTIER**, Gaumont: [Travelogue of Spain's Basque country.] **MPW**:6.18.10, p1059.

[108] **SPANISH LOYALTY**, Gaumont: [King Aflonso XVIII reviewing his troops."The Spanish troops are shown kissing flag" at a military/religious service.] **V**:11.29.10, **MPW**:12.3.10, p.1296.

[109] **A TERROR OF THE PLAINS**, Yankee: [This film presents an uncanny, certainly unconscious foreshadowing of the plethora of super-Anglo versus the 'slimy spics' engaged in all forms

of illicit behavior, fantasies, produced in this past decade, best represented in films which starred Chuck Norris and Charles Bronson. No matter how many Hispanics opposed these two, audiences could watch easily knowing from the start that Anglo virtue would triumph over Hispanic treachery. In this film a young boy tires of his Buffalo Bill dime novels and dreams himself into a western adventure where he save the ranchers daughter from the "evil eyes" belonging to the Mexican "cutthroats" peering through the window. "One shot from our hero's pistol and seventeen Mexican brigands bite the dust." The only difference between this fantasy and the one Norris lived in **Code of Silence**, 1985 where he disposed, singlehandedly, of more than fifty Hispanic drug dealers, is that little Chuckie's father was not there to spank him for swinging on the "gas chandelier" after he crashed through the floor, as the father of the boy fantasist in this film did. He should have been.] **MPW**:12.24.10, p1492.

[110] **THE THREAD OF DESTINY**, Biograph: [This film is significant because it is the first, according to this research, which presents a sympathetic portrayal of, what will come to be called well until WWII times, one of the lower caste Mexicans. It was always considered proper to deal with "high cast Mexicans", or Mexicans "of a better class." In this production, a common Mexican, Estrada, proves to be Myrtle's, the Anglo heroine, salvation. Even more significantly, the two will wed. From the wordy, but colorful, critic's elaborate recounting of the scenario, the young lady seems to have been something of an early 'flower child.' "Myrtle, the orphan girl of San Gabriel, stands at the window of her cabin contemplating the beautiful sun ... the valley out between the hills bedecked by the hand of Flora, iridescent in the morning light, a veritable Iris [as] her pure soul goes out in love to the trees, the flowers and the sun which is responded in the exhilaration of their perfume." Her only concern was not to have ever known "paternal love." As such "her pure tender heart does not concur with those around her for the village is made up of a people abjectly material." [Had she not been the star of this script she could easily have headed for Big Sur looking to join a commune along with the reviewer.] Her "generous" and "affectionate nature" cause her to bring flowers to a sick friend every morning. On this particular morning, her arms heavy with flowers, she "meets a Mexican stranger, Estrada." Somewhat surprised, she drops a few of her floral gifts, and when the Mexican helps her recover them, "their hand's touch." Even more surprised, "she experiences a thrill, such as she had never felt before." More surprised than either of these two, this researcher, knows of no other scenario where a Mexican was allowed to have such an affect on an Anglo lady until Hollywood washed all the dirt out of their "greasers" and transformed them into Latin Lovers. What follows was completely out of character with any of the scenarios written before or for several generations after. It seems that the pretty Myrtle had become the active object of drunken Gus Walter's libido and on this particular day Estrada had to save the lady from the Anglo lout. This of course provoked much anger and forced Gus to gather a bunch of the

local boys together who set out to lynch the Mexican. For what is certainly the first time on film, the Anglo heroine protects the gentleman and keeps him hidden in her house until the mob can be convinced that further pursuit would prove fruitless. Only Gus remains behind and watches as the two run for the local Spanish Mission where the good padre joins them together forever. By then the cowboys have returned and when the "Angelus" tolls, the boys "awaken to their better selves" and demand that old Gus leave the lovers alone and that he buys a round of drinks for everyone. Truly unique for this time and long after.] **MPW**: 3.19.10, pp393-4. LCFL: Robinson Locke Collection Dramatic Scrapbooks.

[111] **A VACATION IN HAVANA**, Edison: [A shipboard romance leads an Anglo boy and Cuban cutie to fall in love despite the objection of the father who refuses to leave the young couple as they tour the city. On the tour Cupids influence prevents the lovers from noticing the still visible wreck of the **Maine**, and other notable sights. But while visiting Moro Castle, they manage to place dad in a cell and refuse to set him free till he agrees to their being wed.] **MPW**:7.16.10, p244.

[112] **WESTERN JUSTICE**, Lubin: [This film opens with a "Mexican" peering through a window, which soon became a commonly used scene to emphasize the Hispanic's sinister character. Doing so, he sees two prospectors dividing the profits of their work. Later he ambushes one of them and pushes him off a cliff. This action is witnessed by an indian girl that he has earlier "insulted" (a then accepted euphemism which covered everything from kissing to rape.) She seeks help from her indian husband and some local Anglos. Although her spouse was able to wound the Mexican culprit, he manages to hide out in a cabin. After a continued search, he is discovered there in the last scene. Screaming and thrashing about, the Mexican is dragged from the cabin by the rope tied firmly about his neck where he is forced "to face western justice of a summary kind."] **MPW**:4.16.10, p613. Lynching or hanging scenes will by the 1920's be one of the most censorable of all film action. After the Production Code was adopted, no such scenes were allowed save in the most distant views. See **Viva Villa** file in Special Collections and the Academy library. This topic is well discussed and outlined specifically in: **John Eugene Harley, World-Wide Influences Of The Cinema**, (A Study Of Official Censorship And The International Cultural Aspects Of Motion Pictures). University of California Press, 1940.

[113] **WHAT GREAT BEAR LEARNED**, Meiles: [The almost weekly reinforcement of negative Hispanic stereotypes merely encouraged their solidification in the viewing public's mind. Comments on this film explained that "the character of the scheming Mexican will be recognized as life like. That sort are much too common in that section of the world." What Great Bear learned was never to trust a Mexican, he "was deceived, as many others have been before and will be after."] **MPW**:12.24.10, p1476.

[114] **WINTER BATHING IN THE WEST INDIES**, Lubin: [Basically a travelogue taken in the Bahamas featuring Nassau's then famous Hog Island where visitors enjoyed the local fruit lunch. Hog islands then is the famous Paradise Island resort center of today, which to some paying guests is about as difficult to take as discovering what Boca Raton means for some citizens of that affluent community.] **MPW**:5.28.10, **p900**.

[115] **THE YAQUI GIRL**, Pathe, [In 1910 the Yaqui were still being transported and sold into slavery for about a dollar a piece to the sisal magnets of the penal colony of Quintana Roo, the cite of present day Cancun. In this typical scenario, a yaqui girl falls for the wrong man, not the Federal officer which lusted for after her. The vengeance he exercised allowed the writer to reflect on what was commonly accepted as "Mexican treachery" and a form of "punishment which lacks proper conception."] **V**:1.7.11, **MPW**:12.31.10, p1548, See also: Honorato Beltran, "The Pacification of the Yaquis,"**The Mexican Review**:2.21, p44.

1911

[116] **ACROSS THE MEXICAN BORDER**, Powers: [Ruiz, an old Mexican greaser, wishes to sell his daughter to Jose, a young Mexican, but she is in love with Jack Armstrong, an all North American soldier. Despite his amorous efforts to the contrary, Jose is unable to win her away from the gringo stalwart. Realizing the futility of his situation, being a Mexican, and possibly, hoping that a change of nationality will help him find true love, he crosses over the border to "live in the country of the free."] **MPW**:2.25.11, p437, 3.11.11, p543.

[117] **ACROSS THE MEXICAN LINE**, Solax: [Reacting to the revolutionary upheaval in Mexico the Solax scripters built this "thrilling adventure" around a female spy and her true love, but the heat of their nationalism could not prevent them from North Americanizing the conflict. To obtain information about United States troop movements on the border Descastro, aid to a Mexican general, suggests that they send, Juanita as a Mata Harista to do the job. In little time she involves herself with "Lieut. Harvey" who teaches her the wonders of telegraphy, but she fails in her espionage. Worse, but nothing could prevent that, she falls in love with our hero. Descastro now captures Harvey and brings him across the line, where the general tries unsuccessfully to torture information out of him. Sentenced to stand against the white wall at dawn, Juanita plans his rescue. Climbing to the top of a pole she calls across the border for the North American troops who arrive in time to save the day for the two lovers. Juanita may have betrayed her cause, but she acquired the affection of her Anglo lover. In a full page ad the Solax people advertised this film as the, "BIGGEST MONEY-GETTING PROPOSITION ON THE MARKET".] **MPW**:5.13.11, p1083 4.29.11, p929, p970, 5.27.11, p1201.

[118] **THE AMERICAN INSURRECTO**, Kalem: [Set in the wild mountains of northern Mexico, this story focuses on Mexican revolutionaries whose number include local indians and a North American hero. When the latter is wounded he is found by an Indian maid who unknowingly takes him to the ranch of a Federalista sympathizer. Only Mona, the darkskinned maid can and does save our hero by bringing the Indian calvary. Though she loves him, she must marry the Indian chief who has saved the hero. Not very impressed with the production another commentator wrote: "If this picture represents the Mexican imbroglio accurately there is little inducement for soldiers of fortune to follow the insurrectos further into the Mexican domain."] **MPW**:12.9.11, p817.

[119] **THE ARGONAUTS**, Selig: [Boy, girl, brother, sister incur the ravages of the early silents on the way to the California gold fields where after much travail they strike it rich. The Hispanic characterizations merely provided atmospheric background.] **V**:1.7.11

[120] **ARMY MANEUVERS IN CUBA**: Imp: [An "excellent" picture of the Cuban troops in review.] **MPW**:3.18.11, p603.

[121] **ARTFUL KATE**, Imp: [A picture which "depicts Cuban manners and customs with close attention to the real truth." "The dash and spirit of the soldier, combined with the lively flirtation which is popularly supposed to be a part of the life of the Spanish and Cuban girl", [all Hispanic girls are easy, Anglos females are all virgins,] provides the basis for this film's scenario. She flirts with anything that moves, and he hurts a lot, but they overcome "the rocks upon which their bark was almost wrecked" in the final scene which features a tender embrace.] **MPW**: 3.11.11, p542.

[122] **AT THE BREAK OF DAWN**, Essanay: [Pepita, the village beauty falls for a young North American surveyor and they marry. But Randel is called back to the north and his wife hears nothing from him for five years. Some screen writers back then were heartless. When he returns, he is seen in the company of a "white lady." It's all too much for Pepita and she strays into a blasting zone where she is blown into lots of little pieces.] **MPW**:7.8.11, 1603, 7.22.11, p124.

[123] **AT THE GRINGO MINE**, Melies: [Love complicates labor unrest at the Gringo mine. After some violence all is resolved, the foreman gets the girl, the miners obtain their raise.] **MPW**:7.22.11, p140.

[124] **AT THE TRAIL'S END**, Champion: [Four years after the first real scripts were translated to the screen, some writers really had to reach to come up with scenarios. This was a tale of hot pursuit by Portuguese Pete and the sheriff who employ ice skates to overtake the villain and save the lady.] **MPW**:7.22.11, p148.

[125] **BESS OF THE FOREST**, Lubin: [While out west Bess was lost to her parents and found by Manuel Garcia who with his wife raised her. Seventeen years later Harry hears the story at a family gathering and as luck would have it, runs across the Garcia cabin. There he sees Bess and from a locket she is wearing recognizes who she is. Garcia's wife begins to realize what is happening and wants to be rid of the young beauty because she knows that her husband lusts for the child. Seeing all of this, Harry "promptly offers to officiate at a greaser "necktie party," unless he releases the girl. He refuses which provokes a fight with what the screen had already identified as the most traditional Mexican weapon, knives. Although Harry is wounded by the blade, the Mexican is shot dead and the Anglo savior is rewarded by winning his future wife.] **MPW**:8.19.11, p476, 9.9.11, p716.

[126] **BILLY AND HIS PAL**, Melies: [Joe, the cowpuncher, is Billy's idol on the ranch. When the former's love for Madge, arouses the jealousy of a "presumptuous Mexican," he attempts to make his move by kissing the "angel" everyone adores. Rising to her defense, Joe knocks the Mexican around a bit

which of course makes him plot his revenge. Luckily for Joe, Billy overhears this "villainy." Although he is unable himself to prevent his hero's capture, he sounds the alarm which brings the other cowboys and together they defeat the Mexican and his "would be murderers." Joe and Madge are very grateful and thank the boy for his heroism.] **MPW**:2.25.11, p434.

[127] **BONITA OF EL CAJON**, American: [Bonita's father was the head of a band of outlaws. After some typical complications, a Texas Ranger appears and wins the heart of the darkskinned lady, but he has an Anglo lady of his own. The father objects and tells her to entice him and his lady to camp where the two can be properly taken care of. This is done, but Bonita, after conversing with the other woman realizes that she and the hero belong together. After helping them to escape, she kisses the Ranger goodbye and tells her father of her action. Later when the camp is raided by the law, she is killed by a bullet from dad's weapon. One exhibitor thought that this was a "commendable" picture and conclusion.] **MPW**:12.23.11, p1014. 1.6.13, p42.

[128] **THE BORDER RANGER**, Essanay: [A lone ranger captures the Mexican leader of a band of border smugglers. His boys retaliate by abducting a local lady. Uncompromising to his principles, the ranger will not deal with the terrorists brigands and mounts a rescue mission in which he is taken captive, tortured and almost killed. Luckily our lady escapes and brings the troops. "This picture is intensely melodramatic, but not impossible." So it would seem, even today.] **MPW**: 1.28.11, p201, 2.4.11, p244.

[129] **THE BROKEN TRAIL**, Kalem: [Taken by Apaches as a child a young man escapes and makes his way to lower California where, some twenty years later, he falls for a girl who is already spoken for. Just before killing his rival, he discovers that in reality, the other is his long lost brother from whom he was separated in childhood. Fantasy challenged reality even in Spanish California days.] **MPW**:2.11.11, p322.

[130] **A BROTHER IN ARMS**, Pathe: [When troops are sent to the border to protect against Mexican Indians, two good friends must go. One promises the other's wife he will protect him, so when Frazer is captured, Hilton must pursue, but he cannot do so as a trooper. So with the help of several others, all that is required against inferior races, as civilians they cross the border and using a new government explosive, "jobite," blow the enemy into oblivion. Little Chuckie Norris must have read the script for this one at the start of his career.] **MPW**:11.11.11, p496, 11.25.11, p638.

[131] **BUD NEVINS--BAD MAN**, American: [When a notorious badman is engaged by a ranch owner to kill his wealthy rival, he meets the intended victim's daughter and falls in love with her. Meanwhile he has had a "fistic" encounter with a Mexican whom he defeats. Ever ready in Hollywood's Hispanics, vengeance is pledged. Unable to fulfill his assignment because of his love, the badman is attacked and shot by the

Mexican. In little time the assailant is captured and justice is meted out "in the stern guise of Judge Lynch."] **MPW**:5.6.11, p1028.

[132] **THE CALIFORNIA REVOLUTION OF 1846**, Kalem: [Promoted as "A love story with a historical attachment" the film focused on the thirteen North American settlers who proclaimed independence from Mexico and "seized the pueblo of Sonoma," raising the "bear flag" and declaring California a republic. A little scripted embellishment for added victory, had the dashing young Anglo hero also managing to conquer the Spanish Commandant's lady along with the real estate.] **MPW**:10.21.11, p207.

[133] **CAMOENS, THE PORTUGUESE SHAKESPEARE**, Selig: [Accused of writing seditious and unpatriotic poems, Camoens was forced to live in exile from his beloved Lisbon, with only his faithful slave Barbara to provide for him by begging food in the streets. This brief clip touched on the broad outlines of his tragic career.] **MPW** 12.2.11. p745.

[134] **CARMENITA THE FAITHFUL**, Essanay: [One more variation of the avaricious Mexican father attempting to "pawn" his daughter to a richer Mexican merchant for as much profit as the flesh would bear. An evil deed which was rarely possible with the omnipresent young North American, ever ready to save the sweet señorita, but this time, the hero must pay a price. He wins the lady but loses the use of his legs while saving her. In the last scene "the bad Mexican is seen dejected and being led away to prison."] **MPW**:2.11.11, p320.

[135] **THE CATTLE KING OF ARIZONA**, American: [The Arizona cattle king plans to merge his vast holdings with Don Romero, a Mexican rancher, who is very much in love with his prospective partner's daughter. She loves another which results in the usual complications. Romero plans to kidnap the girl and take her across the border but is prevented from doing so by yet another young Anglo hero.] **MPW**:2.11.11, p322.

[136] **A CHILD OF THE RANCHO**, Bison: [A rebuffed Mexican confronts the Anglo girl in a park trying to force her to elope at the point of his pistolla. Using a ploy that would be reused countless times thereafter, she tricks the Mexican into dropping the gun by simply looking over his shoulder and shouting "Don't Shoot." With his gun she holds him at bay till help arrives to administer the "well deserved punishment" required for his "impetuosity."] **MPW**:6.17.11, p1395.

[137] **CINTRA, A PICTURESQUE TOWN OF PORTUGAL**, Gaumont: ["Where the wealthy from Lisbon" went to relax, the film features the combination of Christian and Moorish influence on the local architecture.] **MPW**:9.30.11, p990, 10.21.11, p207

[138] **COALS OF FIRE**: [Mexican perfidy knew no geographical boundaries. Some how a Mexican roustabout manages to steal gold from a miner in Nome; he hides it in a local cave. Only

the appearance of the miner's daughter prevented the Mexican from being lynched.] **MPW**:2.11.11, p324.

[139] **COL. E. D. BAKER, 1ST CALIFORNIA**, Champion: [Patriotic love triangle in old California, one of the participants is a veteran from the Mexican War.] **MPW**:5.6.11, p1026.

[140] **A COWBOY AND A LORD**, Champion: [This contest between a lowly cowboy and a wealthy lord involves the capture of the girl by the ever available Mexican abductors. The cowhand chases them, shoots one and forces the other to give up the girl. Still the mother wants her to marry for dollars and sends the hero away. But happy endings came early to the silver screen and in time Mom comes to realize her daughter's preference and has her true love return.] **MPW**:7.22.11, p126.

[141] **THE COWBOY'S INNOCENCE**, [Again a Mexican has an Anglo rival for the little lady. This one is inventive enough to place a few extra aces in the cowboy's boots and have him accused of cheating for which he is fired. This action is witnessed by an indian girl who can clear Jack, but she is captured by the malevolent Mexican and bound with ropes. "Gnawing" her way through them she sounds the alarm which brings Jack's friends to the rescue. It's over the cliff one more time for the Mex and honeymoon city for Jack and Gertie.] **MPW**:1.7.11, p38, 1.14.11, p90.

[142] **THE CRUCIAL TEST**, Edison: [Basically this story has the fortunes of fate placing an Anglo reporter just at the right place at the right time so that he can obtain the big scoop for his New York paper. His good luck allows him to witness at first hand the Battle of Santiago in which the remainder of Spain's fleet not destroyed in Manila Harbor was sunk to the bottom of Santiago Bay.] **MPW**:7.1.11, p1582.

[143] **A CUP OF COLD WATER**, Selig: [When California was still under the influence of Mexico, "before the American influence [exerted] much power over the old and splendid Mexican families", a notorious bandit, Jose, stole Señora Inez's beautiful daughter from her hacienda. Pursued by "rurales", a "sort of Mexican Vigilantes," Jose tried to hide in the Sierra Madres near the Mission of Padre Antonio. Discovered there, Jose was killed as was his wife, who died protecting the stolen child. As a result of this the Padre kept the infant and raised her at the mission. Eighteen years later, circumstances, which of course involved a young North American, falling in love with the land and his recognizing a certain cross, bring mother and child back together. Coincidence came very early to the aid of stranded silver screen scripters.] **MPW**:9.16.11, p822, 10.7.11, p39.

[144] **DEWEY**, Champion: [A historically inaccurate, patriotic glorification of Dewey's destruction of Spain's wooden fleet in Manila Bay at the opening of the Spanish American War. In effect, the story is more humorous than intended as it is an account of the admiral's son attempt to marry just prior to the opening of hostilities. The heroine's father wants her to

marry the son of a Spanish grandee who is forever offering up toasts to "Yankee Pigs" which makes Dewey's exploits in the Philippines seem as much an act of vengeance as one of patriotism. As a result of the heroics, the Hispanic senator is forced to give his consent to the marriage. This is one of the first films to use the actual names of living historical personages which caused some criticism on the part of the viewing public.] **MPW**, 8.5.11, p312, 8.19.11, p466.

[145] **THE DIAMOND SMUGGLERS**, American: [Two Anglos who love the lady are engaged in smuggling diamonds across the border. The lady loves only one and convinces him of the error of his ways. He reforms, the other does not. At the scripter's convenience, the unselected sweetheart sacrifices his life for their happiness by leading a posse away from the lovers to certain death into the heat of the Mexican badlands.] **MPW**:9.2.11, p646.

[146] **A FAIR EXCHANGE**, Selig: [Madge loves George and takes him on a picnic. Pedro and Juan Sanchez are Mexican horse thieves operating near by. Juan is taken prisoner by a local sheriff, for which Pedro captures George. Madge then captures Carita, Pedro's girl in a "thrilling chase." When Pedro tries to exchange Juan ... yup, that's right. Madge, the "spunky [Anglo] sweetheart" orders Pedro to send back George because she has Carita. All of these frenetic exchanges took less than twelve minutes to accomplish.] **MPW**:8.5.11, p308,310.

[147] **THE FLOWER GIRL OF LAS PALMAS**, Pathe: [Serious problems occur when an estranged Mexican husband falls for the local flower girl. The affair infuriates her lover, father and his former wife. After many complications and with the necessary help of the screen writer, the señorita "reconciles the imbroglio."] **MPW**:12.9.11, 832, 12.23.11, p989.

[148] **THE GIRL OF THE WEST**, Essanay: [A basically good Anglo boy falls in with bad company and loses the straight and narrow path. Faced with having to confess all to his father or find some other way to raise the money necessary to appease his new compatriots, fate intervenes. The errant lad is presently introduced to "the Devil, in the person of one Pedro Verez, a Mexican," who offers him a deal he can't refuse. When the two try to steal a bunch of horses, the Mex is caught and treacherously gives the Anglo up. While the former gets his just deserts, the lad escapes, falls for the Mexican's little sister. He is then offered the opportunity to reform. The law worked in rather selective ways for Hispanics and Anglos in the screen writer's west.] **MPW**:1.21.11, p150, 1.28.11, p194.

[149] **GREATER LOVE HATH NO MAN**, Solax: [The action for this story is laid in a Mexican mining town where an unrequited Anglo lover, although heartbroken, accepts the fact that the girl he loves has chosen as her mate the new superintendent of the mines. Unlike a typical Hollywood Hispanic, he does not seek to revenge himself against the lucky fellow. It even works out that when the Mexicans revolt against the new super

desiring to drop him into the nearest mine shaft with a rope tied around his neck, the disappointed lover helps him and the girl escape. He stays behind while the two go for the cavalry, but when they return to quell the rebellion, it is sadly discovered that the "young man has given his life for the one he loved." Hispanic males were also required to give up their lives for what screen writers considered to be their Anglo betters.] **MPW:7.15.11, p40.**

[150] **THE GREAT NITRATE OF SODA INDUSTRY IN CHILE**, Selig: [Essentially a documentary showing the manner in which this valuable commodity was secured and prepared for market. The bulk of the world's supply came from the long and narrow South American nation, but was controlled by two North American concerns.] **MPW:6.10.11, p1322, 6.17.11, p1387.**

[151] **HER CHUM'S BROTHER**, Kalem: [A love story set in Florida and Cuba with "exceptional" scenery filmed on the beaches of that tropical paradise.] **MPW:2.4.11, p243.**

[152] **HER SACRIFICE**, Biograph: [Another version of an aristocratic maternal parent interfering with the offspring's love for someone of a lower class. In the denouement, a young cantina girl who loves her swain so much, takes the bullet intended for her man. Oh! were it only true.] **MPW: 7.1.11, p1524.**

[153] **THE HOME OF THE SEAL**, Edison: [One has to be slightly amazed at some of the distant and isolated locations that many of the early documentary film makers traveled to bring back their motion pictures of the unique and not previously photographed. This crew voyaged to the even for this day, isolated Palominas islands, off the coast of Peru, to bring back flickers of the frolicking habits of the harbor seals in that remote region.] **MPW:1.28.11, p201.**

[154] **THE HONOR OF THE FLAG**, Melies: [Mary's XX ranch borders a ford near the Rio Grande. One day as she crossed into Mexico she hears the scream's of Juanita, a beautiful Mexican girl, who was being "insulted" by Jose, leader of a group of pseudo-guerrillas, that merely assumed this guise to rob, plunder and 'insult' available maidens. Mary saves the girl and brings her to the ranch which is soon attacked by Jose. The two women and Mary's mother hold off the bandits, but their superior numbers begin to tell. As luck would have it, Mary has recently learned to communicate with the nearby garrison by using the new "wig-wag" signals then employed. She calls for help [possibly they could not hear the shots of the fracas because this was still the silent era] and quickly the troops arrive. In the last scene, Jose and his troops are made to salute the Stars and Stripes which they had also insulted. Interestingly enough, President Wilson will send troops to occupy Vera Cruz in 1914, in a vain effort to have the Dictator Huerta "Salute the Flag". The action will be supported by the vast majority of North Americans: See **Richard, The Tampico Incident: Connecticut Almost Goes to**

War," Connecticut History, November 1987, pp1-24.] MPW:7.1.11, p1526, 7.15.11, p38.

[155] **THE IMMORTAL ALAMO**, Melies: [A little history lesson was included in the price of admission for this film which may be considered the first of many to follow, that would glorify the events leading to Texas independence."In 1722 Spain conquered Texas which takes its name from an indian federation, the Tejas." What followed was a fairly romanticized retelling of the defense of the old mission by the immortal 140. In the last scene after the walls have been breached by Santa Anna's cannon, Travis and the remaining four survivors are shown to be slaughtered, but the women are allowed to leave. Although technological advances would greatly improve the cinematographic quality of all subsequent retelling's, culminating in John Wayne's own personal epic production, **The Alamo** 1960 the basic scenario established in this little one reeler remained unchanged. It may well be considered understandable that every one of the more than a dozen productions, have been very one sided, the history that has been employed has told the tale from the Texas point of view. Interestingly enough, at least for this writer, there has never been a **Tora Tora Tora** type film produced about that little Spanish mission where all that sacred blood was allowed to soak into the dry and dirty sand. The battle cry, "Remember the Alamo," a central feature of all the productions, was adapted to undeniably the most deadly and devastating surprise attack the United States every suffered: "Remember Pearl Harbor" was on everyone's lips throughout the war and for sometime thereafter in song and in many, how we came back to beat the Japs, films. The point is simply that although the Japanese were portrayed in an extremely negative light for some time by Hollywood, by the mid sixties, that had changed, they had then become the honorable opposition. And **Tora** actually detailed the history of the sneak attack from the one time hated enemy's point of view. Admiral Yamamoto was actually shown doing some artistic work with a camera on the way to battle. There is some significance to the fact that eleven time president of Mexico, {pronounced in films} Santy Anny, {admitted scoundrel that he was, he actually sold part of his country to the United States to make a few dollars to keep himself in power a little longer} never enjoyed such film luxury. The story of the Alamo has never been told from the Mexican point of view. The very latest Alamo production, **Alamo, the Price of Freedom**, 1988, although somewhat more accurate with the facts, is still basically "goodguys versus badguys" Hollywood history.] MPW:5.27.11, p1204, 6.10.11, p1313. The protest against this last named film is outlined in: "Alamo Film is Under Hispanic Siege," NYT:3.7.88, IV, p11.

[156] **IN BLOSSOM TIME**, Kalem: [The action in this melodrama takes place in Spanish Florida where Dom Pedro, a nobleman finds it temporarily humorous that his son, Victorian, loves Angelica, his gardener's hija. Love may disregard social class in more egalitarian societies, but for Hollywood's Hispanics, Spanish grandees almost always interfered when relationships between their children and the lower classes went beyond the

point of dalliance. In this case the hero was forced to endure exile abroad and wait until the death of his father, before he could be reunited with wife and child."] **MPW**:5.20.11, p1144.

[157] **THE INDIAN MAID'S SACRIFICE**, Kalem: [Filmed on location at the "Gunga Ranchero", this story was based upon an early legend of the San Luis Rey Mission as told by the Paula indians. Wana, an indian girl, is saved from a fate worse than by Don Pablo, a Spanish gentleman who places her in the care of the mission padre. A local halfbreed who seeks vengeance against the Don and his lady for an assumed slight, urges the local indians to exterminate the settlement and "plans to kill [the Don] during the dagger dance at the annual festival." When Wana, learns of this treachery, she disguises herself as a boy, kills the halfbreed Romero and saves her benefactor. The indians, denied their entertainment, demand her blood for betraying her own, but, the padre intercedes and calms their passion.] **MPW**:7.22.11, p138.

[158] **IN OLD FLORIDA**, Kalem: [There was always romance in the Hispanic world, no matter what the time or place. In this film it was to be found in the Spanish Florida of the early 1800's and included a "Don's, proud parents," "duels," and other romantic accessories, all before any Anglo/Englishman ever set foot in that land. Despite the fact that the action projected took place during the 1560's, this film's reviewer felt that the young man who won the duel with "the Spaniard" showed "true American" spirit in doing so and was justly rewarded as a result by being given the hand of dainty damsel despite "parental objections."] **MPW**:4.29.11, p957.

[159] **IN OLD MADRID**, Reliance: [Tragically, the vast majority of these one reelers have not survived. Some may be viewed in the film collection at the National Archives and many others in Rochester, New York which houses, the Edison and other collections. Luckily, for film historians at least, a few trade papers like **Moving Picture World**, and the **Exhibitor's Daily**, carried very detailed outlines of the scenarios these films attempted to project. In reality the trades provided an advertising service for the production companies, in addition to critical reviews for audiences. Yet, without having seen the finished product, it is very difficult to imagine how directors were able to translate to the screen, in one reel, such very complex and involved scripts, as **In Old Madrid**, outlines in print. After a seemingly endless series of complicated intrigues, all designed to obviate the objections of two sets of parents, the two young Spanish lovers finally are allowed to stay together in the final scene. But this is accomplished only after they threaten to take their own lives by plunging themselves into the ocean that surrounds the rocks they have escaped upon to find refuge from all that parental interference. In the denouement the frantic parents plead with the youngsters to come home.] **MPW**:3.18.11, p609, 4.1.11, p720.

[160] **IN THE DAYS OF GOLD**, Selig: [Possibly the most persistent of the scripters fantasies focusing on

Anglo/Hispanic relations is that which mandates in hundreds of different situations an Anglo savior in one form or another. Some how, Hollywood's North Americans have always been able to solve, fix or repair a complicated south of the border situation. This concept, born in the very early days of the industry, was continuously reinforced by films such as this one. The Lopez family is attacked by indians who carry off the mother. With luck, Juanita escapes and seeks help from Sheriff Dick, who with a posse, and some little effort, rescues the about to be barbecued madre from being burned at the stake by the savages. The reward for such heroics was invariably the señorita's favors and affection.] **MPW:11.11.11, p492.**

[161] **IN THE HEART OF PEGGY**: [No information can be found on this, it does not seem to exist.]

[162] **IN THE NICK OF TIME**, Solax: [Once more a Mexican attempts to force his affection on another Anglo girl, which insults her and causes her young army hero to warn the offender. Invariably, such rebuke provokes a call for vengeance which in this case takes the form of a sneak "lariat attack." Tied, bound and dragged away, the soldier is thrown over a cliff, yet fate, not necessarily on the side of the righteous, but always favoring those north of the border, intervenes. The rope catches onto a convenient stump and holds the hero suspended waiting for rescue. His faithful horse provides the means and together with the cavalry buddies just summoned, prevent the lust crazed Mexican from having his way with the helpless lady.] **MPW:5.20.11, p1146.**

[163] **JUAREZ AFTER THE SIEGE**, Kalem: [Significant because it may be the first film of a city under siege taken during and immediately after the battle. Scenes include the "poorly clad Insurrecto Army armed to the teeth with guns and revolvers" taken from the bodies of dead Federalista troops. The machine gun riddled customs house, the cite of Presidents Taft and Diaz's meeting, was also featured. Juarez, as it was pointed out in the title cards, was the first foreign territory visited by a North American President.] **MPW:6.17.11, p1459, 7.8.11, p1585.**

[164] **LAUNCHING OF THE BATTLESHIP RIVADAVIA**, Edison: [National pride and armed strength would continue throughout the century to be a major factor in the tumultuous histories of all the Latin nations. One of the major factors influencing relations between the two hemispheres would be the sale of arms. This documentary covers the building of the Rivadavia for Argentina at the Quincy Ship Yard outside Boston, Mass.] **MPW:10.14.11, p152.**

[165] **THE LONG ARM OF THE LAW**, Kalem: [Sancho is an illusive and clever Mexican outlaw who outwits the local authorities making his escape. Crossing over the Rio Bravo to obtain work and hide out on a North American ranch, he soon makes his move for Olivetta, the local lovely, but is of course refused. The lady, in all such circumstances, invariably had a thing for

the Anglo ranch foreman. When all are invited to a fiesta, the local sheriff attends and recognizes the bad man. Knowing he has been identified, the bandito tries to use Olivetta as a shield, escapes temporarily, but is eventually driven off "the edge of a precipice" by the posse in pursuit.] **MPW**,12.2.11, p748, 12.16.11, p905.

[166] **LOVE IN MADRID**, Pathe: [Juanita Maria Del Carmen, a lovely lady looking out from her balcony, espies Enrique and drops him the traditional rose. Later they attend a dance together where she entertains all with a beautiful "jota." Taken by her grace, a bystander makes unwelcome advances which causes Enrique to challenge him to a duel. The young boy wins and in doing so acquires the admiration of the young woman's father who, because of his successful defense of his daughter, consents to their marriage.] **MPW**:4.1.11, p722, 4.8.11, p782

[167] **THE LOYALTY OF DON LUIS VERDUGO**, Kalem: [By this date, the transfer of California's colors from Mexican to United States control was already a popular subject for film. During the next eighty years, it would continue to be used in more than a hundred other screen scenarios. In this one a young Lieutenant Malcolm is forced to read the proclamation, "authorizing the occupation of Southern California by the United States," to the old Don who refuses to haul down the Mexican flag. Lucky for the Don, the Anglo lad falls for his "little [sic] signorita," which allows the patriotic "Spanish Grandee" to keep his flag flying. But, when the Cohuilla indians attack his hacienda, the U. S. cavalry defends him and he gratefully "surrenders to the Stars and Stripes."] **MPW**:5.13.11, p1084, 5.27.11, p1200.

[168] **MADEIRA, PORTUGAL**, Eclipse: [A travelogue of "more than ordinary interest" showing a wide variety of local activity including the lively streets, beautiful surf, the wicker chair industry and pineapple growing.] **MPW**: 10.14.11, p150, 11.4.11, p378.

[169] **THE MAIDEN OF THE PIE-FACED INDIANS**, Edison: [An intended parody of the "usual indian maiden and cowboy rescue" scenario. Apparently these indians love custard pie and baked beans, and while one particular indian maiden is indulging her gourmet delight, a "wicked Mexican attacks her." She is rescued by an Anglo boy named "Fauntleroy" with whom she immediately falls in love. But the vanquished Mexican wants his revenge and convinces the maiden's father to have the cowboy tortured "in a most ridiculous manner." Ha-Ha-Minnie intervenes by declaring her love for her savior and it all ends well. Exhibitors commented that, this film "deserved to be popular since it containe[d] humor of a rare and altogether commendable sort," and it "clearly illustrate[d] the absurdities which often [found their way] into usual indian stories."] **MPW**:9.30.11, p988.

[170] **MANRESA, A SPANISH TOWN**, Gaumont: [Scenes from a little village near Barcelona which afford the viewer "an excellent

idea of the peculiar characteristics of the district."] **MPW**: 11.4.11, p412.

[171] **THE MEXICAN**, American: [Most of these early scenario's were unconsciously racist, they merely reflected commonly accepted attitudes of the time. This is one of, if not the very first to deal with Hispanic racism as its basic theme. Joe Curvey, a Mexican, finds a baby girl in a basket, adopts her and brings her up as his own. Eighteen years later, race hatred causes the local toughs to attack the father and daughter. Clarence and some of his more enlightened cowboy friends rescue them, but the father's anger provokes him to retaliate against the other Anglos. He enlists the aid of some Mexicans, who have also suffered racial attacks, and together, they attack a neighboring Anglo ranch. Some are killed, the father is captured and along with the daughter, both are to be hanged, but Clarence comes once more to rescue his love [471].] **MPW**:11.11.11, p498, 11.18.11, p552.

[172] **THE MEXICAN**, Lubin: [Rose who loves Tom, presently on active duty, lives with his mother. They rent from a "crafty" and avaricious Mexican who demands his rent. On the day of the crisis Tom returns home to help. Now a sergeant the soldier has earned more than enough money to square the debt, but also enough to excite the Mexican's greed. To provoke Tom, the evil landlord demands his money in an "insulting" way, which causes the son to strike him. Of course he gathers up other Mexicans in the bandit business and an armed struggle ensues. Almost out of ammo, Rose takes one of the bandit horses and is able to bring the ever ready troops who quickly dispose of the baddies.] **MPW**:10.28.11, p314, 11.4.11, p348.

[173] **MEXICAN AS IT IS SPOKEN**, Melies: [There is probably more truth than humor in the story about the displeasure experienced by North American tourist's who travel across the border and elsewhere and find themselves faced with the fact that 'those people' speak a foreign language, not 'American.' In this comedy an Englishman is "in the predicament of a man who cannot understand Mexican," spoken by the two bearded Mexicans, "horrid men" gesticulating violently as he approached. Ignoring them contemptuously, he attempts to proceed, but they tie him with rope. He then discovers that he was in a blasting zone and the locals were trying to protect him from injury. This same problem with language will provide the theme for **The Unexpected** [719]] **MPW**:10.28.11, p318, 11.18.11, p549.

[174] **MEXICAN FILIBUSTERS**, Kalem: [One of the first controversies created by the incoming Wilson administration in 1912 was the reopening of the border for the sale of arms to various Mexican revolutionary groups. The new President's animosity for the Huerta dictatorship was intense, if Villa or Zapata could overthrow him, all the better. In this film the insurrectionists are loading guns and arms into a train ready to cross over the border. One disgruntled revolutionary tries to tell the Secret Service about the activity. They treat the traitor with contempt, but must act on his information.

Luckily, Blanca, a fiery female freedom fighter saves the day by sounding the alarm and rides the train across to Mexico.] MPW:3.4.11, p491, 3.18.11, p603.

[175] **THE MEXICAN JOAN OF ARC**, Kalem: [Two refinements that would become a standard part of the trade begin to take place in 1911: Reviews for certain films will identify their authors and the specific performance of a particular player/actor will be evaluated. **Joan** exhibits both. Stephen Bush was taken with this film of the "great empire to the south ... the theater of bloody and stirring events [of] elemental tragedy." He claimed that it was a true story taken from the pages of the daily press, a Mexican tragedy perfect for the screen. It would seem that dictator Diaz's drunken tool, Zefas was responsible for legal execution of Talamantes's husband and son. Caring nothing for the revolutionary movement herself, she merely employs it to achieve her vengeance. The widow forms a group of Insurrectos, which include many indians and halfbreed Mexicans and devises a plan to lure Colonel Cephis [sic] to a town where he is taken prisoner. He then is tried as was her husband and shot in a similar fashion. The heroine was now free to return to her people. By this date Kalem was responsible for producing a significant number of films with Mexican themes and for this one they employed Hispanic locals to play the extras. But an Anglo gal, Jane Wolf "essayed the difficult role" of Talamantes. Bush ended his review with a prophetic statement, one which is, in effect, the central focus of this work: "We know to-day but little more than our grandfathers about the land of the "conquistadors," but with the modern moving picture this will soon be changed."] MPW:7.15.11, p19, 7.29.11, p181, p223.

[176] **A MEXICAN ROMANCE**, Urban: [An inferior production, even for the times. A young Mexican girl is heart sick because of her family's objection to her choice of lovers. The doctor diagnosis the cause and talks her parents into the cure.] MPW:1.14.11, p88.

[177] **A MEXICAN ROSE GARDEN**, Kalem: ["Heart breaks and heart throbs a plenty", [the silver screen] Spanish style. A wealthy señorita, sought after by many aristocrats, loves her gardener as he loves her. His loving gift for her is the rose garden, but he despairs that she will never be his because of his poverty. His despair drives him to enter a monastery and forces the lady to search for him for the next fifty years without success. Having learned a lesson screen writers sought endlessly to teach, as she approached death, she wrote a will that would force her niece, Bonita, to select love over the security of material possessions.] MPW:6.17.11, p1353, 1391-2, 7.8.11, p1584.

[178] **THE MISSION FATHER**, Melies: [Set in California still under Mexican rule, a local Hacendado, Don Hernando "is a powerful feudal lord", arrogant and cruel, the owner of many slaves. While trying to punish one of them, Pedro an indian, the local beloved padre is struck by the Don. Unbending in

his duty the padre tends to the wealthy ranchero when he is stricken by smallpox which produces grave consequences as the illness kills the faithful priest the grateful Pedro swears vengeance. But just as the indian is about to plunge his knife into the cruel Don's back, the latter repents, pleads for forgiveness and master and slave are reunited.] **MPW**: 12.9.11, p827.

[179] **THE MISSION IN THE DESERT**, American: [This little lesson in morality provides an excellent example of the most melodramatic of these early screen scenario's. It may have been easier for the scripter to use a Hispanic character as the object of his pathos, but the story could have been universally applied. Nell, a Mexican girl loves and trusts Ned who is Joe's partner. Joe is much older than his young friend and understands the hopeless situation he is in. The first problem is that he secretly loves the young lady even more than the boy does, but lets no one know. The next problem sprouts from the desire Ned has for Nell: "Youthful love is sometimes impatient and impatience conquers discretion." So it was that Nell found herself in a delicate condition asking Ned to do the right thing. But Ned cherishes his freedom more than the girl and refuses to marry her. His refusal causes Joe to rebuke him, and Nell's hot tempered brother Jose to kill him. Now alone she plans suicide but is prevented from doing so by the mother superior of the convent next to the Spanish mission in the desert. Having left before the tragic events, Joe returns after some time and finds little Spanish Nell placing flowers on Ned's grave. Moved with affection and still in love, he offers his hand in marriage. She expresses her gratitude, but her desire to cleanse her soul forces her to refuse. She has chosen the convent as her way of the cross, her penance to atone for her sins.] **MPW**:2.11.11, p322.

[180] **"THE MYSTERY OF THE MAINE"**, Raising-the-Maine Film Company: ["Looking for sure Money? Then **"Remember the Maine"**. "The Most Successful Feature Film in Existence." "Appeals to All the Classes, from the Newsboy to the Millionaire." A little historical mystery, who blew up the Maine? properly advertised turned a nice profit for exhibitors. Interest in the mystery was rekindled by the removal of the remains of that famed but ill fated warship from Havana harbor in 1911.] **MPW**: 12.16.11, p921, p999.

[181] **NEVER TOO LATE TO MEND**, Solax: ["Jack moves out to the Mexican border for his military duty" and stays in an old Mexican inn long enough to marry the señorita that runs it, he was either a fast Anglo or she was an easy Chiquita. Called to duty immediately, he is away twenty five years--fidelity was really given the acid test in those early silver screen years. Having planted the seed before leaving, his son soon grew to manhood without benefit of fatherly advise. The Mexican madre did her best but Juan grew to be a wild lad and in time joined a band of Mexican horse thieves. Having returned with his cavalry troop to assist the sheriff in the next county, his father was responsible for tracking down the outlaws and

actually capturing his own son. Viewer credulity was also tested, for the errant father recognizes him, and all of a sudden remembers he had left his wife some time ago. Also realizing that he faces a possible conflict of interest, he decides to leave the service and frees the boy. Amazingly enough, the only criticism one reviewer expressed for this production was that when actor Jack saluted "Old Glory," he did so in a very sloppy fashion. The real important things were much easier to identify back then.] **MPW**:6.3.11, p1265, 6.17.11, p1387.

[182] **THE PANAMA CANAL IN 1911**, Edison: [By 1911 the work on the waterway that would benefit the "ships of all nations" was making great gaps in the continental divide. A proud people demanded more footage from Panama. This movie reviewer's faith in his nation's ability and the canal's future certainly proved prophetic: "The film depicts the most wonderful piece of engineering work which the world will never forget." [384]] **MPW**:5.6.11, p1022, 5.20.11, p1140.

[183] **PASTIME IN CHILI**, Pathe: [Realistic scenes of bullfighting in far away Valparaiso. Some viewer comments registered a touch of disapproval for the art of the corrida: This is "scarcely the thing to be presented to American audiences." The Humane Society frequently espoused this view.] **MPW**:5.13.11, p1081.

PATHE'S WEEKLY

[184] #47: [Audiences were apparently becoming more sophisticated or at least more demanding by 1911, judging from their reaction to these news clips of "scenes of a burnt out building in Rio Janeiro [sic], Brazil." No picture of "a gutted out building is interesting unless it happened to be a cathedral, a capital, a famous city hall or something of the kind."] **MPW**:12.2.11, p724.

[185] #51: [Lisbon, Portugal: The clips show Republican soldiers conducting Royalist prisoners to the fortress of del Duque.]

Havana, Cuba: [This sequence describes the work of raising the remains of the Maine from the mud of the harbor.]

[186] **THE PENNILESS PRINCE**, Reliance: [When a dispossessed German prince jumps ship in Cuba, he goes to work for a tobacco plantation and is pursued by two local ladies, one a flirtatious vamp, the other sincere. When he comes into his inheritance, he of course selects the latter to be his bride.] **MPW**: 3.18.11, p609, 4.8.11, p782.

[187] **PICTURESQUE WATERFALLS OF NORTHERN SPAIN**, Gaumont: [Documentary featuring the famous waterfalls of the Monastery of Piedra near Saragossa.] **MPW**:4.22.11, p904, 4.29.11, 956-57.

[188] **THE POISONED FLUME**, American Film Manufacturing Company: [As with many of the earliest of the film makers, this film

was based on the assumption that all those considered to be darkskinned men spent most of their languid days lusting after lily-white Anglo women. It might well be considered a universal assumption among these film pioneers and one that was from the start transferred from the nether lands of insecure ego's to transparent film that would continue to be projected throughout the century. In this childlike moralistic warning, the message was clear: White women needed strong Anglo men to protect them from the evil desires of Mexican males. After the man of the house was killed, an attractive widow and her pretty daughter did their best to keep the old ranch going. Martinez, a local Mexican, had always wanted that property and now felt he had two possibilities to achieve his goal. One of those two was sure to accept his offer. But no Anglo writer at that time was ever going to let that happen and when the prospective, but avaricious swain was rejected by both of the then virginal ladies, it should be no surprise that he was infuriated and sought revenge. His anger provoked him start poisoning their cattle. Had it not been for Joe, the handy ranch hand who killed the Mexican for the lady, there is just no telling what might have happened, at least not at that time.] Mention of this film can be found in another very useful compilation: **National Film Archive Catalogue: Silent Fiction Films, 1895-1930**, London: British Film Institute, 1966, p180.

[189] **THE PORTUGUESE CENTAURS**, Eclair: [The "dash and execution" of this "crack regiment" of Portuguese cavalry was featured in this documentary. "After a precipitous flight down a stone staircase they speed away climbing mountains with the ease of antelopes."] **MPW:11.25.11, p660.**

[190] **PORTUGUESE JOE**, Yankee: [Young Ned Bunting has signed on as a seaman to fill out his manhood, but is revolted by the abuse one of his mates, Portugee Joe, is forced to endure, which is administered by the crew for no apparent reason. Ned rises to Joe's defense, but the leader of the toughs has Ned charged with insubordination for which he is severely flogged. In appreciation and out of friendship, Joe kills the mate and jumps ship. But Ned is blamed for the crime. When the faithful friend learns of this, he returns and confesses. More than grateful and appreciative of the selfless act, Ned's family, which has connections, intercedes and Joe is acquitted. "He also finds a new home with his benefactors."] **MPW:7.8.11, p1608, 7.22.11, p126.**

[191] **A PRISONER OF MEXICO**, Kalem: [Revolutionary turmoil and the over throw of Porfirio Diaz in Mexico coincided almost perfectly with the birth and rapid expansion of the motion picture industry. War and revolution were perfect subjects for film. From those early times to the recent issuing of the **Old Gringo**, screen writers have had to take a point of view, usually siding with the insurrectos. This early production identified Mexico's social revolution with the North American struggle for freedom in 1775 and romanticized Madero as leader of his troops in battle. A spirited North American youth who sides with the rebels forms an "American Legion" to help them

win. Leaving his true love to fight for the right, she by accident gets caught in a train heading across the border where she is taken prisoner by a Federal officer. Paul Mason is subsequently captured and reunited with his lady. She effects their escape with the help of the rebels, and "The American Legion [comes] to the Rescue." In contrast with later productions, **Viva Viva** and **Viva Zapata**, the heros and heroines of these early Mexican Revolution films were almost invariably North Americans. Scripters always found it easier to solve Mexican problems with gringo help.] **MPW**:10.21.11, p226, 11.4.11, p380.

[192] **RAMONA'S FATHER**, Selig: [Set in a Spanish California community just prior to the transfer of title, this one reeler touched on the cross cultural complications which frequently occurred when an Anglo boy attracted the attentions of a Mexican girl. At this point in time, it was never allowable the other way. When a young North American sailor disembarks from his ship in the harbor he becomes involved with a little señorita and the customs of the Hispanic community. The scripter refers to the object of his infatuation as a "Mexican indian girl," reflecting an attitude that was commonly accepted throughout the United States, but especially true in the southwest. For many, the terms "Mexican" and "indian" were interchangeable: More accurately, it was understood that all indians were not Mexicans, but most Mexicans, were indians. Although some North Americans would have had a problem with the fact that a naval officer might have wanted to do more than spend a little pleasant time with such a señorita, many more may well have been insulted that Ramona's father objected strenuously to the affair. Many whites were taken aback in a similar fashion when the black father a half century later in **Guess Who's Coming to Dinner**, was more angry than Spencer Tracy was worried that his daughter was in love with a black man.] **MPW**: 1.28.11, p194. **V**:1.14.11.

[193] **THE RANCH MAN'S DAUGHTER**, Lubin: [When Jose tires of his wife and child, he leaves them for employment North of the border. There, his natural lust is stirred by Rose, the ranch owners's daughter. She is very much in love with cowboy Sam and so when the Mexican makes his move, she rejects his advances in an outright fashion. Undaunted, and bent on revenge, Jose steals a picture of the little lady and brags about her in the local saloon where Sam overhears all and has to hold back his fury. Meanwhile, Jose's wife who has finally tracked him down, greets him as he returns to the ranch. So does Sam, who threatens him with his gun in order to recover the picture of the woman he loves. Having done so, the cowboy leaves, but forgets his gun. Seizing the opportunity the vengeful wife uses it to kill her errant Jose. Although Sam is accused, the wife admits having shot her not so nice husband and the Anglo lovers are left free of further complications from across the border.] **MPW**:11.18.11, p572.

[194] **THE RANCHMAN'S VENGEANCE**, American: [This was one of the first and very few of these early films involving a Hispanic character in which the Anglo was given the negative

characteristics usually ascribed to the former. Such ethnic role reversal was rare for this time. In this scenario, the Anglo, not the "greaser" was the ingrate. Pedro, a Mexican half-breed finds Tom Flint near death and brings him home where his wife Marie nurses him back to health. A cad to the core, Tom makes love to her while Pedro is working in the fields. Manuelito, her father, tells Pedro about the affair. To resolve the problem, the scripter gave Pedro uncommon understanding by having him love his wife so much that he wanted only her happiness. And so he sends her off with the Anglo, but with a warning that he must be good to her, or else. Five years later, the cad has taken to beating Marie and is living a life of debauchery. Once more Manuelito's message brings Pedro. Tom is terrified upon seeing him and Marie dies on the spot. Pedro now proceeds to thrash the blaggard and in the process, pushes the wife beater off a convenient cliff. Avenged, he cries and recrosses the Rio Bravo.] **MPW**:5.20.11, p1148.

[195] **THE RENEGADE BROTHER**, Pathe: [A Hispanic variation of the prodigal son set in Californian-Mexican times. Tony is the renegade, though loved by his father, Don Luis, he is a terror and even steals his brother's fiancee. In the last reel, after years of beating her up and "having gone the downward path to the very depths," his brother, now a priest helps him climb out of the slimy abyss he has inhabited and helps him clean up his act.] **MPW**:10.14.11, p150, 11.4.11, p378.

[196] **A ROMANCE OF THE RIO GRANDE**, Selig: [Pedro, the Mexican bootlegger, provides the means for this melodrama to unfold. He sells fire water to the indians who immediately tie him up and go on the warpath. This provides the Ranger hero the opportunity to save and win his lady fair [1354].] **MPW**: 2.9.11, p83, 12.23.11, p989.

[197] **THE ROSE OF OLD ST. AUGUSTINE**, Selig: [A love triangle in which Captain Lafitte, the pirate, prevents the Spaniard, Alicante, from marrying, Dolores, the Rose, by posing as her betrothed and capturing her love. This causes her father to send the Spanish soldiers into the privateer's camp to capture the newlyweds. A loyal indian friend helps them escape, but they are pursued by bloodhounds until they reach the Captain's boat where his men help to capture the pursuers. All are released save the real heavy who is made to walk the plank.] **MPW**:6.3.11, p1263, 6.17.11, p1386.

[198] **THE RUBBER INDUSTRY OF THE AMAZON**, Selig: [Before the discovery of synthetics, rubber came from the Brazilian Amazon. It's profits made Manaos one of the richest boom towns in the world. That city, 1500 miles from the river's mouth, still boasts of having the largest opera house in the Western Hemisphere. This documentary depicted the various phases of producing rubber, from taping the trees to producing the giant "biscuit" sold in the open market as Manaos.] **MPW**:7.22.11, p142, 8.5.11, p293.

[199] **SAVED BY THE FLAG**, Pathe: [Taking into account the most recent furor over the desecration of the flag, it should not be difficult to understand the reverence that symbol commanded at the beginning of this century. In 1914 Huerta's refusal to salute the colors provoked Wilson to send the fleet to Vera Cruz: See: **Honor of the Flag** [154]. Yet, even this film reaches for the outer limits of patriotic veneration. While in Mexico a young Army officer falls for the lovely dark skinned lady who belongs to the Mexican general. She immediately responds to the Anglo's charms and they marry. The lieutenant resigns to become a local businessman, which allows the General to seek his vengeance. Trumping up the traditional charges, he plans the arrest of the newlyweds, who luckily are warned in time. Now begins a mad dash for the border with the Federalistas in hot pursuit. As the two lovers cross over, the former officer grabs the Stars and Stripes from the customs house staff and wraps the flag around the two of them, taunting and "defying the representatives of Mexico" rendered helpless by Old Glory.] **MPW**:10.21.11, p232, 11.11.11, p470.

[200] **THE SECRET OF THE PALM**, Imp: [Produced in Cuba this tale of one lady and two lovers was destined for tragedy from the start. But the contest for the señorita was also predetermined by the Anglo scripter. The Spaniard, who is part of the triangle, cannot play fair and tries to cause the ruin of the North American swain. Successful at first, the deities were with the writer and more inclined to favor the North American; their intercession somehow cause the Cubano to die. To save something of his honor, just at the moment of his death, he confesses all, which allows the wedding bells to be prepared for the coming nuptials.] **MPW**:3.25.11, p658.

[201] **THE SEÑORITA'S CONQUEST**, Lubin: [The sheriff of a Texas border town was determined to rid his region of a "notorious gang of Mexican brigands." Offering a $500 reward for their leader's capture, Dolores, a young Mexican girl, "in the spirit of dare-deviltry" determined to deceive and deliver him into the hands of her chief, Juan. Arriving in Juarez during the ever on going festival, she was annoyed by the attention of a cowboy. Seeing this, the sheriff stepped in to protect her. Almost immediately he falls in love with her and she responds, feeling a "strong turbulence in her heart." Meanwhile, Juan, the bandit chieftain, has sent his subaltern, Pedro. to check up on her. He sees immediately that her affection has shifted to the Anglo's side, further, she prevents him from returning to the bandit camp. Angered, Juan orders both captured and sentences the sheriff to death. Because the bandita effects her Anglo lover's escape, she is her self sentenced and in turn rescued. For the audience, all was well that ended in the final reel in which the Mexican bandit was killed.] **MPW**:9.6.11, p820, 9.16.11, p766, 9.30.11, p972.

[202] **THE SEÑORITA'S SACRIFICE**, Yankee: [Brigands were forever attacking North Americans whenever they traveled to Hispanic lands. This time it happened in Spain, where the Anglo was

left for dead until Papinta discovered the wounded man while gathering her morning flowers. Applying a little tender loving care, she brings him back to life.] **MPW**:3.4.11, p494, 3.25.11, p658.

[203] **THE SHERIFF'S DECISION**, Essanay: [With the rapidly growing number of scripts required to feed what seemed to be an insatiable appetite for these one reelers, coincidence became an most necessary tool for the hard pressed scenarist. In this one a sheriff with a very long memory, apparently never forgets a chance meeting he has had with a suspicious looking Mexican who might have been on the run. As the years passed Steve becomes a sheriff and falls in love with the natty Nita. She fails to see his charms and chooses Manuel Garcia from among her many suitors, to wed. But just at the moment the nuptials were taking place, sheriff Steve receives a telegram from the neighboring law asking him to arrest Manuel who committed a murder some ten years ago. Remembering the incident from long ago, Steve recognizes Manuel as the Mexican on the run and drags the culprit away before the couple could finish saying they did. It was too early in screen history to allow any Mexican to be chosen over an Anglo.] **MPW**:9.30.11, p988.

[204] **THE SHERIFF'S PUNISHMENT**, Pathe: [One of the first westerns in which the sheriff is a heavy. He and a cowpuncher seek to woo a Mexican bar-keeping heroine, but the law oversteps its authority in the heat of pursuit.] **MPW**:8.12.11, p376.

[205] **THE SPANISH GYPSY**, Biograph: Vengeance continued to be one of the most persistent themes for Hollywood's Hispanics in both the silents and sound films. Here, Pepita was anxious to avenge herself against Jose "for the jilt she suffered." The fickled Jose needed only "a pretty face and trim figure" to make him forget the very existence of Pepita. Spying Mariana he made his move, so did Pepita. From inside her dress, she drew the traditional Mexican weapon, the ever present dagger, and causes the coward to run. Now, in quick succession, Jose is blinded by an accident, left by the other lady and is forced to wander blindly about helplessly. Seeing him in this condition calms Pepita's anger and she vows to care for him forever.] **MPW**:4.1.11, p722, 4.15.11, p842.

[206] **A SPANISH LOVE SONG**, Melies: [For whatever reason, misinformation about Puritan heritage, or fear generated by inhibition, the generally accepted by the public, folk mythology about the sexual prowess or physical endowments of races and nationalities other than white, found it's way quickly into film. In some of these earliest films, Anglo scripters seem to feel that there was something in a Hispanic's ability to make love that was apparently lacking in their own people. Latin's always loved with more passion, fire or fierceness than the Anglos apparently seemed capable of. In this one an Anglo boy who has a problem with the girl he is engaged to, is sent across the border to resolve his problem. There he encounters a Mexican girl, Juanita, who has

been cruelly mistreated by her parents. Worse, they want to sell her to a rich local, Don Jose. He loves her in "fierce fashion", but unsuccessfully, for the señorita scorns him and prefers the Anglo boy. He, meanwhile, has become a real cowboy as a result of her loving, but in doing so has incurred the wrath and vengeance of the Don. Try as he may as treacherous as he was, Don Jose was unable to do the boy in, Juanita forever saves him. But, while the Anglo was allowed to play in Mexico, he was not allowed to stay, he was summoned back to marry the white girl. Filial piety forces him back across the border which causes Juanita's heart to break, but all is saved when the fiancee runs off with another man, allowing the lad to return to his Mexican therapist. In terms of love and passion, the lure and mystique of the Latin lover or loveress was born early and remained consistent throughout all film history.] **MPW**:8.19.11, p478, 8.26.11, p561.

[207] **THE STAGE ROBBERS OF SAN JUAN**, American: [A pair of outlaws fall out over the fact that the plunder must be shared with a wife. The wife wishes no part of the loot and finally convinces her husband (Slippery) to give up his life of crime and go to Mexico where they can start a new life.] **MPW**:9.16.11, p826.

[208] **THE STAMPEDE**, Imp: [Marie Almedo, the wife of Jose the cattle thief, tries to warn the rancher her husband plans to rob that night. She fails in her intent and is trampled to death by a stampede for her trouble, but divine intercession saves her daughter, Nello, from the killing hoofs. Some twenty years later the girl falls in love with the son of the very rancher her mother tried to warn. Moreover, Jose has not renounced his life of crime and is still out on the range taking the rancher's cows. In one of his raids, he also manages to capture Nello, upon whom he tries to force his attentions. But when he sees the locket she wears about her, he realizes that she is his own flesh and blood. Overcome by remorse he willingly rushes to a window to be shot by those who have come to rescue the little lady.] **MPW**:4.15.11, p484.

[209] **THE STRUGGLE FOR LIFE**, Eclipse: [Inez, a Spanish girl, despises Jose who is courting her. She really likes the young Anglo artist, George Barnes, who accommodates her by frightening Jose away. This of course necessitates vengeance which Jose plans to achieve with the help of certain compatriots. But when they attempt to holdup the stagecoach the young couple are heading north in, and despite the fact that Jose has the help of several friends, George proves too powerful and hurls Jose off a cliff. Seeing this, his friends flee.] **MPW**:7.29.11, p224.

[210] **THE SUBSTITUTE**, Lubin: ["A very commendable picture in which the heroine, who will strongly appeal to spectators, saves a large invoice of gold from Mexican bandits." When she discovers her male counterpart in a drunken stupor, she climbs a pole and calls for the troops. The calvary comes into the picture in a "thrilling style" "that does credit to Uncle Sam's boys."] **MPW**:12.30.11, p1071.

[211] **THE TERMS OF THE WILL**, Pathe: [The Mexican Constitution of 1917 includes specific provisions against the outright foreign ownership of property in Mexico today, but even in 1911 such ownership could cause problems for an Anglo. Having been left a large Mexican estate, our hero finds himself forced into marriage at gun point by the brother of a pretty Mexican señorita. It would seem that the boy could only inherit the hacienda if he were married within thirty days of the old Don's death. The Mexican brother who felt excluded by the terms of the will, seeks to profit through his sister marriage to the gringo inheritee. All works well until the arrival of the North American's sweetheart which compels the Mexican to abduct her to save his ill gotten gains. In the final scenes, to tidy everything up, the Anglo scripter has the unfortunate sister accidently shot by her conniving brother, thereby leaving the way clear for his Anglo lady and lad to marry.] **MPW**:11.25.11, P636.

[212] **THE TEST OF LOVE**, Yankee: [Carmencita was a "wild, carefree daughter of Spain, fair of face and with voluptuous form; "the favorite dancer of Madrid's wine gardens," all came to enjoy her charms. One day she becomes fascinated with a certain North American tourist. She knows the attraction is only momentary, but realizes she can use the affair to her advantage. Like so many other later Latin vixens, she plans to make her man a little jealous with the flirtation. She succeeds well, which causes near fatal results for the chagrined traveller.] **MPW**:3.11.11, p548, 3.25.11, p658.

[213] **A THWARTED VENGEANCE**, Essanay: [Nell, proprietress of the local bar and gambling establishment, has many admirers, but she forces them all to keep their distance, saving her virtue for a special cowpoke. When a Mexican comes to town, he crosses the line and makes a move for the much desired miss. Bob boots the bastard [few silver screen Mexicans ever had legitimate fathers] out, which provokes the ever eager vengeance of the insulter. Later, when Bob is injured, the Mexican captures the lady and ties her up in view of her bedridden lover, planning no good. Some of these early Mexicans were almost as bad as the entire company, save one, that were characterized in 1967's **Wild Bunch**. But as this villain was about to use his "gleaming blade" on Bob, a friend saves him. Escaping momentarily, and crazed with anger, the Hispanic rotter now tries to use his knife on the defenseless Nell, but is finally shot.] **MPW**:3.25.11, p666, 4.8.11, p780.

[214] **TONY THE GREASER**, Melies: [This film would be remade in 1914 and is significant for its sympathetic treatment of its main character, a Mexican. Although cited by various authorities as an example of typical negative stereotyping, this is inaccurate. Apparently those researchers were misled by merely reading the title of this film. Although no print of this film seems to have survived, it is clear from the review that sympathy was cast with the Mexican, although some might consider him an uncle-Tomista: "From force of habit some might call him a "Greaser." True, he is a Mexicano--he is no more. [sic] a man of nobel instincts and chivalrous nature."

He loves the rancher's daughter, but "will not inflict his attentions upon her." Overhearing a conspiracy among a gang of "dissolute Mexicans" to attack the ranch and their insults to the "stars and stripes", he grabs the flag they are about to desecrate and races to sound the alarm. The lady runs for help while Tony fights the "black hearted devils" who slay him as he clutches her bandanna, evidence of his eternal devotion and love [522].] **MPW**:2.18.11, p374, 2.25.11, p430.

[215] **TRACKED**, Imp: [This production company was one of the first to announce their plan to make a series of films staged on location in the "Pearl of the Antilles." Their first film with a Cuban setting used the islands lush tropical scenery as a backdrop for a "perfidious wife" who is accused by her husband of" villainy" as "the dramatic story unfolds." Wives, especially Hispanic ones, were not allowed such latitude in 1911, and scripters along with audiences, universally demanded their punishment in the final scene.] **MPW**:3.18.11, p603.

[216] **THE TRAGIC WEDDING**, Pathe: [A Mexican girl living in a "marble palace" falls in love with a local gypsy. Her family wishes her to marry wealth which she refuses and begs her lover for rescue. To insure that their daughter does the right thing, the parents plan an immediate ceremony. South of the border romance was always complicated and passionate. Upon learning this the gypsy and his trusty band of bandidos ride hard after the wedding coach, save the señorita and, in a raging gun battle on the beach, slay the other suitor and his retainers. One assumes the reunited couple lived happily ever after enjoying the slightly soiled sand and surf.] **MPW**:7.29.11, p211.

[217] **A TRIP THROUGH MEXICO**, Powers: ["A scenic picture of value presenting varied scenes of Mexican life, accurately and interestingly."] **MPW**:2.18.11, p431.

[218] **TWO DAUGHTERS OF HAVANA**, Pathe: [Set in Cuba, the story involves the romantic complications which arise when two señors realize they are in love with the same girl. Under such circumstances, Anglo scripters had but one solution. The film ends with a "typical, but thrilling" fight/duel, between the two hot blooded Hispanics.] **MPW**:11.18.11, p570, 12.9.11, p816.

[219] **THE TWO SIDES**, Biograph: [This work was one of several sympathetic portrayals of Mexicans lensed by this production company before the heat of the Mexican conflict and North American newspaper war turned the public against the entire nation. Both good and bad Mexicans inhabit this film, one is rich, the other poor. Both have children, one sick, the other healthy and unhappy. The wealthy ranchero has fired the poor peon and is unsympathetic to his child. The rich rancher was merely trying to cut corners and make a few extra dollars by firing one of his Mexican helpers. Soon the situation grows worse for the peasant because his child's condition deteriorates and only medicine will save its life. In his despair the Mexican peon plans to go to the rancher and beg for his job or some assistance, but circumstances allow him to

rescue that individuals child from a fire for which he is duly rewarded. Heroic deeds performed by Mexicans in the service of either Mexican or Anglo masters will stop being portrayed in the following year when the call for intervention in Mexico gains increasing momentum.] **MPH**:5.6.1911, p1023.

[220] **UNCLE SAM WATCHING THE MEXICAN BORDER**, Motion Picture Distributing and Sales Company: [With the growing unrest in Mexico, the overthrow of the Madero government by the Dictator Huerta, President Wilson ordered more troops to the border. From this date through 1916, many if not most North Americans wanted armed intervention in Mexico. This film depicts "all phases of military life as pertains to the preparation for actual warfare", mobilization scenes, cavalry, artillery, comedy camp-life and "the first moving picture of aeroplanes in active military service."] **MPW**: 4.8.11, p747.

[221] **UNDER THE TROPICAL SUN**, EDISON: [The new American foreman in the Cuban cane fields of course attracts the attention of Marcadies, a lovely worker. Later he takes her to a dance, not realizing she belongs to Morales. When he does so the next day, and understands "the great wrong" he has done, he attempts to rectify it. Few of the early silents allowed the North American protagonist to give way to the Hispanic, but it was a chivalrous thing to do. Exhibitors felt that the story line was thin, but the pictures depicting various aspects of Cuban life were "highly educational" and worth while for audiences.] **MPW**: 9.9.11, p724, 9.30.11, p972.

[222] **A WARTIME WOOING**, Thanhouser: [Even today, among Hollywood's favorite scenarios involving any nationality, including Hispanics, is that which has them betray their nation for the United States. In this film a Spanish nobleman living in Cuba joins in the war against the United States. His death incurs a desire for vengeance on the part of his daughter who now becomes a dancing girl to disguise her real function as a spy. She is quite successful using her seductive ways, in obtaining information until she meets the young Anglo hero who makes her love him and shows her the error of her ways. When he is captured, she denies her cause and twice is responsible for effecting his escape.] **MPW**:5.27.11, 6.10.11, p1319.

[223] **A WESTERN HEROINE**, Vitagraph: [The formula well established by now, Miss Story, our western heroine is intrusted with a large sum of money which is coveted by the ever present Mexican thief. With some effort and dash, she easily thwarts his evil intentions, saves the dollars and returns them to the rightful owner. As always, the Mexicans receive what they deserve]. **MPW**:10.14.11, p128.

[224] **WHEN CALIFORNIA WAS WON**, Kalem: [A slightly romantic interpretation of how California gained its independence from Mexico. When Commander Sloat of the American Navy sends his lieutenant ashore to demand the Mexican governor's surrender, the young officer falls for his beautiful daughter, Manuelita. She returned his affection and later, when he the authorities

captured him as a spy know she must try to save him. Whereas the only help she can depend on is in the harbor, she rows out to his ship to bring the bluejackets for his rescue. Having saved their fellow officer from Mexican tyranny, the group now decides to continue the conquest which effectively brings the former Mexican territory, it's independence. All of California was acquired as simple as that. For the very early silver screen it is understandable, even a little less naive than having Silvester or Chuck bring independence to Afghanistan or Vietnam.] **MPW**:11.11.11, p494, 11.25.11, p636.

1912

[225] **ACROSS THE ISTHMUS 1912**, aka **PANAMA CANAL--ACROSS THE ISTHMUS IN 1912**, Selig: [Basically an up date of Selig's fine work in 1909 [38] Jason S. McQuade's review of the production was very detailed and laudatory [38].] **MPW**:3.16.12, p952-3.

[226] **THE ADVENTURES OF AMERICAN JOE**, Kalem: [Known in Southern California as "Jose de Ingles," Joe is shipwrecked and picked up by Bouchard, a local pirate who wants his help to attack the Ortega ranch, home of a reputed treasure. Grateful, but not willing to sign on as a privateer, Joe warns the lovely daughter of the Ortegas and helps thwart Bouchard's raid. Deciding to stay with the family, he "instituted many progressive measures and built the first mill in California." This scenarist may well have been a full blown Bull Moose progressive, because, his main character's reforming was still unfinished. Joe rescues his lady from the evils of the pirates and establishes himself as the defender of the right.] **MPW**:4.13.12, p158, 5.4.12, p425.

[227] **THE ALCALDE'S CONSPIRACY**, Kalem: [Basillo works while Melitta strums her guitar; her Hispanic carpenter is the only one that can really make her wood work. One day the Alcalde and his sister pass by and ask for water, but the Spanish official wants a lot more than water when he sees the sweet Melitta. A few days later he sends the lady a note claiming that his sister needs help, but when the unsuspecting samaritan arrives, 'there are no etchings.' Forced to defend herself with a sword, the skillful señorita drives the dirty deceiver away and returns home to Basillo. Yet, there was some honor in Mexico's colonial period, when the sister finds out what her bad boy brother was about, she forces him to send a note of apology.] **MPW**:2.17.12, p610, 3.2.12, p867.

[228] **AN AMERICAN INVASION**, Kalem: ["A dramatic picture of life in Southern California just before the Americans came." Alice Joyce plays the Mexican heroine who saves three North Americans from trouble and falls in love with one of them.] **MPW**:2.24.12, p690.

[229] **AN ARIZONA ESCAPADE**, Essanay: [Brig Harris a "renegade Mexican" tires of his sweetheart and dumps her. With time on his hands he now plans to rob the Catspaw mine. But the scorned Mexican señorita discovers the plot and is responsible for his arrest. Her vengeance satisfied, she laughs as he is put behind bars.] **MPW**:3.23.12, p1092.

[230] **THE BAG OF GOLD**, Kalem: [When the brig, "Danube" sank off the coast of San Pedro near the pueblo of Los Angles in 1838, Sam Prentiss managed to make it to shore with his savings strapped to his waste. There, exuding all the brashness of North American youth, he was saved from various imprudent actions by Antonio Lugo one of the pueblo's

prominent men. This of course was done because the Anglo had captured the heart of Rafaela, Antonio's daughter. Historical notes frequently affected the hearts of Hollywood scripters.] **MPW**:6.15.12, p1056, 6.29.12, p1227.

[231] **THE BANDIT'S MASK**, Selig: [Exhibitors complained that there was not much originality in this photoplay. Yet it did present a variation from the established norm. In the end the love of the every ready dark skinned Mexican maiden saves an Anglo hero, but in this case, he is saved from a Mexican posse, which is chasing North American bandits operating south of the border.] **MPW**:2.3.12, p393.

[232] **THE BANDIT'S SPUR**, Pathe: [The silver screen's Hispanic women could prove very resourceful, if one really captured their hearts, it was best never to cross them. Although this Mexican lady loves her Anglo man, he makes the mistake of making her jealous. To avenge herself, she has the crime her father was accused of pinned on her lover. Luckily for all, the Anglo's implication results in the apprehension of the real criminal and the North American is eventually freed. It was discovered that "Manuel Garcia, a bandit" had had a fancy set of spurs made by an indian artisan, but refused to pay for them. For good measure he had robbed the Overland stage. When the indian told the sheriff about the incident, both men were cleared and the proper Mexican hanged.] **MPW**:9.14.12, p1106, 10.5.12, p40.

[233] **BETTY'S BANDIT**, Nestor: [This scenario was somewhat more sophisticated, but it contained the essential identifying props, especially the Mexican's favorite weapon, a "jeweled dagger." Somewhere just north of the Rio Grande, a Mexican bandit had attempted to rob the North American hero with the help of his prized possession. Wounded during the struggle, but still alive, the victim picks up the knife that his assailant has left behind and somehow makes his way to Betty's ranch. There she tends to his wounds and of course, immediately falls in love with him. As she works on him it is impossible for her not to notice and admire the dagger he has in his possession thinking it is his. Later, when she learns that a reward has been offered for the owner of the easily identifiable knife, Betty is torn between duty and love, believing that the boy of her dreams is really a bandit. She chooses the latter and audiences did not have to imagine her elation when she discovers his innocence. The Mexican is brought to justice.] **MPW**:10.26.12, p386, 11.2.12, p451.

[234] **BLACK SHEEP**, Biograph: [Not a "western", but a "Californian", with a "weak" wayward son who has been reprimanded at the same time a Mexican decides to rob the fathers ranch. The bad boy is blamed for the crime. The exhibitors criticize Biograph for indulging in the techniques of "lesser contemporaries" by using the "near lynching" ploy and a Mexican's confession as he lay dying on the gambling house floor where he has just been shot. All of this takes place just as the rope is being placed round the innocent Anglo's neck [852].] **MPW**:8.10.12, p546.

[235] **THE BORDER DETECTIVE**, American: [Significant because it is the first film in which drugs, at that time it was opium, are intercepted at the border by agents of the U. S. Government. "Uncle Sam has many representatives in various vocations paid to guard his interests." This story described the work of the Secret Service and border customs officers.] **MPW**:10.19.12, p278, 10.26.12, p344.

[236] **BRONCO BILLY'S MEXICAN WIFE**, Essanay: [The faithlessness of the silver screen's women knew no race, but woe to the man who weds such a Mexican maiden. By 1912 Broncho Billy Anderson could claim to be the nation's most easily identifiable and popular moving picture star. This film merely improved his image: "G. M. Anderson should please his multitude of followers with this exciting episode." "A faithless woman is more than a match for the wisest man in cunning." "Billy's Mexican wife makes him appear like a deuce spot, when measuring his craftiness against hers." She marries Billy to please her father but knows she will keep her lover. When her cupidity is discovered she cuts herself with "a large knife," and has the star arrested. While behind bars she "tantalizes her imprisoned husband by kissing her Mexican lover [and] expresses the lowest depths of woman's self abandonment and fiendish cruelty." It takes another woman to resolve the situation. The Mexican has himself done a lady wrong and when she discovers him with Billy's wife, she kills them both and clears Broncho.] **MPW**:11.30.12, p867.

[237] **THE BURIAL OF THE MAINE**, Comet: [Comet took out a full page ad for this topical feature advertising it as "another victory for the sales company." Among its features were "Cuban soldiers carrying the caskets containing **Maine** victims" and U.S. Sailors placing them on the Battleship North Carolina.] **MPW**:3.30.12, p57.

[238] **CAPTAIN RIVERA'S REWARD**, Kalem: [Set in Spanish California, the Captain works for the Viceroy who wants to increase the size of his little pueblo, Los Angeles. On his way to Sonora to seek more colonists, Rivera performs an act of kindness by saving Meta's child, unaware that she is the wife of a local bandit. Because of his heroism, the señora pledges eternal gratitude. No sooner than that, the Captain is captured by the notorious, Palomare, the bandit leader, who sentences the young soldier to death for being Spain's representative. Meta, not forgetting her obligation, enlists the aid of the Viceroy's daughter, Ermins to save the officer. Two months later, having successfully completed his mission, he returns to the pueblo with many more settlers and the Viceroy is so pleased, he gives him his daughter. And that's how LA's population boom began.] **MPW**:3.2.12, p796, 3.23.12, p1063.

[239] **CELEBRATIONS ON THE RANCH**, American Kinema: [This neat little cinematic stereotype enhancer was about as concise a prejudicial package as you could get. With slight subtle and more overt changes in wrapping it provided the silver screen with hundreds of apparently different scenarios, all basically

the same story. Anglo Bob and Mexican/Hispanic Sanchez both love the same little filly, cute little mare that she was. Sanchez though, does not like the competition and determines to have it removed. He uses as a vehicle for the transfer, a card game. Having previously planted several aces in his rival's boot, he proceeds to discover that there are too many aces in the desk and immediately accuses Bob, pointing to the cards sticking out from his boot. In disgrace, Bob rides off the ranch leaving the range wide open for the Mexican to do a little roaming on, but to no avail. Bright as he is Bob soon discovers that he been a real dupe and returns to tell the lady everything. She of course accepts his explanation and all is well until the Mex decides he must possess the object of his lust. He kidnaps the sweet innocent thing and takes her to his cabin where he has decided he will have his way with her, but he has misjudged his quarry, western women were hardly frail females. Without much trouble she outwits the stupid Mexican, escapes and tells good ole Bob all about the unpleasant event. In anger, seeking justice, not revenge Bob rushes to the cabin to beat the dirty Mex to within an inch of his life. They fight and fight and fight, eventually falling off a cliff as a result of the blows. Of course the Mexican was killed by the fall, but with a little bit of Tarzan in him, the Anglo managed to grab onto a vine and save himself for the prize that was waiting for him back at the old rancho. And there you go, dress it up a bit, change a few of the unessentials, move the location to the streets of LA and you can do it a hundred times.]

[240] **CHIQUITA, THE DANCER**, American: [The scenes for this story take place "near one of those border towns near American and Old Mexican territory where Americans and Mexicans fraternize." After a lot of stuff happens, with good and bad Americans and good and bad Mexicans, and despite Chiquita's "half witted brother," another Mexican señorita was afforded the opportunity to save her Anglo lover, this time from the nefarious designs of an "evil Justice of the Peace."] **MPW:10.26.12, p337.**

[241] **THE COMING OF COLUMBUS**, Selig: [Certainly one of the major productions of 1912, this three reel historical drama represents the first serious attempt to bring the discovery of the new world to the silver screen. In contrast with the 1910 Gaumont production, [qv] extensive historical research was conducted to insure accuracy. The production costs were also significant. A $100,000 bond was paid to the Commissioners of the Columbian Exhibition for the use of the three vessels, duplicates of the originals, the gift of Spain in 1893 to the great fair celebrating the New World's discovery. Selig, the films producer, exhibited an early flare for flamboyant exploitation when he employed a Catholic friend of his to have a copy of the film given to Pope Pius X. The Pontiff, who had ordered all the priests in Italy not to attend moving picture shows, was so pleased with the film that he presented Selig with a commemorative medal which the producer exploited to the fullest. European orders for prints of the film were so numerous there were long delays. The picture's success helped

pave the way for future historical epics each with its own unique interpretation. Certainly, Hollywood never let historical accuracy get in the way of a good picture. In this one the native indians, who have grown to love Columbus so liked the great white father, they have to be stopped from killing the new Spanish governor who has arrested him and placed him in chains.] **MPW**:5.1.12, p58, 5.4.12, pp407-410, 521.

[242] THE COWARD, American: [In future decades Hollywood will require the bodies of some new nationality to use as cannon fodder. As has been traditional, they will be portrayed as inferior who can be terminated without much fear that the required bloodletting will cause significant protest. Almost invariably these bodies will be of some considered inferior race, slaughtered in selective scenes by scripters and scatter between lines of inane dialogue. Beginning in the silent era, these disposable bodies, were most frequently, hispanic, black or oriental. Things would not change much with the coming of the talkers. In this film the major action revolves about a pansy cowboy that all the Anglo's ridicule. But it takes an insult from a Mexican cowhand to provoke him to action. He shoots the Mexican dead, is pursued by the posse, but is allowed to redeem himself by saving the sheriff's child. He tells the grateful father where he will be hiding, but the sheriff never travels there, it was not an Anglo that had been killed.] **MPW**: 3.30.12, p1178, p168, 4.20.12, p231.

[243] THE DAUGHTERS OF SEÑOR LOPEZ, American: [The complications in this Spanish love affair are caused, as the reviver put it, by "the custom of their people." First a "worthless" farm hand is discharged, [that will be important later.] The primary plot focuses on the problems created by the fact that the father has two daughters and requires that the eldest must be married before the younger one can be courted, an old Hispanic custom. To complicate this situation the scribe has, the attractive young suitor, Trevino, fall for the younger señorita. To make matters worse for her, he has her punished by her father for being on the street without her duenna and enticing the señor. When the romantic suitor sends a note suggesting a pleasant meeting, the elder daughter keeps the assignation. Meanwhile, the younger one escapes the confinement of her room and runs from home only to be captured and held for ransom by the fired workman who was seeking to revenge himself against her father. All is resolved when the Señor Trevino rescues the girl and is granted permission to marry her as his reward.] **MPW**:12.16.12, p1122.

[244] THE DIVINE SOLUTION, Lubin: [Exhibitors had problems with the morality implied in this production. The story features the "lowly folk of a Mexican village," where a wife who is brutalized by a boorish husband, is also loved by a nicer man. The exhibitor's review found fault with the fact that the wife returned the affection. This was a time when wives on either side of the border were forced to endure. But the reviewer's biggest problem with the scenario was the fact that the brutal husband, also a thief, was struck dead by the

image of Christ as the brute attempted to steal a golden chalice from the local church. Apparently, at the moment of the robbery, his wife was at home praying in front of a crucifix. That she had clearly considered eloping with the other man, provoked the ire of the writer. But worse, that the divinity should intercede on her behalf was not considered acceptable, and should not have been shown to be so on film, even south of the border. In final judgement, "this" was not considered "a pleasant picture." Scripters were not to use a "Divine Solution" to solve domestic troubles on either side of the river.] **MPW**:7.27.12, p314, 8.10.12, p545.

[245] **DON CAESAR DE BAZAN**, Reliance: [Very complicated at court drama centering on the problems faced by Don Caesar who, before being executed is forced to marry a young flower girl so that his title and line can continue. The various intrigues at the Spanish court eventually result in his being shot, but he survives and escapes which allows him to eventual return and claim his rightful place, this time with the King of Spain's blessing.] **MPW**:11.16.12, p704.

[246] **DON JUAN AND CHARLES V**, Pathe: [This was the second important historical drama with a Hispanic theme produced in 1912. As would forever be the case with history adapted to the screen, the scripters took certain liberties with the facts, although there is evidence of some in depth research for this production. The story opens with the abdication of Charles V, "whose vast and scattered territories had cursed his country with a foreign policy in nearly every corner of Europe." This was true enough, but more to the point were the reviewer's attitudes concerning the Spanish personality: "This [photo]play boldly presents the contrasts and contradictions of Spanish character ... it follows closely our own conclusions that the Spanish are proud, courteous and brave, but given to intrigue and [are] magnificently impudent." "The photo-play well brings out the half-vindictive, half-voluptuous nature of court life at the time of Philip II." To promote this "two reel" historical epic, Pathe took out a lavish two page spread in several of the trade journals.] **MPW**:7.20.12, p286-7, 7.27.12, p330-1.

[247] **THE DOVE AND THE SERPENT**, Imp: [The title refers to the lady and one of her slimy Spanish suitors. Tortola, the dove, chooses the less worthy of two admirers and thus falls into the clutches of the snake, Luis Arguello. Meanwhile, he and the one she rejected, Pablo, are under the influence of the local cantina cutie who makes them cut cards for her favors. Luis wins and plays out the hand, but soon discovers that the chips he left on the mesa at home were worth more than these. But its too late for Luis, Tortola has reunited with Pablo and all is forgiven. Things were simpler then.] **MPW**:3.30.12, p1202.

[248] **FANTASCA, THE GYPSY**, Kalem: [The beautiful "gipsy" who is part of the troop entertaining at the lawn party for the very rich, falls for the master of the house, Neville. He is repulsed by her show of affection, someone so beneath his

class should have known better. Meanwhile, the other gypsies have planned, which was generally accepted their tradition, to steal Neville's child. But once the infant is led away, Fantasca realizes how much pain and suffering this will cause the father, and though her love is unrequited, she returns the child to the happy parents.] **MPW**:7.20.12, p270, 8.10.12, p546.

[249] **THE FILIBUSTERS**, Kalem: [In this action drama the Spanish American war provides the opportunity for our young newspaper hero to obtain the proverbial "scoop" that would forever ensure him a place on one of the big New York daily's. Don, the reporter, enlists the help of Daisy, the daughter of a tugboat captain who is smuggling arms to the Cuban insurrecto's. When the plot is discovered by Anita the sinister Spanish spy, she informs her people and they pursue the tug in an exciting chase. Just as they are about to be captured, the Spanish gun boat is blown out of the water by the rebel Cubanos who control the beach. It made a great story for the paper, helped the cause of Cuban independence and provided the humble reporter with a bride. Kalem productions invariably supported the rebel cause in Cuba and in Mexico.] **MPW**:6.28.12, p1264, 7.20.12, p243.

[250] **GERONIMO'S LAST RAID**, American: [This melodrama set in the southwest, is less a story of the great Apache warrior than it is a love story between the pretty young thing and the two officers that crave her affection. Geronimo's role in this film is simply to escape, thereby providing the two soldiers an opportunity to prove their heroics by attempting to recapture him. The fiercely portrayed indian warrior provides added drama to the production by attacking a settlement and slaughtering all including the soldiers who have come to the rescue. Only the lady and her lover survive. Indicating a growing interest in such productions, there were three different reviews for this film in the one trade journal cited.] **MPW**:9.21.12, p1176, 9.12.14, p1054-5, 9.24.12, p1204.

[251] **THE GIRLS OF PINE TREE RANCH**, Cosmopolitan Film Co: [Once more the evil character of the western half breed, certainly it's darker side, could be found lurking about with another scripted creation, a really dirty Mexican. The latter, when scorned in his desire for a pretty white skinned Anglo girl, devised a certain plan for revenge, one which was aimed directly at his Anglo cowboy rival. This Mexican villain was created a cut above others in intelligence, and was naturally shrewd. Not wanting to be found out, he decided to use his halfbreed friend as the unconscious stooge, to do the dirty work. Even by 1912 audiences knew that horse stealing was considered to be a serioussss violation of the silver screen's western code, a real hangin' offense. It was made obvious to all that the offended Mexican knew it too, so when he steals a horse and graciously gives it to his dummy friend, all could see that he was a real bad hombre. To make it even worse, he instructs the boob to tell all that the cowboy had sold him the horse. Obviously enjoying being in on the action, the breed does as he is told and for a while it looks bad for the cowboy, but no scripter could let an Anglo

be beaten by two such as these and in the final scene both are seen being beaten and driven out of town. A simple film like this was one more reaffirmation that the screen character ascribed to halfbreeds and Mexicans reflected real life.]

[252] **THE GREASER AND THE WEAKLING**, American: [All but one of the big N Ranch hands mourned the death of its owner. Only a Mexican greaser, "generally disliked for his bullying ways," was unmoved. When the latter discovered that the two daughters were returning to run the ranch, he devised a plot to marry one of them and gain control of their assets. Enlisting the aid of a confederate, he attempted to force his affections on one of the girls who promptly spurned him. Forced to take more direct action, he abducted the other sister. He is of course thwarted in his intent by the Anglo hero who, subscribing to the very well understood law of the silver screen scripter, rescues and thereby wins the lady for himself. In the final scene the mortally wounded greaser sinks to the ground and dies. Anglo justice always triumphed, it was prescribed by the writers.] **MPW**:8.31.12, 885, 9.14.12, p1108.

[253] **THE GUN SMUGGLERS**, Kalem: [Another "educational" view from Kalem's perspective of the Mexican Revolution. Steve Jarrow is running guns to the insurrectionists. It is left to Col. Valdez as a Federalista officer to stop him. Steve's son is unaware of what his father is doing and loves Valdez's beautiful daughter. True to his word, the officer stops the gunrunner and kills Steve, which causes his son to seek revenge, a la Mexican style. Luckily, he is saved by the "cool-headedness of the brave colonel," who explains that he was only doing his duty and that when you by a ticket, you have to expect to take the ride, no matter where it leads.] **MPW**:6.8.12, p650, 6.29.12, p1226.

[254] **THE GYPSY FLIRT**, Crystal: [Chester and Mable, while strolling, run across Carlotta and Pedro, wandering gypsies. As Carlotta tells Mable's fortune, Chester is taken with her. Later Chester and Carlotta get it together and Mable sees them. She now pays Pedro to make love to her in front of Chester. The gypsy is willing, but when he sees his lady kissing Mable's man, a fight breaks out. In a moment all are exchanging blows with the gypsies gaining the victory and each other. If there was a moral in this one it was something like: Anglo's should never mess with Spanish gypsies, they carry knives, even the ladies.] **MPW**:11.9.12, 592.]

[255] **A GYPSY'S LOVE**, Shamrock: [A beautiful gypsy falls in love with a boy who loves her for a while, as boys often do. But boys should not trifle with the affections of a Spanish gypsy. After he has married another, one of his own kind, and helped produced a little girl, she unknowingly falls into the hands of the scorned and colorfully clad lady. Realizing that the babe is lost and knowing who she belongs too, Leila takes her to the good sisters and works hard providing for her during some eleven years. Possibly feeling that that was enough punishment for the poor parents, she tells all to the

sisters who return her home, hopefully a more reverent adolescent.] **MPW**:5.4.12, p462.

[256] **THE GYPSY WIFE**, Champion: [A beautiful young gypsy girl falls in love with one who is not of "her tribe." His mother opposes the union, but they are wed, first by the "quaint customs" of her people, then by the church. All goes well for six years, a lovely child is born, but when the wanderers return, the girl is tempted back to the free life without responsibilities, but only for a while. This is one of the few gypsy stories that ends well for all.] **MPW**:7.6.12, p78.

[257] **THE HALF-BREED'S FOSTER SISTER**, C. G. P. C.: [From today's perspective it may be difficult for some to believe how class conscious early screen writers were, it maybe even more difficult for others to imagine why so many early film heroines were portrayed as selfless and selfsacrificing. In the film the beautiful Mexican half-breed was imbued with both characteristics. Displaying great heroism she saves the child of a rich Castilian family. She is rewarded by being adopted. Now moving in better circles, she is introduced to the son of the Governor who falls in love with her immediately. But considering her former station, she refuses to "sacrifice his life for her" own happiness and enters a convent. This one was not for the feminist.] **MPW**:7.20.12, p274.

[258] **THE HALF-BREED'S SACRIFICE**, Lubin: [Manuel's father was a Mexican, his mother an indian, from the first he had little chance. As his life unfolds, he falls off a cliff, is saved by the Governor of Sonola, becomes his "dog" like slave, saves him from the evils of Castinette and her lover and dies for his trouble. And for all of Manuel's travail, the exhibitors complained that the production lacked continuity.] **MPW**:2.21.12, p1176, 9.7.12, p998.

[259] **THE HALF-BREED'S TREACHERY**, Lubin: [Elsie's dad had no luck with his prospecting and died leaving the girl penniless and alone. Pedro, the drunken Mexican half-breed tries his luck but is refused. He then attempts to force himself on Elsie, but is beaten away by Joe, the mining engineer. Later, even more inebriated, he shoots wildly at the young hero, misses him, but hits the gunpowder that blows up the mine. Joe is buried, but a rich vein of gold is uncovered. Pedro ignores Joe's problem and is scooping up the yellow stuff just as the heroine comes with the boys to rescue her man. Pedro of course receives his just deserts, and the two lovers find themselves richer in the bargain.] **MPW**:7.6.12, p70, 7.27.12, p343.

[260] **HAVANA, ITS STREETS, BUILDINGS AND FORTRESSES**, CGPC: ["An entertaining series of views, showing the quaint beauty in the capital of the Star of the Antilles."] **MPW**:7.27.12, p376.

[261] **HER LAST RESORT**, Bison: [With the advent of the second world war, Mexican bracero's would be welcomed into the United States with open arms, but in the early part of the century

those that could find day labor, or any at all were treated more like Hispanic slaves than anything else. This fairly early film was a fairly sympathetic portrayal of their plight. Pedro was unable to find work at any of the local ranches, so when cattle started disappearing, he was the natural suspect. One day, on his way back home to his hungry family from a day of unsuccessful job hunting, he heroically saves the life of one of the ranchers who had denied him work. He leaves immediately after the act without having been compensated, hurrying home. There he discovers that his wife has stolen a cow to get milk for the little nino's and when the local's arrive, despite his wife's confession that she had borrowed the animal, they plan to string him up. They would have done so had it not been for the grateful rancher who arrived in time to tell of Pedro's heroic deed. In the last scene, a grateful Pedro, wife and the kiddies are shown being rewarded with a cow and a new job opportunity. This type of portrayal was quite uncommon.] **MPW**: 9.7.12, p1012.

[262] **HER OWN COUNTRY**, American: ["A superb presentation of sentiment and natural beauties." The players included the Señor and Señora Mendez, the señorita, their adopted daughter, Juan Cortez, the wealthy Spaniard and Charley Dexter as the Ranger. Guess who gets the girl and why. All the characters, as had been the case since the primitive beginnings, were played by Anglos.] **MPW**:11.23.12, 734.

[263] **HIS MEXICAN SWEETHEART**, Pathe: [A young lieutenant in the U. S. Army is serving on the border waiting for war to break out with Mexico. While waiting for what many North Americans then considered an inevitable occurrence, he falls in love with a Mexican maiden. Once war is declared he is sent as a spy across the border and is captured. He easily escapes from his inept captors and makes it to his lover's home. She is patriotically at work and hides him beneath the folds of the Mexican flag she was making. Secured by the enemies colors, they cross the border to safety and are immediately married by the company chaplin. It could happen! From earliest times it has been almost impossible for scripters to avoid nationalistic pride and patriotism. Some time later those few who did, experienced the consequences of HUAC, film critics with a purpose.] **MPW**:2.22.12, p712.

[264] **THE ISLE OF STRIFE--CUBA**, Comet: [An instructive travelogue beginning at the historic Moro Castle, passing through the streets of Havana, stopping at the cathedral, which like many others throughout the Caribbean claimed the bones of Columbus, and with a final stopover at, the North American run, "largest sugar plantation in the world." Such "entertaining" short subjects of our "Cuban Colony" were very popular.] **MPW**:6.15.12, p1068.

[265] **JUAN AND JUANITA**, Lubin: [Note worthy because it is one of the few and possibly the earliest scenario in which a Hispanic is the hero that is responsible for capturing the Anglo bandit. A very romantic story which "bristles with the atmosphere of the land of the cactus and palm tree ... the

types are Mexican, but the story is told in our own country." Two lovers are prevented from courting until the poor peon, Juan, acquires a job, which he does at the local mine. He works well but is faced with dismissal when a consignment of gold is stolen. Determined to win his lady, he and the station master who was assaulted, pursue the baddies. The crooks had escaped in the company engine, which forces the two pursuers to use a simple hand pump car. After a lot of pumping Juan manages to brings the culprits to justice which prompts the mine owner to double his salary and provide a proper place for he and his bride to reside in. Juan an his lady were very pleased that the Horatio Alger thing also worked for Hispanics at times.] **MPW**:11.2.12, p474, 12.2.12, p459.

[266] **LAND BARON OF SAN TEE**, American: [A wealthy land baron controls the local's water rights and is forced to share his water by the intercession of a Mexican who captures him.] **MPW**,2.24.12, p748.

[267] **THE LAST RITES OF THE MAINE AND THE BURIAL OF ITS DEAD**, Selig: [Selig claimed to have scooped the competition with this film, another of his "Topical Features," but the Comet production was out first. Yet this production had features not found in the others. It showed "the building of the great water tight bulkheads necessary for the operation" and the raising of the unfortunate ship as it came to the surface for the first time in fourteen years.] **MPW**:4.13.12, p145.

[268] **MAN'S LUST FOR GOLD**, Biograph: [Something of a morality play emphasizing the difficulties created by man's transgressions and the problems that result. This one was more or less a loosely connected series of semirelated scenes with both Mexican and Anglo characterizations, all searching for gold, with the Hispanics somewhat more sleazy than any of the others.] **MPW**:7.13.12.

[269] **THE MASSACRE OF THE SANTA FE TRAIL**, Universal-Bison: [An elaborate scenario describing frontier life near the border prior to the Civil War. The Rosarro's are wealthy Mexicans who must leave their "palatial estates" to go north for reasons of health. On the way they are attacked by drunken indians crazed by fire water. Only young Juanita escapes with the family treasure. She grows up at an apparently remote army camp where the captain and colonel still hold the same rank they had twenty years earlier. Complications arise involving just who the little lady will marry. But in the final reel she finds true love and he uncovers the treasure which had remained buried since her escape as a child from the savages.] **MPW**:9.14.12, p1058-9.

[270] **MELITA'S RUSE**, Melies: [Melita, a resourceful love mate, manages to save the inept Pedro from the law twice in one reel. First she uses a disguise to lead the posse astray, then she employees jealousy to fool the sheriff. In the end she and true love Pedro manage to make it across the Rio Grande where

the good padre, [there was never a bad one at this point in time], makes the two one.] **MPW**:2,17,12, p635.

[271] **A MEXICAN COURTSHIP**, Lubin: [By this date certain directors were achieving notice in some reviews. Known for his "interesting" Mexican subjects, Wilbert Melville and a Company of Lubin players working in the El Paso/Juarez area, filmed this story of a brave matador, Alonzo, and his attempt to have the beautiful Dolores marry him. Dolores desires instead a poor employee of the "Plaza el Torres," who is devoted to her. On this particular sunday when Alonzo was to fight the fiercest bull in all of Chihuahua, the unhappy matador arrives drunk and unable to meet the challenge. Juan, knowing that Dolores' parents want her to marry the rich bullfighter, volunteers to fight the bull himself. Laughed at first, he is allowed to prove himself and is well on the way to becoming Mexico's top toreador in the final reel, which makes his señorita's smile as warm as the sun side in the corrida on a sunday afternoon at the fights.] **MPW**:2.22.12, p710, 3.2.12, p769, 3.16.12, p.962.

[272] **MEXICAN ELOPEMENT**, Pathe: [Once more dad does not like the daughters choice of suitors, but in this "beautiful love" story, the two young Mexican lovers manage to escape in time and get married before the father can prevent it. As frequently as this scenario would be used in future films with lovers of many different nationalities it was hardly original in 1912.] **MPW**:3.23.12, p1096, 4.13.12, p137.

[273] **A MEXICAN MIX-UP**, Nestor: [The heavy in this photoplay is Don Pedro, rival mine owner and "a villain at heart." Avaricious, as most Hollywood Hispanic villains were scripted to be, Don Pedro wants the neighboring mine which belongs to Mrs. Rice. To do this he has his henchmen steal the deed to mine just as our Anglo hero, Jack, and his boys arrive on the scene. Needless to say, they sum up the situation quickly and foil this plot as well as all the others that the Don can devise until he and his bandito's are safely behind bars. But it was no easy days writing to get them there.] **MPW**:8.10.12, p580, 8.17.12, p674.

[274] **THE MEXICAN REVOLUTIONIST**, Kalem: [The scenario of this film is incidental in comparison to the significance of the exhibitors comments which praised it and its production company. The pictures political orientation is liberal, favoring the Maderista revolutionaries. More often than not, the silver screens sympathies sided with those groups who were fighting to overthrow an established dictatorial regime. In this one, Juan is a revolutionary who volunteers to assess Federalista troop strength in "Guadalyayra" [sic]. While there he falls for the lovely [there were very few ugly screen señoritas] Marcella. Eventually recognized by a drunken Federal officer, he is arrested and jailed. His lady helps him escape in time to join in the capture of the city. True love and justice triumph in the last scene. The exhibitors loved this film as they did most of the Kalem productions, some of which were responsible for perpetuating the harshest

of stereotypes. Their comments emphasize the central focus of this work: "A splendid Mexican Kalem. Because of their absolute fidelity to truth, their correct rendering of every detail and the charm of their outdoor settings, these [films] have justly become very popular with exhibitors. Their educational value is considerable. Americans have learned more about conditions as they exist in the sister republic through these pictures than through any other medium ... The correctness of these pictures from a military point of view is surely not the least of their merits." It would be difficult to find words more to the point.] **MPW**:4.20.12, p256, 5.11.12, p528.

[275] **A MEXICAN ROMANCE**, Lubin: [For those ready to believe that the Latin character was nothing less than lascivious, this was a perfect little photoplay. The characters included Don Juan, Don Jose, Dolores and Pepita: Don Jose loves Peptia and proposes under the big cactus in the court yard of the "Grape Vine" cantina. But as he is slipping the ring on his true loves finger " with one eye," the other encounters Dolores, the dancer and he is immediately smitten. Finding a way to bring his fiancee home, this early hot blooded Latin lover, now returns to the scene of his infatuation. Pepita has followed with the traditional knife to plunge it in the traditional back, but is stopped from doing so by Don Juan, who loves, and apparently understands Dolores, his not too faithful lady. After much more confusion and delay, Pepita discovers that Jose really loves her was only interested in a momentary flirtation, and that's Hollywood, even back then. The mythology of Hispanic hot blood, sexual ease and easy virtue has persisted to present days. Audiences loved the simplistic scenario, and exhibitors reported that these "romances in Mexican costume" were very popular.] **MPW**:5.11.12, p556, 6.1.12, p831.

[276] **THE MOORISH BRIDE**, Cines: [Interracial romances provided problems and pathos for almost all film scripters, understandably, these writers were a product of their times. The problem for the scenarist was eased for a while in 1927, when such interracial relationships were forbidden by the Production Code. Throughout film history it mattered not who wanted who unless they were of different, imagined, colors. This historical epic chronicled some of the eight hundred year conflict between Islam and Christianity fought on Spanish soil until the final expulsion of the Moors in 1492. Only in this past century have historians begun to see the more positive consequences of such a long engagement. The two races were not locked in lethal combat continuously throughout that time. During periods of peace, there was much commercial, intellectual, social and even, sexual intercourse between the two peoples. All of this led to a greater tolerance and understanding of each other. At times, some of these differing peoples fell in love. This films describes the complications of such a illicit affair. Luckily for the two of different faith and color, the celluloid medium of their affair allowed its acceptance in the final reel, at that point in time. When the Production Code came into existence such interracial

unions would be forbidden.] **MPW**:2.17.12, p599-60, 3.23.12, p1063.

[277] **NELL OF THE PAMPAS**, American: [The American Western company in an attempt to achieve some variation of the so similar and by now very familiar love story plots, shifted the local for this scenario to the Argentine Pampas. There on that "treeless plains of South America where the tall and graceful stems of pampas grass with their panicles of silvery whiteness undulate over a sea of tremulous green," the lover would meet. Although this was one of the first such films to claim so distant a location, the scenes were shot outside American's studio in Southern California. Again, there are no Hispanics playing the parts of Juan Cardoza, Pedro Villar, Nell Villar and the half-breed girl. There is an "orphan idiot" who lives off the largess of the Cordozas. The action is quite typical of what usually took place 5000 miles to the north in Mexico, but all Hollywood Hispanics were the same. Nell is loved by all, but she cares for Juan, who is the focus of the half-breed beauty's existence, though unknown to him. This could only end in tragedy and it does. The unrequited lover takes a bullet for Juan, but he is killed anyway. Only Nell and the idiot survive. Such was life on the silver screen Pampas.] **MPW**:12.7.12, pp965-6, 12.14.21.

[278] **THE NEW RANCH FOREMAN**, Lubin: [Jack Walton, a renegade and a gambler shoots a Mexican for accusing him of cheating. Forced to run he obtains a job by dirty doings at another ranch. Eventually a price is put on his head for the killing. The remainder of the story merely involves the manner in which he is brought to justice. Eventually he is, which must have surprised some, for he had only shot a Mexican. Screen Anglo's were rarely severely punished for such actions, but Jack was a real bad hombre, so that might have helped put him behind bars.] **MPW**:8.17.12, p686.

[279] **ON EL MONTE RANCH**, Essanay: [Mary is nice, Jim likes her. Dave, Mary's brother, is not nice, he gambles and cheats. Caught doing so, Jim is forced to fire him. Mary believes the lies Dave tells and gives Jim back his ring. Unable to do anything right, Dave falls in with a thieving Mexican and the begin rustling cattle. Of course they are caught, but Jim is able to save the prodigal from being strung up. Grateful, Dave writes a note saying he lied and heads across the border. The lovers are reunited. Audience realized the evils of bad company, especially if he was Mexican. It was all that simple.] **MPW**:6.1.12, p854.

[280] **ON THE CACTUS TRAIL**, Essanay: [The problems one faces when moving west to find fortune cannot be overcome if you fall in with a bad crowd and marry a Mexican girl. Dan leaves his sweetheart back east and heads west where everything turns bad after his marriage to the dark skinned lady. He kills a "puncher" over a card game, turns to crime and displays a treacherous nature. When the girl back home comes to save him, its all too late; the negative infection has led to his incarceration.] **MPW**:6.29.12, p1256.

[281] **THE OUTLAWS'S SACRIFICE**, Essanay: [Characterized by the exhibitors as a "good western" the cast includes a "Mexican marauder" played by an Anglo actor as was still universally the case. The twist here is that it is a good Anglo outlaw who shoots the Mexican as he is attacking the sheriff's wife. Not only that, he then rushes in and saves the child from the "marauder's evil intent."] **MPW**:11.2.12, p450.

[282] **THE PANAMA CANAL**, Aviation Film Sales Company: [One of the first films taken from the air of "The Greatest Engineering Feat Ever Undertaken." "Shown in two reels of Motion Picture Film." [383]] **MPW**:6.22.12, p1133, 7.27.12, 381.

[283] **PANAMA, THE EARTH DIVIDED, THE WORLD DIVIDED**, Shown by Kinemacolor: ["On the afternoon of Monday, November 25 at the Belasco Theater in Washington, President Taft, with members of his family and official staff saw the first showing" of this film. The gala production was repeated the following Friday for members of the National Geographic Society at its headquarters in Washington. One of the most elaborate of the Panama documentaries, the film took two hours to show and covered the complete fifty mile expanse of this incredible project. Much of its footage can still be seen in more recent historical surveys, including the "Panama Canal", a Public Television production.] **MPW**: 12.14.12, p1090.

PATHE NEWSREELS:

[284] **#13: El Paso, Texas**: Scenes of the Mexican Revolutionist in Control of Juarez. **MPW**: 3.25.12, p.1200.

[285] **#22: Del Rio Texas**: Film of ranchers driving cows across the Rio Grande to save them from the Federalista and revolutionary troops.

[286] **PEPITA'S ESCAPADES**, C.G.P.C.: [Exhibitors reported that this was an "excruciatingly funny" burlesque of the usual Spanish drama which climaxes with a mock duel that kept the audience howling." No intended to be a comedy it was certainly an indication that there was a real need to find new material for the already to very similar scenarios.] **MPW**:6.29.12, p1227.

[287] **PORTUGUESE JOE**: [The sailors who patronized Portuguese Joe's and his pretty wife's saloon, loved to "put it over the simple dago in a peculiarly sailor fashion." They taunted him by insulting his wife forcing him to defend her with his own. Although the term was usually used to describe Italian ethnics, the writer apparently thought it applied here, and expressed no reservation at their teasing "the dago" to distraction or death.] **MPW**:6.22.12, p1162.

[288] **THE PRAYERS OF MANUELO**, Vitagraph: [Manuelo and his wife are impoverished. Attempting to steal a few beans for her meal he is kicked and called a "lazy greaser." The job he is offered as a sheepherder turns him into a slave. Attempting to return home to his pregnant wife, he takes a horse that is not

his. Pursued, he is also shot, but when the cowboys enter his humble mud hut, they discover him with his good arm about his wife who is holding their new child. A picture of the Virgin is seen above the bed. Either out of bullets or feeling that he has had enough, the cowboys return to other pursuits. Such stark attempts to illicit sympathy for Mexicans, although condescending, were rare.] **MPW**:6.1.12, p852.

[289] **PUEBLO INDIANS, ALBUQUERQUE, N.M.**, Lubin: ["One of the most interesting educational pictures ever taken in the semi-Mexican Atmosphere of this country." Another example of the blurring of ethnic/racial line in the popular mind. Mexican and indian were for the most part interchangeable.] **MPW**:7.27.12, p545, 7.27.12, p314.

[290] **QUEEN ELIZABETH**, French: [Significant for its association with the birth of Paramount studio, but more so because it was the first attempt to picture the life of the "Virgin Queen" whose refusal to accept the advances of Philip of Spain was responsible for creating the centuries of animosity that resulted in the solidification of "la leyenda negra."] **[MPG]**

[291] **RAIDERS OF THE MEXICAN BORDER**, Warner: [As tensions increased along the Mexican border, almost anything that brought distant audiences a little closer to the action was easily saleable to exhibitors. This clip was advertised as showing "over a 1000 soldiers. Cavalry. Artillery and field guns. The most remarkable feature ever produced. You are losing money by not booking" this picture. In reality it simply involved the movements of some of the border guard from one encampment to another.] **MPW**:10.26.12.

[292] **THE RANCH WOMAN**, Champion: [Peggy Wilson has it hot for a real nogood Mexican gambler, Juan Gonzales, who has a beautiful señorita as a "side diversion", another "string to his bow." Unaware of all this, the lady gives him money which he squanders. Bill, a righteous Anglo, likes Peggy and feels bad for her being deceived but thinks it best to let events unfold. When they do, it's Juan's fiery fluff that explodes his powder. Now scorned, he seeks revenge, but as the writers would have it, Black Cloud, a faithful Chippewa friend of Peggy's, saves her from peril. The vile Mexican had chosen the hour of the Angelus for his dastardry. Instead of doing his former benefactress, he finds himself flying off the face of a cliff at the hands of the indian. Interestingly enough, Bill has nothing to do with the rescue.] **MPW**:5.25.12, p766.

[293] **THE RANGER'S REWARD**, Lubin: [Ranger Romaine guards an isolated district on the Mexican border. His orders include the capturing of Surrento, the local Mexican bandit. One day, the Ranger, happens onto the baddie as he is "insulting" the beautiful Bonita. In the struggle the señorita is saved, but the bandit escapes and plans his revenge against the lawman. But the writer could not allow this to happen, and as the bandits hangs from a tree with his knife ready to plunge into Romaine's back, Bonita shoots it out of his hand and gives her

own to the ranger, an added reward for his earlier service.]
MPW:7.20.12, p270.

[294] **REVOLUTION IN MEXICO**, Mexican Film Co: [Revolutionary unrest in Mexico had many production companies sending crews south of the border to feed the North American public's ever increasing appetite for almost any film concerned with such activity. This one was advertised as: "General Orozco on the Warpath" [after all they were indians] "two reels of the greatest picture ever filmed taken during actual battle."] **MPW**:11.23.12, p801.

[295] **THE REVOLUTIONIST**, Lubin: [A romantic young doctor loves a certain lady, but is rejected and so joins the Revolution to hide his sorrow. She selects a federal officer to wed. Later, in a battle between the opposing forces, the revolutionist survives the carnage and escapes and finds refuge in you know who's house. As it happens, the marriage has produced a young "señor" who happens to be mortally ill. The doctor of course saves the baby. But when the federal officer returns home, he makes the rebel his prisoner. Upon learning what the medico has done, he is forced to provide him with his freedom for services rendered. If everything in life were so well balanced, the scripters would really have to scramble to create a little challenge.] **MPW**:3.16.12, p994, 3.30.12, p42.

[296] **THE RING OF A SPANISH GRANDEE**, Thanhouser: [The script for this romance might well be considered a cynical commentary of what many screen writers considered the materialist nature of the Anglo females heart. While visiting the castillo in St. Augustine, Florida, a pretty young thing has to choose between the wealthy Anglo lover and the romantic young Hispanic who only has his love, affection and ancient heritage in the form of a ring, to offer. The poor Hispanic claims that the ring he would seal their love with has been given to his "great, great, great, great" grandfather by the then governor of the colony for his help in saving the city from British attack. Very impressed, the virgin considered the romance of his offer, but was brought back to reality by a vision that told her his revered ancestor had merely been the cook for the fortress guard. With the illusion exposed by the dream, she comes to her senses, "end[s] the infatuation", "stop[s] being romantic," and elects to wed the "good American" who could supply her with affection but also "new gowns, opera tickets and a steam heated home with all modern improvements." **Thirty Something** came early to the Cape Canaveral coast."] **MPW**:5.18.12, p660, p668, 6.1.12, p831.

[297] **A ROMANCE OF THE BORDER**, Lubin: [This script did not follow the usual formula of Mexican boy loves Anglo girl and its conclusion would certainly have given the Production Code censors some concern. Pedro, a young Mexican rancher, loved Rita, the daughter of Sergeant Blake who admired the hard working Hispanic lad. The heavy in this piece was an officer who tried to force his intentions on Rita causing both father and Pedro serious problems. The dirty doings of the officer

provoked a fight in which Pedro, to save the Sergeant shoots the officer. The Mexican manages to escape, but in doing so the old man is blamed for the crime. At the court-marshal the sergeant is convicted. When everything looks bad, at the very last moment, the loyal Pedro reappears, confesses to the crime, and clears the accused. Here the writer allows Pedro to escape again making his way across the border to safety. Scripters, after the Code came into effect, would not have been able to save Pedro, he would have had to be punished, but maybe sending him back to Mexico was considered punishment enough?] **MPW**:6.1.12, p856.

[298] **THE ROSE OF CALIFORNIA**, Imp: [A father, a wealthy Spanish ranchero, objects to the wedding of his daughter to the young government official from Washington. As it frequently did on the screen, love triumphed over parental devotion and the two are married by the local padre who approves of the union. All seemed well until the inflamed father attempts to plunge his dagger in the bridegrooms back just as they are leaving the church. Only the intercession of the good padre, whose authority was feared, allowed the two to escape.] **MPW**:2.24.12, p718, 3.2.12, p868

[299] **THE SEÑORITA'S BUTTERFLY**, Lubin: [In the fifties many new television owners may have wondered why they found themselves watching the test pattern after eleven or twelve o'clock as broadcasting ended for the day. It was at least something. In the same way, one may well wonder how audiences at the birth of the motion picture industry could enjoy what must have seemed like such small variations in so many similar scenarios. The most frequently used for Spanish señoritas was, of course, the prearranged marriage which the lady refuses to consummate. This one makes the prospective suitor somewhat more inventive than most. When he realizes that the lady he has yet to meet, the object of his affection, strongly opposes her father's choice, he feels he still has a chance. Learning further that she loves butterflies he borrows his own gardeners garb, catches one of the little winged creatures and strategically places it on his head as he sits behind a bush in her garden. Out gathering her own specimens, the lovely miss nets the inventive fellow. Once their eyes meet, it's love at first sight and 'adios' to the rich and fat father's choice. And you thought there was no romance left in the world.] **MPW**: 5.25.12, p756.

[300] **THE SEÑORITA'S REMORSE**, Lubin: [And you may very well have thought that **Waterloo Bridge** was an original Anglo script .... Perdita loves Trovio, which pleases him beyond belief. But the pernicious Alfonso also has intentions for the pretty little Spanish rose. Attempting to force his affections on her, worse, trying to take her to the local tavern, Alfonso is thrashed by Trovio. Employing Manuel, the former devises a plan to have Trovio sent up for five years. It works, which causes Perdita to faint when she learns that her lover has left. The two culprits now take her to the tavern and fill her with wine. Her mother is called and she rebukes the girl. "Perdita's only course now is the life of a coquette." Her

unfortunate spiral downward is unavoidable. Five years later, Trovio returns looking for his love. When she sees him she is over come by her detestable condition and plunges a dagger into her heart so that her true love will not have to bear the shame of her existence. Close enough?] MPW:7.13.12, p170, 8.3.12, p445.

[301] SMALL TRADES IN HAVANA, Pathe: ["A very interesting glimpse of street life in the Cuban capital.] MPW:3.23.12, p1062.

[302] THE SMUGGLERS'S DAUGHTER, Essanay: [Jason McQuade who began more comprehensive reviews of some of these one reelers in 1912 was filled with praise for G. M. Anderson, his production company and all of his films, especially this one. Here the Anglo hero loves a local girl whose father smuggles goods back and forth across the border. The problem is that the hero is made sheriff and ordered to stop the smuggling. The lady unaware of her father's activity until told by her lover, Anderson, is forced to choose at this moment of crisis. Luckily for the major players the problem could be handled by the writer with relative ease because of their close proximity to Mexico. The sheriff captures the lesser bandits and allows dad to fly across the border where, though he is exiled, he is safe from the law. For this the daughter's gratitude was forthcoming.] MPW:7.20.12, p233-4, 7.27.12, p344.

[303] A SPANISH CAVALIER, Edison: [Set during the time of the Inquisition, this love affair between the Spanish cavalier and a lady of noble birth is complicated by the adoration that the Grand Inquisitor also shares for her. For the nonCatholic, the Inquisition has always been considered brutality difficult to understand, it may well have been seen in a similar light by the thousands of Spaniards and Jews who died in the flames of the auto-da-fes. Here, the reviewer betrays a similar bias: "The shadow of the Spanish Inquisition with all the cruelty and ignorant conception of misguided Christianity," falls across the lovers path. It was simple enough for Spain's opponents to use this medieval cruelty as simply another aspect of the "Black Legend." Spain and Catholicism were demonstrably bad, England and Protestantism the reformers opposed to such evils were good. Under most circumstances, unless one is a religious zealot, it is/was difficult to defend the Inquisition, it is much easier to emphasize its dark side. In this film, the Grand Inquisitor, who's powers over life and death were almost limitless, used the "holy office" to torture a confession from the lady's maid which allows him to condemn her, his true love, to death. But in the last scene the maid manages to escape her confinement and she brings the cavalier and calvary to rescue her mistress from the purging fires of truth.] MPW:3.23.12, p1079, 4.6.12, p64.

[304] A SPANISH DILEMMA, Biograph: [Audiences seemed to love Hispanic love triangles, possibly any love triangles, it was certainly one of the most frequently used ploys in these early films. This variation on a theme was played for its humorous

and farcical aspects. A sweet señorita could not decide between two suitors. She wants to hurt neither, but what ever ruse they use to win her keeps them ever even in her eyes. In the finale the two señors decide to leave it to destiny and cut cards for her favors only to discover that she has, in the meanwhile, given them to another not even in the competition. Mujer, su nombre es, fickalita.] **MPW**:3.9.12, p3.23.12, p1063.

[305] **THE SPANISH REVOLT OF 1836**, Kalem: [It would seem according to this account that California gained its independence from Mexico because Alvarado was deeply in love with Isabella the daughter of the Alcalde of Monterey. She returned his affection but then Chico the "cruel and irascible governor" of the province, wanted the beauty for his own. Scorned, he removes the Alcalde from office which provokes Alvarado to lead the local citizenry into revolt, they loved him too, and remove the offensive tyrant from office. And this is only a brief second, momentous as it's consequences were, of Hispanic history according to Hollywood.] **MPW**:3.9.12, p877, 3.20.12, p1196.

[306] **TOMMY BECOMES A TOREADOR**, Gaumont: [A comical farce played at Tommy's expense. When a rich young lady is willed a fortune if she can marry a toreador she starts seeking suitors. Tommy enters the ring on try out day and is quickly laughed out of the corrida. Then, the real bullfighter comes in and takes over, his thrilling performance takes the girl's heart. Tragically, Tommy goes back to delivering meat and suffers, his heart is broken when he sees the newlyweds pass by.] **MPW**:5.18.12, p660, 6.1.12, p831.

[307] **THE TRAIL OF GOLD**, Kalem: [When Mary's granddad became ill she sent for the doctor, her sweetheart, to treat him. In failing health the old gent disclosed the hiding place of two bags of gold he wishes the lovers to have. As luck would have it, a malevolent Mexican, Tony by name, witnessed all through a side window. Waiting for his chance he enters the cabin and goes for the gold. A struggle ensues, but the grandfather is too weak to prevent the theft. As he is escaping the Mexican unconsciously rips one of the gold dust bags leaving a trail directly to his cabin. At first the doctor is accused of the crime, but our heroine discovers the trail and the "cowardly Mexican" criminal is brought to justice.] **MPW**:4.13.12, p158.

[308] **TRAINING FIGHTING COCKS IN CUBA**, Pathe: [Hollywood has helped fix certain immediate identifiers in the minds of their audience which instantly call certain Latin nations to mind, Tia Juana's zebra painted donkey, the corrida, hugh sombreros, señoritas clenching a rose in their teeth and the like, quickly call Mexico and Spain to mind. For Cuba, the identification has always been, fighting cocks and chickens in general. One might remember the press accounts revolutionary Cubans cooking chickens in open fires on the tenth floor of the Tereasa Hotel while Castro was in New York addressing the United Nations. Since earliest days it is almost impossible to find a film with Cuba as its central focus that does not have a gratuitous scene involving a cock fight. This was

merely a brief documentary showing how the fighting birds were trained.] **MPW**:4.17.12, p162.

[309] **A TREACHEROUS SHOT**: [Unconsciously touching on various degrees of racial prejudice this film has a southern aristocrat's daughter scorning a true blue son of the south for her recently acquired affection directed at a Spanish gentleman, Roman D'Arville. Over the objections of her father [few Hollywood daughters were dutiful when it came to affairs of the heart] she plans a tryst, but can only escape from her room by assuming the guise of a negress. Accompanied by her mamie, the two are captured as escaped slaves just as Roman appears. Thinking her now to be a mulatto, he insults her and her ancestry. Still in love with the lady, the former suitor challenges the Spaniard to a duel, which honor dictates must be accepted. Obviously worried about the outcome of the mortal contest, the Spaniard takes advantage of the chivalrous southerner's distraction by attempting to plunge his knife in what by then Hollywood had identified as the favorite Hispanic target, the boy's back. Having shown his true colors while only wounding the boy the Spaniard is driven from town. The young but foolish belle, now appreciates what she almost threw away.] **MPW**:12.28.12, p1328.

[310] **UNCLE SAM'S BOYS ON THE MEXICAN BORDER**, Powers: ["A picture of soldiers in Texas pretty well photographed and very interesting." There would be even more interesting documentary footage two years from this release date]. **MPW**:3.30.12, p1175, 4.20.12, p231.

[311] **UNCLE SAM'S TRIBUTE TO THE HEROES OF THE MAINE**, U.S. Navy Dpt: ["Another great topical subject" showing the ceremonies honoring those who died in the sinking of that battle ship in Havana Harbor]. **MPW**:5.4.12, p448.

[312] **UNDER MEXICAN SKIES**, Essanay: [One more variation on Mexican loves Anglo maiden, but with a twist. Pasquale, a Mexican half-breed, whose father must have been an Italian, falls for Vedah, the daughter of the ranch. She "repulses his attentions and tries to show him the error in loving her." He persists which forces her to employ that prop most necessary in later vampire films, the crucifix, which of course terrorizes the Catholic Mexican. When dad discovers what has happened, he rounds up the boys who want to string Paquale up. He is saved by the girl who not long after attracts the attention of an "Easterner." Also repulsed he takes her to the Mexican's cabin and with the help of another tries to force his intentions on her. Pasquale returns to save the maiden's honor and has his satisfaction as a reward.] **MPW**:3.30.12, p60.

[313] **THE VOW OF YSOBEL**, Selig: [Possibly easier to understand now than in less enlightened times there still persists today, for many North Americans, questions over the nature of Mexican race. As today many Anglo's perceive Puerto Ricans and Panamanians as predominantly black, few would consider the Mexican to be mainly white. Such racial perceptions were even

more harsh eighty years ago. Hollywood whites were always the prize for romantic conquests by any Hispanic and such scenarios remained a persistent theme from then until today. "With the advent of the Gringo, or white people, into old Mexico, many picturesque, and often-times, thrilling romances took place." One especially long remembered was that between Ysobel, Juan and Doctor Livingston. By now a stock formula for most film writers, the daughter of a rich Don refused to honor the marriage her father arranged. She wanted the man she had fallen in love with, the handsome young Anglo doctor. The rejection of course required the suitor to revenge himself against his "white rival", so he maliciously cuts the cinch of the medical man's saddle which causes him to nearly be killed. Offering to rescue the injured doctor only if he agrees to let the pretty young thing marry him, Juan leans too closely to the edge of the cliff and falls to his death next to the doctor. Apparently, some screen Hispanics were more fragile than Anglo's because the doctor survived the fall and the señorita becomes his prize in the last scene.] **MPW**:7.6.12, p70.

[314] **THE WAYFARER**, Selig: [As the most ubiquitous of early film villains, the Mexican was forced to travel far to do his dastardly deeds. This one could be found on a Colorado ranch peering through the tradition window's as the ever present unsuspecting was wife hiding the family treasure behind the loose bricks of the fireplace. Lurking, stalking, waiting for his chance, usually for the husband to leave the damsel alone to deal with her distress, but in this case, waiting for the couple to retire, he makes his move. Having suspected Pedro simply because he was a Mexican, the wife catches him in the act and rouses her man. After being wounded and felled to the floor, by the Mexican, who was "on the very verge of killing him", the loyal wife arrives just in time, with the sheriff and the posse to deal with the villain.] **MPW**: 8.10.12, p570.

[315] **A WESTERN CHILD'S HEROISM**, Champion: [One of two Mexican cattle thieves is shot escaping. As the posse continues in pursuit, the wounded man begs a local miner to hide him. The miner's wife convinces her husband that they should help the poor unfortunate. Later, the miner strikes a rich pocket of gold and is overheard by the ungrateful Mexican who pretends to be asleep. Feigning illness, he pleads for a doctor and when the man leaves the house the vile ingrate attempts to steal the gold. The wife and daughter manage to stop him and drive him off, but now he's really mad and when he encounters a handy band of marauding indians, together they attack the cabin that once was his refuge. As the women did their best to fight off the attackers, the child manages to steal one of the indian ponies and rides for help. In the end the perfidious Mexican is captured and his indian allies dispersed. The child has beaten the worst of the silver screen's baddies.] **MPW**:6.8.12, p960,961.

[316] **A WESTERN EPISODE**, Bison: [Absolutely stock formula by this time. The lady does not want the advances of the wealthy Mexican. An easterner saves her from his clutches and is shot

from ambush for his favor. The boys round up the culprit and he is allowed to "git" over the border before dawn.] **MPW**:10.5.12, p80.

[317] **WHEN CALIFORNIA WAS YOUNG**, Vitagraph: ["In days of old, when California was young, it was riff with chivalry and romance. No story more beautiful and pathetic has ever been know than that of Rosita Peroso and Jose Martina." The two fall deeply in love as youths and all is well until a "knight of the Spanish nobility" catches the girls fancy. He plys her with fancy words and jewels which allows her to shift her allegiance and she pledges herself to the suave and well to do scoundrel. Heartbroken, Juan warns her parents that the other is a "profligate and libertine," but in their greed, they see only his wealth and position. Juan now joins a monastery of ascetics. The two wed, but immediately true colors are exposed. The beast beats his beautiful wife, gets drunk, insults the governor and drops dead from heart failure. Rosita now runs to the monastery only to pass away herself as she contemplates what she has done and watches Brother Jose ring the last bells she will ever hear.] **MPW**:10.5.12, p70.

[318] **WHEN HEARTS ARE TRUMPS**, Nestor: [One of the best examples of true love conquers all in old Mexico. All of the standard cliches are present. Dad wants daughter to marry for dollars, she wants to for love. Her affection belongs to a dirt poor peasant. In their first try to elope, a note is discovered which thwarts the plan; father, wealthy suitor and padre bring the lady back. Then the ladder is used to free her from her second floor prison. Once more the girl is recaptured. In the final scene, the boy uses a horse to snatch her from the alter and effects a **The Graduate** like escape. Grief stricken, the father is filled with remorse because of the loss only to discover the newlyweds returning home for his blessing.] **MPW**:7.6.12, p78.

[319] **YOUNG WILD WEST CORNERED BY APACHES**, Nestor: [Young has left the east to go find adventure in the west. He does. In this episode, one of his first encounters involves the border Apache where he saves "Starlight" from her "savage adorer", Young Bull. Angered, the indians attack his camp, but he and his sweetheart, Arietta drive the savages away.] **MPW**:7.13.12, p182, 7.20.12, p245.

[320] **YOUNG WILD WEST ON THE BORDER**, Nestor: [Young and friend inhabit a deserted hut on the Mexican border and hold a Forth of July celebration. Pedro, the owner, is paid off and driven away. Later the boys go to a cantina in town and discover that the locals are displaying the Stars and Stripes beneath the "Mexican banner." Hot blooded patriotism pours out of Young as he rectifies the offensive arrangement. This of course provokes the local Mexicans and a miniwar breaks out in which Young and the boys are victorious. But Pedro is a sore looser and determined to revenge himself, so he heads for the cabin to do damage. Ever ready, Young and Arietta, with whom he still keeps company, arrive in time to save the goods and the "chinaman" that had been left behind. Pedro was brought to

jail. All was well that ended the white man's way, they were writing the scripts.] **MPW**:7.6.12, p6, p78.

1913

[321] **ACROSS THE RIO GRANDE**, Essanay: [It would seem that you had to do a lot less to keep a woman's fidelity in the earlier part of this century. Brinsley Shaw loved Evelyn Selbie, but he was poor. After they marry the husband decides to go west to make his fortune for the two of them. Evelyn promises to wait. Twenty years later he has not returned and she is still waiting. Apparently thinking that sufficient time has elapsed, the wife sends the son to the border country, with a few questions for the father. Possibly because of Mexico's proximity, dad has become a degenerate gambler, but with some parts of his memory unaffected. He recognizes the ring his son is wearing as that which he had given his sweetheart long ago, and sacrifices his personal freedom to save him from an unpleasant posse bent on revenge for his own cheating ways 630].] **MPW**: 6.21.13, p1278.

[322] **AN ADVENTURE OF THE MEXICAN BORDER**, Lubin: [Romaine Fielding and his Lubin troop produced this border love tale in Nogales, Arizona. It is almost unique for this time, because of the denouement. United States and Mexican Federal troops are standing eye ball to eye ball on the border line. Each protecting against the other. "One of the bright-eyed señoritas of the southern race captivates two officers", one on either side of the dividing line. The Mexican is older and a captain, the brash young North American is lower in rank, but filled with ardor which causes him to lie about the other. The lady has chosen the older man because of his kindness and gentility and in the end the lieutenant accepts his loss and apologizes to the captain in the spirit of fair play, of course. There are very few films in which the dark skinned lady chooses the equally dark skinned man over the paler blond Anglo.] **MPW**:3.8.13, p1018, 3.15.13, p1113.

[323] **THE ALTAR OF THE AZTECS**, Selig: ["A picturesque and romantic story dealing with the strange adventures encountered by Edwin Dalton, a young mining engineer in the ancient silver mines of the Aztecs in Sonoma, Old Mexico."] **MPW**:1.31.13, p390.

[324] **THE APACHE KIND**, Lubin: [Joe is a bandit of the "Apache kind" that infests the region around the Sabinia Canyon. His lady is Loretta, an attractive Mexican halfbreed. Joe's major occupation is playing poker, but when he loses he cannot control his hot temper and robs the game. Having had enough of this the other players call in the law, the handsome sheriff, Bud Jones. This film differs from most in that Joe is able to revenge himself against, Silver Jack, who turned him in. Possibly as compensation for allowing Loretta to fall in love with the sheriff, Apache Joe is permitted by the writer and the law man to make good his escape across the border.] **MPW**:7.12.13, p228.

[325] **APACHE LOVE**, Nestor: [An excellent example of the blurring of Indian, Apache, and Mexican identities in the writer's mind. All were considered to be of the same race. The Apache's were Mona and Ortega, the Hopi was, Blackhawk who lived in a "wickiup" and wants Mona to be his "squaw." Mona wanted to be Ortega's woman. The men fought, the tribes fought, the men, women and tribes fought. In the last reel Blackhawk found himself flying off a high cliff, possibly praying that his namesake would be of some assistance. Killed by the scripters fall, Mona and the Mexican Ortega were left alone to be one intent upon the other's pleasure.] **MPW**:6.14.13, p1178.

[326] **ARIZONA**, [On the border western with Mexican peons as incidental characters. No further information.]

[327] **THE ARMADILLO**, Eclipse: ["A worthy picture of one of the queer but well-known little animals of South America." It resembles a rhinoceros and has the mouth of a pig, it eats mainly worms, insects and roots. Although not presented in a threatening manner, much of South America's wild life, in later productions, would be. If it came from South America it would be deadly, from man-eating piranhas to deadly killer bees.] **MPW**:6.7.13, p1048, 6.21.13, p1251.

[328] **[A Trip Through] BARBAROUS MEXICO**, America's Feature Film Co:["One of the better productions hastily put together by the independents who went to film revolutionary upheaval in Mexico. The title has no relation to the book of the same title. "Mexico as she really is today, mingling together it's beauties and it's turmoil. A country full of wonderful scenery, interesting pleasure resorts and amusements that have not changed since the days of Nero." Even forgiving the ad copy's historical latitude, it should be pointed out that despite the in depth coverage of Mexico's social revolution that daily filled this nation's press, for this ad man, as it would remain for some unconscious segments of the general public throughout the century, Mexico was a land of fiestas and siestas, a land of beautiful scenery where a not overly ambitious or industrious fun loving people did a lot of celebrating and sleeping which could at anytime be interrupted with a lot of shooting. Whatever else took place there was merely added material for filming. The title was taken from John Kenneth Turner's, **Barbarous Mexico**, Kerr:1910] **MPW**:3.15.13, p1142, 3.29.13, p1356, 4.12.13, p228.

[329] **THE BATTLE OF SAN JUAN HILL**, Bison: [Involved but by now a predictable plot which pleased the audience, but left some exhibitors critical. A few criticized Bison for its lack of production values in some scenes. They considered the costuming of both soldiers and civilians somewhat sloppy. It did not take long for the young industry to develop its home town experts. In reality the famed battle was incidental to the love story which unfolds, one exhibitor thought it detracted from the main plot. It would seem that Cuban Dr. Lopez mistreats his wife and frolics with ""the other woman"" Dolores, the sensuous lady of his late night love. While

tending a wounded rebel soldier, he learns something important and discloses the valuable information to his wife. When Simmons, a "virile" Anglo soldier of fortune, learns of this, he realizes she must be taken captive to prevent the Spaniards from learning these facts. Her sympathies then were with Spain and not the "Coubo" rebels. As his prisoner in his "luxurious quarters on the edge of town", Simmons falls for Inez Lopez the wife, and she for he, but does not tell him so. His affection for her allows her to leave, which she does reluctantly. As the time for the famed battle approaches, the Doctor is found smooching with his sweetie in a local cafe. Worse, he is drunk and discussing the defenses of the San Juan block house. For this the Spanish soldiers tie him up in his home and dynamite the place. Simmons has over heard all, but must go to battle. After having been heroic and wounded charging up the hill, the soldier of fortune returns to the wife's home and mourns, thinking her dead. When she appears, all is well. Teddy's exploits would live forever, immortalized in countless retellings, not one of which, until this film was made, disclosed that all was made possible by love of a simple soldier for his lovely Cuban lady.] **MPW**:5.31.13, p950, 6.7.13, p1032.

[330] **THE BLIND GYPSY**, Patheplay: [Not all Hollywood gypsies were all bad. She loves "Minola", who loves her until he is vamped by a more alluring, but transient beauty. In the fight that follows, the cad's lady is blinded. Exiled by the king of the gypsies for his heartlessness, the lover leaves to make his fortune elsewhere He does and returns home with his wealth to help his former lady regain her sight.] **MPW**: 9.23.13, p1402, 10.4.13, p48.

[331] **BRONCHO BILLY'S STRATEGY**, Essanay: [Tom Morgan is corrupted by a dirty "Mexican greaser." Under his influence he steals money from his wife and loses all of it gambling. When the greaser wants help in robbing the express office, Broncho intercedes and saves the errant husband from further grief. In no time at all the greaser gets his just deserts, and is sent to prison. Sometimes, in Hollywood, it was a simple a having a good Anglo friend.] **MPW**:6.21.13, p1278.

[332] **BRONCHO BILLY'S WAY**, Essanay: [Once in a while, timeless wisdom flowed from the scripters pen: "When a woman's heart turns to stone, that is the time to watch out for her." This film may be unique in that an Anglo, and a heroic one at that, loses not his sweetheart, but his wife to a Mexican. Broncho had been warned that this Mexican lusted for his wife. He trusted her completely, naught to worry. But upon returning home unexpectedly one day, he discovered the Mexican hiding in the closet. A little upset, he pumped a few bullets into the door, just above his head. Simply to get his attention. To let "him know that this had hurt him beyond expression." Now, man that he was, he allowed the scoundrel to leave, but he placed "the weeping form of his wife up on the horse" with him, advising her never to darken his door again. Men were real men then.] **MPW**:3.29.13, p1355-6.

[333] **THE BUCCANEERS**, Gold Seal: [The second of this production company's pirate features focused on the rivalry between the celebrated "La" and the infamous Blackbeard depicting their activities on the Spanish Main.] **MPW**:12.29.13, p1545.

[334] **THE CALL OF THE ANGELUS**, Frontier: [Exhibitors panned the poor acting in this production: "This picture might have been made convincing by strong acting." The story is one of conscience. Two Mexican rivals have fought a duel, one thinks he has killed the other. When the Angelus sounds, his remorse and grief make him want to confess. Upon returning to his native village he discovers that his former foe is still alive.] **MPW**:6.21.13, p1254.

[335] **EL CAPITAN AND THE LAND GRABBERS**, Bison: [Set in California's transitional period, the film focuses on the activities of those unscrupulous individuals who sought to take land from the established Spanish residents and a local hero who fought for their rights. This same scenario would become the basis for more than twenty five future productions, basically a Zorro type character, the hero championed the cause of the oppressed.] **MPW**:1.4.13, p52.

[336] **THE CAPTURE OF AGUINALDO**, Bison: [Essentially this was a love story set in the Philippines using the capture of the "redoubtable leader of the Filipino forces" as its background. The battle scenes were considered commendable, but one of its better points was a "glimpse of the headhunters." Of all the Hispanic regions which became locations for silver screen productions, none was portrayed as being more savage and underdeveloped than the Philippines. It was important for audiences to know that the agents of civilization and christianity were at work in the darker parts of North America's domain. This type of portrayal for these islands on the screen, would not change until the advent of WWII. See: **The Real Glory**, 1939.] **MPW**:6.21.13, p1253.

[337] **CARMEN**, Monopol Film: [At least for the **MPW**, the review for this film presents the reader with something new, a truly critical review. Most of the scenarios and story outlines appearing in this invaluable source for the early days of silver screen productions, were just that, detailed outlines of the action. One could begin to gauge exhibitor and audience reaction to these productions by reading their submitted comments. H. C. Judson's piece on **Carmen** represents a marked departure from the past practice of merely providing added promotional praise to induce more exhibitors to purchase the productions. He mentions the three existing versions [qv] of the Prosper Merimee novel outlining the merits of each and praises Monopol for its pluck and boldness in attempting to produce still another adaptation. But he is very critical of the final product. While heaping praise on Marion Leonard for her effort he considered the important scene where she tempts Jose to sacrifice his honor, as "badly connected, spoiled, hurried and incoherent." "The spectator [could] feel nothing of the tragic intensity" and pathos required to understand the

story as a whole. He concluded, "I confess my inability to characterize such ghastly perversions of the first principles of dramatic art. There are said to be no less than four hundred and twenty-six scenes--this is enough to make the most hardened critic shiver. How much better it would have been if there had been less riding and stage coach robbing and more of Marion Leonard." Some more modern directors so in love with slightly more sophisticated special effects may not have read this eighty year old criticism.] **MPW**:3.29.13, pp29-30, 5.31.13, p956.

[338] **CITY OF MEXICO**, Essanay: [This scenic presentation of beautiful Mexico City, now the topic of every newspaper", featured what every North American tourist then and now expected to see and firmly believed to be the major preoccupation of most Mexicans, begging for handouts: "The audience will see the Peons, natives of Mexico, scrambling for a few centavos [pennies], their adobe dwellings and the market place." As an added attraction, it was apparently still alive in 1913, this clip claimed to show the very tree under which Cortez wept on "La Noche Triste" when he experienced his first defeat at the hands of the Aztecs.] **MPW**:4.19.13, p300, 5.10.13, p594.

[339] **THE CLOD**, Lubin: ["Pedro Mendes ... a big simple minded Mexican farmer [is] so dull mentally as to be called a clod." While obtaining supplies in town he learns of impending revolution which he cannot comprehend. Unable to enlist he returns home to discover rebel soldiers in battle which results in the death of his wife and mother. With his house in flames he goes berserk and is killed understanding nothing of what has transpired. Exhibitor reaction to this film produced a significant insight as to what, at least some North American viewers felt about events in Mexico, the character of its people, and their capacity to endure intolerance: "An impressive story of Mexico. Its central character is a peasant who is badly misnamed the "Clod"; for he has a rich farm which he has cultivated ... He is stolid, but this is a 'typical stolidity' and his attitude toward the revolution is chiefly conservative, a landowners' instinct. The impressiveness of the picture comes from the showing of how deep the iron of tyranny can go before such a man becomes a true revolutionist. Revolution founded on such wrongs as the man suffers can't be blown out easily. The picture's mistake, it seems to us, lies in the failure to turn the man into a consistent revolutionist at the end." Certainly a strong indication of the power of film at this early stage of its development. If one assumes that business interests are by nature not easily predisposed to destructive revolutionary activity, this merchant was apparently convinced of the need for significant change in the Mexican social and political structure. He sounded like he was ready cross over and sign up with as one the boys.] **MPW**: 9.20.13, p1293, 10.4.13, p49.

[340] **DOWN ON THE RIO GRANDE**, Lubin: [You can't have enough friends on the border. Bob loves May, she loves him. The Army captain has the hots for her also, that is a problem. All

this on the Mexican border where animosities flourish like loco weed. Bob fires two drunken Mexican brothers who later accost him, the younger brother is killed. The older one now enlists the aide of the Mexican Federales who pursue Bob for killing a national on Mexican soil. The dirty greaser had lied. After some hot pursuit, as Bob holds off a horde of Mexican regulars who have cornered him in a narrow gorge, the faithful May manages to make it to the Army camp where she pleads to the rejected Captain for help. What an opportunity. But man that he is, he cannot let the Mexicans do his dirty work and duty requires him to rescues May's true love. Bob thanks him. Sometimes, back then, it was as neat as that! Maybe. Well at least on film.] **MPW**:2.10.13, p600.

[341] **THE END OF THE TRAIL**, Powers: [The heavy in this work is a scorned Anglo who does his best to incriminate his lady's true love. Carlos the halfbreed is the good guy who tries to intercede for Dolores, the woman he wants, but knows he cannot have. There are incidental Mexicans who are used for dirty dealing, but Carlos is close enough to them to prevent them from doing harm [1605].] **MPW**:5.24.13, p846.

[342] **EPISODE OF CLOUDY CANYON**, Essanay: [Although G. M. Anderson had already established the popular character of Broncho Billy with the public, and possibly because he had a significant financial interest in this production company, he also portrayed other roles which did not have him cast as the hero. Most of these productions were filmed within a single week of shooting, so there were opportunities to step out of character. In this brief bit, Anderson played a really despicable Mexican half- breed with absolutely no saving graces, his clothing was dirty, his hat old and beat up and pulled down to hide his evil face. Worst of all, he beat his horse, an unforgivable offense for silver screen baddies. For this he was severely admonished and in public. Having suffered this humiliation by the hands of the local sheriff's son, even having had his gun taken from him, the ultimate emasculation for the man out west, he burned with desire to revenge himself. His opportunity arrived after a card game in which the son was a player and hard drinker. Only one other had consumed more of the spirits, the heavy loser. When this drunk left the saloon, he passed out providing the half breed with the opportunity to steal his weapon with which he promptly shoots the sheriff's son, leaving the other to be blamed. Not nice, he enjoys watching the events unfold. The dad was so angered with the boy's being wounded that he set out to strangle the drunk with his own hands, but was prevented from doing so by the son who managed to revive long enough to save the innocent inebriate. Then, swift western justice was meted out to the most deserving Mexican.]

[343] **THE EVIL EYE**, Lubin: ["A very strange story of old Mexico and the dangerous superstition of the Peon classes of years ago. The scenes are truly Mexican ... The picture is made at the Lubin studio on the Mexican border and employs a big number of the native peasantry." Don Alma Bondadosa, long away, now returns to "his castle" to erase superstition and

teach the word of god to his people. The locals remember that as a child he had encountered an enraged mountain lion and subdued him with the power of his eyes alone. This cast him as, "He of the Evil Eye," to be feared by all. His chief rival in everything was Don Immenso Superstisioso, and his trusted but apparently stupid friend, Ocioso Ignorante. [Hard to believe sometimes, isn't it?]. Don Immenso has a daughter who ignores her fathers advice by looking "He" straight in the eyes for which she is blessed with his proposal of marriage and thereby "rises clear above the darkness and ignorance of the people." [649]] **MPW**:10.25.13, p390, 11.8.13, p613.

[344] **THE EVIL ONE**, Lubin: [Little Wild Cat was a Coahuila indian maiden accused of witch craft for which she was not a "good squaw" and sentenced to die. She manages to make it to an Indian agency and ends up marrying the local minister. Now that could not have happened in Salem.] **MPW**:4.5.13, p77-78.

[345] **THE FIGHTING LIEUTENANT**, Selig: [Ronald Regan may have had this imaginative scripter as an adviser.] [Don Arguello, an old "roue" wants his ward's dineros. She, the Princess [of what, is not disclosed] Irma, considers him unworthy of her love. Not so are her feelings for Captain Falconbridge of the US Calvary stationed on the Mexican border, who is introduced to her by Don Carlos, "a high-grade young Mexican who consorts with Americans." The officer likes her immediately and to show her, he gives her the North American flag, which she takes instantly "to her heart." Because of this, the other Don, is angered and has the effrontery to insult the Stars and Stripes. This the young officer cannot allow. After losing the fight Arguello gets the rurales after the soldier and Irma joins him in his flight. They make it to the shores of the Rio Bravo and from an adobe hut make a stand. Luckily the shots are overheard by the Captain's detachment and "scenting trouble, ride over the border," to make a daring rescue, dispersing the dirty "greasers", or A-rabs, or gooks, time and circumstance determined Hollywood's ethnic preference.] **MPW**:6.14.13, p1166.

[346] **THE FLAG OF TWO WARS**, Selig: [The South might have lost the war, but in 1913, there were still many who might argue the point. This film is truly interesting because it unconsciously reflects a reality that the people of that time were unconscious of. The great Civil War divided this nation like nothing else ever had. The period of reconstructing the south was greatly offensive to much of that area. The first truly national undertaking, one which roused the patriotism of the entire nation, was the Spanish American War. Men from all parts of the United States enlisted to help Cuba achieve her freedom, but especially so from the south. In this production, units from the north and south are assigned to protect a certain block house. The men from Dixie have with them the Stars and Bars of the Confederate States of America, when the Stars and Stripes gets blown away, the former is raised and all fight proudly to defend it. The Spaniards are soundly beaten through the combined efforts of the former enemies, now symbolically and in reality reunited in common

effort against a foreign foe fighting for one nation.]
MPW:6.21.13, p1251.

[347] **FLAMING ARROW**, Bison: [This film includes a number of anomalies, characterizations uncommon for the time, not the least of which is that its hero, the main character is a halfbreed Apache indian named, White Eagle. On the other hand, the individual that might be considered the major villain, because he betrays his own race, was an Anglo Officer in the United States Cavalry. Only the Mexican was as he had become by this time, the threat, the essential villain. The hero had been born of a white father and indian mother, both had died some ten years prior to the major action in the film. The lad, because of his mixture had been provided with the benefit of a white man's education and returned to his tribe once it was completed. The symbolism of having him named White Eagle as opposed to the tribe's chief being called Black Eagle may not have been lost on audiences even then. Back at the fort, the young brave/boy becomes attracted to the colonel's daughter. This angers the officer who loved her and causes him to join forces with a nefarious Mexican who is feeding the rebellious braves fire water and fomenting an uprising. There was no apparent reason for the Mexican's behavior save that he was a Mexican trouble maker. When White Eagle discovers that the officer is involved, he tells the Colonel which causes the soldier be placed in the brig. Possibly the scenarist liked a lot of heavy symbolism, because he dresses the officer in Mexican clothing to facilitate his escape. Once free the officer/Mexican and his compatriot attempt to make the indians attack the fort, and kidnap the daughter. White Eagle once more comes to the rescue, giving the alarm and killing both Mexicans. Having saved the girl, he sends a flaming arrow into the air to tell the Colonel that his daughter is safe. The two are pictured together in the last scene. There is no other film in era that provides any half breed with such a prominent and heroic role. All others exhibit the conventional view that a person of mixed race inherits only the worst characteristics of both races, all of the vices and none of the virtues are the product of such unions.]

[348] **FOR THE FLAG**, American: [This film presents us with a good example of how some of the more creative of the early production companies expanded their offerings by using already established and proven formulas and applying them to different locals. The major territorial acquisitions resulting from the United States brief love affair with imperialism all came from Spain. Those lands understandably enough were filled with Hispanics, then considered conquered inferiors. It was not difficult to transfer a formula which worked well on the Mexican border, or in Spanish California, Cuba or Central America to the Philippines. This particular patriotic fluff brought its audience close "with fighting as it [was] done by Uncle Sam's regulars [against] the bolo men in the Philippines." The formula was simply shaped and constructed to fit the easily recognizable local filled with warm sun, palm trees and lovely señoritas. In this film an unfairly

disgraced officer goes to Manilla where he signs up under a different name as a private. Luck brings his former regiment to fight the Filipino insurrectos which presents him the opportunity for the required heroics. He saves the governor and his daughter from the revolutionists, is reinstated and wins the lovely dark skinned lady for his own.] MPW:9.16.13, p723.

[349] **FOR THE LOVE OF A TOREADOR**, Kleins-Cines: [Since the very beginning, Hollywood's toreadors have had a much easier time with the bulls they must fight to challenge fate and destiny, than they have had with the women who want them for other services. This is one more of the many that would follow the earliest clip produced by Edison in 1902. You would think it was easy to do this, but, always there are two or more women and only one Toreador. Always the love of one provokes vengeance by the other. In this bloodier than most entries, before 30,000 aficionados, one matador is killed along with two horses, and Francisco, who loves Lolita, not Carmen the dancer, takes a knife in the shoulder intended for his lady's breast, administered by the rejected Carmen. All this in the heat of the Sunday sun in "la Corrida." Certainly worth the price of admission, even if one had to sit on the sun side.] MPW:11.8.13, p581.

[350] **THE GHOST OF THE HACIENDA**, American/Mutual: ["Zaptos doos yur stuff!!!" Enid and dad buy a new hacienda south of the border. Billy also joins them. The peons on the new rancho soon tell the owners of Señorita Ysolda, who was killed as a child by "El Capitan," the Mexican Bandit. The story is that she still walks the white halls of the old place late in the evenings. Meanwhile, dad is foolishly putting gold away in front of Señor Tocquinado, just visiting now, but a bandit by trade. Later he and the boys decide to relieve the rancho of the gold and attack in force. Just as the burly banditos are battering down the front door, Enid, having run out of ammunition, remembers how innately "superstitious the lower class Mexicans are." She now dons white robes and a candle and as the baddies burst through, she appears on the veranda in this ghostly garb, which of course sends the dumb Mexicans yelling and screaming in all directions. You had to know those local customs to survive back then.] MPW:9.13.13, p1154, 9.20.13, p1244, p1324.

[351] **THE GIRL AND THE GREASER**, American: [Those frontier women were really something back then. When a "greaser invades" Dave's home, his wife and his sister are there, but he is ill elsewhere. Successful at first, but not satisfied with merely stealing the money the Mexican attempts to set fire to the house. This really angers the Anglo lady. To quick for the slow moving greaser, the wife reacts. She stamps out the fire, pursues him as he runs away and holds him at bay with her own revolver until the authorities arrive. In time, Dave recovers and the Mexican is behind bars.] MPW:11.1.13, p528, 11.8.13, p613.

[352] **A GIRL SPY IN MEXICO**, Lubin: ["A Powerful Two-Reel Story of the Mexican Border." Capitalizing on the success of these films, Lubin pushed out [most of the time in one week] another version of the war "between the insurrectos and Federal troops in Old Mexico." Sympathy here was for the rebels. The señorita, not having heard from her man for too long, enters the Federal camp as a Red Cross nurse but is quickly identified and arrested as a spy. When her lover, Armaje Blanco, discovers this he uses a captured Federal spy as a guide to go to her. They escape, but the federalista general vows to recapture them and does. Uncharacteristically for Lubin, possibly searching for a new ploy, their fate was left for the audience to imagine.] **MPW**:5.3.13, p460, 504.

[353] **THE GRAND OLD FLAG**, Bison: [Rich old Don Lopez had tried to stay loyal to the Spanish King, but "the cruelty of Weyler" against the Cubans had driven him into the insurrectos camp. He now purchased arms for the "down trodden" rebels. His beautiful "dark eyed daughter", was courted by El Donza, a suave, polite Spanish spy, who was of course, denied his intent. Into this picture arrive two wet Anglo soldier's of fortune; their boat had been wrecked in the rocky surf. After a lot of action, all are captured by the ever vengeful El Donza, who desperately wants them to salute and pledge allegiance to the Spanish Flag. Refusal results in the branding of one of the Anglos, but the resourceful Hispanic heroine sets fire to the prison which attracts a North American Gun boat, the marines and eventual rescue. In the final scene, Old Glory is seen waving proudly over the Spanish block house. It might be difficult for some today to understand the importance the flag represented as a symbol to the North American public at this time, but the recent demand for a constitutional amendment to protect it from desecration finds its roots in much earlier times than these.] **MPW**:6.7.13, p1064, 6.14.13, p1138.

[354] **THE GREATER LOVE**, American: [By 1913 certain formulas had become stock fair. If you needed a picture turned out in a week, it was not difficult to change the names and the local, ad a little something new and there you go. Among the most favorite plots, guaranteed to "WOW" them in Woonsocket and everywhere else, was the one in which the ethnic beauty sacrificed her life for her Anglo man so that while she died, he could live happylieee ever after. This American Western production is pure self sacrifice. Evan kisses Betty goodbye and goes west to make the dollars so he can call for her later. There, he meets Conchita, who immediately falls in love with him. Meanwhile he suffers a bad accident which brings his lady to his bedside. Unbeknownst to her, Evan has incurred the wrath of Conchita's scorned Mexican lover who now seeks to stab him while he lies helpless in bed. Conchita, knowing that she can never have a chance for his love, throws herself across his body and lets the knife intended to kill him, "plunge deep in her back." Some women could really care back then.] **MPW**:3.1.13, p926.

[355] **GROWING AND GATHERING CACAO BEANS**, Lubin: [Showing the folks back home how and where the raw material for their chocolate bars was produced. Filmed on one of the largest of the West Indian plantations, it featured "negroes cutting the cones" from the trees, splitting them to separate the beans and laying them out to dry.] **MPW**: 12.13.13, p1320.

[356] **GYPSY LOVE**, Patheplay: ["A tale of untamed passion and ruthless determination to win a lover at any cost." More of the same.] **MPW**:10.18.13, p286.

[357] **THE GYPSY'S WARNING**, Melies: [A guy named Smith is the heavy here. He woos a lovely gypsy girl away from her "tribe," loves her for some months, then sends her back to the caravan after he has met a beautiful North American girl. The gypsy dies of a broken heart and her mother never forgets. When presented with the opportunity to ruin the wretch's wedding plans, she does.] **MPW**:12.5.12, p388.

[358] **THE HEADHUNTERS**, Bison: [Any violation of certain Christian taboos universally causes revulsion among the believers. Incest and cannibalism were two of the big ones that Hollywood's scripter could be positive would immediately condemn whoever might be accused of indulging in either practice. Certainly the Spanish conquistadors accompanied by their prelates used and misused the accusation of cannibalism against the native populations they were conquering. The term itself was derived from the Carib indians. This film set in the Philippines, featured what the writers called "one of the most feared tribes" in the uncivilized world anywhere, "the Igorrote," well known for their headhunting and other unmentionable practices. It is essential for the conqueror or the colonial power to condemn his enemy. Silver screen productions have certainly helped perpetuate the idea that the more enlightened Christian community rid the pagan [nonChristian] world of such nefarious practices even when there is serious doubt that they ever were practiced or even existed.] See for example: **W. Arens, The Man Eating Myth. Oxford University Press, 1979.** "Both Europeans and Arabs seem to have a morbid interest in cannibalism and tend to accept almost any tale told them about it." E.E.Evans-Pritchard.

This one reeler featured some actual footage shot in the islands, but most of it was studio fabrication, but real good boxoffice. Its extremely complicated scenario focused on the love of a North American girl, Margaret for her soldier boy. While there, she rejects the advances of a wealthy, "hot blooded" Spaniard who pays her a great deal of attention during the day, but services Lilita, a notorious woman known to all as the "Firefly of the Philippines," at night, when he is refused favors by the Anglo lady. Lilita herself is jealous and equally hot blooded. Unhappy with the possibility of competition, she has Margaret and her dad kidnapped and then given to the headhunters. Luckily, Aguinaldo decides to revolt against United States control of his island at this time, because this requires that more troops have to be called to help put down the insurrectos. This provides an opportunity for the soldier boyfriend and his comrades in arms to rescue the lady of his heart, before the cannibals could consume it.] **MPW**:7.5.13, p80.

[359] **IMPORTING CATTLE FROM MEXICO INTO THE UNITED STATES**, Lubin: [An "educational picture showing the system of passing cattle across the line ... the inspectors are on the job." The United States government has forever worried about the dreaded hoof and mouth disease, anthrax and other maladies which Mexican [and Argentine] cattle seem to suffer from. Traditionally, it has been easier for people to make it across the border than Mexican cattle.] **MPW**:2.25.13, p804.

[360] **IN THE LAND OF THE CACTUS**, Lubin: [By 1913, Romaine Fielding had established himself as Lubin's premier actor/director used almost exclusively for Mexican characterizations. He was considered an individual, but "natural and human" in the roles he played. He was so seldom "theatrical" that some thought him "queer". But like Grant's love for liquor, the exhibitors wished that there were more queer producers, writers and actors like him. In this near the border production his role was that of "a Mexican who ha[d] fallen in love with an American girl who thinks she is sick." Romaine knew it was all in her head and provided the loving she needed to cure her.] **MPW**:4.12.13, p164.

[361] **IN OLD PANAMA**, Imp: [The exhibitors liked it and described it as a "Good scenic, containing among other features, a novel sunrise, street scenes, ruins crumbling since the British attack" in 1671 and native life. There is "a bit of comedy at the end."] **MPW**:3.15.13, p1105.

[362] **THE INFAMOUS DON MIGUEL**, Kalem: [Dixie Hardie is invited by a former school chum to visit her father's sugar plantation in Cuba. Although war clouds 'ara loomin on the horizon' her parents consent. Once there the days are spent enjoying the elegant estate, but in a while, a party of Cuban refugees breaks into the pleasant pastimes of the idle rich with news of "War." Hot on their trail is the infamous Don Miguel, in some ways not as bad as the "Butcher" Weyler, but in other ways worse. The Spanish officer could not hide his "hot blooded" lasciviousness. Although the Anglo girls escape disguised as Cuban servants, the crafty Don captures them. Showing his true colors, he offers all the prisoners their freedom for the southern bells hand, at least. Proper as she is, she scorns him. All of this has taken some time and by now the United States has come to liberate Cuba from the Spanish yoke. Included among the liberators, as the writers would have it, was Dixie's brother, just one of the many patriotic southern volunteers. When he discovers her plight, he and the other boys quickly rescue her. The hapless Don Miguel is placed in prison guilty of unspecified charges.] **MPW**: 5.10.13, p570, 5.17.13, p734.

[363] **THE JEALOUSY OF MIGUEL AND ISABELLA**, Selig: [Jack loves Vira. Miguel, though unencouraged, also loves Vira. Isabella, a fiery Mexican maiden, loves Miguel and hates Vira

which causes the "green eyed monster" to run rampant through the Mexican country side. Isabella wants her competition whacked so her father Pedro, a local bandito, captures both the Anglos, just to make sure. He then ties them up in a cabin and sets fire to it. Seeing all this Miguel rescues the Anglo lady and the now remorseful Isabella does the same for Jack. The bandit, made even more unhappy by the scribe's pen seeks redemption for his actions by allowing himself to be captured and jailed. It did not always have to make sense to for the audience, but it was essential that the Mexicans knew their place.] **MPW**:6.7.13, p1050, 6.28.13, p1359.

[364] **JUGGLING WITH FATE**, Selig: [The emphasis in this brief clip was placed on the fact that not only did the Mexican-American male have to be constantly kept under supervision, but the female was equally if not more dangerous to Anglos that might have to deal with her. Working in conjunction with one another, the team could be deadly.] The Arizona State University has a collection of some film material dealing with the Southwest and other areas which is valuable for those concerned with studying local stereotyping. Much of it is even organized in workable fashion. Friendly assistance can be obtained. **Hayden Library, Arizona Collection, Grace Sparks Collection, Box 22.**

[365] **THE LOVE OF CONCHITA**, Majestic: [Even in Mexico, if it wasn't meant to be ... sadly, hearts are broken all over. While Conchita and Miguel are attending a fiesta, she becomes intrigued with a masked figure who follows them all around the plaza. Miguel is peeved that the lady tosses a rose to the romantic fellow. When it is discovered that he is none other than Ramirez the ever present, but lovable notorious bandit leader, Miguel vows to bring him to justice. Conchita's father chides his child and demands that she marry the proper Miguel. Risking his very life, Ramirez appears at her window the next evening and the two promise to love forever. Unknown to them, Miguel is in the shrubs, Miguel, and he overhears all. A fight was required, but it proves of no consequence, the lover escapes. Later, the lady discovers that father and suitor are forming a posse to capture the brigand and she rides out to warn him. Too late for anything but the last scene, she arrives only in time to have her lover die in her arms after which she accedes to her fathers wishes and marries Miguel.] **MPW**:10.4.13, p84.

[366] **LOVE LIFE AND LIBERTY**, Bison: [Even as a two reeler, it seems impossible without having viewed the film, to understand how this intricately complicated scenario could have been projected in so brief a time. The Cuban insurrection provides the background for this tale of love and war. Anita, the beautiful Cuban girl, loves Captain Mario of the Spanish Army, but loves her country even more. She really hates Captain Zertuchia, a rebel commander, but only because of his cruelty. She is very much a patriot and a revolutionary. Most of the action revolves around the two men who attempt to woo the patriotic lady. Her primary concern is not necessarily romantic, she insists that Mario join the rebels. Zertuchia

is so jealous and vengeful, that he posses as a Spanish officer and denounces Anita's father as an insurrecto. Not satisfied with that, he kills him and destroys the palatial estate. The blame falls to Mario who was just in the process of changing sides, but first he felt he had to resign his commission to General Weyler--the Spanish were always very formal to detail. On his way to headquarters, with his sword in hand, he is captured by the evil Captain and sentenced to death. He would have been executed save for Anita's intercession. The price of his life was truly dear. The gallant señorita was forced to vow on a crucifix that she will marry the baddie if he spares the others life. In the process of doing so, it is discovered that her prospective husband has killed her father, but as the good Catholic priest explains, any deal made on a crucifix must be honored, very Catholic, very obedient and very religious, those Spanish. Luckily, Pedro, the father's faithful servant, stabs the foul Zertuchia in his most deserving back and the ceremony continues with the real lovers joining hands and forces against Spain to make Cuba Libre.] **MPW**:5.24.13, p846, p848.

[367] **LOVE AND WAR IN MEXICO**, Lubin: [Marrying a Mexican maiden in films usually worked out alright, but sometimes it could drive one to drink. Lubin productions were frequently sympathetic in their Mexican portrayals, but in this one the consequences of the across the border union cause a temporary breakdown in the North American's character. The production company advertised its film as follows: "... a Mexican war drama [although the action took place in Southern California] of more than usual interest .... A young American civil engineer, makes the fatal mistake of marrying the daughter of a Mexican farmer. They quarrel and he strikes her, leaving her for dead. Years later [twenty], he does penance for his crime by giving his life for his son, who he has recognized and who has been captured as a spy" by the Federalistas. The exhibitors who usually praised Lubin films criticized this one in all aspects save the story line.] **MPW**:5.24.13, p781, p832, 6.14.13, p1135.

[368] **MADERO MURDERED**, Universal: [This production is significant because it is the first film to be officially protested by a representative of the Mexican government who demanded that it not be shown any further in Los Angeles film houses. Because the reasons for the demand were political and not moral, the local authorities felt that they could do little to prevent its exhibition. It continued to be shown in the major metropolitan areas on both coasts to large and receptive audiences. One of the problems the Counsel General had with the film was his claim that the individual represented as Felix Diaz was not that revolutionary general at all. More significant was the controversy centering about where President Madero had been shot and buried.] **MPW**:3.22.13, p1206, p1245, 4.19.13, p268.

[369] **MARGARITA AND THE MISSION FUNDS**, Selig: [Sometimes the powers of the Spanish señoritas were staggering. North American adventurer Steward Hopwell works for the Governor of

California and is forced one day to collect the tribute from the San Gabriel Mission which does not please Father Sandez. While attending a local fandango he falls for Margarita Foquerora. But Ramon Valenzuella, a dashing outlaw attending the festivities incognito, also likes the lady. He has no chance against the Anglo and revenges himself by stealing the mission funds. In the denouement, our hero defeats the bandit, returns the funds to the mission, pays the governor the tribute from his own funds, resigns his commission, joins the church and marries Margaritta. There's powerful stuff in those Spanish eyes. Al Garcia played the bandit, one of the first Hispanics to receive credits as an actor at this time.] **MPW**:3.29.13, p1352, 4.12.13, p165.

[370] **THE MARSHAL'S CAPTURE**, Selig: [The plot here revolves around a sheriff's brother who accidently kills a Mexican, and who is aided in his escape by a halfbreed that steals all the horses, leaving his mates to die in the desert. They don't, the brother makes it across the border and the breed is caught.] **MPW**:6.21.13, p1276.

[371] **MELITA'S SACRIFICE**, Lubin: [Once more the kindness shown a Mexican maiden is mistaken for love rather than the friendship that was intended. In this case the altruistic cowboy goes so far as to beat up a brutal father and prospective suitor who are trying to force the little beauty into a marriage she does not want. Angered by this interference the two capture the cowboy and his Anglo lady and are only prevented from doing them harm because the unrequited señorita had gone for help. Melita's only reward for her brave action were "thanks". "Jess would never know the love that prompted it, nor the sacrifice she made in saving his life, only to lose him."] **MPW**:11.22.13, p1042.

[372] **MEXICAN CONSPIRACY OUT-GENERALED**, W: [Sympathy in this scenario attempts to take the middle ground, but favors the Federalista cause more than the rebels. General Galvez, commander of the "loyal Federal troops," applies to Harriman and Tipps, Wall Street bankers, for a loan. An insurrecto maid overhears the conversation and the rebels send their own man, Karr a soldier of fortune, to New York to obtain the loan for the Rebels. Unsuccessful, he robs the firm of a large sum which results in the sending of Pinkerton agent, Martha Langley, to reclaim the stolen funds. Tipps also heads for the border to find his money. All back in Mexico, Karr kills the General, has Tipps blamed for the offense and escapes punishment until the liberated lady shamus apprehends him and brings him to justice. Tipps is her reward, but the rebels still lack funds.] **MPW**:4.19.13, p314.

[373] **A MEXICAN DEFEAT**, Patheplay: [Out of sheer vengeance and meanness, a Mexican Federalist army Captain "frames up" a North American and his wife with evidence that the two were conspiring against his government. The lady had simply refused! Inviting the lecher to their home, it would seem that the Captain would have his way, but the two smoothies outfox him and break for the border. Once on the other side

of the Rio Bravo, they taunt and tease their pursuer, knowing "that Old Glory", which flies high above the U.S. Cavalry fort just to their rear protects them, and the good wife's virtue.] **MPW**:4.26.13, p412, 5.17.13, p704.

[374] **THE MEXICAN GAMBLER**, Patheplay: ["Clara was the apple of daddy's eye," he liked her a lot. She was the real boss of the ranch, but one of these two apparently had little business sense, he or she did not run it real well, there was never enough ready cash. This proved to be no problem until a double-crossing Mexican gambler swindled the dad out of a sum he could not pay. Ever lustful, the Mexican offered to take the daughter in lieu of payment. Hesitantly, the father asks Clara if she will pay. Reluctantly, the dutiful daughter agrees to submit to his evil design. No rotten core here! On the way to the alter dad discovers the duplicity the bounder has effected, and with the help of Clara's true love and a posse they find the Mexican "and justice is meted out to him in a manner that provides a novel punch."] **MPW**:8.16.13, p766.

[375] **MEXICAN INSURRECTION**, Angelus Feature Film Co: [Many independents were very quick to capitalize on revolutionary upheaval in Mexico. Frequently film crews went without any knowledge of what was really happening or even where the action could be found. At a later time, Raoul Walsh would be a part of such a venture, and would ride at the side of Pancho Villa. These earlier adventurous cameramen had but one purpose. They were instructed to shoot a thousand feet or more of some kind of action and return it home for the promoters to market it. "WAR! WAR! WAR! Real motion pictures of the MEXICAN INSURRECTION," filled full pages of advertizing in many of the trades. Smaller such ads, could also be found in major metropolitan dailies, especially by 1914 when it became more common for the papers to provide listings of films to be shown in their cities.] **MPW**:3.1.13, p905.

[376] **THE MEXICAN SLEEP PRODUCER**, Apollo: [Although this was characterized as "a burlesque on the Mexican Revolution," it was may well have been more a reflection of what North Americans wished would happen in that troubled land to the south. When the necessary Anglo hero has to rescue three North American beauties from General Youhurter, he does so by placing the entire Mexican Army into a deep sleep with his "medicated bombs."] **MPW**: 12.6.13, p1152.

[377] **THE MEXICAN SPY**, Lubin: [At times the Mexican border offered the opportunity for rejuvenation. Tom, the Colonel son's, was a "dissipated youth", but loved dearly by Mary the daughter of the post paymaster. The situation worsens when the spineless lad falls under the influence of Luis Rivera, "polished and apparently wealthy", but in reality a Mexican spy. Luis wanted the plans for all the border forts and Tom owed him mucho pesos for his gambling debts. Corrupted by his association, the foolish Anglo agrees to obtain the desired information. Mary prevents this treason by pawning everything she owns, save her body, to pay the Mexican off. Saved from complete ruin but shamed, Tom leaves and reenlists under a

different name Mary becomes a Red Cross nurse. But both are sent back to the border to wage what one exhibitor called, "the war with the Republic of Mexico, that we did not have." Of course, the two become hero and heroine and plan a life of love together. Another reviewer referred to this tale as, "a dramatic story typical of the army life of Mexico and the United States." [476]] **MPW**:1.4.13, p63, 1.11.13, p.184, 2.1.13, p464.

[378] **A MEXICAN TRAGEDY**, Lubin: [Father and son find themselves on different sides of the Mexican Revolution. The father's motive is avarice, the son is dedication to the cause. In sympathy with her brother, Teresa loves the insurrecto leader, General Laredo. Bribed by the Federalista to betray the revolutionary hero, the father uses his daughters love to lure the unsuspecting suitor to his inn, where he is to be knifed in his sleep. The children learn of the foul plot and try their best to prevent it, but both are bound and gaged. Escaping from his ropes, Miguel the inn keeper's son, is struck almost unconscious, but manages to wander into the general's room where he falls to the bed dazed and unaware of where he is. Seeing that his room is occupied, the general chooses another. The Federals now choose the father to do their dirty deed and when he does, he unwittingly slays his son. A fitting punishment for having tried to betray the cause. Exhibitors considered this a solid entry for their trade, but did not think it quite as good a version of the formula as had been applied "in the story of the North American Revolution," some two years prior. In that one, the hero had been, George Washington, and the enemy innkeeper, a Loyalist. It is significant that some North Americans could draw at least a simplistic analogy between the two revolutions, different as they were in causation.] **MPW**:9.20.13, 1308, 10.4.13, p48.

[379] **MIKE AND JAKE IN MEXICO**, Joker: [An other indication of the cavalier, if not contemptuous attitude that many contemporary screen writers held for the dramatic social upheaval taking place in the Mexico of 1913. After "stealing across the border," this early comedy team, learns that the wicked Bumbo, leader of the rebels has abducted "Chilita", daughter of the Federalista general. Falling immediately from favor by accidently blowing up the Federal ammunition dump, they regain prestige by effecting the rescue of the lady in distress. Although they are captured by the rebels, their torture is ineffective, even their cannon merely bounce balls off the chest's of the Anglo heros. The technique they use to subdue the enemy was unique, but understakable to North American audiences. Taking advantage of the Mexican culinary habits, the two clowns employ large quantities "red pepper" on the rebel forces which makes all save their leader sneeze themselves to death. With love in their hearts, they give Chilita back to Bumbo the bandito and depart. From exhibitor's reports, "The results [were] fun galore." Audiences wanted more of the same.] **MPW**:12.6.13, p1204, 12.6.13, p1152.

[380] **THE OATH OF CONCHITA**, Nestor: [Another indication of the blurring of Mexican and indian in the North American film makers minds. The 'better class' of Mexican usually meant pure blooded Spaniards and the 'lower class' were usually considered pure indian. The mestizo, the great majority of the Mexican population fell under the approbation, "halfbreed." When a good padre felt the call to preach to the "wilder tribes" he ascended the tortuous trail up to the mountain village of Conchita, daughter of Pedro. But as the days pass, forbidden love stirs beneath the cassock of the good priest, and only the arrival of a Spanish grandee who wins the maiden's love, saves his priestly vows. But another, the savage El Sombriado, "the black one from the mountains" who also loved the busy lady, vows vengeance and actually slays the groom at the wedding. Conchita wants the indio dead, but the good father, demands she get a grip, and makes her renew her pledge to be good. It all ends with a knife fight between the killer and Conchita, with bodies left all around. Even the best of religious intentions could not cool the "hot blood" of Hispanic vengeance when it was brought to a boil with the stirrings of primitive passion.] **MPW**:8.30.13, p994.

[381] **ON THE BORDER**, American: [American's full page ad described this production as follows: "the pretty dancer and the casual cowboy visitor at the cabaret fell in love. A Mexican waiter loves Chiquita with the passionate ardor of his race. A gringo get this dainty bundle of Spanish nerve and beauty? Never." "As Chiquita danced merrily to the sound of her tambourine and the soft twanging of guitars", the handsome Bill fell in love. But Pedro, "who hated all gringos" swore he would never have her. He attempts to poison the good looking Anglo, but fails. The local sheriff having seen Pedro's eyes "glittering" with rage and vengeance, knew that some foul deed was afoot. Instinctively realizing what the Mexican plans to do, he moves quickly, swats the deadly cup from its intended victim's hand, just in the nick of time, and then leads the culprit away. Chiquita, the cantina cutie, continues her sensuous cavorting as the drama concludes [58, 597, 1430].] **MPW**:5.24.13, p772, p852, 5.31.13, p921.

[382] **THE PADRE'S STRATEGY**, Lubin: [Ramona Martinez, a beautiful Mexican girl supports her poor mother. Jose loves her. One day, Manuel Vasquez, the leader of a band of Mexican guerrillas, comes to a cantina frequented by "a better class of Mexicans." The better class did not do manual labor, they were simply wealthy, and enjoyed greatly doing nothing. Manuel wants the little lady, but she refuses all his advances. Of course he is insulted and enraged, so he merely has his men abduct her. Jose, her poor but honest lover, sees the "bandits" take Ramona away and being pious, goes to the local padre for help: No one else in the cantina cared, they were to busy entertaining each other. As Jose arrives at the monastery, so does a message from the bandit chief, expressing a desire for the services of the Padre. Formulating a plan, the two put on religious robes, go to the mountains to try to rescue the lady. As the two heros hold off the captors,

Ramona rides to the capital to get the troops and does so. All the "bandits" are captured, and the two lovers reunited.] **MPW**:5.10.13, 613.

[383] **THE PANAMA CANAL**, Vitagraph: [Presented as a public service by the producers because they claimed that there was too much demand for such films of the United States' great triumph and too few "panoramic films" "on the that important subject." [282]] **MPW**:2.8.13, p598.

[384] **THE PANAMA CANAL TODAY**, Patheplay: [National pride nearly burst as the canal approached completion. This clip showed how "the most gigantic engineering project in the world's history [was] almost completed [182].] **MPW**: 4.26.13, p412.

[385] **PANAMA HAT INDUSTRY**, Lubin:["An excellent industrial picture showing the evolution of the fashionable [to say nothing of extremely popular] Panama hat."] **MPW**:9.6.13, p1084.

[386] **PAPITA'S DESTINY**, Lubin: [It's nice when you can make things neat, and tie it all up in a pretty package in the last reel. Some scripters, with bizarre imaginations, had that talent. Infrequently, but beginning at this time, reviews mentioned the names of some of the main characters. Few of these are included here at this time, because the vast majority of Hispanic characters were still being played by Anglo actors. This one reel neatly scripted package has Papita, [Clara Williams], marrying a wealthy Mexican, [Franklyn Hall], who by his nature mistreats her from the very first. Luckily, the unfortunate Mexican bride, has two old lovers still hanging around hoping for an opportunity, after all, she was a Mexican. One, even more fortunately for the plot's development, was "a cripple", the other merely suffered from a broken heart, which could be repaired. By this time the infirmed knows that he and his broken legs has no chance with the healthy and still very active Hispanic lady, so he does what he can for her. He kills her husband and wheels himself off to the desert to die. This leaves the way open for number three to move in and they live happily, you know.] **MPW**:6.28.13, p1359.

PATHE'S WEEKLY:

[387] **#31**: Scenes of the fighting in Mexico City, showing "pitched battles among the city houses--a rather illuminating series of views." **MPW**:4.12.13, p164.

[388] **#50**: Clips of the more than 150 people who were killed and 300 wounded by the explosion of 2300 pounds of dynamite, when a munitions train blew up outside San Juan, Mexico. **MPW**:9.15.13, p1420.

[389] **#76**: Hermosillo, Sonora, Mexico. General Carranza, "leader of the Constitutionalist Army that is sweeping over revolution torn Mexico, has chosen Hermosillo, meaning "Beautiful Little City" for his capital." **MPW**: 12.29.13, 1580.

[390] **PEDRO'S REVENGE**, Majestic: [Pedro works as a fruit picker on Mr. Bernard's ranch. One day two tramps are hired to help out, but they try to be too friendly with Pedro's girl. The fight that follows has them all fired. The tramps now plan to rob the daughter, while Pedro looks for other work, certainly a sympathetic characterization for the time. Discovering their plot, Pedro saves the lady and is rewarded with his old position as a fruit picker. What could be more fair? This was the first of many to follow films that would employ migrant Mexican labor as characters for the scenario.] **MPW**:4.19.13, p310.

[391] **PEDRO'S TREACHERY**, Lubin: [Once more Romine Fielding was on the border with the Lubin players filming a tale of the "treachery of a Mexican cowboy." Pedro, in character, was not nice. Vengeful because Bob had given him "a just beating," he implicates the Anglo in a robbery/murder. This drives our hero across the border to seek refuge until he can clear his name. Once there Bob falls for a lovely señorita, what else could he do? Meanwhile, Pedro's character will not let him stop his evil ways, he "is caught being cruel to an animal" and is fired. He also crosses over and just happens to find work at the very same rancho where Bob is so happily employed. Unable to pass up the opportunity, he immediately tries to blackmail Bob. In a fierce fight, the malevolent Mexican is wounded. Just then, the sheriff arrives, it is uncertain from what side of the border, to arrest the killer. It would seem that because of constant mistreatment, "Pedro's squaw" had squawked. Bob and his lady were now free to continue without the interference of what was really one of Lubin's worst Mexican's ever.] **MPW**: 5.3.13, p504, 5.17.13, p703.

[392] **THE PENALTY OF JEALOUSY**, Lubin: [An involved plot where an Anglo fugitive has to cross the border to escape capture by the law. Once there he wastes little time. He first steals a lovely señorita, Carmelita, from her lover, Ramon, and then marries her. But soon his activities and his treatment of her, causes Ramon's former sweetheart to commit suicide. When he crosses back over the border and finds Ramon romancing his old girl, a fierce fight develops, after which, for some unapparent reason, both men find themselves in a cabin which is dynamited by their pursuers. Although the film's sympathy was cast to Ramon, who was "justly" seeking to revenge himself against the Anglo, both men were blown to high heaven in the blast.] **MPW**:5.31.13, p942.

[393] **PRESIDENT TAFT'S TOUR OF THE PANAMA CANAL**, Feature Films: [Featuring "every event of the entire presidential inspection" it included spectacular views of the "Magnificent military pageant to honor the President, the mammoth locks in actual operation and the meeting of the waters of the Atlantic and Pacific." Exhibitors claimed that is was among the most popular of short features ever exhibited.] **MPW**:1.4.13, p11.

[394] **A PRISONER OF CABANAS**, Selig: [Even by this early date, many of the stock formulas had been developed, this time it was applied to Spanish American War days. The North American

hero who slaps a villainous Spanish officer for trifling with his lady seriously offends his honor and pride. When the marine is later captured by the same 'slapee', the Anglo is take to the prison at Cabanas to be tortured. But right on time the Cuban cutie brings the freedom fighters to rescue her man. "It seemed to please the audience." It always did, and would continue to present times.] **MPW**:4.12.13, p165.

[395] **A PROPOSAL FROM THE SPANISH DON**, Edison: [This film adaptation was an attempt to exploit the popularity of a then novel, **Who Will Marry Mary**. Mary loves the Don's manners and his "nicely modulated accents." Aboard the streamliner heading west, he had made a fine cross country companion, but she also knew that for various reasons, her wealth being not the least consideration, that she could wed who ever she wished. Although the Spaniard had twice proposed, she felt she could do better. Infuriated because he felt she had trifled with his affections, he decided to uncouple her private railroad car and let it smash down a dangerous grade. Luckily, Captain Justin Bradford, U.S.A. was there to save the day by jumping onto the runaway car where his noble strength and youthful vigor allowed him to fight the breaks and stop the runaway car. You can guess what happens to the Spaniard and who gets the lady.] **MPW**:8.16.13, p760.

[396] **THE ROSE OF SAN JUAN**, American: [Ben Cameron moves to California in the early fifties. His first encounter upon arrival involves saving the life of a young Hispanic peon, Ozozco, who he leaves at a local mission. His second encounter is some what more satisfying, possibly a reward for his earlier good deed. At an evening fandango, he falls in love with Inez, a Spanish beauty. She has been the local lovely for a while and is already the object of much attention. One in particular is a "drunken Spaniard" who has "lusted" after her for some time, waiting for the opportunity to make his move. In those transitional days, California was filled with land grabbers "everywhere" whom the local Spaniards hated as "thieving gringos" to be killed whenever possible. It was Ben's job was to stop all that animosity and make things right between the two different cultures. His first real crisis comes when the drunken Spaniard threatens his life and that of the señorita. He captures Bob and turns him over to the local Spanish commandant who condemns him to death. It is only through the intercession of the starving peon that Bob's life is saved. With the grateful peon's help, he manages to escape with Ines over the mountains, realizing possibly that there was still a lot of work to be done back there before the two cultures could get along together.] **MPW**: 12.20.13, p1476.

[397] **SARAGOSSA**, Patheplay: [A brief documentary showing the capital of the ancient province of Aragon, "a reminder of the golden age of Spain" el siglo de oro, when "she was the greatest power in the world."] **MPW**:5.10.13, p624.

[398] **SCENES IN MANILA**, Selig: [This production company in its early days did a lot of globe trotting documentaries, many of

which were south of the border, and in other formerly Spanish held territories. The only complaint that the exhibitors expressed over this one was that it was too short in its presentation of "impressive sunsets' and an "instructive views of the chief city of the Philippines."] **MPW:6.14.13, p1135.**

[399] **THE SECRET OF PADRE ANTONIO**, Frontier: [Exhibitors considered this a poorly made Mexican love story in which the relationship between Ramon and Carmel was not made clear throughout their five year affair.] **MPW:7.12.13, p206**

[400] **THE SECRET TREASURE**, Patheplay: [Pete hides a fortune. Always with an ability to smell out some Anglo's treasure, his Mexican neighbors "are very anxious" to find it. Pete's loyal "redman" servant is the only other who knows where it is, so the sly Mexicans, ever ready to use flesh for their advantage, send the beautiful "Delores" to seduce it out of him. True to his master, she fails despite her best efforts. Most pleasing to the audience, she betrays her own people, by becoming a loyal friend to Pete's family.] **MPW:9.24.13, p1420**

[401] **A SISTER TO CARMEN**, Produced in Miss Gardner's Studio, at Tappan-on-the Hudson]: ["The most beautiful and dramatic picture ever made in three parts, showing Miss Gardner in a most captivating role. Picturesque in costume and setting." Somehow, Carmen on the Hudson may make some smile, but should indicate how ingrained the lovely hot blooded Hispanic temptress and, apparently her relatives, had become in the public's mind by this early time. Some of the title cards read: "I'll Blow Smoke in His Eyes", "Three Men and a Woman", "This Shawl is Worth Twenty Men," "I Could Wear These", "When You Trick a Woman, You Trap a Man", and "Never Mind--I'm Not as Wicked as I Look."] **MPW:8.16.13, pp864-5.**

[402] **SOMETHING'S ROTTEN IN HAVANA**, Essanay: [It was not always easy to know in what form malevolence from South America would make its way north. In this production it took the shape of some rotten Cuban cigars, which when disposed of in the back yard, and after a neighbor's complaint, caused the local constable, to accuse the displeased smoker of having killed his wife and buried her body. And you thought you had to be real bright to write scenarios.] **MPW:7.12.13, p230.**

[403] **THE SPANISH PARROT-GIRL**, Selig: [It would be difficult to find a better example of the formula, rich Spaniard loses lady to Anglo from the north, than is presented in this film. The beautiful parrot girl loves dad, who was at best a poor money manager. To pay his debts, the Spaniard demands the daughter. She accepts, but only out of parental love. Along comes the Anglo, in this case, he is also rich. After a little action, he has her at the altar and pays dad's bills with a "certified check." The fruits of an industrious capitalism have sent another wealthy, but worthless Spaniard packing.] **MPW:3.6.13, p916.**

[404] **THE SPIRIT OF THE FLAG**, Bison: [Two young North American nationalists, who were "very patriotic" find

happiness with one another through a shared love for their country. In 1913, that was a sure sale scenario. The story opens with a young doctor treating the "natives" of "this primitive land," it is difficult to know whether it was before or after the colony's take over. Either there were some Spanish troops still there at the time, or the State Department was giving its permission to "train Filipino natives in the way's of North Americanism" before hostilities broke out. The young lady is a teacher, teaching them all that the flag of the United States means to her. The problem is Bonita, who is hopelessly in love with the doctor. Her father is too old to be in his battalion of natives, but the kindly doctor gives him a gun to play with anyway. Because of the Anglo lady, Bonita's fiery love turns soon turns to jealousy which unthinkingly forces her to seek assistance from Spaniards. But fortune, which was most frequently on the side of the North Americans turns that against her. The Spaniards find her father fondling his gun and summarily shoot him. She protests. The teacher protests. But the doctor gets his boys together and with the help of a handy detachment of bluejackets, Philippine independence is born. Bonita willingly dies clutching the folds of Old Glory. Many of these same, almost exact scenes, filmed with about the same amount of subtlety, will be duplicated in 1945's **Back to Bataan**, with the Duke in charge of his Filipino scouts.] **MPW**:5.31.13, p950.

[405] THE SPONGE INDUSTRY IN CUBA, Patheplay: ["An interesting study of all the phases of an unfamiliar although thriving industry."] **MPW**:4.12.13, p200, 7.3.13, p488.

[406] A STORY OF THE MEXICAN BORDER, Frontier: [Again, the intricate intrigues of love in Old Mexico: two Mexican swains who have no chance against the Anglo who just happens onto the scene, accuse him of murder, lying, false accusation and eventual resolution. "Luis" of course [the Anglo] is cleared and is "married to Marguerita."] **MPW**:6.14.13, p1180, 6.28.13, p1360.

[407] SUGAR MAKING IN CUBA, Pathe: [A more cynical historian once observed that Cuba suffered from two major problems, all of her others could be directly related to these: The fact that the United States coast line was only ninety miles away and the island's single crop economy. It would be difficult to argue the point. In the twenties, Jenks would write a history titled, **Our Cuban Colony**, and so she was. This educational feature claimed to present, "an interesting bit on the production of sugar from the gathering of the sugar cane to the finished product ready for market."] **MPW**:1.9.15, p221.

[408] A TANGO TANGLE, Essanay: [The tango craze would reach its first peak in 1914, but by the summer of 1913, it was already gaining in popularity. This film was the first to feature the new Latin rhythm which seemed to legitimize or at least recognize the undulations of libido on the dance floor. In film the tango invasion created all manner of complications for those that were smitten by its salacious strains. In this

production a happily married couple are bitten by the "tango bug." Secretly, they take separate lessons, but become suspicious of each other's absence. The man wants to know where Mrs. Jiggers has been jiggling. She threatens to go home to mom, just as an organ grinder's music makes its way through the window. To their mutual surprise, they find they cannot control themselves and are soon dancing the tango together, and happily ever after.] **MPW**:5.3.13, p504.

[409] **THE TARANTULA**, Powers: ["A Spanish-Mexican girl known as the Tarantula, [was] coolly polishing the blade of a stiletto with which she has just killed a lover she was tired of--her new lover being a young Mexican boy whose beauty and innocence appeals to her." Need we say more? The North American who rides into the town to report finding the body, has the murderess and her intended victim pointed out to him. Deciding to resist her advances, he befriends the boy, and is very cautious not to look the lady in her deadly eyes. Angered by his rejection and her intended victim's respect for the gringo, she plans a revenge which involved "one of her kind." She selects the biggest and deadliest of her namesakes and places it beneath the sheets of her victim's bed. But, as the writers would have it, it must have been an Anglo tarantula, with a conscience and a little lust at that, for the next morning, the lady runs screaming from her tent, clutching her breasts where the deadly venom was injected [717].] **MPW**:5.10.13, p626.

[410] **THE TOBACCO CULTURE IN CUBA**, Pathe: [This offering was filled with information showing the public "process of growing" and cultivating "our smoking" and "our chewing" needs.] **MPW**:4.12.13, p163.

[411] **THE TOLL OF FEAR**, Lubin: [It may be a truism that the greatest fear is generated from the unknown. It may well be nickel psychology to imply that many North Americans, then and now fear our neighbors to the south because of an abysmal lack of information about them. Frequently what passes for truth is less than collective folk mythology an intelligent three year old would discount. At any rate, it is generally assumed by many who have never had to good fortune to visit there, that Mexico is filled with mystery, even danger. Once you cross that line, you must beware. If you have a blond hair blue eyed little sixteen year old daughter, you must be doubly careful. Of course you can just leave her out on the street of New Rochelle at any time.

This little piece of nonsense was supposedly taken from an incident that actually occurred near Nogalas, Arizona, it was "vouched for by local authorities." The Lubin players, with Romaine Fielding in the lead, brought it to life. The incident was generated by some Mexican cattle rustlers who raided across the line and then returned with their profit to the safety of their homeland. But what is safe for some can be hell for others. With the local sheriff out of town, his brash younger brother decides to go after the thieves. But once in the Mexican badlands, strange occurrences begin to

take place. Quickly disoriented, things are made worse by the
discovery of a note pinned to a tree which warns: "Go Back or
You Die With the Sun." Bravely he continues, but the words
begin to burn into his brain. Now every little noise rattles
his nerve "worn to a raw edge by the fear which the words
signify." Unable to bear up he shoots himself in the head.
When his older brother goes looking for him, basically the
same things happens. Mexico's mysterious phantom had
activated some really bad monsters from those id's to say
little of the screen writer's condition.] **MPW**:3.29.13, p28.

[412] **TO THE BRAVE BELONG THE FAIR**, Nestor: [The preoccupation
with placing Mexicans in films as necessary foils at times
took on bizarre proportions. In this beauty a father offers
his daughter's hand to whoever can cross the border and
capture a Mexican. "Hiram, John and Eddie," the suitors,
start immediately and cross over. Eddie is the first to
encounter his possible quarry. At first he's afraid, but when
the hombre merely wants a match to light his cigaro, Eddie
obliges. Besides, he is holding him under the cover of his
pistol. Learning that the Mex is really a general, he makes
him exchange clothes and leaves him in the bushes. He then
encounters a band of banditos pulling a gatling gun, who
mistake him for their leader. As such, he heads them north.
In the meantime, John has dressed a tramp up as a Mexican and
for this was awarded the girl, but at the ceremony, when Eddie
is seen with his captives, little Alice is given to the proper
hero. All in all, one supposes, its not much different from
any present day superhero scenario ... any Anglo is worth
several hundred Hispanics. It boggles the mind though, when
one considers the relative sophistication of the audiences,
then and now.] **MPW**:6.28.13, p1398.

[413] **THE TROUBADOUR OF THE RANCHO**, Powers: ["Pedro, [the]
irresponsible rascal, albeit a lovable one, is better at
playing his guitar that at work." He loves his master and
mistress and plays for them seductive tunes to sooth them as
they make love. But as it is all over, a little neglect
tempts the master's lady into other arms. Meanwhile, Pedro,
still "unable to appreciate the dignity of toil," [a popular
view among Anglos even today] was discharged by the Don.
Blithely on his way, he spies his former mistress and another
man and grasps the situation immediately. A few soft strains
from his magical guitar outside the window of the now
remorseful señora, sends her scurrying back home to the señor.
Reinstated for the service, Pedro continues to strum away the
hours still free from manual labor.] **MPW**:4.12.13, p202,
4.19.13, p282.

[414] **THE TWO BROTHERS**, Vitagraph: [Let the exhibitor speak:
"A very tragic picture .... Mary Charleston plays a Mexican,
the younger brother's sweetheart, who sees the old father
killed by the older brother. It is moonlight, and she has to
testify against her lover, who is hanged. Later she finds
that it was the other brother, so she stabs him." Enough, it
was tragic, it was Mexico.] **MPW**:4.12.13, p164.

[415] **UNDER THE BLACK FLAG**, Gold Seal: [Most young lads some few decades ago dreamed of sailing under a flag that proudly displayed a white skull supported by crossed bones on a black banner. That would have made us pirates operating somewhere in a place called the "Spanish Main." Few of us knew just where that was, but we knew that the Spanish were the enemy. The movies told us that they were treacherous and evil and it was ok to fight them. This fanciful tale of pirates operating on the Spanish Main was another in a significant number of productions that would justify attacks against Spain and her ships sailing in the Caribbean. This one featured the rivalry between two legendary figures, Morgan and Teech who sought to out do one another in the taking of Spanish gold. In this three reeler the action moved quickly, when Morgan captured Captain Mardo's ship all the Spaniards save the padre and a boy name "Juan" were killed. Death was the price paid for being a Spaniard in this film. Holy terrors at sea, on land the Sea Dogs were just as deadly. With little trouble, the brave mates destroy a Spanish colonial town, in what was the first film version of the sack of Porto Bello. Nothing was shown to be left standing. As the booty was being divided, Morgan's only worry was his dangerous enemy, the Pirate Teech. A good days work had been done, good enough to be made Governor of Jamaica. The exhibitors commented, "Here is a praiseworthy three-reel production concerning the career of Sir Henry Morgan, celebrated in history as a pirate, one of the worst, who ever sailed the Spanish Main."] **MPW**:11.22.13, p1050, 12.6.13, p1152.

[416] **VENGEANCE IS MINE**, Selig: ["A Mexican or perhaps Spanish story of a hunchback painter." {What difference was there between the two nationalities ? all of them looked alike, or so it would seem to this reviewer.} The scenario involved a simple story of poetic justice, where a Hispanic rouge sees the picture of a sweetheart, {actually it's her daughter,} that he had heartlessly discarded long ago, and justly, the shock kills him.] **MPW**:4.19.13, p280.

[417] **WHEN LUCK CHANGES**, American: [Interesting because a gratuitous Mexican kills an Anglo and no one cares. Two young men go west to find fortune. One gets the girl and becomes a gambler, the other merely works hard. The gambler beats the wife and incurs the hatred of a Mexican and most of the town. When the Mexican kills him, no one pays attention. The other boy then finds the widow and they wed. This is one of the very few of these early productions where such action does not result in the Mexican being killed. Possibly the cast felt he was performing a public service.] **MPW**:5.31.13, p954.

[418] **THE WHITE VAQUERO**, Bison, [The overwhelming majority of Mexican bandits who had appeared on the silver screen by 1913, were malevolent in nature; this film introduced a new characterization and represents the earliest appearance of the loveable rogue, a good-badman, something of a Cisco kid. Exhibitors reacted to this production in the following manner: "A hold-up in this two-reel drama of Mexican bandits and soldiers sent to capture them shows an exceptionally good

piece of photography." By this time, the Mexican as a bandit was firmly ingrained viewer mind's. The terms were thought to be interchangeable, Mexican equalled bandit. Certainly that was so on the silver screen. Reviewers accepted the idea implicitly, one merely commented on the above average technical expertise and technique of filming this production. But another noticed the something different: "The White Vaquero, a very romantic Mexican bandit, is a character who will win many friends." Possibly not among his victims, but apparently with the audience safe in their seats. That would certainly be the case in 1929 when **In Old Arizona** [1338] introduced the Cisco Kid and the Academy gave him its highest award.] **MPW**:11.29.13, p1009.

[419] **A YANKEE IN MEXICO**, Patheplay: [John Harvey is a chivalrous young American who witnesses a Mexican "brutally maltreating a Peon woman." He beats the brute which incurs his vengeance, but gets to meet his lady and take her from him as a reward. A duel must be fought which cannot be "on the square." The malevolent Mexican plans to remove John's bullets, but the señorita overhears and does the same to the scoundrels gun. Exposed and dishonored, the culprit is shamed out of the last reel. Boy gets girl. More significantly, the exhibitor comment: "A Patheplay of peculiar interest not only because of its intrinsic merit, but in view of the present prominence of Mexican troubles." Mexico was on many peoples minds in 1913, in the following year, especially from April to May, the vast majority of the North American public would want the United States to go to war with that nation.] **MPW**:10.18.13, p286, 10.25.13, p380.

[420] **THE YAQUI CUR**, Melies: [A full time prospector operating near the border, was apparently also moonlighting as a part time philosopher. One day he meets a young Yaqui boy, and possibly because he knew that Mexican tribe to be among the fiercest of all indians, he decides to teach him a bit of pacifist wisdom and some Christian ethics, neither of which will serve him very well. Having convinced the cur to "give peace a chance," he move on. Later when the indian's tribe is attacked, the student applies what he has learned and is branded a coward for his effort. As luck would have it he is presented with a chance to redeem himself when his tribe is once more attacked, but "the white man's wonderful doctrine" which he had learned, "Big love man lay down life for friend," leaves him biting a a lot of dust. There must be a lesson in there somewhere.] **MPW**:5.10.13, p624, 5.31.13, p919.

1914

[421] **ACROSS THE BORDER**, W: [A three reel adventure which features the experiences of Curly Smith, Texas Ranger, as he struggles with a band of Mexican/American arms smuggler's who are providing the rebels across the border with guns and "Lydite" bombs. Anita, daughter of Amador, the smuggler's chief is caught between her filial piety and her growing love for the young Anglo hero. The heavy in this piece is Dean, a "renegade American" whose jealousy drives him to tie the hero up next to a live rattlesnake to die a horrid death. In the end, the lady saves him, he captures the baddies and they march to the altar. The **New York Telegraph** felt that this work had "the obvious advantage of being a timely play."] **MPW**: 8.8.14, 788-9, 9.15.14, p970, 9.22.14, p1156.

[422] **ADVENTURES IN DIPLOMACY**, Eclair: [Interesting also because it may be the first to employ James Bond like special effects and secret devices. Two Spanish spies are hired to obtain the secret treaty signed between Venezuela and Mexico involving their internal affairs. The two leave Spain to complete their task and plant a bomb in the Embassy which, if they were caught, could be triggered by a "secret mechanical contrivance" still in their rooms. One of the baddies is an expert in "analytical chemistry." The good guys, the secret service, are led by Grimm, who has intercepted a message from Barcelona. After some Embassy party intrigue, where the Mexican Ambassador is knocked out, the plot is uncovered, the evil count exposed, and his sister is "reformed" by our hero Grimm, who, as is tradition in JB movies, gets to spend the last scene with her alone]. **MPW**:9.12.14, p1552.

[423] **ANDY GOES A-PIRATING**, Edison: [Young Andy dreams of being with the English Buccaneers raiding the Spanish Main.] **MPW**:6.10.14.

[424] **ARMS AND THE GRINGO**, Majestic: [In 1914, almost all the developing production companies rushed their stars, or sisters there of, to the border for a little exploitative drama, even the very big ones went south. Dorothy Gish starred in this "interesting subject telling of an episode of present conditions along the Mexican border."] **MPW**:4.4.14, p1902.

[425] **AT DAWN**, Mutual: [Sykes, a North American boy leaves his lovely for the Philippines where he has been employed to teach. He plans to send for her later forgetting what the tropics can do to an unattended with man, even one whose heart is pure. "Succumbed to the tropic influences", later proves to be a lot longer than anticipated. Meanwhile, our boy passes the time with a local lovely native lady. Tired of waiting and having inherited a fortune, the Anglo femme sends news of her imminent arrival. More interested in "coin" than he is in continuing what had become a distasteful necessity, Sykes tries to send the girl back to her tribe. When she refuses,

he poisons her and is in the process of disposing of the body when some of the North American occupation forces come by looking for "the way to the trail of Indians." Not really fools, they suspect something is amiss when they notice the gone bad lad carrying the dead native girl's body. "What's another Filipino, more or less," offers Sykes. Apparently, no one in the company can answer the question, and the soldiers head down the "Indian" trail without further delay. Only later, when the Anglo lady arrives and notices that her Sykes may well have gone native, and off the deep end, does the baddie gets his. The stupid sergeant, who finally realizes that the Anglo might well have done something wrong in killing the native girl, brings in Sykes and takes his former girl to Manilla. Racism in the Philippines, if one gauges it by the number of bodies left dead by North American occupation troops, was harsher there, than even it would be throughout the Haitian intervention which left more than three thousand locals for burial. See references to "Killing Niggers in the Phillipines," **Real Glory**, 1939.] **MPW**:12.12.14, p1582.

[426] **AT MEXICO'S MERCY**, Victor: [The title quite possibly reflects a feeling held by many North Americans prior to the direct action taken against Mexico in April of 1914. Here an Anglo is in charge of a Mexican mine when Romero, a local bandit, demands part of the payroll as tribute for allowing the mine to continue operations. Jack Desomod, unwilling to pay one peso for tribute, is shot for his bravery, but not killed. Brenda, his lady, goes for help, but meanwhile, General Cardillo, portrayed more as a bandit than a revolutionary and Romero's rival for leadership, discovers that his little child wandered out of the neutral zone and is lost. Having recovered from his wounds and not one to keep a grudge, Jack saves the child, but is captured by the general's men who are about to shoot him more officially, [with his back to a white wall] when his kindness is explained. Quickly, his sentence is reduced to prison, where we also find his lady, Brenda, who had been captured before she could make the border. As luck would have it, she escapes, just as Romero was about to blow both Jack and the General to eternal salvation. In time she returns with a detachment of Uncle Sam's best cavalry [which we must assume were operating in Mexico] to rescue Jack just before the place blows up. The lovers were rejoined, but the general blew into a lot of little pieces. Once more the negative influences of Mexico's revolution had been overcome by simple Anglo's just trying too do their job, taking much of Mexico's subsoil riches North of the border.] **MPW**:7.18.14, p478.

[427] **THE AZTEC TREASURE**, Eclair: [Miguel Perez, the bloody butcher tyrant of Mescalito, knows that somewhere in his province is hidden the treasure of Montezuma. Meanwhile, he has "oppressed and enslaved the peons [until] they face starvation." Dolores is the daughter of the local head man, Juan Icaze, who knows where the treasure is, but waits. Miguel desires to "annex" the beautiful Mexican/indian, but is momentarily deterred from his evil design, by the Yankee insurrectionist, Dick Henshaw. He is leading the

revolutionary activity against the evil oppressor. Dick's capture would be more important to Miguel than the lady because "it would place the revolutionists in a precarious position as they [were] entirely dependent upon their Yankee leader for success." [It had been established much earlier by the scripters that it was essential to have an Anglo to get things done right, or at all.] Miguel settles for taking Juan captive and torturing him to death without learning the treasure's whereabouts. Eventually, he captures the hero and heroine and just as he is about to kill them, his guards and the peasants revolt out of respect for the young Yankee insurrecto. Miguel tries to escape through a trap door, but discovers a pit filled with snakes awaiting to provide him with death. After the snakes slither away, the treasure is rediscovered and the lovers wed. Exhibitors considered this a "strong offering" with a "fine historical flavor." Audiences were as pleased with this then as they would be later when Yul Brynner plus six other's, Robert Mitchum and several score of other Anglos performed similar services.] **MPW**:9.19.14, p1686, 9.26.14, 1778.

[428] **BAD-MAN MASON**, Reliance: [For this writer, two wrongs could make things right. Bad Man gets into a scrape one evening and "shoots himself a Mexican." The sheriff, being fair, explains that even though Bad Man has saved his daughter from a raging torrent and the town from destruction, that he must be exiled. Understanding the situation, the antihero head's for Sonora where he takes a tenderfoot under his wing and attempts to deliver him to the local school marm. Shot by the Mexican's brother, he awakens to find a lovely teacher, nursing soothing life back into his body. Better, the sheriff explains that whereas the Mexican's brother attempted to murder him, he could now return to town. Well, there was some fairness in it.] **MPW**:10.10.14, p248, 250.

[429] **THE BARGAIN**, P: [Seven reels of revitalized western with W. S. Hart as the star. The film is significant here because, the bandit makes a deal with the sheriff to give him two hours to head for the border where he will hide out in Mexico, as so many much later criminals will do. Using Mexico as a hiding place will become so commonplace with scripters that by 1941, Will Hays, the industry's number one watch dog, will have Joe Breen, his top hand, issue a general communique to those production companies making western's, banning the use of the term "Ok boys, lets head for the border" or any other such variation. With WWII to consider, no offense could be tolerated that might insult our next door neighbor. Interestingly, the reviewer for this film, taking these seven years during which westerns were the predominate screen genre, considered it not only bad form not to punish the baddie, but a "dangerous weapon" in the hands of our enemies to show that our "National Censors condoned such action." This critic states that there was no doubt such films gave a message to the youth of this nation that crime could pay, when neither of the two men were punished for the crimes they had committed.] **MPW**:12.3.14, p1390.

[430] **BASQUE WEDDING**, Pathe: ["No one knows to what race the Basque people belong or how it was that they got their place in Europe. They live in the Pyrenees between France and Spain. They are all novel men, for once in the Middle Ages when they came to the rescue of a Spanish king, he ennobled the whole tribe ... this picture of their marriage customs is, we think, an especially worthy offering." So the exhibitors thought then.] **MPW**: 9.5.14, 960.

[431] **BATTLE OF TORREON AND CAREER OF GEN. VILLA**, Mutual: [**Variety** questioned the authenticity of the Torreon segment of this film claiming that it was put together from clips of the **Career of Gen. Villa** and location shots taken in Torreon. They further complained that the word descriptions did not coincide with the actual scenes and warned that if the Mutual company planed nationwide distribution for this production, its reputation will "receive a severe bump." The **Moving Picture World** made no such qualifications claiming that the film did show actual scenes from Torreon and of General Villa himself. "Two thousand feet of actual battle scenes have been selected." **V**:5.15.14, **MPW**:7.18.14, p10, p1312, 7.11.14.

"Film Institute Presents Old Border Films to Mexican Archives," More than 15 reels of original nitrate film were presented to the Cineteca Nacional and the Filmoteca de la UNAM. The work was that of Charles Pryor and includes footage of General Villa taking Juarez and General Pershing. **V**:12.11.85. "General Villa in the Movies," **NYT**:5.10.14. IV, 4.

[432] **THE BATTLE OF VERA CRUZ**, Sawyer: [For almost a full month, throughout most of April 1914, the vast majority of citizens north of the border, wanted Woodrow Wilson to declare war against Mexico. There was talk of sweeping all the way to Panama. Two years of revolutionary activity in that troubled nation, frequent border incidents and now, the insulting behavior of President Huerta who had refused to "Salute the Flag" of this superior nation provoked a nationwide demand for intervention and occupation. When the marines were landed in Vera Cruz, seventeen of "our boys" were lost, several hundred Mexicans, mainly youths lost their lives defending their homeland. Huerta never did salute and we occupied that city for almost a year, but we showed em. This production was advertized as "the _real thing_ in the _real place_ ... the first real, genuine pictures of the taking of Vera Cruz by Uncle Sam's sailors and Marines ... Taken on the spot during the fiercest fighting, amid a hail of bullets and showing "our boys" taking the city [by] assault [featuring] our boys working their machine guns with deadly effect ... them squirming up the street flat on their faces driving the enemy before them [and] the refugees getting protection under the Stars and Stripes."] **MPW**:6.13.14, p1639.

[433] **THE BLIGHTED SPANIARD**, L-KO: [Another film in which we find Spaniards confused with Mexicans by the writer. Two Spaniards, Tomalio and Bombardio, are in love with Sunshine, the village beauty, and a real sweet señorita. The lady favors the former and scorns the other. After witnessing

Tomalio serenade his lady, the rejected lover happens onto a cave filled with Federal spies and a lot of dynamite. He plots to blow up the competition, but is himself the victim. I know, it doesn't make a lot of sense, but that's how the writer envisioned love in 'ole Mehico'.]**MPW:11.21.14, p1126.**

[434] **BRONCHO BILLY--OUTLAW**, Essanay: [When a "refractory" "greaser" named Carnos, is sent to prison by the law, he vows to get even with the sheriff if he ever gets free. Broncho Billy himself, not always a good boy and frequently on the very edge of acceptable behavior, is captured by the same sheriff, who he likes. Upon learning of the mad Mexican's plan, he escapes in time to save the sheriff's wife from the clutches of the vengeful greaser. Grateful, the lawman obtains a pardon for Billy and reincarcerates the Mexican. It was that simple if you were an Anglo.] **MPW:6.20.14, 7.4.14, p64.**

[435] **BRONCHO BILLY AND THE GREASER**, Essanay: [By 1914 Broncho Billy was so popular with his public, that the demand for his films were almost impossible to meet even though his production company, Essanay, turned out almost one a week of these most successful single reelers. The plots were at times, very simple but the action, hard and fast. In this one Billy ejects a greaser from the Post office because of his rudeness to a young woman. The "halfbreed" swears revenge, but is foiled in his attempt to stab Billy as he slept by the grateful young woman. All that in about twelve minutes.] **MPW**:10.3.14, p90, 10.10.14, p90, 10.24.14, p492.

[436] **THE CABALLERO'S WAY**, Eclair: [This is the first film in which the main character is called "Cisco." This Cisco is loved, feared and hated for his activities and his very deadly aim. He loves Tonia, the sly, but capricious coquette. At times Cisco's behavior is not so lovable, he takes what he wants at will from the general store, shoots sheriffs "through the badge" and is always very jealous. Much of this upsets the town and in as much as the local law cannot bring him in, the Army is assigned the task. A handsome young Lieutenant Sandridge is given the job to deal with the badman. Some problems develop, the soldier falls for Tonia and she for he, that was required, but it works to everyone's advantage. When the bandit learns of the affair, the brave Cisco has no chance, his spirit is broken and he is brought to justice submissive and seeking punishment. The scripter must have had a very catholic upbringing. Betrayed by his woman, he wants the rope that the sheriff has for him. The lieutenant gets the señorita's rose, and maybe more, but not on the screen in 1914.] **MPW**:3.28.14, p1734.

[437] **CAPTAIN ALVAREZ**, Vitagraph: [Had this film played in downtown Buenos Aries anytime after its production, it would have been considered sufficient reason for demanding a declaration of war. Even those Argentines with the lowest boiling point in terms of national pride would have been offended to discover that a North American Yankee, who just happened by and decided to become a soldier of fortune siding

with the rebels, was responsible for the birth of the Argentine nation. No other country in South America was more fiercely nationalistic in the first fifty years of this century than Argentina. The scripter for this one had to have had some familiarity with Argentine history, but little knowledge of the national character. His protagonist, Rosas, the Federalist tyrant, was responsible for one of the most brutal dictatorships that nation ever experienced. His rival, "Urquiza," [Urquiza] was what we would call in the United States, his states rights opponent. Rosas was a centralizer, the other for provincial rights. Into this fray supposedly arrives the Anglo hero who become Captain Alverez, the savior of the provinces, foe of Rosas and lover of Bonita. In the final reel, the tyrant is deposed and the Yankee wins the rebel lady, the product of their union is Argentina. Myrtle Gonzales, the first woman with Hispanic heritage to receive film credit, played the seductive rebel heroine.] **MPW**:5.9.14, p799, 6.27.14, p1880.

[438] **CAPTURED BY MEXICANS**, Kalem: [This film scenario provides an excellent example of the what early screen writers considered would play well with the general public. It exhibits the general contempt that many North Americans at the time, held for the Mexican character, one that was not acceptable in civilized society. Pete, the Mexican, was rescued from sure death on the Yuma desert by a couple on their way to California. He is nursed and cared for, but after his recovery, he shows his "supreme ingratitude" by shooting at and wounding "his benefactor." Worse, he steals the samaritan's horse. Leaving the two almost helpless, Pete rides off to join his revolutionary friends, yet soon returns to capture the man that had rescued him. Having been accused of insurgent activity, to save his own life, he turns the Anglo over to the Federalistas and accuses him of being the real leader of the rebel band, who are in reality, merely his bandit buddies. Luckily for the North American, his lady's "pluck" allows her to rescue him with the aid of her faithful dog and the American Consul. In the final scene the "American is freed. Pete, however, meets the fate he deserves."] **MPW**:4.4.14, p98, 4.25.14, p517.

[439] **CARMELITA'S REVENGE**, Selig: [Any Anglo, especially one on the silver screen should well have known, even in these early days, that it was at best a chancy situation to keep company with a señorita named "Carmen" or any derivative there off. Crossing any one of them was certainly suicidal. Ah!, but without spice, where was the life? For the scripter, it was easily found in Mexico. This film detailed: "A lost love romance [very conventional.] A story of hatred and jealousy which has been used many times, "which North Americans by 1914 may well have considered to be the norm south of the border. The scenes were set in Mexico and New York. He does her wrong, she does him in, her "hot blooded" nature demanded revenge. But it was not done with knives in this one. "The audience received it with favor."] **MPW**:9.22.14, p1099.

[440] **CLASS MATES**, American Biograph: [In this little piece of fantastic fluff, a few West Point cadets try to outbrave each other in the dangerous wilds of an unspecified South America jungle filled with all the accepted and required misinformation designed by the imaginative screen writer to really impress a pretty girl. Why else? In 1924 this film will be remade with the same dangers implied but with story line updated [1034].] **MPG**.

[441] **COCAINE TRAFFIC** aka **THE DRUG TERROR**, Indy: [The drug traffic provided the major theme for first of what would be later called, "exploitation" films. **Variety** voiced its serious objections to such productions from the start. They accused the police of being lenient in allowing them to be shown to "weak minded people who endorsed them." Such films included coke sniffing, white slavery and the destruction of lives and property. Their modern counterparts merely identify the problem as generated by Hispanic influences. It these earlier times, the culprits were usually oriental. The problem with drugs, from the first, was rarely considered a North American one. The supplier was always the villain, the user, a victim. No one cared to imply that if the market was not present, the suppliers would go out of business.] **V**:2.27.14.

[442] **COL HEEZA LIAR IN MEXICO**, [The ever increasing swells of the social revolution Mexico experienced in 1910 could not help but spill over the Rio Bravo's borders affecting North American life on an almost continuous basis throughout this decade. Between 1912 and 1914 the presidents of the two republics vied with words and watchfully waited, until April 1914. At that time President Wilson's blue jackets took the port city of Vera Cruz and occupied it for almost a year. At the very moment the marines were taking Vera Cruz, this nationalistic fantasy, an animated cartoon, was released. Heeza's purpose was to singlehandedly quell the revolution in Mexico, after some trouble with a burro, he steals a plane, captures President Huerta, flies him to Mars, presents Wilson with his sword and receives the "medal of Legion of Watchful Waiting." Heeza would continue to lampoon the governments Mexican policy for the next two years in subsequent forays against Villa, but the stereotypes he employed to do so were at best offensive.] **MPW**:4.22.14, p820.

[443] **THE COMING OF THE PADRES**, American: [A historical documentary featuring the bicentennial celebration of Father Serra who, having journeyed from Mexico City, celebrated his first mass at the Santa Barbara Mission in Spanish California in 1714.] **MPW**:4.4.14, p58.

[444] **'CROSS THE MEXICAN LINE**, Nestor: [A very young Wallace Reid, Anglo hero, and destined to act in numerous productions featuring south of the border locations, led his troops south of the border in this production. Wounded he is nursed at the hacienda of a Mexican officer where the wife falls immediately in love with him. It would have been impossible for her not to, but when she discovers that he has a lady waiting for him

somewhere to the north, she is most displeased. Now vengeful, what else could she be, she lures the innocent into a trap where the hero, the girl and her father are all captured by prearranged agreement with more traditional Mexican bandits. In the end she is repentant, but unable to secure their freedom. As such, it was not necessary, the Anglos relying on their pluck and ability, manage their own escape, albeit with the aid of the ever ready United States Calvary. Exhibitors reports indicate that audiences bought this every time.] **MPW**:6.13.14, p1590, 6.20.14, p1690.

[445] **THE DEAD LINE**, Princess: [A heart sick Anglo lover uses the possibility of a Mexican raid across the border to win back his lady. Those early scripters certainly took every possible advantage of the Mexican situation to find material to put on film.] **MPW**:11.7.14, p834.

[446] **THE DESPERADO OF PANAMA**, Balascop: [The international significance of the Panama Canal, its importance to the United States and world maritime traffic was not lost on film makers. Almost before its final completion, this was the first film to plan its destruction. With an almost all male cast North American audiences cheered its successful protection by United States soldiers.] **V**:11.28.14

[447] **DOLLY'S DELIVERANCE**, Frontier: [Anglo, Hispanic, White Woman triangle again leads to Mexican seeking revenge. He and the Anglo end up fighting it out in a mine shaft after "the greaser's gun" clogged. Fred and Dolly happily ever after it as Jose is on his way to San Quentin. In an attempt to fill the skyrocketing demands of audiences for new productions, some duplicity occurred. A few producers attempted, with success, to sell the very same film under a completely different title. This film was also distributed as the **Greaser's Revenge**, [454]. **MPW**:10.17.14, p400.

[448] **DOLORES DE ARANDA** aka **THE LADY OF SORROW**, Bison: [The action in this film developed quickly and steadily. The scene was set in a Mexican border town where the sheriff was a gambler. The local Don Miguel was the big hacendado who, while waiting for his Dolores to grow out of the convent she was placed in to keep her a virgin, had impregnated Nita, kicked her in the stomach and left her to die. Just another day south of the border. After being rejected by his arranged bride, he rampages through the town killing all but the Anglo sheriff who does him in and wins the girl for himself. The reviewer refers to the Hispanics in the cast as "Mex or Spaniards" illustrating what was/is a continuous problem for Anglos. All Spaniards are/were the same, Mexicans, Spaniards, Colombians, Puerto Ricans, indians, the idea of nationality was/is apparently difficult to grasp. Hispanic character is more universal and identifiable.] **V**:4.24.14, **MPW**:4.18.14

[449] **DOPE**, [Another of the drug exploitation films which gained popularity in 1914. This product attempts to be more educational and informative as it outlines the problems created by the use of cocaine. A mother leaves home to become

a street walker to support her habit. While not as lurid and sensational as **Cocaine Traffic** [441] it includes scenes not unfamiliar today, including a New York "coke sniffing party."] <u>V</u>:4.3.14.

[450] **THE DREAM OF LOCO JUAN**, Box Office Attractions Co: [Some scripters simply could not hide their feeling for the peoples south of the border. "Loco Juan, a peon woodchopper has no chance with Carmencita but spent most of his time fantasizing about her. In his dreams he saved her from the wealthy Señor Domingues, owner of the Cantina El Toro, by becoming a dashing young macho with "newly attained manhood." One wonders what freudian log this writer slept with. Always Juan overpowered the other suitor and always the señorita succumbed to his desires. But reality was only a wake up away and when he did he forever found himself to be the simple "half-witted wood chopper" daydreaming "under the sun-flower in the wild-wood" that he was destined to be.] **MPW**:12.12.14, p1592.

[451] **THE ETERNAL DUEL**, Lubin: [One more Lubin production which utilizes the conflict between the Federalistas and the revolutionaries as the background for a love triangle. Modesto and Martinez although publicly vocal in support of the government are in reality in sympathy with the rebels and working for them. Don Alfredo, who supports the Federal government, loves the Martinez girl. His affection is not returned because she wants to marry Modesto. Although the latter is a soldier, he was not the best shot in all of Mexico and proves this conclusively dueling with Don Alfredo for the lady's affection. He loves her a lot, but misses his target five times. This allows his opponent to use his riata to capture and tie him up. Not only does he bind him, he leaves him suspended over a cliff, with the rope on fire which will eventually burn through drop him to certain death. Having done so, the Don goes to claim his prize. But nature, not a North American intervenes this time, and at the last moment Modesto is saved. Don Alfredo is then captured, and the groom to be, for no apparent reason, becomes the new revolutionary governor. The Federalista receives the punishment then afforded to those of his class. Although confusing in parts, the film cast sympathy to the rebel cause.] **MPW**: p324.

[452] **A GAME OF WITS**, Eclair: [It's only international intrigue with Inez the beautiful Mexican adventuress spy, who lures the easily afflicted secretary of the American Ambassador to Mexico City with promises of heaven if he will part with certain secrets desired by her corrupt government. Luckily our secret service boys are right on the spot to prevent any damage to national security, to say nothing of the poor fool's trip to paradise.] **MPW**:12.19.14, p1681.

[453] **THE GREASER'S REVENGE**, Frontier: [Also issued under the title with slight variations: **Dolly's Deliverance**, [447]. Dolly and Fred met by accident on a ranch out west but liked each other from the start. Jose liked Dolly also, but when the "greaser" had the effrontery to try to "make love to the lady", Fred intervened and the Mexican was immediately fired.

Jose was angered at being fired and stole Fred's horse. Fred was of course required to chase after his property and the culprit, but when he cornered the greaser, his gun jammed allowing the Mexican to pull his knife. Forced to run, Fred only managed to escape by hanging from a rope down a mine shaft. Seeing this the Mexican cut the rope, but in doing so he fell to the bottom of the pit where the two struggled. Fred quickly overpowered him and brings him to justice. Mexico was daily news throughout 1914, even some of the more responsible and less sensational metropolitan dailies used the term "greaser" to describe the citizens south of the Rio Grande. That would continue in some areas until WWI.] **MPW**:10.3.14, p69, p96, 10.10.14, p189.

[454] **THE GRINGO**, Kay-Bee: [Not very often the case, a North American couple are the heavies in this tale of greed and treachery. Looking to purchase a gold mine near California's Mexican border, the two ruin the reputation of a pious monk who had advised his Hispanic nephew against the sale. Angry because their plans have been thwarted they try to make even more trouble which provokes a little Spanish vengeance and results in the Anglo male's death and threatens the woman's life. The only one that can save the Gringa is the good Father Bernardo, true to his vows he of course does. See **The Greaser**, [568].] **MPW**:3.27.14, p116, 4.4.14, p59.

[455] **THE GRIP OF THE PAST**, Lubin: [Certainly a spin off of the **Octoroon**, [57], this epic staged on a southern plantation has as it's protagonist a Spaniard named Pedro who loves a local Dixie beauty, Jane. When she inherits the plantation and all those acres, her childhood beau, properly named Craven plots to do Pedro in. He plants the rumor that the señor is not a Spaniard, but actually a light skinned black man posing as one. Jane is "over come by the horror of the thought ... [that] it may be true." Especially since she has just kissed him, and on the lips too! Of course it is proven by Jane's sister that Pedro is not a negro, but is really Hispanic. But by then the whole distasteful affair has soured him on the not so sweet southern lady. It was Belle that he really loved, the sister who had defended him with dear dead ole dad's diary, which proved he was the proud Spaniard he had always claimed to be. Yet, as was so often the case for the screen's women, all was not lost for Jane, she simply marries someone else, and soon thereafter.] **MPW**:11.28.14, p1268.

[456] **THE GYPSY GAMBLER**: Kalem: [It was not only the Anglo's that could exercise their prejudice against the Spanish. Espan, the gambler, loves Pardena, daughter to Romano, the king of the Gypsies. The lady says "no", but later, Espan wins her in a card game, a crooked one. What could be more fair? When that is discovered, the two men "engage in a knife duel," and the dad gets killed. Meanwhile, the lady has wandered in to the badlands where she is discovered by Light Cloud, an indian, who immediately falls in love with her. Somewhat grateful to be saved, she responds, but his family, and the tribe in general, hate the nomad lady and reject her. True to his love, the indian makes her his squaw anyway and

leaves his people so that they can share a life together.]
MPW:6.20.14, p1724.

[457] **A GYPSY ROMANCE**, Nestor: ["A story of the inside life of nomads who live in the shadow of civilization worshipping their own goods [sic] and cling to their ancient rites." Just before the old king dies, he appoints Jose his successor and gives him his daughter to wed. Not all are happy and rivals appear who intrigue against the new rulers, unsuccessfully.]
MPW:4.4.14, p112.

[458] **HER SPANISH COUSINS**, Edison: [A wealthy New England spinster, Hepzipah Perkins, is invited to Spain by her aristocratic, but impoverished family merely for the purpose of acquiring some of her wealth. They do not, and she meets the man of her dreams on the steamer home.] **MPW:7.4.14, p102.**

[459] **HE WAITS FOREVER**, Lubin: [It would seem that some exhibitors wanted scripts that provided what might be considered acceptable justifications for the actions their stories described, and which discounted the turmoil in Mexico as the primary reason for an unhappy photo play. This film set in Mexico "has to do with the petty insurrections which are continually occurring there" The love theme has such a sad end, why the author should have Jose killed, "when he has done nothing to deserve it," seems unfair. Once more, poor boy loves rich girl, but dad objects. Off to seek his fortune, she waits six years before marrying the wealthy Andres de Romar. Immediately thereafter Jose strikes it rich and is asked to join as well as finance part of the rebel cause. Assuming that if he is both rich and famous as a revolutionary General, the lady will be really pleased and remain his forever, he heads back to tell her the good news. When he discovers what has happened, his disappointment knows no bounds, it fills him with hate. Because of his new wealth he now has the power to order all of the principle players to a fiesta for a macabre celebration where he plans to poison the lady, her father, her new husband and himself. But as the scripter's fate would have it, he accidently drinks the deadly potion himself and dies before the others can do the same, a victim of his tragic love and unfamiliar hate. Apparently the above was a something of a practical romantic.] **MPW:11.21.14, p1116, 12.12.14. p1523.**

[460] **IN THE DAYS OF THE PADRES**, Domino: [Inez, daughter of Don Luis, agreed to marry Jose Sepulevada because dad wanted her to, but she was really in love with the bandit, Juan de Lara. Juan had met the little señorita when he had robbed another Spanish Grandee who happened to be carrying a letter of introduction which allowed him to go to Inez's hacienda because he needed medical attention. When the romantic bandit assumed the identity of the patient, she applied the bandages and her tender loving care. That's all it took, the bandit was then her captive for life. But there was a problem, dad needed the dineros and insisted she marry the more prosperous Don. But the screen writers had established the formula long before, the father's desire and need proved secondary to true

loves dictates. When Jose promised to give up waylaying señors on the camino, the lady said "si" ya later to the other suitor.] **MPW**:3.27.14, p116.

[461] <u>IN THE LATIN QUARTER</u>, Vitagraph: [The scene was Paris's Latin Quarter with the French doing most of the operating, not the Hispanics, there were none included in the action.] **MPW**:12.26.14, p1872.

[462] <u>THE KEY TO YESTERDAY</u>, FP: [A simple story of mistaken identity and lost memory. A noted French artist temporarily loses his memory when beaten by roughnecks out west, but he know that the key in his pocket is the key to his future if only he can find the lock that will open his past. Meanwhile he travels south of the border where he is mistaken for a South American revolutionist that has suffered a wound in his left hand. Luckily someone notices that the wounded artist has an injured right hand and so he is released after partaking in several revolutionary adventures. In time he finds his key hole, his past and himself.] **MPW**:10.17.14, p348, 12.19.14, p1784.

[463] <u>THE LAST DANCE</u>, Picture Playhouse Film Co: [Conchita Ledesma plays a "rather buxom" Spanish dancer who entices a young artist away from his true love for a brief but passionate affair that ends in an equally brief marriage. Broken hearted at the broken marriage the artist falls apart very quickly and dies in the naughty lady's arms. In his memory the Carmen like dancer performs a last provocative dance for him as he lies dead on the floor, she was all heart.] **V**:11.28.14.

[464] <u>THE LIFE OF GENERAL VILLA</u>, Mutual: [The Mutual company scored a first for the film industry when it contracted with the leader of the Army of the North, which controlled more than half of Mexico at that time, to provide exclusive film coverage of his exploits. The advertising campaign promoting the venture was extensive. This production used actual footage of various successful encounters and provided a justification for Villa's exploits that none of the subsequent productions would deviate from. When Villa was very young, Federalista soldiers came and "ruined" his sister. Thereafter, all was justified. He killed one of the officers responsible for the outrage to his sister and then sold his rancho vowing eternal revenge and not to stop until the Porfirioato, the Diaz regime, was brought down. "He became a bandit and by meeting and defeating other bandits, became the chief of a great band" and ruled Northern Mexico. This film ends with his successful revolutionary activity being responsible for placing him in the Presidency. A memorable scene in both, <u>Viva Villa</u> and <u>Viva Zapata</u>. **MPW**:2.7.14, p657, p705, 5.23.14, p1215, p1312, 6.20.14, p1646, 7.4.14, p341.

[465] <u>THE LITTLE SEÑORITA</u>, Princess: [Quite interesting because it is the first film in which an exiled "mysterious" South American leader seeks refuge way north of the border from those who would kill him. "Señor Carraza" has purchased

Hendricks Island in the middle of a river up north and lives there with his wife and attractive daughter. Tom, the neighbor, is curious and visits the secluded place where the lady likes him. The father does not and refuses to allow any of his progeny to marry or even keep company with an American. Later, the Latin assassins have found the señor and when Tom comes to the rescue, repelling the killers, "the despised "Americano" wins Carraza's respect and the lady for his wife.] MPW: p6.27.14, p1876, 7.4.14, p65.

[466] **LOVE SACRIFICE**, Kay-Bee: [The only connection is that Don Jose, a wealthy Spanish grandee is exiled from Mexico because of his political belief's and once across the border, he and his child are captured by indians who bring up his child.] MPW:5.9.14, p868.

[467] **THE LOVELY SEÑORITA**, Edison: ["Wood B. Wed" inherits money and decides to go to "romantic" South America to find a wife. Arriving in Santa Marina, he immediately meets Paprika, a fiery, "dusky Señorita." Pleading for her hand, she forces him to dress like a local before considering his offer. Looking like a "vaquero or a toreador or whatever the proper word is" she is charmed. But former suitors, Tomale and Tobasco, accost our hero with a long and ferocious knife and threaten his life. His up north response is money which buys them off easily. The fair Paprika, "like Desdedemona, loved him for the danger he had passed." She weds him and initiates him to the "spicy mysteries of the hot tamale." Later caught in a revolution, he is saved first by the indecision of the Hispanic officer who cannot decide where to shoot him and then his lady who brings the rebels to the rescue. But she is disappointed with his behavior and so rides off with the insurrecto leader. No comment, it speaks well enough for the scripter's personal conception of life south of the border.] MPW:1.31.14, p576.

[468] **THE MAN FROM MEXICO**, FP: [A pleasant comedy in which a fun loving husband [John Barrymore] uses his wife's absence to plan a big night out. Fun leads to arrest and he is sentenced to a month in jail. To cover his absence he tells her that he is going to Mexico.] MPW:11.14.14, p941, p996. V:11.21.14.

[469] **THE MAN FROM THE WEST**, Lubin: [Some time in the past a mysterious easterner came west and became loved and respected as the "Man from New Mexico." Years later a nice eastern lady also comes west to visit her dad's mine and the two meet when "the man" saves the tenderfoot that is threatened by Mexican Joe. Love at first sight sends her home, but he goes to fetch her and she comes as willing as if she'd been tied to his horse. Mexican Joe ceased to be a local problem.] MPW:1.22.14, p324.

[470] **THE MASKED DANCER**, Vitagraph: [A mining engineer in Mexico becomes infatuated with a pretty señorita who works at the local cantina. His wife to regain his affection learns to dance like the bonita little beauty. The exhibitors considered that some of the scenes were "pretty sensuous."

The credits include Myrtle Gonzales and Beatrice Dominguez, but also "George Cooper who is the greaser divekeeper in as convincing a role as any we have seen." Apparently, it took an Anglo actor to really bring the slime out of a "greaser" characterization.] **MPW**:1.24.14, p544.

[471] **THE MEXICAN**, Selig: [A "nobel act is a courageous revenge." Tom Mix starred and directed this melodrama in which a Mexican crosses the Rio Bravo to seek employment at an Anglo ranch so that he can feed his starving family. While there he is mistreated by the cowboys and seeks revenge by burning down the bunkhouse and a lot more. Meanwhile the ranch owners daughter is bitten by a rattler and forgetting his vengeful way, the Mexican rides for help to save the child. He does and is rewarded by the grateful rancher who provides for his starving family. Not all, but most of Tom Mix's films [with Mexican scenes] presented generally favorable or sympathetic views of the Hispanics [171, 172].] **MPW**:10.10.14, p230, 10.31.14, p640.

[472] **THE MEXICAN HATRED**, Warner: [The Mexican revolution exerted many influences north of the border, even the scripters were affected. This fantasy focused on the Mexican's hatred for United States soldiers, especially one mother whose son had been executed as a spy. When circumstance provided her with the opportunity to avenge herself, she did. One day the officer responsible for her son's death was close enough to be hit by a rock she threw at him. When he awakened, his memory was gone. Now all of the hatred that she felt, she poured into his blank mind, creating a fierce fighter of the despised gringos. Leading rebel forces against his own men, he is revived at the last moment. No good North American soldiers would ever shoot their own, in Mexico, Panama or anywhere else the flag of freedom is unfurled.] **MPW**:11.14.14, p934.

[473] **A MEXICAN MINE FRAUD**, Pasquali-American: [Mr. Starey, a North American banker, is selling phony stock in an even phonier Mexican mine. George, a reporter for the **Daily Truth**, recently returned from the Balkan Wars, is sent to Mexico to make sure that there is no fraud involved in the riches the Banker is acquiring. Before going south, he falls in love with the bankers daughter and refuses an offer from the corrupt banker, that was really difficult to refuse. Realizing that the honest reporter can not be purchased, banker Park travels south to stop our hero. There he "visits all the dives and makes the acquaintance of many bandit lion tamers", [yes, lion tamers.] George is captured and placed in a cage with 10 lions, but escapes miraculously in time to tell the truth about the fraud. The banker, after his flight to Switzerland now returns all the money, and George gets the lady. Some reviewer criticized this international effort because of its lack of familiarity with the Mexican characterization, which they considered burlesque and like scenes from a comic opera. They felt that the local lions would have been more at home in South Africa.] **MPW**:6.13.14, p1604, 7.4.14, p84

Feature Film List 1914   125

[474] **THE MEXICAN REBELLION**, Ammex: ["Thrilling Adventure of an American in Mexico" "A sensational story of romance and war, showing how an American soldier of fortune joined the Mexican rebel army and had many narrow escapes from death. A timely subject, right up to the minute, regarding which columns and columns are being written in the daily papers." Aside from saving the revolution for the Mexican rebels, he wins the wonderful little señorita for himself ... sound familiar. By this time this formula was absolutely ingrained in the minds of the movie going audience. The added twist was Mercedes, the daughter of a fiery Federalista general, "who longed to lead a desperate charge ... and transform retreat into victory." Her change of sides was of course affected by her heart, which she was forced to give to the Anglo hero by the screen writer, it was his fantasy.] **MPW**:1.24.14, p396, 1.31.14, 573.

[475] **MEXICAN SNIPER' REVENGE**, Canadian Bioscope: [Exhibiting what may well have been generally accepted North American attitude toward all other races, and a particular contempt for our southern neighbors, **Variety** felt that the Mexicans in this film who were supposed to be "Federals and Revolutionaries" looked "like a bunch of Japs impersonating giants." In this production the American hero is shot by a Mexican sniper as his "olive-skinned sweetheart" falls prostrate across his body. Even before the Production Code was instituted, inter-racial relationships were rarely allowed. For all his trouble **Variety** considered the dead man the "most unAmerican like movie hero yet cameraed", possibly because he had allowed himself to be killed, a feeling more than likely shared by most of the audience.] **V**:7.31.14.

[476] **A MEXICAN SPY IN AMERICA**, Bison: [Another timely tale of intrigue and espionage in which a Mexican woman tries to take advantage of a defenseless Anglo lover. The friendship between a border commandant's son and a Mexican Federal Officer, Captain Huraz is used to try to obtain the secret code of the signal corps. It is well known that a young Army officer is in love with a local lady and she he. In an attempt to use this, another Mexican woman disguises herself as his true love to steal the document. This of course fails, and the officer is most pleased to have his sweetheart vindicated in the last reel. The inventive spy, Madame Solez was brought to justice [377].] **MPW**:7.11.14, p340, 9.22.14, p1101.

[477] **A MEXICAN WARRIOR**, Imp: [It would seem that revolutionary activity south of the border served many functions. A northern dipsomaniac to evade the clutches of his grasping mother in law tells his wife he is about to join the army to go fight the Mexicans. His buddies place him in a uniform and set off for a rollicking good time. Meanwhile his meek wife decides to shed her fear for her husband and serve her country at the same time. Bravely she enlists as a Red Cross nurse in a group to be sent to the border. When the drunk returns home "non compos mentas," the mother in law, discovering the duplicity, marches him down to the recruitment

station and forces him to really enlist.] **MPW**:6.6.14, p1409, 6.13.14, p1590.

[478] **THE MEXICAN'S GRATITUDE**, Edison: [Mexican Frank, a notorious bandit is the hero of this piece. His friend and deep down no gooder is the Frio Kid, who especially loves killing at Christmas weddings. He is personally infuriated at the man who marries Rosita, the lady he loves. Staying away for three years he "embarked on a fervid career" along with his Mexican friends. He "dynamited trains, shot bank messengers and did other things incompatible with good citizenship." But when "the kid" planned to kill the real Santa Claus so that he could have his outfit to gain entrance to Rosita's home, Mexican Frank remembered the service that lady had once done for him. He saved Santa and laid out the Frio Kid under the stars with a bullet in his head [54].] **MPW**:3.7.14, p1284.

[479] **THE MEXICAN'S LAST RAID**, Nestor: ["An early Southwestern drama set at a time when Mexican bandits held forth in mountain strongholds and hurled defiance at gentlemen and miners alike." A little historical introduction, set the scene. The bandits are real active in this one. First they try to rob the store belonging to the father who will not let Bill marry the beautiful daughter, even after he has saved him from the first set of Mexican bandits. Luckily more Mexican bandits show up and kidnap the girl for which the father offers marriage as a reward if he can rescue her. Remember? No number of Mexicans can withstand the assault mounted by a single Anglo. Having dispersed the first set of bandits, the second group presents little difficultly for the hero. His reward, as was traditional, was the lady.] **MPW**:3.2.14, p1298.

[480] **MEXICO**, Al Dia: [Sometime during 1914 the one reel production became a short subject. Following Griffith's lead, many directors used more than one for their feature presentation. The benefits of not being confined between ten to fifteen minutes of film were quickly obvious to all. This across the border feature boasted of, "Four reels of Mexican revolutionary activity" which one reviewer claimed had "an atmosphere that has not been on the screen very often. In getting glimpses of Mexican nooks and corners, in seeing what looks like a revolutionary camp ... the spectator feels that he is getting instruction. The producer of the picture seems to have had a first hand knowledge of things" as they happen south of the border. The story itself involved Lopez, a dedicated peon who wishes to fight for Villa and enlists in Juarez to serve the cause. While he is away, a treacherous Federalist officer tries to have his way with Lopez's woman, but fails. The youth returns to save her and kills the Federal spy sent to turn him in. The last of this four reeler provided recently shot footage of fight sequences between the two opposing forces.] **MPW**: 2.28.14, p1091.

[481] **THE MINER'S PERIL**, Reliance: [Boy! Talk about close shaves! Within a few years the **Perils of Pauline, Liberty** and **Patria** would become much looked forward too weekly fare for

movie goers. The complex problems that the scripters will force these fearless female heroines to face will, with some difficulty, always be overcome. Certain dangerous situations will be standardized, quickly recognized and accepted by the audience all over the Americas. This little one reeler used two of them to enhance the created tension and also, increase the sinister and evil nature of the perpetrators. The problems began when Jimson, the mine foreman fired two slovenly Mexicans for stealing ore. As required by the writers for almost a decade already, Pedro and Madro, the sleazy thieves swore to achieve revenge. Their desire was greatly intensified, when the boss rescued Nina, the beautiful Mexican girl from their evil and unwelcomed attentions. When Nina marries Jimson, the sinister two follow them back to the camp and before their love can be consummated, they capture and tie them up. Nina is left in the cabin which happens to house the mechanism that holds aloft some hundred feet, the huge bucket used to haul up the ore. After the foreman is bound and gagged, they put him in that container and raise it high above the cabin. Then the really bad hombres, tie a rope to hold back the mechanism that will release the iron monster and allow it to plummet to the ground thereby crushing the cabin. Intersecting the rope, they place a burning candle which when it burns down, will result in the destruction of the newlyweds. Not really nice guys, their flashing eyes and gleaming teeth are obvious testimony that their dirty work has brought them pleasure. With one last look back they scurry away certain that the two will be dead by morning. But as each flicker of the flame brings death a little closer, Nina struggles with her bonds. Unsuccessful in her attempt to free herself, she just manages to knock over a board by using her feet. When the board falls it extinguished the flame and the morning crew frees the two happy captives who have a lot to look forward to. After the Mexicans were punished severely, the scripters set about thinking of finding new and even more inventive ways of putting out that candle.] **MPW**:11.7.14, p834.

[482] **NATIVE LIFE IN THE PHILIPPINES**, Pan-American: [As the generally unconscious agent of imperialism, film remained one of its best allies until well into most recent times. It was not only those of us as young Anglo's who sided with the three British stalwarts in **Gunga Din**, even native audiences in India did the same. Psychologists may have clinical explanations for this, but everyone wants to be with the good guys. In most films, it was rather easy to identify who that is. Of all the media, film presented the most idealistic, rose colored glasses, side of North America's brief flirtation with imperialistic endeavors, it still does. This production reviewed by Stephen Bush was designed to show North American voters "what their country has done in the Philippines ... how manfully the nation has shouldered the white man's burden and how with infinite patience and toleration, it has conquered the superstitions and evils and the crimes of savagery [of a people for the first time] under the influence of Christian Civilization." Apparently the more than three hundred years of Spain's Roman Catholic influence had done little to enlighten the dark skinned savages.] **MPW**:4.18.14, p365.

[483] **NEPTUNE'S DAUGHTER**, Universal: [In recent times many North American's earned a dubious distinction for their notorious lack of geographic knowledge, so far as what nation is where in the world. This failing not only applies to exotic place names like the Sanjack of Novi Vazzar, but sorrowfully to New World nations. I have known students in college classes who thought that Nicaragua had to be reached by crossing an ocean. One even placed it just south of Kansas. Bermuda is a bit of a bug a boo for many. Most people consider it a tropical isle, somewhere in the Caribbean, and are amazed to discovery it off the coast of North Carolina, well, a few miles out. This Bermuda entry may be considered a self indulgence to indicate there is a need for broader geographic knowledge, a fantasy filmed in the Crystal Cave on that beautiful island. In more recent times that location was used film an incredible piece of nonsense, **The Bermuda Depts**, which has a monstrous turtle threatening the happy islanders.] **MPW**:5.9.14, pp796-7.

[484] **NIPPED**, Domino: [The ethnic pun used as a title for this film along with its content, may well have been noticed by one whose nationalist xenophobia would later prompt him to produce one of the most racist of invasionary scenarios. W. R Hearst would finance the production of **Patria** [699] in 1916. Here, the concern was merely the Japanese who were swapping arms for a land concessions around Magdalena Bay, Mexico. Luckily for those with dual concerns about the "nips" and the "Mex", a North American artist happened to be using the daughter of the Mikado representative as a model. She falls for him and tells of the plot. He and his buddy immediately go to the Japanese/Christian mission being used as a store house for the arms and blow it up. The little daughter of Nippon is shot by accident, but this was justified, because "she had betrayed her country," even if it was for a superior cause. See also: **Pride of Palomar** [940]] **MPW**: 11.21.14, p1138.

[485] **NUTTY DELIVERS THE MESSAGE TO GARCIA**, Universal: [This nonsense has nothing to do with the Spanish American War, it merely capitalizes on the popularity of the then well known phrase.] **MPW**:1.3.14, p82.

[486] **OLD CALIFORNIA**, Bison: [This little racist melodrama set in Spanish California had all of the ingredients that would, with frequent repetition, be used to characterize the Hispanic character in later productions, faithlessness, violence, brutality, weakness, mistreatment of women and infidelity. Dolores marries the wrong man, he brutalizes her for twenty years, she suffers for her son, he proves no better than his father and betrays his king, Philip of Spain. His only redemption is that he begs the authorities not to tell his dying mother of his misdeeds.] **MPW**:4.25.14.

[487] **THE OPENING OF THE PANAMA CANAL**, Hagy Feature: [The result of over six months work in the Canal Zone, scenes include Panama City, the markets, the fortifications on Naos Island, the flooding of Culebra Cut and the initial passage through the Gatum Lock "lifting a tug more than 85 feet above

sea level." Even after the outbreak of WWI, Panama shorts and features were among the most popular of 1914.] **MPW**:6.13.14, p1519, 1586.

[488] **PANAMA-PACIFIC EXPOSITION**, Victor: [Immediately after the great success of the Crystal Palace exposition in 1851 the world looked for reasons to hold international fairs, certainly the opening of the canal that would be for the benefit of the "ships of all nations" was sufficient reason for another such celebration. Sadly, Panama-Pacific Exposition coincided with the outbreak of great world war which inhibited some of its success. This presentation showed "how work on the mammoth exposition was progressing."] **MPW**:7.18.14, p434.

PATHE NEWS REELS:

[489] **#6, Neuevo Laredo**: "Mexico: Mexican Rebel Army leaves for the front."

[490] **#7, Colon Panama**: "Cleaning up the Cucaracha Slide."

[491] **#24, Mexico City**: "Huerta's army alleged at 20,000 parades in the capital."

[492] **#27, Mexico City**: "General Rincon Guallardo directs the defense of Torreon against Villa's onslaught from an arm chair in the Capital."

[493] **#28, Mexico City**: "The flower of the Federal Army head to defend Torreon."

[494] **#32, In the Gulf of Mexico**: [Mainly Uncle Sam's war ships patrolling Mexican ports.

[495] **#32, Washington, D.C.**: "John Lind, President Wilson's representative in Mexico confers with Secretary of State Bryan."

[496] **#33, Mexico City**: "Here is a crack troop of Huerta's army men and boys torn from their homes and forced to follow their dictator's flag."

[497] **#33, Vera Cruz**: "Uncle Sam's men-of-war [which included the Connecticut, Admiral Mayo's flag ship] in Vera Cruz, with their decks cleared for action." The Louisiana was off Tampico.

[498] **#35, Havana, Cuba**: "Four blocks of the city burned down to kill the rats that carry bubonic plague."

[499] **#35, Chihuahua, Mexico**: "Look who's here. Carranza and his whiskers demanding that the United states get out of Vera Cruz."

[500] **THE POWER OF THE ANGELUS**, Mutual/Domino: [Nineteen twenty seven will bring revolutionary developments to the

silver screen. What had always been silent would now talk. But that would create more problems, especially for the many ethnics, usually Anglo actors and actresses, who never had to speak their lines. The situation will be even more severe for the scenarist faced with the inventing dialect and dialogue. At this time the North American consciousness tended to group all Latins into one giant Hispanic lump. Although this was frequently done throughout the silent era, in 1914 it was evident that some screen writer had little knowledge of even the most basic world geography. This film, intended to be a pious reflection of the power of prayer as exhibited in our most southern neighbor, confused Spain and Mexico as one nation. The leading characters are identified by title cards as being in Spain, some short time later, most of the action takes place in Mexico. The eternal triangle causes the señorita to elope with a fortune hunter, Carlos, who is more than disappointed when dad the Don disinherits his daughter. Her former suitor becomes a monk at a Mexican monastery which is awaiting the delivery of a holy challis. The unhappy groom now plans to rob said golden artifact, but he is prevented from doing so by our lady who rings the call to prayer, the Angelus, reminding the culprits, Carlos's men, of their piety, and possibly that they shall certainly go to hell unless they tear him apart. They do. Having taken vows, the rejected suitor must remain married to the church. Realizing this, the rejected lady prostrates herself at the feet of Christ, contemplating a life of prayer, alone.] **MPW**:10.24.14, p493, p542.

[501] **PRIDE OF JENNICO**, FP: [This early swashbuckler was the film version of James K. Hackett's play included beautiful location shots taken in Cuba. The scenario involved a high born señor who had given his word to his aristocratic family that he would not marry below his rank. A perfect promise for a silver screen script. Of course he falls for a lower born princess and must sorrowfully sacrifice love for duty. The sad tale worked very well with audiences in 1914 and the formula may have been reused not a few times throughout the next seven decades, several hundred times.] **MPW**:2.28.14, p1071.

[502] **THE QUICKSANDS**, Kalem: [Few North American's in 1914 were conscious of the Philippines essentially Hispanic character. The only Roman Catholic nation in Asia, the islands named after Philip the Second were then a miscegenetic combination of pure Spaniards, natives including the Moro and an endless variation of that mixture. With the advent of the Spanish American war and the acquisition of these islands, all of the negative characterizations associated with Hispanics in general were combined with the assumed savageness of the natives and applied to the general population of these islands. This film of the North American occupation exhibits the same superior attitudes of those in any occupied territory. Native girl falls for young officer captured by savage locals and as is invariably the case, gives up her life trying to save him despite her awareness of his Anglo sweetheart [1001].] **MPW**:5.9.14, p821, 6.6.14, p1434.

[503] **THE RENEGADES VENGEANCE**, Selig: [A hard working Anglo falls upon hard times and chances across a Mexican beating his wife. He thoroughly trounces the brute and takes his lady home to care and be cared for by his wife. The Mexican now embarks upon a career of vengeful actions all directed at the husband, the two wives and a small child. In the last reel he evens runs off with all the horses. But it ended well for the audience, Mexicans were always punished before the final fadeout.] **MPW:3.2.14, p1290.**

[504] **THE RETURN**, Eclair: [Another love triangle, but this one ends in redemption on the Border. Tom lost the lady because he drank his inheritance out of one big bottle and ignored her. Moving west to find himself again, he becomes a Texas Ranger and is responsible for capturing a notorious gang of gun-runners providing the warring forces in Mexico with arms. Yup, the lady soon follows and saves him from being shot dead by one of the smugglers who had him dead in his sights. Anglo women were tough and faithful on the silver screen back then.] **MPW:10.31.14, p680.**

[505] **THE REVENUE OFFICER'S DEPUTY**, Reliance: [A very complicated love story involving Jason, "the revenue officer's" deputy who discovers that Mexican whiskey was being made in his district. The action revolves about complex love interest, more than the making of the illegal alcohol.] **MPW:10.10.14, p248.**

[506] **ROSE OF THE RANCHO**, Belasco-Lasky: [Destined to provided the formula for numerous screen plays [including **Kit Carson** which would be banned by the Mexican government in 1941] **Rose** tells the story of the United States take over in Spanish California and the subsequent problems this created for the established Spanish population. Here the Castro family refused to obtain a new land grant and leaves itself open to land grabbers. The new government sends an Anglo savior who rights wrongs and wins the heart of the Spanish beauty. A young Cecil B. De Mille directed this production and was one of the first to realize that using actual Mexicans in the production could only enhance its value. For this reason he and Wilfred Buckland "made a trip to Guadalajara, Mexico, and there engaged forty native actors to appear in the roles of Vaqueros, Caballeros and Mexican indians." The director "prevailed upon the Mexicans to bring their native costumes and characteristic mantillas and multi-colored gowns." Certainly one of the reasons for his later success, he considered this atmospheric research necessary and later made trips to Old Montery, Aguas Caliente and Nogales, Mexico to obtain necessary material.] **MPW:10.10.14, p203, 11.21.14, p1078, 11.28.14, p1294, V:11.21.14.**

[507] **THE SECRET TREATY**, Eclair: [George Howard, secretary to one of the officials responsible for formulating a new treaty with Great Britain, was handsome, but had no character. When presented with the opportunity to sell out for a fortune, he was willing. Vamped by Donna Inez, a lovely Mexican spy, he is told to go to Tucson, Arizona with the secret papers for

the payoff. Meanwhile, Steel, of the Secret Service, who has been closely following the events shows the young rake the error of his ways. Realizing that he has been used, and that Donna is now on a wagon train west with Pedro her lover, and that the sneaky spy held him in "contempt," he returns the papers with the assurance that "no eyes" save the pursued and pursuee have "ever read its lines."] **MPW**: 10.3.14, p97.

[508] **SHORTY'S TRIP TO MEXICO**, Broncho: [Pedro Sanchez, the border smuggler, enlists Shorty's help in moving arms across the border. To help sooth his broken heart he accepts because this will all so give him the opportunity to see Anita in Mexico. As someone would have it he arrives there just in time to save her and her family from the evil Mexican general, Carramba.] **MPW**:6.3.14.

[509] **SOLDIER OF FORTUNE**, All Star: [Because of its influence, this is really the most important of Richard Harding Davis' entries to be translated to the screen. The reviewer in 1914 praised the author, but pointed to the difficulty of making a film from his work. That might have been so, but the producers managed to over come the obstacles, as others would numerous times in the years to follow. Possibly taking their cue from the State Department, Hollywood will create the necessity for the Anglo hero to go south of the border to save the situations for the macho Anglo Author's always inept Latin American dictator providing the Anglo with various justifications for his actions. Made first in this year this scenario will be reused many times, under many different titles, but will remain essentially the same story, all the way down to **Moon Over Parador**, 1988. To aid in this production the Cuban government, apparently still grateful for services rendered in the cause of Cuba Libre, provided the film makers with "an Army to do any thing" that they might have wished them to do. Times certainly change, one might smile at considering the consequences, had the producers of **Cuba Crossing**, 1980, asked Fidel for a little help with piece of right wing Miami paranoia. And from this side, the producers of **Havana**, 1990 were unable to obtain United States State Department permission to film that production in that same city. The refusal forced them to use the Dominican Republic as the new location for the Cuban capital. That only makes sense because it involves Hollywood and the State Department.] **MPW**:8.30.13, p969, 1.10.14. **NYT**: "Mimic War in Cuba For Yankee Movie," 11.6.13.

[510] **THE SPANISH OMELET**, Biograph: [Barney O'Malley, owner of the Tarantula Cafe, "makes Spanish omelets of antique eggs". His daughter, Carmen, is a faithless flirt who fools around with anything that moves quickly. Almost immediately after the dashing Don Jose, "a tabasco Spanish lothario, elopes with her she transfers her affections to Don Bullo, a bull fighter, which provokes a duel. Dad intervenes by pulling off the bald headed lady's whig, showing the foolish lovers the worthlessness of their anger. "The surprised duelists embrace and congratulate each other on escaping conjugal relations with one so false as Carmen." One wonders what message the

scripter had in mind: Dad may have dealt in damaged eggs but he could not let two such gentleman die over his apparently damaged daughter?] **MPW**:6.27.14, p1860.

THE TAMPICO INCIDENT, Pathe Newsreels:

[511] **Tampico Incident**:4.23.14.
  Lind confers with Bryan.
  Crack Huerta Troops forced to serve Dictator's flag.
  Fleet at Vera Cruz.
  Louisiana steams to join fleet at Tampico.

[512] **Tampico Incident**:5.27.14.
  American troops at Vera Cruz.
  Hospital ship reaches Ny from Vera Cruz.
  Gen. Bell takes command of troops on Border.
  ABC, Niagara conference.
  Vera Cruz prospers under the firm kindly rule of the American occupation.

[513] **Tampico Incident**:5.20.14.
  How men on NY prepare for war on way to Mexico.
  American refugees escape from Mexico City.
  Vera Cruz turned over to Funston ... San Juan prison emptied.

[514] **TANGLED TANGOIST**, Vitagraph: [The influence of the tango new no bounds. Having been responsible for bringing two lovers together they decide to celebrate the dance by being married "a la tango." In a bizarre scene the Justice of the Peace, the bridesmaids and the couple keep time to the Latin beat as the entire marriage ceremony takes place.] **MPW**:4.24.14 p394, 5.9.14, p820.

[515] **THE TANGO CRAZE**, Biogaph: [Producers quick to take advantage of the North American love affair with the tango devised outlandish scenarios to provide vehicles for the dance film. In this one an overly enthusiastic participant dances himself into a dream wherein he discovers the "tango microbe" which infects all who hear the music causing them to sway to its rhythms "involuntarily leading to endless mayhem."] **MPW**:4.23.14, p412, 5.9.14, p820.

[516] **THE TANGO FLAT**, Biograph: [In this one the tango craze was responsible for driving the newly arrived occupants of an apartment house crazy. All of the other guests are forever doing the tango, including the cook, house keeper and janitor.] **MPW**:4.23.14. p572, 5.9.14, p820.

[517] **A TANGO SPREE**, Edison: [By mid 1914 the tango could melt the coldest heart. Mr. Sparks hated the tango, he only sold slippers to girls who promised not to use them doing the dance. He was a one man army dedicated to riding his beloved town of the terrible tango, but when he discovered his wife and dear old mother doing the 'forbidden dance,' he had to accept it. For those who were still making one reelers, it did

not take much to produce a film.] **MPW**:8.1.14, p731, 9.5.14, p960.

[518] <u>A TANGO TRAGEDY</u>, Lubin: [Pat Muldon hated the salacious strains of this dance import and threatened to kill anyone who might teach it to his daughter. He gets so angry one evening that he sets his socks on fire. Dick who likes the daughter, wants to take her tangoing. To do this he plans a ruse where by the father thinks he has killed a tangoist. Dick now dresses as the ghost of the departed dancer and drags the father to a dance hall where he makes him learn how to tango. When he does, he loves it. Sure, that worked for the tango, but it would never work for Rock and Roll.] **MPW**:5.23.14, p1158.

[519] <u>TANGO TROUBLES</u>, Royal: [Just one more of the same genre, considered by the exhibitors as "a serviceable, commercial offering." When those affected were not dancing the new craze, they were watching it done in play houses.] **MPW**:6.2.14, p1689.

[520] <u>THE TANGO IN TUCKERVILLE</u>, Edison: [The first of the dance crazes to come north from south of the border was the tango. Sailors danced it with their sweethearts as they left the docks of Boston and New York for duty in Mexican waters of Tampico and Vera Cruz. This year produced a rash of such films as all other Latin rhythms, from the conga to the Lambada. In this light fluff, the wives revenge themselves against their husbands other than matrimonial interests by starting a Tango class with a Latin type to make them jealous. It works to perfection, but threatens the dance instructors very life.] **MPW**:6.8.14 p1436.

[521] <u>THE TEST OF MANHOOD</u>, Box Office Attraction Co: [A ranch owner decides to teach his drunken gambler of a son a lesson by making him earn his own way. He replaces him as foreman with a Mexican, not knowing that the greaser is in league with a local land shark. In time they wrest the mortgage from the father, but when the son is reborn and returns he wrests it back from the baddies.] **MPW**:11.28.14, p1283.

[522] <u>TONY THE GREASER</u>, Vitagraph: [This remake of the 1912 film with the same title is essentially an updated version. The characterization and the sympathy are the same. A young Anglo beauty, attracts the attention of a guitar strumming Mexican who immediately falls in love with her. Hired to work on her fathers ranch, he is mistreated by the other help and rejected by the girl. Despite this, his character is sympathetically portrayed. In the denouement he returns to save the girl from across the border insurrectionists losing his life as a result [214].] **MPW**:4.30.14.

[523] <u>THE TOREADOR'S OATH</u>, Pathe: [The authentic locations for this bull fighting film provide a realistic background for the tragedy that unfolds. Such films always required unhappiness in varying degrees, this one had two brothers in love with the same young Spanish beauty. The denouement has the two lovers dying in front of a crucifix falling over each other and

forming a cross. The Roman Catholic characterization has always been another significant motif used by film makers to identify Hispanics, especially when it could be blended with a little indian [Aztec or Inca] religion.] **V**:11.28.14. **MPW**: p1290.

[524] **TOREADOR'S ROMANCE**, Kleine: [Jose a "rancho" cattle herder loves Rosita, "the village coquette" who has enticed the hacendado's son, which causes the two to quarrel. Unjustly accused of robbery, Jose leaves seeking his destiny which he finds in the corrida. Recognized by his former employer he is entertained at he rancho where the wife becomes interested in him, a mutual feeling. To prevent unhappiness the toreador returns to the bull ring and is killed in his next fight. Honor was important to at least some screen Hispanics.] **MPW**:4.25.14, p682, 5.12.14.

[525] **A TRAITOR TO HIS COUNTRY**, Lubin: [Once more in the Philippines, this familiar Hispanic love triangle involves an insurgent leader, General Gonzales, Maria, the lovely señorita he loves, and Manuel, a more romantic than patriotic Filipino. For one of the first times, the young Anglo, Carter, does not get the girl. As the hero, he is responsible for saving Maria's chosen from the rejected suitor, Gonzales. Understandably, for the flag and local audiences, sympathy is cast more to the lovers, than to the rebels who are still holding out against the Uncle Sam's occupation forces. Manuel is branded, "Traidor ala patrie," by the insurgent General for having brought the United States soldiers to his camp. When the young lieutenant explains what this means, to Maria, she accepts Manuel's lack of nationalism and apparently, the North American occupation of her homeland. This script certainly has to be considered a product of its times. Few North Americans outside of the Anti Imperialist League could imagine this government's role in that part of the world as a negative thing in 1914. Save for a few idealist intellectuals in that noble sounding organization, the League's real objections to this nation's ownership of those islands can be traced to racist roots. Some felt there were already had too many little brown brothers. Much would change with the Japanese invasion in 1941. **Back to Bataan**, 1945 also includes two island lovers, but their patriotism, which included a respect for the United States was portrayed in a significantly more nationalistic fashion.] **MPW**: Volume XXI, p472.

[526] **THE TRAP**, Lubin: [Rita Hermanez is responsible for a lot of trouble, of course two men love her. One is a soldier, Orizaba, a mountain of a man, the other, just plain Anglo Charly Ross. Her father, an important general, hates gringos and wants the young North American out of town by sunset. Unbeknownst to the general, he has an even more pressing problem. It happens that he is also shipping a lot of gold out of town which the Mexican suitor plans to rob with the help of some local bandits he happens to be friendly with. Although the Anglo helps foil the robbery, the general's men attempt to take him captive, not for the attempted robbery of the gold, but as the gringo who is eloping at that very moment with the

señorita sitting beside him in his auto. Their mad dash to the border is successful and Orizaba is shot at break of dawn.] **MPW**:11.7.14, **p820**.

[527] **UNCLE SAM IN MEXICO**, Victor: ["A purely descriptive number, showing scenes in Mexico particularly in the vicinity of Vera Cruz." Although issued a month after the occupation of that city by United States Bluejackets and Marines, this clip still showed them fighting the locals. It claimed to give "a good idea of conditions in Mexico," but was obviously taken during the April invasion.] **MPW**:6.2.14, **p1689**.

[528] **UNDER FIRE IN MEXICO**, Warner's Features: [Produced by the United States Film Corporation operating under the direction of J. Arthur Nelson who somehow obtained permission to utilize "the 5000 Mexican prisoners being held at Eagle Pass", for the cannon fodder in this film. One contemptuous reviewer reported that where as "there were no bullets flying recklessly about, they were very brave--who wouldn't be." Yet they produced a "thrilling, stirring story of Mexican warfare, to the staccato accompaniment of hair-breath escapes, dark conspiracies, wholesale massacres and daring rescues." "A powerful story of guerilla cruelty and American heroism. It will thrill the heart of every American patriot."] **MPW: 7.11.14, p454, 7.18.14, p479, Motion Picture News, 8.1.14**.

[529] **URIEL ACOSTA**: Great Players: [A film designed to show "the brutality of medieval Roman Catholicism" as is functioned through the Inquisition in an attempt to maintain the purity of the faith and persecute and purge the Jews out of Spain. Uriel, was a Spanish Jew whose family was forced to go to Portugal to escape being burned alive as a heretic in Spain. Once there, the family must still accept Catholicism to prevent a similar fate. This film focuses concern on the problems that all such exiles experienced, but specifically on Uriel, who first accepts the new faith, but later is drawn back to his roots in the Talmud. Unable to deny his heritage, he is exiled for writing heretical works and eventually, "despondent and grief-stricken ... dies by his own destruction."] **MPW**:7.4.14, **p120**.

[530] **THE VENGEANCE OF NAJERRA**, Majestic: [Najerra, a humble indian loves Tula, a lovely local of the village. She loves him until a dashing Mexican youth steals her away to the city. Punished for her fickled nature from the very start, she is mistreated immediately by her faithless lover who "consorts" and a lot more, with the other señoritas who are shown "smoking cigarettes on the tables under the vines or shade trees." Broken in heart and body, Tula attempts to return to her village where she dies in her former sweethearts arms. Najerra, who had accepted his fate with "stoical resignation" wanted revenge, but is saved from "soiling himself with blood by an accidental explosion which kills the victim." A blasting powder vendor happens to leave his cart filled with explosives beneath the window of the lady he is seducing and when the faithless swain throws out his cigaro, the whole building goes up. The scripter's fate was sometimes with the

good guy, even in Spanish California.] **MPW**:2.7.14, p720, 2.14.14, p809.

[531] <u>THE VENGEANCE OF THE VAQUERO</u>, Kalem: ["A Mexican love story, melodramatic, but pleasing." The very familiar formula is all in the title.] **MPW**: 6.6.14, p1408.

[532] <u>THE WAR EXTRA</u>, Solax/Blanche: ["16,000 Mexican soldiers in action", were used in the advertizing, for this production, but not all received payment for appearing in the film itself. "During the staging of "THE WAR EXTRA," the BLANCHE players suddenly found themselves in the midst of the bloody battle of Monclova. Cameraman Charles Pin succeeded in photographing the terrible onslaught of the Constitutionalist army upon the doomed city, smoking ruins of which are also seen in this remarkable photodrama ... Following the battle the actors were placed in a special train by General Francisco Murguia and sent under heavy guard to the US Border Post at Eagle Pass, Texas."] **MPW**:9.22.14.

Prior to the above advertisement, **MPW** devoted space to the incident describing the problems of staging some of the action sequences using Mexican and North American cowboys. The former resented the idea that they were to be captured by the gringos so severely that they "discharged" their pistols in the faces of the part time actors which caused a mini war on the set and took the combined efforts of the diplomatic service and director Schenck to settle the issues. The general contempt for all things Mexican held by many is reflected in the following: "Miss Vinnie Burns is the only member of the company who is anxious to return to the land of strife. She brought back to the Fort Lee studios a little Mexican dog which bears the name of Jesus Carranza and says she is going to return ... with a pad and a pen and make a million dollars of Mexican legal tender [Constitutionalist] which any school girl ought to be able to make with the aid of a twenty-five cent rubber stamp. But as the million dollars is only worth about two dollars and thirty-two cents [Broadway], making Mexican money is not as attractive as it might seem to the casual observer."] **MPW**:7.4.14, p80.

[533] <u>WAR IN MEXICO</u>, Al Dia Feature Company: [The Tampico crisis heightened even more, the North American public's desire for news from what was now, an occupation by Marines and Bluejackets of Mexico's most important Gulf port city. Independents attempted to rush one and two reelers home for exhibition. This one was advertised as: The "film of the moment" with "striking events of the present War." Like many others, this early example of exploitation, successfully capitalized on what the public certainly considered the most significant current event taking place south of the border.] **MPW**:5.9.14, p1167.

[534] <u>WAR WITH HUERTA</u>, Mullin and Tisher: [This timely production derived "its principal interest from the daily newspaper reports of the Mexican situation and [was] calculated to provide those who witnesse[d] it with a better

understanding of existing conditions in the territory for the control of which the Federals and the Constitutionalists have been battling for so long. In this sense ... [it] is certain to prove a big success." The film began with pictures of "Huerta posing for the camera, federal troops leaving the capital and featured the positioning of the U. S. war ships off Tampico" just prior to the taking of Vera Cruz. The final sequence featured the North American troops guarding the border ready to prevent any possible attack by Mexican forces.] **MPW**:5.23.14, p1155, p1202, 6.6.14, p1417.

[535] **THE WINNER**, Box Office Attractions Company: [Tex and Jack are rivals for the big job on the ranch and the owner's daughter. She likes Jack, her father would prefer her to like Tex who does not drink and gamble like the other. Jack does not like Mexican halfbreeds and was about to give the one they kept on the ranch another beating, when Tex saves the unfortunate one from suffering again. That night Jack drinks himself into another county and were it not for the clever horse who enters the saloon to knock the drinks out of his hand, he might never have been heard from again. After a lot of action which has Jack selling Tex's horse without permission, Tex being accused of a crime he did not commit, namely, shooting the drunk, and more, the Mexican who has escaped to another place, returns the favor for Tex by writing a letter explaining that he was the one who shot the not so nice friend thereby clearing Tex.] **MPW**:11.21.14, p1146.

[536] **WITHIN AN INCH OF HIS LIFE**, Eclair: [When the foreman of the T Tumble T ranch is mysteriously killed, Searchlight Williams accuses the cowhand best liked on the place, Dan Henley of being responsible. Actually he wants to get rid of his competition for Elsie Brandon. Not satisfied with having Dan arrested he then gathers a crowd to get him lynched. Luckily Dan's loyal friends include Wildcat Thompson and his good amigo, Pablo Wiggins, the Mexican snake charmer. When the crowd gathers to do the dirty deed, Wildcat tells Pablo to use the power he has over his deadly little wiggly friends to break up a lynching, and it works. Then, after lots more action, Wildcat plugs Williams and becomes the new ranch foreman. Dan gets the girl. Pablo is allowed to continue playing with snakes, and all was happy and serene on the serpentine range.] **MPW**:12.26.14, p1886.

1915

[537] **AFTER BIG GAME**, Universal: [Some travelers who were fortunate enough to see Bermuda before the motorcar invasion changed the nature, pace and face of the that lovely island, might well have been surprised and disappointed to discover that they had missed seeing the ferocious crocodiles and the equally dangerous porpoise and the worst of all, the shark. But the big game expedition that left Key West for its adventure on Andros island with camera's turning, was apparently more fortunate.] **MPW**:5.8.15, **p960**.

[538] **THE AMERICANO**, Komic: [After Huerta's departure in the summer of 1914 three dynamic figures dominated the Mexican scene, Carranza, leader of the Constitutionalists, Villa, who controlled most of the north and Zapata, whose power base emanated from the centrally located state of Moreles. The rivalry which developed among these former comrades in arms would keep Mexico in turmoil for another five years and would force the United States to choose which one it would reluctantly support. When this government recognized Carranza, Villa was cast as more of a "bandit" than a heroic revolutionary leader. Eventually this would force him to attack across the border.

One can begin to see a shift of sympathies in the scenarios which included North American involvement in Mexican affairs with films like the **Americano**. Hammon is the manager of the Mexican branch of the Manhattan Oil Company in Tionana, Mexico, where he lives with daughter Elaine. After a "worthless Mexican" named Tonio is discharged he joins a group of "bandit soldiers" who raid the oil works, kill Hammon and kidnap Elaine. The new superintendent, who is in love with the lady now enlists as a scout in the army of the "Constitutionalist" General Ferranda, where he earns a position of trust. When it is learned that the "bandit chief" is running low on ammunition, a plan is devised to prevent his resupply that incidently throws the two lovers back into each others arms. In the second reel Tonio is killed, the bandits have no arms and the lovers have theirs around each other. The Constitutionalists are in control.] **MPW**:7.17.15, **p564**.

[539] **AN ARIZONA WOOING**, Selig: [Manuel Paquito and Tom Warner both love Jean Dixon. Because the lady knows Manuel to be an outlaw, she favors Tom. Somehow Tom gets staked out in the desert by some angry cattlemen and is found by Manuel, who having the obvious advantage of being a treacherous Hispanic, begins to torture him. When little Jeany wanders onto the scene, she is forced to promise herself to the torturer, or have her true love killed. But this was the west, and when all is discovered by Dixon, the dad, he and his boys chase down the despicable Mexican and arrive just in time to prevent the wedding ceremony. After a gun duel, Manuel, for his

punishment is forced to watch a real wedding between Tom and his willing lady.] **MPW**: 5.8.15, p960.

[540] **AT THE STROKE OF THE ANGELUS**, Majestic: [The only survivor of an indian attack on the wagon train heading west is a small child who is saved by a Mexican Bandit who then raises her to womanhood. Later she falls in love with the one whom "she learns is falsely her father." When the truth is told, the wedding bells are heard. In those early days it was somewhat easier for the scribes to solve very delicate problems.] **MPW**:5.29.15, p1432.

[541] **THE BATTLE OF AMBROSE AND WALRUS**, Keystone: [One of many early Keystone comedy teams Ambrose and Walrus journey to Mexico as buffoon like military leaders, exaggerating every commonly accepted stereotype and caricature of the revolutionary upheaval. The final scene involves a girl tied to a target as cannons are ineptly fired by obviously more inept peon soldiers.] **MPW**:9.4.15, p1645.

[542] **THE BLACK BOX**, Universal: [The early cliff-hanger serials would truly come into their own in the following year, but 1915 witnessed the real beginnings of their popularity. **The Black Box** was multi-episodic [14] and a good example of the developing genre, it was at first produced in two parts. In the first installment the main characters are introduced, a wealthy and aristocratic English family who are sending their daughter to the States. There she suffers the robbery of a great diamond and is killed. The father crosses the pond to pursue the culprits and is partially successful, North American law has not let him down. Another baddie has learned through "hypnotism" who else was involved and where the jewel was hidden. Meanwhile, "down in South America, Prof. Edgar Ashleigh, anthropologist, a twin brother of Lord John, is caring for his fever-stricken servant, John Craig. Their researches through the dense jungles have led them into dangerous climates and Craig succumbed. ... [The dedicated doctor has knowledge that his man is an evil deed doer] the fever crazed brain has but one thought ... cunningly waiting till the scientist has gone from the tent, the servant feels under his pillow and brings out a small black box. With glazed eyes staring he fondles the box and hides it once more." Enough, those South American jungles were enough to drive anyone crazy. Episodes #12 and 13 include scenes shot just south of the border with drunken Mexicans who have the effrontery to attempt to kiss the Anglo heroine, but she has the strength to ward them off. They have knives to employ for such purpose, but she proves more resourceful. All the familiar identifiers and stereotypes were present to reassure audiences of where they were watching the action take place.] **MPW**:3.13.15, p1677.

[543] **THE BORDER RUNNER**, Kriterion-Navajo: [A significant entry because it is one of the first two films produced dealing with smuggling drugs from Mexico into the United States. In recent years the number of films identifying drugs and Hispanics has increased tremendously. It may well be

universally accepted throughout this nation that the drugs are a Hispanic and black problem, that if these minorities could be controlled, the drug problem would disappear. This attitude represents a massive displacement, a comfortable delusion for the Anglo majority which does not want to face the reality that three-quarters of all drug users in North American are white. The cocoa leaf has been cultivated in the Andean region for several thousand of years. It was not an export item until the demand in the United States made is a profitable commodity of trade. As early as August of 1919 the **Revista Mexicana**, editorialized on what would continue to be a growing problem: "Investigation with regard to the growing use of opium and other narcotics in the United States discloses the astonishing fact that from ten to sixty times as much of that drug is used there as in Austria, Italy, Germany, Portugal, France or Holland. A grand total of 470,000 pounds is consumed annually in the United States ...It is claimed (by the Treasury Department) that opium has increased extraordinarily in those States where prohibition has been in force the longest."

Gay Sherman's unscrupulous guardian uses his ward as a cover, and as an unsuspecting "mule" for his drug running operation. His Mexican connection is Peto Montery who places the drugs in water canteens. Gay carries the opium across the border without knowing that she is doing it. Frank Weldon, ace government agent, suspects that Gay is the ringleader of the operation, but knows that Peto is involved. The latter, to prevent further investigation captures the agent but the "G-man" escapes and confronts Gay with his fears that she is involved. She immediately returns his ring, but questions her guardian about his possible duplicity. Faced with possible exposure, the apparently spineless drug king dies of a heart attack. Montery then abducts the lady and heads for the hills. In time Frank realizes that Gay is innocent and he rescues his lady and brings the baddie to justice.] **MPW**: 2.27.15, p1360.

[544] **THE BOWL-BEARER**, Thanhouser: [A young Anglo rides into Mexico where he meets with numerous adventures while visiting a wealthy Don. Of course the scripters force him into an attraction for the lady which provokes the usual vengeance from the discarded Hispanic suitor. By this time it was dictated by the formula that the young dark skinned, brown blazing eyed beauty would have to save her man from her fellow countryman's desire to do him in.] **MPW**:9.18.15, p1996.

[545] **BRAGA'S DOUBLE**, Essanay: The writer for this one certainly had a colorful conception of what his Hispanic characterizations should be. "Dominica Mendusa, a beautiful and unusual heroine ... has her own code of morals, elastic as to the property rights of others, rigid as to her own personal conduct." "Emilo Braga, a saturnine-faced Argentino, [was] a criminal by instinct, training and desire." To evade the wrath of the vicious Legrand who was as "unscrupulous as Braga", he sends his trusty tonto to find him a double that can unsuspectingly take the blows for him. Dominica finds the

double in the person of Taylor, a mining engineer from El Paso, Texas, but he proves to be a "rough and tumble" fighter who assaults the ruffians when they attack. This of course impresses Dominica, but when Braga becomes jealous, this turns her against him and she leave him "in rage and disgust." Some of the scribes allowed Hispanic ladies to have a little honor.] **MPW**:6.19.15, p1980.

[546] **THE BRIDE OF GUADELOUPE**, Domino: [In the mythical Spanish California village of Guadeloupe resides Berta and her true love Ricardo, but also Felipe, whose passion burns for the same lady. Unsuccessful in his attempts to win her with affection, he has his rival abducted by local bandits who force him to write a letter claiming he has gone to Spain to marry his childhood sweetheart. Berta now attempts suicide, but is prevented from her intention by the Padre Sebastian who convinces her to enter a convent and consecrate herself to the work of the church. Meanwhile Ricardo escapes and has the sheriff do his duty. The good padre tells our hero where his lady is and through the convent gate, the lovers are reunited.] **MPW**:2.13.15, p1048.

[547] **BRONCHO BILLY'S BROTHER** aka **BRONCHO BILLY'S COWARDLY BROTHER**, Essanay: [Apparently, Broncho's brother was not cut from the same clean sheets that our hero was conceived on. In this film he quarrels with and beats up a greaser who swears he will be avenged. Returning home drunk, the brother now beats up his mother. Broncho of course comes to the rescue, finds the baddie has stopped his inebriated behavior, but is not repentant. Broncho then beats him up. The greaser who has witnessed all this sibling slugging sees his chance to shoot his former aggressor and does. The brother falls dead in Broncho's arms. Horrified, Billy is too stunned to react and is quickly arrested by the sheriff who was brought to the scene by the vengeful Mexican, who further complicates the tragedy by identifying Broncho as the killer. God could not allow such injustice and neither could the screen writers, in the final reel, in a saloon under pressure from the other Anglo's, the greaser breaks down and confesses his crime. Billy is freed, the Mexican punished and the audiences cheered.] **MPW**:2.20.15, p1186.

[548] **BRONCHO BILLY'S GREASER DEPUTY**, Essanay: [Broncho Billy, true to the code of the west he was helping establish in the North American consciousness, never had real good luck with the ladies, he fared much better against a variety of opponents. But in this reel, having lost the lady that he loves to a real no good, a drunk and a thief, who was even required by the writers to beat her, and being unable to reform the wretch, Billy is finally required to arrest him. After a lot of crying and pleading by his former love, not to put the husband behind bars, the old tough guy softie lets him escape. But only momentarily because the greaser deputy shoots him. Early women's liberation, Hollywood western style. Exhibitors felt, that the film had "considerable realism."] **MPW**: 1.30.15, p712.

[549] **BRONCHO BILLY'S MEXICAN WIFE**, Essanay: [This reissue of the 1912 version was precisely the same film. Losing one's woman is bad enough, but losing your wife to one of her own race, was a real trial for Broncho. Worse the lady falsely accused him of having stabbed her so that he might be arrested and the way be cleared for their illicit tryst. It took the fire and passion of another brown skinned dark eyed lady to clear our tender hero, the Mexican's lady slays both the lovers and then clears Billy so that he might continue in the way of truth, justice and the North American way. In the final scene, our hero forgives all and placed the dead lovers hands one in the other and walked away without ever looking back.] **MPW**:11.13.15, p1311, 11.20.15, p1538.

[550] **CAPTAIN COURTESY**, Bosworth: [The story is laid in 1840 California, "when that part of the country was under the rule of Mexico," and only a few North Americans lived there. After the Davis family was killed by bandits, the one surviving son became the avenging "Captain" who cleans up the marauding gangs of Mexicans jeopardizing the Anglos. He also robs the rich Mexicans, a la Zorro style, giving the proceeds to the American community to help solidify their position in the territory. With just a little help, he could have brought an end to Mexican control. Needless to say, he did win the heart of Spanish beauty in doing so.] **V**:4.16.15.

[551] **CAPTAIN MACKLIN**, Majestic: ["A story which" gives vent to the prevailing military spirit" by Richard Harding Davis. "South American republics, like "Zenda" kingdoms somewhere in the Balkans ... permit the intrusion of love stories into affairs of state." "We cannot locate modern romance within our own boundaries and get away with it ... because it would be incongruous ... and then revolutions are altogether too infrequent for the purpose of a story. Why bother about it when the republics of Central America furnish an abundant supply of battle scenes and swift change of governmental control?" It might be difficult to find a more unconscious and generally accepted statement of contempt for the workings of Latin governments than this. Macklin can't do it the West Point way, the enforcement of strict discipline interferes with his demand for the daughter of a coast steamship line, but inspired by the achievements of his military ancestors, he seeks redemption in the mythical republic of Anduras. There, along with General Laguerre who displays his "military ardor on a prancing charger at the head of his troops", he will help restore the rightful government of General Garcia, "known to all cigar smokers" who had his presidency wrested from him by the usurper Alvarez. Yet his real object is to rescue his new found sweetheart, the deposed leader's daughter. Arriving "at the nick of time to save his struggling" sweetie from the clutches of a brute, he also manages to rescue the father who is about to be "dishonorably executed by some unwashed Peons." The reviewer was pleased with all this, even though by this time the same story had been "visualized several times under various titles ... proving its merit." He also accepted with a bit of sarcasm the fact that there was some "remarkable shooting done at close range without scoring many clean hits,"

but as he explained with a little more Anglo condescension, that "for all we know it may be characteristic of Central American revolutions."] **MPW**:5.1.15, p739.

[552] <u>CARMEN</u>, Essanay: [Chaplin was achieving significant popularity when he decided to present his version of the opera. It was considered one of his very best efforts, a brilliant satire of the other productions. Edna Purviance was his leading lady. Charlie not only captivated North American audiences, he was also very popular south of the border: "Your little Pepita or Manoel of Brazil begs just as zelously to be taken to the movies ... as Mary or George of Buffalo [and they pay prices] far in advance of ours ... from forty cents to two dollars for an evening of film fun." Among their favorites were Charlie Chaplin and Mary Pickford.] **MPW**:12.18.15, p2211, "Film Fans in South America," <u>Literary Digest</u>:10.14.16, p988.

[553] <u>CARMEN</u>, Fox: [Although <u>Variety</u> considered Raoul Walsh's directorial effort just shy of being a "masterpiece", they felt that Theda Bara lacked the "physical allurement of the Spanish cigarette girl." While they were satisfied with all other Hispanic characterizations, all of them played by Anglos, Miss Bara's eyes and body were not enough to portray what they considered the "standard characterization" of Carmen as, "a slow moving, lazy, listless, shambling, warm blooded girl, concealing beneath a phlegmatic exterior an intensity of passion only fanned to life by jealousy ... the Spanish make up is merely one of mechanics with which any actress [must be] familiar." For its part the **NYT** considered the Vamp mechanical in her seductiveness and objectionable in her behavior.] **MPW**:11.13.15, p1319, **V**:11.5.15, **NYT**:11.22.15.

[554] <u>CARMEN</u>, Lasky-Paramount: [DeMille's interpretation of Bizet's opera had Geraldine Farrar as Carmen, the archetypical Spanish gypsy vamp who ruins Don Jose, consorts with Pasita, tavern keeper, smuggler and who loves Escamillo, the Toreador, played by Pedro de Cordoba, the only Hispanic in the cast. As always the Spanish gypsies, when not stealing children for resale were smugglers or thieves living outside the law enjoying the entertainment of numerous, lascivious and exciting dancing girls. This Lasky production enjoyed enormous success in the United States, solidifying accepted stereotypes and the screen scenarios which would vary only by technological improvements in the many subsequent remakes of this classic. But the film ran into severe problems in Canada because Ms. Farrar was considered to be a German sympathizer. Canadians boycotted the film choosing to attend the Fox version [qv] in its place. An early indication that the sensitivities of some foreign nations would have to be taken into consideration by future film makers. Yet, in the States, some exhibitors charged as much as two dollars (at a time when many did not make $15.00 dollars a week) for the first run showing, an enormous sum for that time. Lasky bragged in some of his advertisements that in a single day, 24,211 paid to see the film. The heartless little señorita made a significant profit for the film maker as she firmly established herself in the public's mind. The success of her characterization

allowed the producers to reissue the film in it's original form once again in 1918.] **MPW**:8.14.15, p1182, 10.1615, pp420-21, 11.13.15, p1242, 11.20.15, p1501, 12.11.15, p2052, 10.12.18, p273, **V**:11.5.15, **NYT**:11.22.15, **MPG**.

[555] <u>**CIPHER KEY**</u>, Lubin: [This one could be revived as a training film for the present day yuppies to provide them with inspiration as they sit in their LaSalle Avenue offices in Chicago wondering what to do about lagging sales. Certainly at its issue, it was an expression of the satisfaction and confidence some scenarist felt over the success North American capitalism was experiencing south of the border. Two companies, an "American" firm, and a "South American" one were in competition to build battleships for Argentina. The United States Corporation sends it's messenger with their proposal, but he is almost murdered by the South American company's spies. Luckily, one of the spies was a lady and she fell for the "American" messenger. She then betrays her own company and country to help the Anglo place his bid before the commission and win the contract. In two chase scenes between a car and plane, and a plane and speed boat, the other Latin spy is killed. All of this enterprise results in success for the North American firm and the young apostle of the Gospel of Wealth.] **MPW**:4.10.15, p247.

[556] <u>**CIRCUS MARY**</u>, Victor: [Pedro is merely a handy Mexican gambler who proves to be the Hispanic foil in this melodrama. A rich aristocrat who seeks power cannot wed the lady he has loved if he wants to be governor. She is beneath his station in life, but she is also with child and broken hearted when forced to leave. Managing to survive, the madre brings up the unrecognized daughter to be a successful high wire artist. Pedro now happens into the scene as a dirty gambler and killer. He even tries to kill the governor, who has power but little else, but is prevented from doing so. When Pedro and his knife pass away, the now penitent politician is pleased to discover his progeny and a family reunion is effected.] **MPW**:7.10.15, p376.

[557] <u>**THE COWBOY PASTIME**</u>, Lubin: [Romaine Fielding, the driving force behind Lubin's prolific output of Mexican border productions, offered still another for the apparently pleased public to consume. "This is certainly a rough and tumble comedy in which cowboys, Mexican highwaymen and police [rurales] go through some strenuous stunts winding up in a wild chase," which results in the capture of some real baddies.] **MPW**:1.16.15, p368.

[558] <u>**THE DEATH DICE**</u>, Reliance: [Any little variation of a standard formula was reason enough for a new film. Baptismo and Sellers quarrel over cards; Sellers beats the Mexican up. Revenge is called for. Bass and Sellers love Florence, she only loves Bass, it was 1915. The eternal triangular rivalry could be naught, but bad. Using Bass's knife to defend herself from Sellers, she drops it after he has been repulsed. As he departs he is heard humming the mournful strains of the "The Dying Cowboy." Witnessing all of this, the Mexican picks

up the knife and stabs Sellers in the you know where, it was mandatory. Bass thinks Florence did it and takes the blame. The sheriff know the Mexican did it because he saw that look in his eyes when Baptismo heard Sellers humming the "Dying Cowboy" song. The town "jeers" at his naivety, but the sheriff is sharper than the people know. Using fixed dice he has the two suspects leave it up to fate. The pressure cracks the real culprit and the Mexican confesses. Simple superstitions would do in simple people every time.] **MPW**:2.20.15, p1194.

[559] **THE DICTATOR**, Famous Players: [Richard Harding Davis had thrilled his readers with accounts of heroics during the Spanish American War. He was still wearing his long white duster, and still writing about the adventures of North Americans south of the border during the Mexican intervention, but that proved too tame to keep his interest. He would be pleased to know that the fantasy he found more exciting in his novels, the film going public did also, once translated to the screen. Basically he had but one story to tell. Any North American adventurer, whether a **Soldier of Fortune** [509, 834], or just an ordinary citizen off the street, could take care of any problem that might confront any South American political leader. In this variation of the above, a young local flees to Central America to escape possible arrest. While there he exchanges identities with the dictator which cause endless humorous complications. If it sounds like the above film or **Moon Over Parador**, again, it should. Most of this production was shot in Cuba with the aid and permission of the government. **Variety** praised the female lead, Ruby Hoffman as the Spanish señorita: "She not only looked the part, but acted it to perfection." There were still no Latin ladies that directors considered competent enough to play themselves, something akin to painting white actors black for their roles in **Birth of a Nation**. Remade in 1922 [909].] **V**:6.25.15.

[560] **THE FEAR WITHIN**, BIG "U": [The Mexican revolution was responsible for many a broken heart. Brother Gregoire, a Spanish monk in a Mexican monastery was very devoted to young Pedro, a local boy, as was his mother. When the need came for him to defend his country, he volunteered, but with the first cannon volleys, he ran back home to find his mother and the good monk praying for his safety. Soon he was discovered AWOL and the camp commander came looking for him. Mother had by then hidden him behind the Brother's altar, where Pedro learned that the two had once been lovers also separated by war. Renewed with religious strength, he bravely confronted the officer and returned with him for the sake of his country. The Brother then dropped to his knees in thankful prayer that "the boy ... proved to be a man."] **MPW**:4.17.15, p456.

[561] **FIGHTING BOB**, Rolfe/Metro: [Five reels of justifying North American intervention in Central America where United States aid was absolutely essential for the establishment of democracy. Although the **Motion Picture Guide** places the action for this film south of Mexico, that is not correct. The scenes take place in Juarez, Mexico, at that time under

the complete control of Pancho Villa, whose permission was granted for that city to be used as the backdrop for this photo play. The revolutionary general loved North American films, especially those he could be in and proved to be most helpful in this production. "Orrin Johnson, who play[ed] the title role, procured from Rodriguez Gonzale [Villa's social secretary] use of arms and riding accoutrement for the ... picture, with the result that historically and atmospherically [it was] as perfect as it is possible to make." " **Fighting Bob** is a most timely subject. President Wilson has just delivered his ultimatum to General Villa, Carranza, Zapata and Jara and trouble is anticipated by Washington officials." The reviewer's copy was exciting, but there was no real problem at the time save that Washington was leaning more toward Carranza than Villa. When Carranza was recognized by Wilson as the head of the Mexican government, Villa would be very upset [47].] **MPW**:6.19.15, p1952.

[562] **FLAME OF PASSION**, Terris Film: [Without a scenario this film could have made a beautiful travelogue of Jamaica's natural beauty in pre-automobile times. The story has a trained southern temptress seducing an innocent northern boy out of his inheritance while visiting that tropical paradise. Native representations reflect the white man's assumed superiority. More over, it emphasized the idea that the further south one travels the more primitive passions control behavior. "Passion is the motif running throughout the story." "The woman [in question] is the embodiment of passion ... we see how passion is born in the heart of the young man, how it asserts an irresistible power and how the victim is released only by death."] **MPW**:10.23.15, p630, **V**:11.5.15.

[563] **FOOL'S GOLD**, Biograph: [A proximity to the border can have a negative affect on even the best of Anglo's. An ole sourdough has searched for years seeking the elusive "El Doroado," now quite mad, he discovers a vein of iron pyrite and thinks he has struck the mother lode. In the local saloon he brags of his find. Two there love his daughter, the sheriff and another, a poor miner. To save his feelings they substitute a real nugget for his fools gold. When the old man buys drinks for all, a "greaser" plans to rob him of his assumed riches. Problems arise from the rivalry for the daughter. The sheriff cannot stand the rejection and when he goes to the cabin to plead once more, he discovers the old man and the Mexican both dead. Seized with the opportunity, he forgets his duty and blames his rival for the foul deed, "he protests that border law justifies his act." But the border also betrays his evil intention. Returning with his prisoner, he stumbles and falls to his death. The lady sees this and saves her true love. Every border loves a lover. So did audiences.] **MPW**:4.24.15, p626.

[564] **FORKED TRAILS**, Selig: [The path not taken might have avoided this encounter between a Mexican bad man bandit and the pretty young thing who was a bit dumb because she left a gun where the bandido could take it and hold her at will, but only until the Anglo hero saves her.] **MPW**:2.20.15, p1139.

[565] **THE GHOST WAGON**, Bison: [The question of mixed race, halfbreeds, whether half Mexican or half Indian is central to a significant number of motion picture scripts. Rarely, until the fifties, was such a halfbreed presented in sympathetic characterization: He was usually scorned by members of both parts of his ancestry. In this early Bison production although a halfbreed is responsible for saving the heroine, his role was secondary and he received no mention in the credits.] **V**:7.14.16

[566] **GIRL OF THE GOLDEN WEST**, Knickerbocker Star Feature/Lasky-Belasco: [Serious complications arise when Nora is favored by Lopez on her now dead father's ranch. He makes advances and she of course refuses. He persists and she shoots him, thinking that she has killed him. There is an Anglo boy, wealthy, but mom disapproves of our heroine and she is allowed to believe the Mexican was killed which causes her to flee. Yet her character will win out and when she returns some years later to face the consequences, she is relieved to discover that she was not a murderess at all and that she can have the rich young man, who waited all that time. Some men are very faithful. Art Ortega received credit for playing Antonio. The **MPG** claims that DeMille helped "revive the western genre" with this melodrama employing gold rush days in Spanish California as its backdrop. The evidence presented in these pages may well indicate that it had never perished. It is more important to realize that there is significant justification for considering the western the first true genre in motion picture history, one that has outlasted all others, and one in which Mexican/Hispanic characterizations were an essential ingredient in its creation and continuation. A similar argument is put forth by: **Peter Stanfield**, "**The Western 1909-14: A Cast of Villains**", *Film History*, Volume 1, 1987, pp97-112. Remakes: [982, 1405].] **MPW**:1.16.15, p381, **V**:1.8.15, **MPG**.

[567] **THE GRANDEE'S RING**: Interstate Feature Film: [Life just across the border was almost always filled with the adventure that a healthy eastern girl was looking for, but she found more than she wanted in this brief clip. Required by the scripter to refuse advances by the locals, she just managed to escape from Mexican bandits, kidnapping and all that, and a little more]. **MPW**:11.20.15, p1507.

[568] **THE GREASER**, Majestic: [It would be interesting to discover why script writers exercised what might be described as a need, to write scenarios for themselves and whatever race was carrying the white man's burden in those primitive unChristian areas, which for many included Mexico, that portrayed the locals as willing to give their lives to allow their superiors the uninterrupted pleasure of keeping them, the inferiors, servile. Gunga Dinistsa, did not overpopulate these early days, but were not difficult to find. More often they were female, but there were also males who were forced to suffer the scripters assumed superiority. This scenario of selfsacrifice had been used several times before, but not in this extreme. Manuel, although an average ranch hand was just

a "greaser" to Mariam. She was nice, but very distant. One
day her father actually kicked the greaser because he had the
effrontery to kiss a discarded rose she had once touched.
When young Clifton was discovered outside the ranch wounded,
Miriam nursed him to health and they fell in love. Deeply
hurt and very vengeful, Manuel was most pleased to see the
Anglo accidently kill one of the extras, and although he
realized Clifton was innocent, he compounded his treachery by
helping to lead the lynching party in pursuit. But hanging the
Anglo could not be allowed, audiences would have rioted,
demanded a reinvasion of Mexico, something. So when the
Mexican sees how troubled the little lady has become because
of her fear for her man, a complete transformation comes over
him. He had to do something, to prevent the lynching of the
innocent Anglo, maybe even climb the minaret and blow a bugle
to warn the troops. Unable to do that, Manuel, settled for
putting on the pursued's clothing which of course fools the
posse and leads them away in the wrong direction. It also
provokes them to shoot him dead, which allows the Anglo
lovers to continue carrying on the burden of his race as they
happily added a few new little buckaroos to their own. See **The
Gringo**: [454].] **MPW**:3.27.15, p1988, 4.3.15, p64.

[569] **THE GRUDGE**, Broncho: [A two reel western in which the
legendary cowboy hero who would replace Broncho Billy in the
hearts of youthful North America, William S. Hart, stars. It
happened that there was a brash and offensive youth, also a
bandit and a Mexican. The three make up the mainly male cast.
Unintentionally the youth offended the bandit who refused to
seek revenge until the boy who was ill, could get better. Part
of the still being written code of the West. Meanwhile a
Mexican complicated the conflict and was necessarily killed by
the bandit. By the time the boy recovered, the bandit is
ready to forgive, so they became friends. Sometimes it was
that simple where the loco weed grew wild, in this case, that
may have been in the writer's back yard.] **MPW**:2.27.15, p1290.

[570] **THE GYPSY TRAIL**, Vitagraph: ["A wonderful tale of
romance and adventure is told by a young Gypsy to his white
friend, how his life was saved from folly and disgrace and
brought out into the sunlight of happiness and love." Antonio
Moreno played the grateful lead.] **MPW**:11.13.15, p1268.

[571] **THE HEART OF A BANDIT**, Biograph: [A Mexican half-breed
chases a bandit for his reward money, but he is too cowardly
to face the bad man head on. He even tries to use his wife
and child to capture him, but this also proves unsuccessful.
In the end the slimy breed is killed, but so is the bandit,
some what more honorably. He sacrifices his life for the
rancher's family.] **MPW**:2.27.15, p1331.

[572] **HER OWN WAY**, Metro-Popular Players: [Yet another love
affair set against the background of the Philippine war. Yes,
the native girl loves an Anglo officer in this one also, but
the Anglo lady overcomes his attraction for the primitive
savage. All the occupation soldiers were valiant.]
MPW:6.12.15, p1856.

[573] **IN THE AMAZON JUNGLE**, Selig: [For the great majority of screen writers without any certain knowledge of those nations to our south, all Latins were alike. Even major differences in national character escaped their writings. Well until the talkers arrived, when the problem between Castilian and South American Spanish presented even more complex problems, many North Americans including screen writers, considered all those inhabitants who lived south of Texas to be basically the same. For the unschooled, even Brazil was little different, even though that nation then was larger than all of the continental 48 put together. Most United States citizens would have had trouble believing that fact. This scripter's lack of information was more ethnic than geographic. His characters are Spanish, but he places them in the Brazilian Amazon looking for rubber, some of their names are Portuguese, but they are apparently not. "Silva, a young Spaniard" along with Lineres and Arevalo, "a Spanish half-breed" are all deep in the rain forest seeking to make their fortune in rubber. Two of the men love the same lady. While there, Silva is attacked by a jaguar and wounded. Possibly assuming that the divinities have intervened in his favor, the friend abandons him. But he soon suffers the same fate himself. It was either a section of the Amazon infested with a lot of jaguars, or the writer ran out of information, although, he is more seriously wounded. Silva recovers in time to help his treacherous companion who, beneath the rain forest tent is heard to say, "And in return for my treachery you saved my life." Even if he was not a Brazilian. This type of misinformed misrepresentation would continue well into the war years until Addison Durland joined the PCA. See **Now Voyager**, 1942. In 1925 a concerned North American of Brazilian decent named, Francisco Silva Jr., wrote to the **NYT**: "Some months ago I saw a motion picture supposed to have been taken in Rio de Janeiro, Brazil. However, the "Rio" shown in it was like a Spanish village some centuries ago, with a Spanish aspect in everything--even Spanish names and phrases were used in it. ... I feel greatly surprised at this ignorance of geography when I remember that any seven-year-old child in Brazil knows that in the United States English is spoken, that New York is not a Federal capital and that New England is not a British State ... Spanish is not even spoken in Brazil".] **MPW**:5.29.15, p1488, **NYT**:3.17.25.

[574] **IN THE LATIN QUARTER**, Vitagraph: [Although he was not referred to as such at this time, Antonio Garrido Monteaguado y Moreno, born in Spain in 1886, was Hollywood's first Latin Lover. In a career that spanned fifty years, he would make a hundred and thirty five films, the last one, **El Señor Faron Y La Cleopatra**, 1958, made in Cuba just before the Castro take over, was never released in the United States. In the silents, along with Navarro and Valentino, he was the Latin lover, later in the talkers, he became the identifiable Hispanic. In this little fluff two lovely ladies want to be his significant squeeze, actually one wants to be his slave, whatever that could mean back then. When he passes on the opportunity to be master, she tries to destroy his art work which the other saves for him. Throughout the silent era

Hollywood scripters made a lot of ladies susceptible to his Latin charms.] **MPW**:1.16.15, p369. For a complete list of his films see: DeWitt Bodeen, "Antonio Moreno,"<u>Films in Review</u>, June-July 1967, pp325-44.

[575] **IN OLD MEXICO**, Reliance: [A typical day in this scripter's Old Mexico involved a husbands passion for his wife, his gift to her of a colorful shawl, a jealous suitor rejected, incriminating lies told the husband to provoke revenge designed to "remove the stain upon his honor," and finally, remorse, at just the right moment to prevent the killing of a innocent party. Certainly not an uneventful day in upper middle class Upper Saddle River.] **MPW**:7.3.15, p140.

[576] **IN SAGE BRUSH COUNTRY**, Kay Bee, [Frank was the proud and successful owner of the Lost Hope Mine and was just about ready to go there to pay the help when he hears that the local Mexican bandito was once more in business. Apparently thinking that this bandit was chivalrous, he sends his wife with the money. When the Mexican stops the stage, he robs everyone but the lady, demanding only a kiss which she refuses to give because of the insult. The plucky lady then slaps the bandit for which he forces her to his cabin, but Frank arrives in time to prevent too much damage. No one will refuse **The Kissing Bandit** when Frank Sinatra plays him at a later time.] **MPW**:1.2.15, p135.

[577] **THE INSURRECTION**, Lubin: [Lubin, responsible for so many border melodramas, this successful production company attempted to vary it's local with this presentation of revolution in an another South American nation. The exhibitors applauded the film and explained that while such occurrences were frequent in those sunny but dangerous climes that this was not simply one of fighting factions but "one of love and strife in some South American capital, [where there was] "no lack of stirring realism and dramatic incident." Yet there still were no Hispanics in the cast.] **MPW**:6.19.15, p1953, 7.3.15, p65.

[578] **THE JAGUAR TRAP**, Selig: [Selig either had a surplus of jaguars or he was trying to make the most out of the one he had acquired. This was his third feature in 1915 in which he used the beautiful cat as a main character in one of his single reelers: This production was released seven days after **In the Amazon Jungle** [573]. His writers also need serious lessons in geography. "Joe Grant [was] the renegade husband of Lengus, a beautiful South African [sic] native girl." John Lewis, was a South American trader. Grant steals from Lewis's trading post, while the other is taking medicine to some stricken natives. While in the jungle, Grant wounds him, but not critically. Apparently the latter has a way with big cats because he ties his scarf around a Jaguar's neck and sends him for help. Meanwhile, Lewis falls into another trap and finds himself fighting a losing battle with the jaguar already there. The two eventually reach an understanding. Audiences must have loved this one.] **MPW**:5.29.15, p1488.

[579] **JEANNE OF THE WOODS**, Victor: [One of Pedro de Cordoba's first films in which he is involved with diamond smugglers.] **MPW**:7.24.15, p651.

[580] **THE JEST OF JEALOUSY**, Selig: [The sheriff of this border town was having a tough time catching any of the baddies, he could not even get near Mexican Pete, the notorious bandit, who hardly bothered to hide. Worse, his girl who is back east has just informed him that she is bringing home a another boy to marry. It gets even worse for the poor law man. The citizen committee informs him, formally and in writing, that if the Mexican is not captured, he can turn in his star. Luckily as the last reel approaches the little lady arrives with the other man, and foolishly, the Mexican shoots at them. Now our hero must act and he does so by capturing the bandit. For his reward he learns that the eastern boy was brought home not to marry his lady, but one of her best friends. Reinstated, all around, the sheriff and his soon to be woman, ride off into the sunset together]. **MPW**: 5.22.15, p1314.

[581] **A JUNGLE REVENGE**, Selig: [Somewhere near a Central American coffee plantation lives an Anglo animal trapper who owns a jaguar. Dais a local native girl, likes the sleek cat, but the trapper even more. Unaware of her affection, he gives her the animal, but his love to the a rich planter's daughter. Realizing she must act if she wants her heart's desire, the dark skinned native lady tries to use the jaguar to get rid of her opposition, but a shot from the trappers rifle, intended to save his true love, kills her instead. After this one, Selig sold the jaguar.] **MPW**:11.27.15, p1710.

[582] **THE KINSHIP OF COURAGE**, Majestic: [Partially set on the Mexican border, this film tells the of the regeneration of a man from his "life as a bandit" to one of honor. It had that effect sometimes.] **MPW**:8.28.15, p1480.

[583] **THE LAND OF ADVENTURE**, Edison: [Some North American fantasies adopted or created by silver screen scripters, span the century. Possibly the most persistent is that which postulates that 'gud ole American' know how is/was required to solve any Latin problem, political, social, economic and especially technical. This concept soon became a firmly fixed feature of North American consciousness on the silver screen. There's a lot of Richard Harding Davis in this fun piece of fluff, which was not played for laughs. When two young Anglos read about a revolution which has just broken out in Panzeulo, situated somewhere south of the border, they consider this an opportunity. As fortune would have it, the very next day [the mails were better then] they receive a written communication from the President of that besieged South American republic asking for the help of the two young stalwarts. On the steamer taking them there, they meet the banker who is apparently financing the president and that nation's economy; as luck would have it he has two daughters. Once there, the relieved president expresses his gratitude that they would take time out of their busy schedules to come save his republic. They do, but it takes some doing: First they

ignore the threats made on their lives by the revolutionary bandit, General Villanz. They laugh, as all Anglo's must, in the face of danger, save the girls from kidnapping and even capture the bandit. Good to the core, the two convince the insurrectionist to disband his men instead of having to face the firing squad. He does, the republic is saved and the boys get to marry the rich man's daughters. And you wonder why kids today aren't happy with their every day lives!] **MPW:10.16.15, pp403, 499-500, 10.30.15, p968.**

[584] **THE LIGHTHOUSE BY THE SEA**, Essanay: [Jack, the sea captain loves the lighthouse keeper's daughter, but he has an unrequited rival. Miguel Fernando, jealous Portuguese trader, pays Jack's crew to mutiny and set him adrift. After two years on a rowboat and desert island, Jack finds his way back, his true love abandoned, dying and her child already dead. When Fernando returns years later, only the haunting vision of his dead wife prevents Jack from killing him.] **MPW:10.30.15, p1016.**

[585] **THE LITTLE GYPSY**, [It should have been a forgone conclusion to audiences in 1915, that even a priggish minister would succumb to the wiles of a pretty little Spanish gypsy. He does, but in the last reel, wishes that he had not.] **MPW:10.23.15, p631.**

[586] **THE LOST LEDGE**, Bison: [Leslie makes and loses a fortune to an oil field fire. While viewing the remains of his wealth he happens to save the life of a wealthy man's daughter who offers him a job in Mexico where he has vast holdings. His purpose is to find the lost ledge of a once rich mine. Arriving on the scene he befriends an old "Aztec" who had been there for apparently, a real long time. [Actually, some newspapers in the United States, especially the tabloids, still used the term "aztec" when they wanted to emphasize Mexico's [savage] indian background.] His problem in Mexico was with Foster, the other engineer who has failed to find the lost ledge himself. Foster's jealousy of the new man leads him to enlist the aid of some Mexicans and together they blow up the entrance of the mine while Lesile and the Aztec guide are in it looking things over. This, by chance uncovers the rich lost ledge and a former Aztec place of worship. When the two trapped comrades awaken, they are at least surprised to see one of the Aztec idol's come to life and point the way out for the innocents. The idol also uncovers his equally long lost treasure which he decides they should have. In the last reel, Foster is punished and our hero of course, gets the girl. But the old Aztec, having served his function for the Anglo, "is seen no more."] **MPW:2.27.15, p1346.**

[587] **LOVE'S SAVAGE HATE**, Lubin: [In 1910, prior to the revolution, ninety percent of all of Mexico's arable land surface was controlled by fewer that a thousand very wealthy and powerful hacendados. That required land holdings almost beyond comprehension. Most of Mexico's peasant population lived and died on these palatial estates, some of which were larger than the state of Connecticut. Control of a man's

means for providing for his family, essentially exercises a control over his destiny. The revolution of 1910 was first and foremost one for land reform, its many social, economic and cultural aspects all grew out of the peons demand for land and ridding the system of the hacendados. The use of extra-legal force on film, has from the very beginning been justified rather selectively. For the North American patriots, to revolt against an unjust system and even destroy the property of the British East India Company, it was all right. Justifications for such force was not always afforded Mexican peasants. In this film, the revolutionist who attacked the aristocratic land owners were typed "bandits," so it was and would remain in much of the North American consciousness. In this piece, for some unspecified reason, the family cannot defend the usually well fortified big house, the hacienda, and so remove themselves to a mountain cabin, mother, father, daughter and the two suitors she has not chosen between yet. The rebel bandits not happy with having taken the hacienda, pursue and a five day battle for survival ensues. Certainly not always the case, but in this film the scripter's sympathy was with the regal foxes, not with the peasant hounds. While the struggle rages, the lady finally chooses one of the two, which enrages the unselected. With no class, and unable to overcome his nature, he seeks vengeance and plots his rival's demise. It all ends with a lot of dynamite which destroys the bandit rebels and the suicide of the suitor who betrayed his former friend. The exhibitors loved this tale of "Mexican love and hatred, which [was] filled with scenes of bloodshed and carnage" and ended with the "annihilation" of almost everyone. It was very good boxoffice.] **MPW**:1.2.15, p120, 1.23.15, p515.

[588] **THE MAN FROM ARGENTINA**, Powers: [Manuel Lopes, a high governmental official wants his son to marry the supercilious and surprisingly shallow Bonita. Out of great reverence for his father, Carlos agrees. At their engagement party it is discovered that the nation's defense plans have been stolen, Carlos knowing his father to be innocent, leaves for America hoping he will be blamed for the theft and not his father. Once in New York he is befriended by Helen and Spike Brooks, brother and sister. Spike, a former gang member, is accosted one evening and Carlos saves him, which puts him in real good the sister. Some months later the padre and Bonita show up to surprise the self sacrificing exile. To celebrate the reunion with Carlos, they go to eat at a fashionable place where who should be performing, but Helen. At once the two realize that they are meant for each other, but there was still duty. For this romantic scripter, duty stopped at the docks after which Carlos decides to take out citizenship papers and marry Helen. It could happen, but maybe only in North America!] **MPW**:10.30.15, p848, 10.16.15, p366, 10.30.15, p969.

[589] **THE MARTYRS OF THE ALAMO**, Triangle: [Supervised by D.W. Griffith this film was advertised as an authentic history of the Mexican Revolution of 1836, "when Texas obtained its freedom" ... "the picture appears faithful to the last detail, including Bowie's slow death by consumption and his last act

of killing a Mexican with the knife he invented." One of the problems with all this alleged historical accuracy was that it was significantly tainted by Griffith's own particular racist interpretation. Although not mentioned in the review, every female, down to the last one was sexually harassed and raped by drunken Mexican soldiers after the graphic and brutal slaughter of the last of the "immortals." Prior to this, possibly in some inane attempt to ease the tension created with a little comic relief, Silent Smith was actually able to "get a laugh," before dying by expressing his "contempt for the Mexicans." Better still for, in terms of "authentic history", the reviewer in the **MPW** blamed the entire war on the outrages perpetrated by Santa Anna on the citizens of San Antonio, and specifically on one of his officers who made "insulting" and improper advances against a local Anglo lady. If the fear of such incidents could justify the birth of the Klan, for the supervising director, why not the birth of Texas? No one questioned such attitudes then, they were accepted as projected reality. Mexicans continued raping Anglo women on the silver screen right down to present times. The reviewer continued with his praise of the patriotic production: The story was filmed with "superior care to detail" and "a great intensity during the supreme moment of struggle [when] the most sublime sacrifice of American blood was made for the cause of liberty." It may well be impossible to gauge the actual magnitude of Hollywood's influence in creating or perpetuating real, unique or bizarre historical interpretations, Hispanic or for any other nation's development, but certainly in the popular mind, it's influence must be considered significant. Few of us as children did not know about Alan Ladd and his [oop's, Jim Bowie] and his famous "Iron Mistress" forged from steel struck by lightening, and that he had been killed by the dirty Mexicans at the Alamo. Yet, not one of us had any idea that Texas was in reality, a rebellious Mexican province, overrun by North American interlopers who gained control over a local population, then considered their racial inferiors, and in the end, illegally separated themselves from the national government in Mexico City which merely sought protection for the local Hispanic population and expressed a desire not to allow any further immigration into that distant part of the Mexican national domain.] See: **The Immortal Alamo**: [155]] **MPW**:10.30.15, 864, 11.6.15, p1155, **V**:10.19.15, **MPG**.

[590] **THE MASTER KEY**, Universal: [It was always handy for these early scripters to have a bunch of Mexicans around to do some dirty deed. In this story three mine owners take a break from their operation in San Francisco and head for the Beverly Hills Hotel in Los Angeles to discuss the possibilities. One of them is a crook, and he enlists the help of a bunch of ready Mexicans to help him rest away the mine from the other two. In the battle which ends up in hand to hand combat, the baddie gets killed, and his Mexicans are dispersed. It was tough to get good Hispanic help even in those days.] **MPW**:1.23.15, p568.

[591] **THE MEXICAN CHICKENS**, Kalem: [Or, political ideology follows the stomach. When Señor Sourface learns that the rebels have stolen his chickens, he joins up with the Federalista's for revenge. Empires have fallen for things less foul. But quickly he is captured by General Caramo and sentenced to death by the rebel leader. Learning of her husband's plight, the wife investigates and is relieved to discover that he will merely be shot from a cannon for his punishment. Having done this as a circus act, she and the daughter merely run to catch him with the aid of a colorful Mexican blanket.] **MPW**:2.6.15, p873, 2.27.15, 1287.

[592] **THE MILL BY THE ZUYDER ZEE**, Domino: [Another pseudo-historical film which provided the audience with the background of Spanish cruelty, this time in their attempt to prevent the birth of the Dutch Republic. Two lovers from opposing sides find it impossible to achieve happiness because their governments want to destroy each other. If this sounds familiar, consider further that this was just 1915.] **MPW**:3.20.15, p836.

[593] **NEDRA**, Gold Rooster: [This comedy involved a "White God" and natives in need of one. Most of the scenes were filmed in the Bahamas using local talent: "Needless to say, the scenes filmed on the [islands were] singularly attractive, and hundreds of natives ... responded with remarkable intelligence to the disciplining of Director Jose." Discipline was usually easily achieved for Hollywood's inferior races. It was almost as if they instinctively realized superiority when confronted with it by the screen writers.] **MPW**:11.20.15, p1503.

[594] **NE'ER DO WELL**, Selig: [This scenario which focuses on the problems of a neglected wife almost compromised by a ruthless political boss is incidental to some of the best film footage ever produced showing the Panama Canal before and after its completion. Producer Colin Cambell took his company to the "Zone" "to create an air of authenticity." The scenes of the native quarters of the city and "odd nooks and corners in the old Spanish quarters" [were] testimony to Panama's Hispanic Heritage." This same title will be remade in 1923, [996].] **MPW**:2.6.15, p844. **MPG**.

[595] **A NIGHT IN OLD SPAIN**, Lubin: [Several hundred thousand young men must have taken their sweethearts to see this object lesson designed to teach their little coquette's to be more attentive to what they already possessed. Mary, a country girl addicted to reading the Harlequin novels of that time, puts off her young lover's proposal with a sly smile. Ignoring his obvious pain, she falls into a deep sleep and travels to the land of love, Spain. There she is advised by a passing padre to pray for love and takes work as a cantina girl. In time a young gallant enters and pays her some attention while being very liberal with his pesos. His pulchritudinous purse attracts the attention of the pretty Paquita and her big boy bandit, El Bevlvidero. Ready for all comers, Alonso's gaze now shifts to the designing lady who asks if he will serenade her in traditional fashion. He of

course agrees and leaves Mary to her tables. Though hurt, Mary follows her vamped dream lover to Paquita's window and witnesses the robbery. Quick to sound the alarm, she runs to the bell tower, pursued by the bandit. Meanwhile, the King and Queen who have come looking for their son, hear the alarm and rush with help to the rescue. Mary has saved Alonso and the baddies are put in the stocks. Anticipating her reward she now looks forward to osculating with aristocracy, but is rebuked for being a commoner. Worse, she is sentenced to be beheaded for her effrontery. She's awakened from her dream by a falling broom handle which strikes her neck, after which she runs to her young man and begs to be his wife. Gosh, if it could only be that simple.] **MPW:10.30.15, p1014.**

[596] **THE OBSTINATE SHERIFF**, Lubin: [By this date very simple and straightforward formulas had become standard fair for silver screen productions. The following is an excellent example of one that would remain very popular throughout the century. At different points in time, the current foil, whoever had the national hatred focused on it, was substituted as the necessary antagonist. In film's first decade, it was of course, the Mexican. Handsome Steve loves the sheriff's beautiful daughter but dad objects. Try as he may to obtain approval, all fails until a bunch of baddies, led by Mexican Pete kidnap the little lady. With the posse in pursuit, the bandidos use the helpless girl as a "human shield." Only Steve's love and ingenuity saves his sweetheart. "Her hand" [and hopefully the rest of her] was his reward for such heroism.] **MPW:2.6.15, p881.**

[597] **ON THE BORDER**, Selig: [This was the second of the two films which began the identification of Hispanics with the drug trade, the Chinese had their traditional "dens", the Mexicans would always have the border. This simple love triangle involves the unhappy loser in the trio bringing the opium across the border in the "tire case of the automobile." The border guards, ever alert search the auto and discover the stash. Repentant, one of the smugglers asks for forgiveness," as he is led away. From such simple beginnings, nine hour miniseries featuring the torture death of Victor Camarena, the United States drug enforcement agent, who was allegedly killed by Mexican drug traffickers with the certain understanding of some Mexican officials, make their way to National prime time television and create a significant amount of animosity between officials of the two respective governments.] **MPW:6.26.15, p2159.** National Public Radio offers a tape cassette **All Things Considered** [900199] which presents the issue clearly.

[598] **THE OUTLAW'S REVENGE**, Mutual/Reliance: [The exhibitor's comments on this film are most instructive: "A graphic four-reel offering picturing [in] a very stirring and convincing way a series of incidents in Mexico. The outlaw's sisters are set upon by the federal officers: one of them shoots herself to escape their clutches and the other dies after losing her mind [at least.] The outlaw then sets about getting his revenge, in regular Monte Christo style. There are many tragic

happenings in this [film] based on real life, and some of them are shocking. At the same time the story adheres faithfully to the way they do things in Mexico, the scenes are actually taken there and no effort has been spared to mount the production on a big scale. The cast ... is in every way a strong one of the red-blooded type." This film was advertised in the **Saturday Evening Post** to "10,000,000 readers," as the "Life of General Villa ... wonderfully and vividly portrayed among the hills and valleys along the Rio Grande." Villa was constantly in the news through out 1915, but he was falling out of favor with the administration. This production utilized part of the film taken as a result of the agreement made between Mutual and Villa wherein he allowed one of their camera crews to follow him and film his exploits.] **MPW**:4.10.15, pp274-5, 10.30.15, p854.

[599] **PANAMA CANAL**, Universal: [Many North Americans felt that all of the attendant press surrounding the outbreak of the great world conflagration had robbed them of publicity which should have been devoted to the opening of one of the "World's supreme engineering achievements." England and Germany had both withdrawn from San Francisco's great tribute to the North American know how and get up and go, the Panama-Pacific Exposition. This film helped swell the publics pride: "An exceptional scenic reel picturing in a clear, entertaining way the important features of the Panama Canal as it stands since completion. This is next to a trip to the scene itself. Views were shown of the steamship "Anchon" passing through on the initial trip, carrying prominent officials and their ladies." Although the great World War had interfered with their celebration, audiences were pleased to have such productions as living testimony to this nation's superior technological achievement]. See: **Panama Pacific**: [448] **MPW**:1.9.15, p222.

PATHE NEWSREELS:

[600] **#66: Juarez, Mexico**: "General Villa, the Mexican rebel leader, and George Crothers, special representative of the United States, leaves the home of J. F. Williams after a conference on the Mexican situation with General Scott. Subtitle: [1] General Villa declared his willingness to join with the leaders of the warring factions to bring about peace. [3] Villa [left] with Mr Crothers and Col. Michael at Villa'a home in Juarez, Mexico."

[601] **PAWNS OF FATE**, Rex: [The lengths to which some writers would go to include a Mexican scene were at times extreme. At a fashionable dinner party given by a successful man, one individual is in a room by himself looking at a fancy chess board. Surrealism came early to the silver screen, in an instant the pieces are seen to move, white queen, white knight and black knight all come together. The scene now shifts to Mexico, a flashback of the guest's past in which he rememberers living in the small village of Cocholento where he was awarded a "Zone", by the Mexican government, a large tract of land to prospect and have first claim too if successful.

He remembers more bitterly, a faithless Mexican girl who would not wait for his return. Then, in a blaze of recognition, he realizes that his host was the man who did him wrong. His chance to revenge himself had come, but before the party is over, the offender's lady had her last of too many drinks and falls off the second landing. There was no need to kill the man now, his wife's broken body provided punishment enough. The guest, though a failure now leaves to walk out alone in the snow, satisfied that the wrong done him in Mexico has been wiped away. Justice certainly worked the early screen writer's pens in mysterious ways when Mexico was involved.] **MPW**:1.9.15, p270.

[602] **THE PEARL OF THE ANTILLES**, Picture Playhouse Film Co: ["There are times when the plot of [this film] seems to run into narrative rather than drama," this criticism by the reviewer is an enormous understatement. There is no connection between the title and Cuba, but there are several hundred chance coincidences that must have driven even the most gullible to grab for their seats in dismay. There is a character named Mendoza, but most of the action takes place off the coast of France, where one day the lady chances onto a shipwrecked sailor with no memory of his having spent much of his life in South America with her father the count. A duel in which the more adept Mendoza, who rises from his cripples bed for the occasion, ends this gem.] **MPW**:10.9.15, p282, 10.30.15, p866.

[603] **THE PENITENTS**, FA/TRI: [Set in 17th century Mexico this film describes the practices of a fanatical splinter group of Roman Catholic zealots who enjoyed reliving Christ's suffering passion by crucifying one of their own who was selected yearly on every Good Friday. The film's mood is purposefully eerie, emphasizing the occult overtones of the mysterious Spanish/Papist religion. As was typical during this early decade, all of the Hispanic characters were played by Anglos. An updated version with modern overtones was produced in **1988**, **The Penitent**. The cult has also been used in several other features as a background for the main action.] **MPW**:12.25.15, p2450. **MPG**.

[604] **THE PRETTY SISTER OF JOSE**, Paramount: [The "adorable little star, Marguerite Clark" was featured in this "picturesque romance of old Spain." She was sensational as the "Spanish girl, full of life and buoyancy" with an instinct for romance and a "haughty Spanish pride ... throbbing with the power of love" who came to enjoy the delights and splendors of Madrid, especially its night life. In that most romantic of the early screen's cities, she was soon involved in the "bewitching web of emotion" as she witnesses Sarita die for the hopeless love of Sebastiano. She herself struggled, as many Spanish girls did with her heart, "to maintain a haughty demeanor toward the man she adored, while longing to yield to the impulses of love." With her "fascinating dark beauty and charming grace ... she [was] exceptionally adapted to the role of the exquisite Spanish belle of a thousand moods and whims." All this in an era when

PMS was as of yet, unidentified and there were still, apparently no Hispanic women considered suitable enough to play themselves.] **MPW**:5.22.15, p1278.

[605] **PRO PATRIA**, Pathe: [The first filming of Victorien Sardou, the French dramatist's play, set in the days of Philip II when the Netherlands revolted in an effort to "throw off the iron rule of Spain," and end that nation's cruel oppression. It was the story of "conspiracy and war ... portraying human passions and emotions in the same unchanging aspects as that in which they appear today." Spanish passion, love of intrigue and conspiracy, the talent for treachery and tyranny span Hollywood's Hispanic centuries.] **MPW**:7.31.15, pp835-6, p904.

[606] **REFUGE**: Victor: [Conventional western in which a white child [Baby Early] is the sole survivor of an Indian massacre. When she is discovered alive, she is raised by a Spanish mission indian. As the girl grows, the two learn to love one another, but the inevitable occurs. Not really unsatisfied with her faithful indian suitor, she is completely taken by a Mexican swain who lures her away with tales of the big city, but once there, he proves to be a brutal mate. In the final scene, the compassionate scripter allows her to escape and the two lovers are reunited.] **MPW**:8.21.15, p1318.

[607] **THE RIGHT TO HAPPINESS**, American: [An impossible love affair is generated by a Mexican's declaration of love for an Anglo woman who refuses him. The lady may have had her right to happiness, but at that time, it could not be with a south of the border suitor.] **MPW**: 6.12.15, p1852.

[608] **A ROMANCE OF MEXICO**, Lubin: [If they were all like this one, there would have been a lot of bodies lying around the old scene. Jim loves Carmen, Pablo's sister. Juan the coward, loves Carmen too; though he hates Jim, he is too afraid to act alone against him. Pablo loves Nita which gives Juan the opportunity he needs to have him do Jim in. He tells Pablo that Jim has been doing his lady and uses Carmen merely as a cover. Pablo now gets his knife out and goes after Jim. Jim does not understand, nor does he want to hurt his sweetheart's brother. Believe it or not the writer wrote his way out of this one in the last reel, which was none too easy when, jealousy, passion, knives and vengeance were everyday stuff for Mexicans in love.] **MPW**:8.28.15, p1539.

[609] **A ROMANCE OF OLD CALIFORNIA**, Biograph: [A love story of Old Spanish California, "in the land of the Golden Gate" with Mary Malatesta as the Hispanic beauty. Strictly formula by now: She does not like dad's rich choice, prefers the possibility of a life of poverty with a poor peon and they happily ever-after it together. Mary so far as can be determined had a Hispanic mom.] **MPW**:7.3.15, p64.

[610] **THE SACRED BRACELET**, Edison: [It is at least interesting, for a brief period, to listen to the radio ministries of certain fundamentalist Christian churches

especially when they discuss the vast potential that exist for modern missionaries who want to bring the true light to those unfortunate dark regions of the world. The dark regions referred too are all of the Roman Catholic regions south of the border. Few area of the world appear to be filled with more pious practitioners of the faith than those that are Hispanic. The antagonism felt by the fundamentalist is in essence merely one more reflection of the Black Legend, La Leyenda Negra. Roman Catholicism is also the predominant religious force in the Philippines, another of the regions which fundamentalists consider ripe for revival. This photoplay was set in those apparently godless islands. A young Anglo girl is assaulted by Pedro Ramon. He also steals her new bracelet, but is immediately caught by the United States Marines occupation troops. Yet when his story is heard, it elicits sympathy. It seems the bracelet was originally the possession of the Virgin Mary, and had originally been stolen from her statue because of a dying mother and her children's need for food. For this act of charity, Pedro, not a "half-breed" but an "outcast" was excommunicated by the good Spanish priest. He had sought to recover the holy relic since that time and when he saw it on the arm of Colonel's daughter he had to take it. Hearing the tragic story, the young Anglo girl was understanding and the bracelet was returned to it's original owner. Further, the padre lifts Pedro's burden, and one assumes, there was rejoicing in heaven.] **MPW**:10.30.15, p842.

[611] **THE SECRET OF LOST RIVER**, Kay-Bee: [The one time nefarious act of a "villainous Spaniard" which caused a Spanish Mission to be attacked by angry indians, results many years later in the reunification of a poor miner and his wife from the east. An artist painting the beauties of the Arizona/Mexican border is snake bitten, but saved by Tom and the Padre. His gratitude results in the discovery of a lost painting which he sells in New York and uses the proceeds to effect the reunion.] **MPW**:6.19.15, p2010.

[612] **THE SECRET OF THE DEAD**, Domino: ["Marry me or I'll repossess your madre's hacienda" was apparently a problem on the Mexican border also. Donna Carrillo and the necessary daughter, though once proud Spaniards, were not rich ones. A local "neighborhood" Don held their notes, insisting on the little lady in lieu of payment, a "hateful" prospect to both mother and Maria. Luckily an eastern university professor uncovered a valuable "petrified indian" on their property and was about to purchase it [which would have covered the note] when the Don blew it away. But this was Hollywood, and surprise surprise, inside the chest cavity of the twice expired indio was a treasure map which showed the way to more than enough dineros for all to share. Angered, the dastardly Don rouses the indians against the señorita's new Anglo lover, but the family is "rescued by the rurales." The Don is then "killed by the indian chieftain whom he failed to assist at the crucial moment with his peons, thus resulting in the extermination of the tribe." Lecherous landlords, with long mustaches, Guardese!] **MPW**:2.20.15, p1198.

[613] **THE SEÑOR'S SILVER BUCKLE**, American: [Señor Cabello, a Spaniard, apparently living in Mexico, was threatened by an "invading party of 'Gringos'" for an undetermined reason. Forced to flee, he brings with him the family treasure and his trusted servant Miguel. After they bury the loot under a tree marked with a silver buckle, Miguel proves less than trustworthy, slays his master and leaves, planing to return for the good stuff later. Later, proves to be twenty-five years after. Meanwhile squatters have come to raise a family and fell trees to build a place for forthcoming progeny. Yup, one of them finds the buckle and when Miguel returns, no tree. But George Davis, surveyor, finds it for his lady. There is no moral, simply place your bets on the Anglo if you want a winner on film.] **MPW**:9.18.15, p2066.

[614] **SHAVED IN MEXICO**, L-KO, [Or, in the vernacular, beware of bragging about banging the barber's beauty when you're in his shop and he has a razor in his hand. Señor Buillo, fierce, wild lover and barber has a big "hitio" for Señorita Hitchey Koe, that is until the globe trotting Perkins takes her away from him. Apparently stupid and in need of a shave, he goes to the barber's shop and brags of his conquest. Too late to repent for his "glib tongue" he suffers the razors sharpened edge. But the barber is no better off because the lady was no lady, merely a "fickled jade" in disguise, a classy name for a bad lady back when a shave and a haircut were 'two bits'.] **MPW**:4.24.15, p630.

[615] **SNATCHED FROM A BURNING DEATH**, Vitagraph: [Somehow the ubiquitous Hispanic foil finds itself operating in the great north woods. It's more than your usual love triangle involving a French trapper, an Anglo baddie, the young easterner Joan and Sanchezza. Possibly because she was vengeful or unnecessary the lovely, jealous Mexican señorita was forced to die in a burning cabin. Joan is saved.] **MPW**:3.6.15, p1494.

[616] **THE SPANISH JADE**, Fiction Pictures: [Extremely complicated scenario involving a Spanish beauty who has a mindless brute for a father and the love of all the males in the film including a Spanish Don and a wandering guitarist. She dailies with all, but selects the Englishman who just happens on the scene for a vacation. The complications kill off almost everyone in the cast save for the two lovers [947].] **MPW**: 3.20.15, p1768, 4.24.15, p644, 646, **V**:3.5.15.

[617] **A SPECIES OF MEXICAN MAN**, Lubin: [Certainly unique for its time and interpretation of the Mexican character, this film stands almost by itself as an endorsement of the entire nation. "If the living prototype of the man that Romaine Fielding has made the central character of this three reel drama ... is to be found anywhere in Mexico, the people of that war-worn and misgoverned country would do well to seek him out and following the hint given them by the playwright, seat him firmly in the presidential chair." The reviewer had some problems accepting Fielding's generous evaluation of the national character, questioning how many Mexicans "would be at

home" as leaders in battle or politics, polished courtier and suave ladies man. Revealing his implied prejudice, he wondered how many Mexicans could truly lead their nation as president. Fielding's conception combined a progressive, charismatic Christ-like character with that of the Count of Monti Christo sent to reform all the evils existing, south of the border: "A "Man," born of woman in a republic of darkness walked straight and true, preaching the doctrine of light, intelligence and progressiveness and thereby developed a strength and manhood that the people respected and followed blindly not as fanatics, but as an enlightened race." Heavy stuff for the Hispanic hero who also scored north of the border by winning the hand of the "Powder King's," daughter who he asked to be "Mrs. President of Mexico." It was all right to marry out of your race, even back then, if you're husband was a brain surgeon going back to his roots in Africa to do charity work. Becoming the señora of the senior Presidente, was even more acceptable, how long could it last?] **MPW**:8.21.15, p1361, 9.4.15, p1666.

[618] **STOCK FARMING IN SOUTH AMERICA**, [The parallels between the histories and cultures of Argentina and the United States are many, not the least is that which involves the west and the rise of the cattle industry. This brief documentary shot on the Argentine Pampas and possibly in Paraguay shows scenes, like the breaking of horses to saddle, that might well have been taken in Texas.] **MPW**:6.5.15, p1606.

[619] **A STOP-OFF IN NEW MEXICO**, Biograph: [An inquisitive tourist who disturbs the "siesta" of the local badman finds himself involved in an adventure he had not planned. Possibly to prevent such occurrences, which many North American's still apparently fear, resort cities like Cancun create "Zona Hotelerias" to keep the locals out and convince the tourists that Mexico is not unlike Miami.] **MPW**:3.27.15, p1979.

[620] **THE TERRIBLE ONE**, Lubin: ["The fortunes and misfortunes of war are graphically pictured in this "realistic" story. Men rise wrongly and fall rightly accordingly to the opportunities offered "by rebellion and bloodshed." With this one, Lubin exceeds all expectations that poetic justice prevailed throughout Mexico's troubled times and utilizes the concept of "ley Fuga", literally the law of flight or shot while trying to escape, as a significant incident in the story line. Love triangles in Mexico could apparently have revolutionary consequences. Captain Pireda and Poncho Gonzales both love the deceptively sweet señorita. To rid himself of his rival, the Captain contrives to have him accused of treason, so that he can be arrested and as the traditional "ley fuga" called for, shot while making his escape. He is. With that out of his way, fortune shines on the Captain and he quickly rises through the ranks. On his way up, the lady who mourned ever so briefly for the other, joins him in a marriage of calculated convenience. Circumstance catapults the captain into the presidency which he contorts into dictatorship and all is well for a while. Then, news of the "Terrible One" who is leading an armed

insurrection in the North, begins to filter to the Capital. At first a few trickles, the news becomes a torrent of successful governmental defeats that threaten the dictators very existence. Coward that he is, he still must go forth to Chihuahua to stem the tide. Too late, what seemed at first a revolutionary upheaval, was in reality a personal vendetta led by the very one who had been so grievously betrayed. Shot and left for dead, he had recovered to lead a revolution against the dictator, who when faced with his former rival, saves him the trouble and kills himself. For want of a woman, a new nation was born.] **MPW**:4.17.15, p442, 4.24.15, p573, 5.8.15, p900.

[621] **TIDES THAT MEET**, Essanay: [The silver screen's border almost always bred mayhem. You decide how difficult this confusion must have been to understand for earlier audiences. Estelle, desirous of doing her duty, volunteers for Red Cross service in Mexico because her brother was there. He, meanwhile, has reentered the United States, a survivor of a fierce battle. Safely across the border he learns that the bandits have captured sis. Quickly recrossing the border, he meets Lopez Deligarde, a different outlaw who offers to save his sister in exchange for having the brother kill Bourne Carrington, who has offended him. Filled with mixed feelings, he shoots at his friend, wounding, but not killing him. When sis is saved, she nurses the wounded friend back to health. Meanwhile, conscience has driven the brother to join up with the rebels in order to redeem himself, actually he desires death, but instead, he falls in love with Felicita, who gives new meaning to his life. His brief bout with connubial bliss ends abruptly when he sees that the man he thought he had killed was still alive. Apparently stunned, he tries to surrender himself to the authorities, but is instead turned over to another bandit in what this scripter must have believed was a seemingly endless pool that serviced Mexico's revolutions. This one stakes the unfortunate brother out in the blazing sun, but little Felicita crosses the river and explains the entire story to the sister. Together, all rush to save our early anti-hero from at least severe sunburn.] **MPW**:10.9.15, p317.

[622] **A TRAGEDY IN PANAMA**, Selig: [For once it was not another landslide blocking the canal, but instead the problems created by an illicit love affair. Selig, who was responsible for many of the early canal pictures, used much of the stock footage he had available to provide "the tropical scenery" which formed an "excellent background for the story." Shades of the Production Code, the producer felt that this run-away-wife required chastisement for her transgression. There in the jungle with her man, she was forced to care for him because he contracted a fatal disease. But her husband tracks them to the rain forest and is about to shoot the dying man, when the latter rises and points the gun at the bad lady just as it fires. Both of the sinners are properly chastised, and Will Hays, somewhere in the wilds of Indiana, must have been pleased.] **MPW**: 6.19.15, p1994, 7.3.15, p64.

Feature Film List 1915   165

[623] **THE TRAIL OF THE SERPENT**, Mustang: [An eastern girl, Marguerite, inherits a mine out west. Two suitors help discover it's worth, but one is more moved by jealousy and greed than true affection. He employs the Mexican Pedro, who knows the real wealth of the mine to steal it from the lady. Pedro's lady also gets involved, but the intrigue results in her being forced by the writer to give up her life saving the Anglo for his white goddess. In the final scene, the Mexican mistakenly sees the shadow on the shade as his hated rival, and shoots the baddie responsible for all the trouble in the first place.] **MPW**:10.30.15, p854.

[624] **A TRIP TO THE ARGENTINE**, Roy Chandler South American Pictures: [Part of a travelogue series which was accompanied by a female commentator, [soon to be well known as an actress] Spring Byington. The film took its audience from New York to several Caribbean and Brazilian ports before arriving in Buenos Aires. It provided North American audiences with their first view of the great Falls of Iguazu, and a ride on the Trans Andean Railroad up Mt Aconcagua more than 22,000 feet high to see the famous statue of Christ commemorates the peace between Argentina and Chile. Reviewers remarked that: "The remarkable educational value of the Chandler South America series cannot be overestimated."] **MPW**: 12.4.15, p.1848, **V**:12.3.15.

[625] **THE TROUBADOUR**, Big U: ["A two-reel number featuring Murdock MacQuirrie as a Spanish minstrel" who lures his love out of a convent intending to marry her, but before the affair can be consummated, he is beaten by bandits and his lady forced to marry their leader. The boss bandit turns out to be a drunken brute who beats his wife and child, which allows the troubadour to save her from him, but they can only wed after his death, which happened none too quickly for all concerned, including the audience.] **MPW**:4.17.15, p394.

[626] **THE VIOLIN MAKER**, Victor: [Or, Love's labor lost, returned. Pedro makes violins and cares for his ward who he secretly loves. One day, Maurice comes to the shop and hears the melodious strains of Marguerita's playing. Immediately moved, he offers her a spot in his theater, which Pedro encourages her to take. Of course there's more on Maurice's mind than music. When Pedro discovers the pair walking arm in arm, he confronts them and in front of the girl, destroys the new violin he had constructed for her as a symbol of his love. It was to have been a surprise gift for Marguerita. Time passes and we find Pedro on his way to self destruction, drinking and dejected, he lives in a Latin Quarter cafe. But when that evening's entertainment began, it was you who, who had had you know what fixed, and with that, the ward guardian relationship was over, and a more meaningful one was about to begin.] **MPW**:7.3.15, p128.

[627] **THE WOMAN IN THE BOX**, Vitagraph: ["A story of Mexico during the days when intrigue and war alarms were threatening the precipitation of the present struggle in our sister country." It would seem that the Mexican Secretary of War was

planning somehow to invade the north, but, as our scripters would have it, his wife happened to be in love with a North American Secret Service man. This certainly made planning an invasion of the United States more difficult. And it did, for the love of an Anglo, the wife betrays both her husband and her country, but that made it understandable. For authenticity, the film included: "Typical Mexican street scenes showing the Peon in his home life and pursuits, scenes that picture high officials of the War Department. The men of authority who represent the wealth of Mexico are graphically pictured."] **MPW**: 10.30.15, **p968, 987.**

[628] **THE WONDERFUL ADVENTURE**, Fox: [Five reels outlining the demise of a New Yorker who falls under the control of drugs and the evil Mazora responsible for introducing him to same.] **V**:10.8.15.

[629] **THE YANKEE GIRL**, Morosco: [One of the first Broadway musical comedies successfully brought to the screen with it's stage star, Blanch Ring. The plot focuses on the intrigue surrounding an attempt to obtain a prized copper concession from the rather corrupt president of a not named Latin nation. The pretty lady uses her feminine wiles against the defenseless President Castoba and also thwarts the plans of another North American concessionaire he had struck a bargain with. The rejected concessioner attempts to employ the "ruthless" outlaw Morales and his "band of bandits' to pillage and kidnap, but to no avail. The lovely little lady has El Presidente right where she wants him and with the help of the new American Consul, they win the lucrative copper concession and each other. We assume the President had the memory of what might have been with the Anglo temptress for his troubles.] **MPW**:10.16.15, **p467, 10.30.15, p968-9, p944, p1034.**

1916

[630] **ACROSS THE RIO GRANDE**, Bison: [For many Hollywood writers, Mexico was an ideal place for a dissipated man to rediscover his manhood, so Dixon was sent there after his graduation as a civil engineer having failed to become anything at university but a drunk with a bachelor's degree. Teddy, his lovely lady and the daughter of the Railroad owner pushing a line down into the oil and ore rich nation across the Rio Grande, promises to wait for the metamorphosis she hopes Mexico will regenerate in her man. Once there, Dixon discovers that the "Governor of the province" [state], Jose Morrilla has a cozy deal going with the foreman of the construction crew. His first action though, is to save a "peon, Yaqui Indian" from being beaten by the boss, which understandably earns his undying gratitude. Realizing that their grafting operation is in jeopardy, the two employ Nina De La Guerra to vamp our Anglo hero back to the pleasures of debauchery, which is easily done. But, true North American character will out, and Dixon, although enjoying the favors for a while, plans to expose all. When the governor puts him in jail and plans to execute him, Teddy arrives from the North. Quickly she rouses the indians who rescue Dixon, but the two are trapped until the commander of the Texas Rangers, who is not required to obey the United States border guard, feels his blood boil at the injustice and leads a contingent of his troops across the Rio Grande to save the pair. Sound familiar? Exhibitors considered the last reel "wonderfully realistic." [321]] **MPW**:1.8.16, p263, p290.

[631] **ALONG THE BORDER**, Selig: [Quick to take advantage of Villa's recent raid across the border, Selig placed his skyrocketing star, Tom Mix, across the border to be captured by a superior number of Mexican bandits. Seemingly at their mercy, his charm easily enlists the aid of a willing señorita maiden who helps him escape and save the other "American Adventurers" who had found what they were looking for along the border.] **MPW**:4.29.15, p828.

[632] **THE AMERICANO**, Triangle: [Destined to spend a significant amount of screen time south of the border, this was Douglas Fairbank's first of several films that would require his incredible talents in those sunny climes. This first venture would take him as far to the south as Hollywood ventured in those days, Argentina. There he played a North American mining engineer in Patagonia, "South America", [for those who did not know.] In a plot very similar to Davis's the **Dictator** [909] the stalwart Anglo hero was responsible for reinstating a deposed president of that republic, the father of the girl he loved. Despite the agile dramatics of Douglas's daring-do, the film was played for laughs. **Variety**'s review revealed, what certainly can be considered a typical reflection of the general North American contempt for Latin American politics: "Somehow or other we never seem able

to look upon South American revolutions with any degree of seriousness.] **V**:12.29.16, **MPG**.

[633] **BEHIND THE LINES**, Bluebird: [Harry Carey, who would play his last role south of the border in 1948, at this early time was a National Guardsman fighting for his country somewhere in Mexico. Frequently in films with Mexican themes, his career across the border was ended only by his death in 1948.] **MPW**:9.16.16, p1783.

[634] **THE BLACK BUTTERFLY**, Metro: [All audiences knew by 1916 that Hispanics were passionate in love and life. On the silver screen, they could also be fragile, although not very frequently. This was one of those occasions. Sonia Smirov, was a beautiful and brilliant opera singer. Self-centered, she spurns the advances of an apparently oversensitive Latin lover, Don Luis Meredo. Unable to cope with the rejection, he bolts from her dressing room, goes to a phone, calls the lady and commits suicide as she listens, hopefully not too dispassionately.] **MPW**:12.9.16, p1550.

[635] **BRAND OF COWARDICE**, Rolfe/Metro: [The Mexican border mobilization generated a number of topical film fantasies. This film might not have been released for distribution had Villa not raided across the Rio Bravo. Basically a tale of passage into manhood, Lionel Barrymore plays a weakling, "pantywaist"/"He butterfly" that becomes a man by saving his commandants girl who has strayed across the border and has been captured by Navarette, a Mexican bandit chief. Young Cyril puts up a good fight, but there are too many of the enemy. "At the request of Marcia, he saves his last cartridge that he may prevent her from falling into the hands of the Mexicans." Just as he presses his gun against her breast, "a Mexican bullet reaches him." **Variety** chided the scripter for his lack of knowledge of international law, because in the denouement he does what President Wilson had been unable to at that point in time, that is he sends a battalion of calvary across the border to protect North American lives [1096].] **MPW**: 11.4.16, P 691, **V**:11.3.16, **MPG**.

[636] **BRIDE OF HATE**, Kay-Bee/Triangle: [Certainly one of the best reflections of what Hollywood gauged to be the racial conscience of its potential customers in 1916, this film focuses on the activities of a seducer. Having had his way once too often, the father of one of his conquests introduces him to a voluptuous young woman he cannot resist. After their marriage, the vengeful father obtains his release by telling the rake that he has "married a nigger." Such a sentence of death drives the debaucher to drunkenness in which state he wanders into the yellow fever infected part of town and contracts the dread disease. The final blow comes on his death bed when he is advised that the negress was also part Spanish. The question of race was an acute one for most citizens in the United States in 1917. Hollywood reflected commonly held attitudes, but more importantly, it reinforced them continuously on the silver screen, Hispanics, Indians and Blacks were essentially at their mercy, with little or no

access to any means for presenting contrary views. In 1917 Abrams and Werner, independent producers presented **BAR SINISTER** for white audience approval. Very successful on the Broadway stage, it's plot focused on a heroine's effort to prove that she had no "nigger." blood in her veins which might prevent her marrying a proper Souther gentleman. It was a slightly different time.] **MPW:6.9.17, p1632, MPG.**

[637] **THE BURIED TREASURE OF CORBE**: [A simple film like this gives us a good indication of the general feeling of North American superiority that prevailed throughout this nation after the successful defeat of Spain some years before, the more recent completion of the Panama Canal and the intervention in the Dominican Republic and Haiti. This was a nation that would have its way in the world of nations, especially with those south of the border. It is assumed that President Mendoza of Amapala is a crook himself and that he can be pressured by our new ambassador to sign a treaty of extradition without any trouble. As it turns out, Mendoza is a grafter and enjoys the favors of a rich North American thief, which he repays by granting him residence in his "two bit country." Chester Ward is not only a successful criminal, he has a flair for archeology, and he knows that there is buried treasure to be found in the Corbe site. Meanwhile, an apparently genuine scholar, coincidentally named Peabody (The Peabody Museum's at Harvard and Yale are the results significant discoveries unearthed by Professor Peabody in Mexico and throughout Central America) wants the concession to study the ruins himself. Ward is working for profit, Peabody for science, the concession goes to the former and the latter is threatened by Mendoza. As it turns out in the ruins themselves, Peabody is really a Secret Service man who captures Ward. At this juncture, Minister John Hayden points out the practicality of signing the treaty to the President. He cowers and so agrees. By the way, Peabody gets the girl too.] **MPW:1.1.16, p127.**

[638] **THE CAPTIVE GOD**, Triangle: [Of all the historical facts about the Indians of the Americas that one could be certain would provoke significant interest among students, none were more colorful than those which outlined the practices of human sacrifice employed in the religion of the Aztecs. Such a setting provided the background for this nontraditional western featuring W. S. Hart, who by mid 1915 could write his own ticket with Triangle. His demand for authenticity in this film cost the production company twice the usual price [$50,000] for one of it's usual Hart features. Researcher's studied, (they probably read a copy of Prescott's **Conquest of Mexico**), and translated their findings to grips who reconstructed an actual replica of Montezuma's, capital, Tenochtitlan [Mexico City], the film's major set. The film included the usual Hart one dimensional characters, good guys and bad ones. In this case, they were, good Aztecs, peaceful ones, who lived in cave/cliff dwellings in New Mexico, and bad ones, very warlike, who occupied the capital of the empire. Hart played a Spanish foundling who had been raised by the good guys and who had actually almost become their chief. All

was well until the bad guys from Mexico [even way back then] decided to come raid, rape, pillage and capture all the women who lived in the cliff dwellings. Only Chiapa [Hart] survived and with the help of some other local friendlies, he planed to attack the capital. In doing so he is captured, but wins the heart of Montezuma's daughter, Lolomi, which save his own in the last reel. It was part of the religion to sacrifice all captives, and part of the ceremony to cut out the heart of the sacrificee and offer it up to one of the gods. Lolomi knows the rules and pleads with dad for her man, but to no avail. Hart must lose his, or the gods will no longer shine on the empire. Luckily Lolomi finds enough survivors of Chiaps's tribe to come and rescue the hero, and they do. The lovers head back to the cliff's and Cortez is just landing at Vera Cruz.] **V**:7.7.16, **MPG**.

[639] **CLOUDS IN SUNSHINE VALLEY**, Centaur: [Had the clouds burst, there would have been no story. Jim Car was rich and controlled all the water in the valley. He also had it heavy for Mary Mills, but she had chosen poor Robert to share her water with. Angered, Jim cut off everyone's supply of the life giving stuff, but the locals didn't take kindly to his stupidity. The lynch mob includes a poor Mexican peon who gets killed for no other reason than to have his wife go mad and in her grief, kill Jim. After wandering about the desert for a day or so, she realizes that there is another life within her that she must save. Robert and Mary now share their water with her.] **MPW**:6.3.16, p1751.

[640] **CODE OF MARCIA GRAY**, Morosco/P: [From its earliest days Hollywood has provided all manner and form of criminals, those unjustly accused, runaway lovers and others who just wanted to hide out, with a refuge south of the border. In this film a banker has fleeced his establishment of funds and brought it to ruin. He plans on taking his wife and the stolen money south with him, but she refuses to go with him. He runs, but she rips up her ticket to South America.] **MPG**.

[641] **COLONEL HEEZA LIAR CAPTURES VILLA**, Paramount-Bray: [With little hope of not being considered a cynic, it is postulated that this cartoon, along with that one which focused on Huerta in 1914, can be considered the beginning of an as of yet unrecognized genre, that being, if you can't win the war in the field or save the hostages from the terrorist, do it on film. The self-deception will sooth the psyche. Black Jack Pershing will chase Villa for almost nine months and never once fight a major encounter with him personally. There were significant results from the expeditionary force operating in Mexico during that time: the first use of North American air reconnaissance, the first bombs dropped from a plane in United States service, the first use of armored vehicles [Packard trucks] in pursuit of an enemy, the discovery that Patton was a hell of a soldier, the realization that this nation was not prepared for a minor border raid led by an angry revolutionary leader who felt betrayed by an administration that had once favored him, much less a major European conflict, and preparing Pershing to lead his "Crusaders" across the pond to

make the world safe for democracy. But Pershing did not bring in Villa, he never even saw him. But Heeza did.

Although there may have been other films that propagandized for a particular purpose, this was certainly one of the first to use actual dialogue by well known personages to help popularize with film what many considered a severe problem, "preparedness." The cartoon begins with a debate on being ready for war, between our Secretary of State, William Jennings Bryan [there's a script there somewhere] and the "Bull Moose," Theodore Roosevelt. "Dissatisfied over the attitude shown throughout the United States toward the question of armament, Heeza questions both men. Bryan cries on his shoulder for peace, Roosevelt spurs him on. When he learns [present Presidents take note] that it's costing the government "five hundred dollars a minute" to pursue the bandit ... he immediately invents a "gasoline mule" that will aid in the capture of the bandit. The patriot also invents a formula that will make gasoline only two cents a gallon. With this done, he crosses the border and takes Villa in hand.] **MPW**:5.27.16, p1541.

[642] **COLONEL HEEZA LIAR AND THE BANDITS**, Paramount-Bray Animated Cartoons: [Paramount knew it had a good thing with this cartoon and in the true tradition of sequels that make no sense [you cannot keep a good Jason dead], Heeza is said to have failed in his first attempt to capture Villa, but is here given another chance. Having heard that Pershing and his troops were surrounded by Villa and that his men face possible annihilation, he organizes the remainder of a battalion to rescue him. This leaves miles of the border unprotected, but Heeza gathers all the phonographs in the district and with a special sound affect record, employing psychological warfare, scares the enemy away. Though later captured, and tied to a cactus, he is rescued by an eagle, who take him high in the sky from which vantage point he identifies the enemy camp. Escaping from the bird, he discloses the rebel position to headquarters and collects his reward. It may have been a fantasy, but the North American public really wanted Villa's capture in 1916, if it could only be done on film, at least that was something. Slyvester [sic] Rambo would provide a similar ego saving service for a later generation in a less popular conflict.] **MPW**: 6.17.16, p2065.

[643] **COMMON LAW**, Selznick: [When a beautiful young debutante's mother dies, she becomes destitute. Forced to support herself by modeling, she falls in love with a poor artist, sacrifices herself for his affection and art and is eventually rewarded for having defended her honor by his killing Querida, a "lust-filled Spanish painter."] **MPG**.

[644] **CROOKED TRAILS**, Selig: [Tom Mix was achieving major league Star status at this time, turning out these one reelers for Selig in as short a time as one a week. One of his major foils in these simplistic westerns was the Mexican, any Mexican. In this one it was Poncho, played by an Anglo, who loses a bronco breaking contest to the rising star. Angered,

especially because it happened in front of a lady he wanted to impress, he plans his vengeance and decides to rob a rich visitor to the ranch. With his band of bandit desperados, the halfbreed does his best, but that was hardly good enough for our Anglo hero, Tom. Though wounded, "the desperados [were] overcome," everyone of them, singlehandedly. That technique has remained a requirement down to present times.] **MPW**:6.3.16, p1743.

[645] **EL DIABLO**, Mustang: [No one wants to be the sheriff of Sagebrush, Arizona because the cave dwelling bandit, "El Diablo," who resides there, hates sheriffs. When the new kids in town open up a restaurant and see that there is a municipal opening, one of the boys applies for the job. His sister worries and decides to rid the region of the Mexican baddie herself. Liberated lady that she is, she does. Some of these early screen women were really tough.] **MPW**:8.26.16, p1442, 4.19.16, p1205.

[646] **DON QUIXOTE**, Triangle: [It was felt that this Triangle seven reel production would set a new standard for film excellence in the "adaptation of the classics." Possibly not a first, but certainly setting an example for later directors to follow, this film version used a technical advisor in the person of a "Spanish American clergyman who had lived in La Mancha."] **MPW**:1.1.16, p96.

[647] **THE DUMB GIRL OF PORTICI**, Universal: [Spanish Viceroys everywhere imposed "heavy taxes ... on the poverty-stricken" population so that the Kings of Spain could grow rich at the expense of the peoples they ruled in various parts of the world. This reviewer's condemnation of the Spanish imperial system, was typical of those who unknowingly accepted all of the negative interpretations "la leyenda negra" has been responsible for. In reality the Spanish empire must be ranked as one of the great achievements in the history of imperial [overseas] administration. In the Americas, Spain's empire spanned four centuries ruling over millions of widely different peoples for more than four hundred years. Pejoratives concerning such expansive administrations are almost always the result of nationalistic rivalry, in one form or another. The enemy always has to be portrayed as a real baddie, whether the struggle concerns hugh empires or individual couples.] **MPW**:5.20.16, p1391-92.

[648] **ELUSIVE ISABEL**, Bluebeard: [Certainly a fantasy that all Latin countries at one time or another have entertained: In this 1914 production all the Central and South American nations band together with the Spanish speaking nations of Europe in an intrigue which plans to conquer and control the 'Colossus of the North'. But as was usual, the Hispanics greatly underestimated the North American ability. In the end a single United States secret service man thwarts the entire plan and wins the hand of a Latin female conspirator in so doing. All of the Hispanic characters were played by Anglos.] **V**:5.5.16, **MPW**:5.6.16, p992. **V**:5.5.16. **MPG**.

[649] **THE EVIL EYE**, Lasky/Famous Players: ["Mexican superstition, ignorance and their attendant dangers form the basis" for this production. It would seem that the brave young Anglo doctoress who goes to Mexico to solve their diphtheria problem wears a flashlight on her head when she examines her stupidly scripted patients. In as much as most of the Mexicans working for Anglo mine owner have the disease, they immediately suspect that it is the "mysterious" "evil eye" with which the fair miss can better see their throats that is infecting most of them. "There develops a powerful dramatic situation with swift action." In the final reel her professionalism and feminine charm overcome the native's superstition and the dread affliction is defeated by the determined damsel [343].] **MPW**: 12.16.16, p1666.

[650] **FOLLOWING THE FLAG**, Selig: [When President Wilson ordered the National Guard to the Mexican border to go after Villa in the spring of 1916, it would have been almost impossible to find any voice denouncing this most popular action, even among the loyal opposition. The "invasion" of United States territory by it's former pseudo mercenary fixed and focused public opinion universally against Villa. The entire nation would have followed the flag into Mexico, not a few would have taken it all the way to Panama to end that problem once and for all. This film was one of the many new entries, providing new recently taken material that made up the flurry of reissues flooding the market immediately after Villa crossed the border in hopes of provoking all out war, thereby allowing him to become Mexico's savior and possibly dethroning the recognized Carranza regime. The film itself began with Pershing crossing the border and "penetrating Mexico" with the support of every "man, woman and child in this country." All were proud of the "courage displayed by the indomitable little force which entered alone the deserts of Mexico after the blood-thirsty bandit." The remainder of the film described the daily border activities of the Guardsman, drilling, marching and eating. The exhibitors considered it one of their most popular attractions. "Topical productions" were very successful even at the worst of times."] **MPW**:12.2.16, p1377, 12.16.16, p1658, 11.25.16, p1195.

[651] **FOLLOWING THE FLAG IN MEXICO**: Tropical Film Co: [Issued to the exhibitors in April of 1916, this production was an early example of topical exploitation. Much of the material predated the raid and had been part of other features. The advertising campaign included full page adds in not only the trades but also major metropolitan dailies. It was to be "Villa At Any Cost" a "$20,000 dollar reward, Dead or Alive", "The cruel Mexican Desert of Fever by day and chill by night" and much more! Although most of the material had been viewed by audiences before, taking advantage of Villa's "invasion" allowed them more success than at the time they were first issued.] **MPW**:4.15.16, p515, 4.29.16, p825.

[652] **FOLLOWING VILLA IN MEXICO**, Tropical Film Co: [Produced less than a month after Villa's raid on Columbus, New Mexico, this production company was at the scene before most of the

national guardsman arrived to close the barn door. This review by Margaret MacDonald speaks for itself: In the "series of Mexican pictures which has been showing at Weber's theater ... we have been spared very little and many are the gruesome sights that are reported for our benefit. Having an important place in the history of America they are of exceptional value, bringing home to the spectator more vividly than any word description possibly could the desolation of the country into which our soldier boys have ridden in their search for the bandit Villa. In the march of the miserably equipped Mexicans of both sides, the spiritless horses, the flocking of half-starved refugees into Uncle Sam's Domain, depending like children on his good will for food and shelter, we are reminded of the lack of vigor and of definite purpose that has marked the Mexican struggle from first to last. [If the reader pardons an editorial observation, this copy might have been used on CNN news as coverage for the present ethnic conflict focused on a similar evil deed dooer.] In addition to views of the headquarters of the U. S. troops at Columbus N.M., scenes before and after the raid, instances of Villa's cruelty, such as the bodies of victims hanging by the necks from the limbs of trees, skirmishes between the Villa and Carranza followers, the gruesome toll of the battlefield and the partial burial and final burning of the dead, the films provide a fine insight into the work of the Red Cross in Mexico." The exhibitors felt that it would make especially good viewing for those who had loved ones among the National Guard troops protecting the border. Certainly, much of this should have a familiar ring. The present day Arabs can easily be considered to be in the same situations as the Mexicans of Villa's day.] **MPW**:4.29.16, p817.

[653] **GIRL FROM FRISCO**, Kalem: [**BORDER WOLVES**, was #17 of this serial created by Kalem and proved an instant success, showing, for example, "in 17 New York photohouses simultaneously." It was said to be based on an actual incident which took place during the Madero Revolution of 1911 when Mexican rebels lured a banker across the border to reclaim the body of his dead brother and then held him for ransom. The intermediary used was a half-breed Mexican girl. The attempt to trick the rebels resulted in the death of the Banker. The big battle scene was recreated by using a real "Mexican 'near army'" of more than three hundred locals. But the attempt at authenticity proved to be something of a problem in human nature. "Mexican rebels are not at all adverse to acting in motion pictures" claimed Director Horne ".... but by the time you have greased the officers and met all the demands of the men they cost considerably more than plain every day extras. They also eat up a lot of film, for each of the officers demands plenty of close-ups ... i [sic] wont have the nerve to come down here again" after they discover all of them were left on the cutting room floor.] **MPW**: 12.9.16, p1508, 12.16.16, p1644, p1658, 12.23.16, p1851.

[654] **GOLD DUST**, Essanay: [Traveling to South America for your health could be fatal to your business if you left it in the wrong hands. But if the salubrious climes to the south

cured you in the nick of time, you could save it all from destruction in the last reel and give the evil deed dooers their just deserts.] **MPW**:2.26.16, p1346.

[655] **THE GOOD BAD MAN**, Triangle: [Although this Douglas Fairbanks feature was set in a west with no Hispanics at all, it is listed here because of the force that the influential actor gave to the characterization of the good bad man. By so doing he established him as a western type, moving his activities from Sherwood Forest to the North American west where later, many others, including many Mexicans would also portray loveable rouges who robbed from the less deserving to provide for those in need.] **NYT**:4.22.16. For the complete Fairbanks filmography see: **Louis Devon, "Douglas Fairbanks," Films In Review**, May 1976, pp267-283.

[656] **THE GUNFIGHTER**, Triangle: [With every new film, Triangle's western star gained in popularity. In this one William S. Hart was the Anglo defender who had to fight for the control of a gold rich border town against the evil "El Salvador," the towns brutal oppressor, played by Roy Laidlaw.]

[657] **THE HALF BREED**, Triangle [Douglas Fairbanks in another "sympathy-compelling" role as a "Good Badman" brought this Bret Harte story to the screen. The scene was set in early California where the halfbreed attempted to right all the wrongs inflicted on a poor indian girl [921].] **V**:7.14.16, **NYT**:7.10.16.

[658] **THE HEART OF BONITA**, Laemmie: [Myrtle Gonzales, one of the earliest of the silent screens at least partially Hispanic stars, was the featured heroine here, one more of a seemingly endless series of señoritas who save or sacrifice themselves for the North American hero. William Kern goes to inspect his mine in Mexico where Bonita lives and waits to love. The investment pays off just as the locals are starting a revolution and need money to finance it. The lady has a Latin lover who persists, but she of course prefers the Anglo. Realizing that troublewasabrewin, the Anglo bury the gold, but when captured and forced to trade it for the life of the Anglo girl, it is discovered missing. Juan had taken it, Bonita finds out and with this information saves Bill's life. Of course the ungrateful wretch prefers white skin and having had it with Mexico's travail, travels north. Bonita settles for half the enchilada and the persistent Sanchez, although second best, still gets his satisfaction.] **MPW**:3.4.16, p1496, p1537.

[659] **THE HEART OF PAULA**, P: [There may very well be more hopeless/helpless romantics out there, sincerely seeking that happily forever after, than care to come out of their self imposed exiles, or comfortable closets, knowing full well that the real world simply waits to rearrange the scenario to suit itself. Whether aficionado or dilettante, when one discovers that the producers tried out at least three different endings to Casablanca, that they actually considered sending Rick off with the love of his manly life, it is usually a letdown. How could there be any other ending, lovingly sad as it is? **The**

Heart of Paula was one of the first films to use the market approach to help determine the outcome of the final reel. Lenore Ulrich was considered sensational as a "Spanish maiden, alluringly attractive and thoroughly versed in the art of flirtation." [There were still not enough Hispanic actresses that could fill the bill, according to Anglo production companies.] "Her warm beauty and emotional fervor" were "perfectly suited" to the character of Paula Figueros, the heroine. Set in a Mexican town controlled by revolutionists, it was reviewed as a "timely and authentic story" which offered "occasional glimpses of typical Mexican character." Paula, not unlike the "wicked Felina" regaled in the popular song of a later decade, was giving her Anglo "looks that made his mouth water." But she belonged to that man "Jose," in this case, Pacheco, although she loathed him, preferring the Anglo. What to do with the ending? Paramount tried out two: "According to the tragic climax, the one we imagine originally conceived ... Paula promises to give herself to the revolutionary leader in payment for the life of the young American." Once he is safely across the Bravo, she "goes to the Mexican quarters, reposes on a couch bathed in moonlight and plunges a dagger into her heart. The revolutionist finds her lifeless body." This was considered the logical ending!? But the votes were even when counted and the producer opted for that which seemed to please the audience. Paula lives, rescued by a small band of North American cowboys with you know who on the lead charger. So much for Hollywood reality in either case.] **MPW**:4.8.16, p281, 4.8.16, p463, 4.22.16, p696.

[660] **HELLS HINGES**: [The William S. Hart vehicle is significant because although it has negative Mexican characterizations, so far as this reporter can determine, it is the first Hollywood production with a totally bad all North American character in a major role.] **V**:2.11.16.

[661] **HER FATHER'S GOLD**, Thanhouser: [Her father's stolen gold was from a Mexican mine and that's the only connection in this Anglo boy wants to marry a woman of wealth scenario.] **MPW**:5.13.16, p1221.

[662] **HER MATERNAL RIGHT**, World-Equitable: [Forced to work because his inheritance was less than he thought it would be, Emory Townsend complicates his life by marrying up with the wrong kinda woman. She spends money like a thirsty camel drinks water. Worse, to keep her happy, he turns to the company's funds and then she will not go to South America with him where the extradition laws are lax. She laughs and refuses coldly to help him in any way at all. It all works out. She gets hers. Without leaving for Rio, Emory makes everything right, but not without the help of a new lady who sets him straight.] **MPW**:5.20.16, p1402.

[663] **THE HEROINE OF SAN JUAN**, Big U: [What some of these scenarios needed was a little simplifying: Grace, a Cuban beauty, falls for a young lieutenant, "part of the American Army invading" her island. They learn of a possible ambush

and save the entire regiment. "The American Army wins the day", they win each other. What once could have been done in one reel easily, now took two or three.] **MPW**:11.25.16, p1221.

[664] **THE HONOR SYSTEM**, Fox: [Raoul Walsh had established himself by this time as a dynamic director and man of action. Having spent a significant part of his early career involved in someway with the revolutionary upheaval in Mexico, he was at ease with turmoil. With Villa, he had witnessed the brutality bred by both sides of the border, so the **Honor System** was a natural for him. Although the film's main focus was prison reform, it was staged on the Arizona/Mexican border where it would seem that Raoul could not separate the revolution in Mexico from that which was taking place behind the bars of the old Yuma State Prison. That hotbed of dissatisfaction provided the director with real "atmosphere", for the prison board's new Progressive orientation. To enhance this film with every attribute of real life, "Mexican raids were staged" with real survivors of these earlier incidents which were "absolutely correct in every detail." Thousands of men were shown "taking place in cavalry charges" and in the battles, authentic in every detail, to those "taking place between the warring factions of Mexico to-day."] For some personal insights and reflections on a most interesting, exciting and enjoyable career, see: **Richard Schickel** [Interviewer], **The Men Who Made The Movies**, New York: Atheneum, 1975. "Interviews with ..., Roaul Walsh." **MPW**:11.11.16, p879.

[665] **IN MEXICO**, Falstaff: [In 1915, Mexican bandits could be found everywhere, even in Mexico. When a street car conductor, his daughter and son-in-law go to Mexico on business and are captured by bandits. There is lots of adventure and in the last reel, their natural ability allows them to outwit the banditos and then escape.]

[666] **IN THE LAND OF THE TORTILLA**, Beauty: [Exhibitor's reports indicated that this contemptuous spoof played very well with audiences. Emerson Howe lived uneasily as this government's consul to Mexico, but he never felt safe. One day his front door was assaulted by a bunch of Mexicans chasing an "American" carrying a little black box. Once the consul quieted the crowd, he discovered that the refugee was really "a cameraman for the Associated Press Dispatch." Just at that moment he received a communication from Washington which informed him that "Veeha was captured by Caperanza and was about to be executed." The President wanted photographic proof that this would be done. Knowing that Caperanza was angry because Veeha had beat him to the "generalship of the Tortillian army," the consul realized that one could only attend the execution by invitation. The saved guest offered to get the pictures for him, but was refused entry. What did this all mean? It might have meant that the United States public was so anxious to have the bandit that had actually invaded their country dead, that even seeing it happen in this humorous fantasy would be soothing to the psyche. It

certainly worked for revising who really the won the war in Vietnam.] **MPW**:7.29.16, p838.

[667] **JERRY IN MEXICO**, Cub: [Finding life too difficult in the States, our hero ventures south and finds that there is little of the solace he seeks to be found in a Mexican Cantina. His first intention had been to rescue a sweet señorita from the traditional Mexican bandit, but once he discovers the cantina, it's another story altogether. Being an Anglo the ladies won't leave him alone and their men are continuously trying to kill him. Unable to control his desires, he decides it's better to be alive than, let's say, supremely satisfied, and the wimp winds his way back across the Bravo with less of a desire to be a hero and one of the other lovely ladies.] **MPW**:1.15.16, p445, 1.22.16, p625.

[668] **THE JUNGLE CHILD**, Triangle: [Hollywood was quick to associate the South American jungle with a savageness unknown in North America. The identification was quickly accepted by moving picture audiences and frequent reinforcements have kept it that way until present days. Hollywood's silver screen South American jungle has bred all forms of wild life, some of it highly specialized. That has always been especially true for Brazil with more jungle than any other single nation in the world. There, one could find what exists elsewhere only by transplantation, the wondrous Amazon, superstrong, superlovely and superwhite. In this film a baddie from the States discovers an unknown Brazilian jungle village whose leader is a beautiful Amazon. Realizing that she is the lost child of a rich Spanish [many screen writers were unaware that Brazil was not Spanish] family and presently an heiress, he marries her off to New York. Sometime later, he brags about his good fortune to a friend indicating that his only interest was her inheritance. Having over heard the conversation, the Amazon reverts to her tribal savageness and chokes him to death with her bare hands.] **MPW**:9.23.16, **V**:9..22.16, **MPG**.

[669] **KENNEDY SQUARE**, Vitagraph: [Running away south of the border often provided Hollywood with the opportunity to perform minor miracles to help script writers out of the problems they had created for themselves. Antonio Moreno's, was a dueling Anglo in this film who was forced to run to South America after killing an opponent. Financed by a friend he discovers a ruby mine while hiding out and returns home to share the new found wealth. And none too soon, the friend had fallen onto really bad times. Quick to repay his debt, Moreno bails out the impoverished buddy and also gets to marry the girl who had never stopped loving him.] **MPG.**

[670] **KERNEL NUTT IN MEXICO**, Vitagraph: [By June of 1916, the mobilization "against Villa was in high gear, few in this country did not want to punish the individual now considered to be the archetypal "bandit." Hollywood responded with many patriotic productions showing the way south, but also attempted to provide a bit of humorous release with brief clips like the following. "Why go to war when there is a fine cafe and a pretty señorita handy? No, No, Nutt prefers to

make his permanent headquarters where the red wine flows and the girls amuse him with their wiggly dances." When the sexy señorita's husband shows up, Nutt frightens him with a rubber dagger and resumes his advances, only to awaken in his own bed, where his wife, realizing where he has traveled in dreamland, "starts a real war right at home."] **MPW**:6.17.16, p2120.

[671] **THE KID**, Vitagraph: [Mexico was frequently a haven for real rotters, they could live, even thrive there, without having to constantly worry about being punished. This film's particular degenerate was a debaucher who had fathered an illegitimate child. Some time after he had successfully crossed over the border, he became a very crooked but also very successful cattle baron responsible for fixing the prices of meat in the north. As luck would have it, the investigating reporter sent there to expose him, turns out to be his very own daughter. He attempts to make amends, but she rejects all of his parental advances with the scorn he deserves and returns to the **New York Herald** with the real story.] **MPG**.

[672] **KINKAID, GAMBLER**, Red Feather: [Hollywood scripters frequently placed their characters south of the border to avoid the confines and strictures of Anglo law. One could do things on the screen in Mexico that were prohibited north of the border. This was especially true after the introduction of the Production Code which required that all crime must be visibly punished no later than in the last reel. In this film a woman detective falls for her prey in Mexico and although troubled by conscience, her heart exercises the stronger influence. In this film's last scene, the two lovers escape from the home of the free and the brave to the "land of the enchilada" never more to return.] **MPW**:12.9.16, p1509, p1513, **MPG**.

[673] **LIBERTY**, U: [In a year when serials gained enormous popularity, one of the most successful entries was **Liberty**, nineteen chapters of dynamic virtue struggling against the dark forces of revolutionary evil at work in Mexico. Liberty was the maid, Lopez the bandit. "This startlingly realistic drama of warfare along the Mexican border" as opposed to other multiepisodic photoplays, increased audience interest with every new chapter. The serial "exceeded all promises" and "swept its way into the hearts of observers." Each installment "provided a vivid picture of conditions on the Mexican border." A unique feature of this adventure series was Liberty's right hand man, a sympathetically portrayed Mexican named Pedro who provided protection and broke her out of rat infested prisons in almost every episode. In the final sequence, all details were tidied up, Lopez was shot, Major Winston saved, Pedro shoots the remainder of the revolutionaries and all are reunited at the Hacienda where the insurrection all began. One revolution, one Anglo woman and all was resolved! What more was necessary?] **MPW**:11.4.16, p749, 11.11.16, p839, 11.18.16, p1063, 11.25.16, p1184, 12.2. p1379, 12.9.16, p1513, p1544, p2005-6.

[674] **LIEUT. DANNY, USA**, Triangle/Ince: [**Variety** considered this a "timely feature because of the fact that it deal[t] with conditions along the Rio Grande where U. S. Troopers [were] holding down the border lines." Always with an eye for solid exploitation, producers were quick to point out to the exhibitors that newspaper accounts of the Villa raid provided the film with a significant amount of free advertising. In the film itself, a young Army hero, fresh from the Point, sees immediate action upon his arrival at the border when he saves a pretty señorita from a Mexican bandito, "a la Villa." Pedro Lopez, the Butcher, later captures the young officer and has him brought to the white wall, traditional color for early morning executions. There his life is saved, when a firing squad bullet refused to penetrate the holy medal of St. Francis, that Ysobel has given him. Mexico's Catholic god must have had a problem with that one. But, one must remember that aside from the denominational divinity, the Anglo also had the scripter on his side. In a quick series of events and this time with the aid of mother nature's lightening, the young Anglo officer kills the bandit who was attempting to ravish his lady and singlehandedly routs the remainder of the cowardly Mexican force. The film ends with Old Glory flying high, and in many local houses throughout the nation, the playing of the Star Spangled Banner accompanied by loud cheering. Displaying the colors and playing the anthem first became a common practice in the Tampico crisis of 1914. It was revived again when Villa invaded in 1916.] **V**:8.11.16, **MPG**.

[675] **THE LONG ARM OF LAW AND ORDER**, P: [Paramount was among the leaders in production companies responsible for creating patriotic cartoons not even just shy of propaganda. Utilizing a frame from the film for the advertizing campaign, Uncle Sam's long arm was pictured reaching across the border to capture Villa. He was shown wearing a hugh sombrero screaming like a child. The copy read: "After months of patiently watching and waiting, the boys from the army have invaded Mexican territory with the idea of putting an end to the terrors that have been instigated through the perverted ideas of the bandit Villa ... In this animated cartoon Uncle Sam ... the staid, calm old gentleman [stretches] forth his arm and from out of the mountains brings forth Villa only to crush him and drop him into a rubbish can in which also reposes Aguinaldo." Fantasies abounded in Tinsel Town, even then. The war had to be won, if only in screen dreams.] **MPW**:4.22.16.

[676] **THE LOTUS WOMAN**, Kalem: [Juana was a woman "who lured men's souls to the shores of sin by the light of her wanton eyes." A pretty good line for a silent film. Juana was also a "South American Vampire," the first. Raised and "reared in rigorous seclusion by her haughty old father Don Roberto" she lived alone until the arrival of the rebel leader Lopez. Wasting little time, the following evening found the lady "clasped in the arms of the rebel gentleman," and when the father disapproved, she had him shot. Parental defiance at times took on new meaning in Mexico. Everything was going her way until yet, another arrival in the person of a young American soldier of fortune, Jerry Mandeville. He had left

the security of home for the "adventure of a good revolution" he hoped would heal his broken heart. When the Lotus Woman tried her specialized seductive skills with him, she was repulsed. With some attempt at drama, the reviewer explained that "there now follows a bloody tale" "a perfect whirlwind of strictly melodramatic action." The rebel chief was killed by Don Roberto, [I thought he had already been killed, also] the North American was shot down, but not killed by a firing squad. This forced the vengeful Juana to dispatch him "by the aid of her own stiletto." She herself is sacrificed in the last reel. More bizarre than all of the above, the reviewer in his praise for the film, felt that "the atmosphere of Latin America [had been] sustained." One wonders where he had traveled to south of the border.] **MPW**:6.17.16, p2055.

[677] **THE LOVE THIEF**, F: [The army mobilization prompted by Villa's raid against Columbus, New Mexico provided yet another background for this complex tale of border intrigue. Forced to leave his sweetheart, a young captain arrives at the border to do his duty. There he orders the death of a Mexican spy whose sister heads a guerilla band seeking to buy arms. Juanita swears vengeance, but falls in love with the Anglo captain instead. True to his own lady, he spurns her advances which causes her to have him falsely accused of murder. Now the writers really complicate things. It is discovered that his true love's father is one of the illegal gunrunners. What to do? Escaping to Mexico, the father and daughter fall into the clutches of the vengeful Juanita, but all is resolved when the captain is cleared. With the help of the secret service and United States calvary he crosses the border to save the girl. Exhibitors called it "A rattling good melodrama."] **MPW**:12.23.16, p1825, 12.30.16, p1975._ **V**:12.29.16.

[678] **THE MAN IN THE SOMBRERO**, American: [The man in the sombrero had no connection what so ever with Mexico.] **MPW**:1.22.16, p661.

[679] **MARIA ROSA**, Lasky/Famous Players: [Geraldine Farrar, despite her German sympathies, was Lasky's top attraction and until the United States entered the world war on England's side, this was not a problem. Following her great success as Carmen, the temptress, she was featured here in this tragic tale of Spanish peasant life and love. Her male support was Pedro de Cordoba, destined to be a super star himself in both Hispanic and other ethnic roles. Some of the Spanish peasants in this photoplay suffered a lot, especially the women, that was their scripted role in life, Maria was one of them. "The heart of Maria Rosa, simple and trusting, finds itself cruelly deceived and betrayed, not by her lover, but by a treacherous rival of her lover." Yet, even a Spanish tragedy could end well in Hollywood, in the final scene the suffering señorita saved her man from a false charge of murder and they shared the last scene together.] **MPW**:5.13.16, p1180.

[680] **THE MEN SHE MARRIED**, Peer/World: [Another variation of girl wronged by rotter who heads south of the border having stolen her jewels and later returns north after squandering

all his ill gotten gains in those sunny climes with lots of señoritas. Now without means, he seeks a new source of supply and attempts to reignite the relationship, but fails.] **MPW**: 12.9.16, p1549, **MPG**.

[681] **A MESSAGE TO GARCIA**, Edison: [Sadly, Elbert Hubbard died on the ill-fated **Lusitania**, before seeing his major work begin production, but possibly for the better, reviewers generally considered this screen offering unworthy of the influential essay which touched the hearts of so many at the time of the Cuban insurrection. This production made more of a heroine of Delores, the Cuban lady who sacrificed her life so that Lieutenant Rowan could deliver the message to the insurrectionist leader Garcia that the United States would support him till the end, than it did of the exploits of the Anglo hero himself. Apparently, it also solved the mystery of who blew up the **Maine**, identifying the culprits as Cuban rebels who had suffered the "oppression and cruelty" of the Spaniard and who realized such an atrocity would draw this nation into the war.] [The naval board of inquiry into the affair said only that the explosion was from internal sources. Remade again twenty years later in 1936, the director then played with the historical facts in an even more extreme manner.] **MPW**:4.29.16, p825, 12.9.16, p1507.

[682] **MIXED BLOOD**, Red Feather: [Quite possibly, when many young students of Latin American history first encounter the name Bernado O'Higgins their smiles are more generated by a question than by anything else. The combination of Irish father and Mexican mother, or the reverse is not at all uncommon throughout the hemisphere. The reasons are not difficult to understand, both share an inordinate reverence for Roman Catholicism, and the Irish sent a lot of people to all of the Americas. In this feature the heroine's father was Mexican, the mother, Irish. This combination apparently made her very active, for she had, not two, but three lovers. Carlos was her Mexican bandit, Joe Nagal ran the gambling house and Big Jim was the sheriff. Although George Beranger portrayed the bandit, the reviewer assured readers that "all of the characterizations [were] true to type." The plot is "one of outlawry, jealousy and primal instincts ... given full play" what else could one expect from Hispanics? Yet, for the squeamish, the last reel was considered "too gruesome" but not for the Mexican border.] **MPW**:12.23.16, p1814, 12.30.16, p2006.

[683] **ON THE BRINK OF WAR**, #20: [As a result of a border politician's desire to exclude Mexicans from crossing the Rio Grande, a bitter race riot develops between native Americans and local Mexicans. The incident, a "bloody affair" is felt to be so severe, that the President of the United States sends his Secretary of State to resolve the situation in hopes of averting war between the two neighbors. After evaluating the situation and being unable to convince the crooked bureaucrat to stop his dirty dealings, the forceful diplomat has the politician, incarcerated and further racial bloodshed is averted.] **MPW**:12.30.16, p2003.

Feature Film List 1916   183

PATHE EXCHANGE, INC:

[684] **#30, Somewhere in Mexico:** "Army aviators brave the treacherous air currents of the Mexican desert looking for Villa's bandits."

[685] **Mexico At a Glance:** "An animated map illustrating the rapid advance made by the American troops."

[686] **Guantanamo Bay, Cuba:** "Uncle Sams's Atlantic Fleet steams "majestically" out of the bay "in battle line formation."

[687] **#31, Philadelphia, Pa:** "The Mexican crisis is severe, but it cannot interfere with opening day of baseball season."

[688] **Columbus, New Mexico:** "Troops from interior forts are daily arriving to reinforce the columns penetrating Mexico. Title card: "The sturdy American troopers, knowing no hardships, are still in the saddle as night falls on the barren desert trail."

[689] **San Diego, California:** "Marines of the 4th U. S. regiment, demonstrate the serviceability of elephants for desert warfare as vantage points for machine guns. Title card: "The immense size of the animal offers good shelter."

[690] **Columbus, New Mexico:** "Twenty Apache Indians who were in the party that trailed Geronimo in 1886, are employed to act as scouts in Mexico. Title card: Chief Sharley, who captured Geronimo." **MPW**:4.29.16, p867.

[691] **#32, El Paso, Texas:** ""American troops" build a temporary bridge across the Rio Grande to facilitate communication with troops in Mexico. Title card: "Off duty, our soldiers are big brothers to the poor, unfortunate population of the war-ridden Republic."" **MPW**:5.6.16, p1042.

[692] **#41, Somewhere in Mexico:** "Led by Mexican guides, little squads of American troopers continue the vain trail over the rocky mountain passes which Villa haunts."

[693] **Marathon, Texas:** "Uncle Sam's Cavalrymen "tune up" for their work in avenging the murder of their comrades by Mexican bandits at Glen Springs."

[694] **#55, El Paso, Texas:** "General Bell and a motorcycle squadron go to the International Bridge to meet the soldiers taken prisoners at Carrizal and released by Carranza. Title card: "The freed prisoners, their clothing in rags, are glad to reach American soil again."

[695] **Galveston, Texas:** "Refugees from Vera Cruz are glad to reach "native soil"".

[696] **#56, El Passo:** "The bodies of seven negro troopers killed in the battle of Carrizal are received by the military

authorities. Title card: "Their comrades of the Tenth Cavalry act as pallbearers.""

[697] **#57, Fort Sam Houston:** "The first armored car belonging to the US Army arrives for service along the border."

[698] **El Paso, Texas:** "Pittsburgh's boys arrive for service at the border." **MPW**:7.29.16, p842.

[699] **PATRIA**, International: [William Randolph Hearst was responsible for this bizarre attempt at awakening this country to the possibility of a Japanese sponsored, Mexican supported invasion of the United States. Although the powerful publisher controlled more than a million acres of Mexican land at this time, and possibly for that reason, he consistently, through the facilities of his vast newspaper empire, propagandized for intervention and outright takeover of that war torn nation. Never really satisfied with what he considered his government's lack of adequate response to Mexican aggression, the mere punitive action of taking Vera Cruz in 1914 and what he certainly considered ineffective action against Villa, he provided the funds to produce this invasion fantasy. It featured one of "the best known and best dressed woman in America," Mrs. Vernon Castle, as the star. A wealthy Newport socialite, apparently with not much to do, Patria decides to save her country from the evil intentions of the Baron Huriki and Juan De Lima. The two had forged a secret alliance against the United States. Mexico's lost territories of 1845, the entire southwest, including Texas and California, were to be the reward for such treachery, (shades of the Zimmermann Telegram.) The first episode of the serial, "The last of the Fighting Channings," merely introduces the characters and the plan. Subsequent chapters moved the action from the other coast to Texas and California. By Chapter 11, "Sunset Falls" the scene shifted to the Mexican border and the banks of the Rio Grande, where the Mexican/Japanese troops were gathering, waiting for the right opportunity to invade across the river. In the following sequence, "Which Passeth All Understandings", Villa, played by Wallace Berry [who would portray him with a completely different characterization, a sympathetic one, in 1934], was cast as an arch villain willing to conspire with little yellow men (including Warner Oland as one of the more militant Japanese Barons) to put the lily white American men in the place they truly deserved, beneath the feet of the conquering avengers. This was overt racism, an appeal to the more negative side of human nature and angered some members of the Wilson administration, so that a temporary ban on the film's distribution and exhibition was ordered by Secretary of State Lansing. The State Department's major problem with all this arose from the fact that by the time the film achieved its greatest popularity, Japan and the United States were allies in the united world effort against Germany. It proved embarrassing to officials to have the Japanese portrayed according to publisher Hearst's racist conceptions. In chapter 14, "The Border Peril", the well trained and disciplined Japanese troops, supported by the effective Mexican Calvary, headed for the border to do their

best. Of course they were thwarted in the last episode, "For the Flag," by a small band of Patria's defenders. "The invasion, thanks to Patria ... was a failure." Yet the invasionary scenario was only one aspect of the nonsense which surrounded this production. In 1918 Congress held hearings on the affect of German propaganda during the war just prior to United States entry. **Patria** soon became a major topic for discussion. It was pointed out that because President Wilson was enraged by the very negative Japanese characterizations, that the producers, were forced to make changes, rather dramatic ones. All of the players, whether Japanese or not, no matter what uniform they were dressed in, were identified, by the use of new title cards in the body of the film, as Mexicans. The invasion then became, not a joint effort, but one that the Mexicans were responsible for alone. Despite all of this, and certainly a sound reflection of public consciousness, the production became and remained a tremendous success with audiences throughout the nation. One of the first joint efforts between film and the press, and designed to increase the production's popularity, many Hearst papers carried a weekly running scenario of upcoming chapters.] **MPW**:11.11.16, p876, 12.2.16, 1352, 12,9,16, p1478, p1510, 4.14.17, p328, 4.21.17, p496, 4.28.17, p683, 5.5.17, p854, 517.17, p1000, **V**:12.1.16, **NYT**:12.14.18.

[700] **THE PATRIOT**, Triangle: [William S. Hart in an untypical role finds himself a Spanish American War veteran whose mine was stolen while he fought to help make Cuba free. Unable to obtain justice, his life is further complicated by having his son die. Bitter that his nation has wronged him, he participates in a Mexican Bandit raid on a U. S. settlement. There he discovers an orphan boy, comes to his senses and helps defeat the attackers. Roy Laidlaw plays Pancho Zapilla.] **MPG**.

[701] **PICTURESQUE HAVANA**, Pathe: [Attractive scenes in and about the Cuban capital.] **MPW**:9.9.16, p1689.

[702] **A PUEBLO LEGEND**, Biograph: [Directed by D. W. Griffith this film starred Mary Pickford amid the Indian Pueblo of Isleta, New Mexico "in a story especially suited" to bring out the little sweetheart's "tender charm."] **MPW**:10.7.16, p122.

[703] **THE QUITTER**, Bison: [A young insensitive wife thoughtlessly offends her husband out west where that is not allowed. She returns back east to be entertained by a "society fop", but only until she realizes where her true heart wants to be. Returning to the wide open spaces, she discovers that a Mexican, Martinez by name, wants to do her husband dirty. On the way home she spies a lurking figure crouched at the base of an earthen dam her husband has built. Just as the Mexican lights the fuse, she attacks and he runs. After putting out the fuse, shooting the Mexican's horse out from under him, wounding him and having herself shot up a bit, she walks the culprit back to where her husband is waiting. Remorseful, she pledges to make it all up to him.] **MPW**:4.11.16, p909.

[704] **THE QUARTER BREED**, Bison: [If being a halfbreed was bad, was being a quarter breed only half as bad? It is difficult at times to understand why individuals considered such things, but on the silver screen, as early as the **Octoroon** [57] and the reality was that people were judged by their ancestry. The practice probably predated Adam. In this one the little lady cannot consider the advances of a half or quarter breed, he of course understands the problem and with noble, selfsacrifice tells the pure blood to honor the other she loves, for he has come to understand that he is good for nothing better than driving a stagecoach.] **MPW**:3.11.16, p1703.

[705] **RAMONA**, Clune: [The flickers had certainly grown by this date. What Griffith had done in a single reel in 1910, had been substantially expanded into this twelve reel adaptation of H. H. Jackson's epic defense of native Americans depicting life in lower California between 1845 and 1881. The showings in Los Angeles and New York took three hours and twenty two minutes, the original shooting comprised twenty reels, but was trimmed to this length for exhibition. Reports indicated that no one left the theaters and that it played to packed houses. **Variety** had sincere praise for the authentic atmospheric recreation showing the problems created for the native and Spanish populations during the transition from Mexican to United States control. All of the actors were Anglos. Although the added length allowed for a more in depth picturization of the story, it created problems with exhibitors, limiting the number of times the film could be shown on a daily basis. The product was always film, but the driving force remained, profitability, from first to last. As will be seen later, only when threatened possible profits, were producers prone to altering or shaping the film content, especially where ethnic stereotypes were the issue. In this case it was overall length and nothing more that caused the producers to cut the film [103, 1303].] **MPW**:3.18.16, p1829, 4.22.16, p640, **V**:2.25.16, 4.7.16, "'Ramona' Shown Upon the Screen," **NYT**:4.6.16.

[706] **THE ROUGH NECK**, Lubin: [Because the heroine in this story of South American adventure was rescued by a "rough neck" who unwittingly lends his "sea-going steam yacht" to further a plot for smuggling arms to the revolutionist attempting to overthrow the government of Santa Bana, one reviewer credited the author with the introducing "something new in situations." The heroine's father, John Calkins manufactured firearms and had a taste for filibustering, "providing it promised a large reward." But the deal goes **Down Twisted** and father, daughter, and son, who is a lieutenant on the naval vessel guarding "American lives" in the troubled republic, are all captured by the insurgents. Now the "rough neck "takes over and leading a contingent of blue jackets from "Uncle Sam's" warship, rescues the family. In the last scene the boy and girl are circled by a cheering group of "Jackies" as they kiss while proudly displaying the Stars and Stripes on foreign soil.] **MPW**:7.29.16, p806.

SELIG-TRIBUNE:

[707] **#27, Saltillo, Mexico:** "Carranza troops leave here presumably for Chihuahua to intercept Villa before he escapes into the [sic] fastnesses of the Sierra Madre Mountains."

[708] **Columbus, New Mexico:** Arrival of additional troops."

[709] **#28, Near Guerrero, Mexico:** "In a running fight here General Cavatos, commanding Carranza's troops had a sharp brush with a detachment of Villa's soldiers." **MPW:4.29.16, p850.**

[710] **THE SHERIFF'S BLUNDER**, Selig: [Selig's shooting star, Tom Mix, was becoming a household name by time in 1916; his more frequent appearances on the screen would soon make him one of the most popular and highly paid actors in Hollywood. In this film Tom played a bank messenger assigned to deliver a large sum of money to the next town. Convincing the driver that Mexican bandits were aware of this and that they would surely hold up the stage, he offered to take the money on horseback himself. When the Mexicans attempt their robbery, there is nothing for them on the stage, but neither was there any thing for the sheriff waiting in the town. Realizing that he has been tricked, the sheriff mounts a posse and when they capture Tom, he manages to convinces them that he is really his brother Steve, on his way to see his sick sweetheart. The sympathetic sheriff soon discovers that he had been a real simp, and that all the money was lost because of his stupidity. It didn't take much more than throwing in the fear of a few Mexicans bandits back to then to accomplish ones purpose.] **MPW:11.25.16, p1219.**

[711] **A SISTER OF SIX**, Triangle: [According to this writer, when California was making its transition from Mexican territory to Statehood in the United States during the 1860's, it was still filled with Hispanic intrigue and conspiracy. Don Francisco Garcia was not satisfied with the vast holdings he possessed; he coveted Caleb Winthrop's land which was contiguous to his and had the added attraction of rich mine deposits. In league with a North American engineer, the Don did in Amos, Caleb's brother, as he was trying to warn him of the plot. Prudence, the dead man's daughter had six sisters to care for and only Uncle Caleb back east, but Amos's chief vaquero loved the little lady and offered his protection until Caleb came to California to continue the war and fight for his property. Don Francisco, upset over this development, hires the ever present band of Mexican bandits to attack the ranch by force. The Puritan Anglos hold their own, but it is left to a very small contingent of United States Calvary to effect the rescue. With Garcia jailed, Prudence gets to play with Sepulveda, the vaquero, while Uncle Caleb watched the nieces frolic with fun in the warm California sun.] **MPW:11.4.16, p758.**

[712] **SOMEWHERE IN GRENADA**, Pathe: [This was the fifth episode of the energetic Miss Pearl White's serial, **Pearl of the Army**,

which pitted her against the "Silent Menace" now operating in and on the Mexican border. It was only natural that her many scripters should have her do her part at this time of her nation's great need. The "plucky girl" is thrown from her horse, nearly drowned and taken prisoner by the evil intentioned captors, all of this action in about sixteen minutes. But true to her form, she did not allow the treacherous lechers to have their way with her.] **MPW**:12.30.16, p1972.

[713] **SOMEWHERE IN MEXICO**, Unity Sales Corp: [Another of the many developing cartoon characters who frequently reflected current consciousness on political or topical events Tweedledum was a rotund, inept buffoon who seemed able to accomplish what the more sleek and skilled could not. In this episode he decides to do his patriotic duty and enlists to help capture Villa. He was immediately an impossible soldier, unable to adjust to authority and command, especially when a pretty girl approached. His only ally was fortune. When he disobeys orders, preferring "to go for a smoke," he chooses as his hiding place an ammunition dump which has many Mexicans guarding it. When he carelessly throws away the remains of his cigar, all of the enemy are blown to bits. Rewarded for his accomplishment, he is immediately promoted to General. Have any of our more recent Anglo superheros seen this one?] **MPW**:12.16.16, p1657, 12.23.16, p1839.

[714] **SPANISH COSTUMES AND DANCES**, Pathe Exchange, Inc: [What most North Americans considered the everyday in Spain, this brief documentary pictured a gay celebration which displayed the national costumes and dances of that festive nation, set against the background and gardens of its largest cities.] **MPW**: 12.30.16, p2013.

[715] **STARS AND STRIPES IN MEXICO**, Powers: [The following review captures well the national consciousness, the aggressive spirit and demand for swift retaliation and the anger generated over having been violated by those who most North Americans, considered racially inferior: "The scenes in this release show, first of all, the American army making ready to go after the notorious bandit Villa after his raid ... in which many American civilians and soldiers lost their lives ... the houses where Villa slaughtered sleeping Americans ... where Uncle Sam's troops made their stand against Villa's bandits. There follow views of the ignorant young halfbreeds treacherous and vicious, who supported Villa in his murderous campaign. These young bandits will be tried before Judge Rodgers in New Mexico." Other scenes of a "girl ranger" who equipped herself as well as any of the troops, troop trains, an automobile truck hospital corps, American aeroplanes "spying out" the country side and dropping bombs "on the fleeing Villistas beneath" are also shown. The final scenes show the 10th Negro Calvary, "just spoiling for a fight" hot in pursuit. Sadly, some of these brave soldiers will be the first casualties of this action, not at the hands of Villa, but in a real Mexican stand off provoked by angry

nationals who did not want foreign troops in their town.] **MPW**:5.13.16, p1215.

[716] **THE TAINT OF FEAR**, Universal: [Another story of rediscovered manhood in the face of the Mexican invader. As a boy, young Bob had the spirit beaten out of him by his father. In an attempt to please his parent, he joins the National Guard, unaware that on July 13, 1916, the day President Wilson would order the brave boys to the border to capture Lopes, the bandit leader. Bob, and his none too sensitive friend, now find themselves in the Mexican desert, which proves too much for the spiritless coward. But when he realizes that his company is threatened with annihilation, he rediscovers his manhood. Although mortally wounded, the new found hero rides for the rescue. The last scene pictures "his ghostly shade" appearing before his grief stricken parents, as the father laments his misplaced brutality, too late to make amends.] **MPW**:12.16.16, pp1691-92.

[717] **THE TARANTULA**, Vitagraph: ["No matter how long the payment is deferred, the wages of sin are death." With this moralism as a theme the scripters compelled a northern rake to ruin a young Cuban beauty, abandon her to disgrace and return unscathed to his wife. After her Cuban family disowns her, the marked woman becomes a successful entertainer eventually going to New York to perform. In the nitery where she performs the seducer drinks himself into a drunken stupor providing the Cuban girl with the opportunity to place a tarantula [a Latin woman's weapon] in his open hand. Her honor satisfied, she now returns home to marry her faithful lover, Antonio Moreno and is welcomed back into the family. Some few times, Latin women were allowed to achieve their revenge against Anglo men [409].] **V**:7.21.16.

[718] **UNCLE SAM'S DEFENDERS**, Mutual: [As the serials gained in popularity in 1916, Mutual took advantage of both the general feeling expressed by the nation for the need for preparedness and the Mexican problem by issuing this production. The first number could have been used as an advertisement for recruiting prospective National Guardsmen. It described the fun of camp life at Plattsburg, New York. The second entry was entitled, "Our Boys at the Border," but in reality could have been shot anywhere. It demonstrated the familiarity or lack there of, that the regular army and national guardsman had with their equipment. Some very general scenes of the border were included, as an added encouragement and to provide the title.] **MPW**:12.23.16, p1856.

[719] **THE UNEXPECTED**, Rex: [This one certainly sent mixed messages to the audience, but played on their collective conception of our neighbors to the south. In a scene not necessarily near the border, Mary decides to go for a walk, but is warned that there may be Mexican bandits about, after all, they were everywhere. Chancing onto what she assumes is an abandoned shack she enters to investigate only to discover that there is a Mexican right behind her. He is quickly joined by others, none of which can speak English. She speaks

no Spanish and the wild gesticulations of the darkskinned men serve only to frighten her. When she realizes that there is dynamite in the boxes, she tries to escape, but is prevented from doings so by the men who scuffle with her. Fearing a fate worse than death, or at least being killed, she sees through the keyhole the intimidating men light the fuse to a stick of dynamite. Frantic, she sends her dog for rescue. He gathers her friends, their friends and some soldiers who happened to be visiting and all rush to the camp only to discover that the Mexican foreman of the mine site laughing at them. There had been no evil intent, the Mexicans were merely at work and had placed the little lady in the cabin for her own safety. Exactly the same situation had been used in 1911's, **Mexican As It Is Spoken** [173], save that the threatened character who lacked the facility of Spanish, had been an Englishman.] **MPW**:4.29.16, p853.

[720] **U.S. MARINES UNDER FIRE IN HAITI**, Tropical Film Company: [President Wilson is known to most young students of North American History by certain catch phrases, not the least of which is, "the selfdetermination of nations". The paradox is that in his attempt to institutionalize democracy south of the border, he more than any other chief executive, was responsible for intervening in the affairs of the Latin American republics. He did so with majority support from the citizens of this nation. Sponsored by the American Defense Society, who aggressively lobbied for "preparedness", this film was shown to an "enthusiastic audience" of supporters. It featured black men gathering coconuts and bananas, but more importantly, it awakened the audience to "a more profound respect" for the navy men [mainly southern Marines], and to the "new interpretation of the Monroe Doctrine, which the present war forced" upon the United States. "The efficient manner in which our Marines" demonstrated their skills as "artilleryman, infantrymen and cavalrymen" when actually engaged against rebel Haitians, made "more clearly the meaning of the new interpretation." These early films helped provide visual proof to audiences of the necessity for such armed intervention and continued occupation.] **MPW**:5.13.16, p1179.

[721] **VAMPIRE**, Gaumont-Mutual: [This "supersensational" "photo-novel", a serial, featured the rich, but evil Santanas, exiled from Spain, now leader of "the Vampires" the arch criminals of Paris, and his opponent, Moreno, "the lone bandit," who had "brought about the death of the Grand Vampire." Spaniards, good and bad fought for supremacy across the roof tops of Paris, under starlit skies in this one.] **MPW**:12.23.16, p1824.

[722] **VILLA-DEAD OR ALIVE**, Eagle Film Mfg: [This was the earliest release prompted by Villa's raid. It was advertised also as a plea for preparedness: "Villa-Dead or Alive ... That's what President Wilson said and that's what we are going to do. Is the United States Prepared? GO AND SEE Uncle Sam's Troops in action. SEE your flag cross the border to punish those who have insulted it." As it turned out the photographer that Eagle sent to Mexico to film the raid first

sent back "inferior" material for which the company apologized and promised better.] **MPW**:4.1.16, p149.

[723] **WAR-RIDDEN MEXICO**, Rex: [This was another good example of simply trying to capitalize on the Villa raid. Most of this film had little or nothing to do with the actual events, but were merely semirelated clips, all of which had been previously exhibited and put together to exploit the new situation. It boasted of "views of the fighting going on in Chihuahua between Carranza, Obregon and Villa," and some pictures of American troops now and as they were "several years ago." "The bridge at Columbus," after Villa's raid was included to tie it all in.] **MPW**:7.29.16, p838.

[724] **WATCHFUL WAITING**, Gaumont: [Until President Wilson landed the bluejackets in Vera Cruz in 1914, possibly no other phrase caused so much unhappiness among citizens who wanted Mexico invaded and punished for its behavior. Wilson had waited two years to take action against Huerta, but he reacted immediately to Villa's raid. This little film was produced before Villa crossed over, but proved prophetic and timely, after he did. "An amusing cartoon comedy in which Uncle Sam is represented dreaming in blissful ignorance until a few unpleasant probes from the Mexican side, and from Germany arouses him to exasperation."] **MPW**:4.22.16, p647.

[725] **THE WEDDING GUEST**, Bison: [Panchita Garcia, "the flower of the town" loved by all who knew her, lived in a community that could boast of having, "the squarest sheriff alive." But, lurking in this pleasant setting there was also, "Bad Pedro", a local who one day tried to force his affections on the beautiful señorita. The sheriff who had just come from Pedro's wife to which he had given money so that she might feed her starving children, of course, intercedes. Panchita, is saved and she drops her shawl, which, the now smitten sheriff keeps as a love token. A week later, Jose Del Barra, "a handsome Mexican" is caught stealing cattle and is forced to take refuge with his woman, "Faro Mamie. Wait, it gets better. With the Stephen, who's cattle were stolen, the square sheriff, attacks Mamie's roulette parlor. Stephen shoots her, Jose shoots him and in a fight with the sheriff, the toothy bandit bites him on the head which gives him amnesia. He forgets all except Panchita. A year later he still "worships at her shrine", but otherwise wanders about in a daze. Then, one evening he finds four others there attending services. Jose happens by at the same time and the sheriff sees Panchita fall into Jose's arms. Somehow Jose has acquired the sacred shawl, and when the sheriff sees that, everything is clear, he regains his memory and there are bodies all around. Blood runs hot in Latin veins, but Anglo scripters more often made them pay the price for their passion.] **MPW**:5.27.16, p1569.

[726] **THE YAQUI**, Bluebird: [John Kenneth Turner's **Barbarous Mexico**, first published in 1910, exposed the horrors of the Yaqui transportation [the colonial periods 'mita'] to Quintana Roo on the Yucatan peninsula where these proud fighters were

sold into slavery. Dane Coolidge dramatized the practice in his **The Land of Broken Promises**, which featured the separation of two lovers. In the book's film adaptation the evil and sadistic General Martinez was responsible for the death of Tambor's wife and his entire tribe's being sold to the Yuca plantations of the penal colony. Such action always proved to be a death sentence. Later, Tambor escapes and leads a revolution against the corrupt Mexican official. **MPW** expressed pleasure that the story of the brutal maltreatment of this "down-trodden race" was brought to the screen. Although all of the major characters were Anglos, "genuine natives were judiciously employed" to provide proper atmosphere. It was a beginning.] **MPW**:3.4.16, p1498, 3.18.16, p1847. **V**:3.10.16.

[727] **THE YAQUI CUR**, Biograph: [An attempt to take advantage of the popularity of the above, this reissue of the 1912 D. W. Griffith film, was considered by exhibitors, "well worth reissuing."] **MPW**:6.24.16, p2261.

[728] **ZOO ARRIVALS FROM SOUTH AMERICA**, Rex: [It came from south of the border, featuring the great, giant ground sloth, his friend the toothless anteater and the most ferocious of jungle hunters, the jaguar. And indicative of a general attitude: "Another strange creature coming from South America is the Matamata, a hideous but amusing turtle, which attains enormous size and is provided with a head which is so grisly that it must have been designed to frighten it's enemies to death."] **MPW**:4.15.16, p502.

1917

[729] **ALONG THE RIO GRANDE**, Pathe-Combitone: [A travelogue tour from El Paso de Norte following the river boundary "to the Elephant Bute Dam illustrating its use for irrigation purposes."] **MPW**:6.16.17, p1772.

[730] **THE AMERICAN CONSUL**, Lasky/Paramount: [Attempting to further his own political ambitions, a sleazy senatorial candidate convinces a true blue and honest, old Indiana lawyer, to support his candidacy. After sometime and pressure, the new Senator finally pays off by appointing the gentleman to a diplomatic position in a small Central American republic. There, with his delightful daughter, he attempts to serve his country with utmost honesty and dispatch, but is confronted by even worse corruption from both sides of the always present conflict between the "ins" and "outs." Both the local administration and the revolutionist's who are trying to overthrow the regime, have the consul, "backed against the wall." This scenario might well have been designed to describe the Central American situation of the late seventies and early eighties. Daily press reports then would indicate its timelessness. Of course the presence of the United States Marines was considered necessary and they arrive to save all concerned. After the boys have taken control, the daughter gets the young mining engineer who was attempting to develop the country's natural resources for the benefit of the native population with good ole North American know how.] **V**:2.16.17, **MPG**.

[731] **THE AMERICAN GIRL**, Kalem: [**THE TYRANT OF CHIRACAHUA** was a further adventure of the heroine, Madge King in her continuing problems with the revolutionist across the border. By this time, sympathy was rarely afforded the revolutionist. "Revolutionist" and "bandit" were almost universally used as interchangeable terms, certainly, on the screen this was the case and in the daily press it was reinforced. In this episode, considered by the reviewer as "one of the best of its type," the locale was Mexico, just south of California, an area "infested" with "politicos" whose only purpose was to increase their lot in life." Into this area wanders one of the King ranch cowpunchers who was warm for the Chiracahua Chiquita. Unbeknownst to him, she belongs to the local "jefe" and he is jealous enough to have Pete killed, stabbed of course, not in Mexico, but in the back on the King ranch. Angered by such lawlessness, the dad and the daughter start after Manuel the treacherous. Madge tries a little deception and disguises herself as a "greaser" lad, but fails to fool the jefe and all three wind up in Jail. Pedro, the sympathetically portrayed, sidekick, sometimes hero, had by this time been dropped from the series, and so it was left up to the father and the daring-do-American daughter to save themselves. They do, and in the process the "Tyrant and his lieutenant are captured." The two are then let loose on the

desert, where a righteous fate would deal with them properly. **MPW**:4.21.17, p446, 4.28.17, p673.

[732] **AMERICAN GIRL**: [THE FATE OF JUAN GARCIA, was the next installment of this action packed frequently on the border serial. In this one, the liberated and multitalented adventuress stumbles across a murder mystery. Having had her picture taken, one of her many talents inclued photography and being clever, she plans to develop the wet plate herself. But somehow, the plate she develops was not the one with her picture. The negative she has brought to light is one on which there is a dead man, actually one of her father's ranch hands. It is soon discovered that he was not that at all, but a Mexican spy, working for those bloody revolutionists and planning no good. In the final scene, it is discovered that he had been killed by the representative of an North American mining interest who was worried about his property in Mexico. Some parts of this episode may well have been taken from the front pages of the daily press.] **MPW**:3.17.17, p1759.

[733] **BETRAYED**, F: [A significant departure from the usual love triangle, this border tale attempts to present "the viewpoint ... wholly from the Mexican side." "There is nothing in it to excite a feeling of animosity between Americans and Mexicans." The villain in this effort is as vile to the Mexicans as he to the North Americans, but his señorita loves him anyway. Ms. Cooper, as the local lovely "does a good deal of satisfactory posing in her Mexican way, for while her nature must play at capriciousness, she really is true to her shiftless singing lover at the expense of both the blustering bandit and the young Americano." Apparently the Anglo lady had been well trained in the ways of a Mexican chiquita.] **MPW**:9.15.17, p1700.

[734] **BILL BRENNAN'S CLAIM**, Gold Seal: [The Anglo is a real heavy in this production, but he hires a Mexican to do his everyday dirty work, like kidnapping and threatening the poor miner's daughter, so that he can steal their newly found riches. As he does so, the Mexican ties the daughter up, binds her to the bed and does a great deal of toothy leering until the Wells Fargo man comes to the rescue.] **MPW**:5.5.17, p846.

[735] **THE BLACK MANTILLA**, U: [One might be tempted to look into this scripters life after reading his conception of how love affairs were conducted across the border. Marachita, "the Señorita Shrew," was also avaricious, cold blooded, beyond insensitive, a user and also very jealous. Not necessarily the girl next door, she was not satisfied with one or two lovers, she had four who craved her attention and more. Juan was one of them, a poor wood carver, he had to be satisfied with the images he made of her; yet, to him she was "a saint in disguise", apparently a very good disguise. Huanto, a "ruales", [sic] was more her meat, but Gueila, "daughter of a tortilla-maker," also had designs on the Mexican mounted policeman. The action in this film begins when Huanto gives Gueila's mother a black lace mantilla, he

was crazy for her tortilla's. As soon as he departs, the mother encourages her daughter to wear the pretty gift, thereby establishing her claim on the señor in everyone's eyes. When Marachita learns this, she is furious and picks poor, dumb, lovesick, Juan to avenge herself. If he would only buy her one better, she would tell all, she belonged to him. Forced to sell his soul for the woman he loves, he steals a valuable painting from the mission church planning merely to pawn it, and later, atone for his misdeed. But on his return, with the very gift the not so nice, Marachita has asked for, she has betrayed him by informing the town of what he has done. She has neglected to tell them why he stole the priceless painting. Enraged, the men of the town take action, and slay Juan just outside of town. He is discovered dead by Huanto, who leaves his body, but picks up the mantilla and the few coins Juan had intended to give the poor. The Mexican policeman now returns to Marachita, but she is disinterested in Juan's death. She is interested in the gift, so he gives her the new mantilla in exchange for a kiss. Watching this tender scene unfold is a vulture hovering above who is heard to exclaim that they are all "cursed." Huato leaves. Marachita enters the house. The writer may very well have been sent to a local asylum.] **MPW**:6.18.17, p1832.

[736] **THE BLOOD OF THE ARENA**, Cosmos-Kinema: [According to the reviewer, "a thoroughly Spanish Story." He continues by explaining that the title refers to the fact that for the spectators, the "blood spilled in the arena" even when it is the life blood of a popular hero, means "nothing." "Sand is sprinkled over it and the slaughter goes on." Vincente Balasco Ibanes, destined to have many of his works brought to the screen, authored this early version of **Blood and Sand** [897] It is in effect the same scenario that will be repeated more than a dozen times with only slight variation. It tells the life story of a toreador, his rise to the heights of popularity, his decline "and his ignominious death in the bull ring." It was assumed that because of the long shot employed in the fatal goring and its brevity, that it might have shown "an authentic killing." What is a significant departure here was the use of Spanish actors and "spanish character." Native dances were shown, one by "real Spanish gypsies at the fountain of Charles V." Everything in this film was Spanish, except the title cards. "The only thing that might be revolting to Americans is the thrusting of the fire darts into the neck of the bull in the last reel." Apparently, the reviewer felt that the "authentic killing" and the "blood in the arena which [made] a considerable puddle" could be handled by North American audiences.] **MPW**:6.23.17, p1953.

[737] **BOMBS AND BANDITS**, L-KO: [This seems a good example of how some writers with not much of a story, gave it increased substance by staging part of the action south of the border simply because it was assumed that a Mexican bandit would easily be accepted as the necessary villain. The middle aged mayor and police chief of a small town whose location could have been anywhere in the United States, are both interested in Dolly's affection. Each wages the other that he can win

her love and both wager $10,000 that they will be successful. For some reason they have Sammy, the secretary, hold the money while they set about their purpose. He immediately calls Dolly and tells her that he has won a large sum and will she go to Mexico with him? She agrees and they set off for the land of sunshine and fiesta unaware of the peril they face. In Mexico, it's been a "dull day for Ignats Tamelo and his bandits, ... no one has been either killed or tortured so far, since sunrise." The two Anglos prove an easy mark to Ignats and his men and once captured, they are placed in a room with moving walls that will eventually push the unfortunate pair to a fiery death, unless they are rescued. Looking for a little extra loot, the bandit gets a message to the Mayor that he is holding the lady and the lad for ransom, which reminds the two old fools that their money is probably with the faithless Sammy. In the final reel only Dolly is saved, Sammy is forced over the edge into the fire with the money. Not even the Production Code would have required that, but for some scripters, such punishment was considered to be everyday stuff south of the border.] **MPW**:7.14.17, p286.

[738] **THE BRIDGE OF FANCY**: K-E-S-E: [A society woman's daughter seeks status through marriage to a Spanish count, she admires his title and wants to be a countess. His rival, a North American captain, fights and defeats him in a duel, but the status seeking girl wants to marry him anyway. Her shallowness is repaid at the very last moment "With all the society of the nation present," the Spaniard is exposed as an imposter, not a count at all, he was in reality a criminal and so arrested. Her social climbing efforts stalled on the lower rungs, and without any suitors, Ester "squawks and screams."] **MPW**:8.18.17, p1124.

[739] **BUENOS AIRES**, Mutual-Gaumont: ["Mutual Tours Around the World", provided the audience with a beautiful and descriptive trip to South America's largest city in 1917. From a technical view point alone, photographing far away places at this point in time was no simple task, but the incidents of travel were certainly even more challenging. Some of the problems involved in being a Central and South American photographer were well described in a brief piece in the **Moving Picture World**, "Guetlein Brings Back Many Feet of Film". The hazards included the constant possibility of arrest, especially in those areas where North American occupation troops were patrolling and in Panama. Costa Rica offered assistance as did some of the other Central American republics, but apparently, filming in the West Indies and Cuba was difficult and resulted in arrest if official permission was not granted.] **MPW**:5.26.17, p1266, 6.30.17, p2154, 7.14.17, p257.

[740] **CADIZ, SPAIN**, Mutual-Gaumont: [Another part of "Mutual Tours Around the World", #29, featuring Cadiz, Spain's largest military port, "situated on the bay of Cadiz." This instructive travelogue provided views of that city's narrowest streets and the "ornamentation of palms" which adorned the grounds of Isabella Castle.] **MPW**:6.16.17, p1772.

[741] **CARMEN**, Cine: [Although this Carmen was filmed before those produced in 1915, it was not released for United States consumption until 1917 and previewed at that time by **Variety**. Their assessment was generally positive. They noted that despite all of the other diversions in the metropolitan area that day, "the race track and the beach" it was a bright sunny day, "the film was well attended." Especially pleased with the photography, which they stated "could not have been filmed in some rocky mountain region of the United States," their only criticism concern the title cards. They advised that if the producers hoped for success, that those would have to be changed "from the incomprehensible garble they presently existed in," to something more intelligible. If not, then an interpreter would have to accompany the showings. The cards for this Spanish production were in Spanish.] **V**:6.15.17.

[742] **CASEY'S BORDER RAID**, Bison: [It is doubtful that any of today's super hero's would object to any part of this scenario. Casey, basically a coward until his hormones became active, was on border patrol. One night on guard duty, he understandably mistakes a burro for the entire Mexican army and sounds the alarm. Ridiculed by his mates, he is forced to do all the camp's dirty work, while the other men spend their time admiring the Captains daughter. She promises her love to anyone that will bring back the blanket worn by the brave Mexican bandit, who is planning to attack the United States at any time. Some try, but all are beaten. The men now bribe the camp boob to go for the gold and he accepts. While they accompany the little lady on a picnic, he crosses the border. Meanwhile, the Mexicans have done the same and find the fort empty, so they steal the machine gun. Returning to camp, they find Casey has overpowered a guard, so they begin to abuse him, but make the mistake of trampling our lady's hankie which throws him into a fury resulting in his singlehandedly capturing all of them. Having done so, he ties them all up and make them drag the gun back to the fort. The Captain was pleased, the girl fell into Casey's arms, and the bandits were all placed in the guard house. More importantly, the United States was saved from invasion.] **MPW**:5.19.17, p1176.

[743] **THE COST OF HATRED**, Lasky: [Vengeance was not privy to Hispanics, frequently it afflicted Anglos if they lived in Mexico. Graves worked a lot and was frequently forced to leave his young wife and daughter unattended. Needing no more reason than neglect, the mother falls into an affair with the neighbor who has a son. Passion flares when the husband returns home a bit too early one evening and discovers the lovers. He attempts to kill them both. Thinking he has killed the man, he flees with the daughter to Mexico and in no time, he makes his fortune. After the lovers die of more natural causes, neither had been fatally wounded, their son ventures across the border and soon falls into the clutches of Graves who now ruled a vast estate and controlled the local "politicos". Still holding a serious grudge, the wounded husband convinces them to arrest the boy on trumped up charges. They of course do, and subsequently sell him into slavery on Graves' hacienda. This was just another day in

Mexico in the scripter's mind. Now the hapless boy is taunted and tortured, which apparently relieves Graves' pent up emotions. But his daughter can not stand the young man's suffering and so, falls in love with him. Helping him to escape, the two recross the border into safety leaving the father with his vengeance and grief of a different kind.] **MPW**:4.21.17, p495.

[744] **THE CRIMSON DOVE**, World Film, Corp: ["A complex tale of lost love, theft, suicide, lost position and a half-breed." What else can one expect when people refuse to keep the blood lines pure?] **MPW**:6.9.17, p1668.

[745] **THE DAUGHTER OF THE DON**, Feature Films: [Reviewers considered this "ten-reel" production seriously dated, one "that might have passed a half dozen years prior to the producers spending so much hard cash," in making it at that time. Set in Spanish California, prior to the United States take over, the action focused on the activities of a Mexican heroine, the "beautiful daughter of one of the Mexican Dons." There was the necessary handsome, young North American officer, but also, there was love for Mexico. When the señorita discovered his country's intentions, she felt forced to react. Dressing as a man, she becomes something of a Joan of Arc for her people, leading the attack on the intruders who would displace the Mexicans. Finally in the last reel, she realizes where her heart truly wanted to be, and gives up the struggle. Love frequently conquered national pride in Hollywood. With benefit of hindsight, it seems that the scripters had very little trouble convincing their Hispanic characters that being a North American was certainly better than being a Mexican. Swapping ones ancestral heritage for the opportunity of acquiring an association with an Anglo, was certainly considered worth the price by most of the writers until most recent times.] **MPW**:6.16.17, p1797.

[746] **EXILE**, Lasky: [The action in this drama takes place in a Portuguese colony where a young North American engineer is trying to bring a little light in the heart of darkness, or at least trying to "improve conditions in the lonely place." He is opposed by the "unscrupulous wretch" Peres, who has long oppressed the natives. In the end Peres is lynched by the locals and the Anglo saves his woman for himself. Sounds fair.] **MPW**:9.22.17, p1871.

[747] **THE FIGHTING GRINGO**, Red Feather: [Destined to have a long and successful career in both the silents and talkers Harry Carey, "experienced delineator of Western types" was selected to bring the character of Red Saunders, a popular hero of the "pulps", to the screen. On his way to Panama via steamer, Red meets a quarreling pair of lovers and befriends them. Once they arrive at the port of Caliente, the R. H. Davis like hero, finds employment as a foreman at a local finca. In time he is reacquainted with the couple, but not before he has quelled a local revolution and exposed the corruption and evil designs of some of the top governmental officials. Applauding the performance, the reviewer felt

that, "The general atmosphere of the Panama country [was] adequately suggested and the revolution scenes were well staged."] **MPW**:3.17.17, p1758, 3.31.17, p2131, 3.24.17, 1850.

[748] **FINE FEATHERS**, International: [A "split reel" divided between an educational feature on ostrich feather fans and a "funny cartoon" showing "Jerry on the Job" in uniform as a National Guardsman and his "trials and tribulations" in guarding the Mexican-American border.] **MPW**:9.1.17, p1390.

[749] **A FIVE FOOT RULER**, Victor: [The popular character of Beau Brummel, wealthy in dollars and everything else, was an early film idol every little boy of any age wanted to be. Sent by the writers to many different locals to exude his charm, in this film, he was attending college and invited to all the best parties, all the time. At one of these he chanced to meet a South American beauty named Argo. Liberated for her time, as many film heroines were, she resisted "the constraints placed on young females by the faculty", and elected to go walking by herself. Of course she runs into trouble. Beau comes to the rescue, but is reprimanded by the authorities and reported to his parents for fighting. Desiring to make a man of him, the father tells him that he must make his own way, before he can be reinstated to family graces. So, Beau hops a steamer for South America where he happens to encounter Argo's father in the very city where the lovely lived. Luckily for the daughter's dad, Beau was there to save him also, this time from a mob of angry insurrectionists. When Argo, who has returned home, tells that he has performed the same service for her, Beau is made "prime minister." Meanwhile, Beau's father just happens to be visiting, again, the very same city and is surprised, even impressed that his son has achieved such a high position. With everyone happy and the nation secure, the lad and lady were then allowed to "follow in the way of youth--and romance." It was really a very simple time.] **MPW**:8.25.17, p1262.

[750] **THE FOURTH IN SALVADOR**, Broadway Star Feature/Vitagraph: [For a few months of his life, O'Henry managed to live in Central America. This stint furnished him with the material for this condescending satire of what he considered a typical Latin American revolution. This "rollicking story of a tea-cup revolution" demonstrates what can happen when "a small, but exuberant party of Americans bent on celebrating the Forth" can accomplish. One of the characters runs an ice concession in the republic and is forced to palm off a block of glass as ice, because he has run out of the cooling substance. Of course the stupid natives would never know the difference. Faced with bankruptcy, he still plans a celebration which coincides with a revolution that is just breaking out aimed at overthrowing the government. It fails, but a defeated rebel general manages to escape. He looks to the North Americans for protection and when the regular army comes for him, "our lads give a good account of themselves" by thrashing the army. To solidify things, they now instate the general as president. He rewards the group by declaring that the substituted glass was really ice, thereby saving the

company for the grateful gringos. What do you do with this if you are sitting in the audience in 1917? Enjoy it, one assumes.] **MPW**:12.29.17, p1969, 1.5.18, P137, 2.2.18, p689.

[751] **THE GHOST OF OLD MORRO**, Edison: [A very definite departure from the usual border tale, this melodrama was set in Cuba, with Morro castle as its focus. The story tells of how a cigar smoking witch comes to haunt the battlements of the old Spanish fortress on a nightly basis, when the moon is high. It all began when the disreputable Mother Morro was running an inn for smugglers and taking thirty percent off the top for protection from the customs official. The captain in charge of customs was a flirtatious American who looked the other way because Morro continued to bring him a steady supply of girls to debauch. In an attempt to eliminate the middle woman, there being little honor among thieves anywhere, the smugglers go to a local convent and abduct Mercedes, who the captain covets, without knowing that she is Morro's daughter. When the mother discovers that he has had his way with her, she orders him dead, but the smugglers place the body of the girl in a bag and deliver her to the woman instead. Thinking she is going to kill the captain, she throws the sac from the fortress, only to discover that she had killed her own daughter instead. Driven mad by the deed, she joins the girl in her watery grave. Now a vengeful spirit, she begins her nightly haunts. Another reviewer found a lot to criticize in this film. He objected to the required Cuban cock fight scene, the cutting out of the man's tongue so that he would not betray the conspiracy, and a "detestable comic monk" who danced while Mercedes played and worse, let her leave the convent for her nightly debauchery, for the price of a kiss. He warned the exhibitors that this film could be shown along with one that had "ennobling" characters, but as a single, it would certainly be disturbing to the audience. Under no circumstances should it be shown to children. He had no problem with the Hispanic characterizations, it was accepted that such things went on, even in Cuba under United States administration.] **MPW**:7.7.17, p79, p136.

[752] **THE GUN FIGHTER**, Triangle-Kay Bee: [By this time William S. Hart had "legions of fans" and with this production he certainly increased their number. Here Hart plays "the Killer", leader of a band of baddies operating on the border. But nearby, across little more than a rather damp spot in the river, there lived worse badmen who sometimes crosses the Rio Grande to maraud. Unable to do anything themselves, the local authorities are faced with sending some bad men after worse ones in hopes that all will be killed. Most are, but not before Hart embellishes the action with a little love interest for a darkskinned lady.] **V**:2.23.17.

[753] **HEART OF TEXAS RYAN**, F: [Not the lead in this tale of treacherous Mexicans who take him captive, Tom Mix was saved by a lady who pays the ransom that the dirty "greasers" ask for his release. His performance and that of the Anglo's playing the Hispanics in this five reel saga of the west, helped promote his career.] **V**:2.23.17. The **Texas Monthly**

devoted its July 1991 issue to films dealing with Texas and it's history on film. Some of the articles mention the problem of negative Mexican stereotyping, one by **Larry L. King**, **"HOLLYWOOD, TX"**, included a reference to this film.]

[754] **HIS MILITARY FIGURE**, Paramount/ Kleaver/Komedy: [An early drawing room farce in which the father of an attractive young lady wants her to marry a man of iron, a military man. The traditional two suitors are employed, Tom and Vic. The colonel does not think the former military enough, so he selects Vic. The problem is that Vic's "chile con carne" cousin, who especially likes him, was arriving on the S. S. Brazilian the day before the wedding. Tom is sent to fetch her, but learns that the ship has been quarantined. This provides him with the opportunity to embarrass his rival and at a party given to prove to the old soldier that Vic was made of the right stuff, Tom appears as a "Spanish dancer," which astounds everyone. When Vic tries to end the dance, Tom feels the "ironing board" [apparently well hidden] that Vic has been using to give him that erect look. Still intent on his purpose, Tom, with a stiletto stabs, as any Spaniard would, even one from Brazil, Vic in the back of the board. But all for naught, with the wig torn from his head, Tom is exposed as a bad loser and driven from the premises.] **MPW:4.7.17, p163. LCFL: Victor Moore Collection, Clippings, Halftones.**

[755] **IN MONKEY LAND**, Powers: [This short subject featured, "The saki of Brasil [sic] an extremely rare monkey, clad like an Eskimo." Yet, remembering where it comes from, "The tiny Brazilian marmoset has a savage countenance." **MPW:8.4.17, p843.**

[756] **JACK AND JILL**, Morosco/P: [After killing his opponent by accident in the boxing ring, Jack Ranney goes west to redeem himself. He does by saving the old ranch for the folks from an attack by the rampaging Mexican bandits. He dose so, singlehandedly, of course. All three members of the Cabrillo family, as well as the Mexican marauders were played by Anglos.] **MPG**.

[757] **THE JAGUAR'S CLAWS**, Lasky/P: [Actors from the world over began flocking to Hollywood by this time to seek their fortunes, it had become the acknowledged film capital of the world and would remain that way throughout most of the century. One recent immigrant was the great Japanese star, Sessue Hayakawa, whose career would span decades. Apparently still unable to find a Mexican actor suitable enough to play the leading role of a Mexican bandit, the producers considered Hayakawa close enough. In this film he played the bandit, El Jaguar, leader of rebels who harassed North American oil companies and also the lecher who lusted after several Anglo wives. Having been thrashed for looking with longing eyes at one of the Anglo beauties, he plotted his revenge which involved kidnapping three North American ladies and one husband. To intensify his treacherous character, the scripter made the poor Anglo choose which one of the ladies would be saved and which one would suffer a fate worse than. In the

final reel, the Anglo hero, having escaped, brings the Texas Rangers across the border just in time to save the wife from killing herself before the foul deed could be done. El Jaguar is stabbed by another of the stolen brides, and his woman seeing this, stabs herself. With all of the Hispanics disposed of the Anglos could then resume pumping oil and possibly look into the advisability of opening a cutlery concession.] **MPW**:6.16.17, p1840, 6.1.17, p1799, 6.23.17, p1955, **V**:6.8.17.

[758] **LISBON, PORTUGAL**, Mutual-Gaumont: [Mutual Tours Around the World #23 pictured the Capital of Portugal, built on a series of terraces of low hills backed by the Cintra mountains. "Beautiful scenes of the Tagus river, the garden of Dom Luis and the Rua Aurea, the street for gold buyers" were also provided.] **MPW**:5.5.17, p786.

[759] **THE LIVING BOOK OF NATURE**, Educational Films Corp: [Two episodes provided views of the wild dogs of Brazil and Argentina and in the Andes, the vicunas, llamas and the alpaca. "Their grotesque forms cause them to look more like animated caricatures than wild animals." One wonders why such a harsh description was given of such cute furry little animals.] **MPW**:6.9.17, p1666, 8.11.17, p991.

[760] **THE MAN WHO WAS AFRAID**, Essanay: [More than a year after the Villa raid, Hollywood was still capitalizing on the sentiment it had mobilized in the national consciousness. With the serious possibility that the United States would now enter the world conflagration, preparedness was on everyone's mind. If Villa's raid had done nothing else, it had, for those honest enough to admit it, indicated how truly defenseless even our second most secure border had been against foreign attack. Reviewers indicated the change in attitude: "This production is most timely, now that we are in the midst of martial preparations, with the national patriotism at a high pitch. The story has to do with the preparations recently made to protect our southern border against murdering marauders from Mexico, and the mustering of Nation Guard forces for the front." This film was one more which showed how effective the border was in transforming a "mollycoddled" coward into a vibrant hero who taking the one chance out of ten he was afforded to save his company at the risk of his own life, does so willingly after the heat, Mexico and the love of an honest woman, encourage him to do so. All this and the staged battles between the Mexicans and North Americans, exhibitors promised would provide "a thrill and a realism [to] excite the hearts of every American."] **MPW**:7.14.17, p253.

[761] **THE MAN WITHOUT A COUNTRY**, Frohman Amusement: [The first filming of the Edward Everett Hale story based on the Burr conspiracy which had visions of creating a great empire to the southwest of the United States. The new Republic would have included a significant portion of Mexican territory, stretching from Texas to California [1131].] **MPW**:8.18.17, p1090.

[762] **MARTINIQUE, WEST INDIES**, Mutual-Gaumont: [Another part of "Mutual Tours Around the World", #29 providing views of the town of St. Pierre before and after the destructive explosion of 1902 which took the lives of 40,000 inhabitants and was instrumental in shifting public opinion away from volcano riddled Nicaragua, to Panama, as the route for the new interoceanic canal. This short subject of the greatest cataclysm to have ever struck the hemisphere was one of the most popular presentations of 1917.] **MPW**:6.16.17, p1772.

[763] **PEARL OF THE ARMY**, Pathe: [Episode #8, **INTERNATIONAL DIPLOMACY**. The ever increasing significance and importance of the Panama Canal made it a prime target for Hollywood's scripters. This chapter in what was possibly the most popular serial of the time was primarily concerned with the evil designs of "Bolero" and his "Boleroista" who were forever attempting to acquire the plans of the Panama Canal so that they could destroy it for the foreign powers that wished it put out of commission. Pearl, up to her usual heroics, was more than a match for the Panamanian saboteurs and foreign bosses. "Pearl Preserves the Panama Canal for the World's Prosperity," would have been a more accurate description and title, and more alliterative also.] **MPW**:1.20.17. p355, 1.27.17, p588.

[764] **THE PERILOUS LEAP**, Gold Seal: [The first recognized drug smugglers who traveled back and forth across the Rio Grande were the Chinese. The drug then was opium, to be smoked on either side of the border, in dens, where people reclined on their sides hence the term, 'Hippies.' This melodrama has Mexicans, halfbreeds and the Chinese running the fruit of the poppy into Texas from the headquarters of the operation across the border in Mexico. Nothing much has changed in seventy-five years. If they could only have closed that border, the poor unfortunates of the middle and upper class addiction, would have been spared the ravages of the evil weed.] **MPW**:9.15.17, p1742.

[765] **PERILS OF THE SECRET SERVICE**, Imp: [Episode #5, **THE MAN IN THE TRUNK**, Capitalizing on the success of the serials in general and those with Hispanic foes in particular, this chapter of the Secret Service in operation focuses on an evil Mexican governor, Diego Rey, and his attempt to gain the secret of the new noiseless machine gun. [You had to be able to believe back then.] Having captured one of the North American agents, Huntley, Diego has him held in cuffs dangling from a wall, while his confederates tirelessly tried to torture the secret out of him. They were fools to even try, he kept the only copy of the secret weapon locked in his mind and would have died before divulging the information. To save him his woman, Cissy, and his partner bring a troop of dancers across the border, knowing full well that such bait would entice the warmblooded governor. Cissy, volunteered to play the lead and once alone with him, "she renders him unconscious by the use of ethyl chloride" and then, one assumes, spirits him into the United States where he is later exchanged for the

captured lover. It was that simple for Hollywood, sometimes.]
MPW:4.7.17, p117, p155.

[766] **THE PLANTER**, Mutual: [In some instances the lack of even general information about Mexico, Central America or South America could result in the creation of bizarre scenarios. If the writers location for this rubber plantation had been accurate, it might well have provoked a full scale intervention and continued occupation by this nation in either, 1914 or 1916. The ad copy for this film reads: "A tale of love, adventure and fight [sic] in the rubber jungles of Southern Mexico--A realistic exposition of life in the tropics of America and a romance laden with big moments." One should not really blame the scenarist for this silly fun, in as much as this "strange, exotic story of the tropics" considered to have displayed a "forceful screen delineation," was based on a novel written Herman Whitaker. It starred, Tyrone Power, [senior] looking for rubber trees on the Isthmus of Tuhuantepec.] **MPW**:11.12.17, p916.

[767] **PUEBLOS OF SOUTHWESTERN UNITED STATES**, Selig: [Selig World Library #1: "The Spanish name "Pueblo" was applied by the conquistadors to native communities ... in New Mexico [in this region alone] "they found 45 tribes speaking nine different languages. The Pubelo of Isleta, largest of Tancan Pueblos ... [is] located on the banks of the Rio Grande near Albuquerque. Among Rio Grande Pueblos there has been no progress owing to slow but sure Mexicanization." Hollywood's message here needs no elaboration. Well, maybe just a word or so, if you wanted to keep your indians more backward than they already were, send them to Mexico, where 'progress' was an unknown word. Too harsh?] **MPW**:8.11.17, p986.

[768] **REX BEACH ON THE SPANISH MAIN**: [Shown at the Rialto for record prices to a capacity house every day for eight weeks, this unique travelogue shot in Costa Rica, Nicaragua and Honduras, included what may have been the first total eclipse of the sun, "the first and only moving picture of the total eclipse of the sun." The film also included "the government lottery at San Jose, the native coffee and sugar industry, and many "shots" of strange tropical customs little known to the people of the north." The title may have been only slightly confusing to some of the geographers in the audience expecting to see other territories, but that was Hollywood and exploitation was certainly more important than exactness. Costa Rica was close.] **MPW**:4.7.17, p130.

[769] **SHORTY LAYS A JUNGLE GHOST**, Monogram: [Along with Republic Studios, Monogram would produce the majority of serials in the days of the talkers. This early silent entry was #14 of Shorty's adventures which finds him in the Philippines looking for a spy that is working to have the islands taken out of North American control, surely a general concern among movie going audiences. Deep in the jungle and into his adventure, he also captures the "ghost" who was operating out of the undergrowth and killing natives indiscriminately. The spy was eventually discovered to be

related to the jungle spirit and also put out of commission. Shorty was just slightly less effective than Pearl, but audiences at the local metroplex were pleased to have both protecting the empire in Atlantic and Pacific alike.] **MPW**:4.28.17, p640.

[770] **THE SLAVE MARKET**, Famous Players: [**Variety** panned this production because of its "flavor of piking." They felt it was a cheap production. Using only six or seven pirates and a small crowd in the slave market, was not enough to create the proper atmosphere. But there seemed nothing wrong with the good guy Englishmen taking and burning the Spanish ship. This was the Spanish Main where the Spain was fair game, even their little maidens taken captive, could be sold in slave markets. The comments are not meant to be really snide, but should serve to indicate that no reviewer or any in the audience at this time, would ever question the fact that Englishmen could with all justification, take Spanish treasure, ships, towns and women. They became England's enemy in the 16th century and continued to be so, especially in Hollywood, until most recent times. This traditional attitude was little different in Roman Polanski's, **Pirates**, 1986, although it must be admitted that the Anglo star was no Errol Flynn.] **V**:1.5.17.

[771] **VILLA OF THE MOVIES**, Mack Sennett: [Most of the film producers tried to cash in on the border problems the United States had with the "Scourge of Chihuahua." As the intensity of the problem passed and the possibility of more serious overseas conflict became clear, there was time to parody the proverbial 'tempest in a tequila cup.' Few could have done it better than Sennett and his troopers. Peggy and Bob run a boarding house on the border. Slim tries to get chummy with Peg and Bob gets jealous, ordering the other to leave. He does, but somehow immediately becomes a smuggler. Practical as he is, Bob remembers that he has failed to collect Slim's rent and goes after it. Slim, about to be discovered a gunpowder smuggler, convinces the fool to take the stores across the border for him. Bob is arrested, but soon becomes an officer in Villa's army. Slim protests and has the other placed before the wall to be shot. Peggy is captured by Villa. She escapes and brings the troopers and you know ... It was time to put Villa to rest as a formidable foe. His rehabilitation as a folk hero according to Hollywood would be the subject of numerous features in subsequent decades.] **MPW**:3.17.17, p1828.

[772] **THE WOMAN GOD FORGOT**, Lasky/Artcraft: [Considered by **Variety**, a "truly epic production," the set included an entire Aztec city created with a temple, over two hundred feet high as a center piece. One of the big scenes involved a staircase built up the side of a mountain which was considered by itself, "worth the price of admission," to say nothing of seeing Geraldine Farrar at least, partially dishabille. The critical reviews which appeared in that journal were pleased with everything but the director, Cecil B. DeMille's, battle scenes. **MPW**, at that time, in reality as much an agent for promoting all films as it was a news journal, could not

restrain its superlatives. It had only glowing praise for this epic of Spanish conquest, "a gigantic spectacle, produced upon a scale of magnificence," "of extraordinary interest ... presenting a number of historical facts." That the conquest involved both Spaniards and Aztecs was true, but the facts more or less ended with that. Even in this historical time frame, 1519, it was impossible for the scripter not to have one of the early Mexican ladies betray her people for love. Miss Farrar played Tecza, supposed to be the daughter Montezuma, but her skin was a "resplendent white," while the others of her tribe, both male and female, were noticeably of a darker hue. In the story she falls for one of Cortez's chief lieutenants, Alvarado [Walter Reid] and according to Hollywood's history, was responsible for opening the gates of the city to him thereby allowing her father to be taken captive and killed. In reality Cortez was welcomed cautiously into the city. No matter, the writers needed to make our heroine a Joan of Aztecs who led the opposition against the oppressor, once she realized the consequences of what she had done. The super production also included the necessary human sacrifice sequence, with Alvarado on the bloody stone, waiting to have his heart cut out of his body with an obsidian blade and offered up to the gods, but that could not be allowed, considering that Cortez will appoint him a provincial governor after the completion of the Conquest. The film correctly portrayed the native reaction to the horse, which the locals had never seen and which proved to be a significant reason for Cortez's success despite the fact that there were but nineteen of them. Interestingly enough, more would be brought from Spain during the colonial occupation, and those healthy little caballo's would procreate enough progeny as they moved north, to provide the flickers with all the horseflesh they would ever need for the countless westerns that would be produced.]
MPW:11.3.17, p722, 10.20.17, p334, 414, **V**:11.2.17, **NYT**:10.29.17.

1918

[773] **ANTIGUA**, Post: [This travelogue featured, "for those that did not know" a beautiful little island in "a cluster of the British West Indies" with "unusual historic and scenic attractions". It was explained that Admiral Nelson had once refitted his ships in one of the island paradise's beautiful bays. And according to the film maker, the "idle dockyards" he had had constructed were still there to be seen. Throughout the century, these incredibly beautiful islands would always be paradise for those who visited, but quite something else for the locals. Film for public exhibition almost always emphasized the former.] **NYT**:7.28.18.

[774] **ARIZONA**, Artcraft: [Apparently the athletic abilities and comedic skills of Douglas Fairbanks, as the young North American Lieutenant Benton, were able to save both the Hispanic Estrella and this motion picture from the evil designs of her insidious countrymen. All of his reviewers indicated that any other actor would have taken the role too seriously. He made it fun, and his mates followed suit. Although the star, Estrella, was played by a light skinned Irish lady, Kathleen Kirkham, her foil, Lena, was Marguerite de la Motte, who would provide Hispanic characterizations in a few other silents. All other Mexican characters were played by Anglo actors and actresses including the energetic Marjorie Daw, as Bonita, whose skill with the weapons and agility impressed the fair Douglas.] **MPW**:4.12.19, p241, **V**:12.20.18, **NYT**:12.15/16.18, **MPG**.

[775] **BEAUTY IN CHAINS**, U: [This Universal subject adapted from a novel by B. Perez Glados, set in a small Spanish town, Orbajosa, concerns the problems created when a prearranged marriage between cousins at birth, runs into difficulties. For Rosarito, it was love at first sight when she saw her handsome Pepe Rey, but his unintentional remarks about the bucolic nature of her small town offend the provincial inlaws to be. No worry, it all works out. More interesting was an awareness displayed by the reviewer for the characterizations. The two Anglo's who portrayed the Spanish lovers did so in an "entirely acceptable way", despite the fact that the hero "looked more like a young American than a Spanish gentleman."] **MPW**:3.23.18, p1704.

[776] **THE BIRD OF PREY**, F: [Adele Durant's lover facing disgrace kills himself in her presence. His friend blames her and threatens to implicate the lady less she do his bidding. For her punishment, she agrees to be taken to a remote part of Mexico where she finds herself installed in a disreputable dance hall as one of the ladies. Dissatisfied with her plight, she becomes one of the leaders of a band of bandits who plan to kill the American owner of a Mexican mine. Concerned for her countryman, she warns him, but her rival bandit leader, Pedro, has followed and he threatens to kill

the wife and daughter unless Adele gives herself willingly to him. She agrees, and manages to hold off the fate worse than death until the very man who brought her to this iniquity rescues her. Satisfied that she has paid her debt with selfsacrifice, they leave the land of danger for the north, arm in arm. It was suggested to exhibitors that they advertise the film with the following phrase: "American Girl Leads Mexican Outlaws on Tour of Vengeance" or "Thrilling Story of Mexican Bandit Queen."] **MPW**: 8.17.18, p1019.

[777] **BORDER LEGION**, Goldwyn: [This story of "hard fighting and desperate riding [set in] romantic California in the gold mad days of '49", [when all men refused to eat quiche,] was one of the first of many Zane Grey contributions to the silver screen. In a California predominately Mexican, with a golden prize to conquer, men would do anything to achieve their ambitions. The main characters in this adaptation were Anglos, the Hispanics merely provide the atmosphere for the action, some of which **Variety** questioned. They apparently did not believe that the heroine could become enamored with the bandit that had actually killed her father. So much for their knowledge of Hispanics, but in fairness, they may well have been unaware that passion runs high anywhere there are Hispanics involved. Well, at least according to Hollywood. Remakes: [1023, 1379]] **MPW**: Volume XXXVII, p171, **V**:8.2.18.

[778] **BORDER RAIDERS**, Pathe: ["Ever since the civil war started in Mexico the border has been a hot bed of trouble for United States officials." So begins the tale of Ranch owner Hardy, father of Rose, who goes into town for supplies, but ends up being seduced by an adventurous faro dealer named Cleo, part of the Mock Sing gang of rustlers and dope smugglers. Just another average Hollywood day in town. Now married to dad, the new mistress of the ranch begins to dispose of everyone. When even the husband disappears, Rose, his daughter goes to the faro parlor looking for the "Chinaman." The plucky girl wanted answers, but he was protected by various toughs including Emanuel Riggs, the Mex half-breed, who was the most dastardly of all. Mock Sing beats out Riggs for the pleasure of attacking Rose, but is killed by one of his Anglo dealers. Everything now rights itself, the "Chinaman" is dead, the Mexican is vanquished, Hardy is found and the Ranch is returned to Rose. **Variety**'s only problem was with Mock, they felt he was not portrayed in an evil enough manner, but Emanuel was "sufficiently villainous." **MPW**'s suggested ad copy was, "Cattle Rustling, Opium-Smuggling and Gun Toting Furnishes Basis of Exciting Border Play." [853]] **MPW**:10.5.18, p122, p129, **FD**: 9.22.18, **V**:10.4.18.

[779] **THE BORDER WIRELESS**, Triangle: [Almost always a fugitive looking for some reason to reform and become the real good guy he inherently was, W. S. Hart unwittingly took a page from the famed Zimmermann Telegram in this vehicle as his patriotic reason to give up the bad life. Wanted in many states as a fugitive, he makes his way to the Tex/Mex border and there saves his lady from a tequila drinking Mexican. Learning that

Feature Film List 1918 209

war has been declared, he is refused permission to enlist in active service because of his background. Luckily his liberated lady is a wireless expert and together they uncover a German spy operation which is funneling secret messages from the German embassy in Washington to Mexico and onto Germany thereafter. Using his manly man techniques he begins to break up the operation, but the girl has to bring the troops to save the day. In the final sequence, Hart is shown marching off to war as his woman waits on the sidelines promising to be there when he returns. Gone are the days. The film was promoted with: "Big Bill Hart Handles Hun Spies" on the Mexican Border.] **MPW**:10.12.18, p274, 10.19.18, p451, **V**:10.11.18, **NYT**:9.29.18.

[780] **CACTUS CRANDAL**, Triangle: [When Bob Crandall finds five hundred head missing he crosses over the Rio Grande to find them. Instead, he finds a lady in distress being kept prisoner in a cantina by the rustlers who also have trumped up charges against her father. Bob seeks help from a Texas Ranger friend and working together they free both father and daughter who are taken north to Bob's ranch. Not to be denied his intent, Mendoza the bandit, follows and once more takes the girl. This time Bob simply kills the bandit, he also finds his cows, but is not sorry "for what might have been a useless adventure." So much for "Wild Life on Mexican Border Made More Vivid by Reckless Adventurer."] **MPW**:8.17.18, p1024.

[781] **CAVANAUGH OF RANGERS**, Vitagraph: [Hamlin Garland wrote the original story for this film and probably supplied the title cards for it also. In the Western genre it is axiomatic that sheep and cattle cannot coexist, in reality that is nonsense, but as a plot scenario it remained a standard from that time to this. More significant to this work's purpose was that in the war that develops between the promoters of the two different quadrupeds, a "greaser" is shot accidently. Where once that might have been discounted as more than likely a necessity, the shooter was at this time arrested and jailed.] **V**:2.22.18.

[782] **THE CHANGING WOMAN**, Vitagraph: [The mysterious influence of the high Andes on the prima donna of a touring opera company, provides the basis for this adaptation of still another O'Henry short story. "The subtle danger and the vast solitudes of the mountains" influence the aspiring diva in a negative way. She misses the applause of the great crowds when performing in Macuto where the company is nearly stranded. There was also, a young North American who falls in love with the star and when she is captured by the savage "Carabobo Indians," he is grateful for the chance to rescue her. She is pleased, but what gives her real satisfaction is be in front of her "admiring South American" slaves. Momentarily, the "danger and the strangeness of her surroundings change Nina", she becomes serious minded and favors Johnny. Yet the lure of the grease paint and the applause of the audience provide too much competition. She craves too much the "homage" and adulation of the crowd. The mountains must be left behind, in the end their magnitude

dwarfs her existence. She must also leave the man who loves her, and so she does.] **MPW**: 8.13.18, p1303-4, **V**:8.16.18

[783] **COL. THEODORE ROOSEVELT'S EXPEDITION IN THE WILD**, Luis Reis Distributor: [The vast majority of North Americans experienced their first visual perceptions of South American wonders through film, the first images were stills, but when the flickers became movies the horizons were bound only by the timidity of the cameraman. From the very first film, the vast diversity of flora and fauna, the incredible majesty of the Andean mountains, and the mysteries of the Amazon, may have made some feel that life up north was some what mundane. It was a 'robust' age for some at least, the more well to do or the adventurous, a time when manly men were men of action, action that often involved killing off the more exotic members of the 'lower' species. Many of these early films provide the historian with the visual record of the beginnings of the wholesale slaughter of the great cats and other "dangerous" animals not found back home. Film did much to create and popularize the mystique of danger, the mythology of man alone against the beast. It justified the action. It need not be said that there was little equality involved when one had a Springfield that could shoot a hole an inch wide through an elephant. Enough of pontificating, this particular chronicle of slaughter has the former President, survivor of the "River of Doubt" [now named for him] shooting a variety of jaguars and alligators. It was certainly not as bloody as the films of his African expedition where in one 'orgy of blood lust' he and his son shot more than 240 elephants, lions, cheetahs, antelope/gazelles and other creatures for the reading and viewing enjoyment of public. The pluses for this production include possibly the first pictures of various tribes and customs never seen before inhabiting the Brazilian boundaries of Paraguay and others from the southern Amazonas. The film could be rented for exhibition in schools and was promoted as such.] **MPW**:6.29.18, p1833, **NYT**:6.10.18. A detailed description of the expedition and South American slaughter can be found in: **Rev. J. A. Zahm, THROUGH SOUTH AMERICA'S SOUTHLAND**, D. Appleton: New York, 1916.

[784] **A DAUGHTER OF THE SOUTH**, P: [A tale of southern plantation life, a faithless lover, creole women and a Hispanic foil, Pedro de Cordoba, who appears merely as window dressing, a pretty boy to be used and then rejected by the sweet southern belle who has little more to do than play at making her real man jealous.] **V**:10.18.18.

[785] **THE DISMISSAL OF SILVER PHIL**, General Film Co: [From the leering look in the lecherous Mexican's eyes as he gleams his toothfull smile toward the helpless little Anglo lady, one need not wonder if his intention were pure. It was seriously obvious that he wanted to press his brown skin against her lily white one, which certainly could not be allowed on the silver screen at that point in time.] **MPW**:6.22.18, p1663.

[786] **THE GHOST OF THE RANCHO**, Pathe: [A wealthy father is disillusioned with his son's lack of concern for work and

threatens to disown him unless he changes his ways. The prodigal promises that he will, if he is allowed just one more party. At this gala affair, a friend is shot and the boy suspects the Mexican dancer. Trailing her to the Mexican border [from somewhere up north] he discovers that she has travelled there on an errand of mercy for her dying mother, but there are complications. Another Mexican loves her despite the fact that she loathes him. Angered, he kidnaps and takes her to a deserted Hacienda. When they arrive the scoundrel is displeased to discover that there is an old hermit living amidst the ruins of the once great house, so he kills him. Soon he is joined by a bandit friend and together they plan to keep her there. Meanwhile, all this time, our Anglo hero had been watching and observing, waiting for his chance to act. The killing provides him with his chance. "Knowing of the Mexican superstition" he poses as the dead hermit. Of course the dumb Mexicans run in two different directions when they see the spirit. Killing is one thing, but ghosts were apparently quite another. The clever lad now released the girl and the two head back north to safety. When dad discovers his little Anglo is a hero, he reinstates him.]
V:8.2.18.

[787] **GUNS AND GREASERS:** [This film is significant because it is the last Hollywood feature that uses "Greaser" in its the title. It was one more version of gun running on the border with some not so nice Mexicans in charge of the business.]

[788] **HEADIN SOUTH**, Artcraft: [In an attempt to find more active scenarios for what was one of Hollywood's most athletic stars, the scripters sent Douglas Fairbanks south of the border seeking adventure with Spanish Joe and his gang of bandits. Joe was a "border bandit" and a "thorn in the flesh of all good citizens" on both sides of the Rio Grande. "Headin South" Fairbanks, put brains into "Joe's badness" and operation, but a dispute over the pretty señorita brought a violent end to the partnership. With some justification, one might consider this to be film the very early beginnings of the "Good Bad Man" genre, an anti hero who makes his own personal distinction between good and evil and never betrays his honor by violating this conception. As a bandit, "Doug" was a perfect gentleman. Advertisers offered this film as a "dizzy debauch of daring deeds and startling stunts."]
MPW:3.2.18, p1272, 3.16.18, p1557.

[789] **HEART OF THE SUNSET**, Goldwyn: [Rex Beach author of the "Spoilers," wrote and produced this story in which "real humans do real human deeds." Alaire Austin, who owned ranches on both sides of the Rio Grande, was saddled with a dissolute husband "whose fancy ran free among the native Mexican women." "Left free to her own devices", she fell for a local law man, Dave Law. All might have ended there had not the lustful desires of a Mexican rebel chief, Longorio, who aspired to be Mexico's president, interfered with the affair. To lure the lady across border, the bandit stole some of her cattle and when she followed after them, he captured her. Having killed her husband in the raid, the way is clear for marriage, but

the lady says, "no," with significant emphasis. When Law pursued the bandit who had his lady, he was taken prisoner and ordered to be killed along with his love. The two are momentarily spared by a passing padre who appears to have been something of a political pundit. He explains to the rebel chief that these, call them executions, would look bad, and could interfere with the bandit's plans to become Mexico's chief executive. Longorio then plots to have the killings look like the work of "peons", but help arrives in time to save the lovers. Law who had worried that he might have inherited a touch of insanity, discovers that he was in fact, adopted, clearing the way for happiness ever after. In reality, it may have been the screen writer who was afflicted.] **MPW**:4.6.18, p35, 4.13.18, p185, 4.20.18, p435. **V**:7.12.18.

[790] **HOUSE OF HATE**, Pathe: (Serial, 20 episodes) [Pearl White, the recognized queen of all the Hollywood "Dauntless Damsels in Distress", required little help to extricate herself from the complications the scripters created for her on a weekly basis, but there was usually a man in there trying anyway. In this series, considered by many her best and most successful, Antonio Moreno's Latin allure was used to make a little more of a lady out of the athletic and capable female. Few of her leading men ever registered with the audience, but Moreno made the difference. There was electricity in her eyes when he was around, audiences saw the heroine more as a dynamic woman than a female version of Douglas Fairbanks. The serial was so successful that Pathe tried very hard to have Antonio continue to make a real woman out of the little lady, but he refused. He knew he could have his share in feature films which is what he wanted to do, and he did.]

[791] **THE ISLAND OF CUBA**, General Films: [Part of the Harold H. Horton series of "Travel Impressions" provides a "clear and interesting idea of modern Cuba." North American occupation of Caribbean countries always did one thing at least for the locals, it cleaned and scrubbed the 'dirty little beggars' till they shined, or so official reports would always claim. This film provided the living proof of Uncle Sam's boys as Mr. Clean's advance guard. The photographer "doesn't forget to draw attention to the cleanliness of the streets of Havana against the filthy conditions which prevailed in some parts of the city previous to Colonel Waring's regime." The high points of tourist interest were also pictured for the audience that could not afford such a sea cruise: Morro Castle, Plaza Emperado, the Casa de Bonifaci, narrow streets, and ornate balconies were all shown.] **MPW**: 7.27.18, p546.

[792] **I WANT TO FORGET**, F: [Varda Deering, "a butterfly [who] lives only for the joy and gaiety life can bring" meets John Long who effects a sense of higher purpose in her. When he is called to Mexico on a diplomatic mission, she seems to return to her old ways. But that proves to be mere deception, in reality she was also working as a spy attempting to uncover by the use of her body, "placing her honor at risk," the very same German plot John was working on. When John returned and

thinks she has fallen back to old ways, he was naturally dejected, but all turns to happiness when he discovers that she has killed the Hun he thought she was sleeping with, defending not only herself, but her country as well. It made no difference to him that she and not he had uncovered the secret plot.] **MPW**:12.14.18, p1252.

[793] **THE KAISER**, Jewel Productions: [An interesting and accurate foreshadowing of what would be considered a very serious problem, in World War II times, by the administration and specifically, Nelson Rockefeller, who chaired the Office of the Coordinator of Inter American Affairs. The showing of this anti-German production was protested in 1917 by a vocal group of pro-German Cubans. The controversy arose when the exhibitor had a sign made which read: "The Kaiser, The Beast of Berlin," certainly not unpartisan, but considering that Cuba declared war on Germany, quite significantly, the day after the United States did, it was not unreasonable to assume that antiGerman propaganda might be shown in Havana moving picture houses. The controversy actually reached the office of President Menocal, who promised an investigation as to who in his government had ordered the sign removed. Although there would be no armed combat south of the border during WWII, a major struggle would take place between the propaganda ministries of both combatants, and the ammunition employed would be film. At this time, the United States dominated the world production of moving picture film, the German industry was still developing and even if they had produced for export to the Americas similar propaganda, it certainly could not have been exhibited in what was still essentially, a United States colony.] **MPW**:6.8.18, p1441.

[794] **KEITH OF THE BORDER**, Triangle: ["Jack Keith, a Texas Ranger has been assigned the task of running down the Border Wolves," who have terrorized all on both sides of the Rio Grande. To stop him the bandit gang implicated him in their murders and he is almost lynched, but escapes, "breaks jail", brings in the baddies, and manages to also rescue the "maiden in distress". "She proves to be a "mascot", for he not only wins her sister for his wife, but also brings the treacherous lobos to justice.] **MPW**:2.23.18, p1142.

[795] **THE KID IS CLEVER**, F: [To satisfy the cravings of his adventurous son, Kirk White's father arranges a sea voyage with a motion picture company that guarantees to make the trip a thrill a minute, and put everything on film besides. Problems arise when the company fails to make it on board and some real South American revolutionists do. Keith considers their activities great fun and thinks his floating Hollywood set is filled with great adventure, until he is struck down by the insidious, Ramon Cortez, leader of the band of bandits. Waking up in a Mexican "dungeon," he knows what he must do. He escapes, saves his future wife, puts down the bandits, and tells dad he never wants any more adventure "than running the family business." It was real simple back then.] **MPW**:4.6.18, p133. [A slightly different version appears under the title: **THE KID IS KLEVER**, [Same story, the scene is Rio de Janeiro,

and its a Brazilian bandit named, Jabbzando who is the heavy.]
MPW:7.13.18, p247.

[796] **LESS THAN KIN**, P: [Wallace Reid starred in this implausible bit of impersonation. It would seem that Wallace had been a bad boy back in the big apple, there he was wanted by the authorities. Unable to return he was hiding out and "languishing in" either South or Central America, the reviewer could not make up it's mind. (It might have been a woman. A little be of screen stereotyping there.) In time, Wally comes to make his own world out of that Central American banana republic until one day he chanced to meet his double. The tourist looked so much like him he thought he was looking in a mirror. When fortune intervened and the new friend was killed, what else could the homesick lad do but leave his Hispanic exile for home. After a lot of trouble, it all works out, strangely enough.] **V**:7.26.18.

[797] **LIGHT OF WESTERN STARS**, United Picture Theaters of America: [Zane Grey's novel brought to the screen for the first time in 1918 would be remade again in 1925, 1930 and 1940. The story concerns a "reckless cowboy" who brags that he will marry the first girl that steps off the incoming train. When the unsuspecting miss does, he forces a local Hispanic padre, at gun point, to do just that and then discovers that she is the sister of his boss. The boss thinks he's "plucky," and saves him from the aggressive sheriff. Forced to defend his bride's good name against the sheriff's insults, he crosses the border and is captured by a bad group of Mexican bandits who plan to kill him. His rescue is effected by his lady who now knows that how much he really loves her. This film would be remade three more times. One reviewer claimed that this "production was a masterly one, which display[ed] correctness of development and [gave] a truthful portrayal of the Mexican border."] **MPW**:11.2.18, p624, 10.26.18, p544.

[798] **THE MAN ABOVE THE LAW**, Triangle: [Whenever **Variety** had the opportunity to use the term "Greaser" in its reviews, it did so, describing any one who even lived close to the Mexican border as such. In this story an eastern gentleman, apparently unlucky in love and on the outs with the law, moves to the New Mexico border and opens a trading post where he sells "Pain Killer" to the locals, "half-indian, half-greaser." Although he does not drink the stuff himself, he does indulge his passion with one of the local breeds, which in **Variety**'s view, makes him a "squawman." This activity eventually produces at least one little female half or quarter breed. When sometime later a missionary/teacher comes to bring light to the semidark reaches of empire, the remnants of his eastern character surface and he decides that his daughter should attend school. His regeneration has dramatic results, he destroys his stores of rum and heads back north with his "family" to seek salvation. The locals were left not thirsting for religion, but for a new supply of fire water.] **MPW**:1.12.18, p241, 1.19.18, p412, **V**:1.4.18, **MPG**.

[799] **THE MAN FROM MEXICO**, FP: [Originally issued in 1914 [468] and presently offered by Daniel Frohamn, this farce starring John Barrymore was reissued to exhibitors as "a delightful comedy filled with laughter-provoking situations." It was the same film shown four years prior to this date. **MPW**:11.23.18, p858.

[800] **A MAN'S MAN**, Paralta: [John Webster, a mining engineer, who has made a fortune in Death Valley and is traveling by train to Denver, saves a pretty señorita from the advances of a low born lout. She immediately is taken with her savior and is pleased to discover that they were both going to Sobrante in Central America, one assumes after a few train transfers. But on the way there, John develops ptomaine poisoning and is hospitalized. Meanwhile, Dolores's father has been killed by the ever present local revolutionaries who have "taken power at the point of their guns." Fortune was still with Dolores for during the upheaval, she meets Billy, John's partner, who is smitten immediately, not by the flying bullets, but her beauty. Yet, it was not meant to be. Once John is freed from the hospital, he takes immediate action with ease and Yankee know how. Having saved the daughter, he now must do the same for her motherland. In rapid order, he rids the nation of the usurpers, places the lady's brother in the Presidency and accepts the love she could not give his partner. A good day's work for any Anglo. The film was advertised as: "The Radiant-Teeming-Rattling-Exuberant Story of an American Superman--who has the right ideas about friendship and love" and proves it south of the border. An updated version of this film featuring the Anglo super soldier of fortune solving South American problems will be produced in 1929 [990].] **MPW**:1.12.18, p276, **V**:1.18.18.]

[801] **MEXICO TO-DAY**, Educational Films Corporation of America: [This film represents a new beginning in altering the North American conception of it's neighbor to the south. In the two years prior to its being shown, Mexico had been presented as the enemy, filled with hate for the gringo and a constant threat to those who lived on the border. **Variety** was pleased with this production and pointed out that there had been, discounting those of the Pershing expedition, "fewer motion pictures taken inside the borders of Mexico than in countries like China and Japan." For that reason this film took on a significance which could not be attached to any other series of travel pictures. "The Motion Picture Educator" in **Moving Picture World**, was equally pleased with "at last [being] permitted to learn something of Mexico as she really is." Twelve reels were taken and five shown to date: "The Heart of Mexico," "Mexico's Floating Gardens," "Pulque the National Drink of Mexico," "The Most Useful Plant in the World" and "Necaxa, the Power Plant of Mexico." Pleased as they may have been, they could not avoid an ingrained condescension by noting how nice it was to discover that "there [were] at least a few Mexicans who are not lazy," in the sequence that showed how Mexico City was supplied with fresh vegetables every day. One of the most valuable reels, "Mexico, Historic and architectural" gave most viewers their first views of the

Pyramid of the Sun, in mass, largest such structure in the world. Over all these reels presented the North American public with a more human view of Mexican life and helped dispel the projected myth that all who lived across the Rio Grande were bandits. Schools soon came to realize the film's value and many employed it in their classrooms. It was a beginning [1624].] **MPW**:6.29.18, p1832,_9.7.18, p1416, p1440, 9.28.18, p1920, 10.5.18, p90. **V**:6.14.18 **NYT**:6.10.18.

Another positive sign of recovery was that the silver screen was staging its own quick comeback all along the border and within Mexico itself. "With Mexico finally eliminated from the first page of the metropolitan dailies as the home of banditry, revolutions, murder and sudden death the attention of the film men and exhibitors of the Southwest has been turned to the land of the Aztecs as an almost virgin field for unlimited business. Mexican exhibitors are coming more and more to Texas and a good trans-border trade is being rapidly built up with the advent of stable conditions." That trade would continue to increase down to this day.] **MPW**:7.27.18, p527.

[802] **M'LISS**, Artcraft: [Entered here only as an example of the totally gratuitous use of the Mexican character whose national background was completely unessential to the story's development. A baddie who wants to take over another's property had him killed by an assassin named "Mexican Joe." Played by Monte Blue, a future star of the silents, and the talkers, the necessity, of having a Mexican kill the individual was required only by the writers attempt to capitalize on the public's acceptance of the Hispanic character as sinister.] **MPW**:5.18.18, p1043.

[803] **THE MOMENT OF VICTORY**, General Film Program: [Frequently Hollywood's rejected lovers were driven south of the border to find solace or a new direction in life. This screen adaptation of O'Henry's work told the tale of a young man rejected by the object of his infection/affection who went south and proved himself by capturing a Spanish General single-handedly in the war that freed Cuba from imperial control. Having been made a captain for his heroism, "he return[ed home] and scorn[ed] she who would not be his sweetheart."] **MPW**:3.16.18, p1559.

[804] **ONLY ROAD**, Metro: [Viola Dana, "the poor persecuted child of pictures," starred in this tale of a poor abused little Mexican girl whose father, Manuel Lopez, would "never forgive her" for returning home without his daily supply of "the liquor he craved." Nita thought that all her problems were solved when the local sheriff fell in like with her. But not so. Elated with his affection she danced her Spanish number on the table of a cantina inhabited by a lot of sleazy, appreciative Mexican types, one of which, Pedro Lupo, dared to "press his foul cigarette stained mouth down upon her lips." She "chagrined" him by filling his face with a plate full of crackers, but he swore vengeance. After Pedro had tried to kill her a number of times, a lot more stuff happens, which makes her the heiress of the land that Pedro's father covets.

As foul a Mexican as was his son, he goes after her and is forced to take her captive, but she would not deal. When he learns in the last reel, after having abused the little lady, that there was no way he could get the property, he sells the information of her whereabouts for a few pesos, to those who would save her, and Pedro Lupo runs away.] **Viola Dan, Scrapbook**: Lincoln Center Film Library, Volume 100, pp125-7.

[805] **PEG OF THE PIRATES**, F: [Considered by all the reviewers one of the very worst motion pictures of 1918 in terms of its lack of production values and overall appearance, this is cited merely because of it supposed location, the pirate infested, rum drinking, Spanish Main where Peggy Hyland was apparently no Maureen O'Hara, even as the newly liberated lady, she proved to be no match against the dirty Hispanic, male pirate.] **V**:5.31.18.

[806] **PERU**, Kleine-Lincoln and Parker: ["A splendidly pictured and comprehensive scenic" view of that South American country "with it's rugged coasts, live progressive cities and interesting people." Natives were also shown, but apparently some of them were just visitors in as much as they included, a "Camel, [shown grazing along with] llamas and vicunas."] **MPW**:3.16.18, p1559.

[807] **REVELATION**, Metro: [Few phrases evince more exotic imagery, the possibility of adventure and the intriguing unknown, in the heart of the romantic and bohemian in spirit, and just generally any North American tourist, than the "Latin Quarter." There, anything can happen and usually does. Already established on the silver screen by this time, this presentation starred the incredible Nazimova who models for the American in Paris dressed as a "Bacchante preforming a mad dance," and generally vamping anyone that lays eyes on her. Her Apache number was a "wow," but sadly, she was reformed by a Madonna of the monastery and forced to give up her life of "gaiety and ease" and devote it instead "to one of self-sacrifice, serving others."] **MPW**:3.9.18, p1408.

[808] **RIMROCK JONES**, P: [Rimrock finds a valuable mine. It is stolen. His friend, a Mexican, Juan Soto, along with the aid of his lady friend, helps him recover it. It proves to be a very rich claim. He rewards them both. The reviewer for this classic, thought that the Anglo who played Juan, did a "corking bit of character portrayal."] **MPW**:2.2.18, p686.

[809] **SHAME**, Duplex: [One reviewer felt that there was a message to this film: "There are no illegitimate children any more. That word should be expunged forever." Basically a "plea to make the world safe for children," the Hispanics in the cast were incidental to the film's overall theme. Boy meets girl and they cannot wait to consummate their love. The Spanish American war separates them, and when the lady goes to Cuba to find her man, sadly, she discovers he has been shot. Returning home she tells all, only to be ostracized from the family. Dying at childbirth, the remainder of the story

describes the horrible plight the nameless child was forced to endure.] **MPW**:5.18.18, p1043.

[810] **THE SHE DEVIL**, F: [The original "vamp", Theda Bara, was the lady who could make men to do anything. She loves a French artist, but manages to have some lovesick fool, a Spanish brigand steal money enough for her wedding present. After the ceremony, it apparently occurs to him that he might have been used. Just as the two newlyweds were happily on their way to Spain, he decides to act and follows the two. Once there the bandit captures both of them, but the sexy lady proves too much for this dimwit once more. The lover's escape the sunny climes leaving the bandido scratching his head and wondering what happened to his Latin charm.] **MPW**:10.19.18, p449.

[811] **THE SHERIFF**, P: [Fatty Arbuckle's star was ascending when he filmed this comedy, it would soon turn into a tragic nova, but here he demonstrated what he could really do, which included rough riding and athletic stunts the fair Douglas would have been proud of. He also tried his hand at love which impressed the reviewer enough to say: "His love scenes with a Mexican belle are models of fervent passion, and it is not his fault if any ... chose to laugh."] **MPW**:11.16.18, p759.

[812] **SUCH A LITTLE PIRATE**, Lasky: [The ad copy read: "Thrilling Story of pirates Bold and Buried Treasures." Patricia was the granddaughter of an old salt whose "ancestors flew the Jolly Roger on the Spanish Main." She attempts to do the same. With her true love, she finds the buried Spanish gold. Apparently she was more successful than **Peg of the Pirates** [805].] **MPW**: 10.19.18, p450.

[813] **A SUN KISSED ISLE**, Post Ravel: [Scenes of empire were always very popular. This travelogue took "the spectator through Uncle Sam's island of Porto Rico."] **MPW**:8.24.18, p1135.

[814] **THIEVES GOLD**: U: [When Curt Simons, a highwayman by trade, is caught by "Mexicans intercepting one of the shipments of money which is being smuggled into Mexico to aid the revolution", he is sentenced to death. He escapes by killing one of his guards and crosses north where he comes across Cheyenne Harry [Carey] who runs the Savage ranch for the little lady and her father. Curt convinces Cheyenne that there's money to be made across the border and so he leaves his position, but by chance, later, in Agua Prieta, he is provided with the opportunity to save his former boss and daughter. Now in romantic and revolutionary Mexico together, the two fall in love, but he has to take care of a little unfinished business before he can return back home to her. He does and they do.] **MPW**:3.23.18, p1709, 3.30.18, p1864.

[815] **UNDER THE YOKE**, F: [The "vamp" herself, Theda Bara, chose to step out of character momentarily for William Fox's production depicting "a brief episode in the North American occupation of the Philippines." Aside from the "thrilling

scenes" of US troopers battling native "insurectors", there was included for the price of admission, a love story between a young army officer and a sympathetically portrayed local Spanish señorita. She was described as having all the "salient qualities of Carmen," but much more on the sweet side. Theda, having played the role before, knew that she was a woman who "loved with no regrets," deep passion and would not be denied. As had come to be the custom in the Hispanic reaches of Hollywood, her grandee padre wanted her to wed another, a rich Spanish planter, but she refused, choosing the fair skin and blond hair of the non-native North American. Her suitor, obviously angered, apparently does what comes most naturally in Hispanic lands, he foments a revolution so that he might capture her. He does, but he has failed to take into account the equally romantic disposition of the occupying troops, they come to the rescue, cavalry and all and give the two lovers to one another forever to be one.] **MPW**:6.1.18, p1309.

[816] **UNTAMED**, Triangle: [This film certainly must have reinforced what many north of the Rio Grande Americans felt about Mexican treachery. Jim Jason, white man, is good enough to give, Don Felipe Arrello, with a darker skin, the opportunity to share in the running of a border ranch. Don Felipe is left in charge which pleases him, but what makes him real happy is the survivors clause. If either was to die, the other would inherit all. It's too much for the Mexican's avarice to resist. Being in the occasion of sin, he gives in to it, and plots to kill all members of the family to ensure his inheritance. His plan for murder is foiled by an ancient love who discovers it and brings "the recreant Don to justice." The honorable Jim now profits by the Mexican's plan. A suggested 'ballyhoo', a promotional stunt, for the exhibitors was that they should obtain a copy of a similar clause, and have it reproduced on a large display asking, "With such a clause as that, what could come of a partnership between a Mexican and a white man?" [1361]] **MPW**:9.7.18, p1462.

[817] **WHEN A MAN RIDES ALONE**, American Pathe: [This "crammed with action" western told the story of love, romance and adventure on the Mexican border. There, William Russell, as William Sykes, the chief of the Texas Rangers protecting the Pecos Division territory, was known as Capt. Bonfire to those who would break the law. Those who were forever doing that in his sector were Mexicans and one day, they manage to wound him severely. So hurt he cannot defend himself, the border bandits take him back to their nest where the "Vulture" was the top bird. He decides that the lovely Beatriz should nurse him back to perfect health so that the entire group of killers can really start with a full deck when they begin to torture him to death. Certainly a nice balanced reflection on the Mexican character, a little good, a little bad. What the Vulture had, of course, not counted on was that old Bonfire kindles a flame in the señorita nurse's heart and he is more than willing to add fresh fuel to it. So when the moment arrives to start the fun filled party featuring all manner and form of mayhem, the receptive nurse hides him out. But a jealous, Rudolpho has been watching all and when he rats on

the lady it really ruffles the big guy's feathers. He now orders her kept captive so that she can watch her father being killed. Nice guys this bunch of Mex's. But right on time, the writer delivers old Bonfire and the boys, who without hesitation, have crossed over the Rio Grande to effect the rescue. There was no time to get permission from the state department and besides, with right written on your side, there are no rules.] **Exhibitors Herald and Motography**, Volume 8, p28.

[818] **THE WINDING TRAIL**, Metro: [Apparently the trail led back east for the lady and to a slight regeneration for the Mexican bandit, Waldo. Although he had been softened somewhat by the woman he had captured, he continued in his evil ways because another of her kind had betrayed him, an understandable rational to many in the audience. Enlisting the help of his capturee, Audrey, he discovers they are both looking for the same seducer. In time she brings him the man who wronged his wife. With a flair for the dramatic the Mexican places a gun in his faithless spouse's hand and orders her to shoot the one she does not love. Sometimes Hollywood left it to fate to decide when Latin blood ran hot with passion and vengeance. Not surprisingly the errant wife shoots the seducer, but pride was at issue, Waldo, not devoid of gratitude, sets her free and sends her away. The other lady heads east shaking her head at "such goings on." Reviewers felt that some of the dramatic moments helped to overcome the more "unpleasant points of the story," but after all it was set on the Mexican border. They also raved over "Audrey, Viola Dana's performance, especially because of her "ability as a Spanish Dancer" in the cantina scene."] **MPW:2.2.18, p685**.

[819] **WITHIN THE CUP**, Paralta: [From the Latin Quarter in Paris to New York's city's version, in Greenwich Village, that hot bed of passion, love and lust offered many opportunities for the regeneration of fallen women. This was just one of those thousands of stories that might well have served to prevent just one poor misguided soul from walking into that occasion of sin. But then again, it may have served as an advertisement for, what some might consider, such pleasant debauchery. Whichever, simply designating it as a "latin" offered a mysterious allure, and possibly, a license to be different than one was forced to be by the pressures of every day society.] **MPW:3.23.18, p1702, p1706**.

[820] **WOLVES OF THE BORDER**, Triangle: [When a gang of cattle rustling "greasers" operating on the border steal one too many cows, a local rancher organizes a bunch of the boys to wipe the "greasers" right off the range.] **V:5.17.18**.

[821] **WOMAN AND THE LAW**, F: [Jack La Salle marries and brings home a South American heiress and for a time they are happy, but when "little Jack" comes into their lives, big Jack goes bad and "brings the happy family to near ruin." He should have stayed in his own back yard.] **MPW:3.23.18, p1709**.

1919

[822] **THE ARIZONA CAT CLAW**, World: [By this date, the viewing audience, having experienced the horrors of the World conflagration, needed something more than a Mexican bandit to excite it's fears. In what **Variety** considers a weak offering, those legendary "poverty row" studios still continued to employ the silver screen first racially prescribed villain. Here he was found battling the newly [legally] liberated woman. What was "hand to hand" combat with a Mexican in comparison with the battle fields of the European theater that had earned for all females equality before the law? Many of Hollywood's women had already been among the most brave. For some in the audience the Mexican of the Western genre was necessary, but for others **Variety** claimed, there was "little to command wholesome interest." They felt that the "Western" would need more than a lot of cowboys in a shootemup and a "bad, wicked Mexican bandit" who merely rustles cattle, to maintain audience interest. The war had removed some layers of innocence that would never be replaced. But two dimensional characterizations, good and badguys, would never ever leave those scripters hiding in the Hollywood hills, it was too easy to play on North American xenophobic fears, they would always lurking be there just below a thin surface of respectable security.] **V**:11.21.19, **MPG**.

[823] **DESERT GOLD**, B. B. Hampton/Pathe: [In 1919, it was difficult to keep Zane Grey novels on the shelves, few of his contemporaries matched his popularity. In the western genre, more of his stories have reached the silver screen than any other North American novelist. This production hardly needed the extensive ad campaign it was afforded to make it the success it became, but much of that was due to the popularity of the author. **Variety**'s review criticized the length of the film but more significantly, indicated that, at least some of those who were concerned with the film industry felt that, Hollywood had overused the nemesis to the south: "The long existing problem between border residents and annoyances by Mexican invaders is a trifle bit commonplace." Despite the criticism, Hollywood producers continued to cast the Mexican in a negative light. Grey, wrote of some Mexican badmen, but almost invariably included the self-sacrificing Spanish señorita in his works; in this one she was called Mercedes Castenada and of course falls for the handsome young cavalry officer whose job it was to patrol the border making sure villainous characters from across the Rio Grande did not ford their way north. Destined to be the first recognizable Tarzan, Elmo K. Lincoln, was starred as the lead who loved an Anglo lady. Although the cast included many Mexican and Yaqui indian characterizations, there were no Hispanics employed [1170.] **MPW** 6.14.19, p1579, 6.29.19, p1994, 9.23.19, p1577, **V**:11.17.19.

[824] **DUST OF DESIRE**, World: [When Ruby de Remer marries her new husband she confesses that she had once had a lover, but neglects to tell the spouse that the other was still alive. Happily and with anticipation, the newlyweds journey to South America. Despite the hemisphere's vastness, they happen to visit the very place inhabited by the former paramour. Discovering that his one time lady has married, the villainous Hispanic, threatens to complicate her happy existence, by exposing their once torrid affair. This, she could not allow. Sly little creature that she was, the wife arranges with some willing locals for only a few pesos, to have the former lover experience an accident by which her husband can save him and become his heroic friend. It all worked to perfection. That's the beauty of Hollywood.] **MPG**.

[825] **THE END OF THE GAME**, Pathe: [Those California gold fields in 49 attracted a constant flow of new immigrants looking for immediate riches. This film just related one of those thousands of untold stories these hardy forerunners of Anglo civilization experienced while searching for the rainbow's end. It's only interest for this work was the lust crazed bartender, a Mexican, who goes for the girl, but gets something quite different instead] **MPG**.

[826] **FIGHTING FOR GOLD**, F: [Tom Mix was at this time, one of Hollywood biggest stars. In this film he chose to play a tough, roughneck gentleman who possessed the traditional soft heart that usually went with such a characterization. In no time at all he falls for a darkskinned lady named Moya. As the reviewers explained, "He mined for gold, but found a greater treasure, love," and possibly a few warm nights with a hotblooded Mexican woman. Tom Mix was quite popular south of the border also, he was one of the many Hollywood stars mentioned in the Pan American Union's descriptive survey on the progress North American films were making against foreign competitors in the South American market.] **MPW:4.12.19, p270**, Muriel Baily, "Moving Pictures in Pan America, **Bulletin of the Pan American Union**, V:L, {Jan-Jun}, 1920, pp.606-623.

[827] **HAITIAN NIGHT TALE**, Chester Travel Picture: [Travelogues proved popular from the industries inception, this one featured scenes of old and new Haiti. Considering that United States Marines were occupying the island at the time, it was of significant interest. Included in the film were scenes of the good works that had been accomplished since the landing of United States Marines.] **NYT:7.21.19**.

[828] **THE HEART OF JUANITA**, Indy: [Beatiz Michelena,"stepped from a high position on the operatic stage to enter filmland, in her own production in which she starred as Juanita, the little Spanish lovely who worked in the Mexican cantina. There she falls in a hard way for Jim, respected by all and apparently loved by many including "Blondie" who vamps him right out of Juanita's lovely Irish eyes. The script called for the typical Spanish reaction and Juanita stabs Jim right were it hurts. Taken by the sheriff to jail, his gun explodes as he attempts to incarcerate her. She escapes to find an

Adonis like hermit [if it was your movie, he could look like Adonis] in the deep woods, who hides her out. In no time at all they fall in love, but there was the problem of Jim's body. After, the Adonis fights "a Bowie knife battle" with the sheriff and all is resolved. The two were now free to happily ever after it together.] **MPW**:12.6.19, 12.13.19, p848, 855, p670 **V**:12.5.19.

[829] **KNICKERBOCKER BUCKAROO**, Fairbanks/Art: [Having enjoyed making his first comedy western, **Arizona**, which allowed him to demonstrate his athletic skills, Douglas Fairbanks agreed to star in this fun piece of fluff. The object of his affection was the lovely Mercedes [Marjorie Daw] and his foil, the insidious Mexican bandit, Manuel Lopez [Albert MacQuarrie.] Fairbanks, rides, shoots, jumps and leaps all over his opposition with comedic contempt, and great ease. Everyone expected it. The Mexican bandit was on his transitional way to being less the object of fear, and more one with humorous possibilities.] **MPG**.

[830] **LASCA**, U: [The story and scenario were taken from a Frank Duprez poem of the same title. Lasca was a lovely little Mexican girl who lives with her sometimes quarrelsome brother. The opening scenes show some very attractive western landscapes identified as being on the border. Lasca and her brother have a bit of a tiff and she leaves for a while. Later she falls in love with the Anglo ranch owner who is fond of her but, at least one other also. In the final scene, she honors a tradition now long established, by willingly giving up her life to save him from stampeding cattle.] **V**:12.5.19, **MPG.**

[831] **ODDS AGAINST HER**, Br: [Luckily for her guardian, Nanette is able to prevent the evil designs of Lolita Rios, under whose seductive spell he had fallen, and her conspirator the evil German baron, from coming to fruition. She had suspected the two and upon investigation, uncovers the plot by the combined Spanish/German team, and saves the estate for he who had been so kind to her when she was orphaned. There was justice in Hollywood's world, and always so when North American interest were threatened by foreign nationals.] **MPG**

[832] **THE RANGER**, W. H. Clifford Photoplay Co: [For **Variety**, this western had a "strong story" which "carried a message." The message must have been something like: If you're a German spy posing as a newspaper editor, operating on the Mexican border transferring secret messages to the motherland that might endanger the security of the United States, watch out of for "Shorty" Hamilton the Ranger. And if you have a daughter, plan on her leaving home, she'll be his.] **V**:5.31.18.

[833] **SCARLET DAYS**, P/Artcraft: Scarlet Days, [Displaying not a little snobbery, **Variety**, considered D.W. Griffith's efforts in picturizing this epic of California's gold rush days, "not worthy" of his great talent and certainly a waste of his efforts on what was merely "just another western." They especially objected to "that little piece of business" where

Chiquita buts a rough in the stomach for lifting her dress. The story focuses on life in a California dance hall or cantina, which is owned by a mother who has her daughter back east in a finishing school, unaware of how the selfsacrificing mom is paying for rent. When the dutiful woman's world begins to crumble, she is aided by Alverez the "Spanish Bandit", a character loosely based on the real life character, Joaquin Murietta [qv.] Constantly at her aid, he comes to save her one more time when she is threatened, but fails in this last effort. The mother is finally killed by local toughs and Alverez taken prisoner. Condemned to death, his woman pleads for his life and somehow the two escape, possibly to a better life away from the camps and the cantina. Richard Barthelmes played Alveres and Clarine Seymour was Chiquita. No Hispanics had even secondary roles. Then again, one remembers that blacks could not be trusted to play blackmen in another of the great directors more well remembered movies.] **V**:11.14.19, **NYT**:11.10.19, **MPG**.

[834] **SOLDIER OF FORTUNE**, Indy: [Plans to film this Richard Harding Davis novel of a Cuban cuartalazo had been in the works since 1913, it was first brought to film in 1914, and served as the outline for a number of other spinoff productions. Some of his other adventure tales were brought to the screen successfully and were also imitated by others, but in reality, they were all basically the same film. This screen scenario provided the prototype for many subsequent reinactments of the traditional barrack's revolution where a single disgruntled officer leads his men against the established authority and takes over the government. Davis's hero was always the young North American engineer who happened to be working for the government. In this original version, the troubled island republic was obviously Cuba. There the Anglo hero discovers that one of the officers, Mendoza, plans to overthrow President Alverez. Once the revolt begins, the loyal engineer, leaps into immediate action and musters his miners, intercepts the "filibustered" arms and prevents the revolution from succeeding. In a little while, the guardians of liberty, Uncle Sam's troops arrive to take over. His heroism is of course rewarded with the favors of a lovely Latin lady, an essential Hollywood embellishment to all such traditional disorders. One reviewer, apparently an expert in military tactics, criticized the manner in which the blue jackets and marines marched "in formation" into battle, but, he obviously failed to realizes that those were brave lads, who understood the importance of discipline, but knew not the meaning of fear. Davis always wrote it that way.] **V**:11.14.19.

One enterprising exhibitor used a phoney news item to help promote the film in Phoenix and created a bit of a scare. The copy read: In bold, "Rumored Heading Toward Phoenix", and bolder still, "MEXICAN BANDIT BORDER RAIDERS. The disclaimer announced a $5000 reward, "if" the rumor could be verified or "the attacks stopped." "If anyone wanted to see the type of men it would take to stop the bandits", the they were to come see, the Richard Harding Davis production. "Bandit Scare in Southwest Helped "Soldiers of Fortune.""] **MPW**:4.17,20, 414.

[835] **THE SPITFIRE OF SEVILLE**, U: [This action packed romantic melodrama featured lots of love interest between the Hispanics and Anglos. But serious jealousies were aroused when Carmelita [Hedda Nova] encouraged the advances of two Anglo suitors, a lighter skinned lady is enraged. It all worked out in the last reel when it was settled that Carmelita's heart belonged to Pedro, played by an Anglo.] **MPG**.

[836] **12-10**, British/World: [Maria Doro, a successful star of what was always called the "legitimate" theater, [what did that make Hollywood?], provided the lethal drama necessary in this little film which portrayed her as a secretary with evil intentions focused on her employer's adopted child.] **MPG**.

[837] **TYPICAL MEXICAN ASPECT**, George D. Wright/ Educational Film Corporation: [This seems an attempt by the Carranza government working in conjunction with George Wright's film crews to present to the North American public very different views of Mexico than they were used to. It was a very conscious effort to demonstrate, with more than eighty minutes of film that the military aspect of the Mexican Revolution had come to an end and that the Carranza government had achieved a certain degree of stability in its daily operation. The initial showing was sponsored by the Mexican Consulate General at Wurlitzer Hall in New York City and was attended only by special invitation. The original presentation of the eight reel production had Spanish subtitles, but it was planned to provided English titles for the one reel break down that would be offered to the distributors. The film opened with scenes of Mexico's independence day parade, September 16, showing President Carranza proudly reviewing the troops with his staff. The equipment displayed indicated a modern army. Another sequence presented "specimens of the people of Mexico," from the more primitive to those working in airplane assembly plants. In effect it was an attempt to promote a much more positive view of Mexico than audiences in the United States were used to seeing. Editorially the **NYT** responded: "This kind of propaganda is a plea to the American people to have patience with distracted by slowly recovering Mexico; to put its ways of civilization in to the balance against offenses committed by its insurgents and brigands; to think twice before seeking satisfaction by waging war upon Mexico." Apparently willing to try this for a while, they were encouraged that "some of the films accumulated [were] to be used for the educational improvement of the Mexicans themselves." This use of the motion picture, they affirmed, could not be "too highly commended" because the Mexicans "in their vast country with its backward means [were] intensely ignorant about one another." A nice little exercise in the art of conscientiously condescending criticism.] **MPW**:10.12.18, p235, 10.26.18, p505, **NYT**:1.31.19, 7.31.19, 9.21.19, See also: {editorial} "Films That Are Not Honest Representations of Mexico," **The Mexican Review**:5.1919.

1920

[838] **ALL THE WINNERS**, Br: [The British also liked to use Hispanic foils, not out west, but in the more confined quarters of their drawing room melodramas. Those employed were usually more Spanish and much more sophisticated than the typical Mexican bandit, but whether male or female, they were frequently more insidious and deadly. This English mystery concerns a wealthy "sportsman" who was almost forced by the nefarious, Pedro Darondarez, to give up his loving daughter in marriage for his evil intent. There were certain letters the old roue should not have written, but faced with giving his pride and joy to such a dastardly criminal, a Spaniard at that, he refused. And in the final reel, the English censors required that the baddie be punished to the full limit of his crime.] **MPG**.

[839] **THE BORDER FURY**, Pathe: [This was chapter 6 of **THE ADVENTURES OF RUTH**, in which the heroine was forced to cross over the border, where she had to gain entrance to the hacienda of the evil "Hound," a notorious bandit. To do this, she passes herself off as a Spanish dancer, performs brilliantly and recovers three bags of stolen gold that belonged to Don Justino. Having accomplished her assignment, she starts out for home, but is captured by the angry bandit's men who for the cliff hanger .... Sorry, you'll have to wait till next week to find out if .... The border would remain big with the serials well into the fifties.] **MPW**:1.31.20, p779.

[840] **THE BRAND OF LOPEZ**, Hayworth: [Assuming that producers considered what would be acceptable characterizations by their audiences, it is significant that still as late as this date, they would not search the fledgling Spanish or Mexican film industries to find a Hispanic actor for what was most certainly the most traditional of Spanish roles, the bullfighter. They chose instead the Japanese star, Sessue Hayakawa to portray the much admired matador, he had had Mexican experience before, that was close. **Variety** agreed with this madness and felt that he was quite acceptable as the idol of Seville. "His swarthiness [lent] itself well to the personation" in spite of the fact that "the Oriental ocular slant" of his eyes was "a trifle incongruous." Possibly it gave him a keen view of the bulls. But Sevilla's sweetheart, Vasco Lopez, also had other things on his mind, the matador was infatuated with the coquettish, Lola Castillo, star of the opera company. It worked for a while as she was "much smitten with the lusty toreador." Yet, soon, all was not well in paradise, Captain Pancho, a childhood sweetheart managed to attract her affection with but a few, knowing glances. Enraged, Lopez, brands his lover's back with a cigarette, marking her as his the day before they were to be married. But it's all down hill after that. The inlaws will not accept a common bullfighter into the family, the crowd in the corrida

begins to boo his performances and he is literally "bulled" out of the ring into banditry. As a bandit there was some success, but most of his boys are buffoons who fail to kidnap his wife, they bring her younger sister instead. The reviewer's most serious criticism of this film was that the director failed to establish a distinct sympathy for the audience to follow. When Lopez raped the young woman, he had lost any chance for it. In the end he was killed defending the child he so irresponsibly procreated. For the audience, it was life as usual in Spain.] MPW:4.10.20, p302, V:4.2.20.

[841] **A DOUBLE DYED DECEIVER**, Goldwyn: [O'Henry comes once more to the screen with this short story of a western youth sowing one too many wild oats by leaving the 'leaded' kernel of his last escapade, planted solidly in the heart of his victim. As such, he flees to South America seeking refuge. In no time at all he finds himself conspiring with the American Consul, who has solicited him to pose as the long missing son of a wealthy Spanish couple, for obvious gain. He does so but in the last reel cannot go through with the dirty work. Aside from the involvement on the part of the American consul, this would have been simply another melodrama, but including him in the script caused a protest by officials who were outraged that anyone in the State Department could conceive of such a criminal plot. Outside of Wilson's worrying about Japanese sensitivities in Patria [684], this is, in lieu of this research, the first instance where the State Department expressly protested a production involving South America, but that was more a concern for the image of the State Department than anything else.] **Included in the file of "problem films" listed with comments made by the National Board of Review at the NYC public library, 42nd Branch, Special Collections.** MPW:6.26.20, p1791. V:6.11.20.

[842] **FOR THE SOUL OF RAFAEL**, Equity: [Once more the audience traveled to lower California as they had so many times before in these early days of the silver screen to witness the sorrow of the Spanish señorita as she wept when she was told the news, by an avaricious aunt, of her American lover's death. It was all a lie, the audience knew it, but the trusting lady did not. Interested only in profit, the aunt forces the girl to leave the convent and marry her wealthy nephew, Rafael, the real heavy, who proves to be a despicable lout. But Hollywood would win out and he is killed in the last reel, thereby allowing the star crossed lovers to happily ever after it, this time, forever.] MPW:5.15.20, 6.12,20, pp1453-54, p983, V:5.28.20 and 10.8.20.

[843] **HIS PAJAMA GIRL**, Pricefilms: [A secret service man investigating the smuggling of drugs across the Mexican border discovers that the culprits have abducted the president of that republic and plan to exchange him for a sufficiently sum of money if they find some business man rich enough and interested in receiving the trade concessions in that country as a bonus. From Mexico the action moves to California where the hero foils the plot and finds true love for his efforts.] MPW:5.21.21, p321, V:9.3.20.

[844] **HOT TAMALE**, Universal: [This comedy burlesque of the by now quite familiar "kidnapping and rescue" deep in the heart of mysterious Mexico, was still quite popular. All of the Mexican characterizations are buffoons, and not one is played by a native actor: **Three Amigos**, beware [1413].]

[845] **THE LOST CITY**, Selig/W: [Apparently Africa was considered more mysterious or threatening than South America, or maybe the starker contrasts of black and white, possibly even the need to show lions and tigers, prompted the producer to choose the Dark Continent as the local for this serial starring the semi-Hispanic Juanita Hansen. North Americans might have known that there were no lions in South America, possibly some in Mexico [See: **Mexican Mine Fraud**, [473] but that there were no tigers in Africa may have been considered something understood only by the more sophisticated. It was white woman imperiled by dark lands which would always be a sure thing at the box office.] **MPW**:1.31.20, p775.

[846] **MARIMBA LAND**, Prizma: [This travelogue presented some "picturesque scenes of Guatemala" with many views of "the interesting customs of the people."] **FD**:10.3.20.

[847] **MARK OF ZORRO**, Fairbanks/UA: [Certainly the most enduring of Hispanic heros has been Zorro. From 1920 to this date, the main character of Johnson McCulley's, **The Curse of Capistrano** has been viewed by movie and television audiences alike. Cable TV's Family channel has recently produced it's own version of the hero first made popular by Douglas Fairbanks in this film, it is featured every Sunday evening in continuing adventures. Playing Zorro, the first of the caped crusaders for truth, justice and the Mexican/American way, insured Fairbanks' screen immortality, he would continue thereafter as a swashbuckler defending the right all the way from Sherwood Forest to the Spanish Main. In lower California it was Zorro alone that defended the rights of all Spaniards, wealthy hacendado and poor peasant alike were protected from the tyrannical rule of Spain's corrupt local administrator. Fairbanks played the dual role of Don Diego Vega, the pretentious fop, and Zorro, the dynamic man of action with excellence unsurpassed. He was supported by an able cast only one of which was Hispanic, Marguerite de la Motte, engaged to Don Diego, but in love with the crusader. The evil foil, was the "greasy Capt. Juan Ramon," who's avaricious greed and tyranny made life a nightmare for the Mexican locals. The film was an immediate sensation and must have satisfied some in the audience that there were both good as well as not so good Mexicans whose struggle for decency deserved support. All the Zorro's through 1957 can be found in, **Edward Connor**, "The Genealogy of Zorro", **Films in Review**, August-September, 1957, pp330-333, 343.] **V**:12.3.20, **NYT**: 11.29.20, **MPG**.

[848] **RIO GRANDE**, Pathe: [**Variety**, with a cynical view of Mexican politics and an eye for promotion, thought it an auspicious time for this entry: "Right at this time, with the disturbing elements of the Mexican population fostering another one of the overnight revolutionary productions in

Mexico, the picture should, if properly exploited have a certain amount of drawing power." The story concerns "the misunderstanding that exists in the mind of the Mex regarding his Gringo neighbor." Apparently **Variety** thought that they thought we thought we were superior, and discovered they were right when they saw this film. Once more the North American [of Irish extraction] lad wins the "fiery tempered" Mexican "spit-fire" played to perfection by Rosemary Thebe. The **Moving Picture World** also predicted the film's success: "A remarkable demand for the production is indicated in the cities where the stage play enjoyed exceptional success and in all the States along the border. The interest [there] is undoubtedly due to the fact that the theme of the story is not calculated to inflame feeling, but will rather show the way to permanent peace between Mexico and the United States." It would seem that, the **World** felt that the Mexicans had come to grips with losing their women to Anglos and that border crossings were sometimes required.] **MPW**:5.1.20, p721, **V**:5.7.20.

[849] **VIEWS OF PERU AND BOLIVIA**, [A travelogue showing the majesty of the Bolivian Andes and the poverty of both nation's peon classes.] **NYT**:2.23.20.

1921

[850] **ANNE OF LITTLE SMOKEY**, Indy: [Gypsies were everywhere. This time on government land where the head forest ranger falls in love with Gita [Dolores Cassinelli] the gypsy girl whom he saves from a treacherous lout. Serious complications arise when the scorned lover comes after the Anglo ranger, but the lusty lady helped to save him.] **V**:1.13.22.

[851] **THE AVENGING ARROW**, (Serial: 15 episodes), Pathe: [Ruth Roland was another of the popular heroines of early "continuing stories". In this episodic tale of love, romance, intrigue and adventure in sunny Spanish southern California, she played Anita, the "athletic, but feminine" daughter of Don Jose Delgado. The offspring of this "fine old Spanish family" she has inherited the "proud blood of her race [while] at the same time having acquired many warm and human American traits." Events moved quickly in serials, an immediate crisis developed just as the story opens. At the fiesta celebrating her twenty-first birthday, it was discovered that she was in terrible danger. An arrow shot from the outside hit the hacienda warning of impending peril. Anita was now old enough to know that Delgado women were cursed, when a daughter reached her majority, life became instantaneously dangerous. In an attempt to capture the individual who threatened Anita, Don Jose rode out after Luis, the mysterious bandit, but was himself shot and kept captive. Learning this, the plucky girl was forced to act and in conjunction with Ralph Troy, the handsome young Anglo she would fall in love with, they took only fifteen cliff hanging episodes to thwart the forces of evil. The Mexican bandit who wanted the girl only to obtain all her property, provided most of the problems. But his slippery señorita, Luisa Traganza, daughter of a rival family and seeking revenge almost succeeded in Anita's demise. In the end the combined efforts of the half Anglo girl and her true love defeated the easily identifiable gang of bandidos and their leader saving the dad and the Hacienda for their future adventures.] **MPW**:3.5.21, p46.

[852] **BLACK SHEEP**, Chaudet-Hurst Productions: [**The American Film Institute Catalogue** lists this film as being uncertain to plot line. It did "apparently" involve the necessary cattles and sheeps, a good possibility. Also a son, a real square shooter, who is wrongly expelled from home, and a final reel in which it is discovered that the real culprit was of course a Mexican [234].] **afic.**

[853] **THE BORDER RAIDERS**, Aywon Film Corp. [This Ben Hill five reeler was not a remake of the 1918 picture by the same name but it certainly was action packed from the first punch to the last knock out. Described by **Motion Picture News** as a "sensational melodrama", the action focused on a gang of Mexican whiskey smugglers who brought the stuff across the Rio Grande at night. There were a series of terrific fight scenes

in the cellar of the more modern Mex bandit's house, a pistol duel across the Arizona mountains, the blowing up of a house with a barrel of powder and a hand to hand fight in the bandits mountain cave where the baddie was finally subdued [778].] **afic**.

[854] **BURIED TREASURE**, P: [W.R. Hearst was beginning to spend a lot of dollars on Marion Davies's career at this time and the production values of this film indicate the extent of his lavishness. Basically a reflection of the public's interest in the latest fad, reincarnation, the star defies her father and accepts the affection of one he strongly disfavors. The action begins in a "lavishly reproduced" Spanish garden "filled with Spanish types, singers and dancers," and leaves the "spectator's mind in the land of the señoritas." From there the story plunges into Spanish Main days with bloody pirates and buried treasure. In her dream Davies discovers the location of the valuable gold and instead of leading her father to it, she tells her lover. Finally realizing where her true affections lie, the wise father gives the couple his permission. Hearst had a curious ambivalence for south of the border, he certainly liked, for lack of a better word, a lot of things there, but was contemptuous of Latin politics and governmental institutions. In backing this film he may have been fulfilling some romantic fantasy.] **V:2.18.21**, **MPG**.

[855] **THE CONQUERING POWER**, Metro: [That was the power of love which could span the oceans, all the way from France to her island colony in the Caribbean, Martinique. This tale was taken from Balzac's **Eugenie Grandet** and focused on the daughter who was forced to live like a near pauper by her wealthy, but money mad father. When she meets and falls in love with her young man, she finances his trip to the colony, where many French aristocrats went to make their fortunes. The father discovers the loan and in a fit of rage promises her to one she hates. The writer's ironic fate comes to the lady's assistance by having a chest of gold crush the old miser, and her lover returning home with newly acquired wealth from the colony was just in time to save her so that they could return to that beautiful tropical paradise and live happily ever after.] **V:7.8.21**.

[856] **CRAZY TO MARRY**, FP/P: [This was "Fatty" Arbuckle's last film before he was unofficially banned from working anywhere near Hollywood. An excellent and very popular comedy, it included a lovely Spanish type, Estrella De Morgan, who played to all the accepted stereotypes of the señorita vamp.] **V:8.5.21**.

[857] **THE CRUISE TO VERA CRUZ**, FP: [Produced by Burton-Holmes this travelogue included "interesting views of Havana," and "cosmopolitan types on the promenade deck" as the ship arrived in Vera Cruz. There, the photographer took pains to show the remnants of the recent occupation by United States Marines, where the fighting had taken place and the captured fort. Formerly Carranza's capital, the President had spent significant amounts modernizing the dock facilities of

Mexico's most important Gulf Port city. All this, plus a significant amount of local color, was captured on film for the benefit of North American viewers who could not afford such sea voyages.] **MPW:10.15.21, p810.**

[858] **DIAMONDS ADRIFT**, Vitagraph: [Having disappointed his father by overdrawing his account some $5000 dollars, dad gives his son the opportunity to make good, if he can repay the money. Bob seeks to redeem himself and signs onto a trap steamer heading for the "Tropic of Cancer." On board ship he beats up the boiler room bully and wins a Persian cat in a card game. Once in Mexico he is smitten by a sweet señorita, Consuela Velasco, and both pledge themselves to each other. The problem arises when her former lover objects and calls Bob to task. Bob is more than up to it and when it is discovered that the man he had bettered was a fugitive with a price on his head, they head north to collect the $5000 dollar reward. Surprise, surprise, that the kitty was worth an other five, because of the Diamond necklace that imaginative scripter placed around his neck. Dad welcomes all, and why not, he was $5000 ahead. Although the son had become a man south of the border, all Hispanics were still played by Anglos.] **V:2.11.21, MPG.**

[859] **A DIVORCE OF CONVENIENCE**, Selznick Pictures: [From the first decade of the flickers, down to this present time, one of the most frequently featured screen stereotypes has been that of the Hispanic whore. In the early days she was simply a naughty lady, a cantina cutie of easy virtue. With the easing of censorship restrictions in the late fifties, her character became more harshly portrayed. More often than not she was viewed as drug addict supporting her self and her usual several children by selling her body. Such depictions make/made it easy for whites to assume that most welfare mothers are/were some kind of Hispanic and that Spanish/Mexican girls all become pregnant before they turn fifteen.] In this piece, "Tula Moliana" was a pretty "Spanish coquette" who one day happens to realizes that she is "encumbered" with two husbands. One of these unfortunates was a United States senator, but he is the one that Tula wants out. To accomplish her plan she engages the services of young Jim Blake, an innocent Anglo. He agrees but wants to make sure that his girl Helen does not become involved. After a series of incredible adventures, which almost take his life because of another jealous Hispanic suitor, Helen forgives all because Jim has been victimized by the adulteress who settled for the Senator and apparently, business as usual continued in the Nation's capital.] afic.

[860] **FIGHTING MAD**, Metro: [Promoted and advertised as "American Musketeers on the Mexican Border," this film adapted Dumas's famous four characters to duty along the Rio Grande. Popular leading man, William Desmond as Bud McGraw, heading out west, after having served his time in WWI, found himself enlisting in the service of the border guard where, because men were men, he quickly had to defeat the three best hombres in the outfit. This impressive feat established a macho bond

which solidified the group and carried them through all of the problems they faced when "a Mexican plot" was uncovered to capture and ransom the wife of a local revenue officer. Rosmary Theby, as Nita De Garma, was featured as the attractive but, "crafty Spanish" señorita whose flashing eyes try to tempt the hero from doing his duty. The seductive looks were certainly tempting, but failed in their purpose. Actually Nita kills her lover, Lazaro, who had posed as a Secret Service man, when he refuses to give up the pretty Peggy he had taken captive. In the end, Bud and the boys capture the more modern Mexican baddies. With all their plans foiled by the four friends, in the last reel the Mexicans find themselves looking out from behind the bars.] **FD**:10.30.21.

[861] **THE FIRE CAT**, U: [Any film that could boast of a cast of characters like, Dulce, Gringo Burke, Cholo Pete, Mother Alverez, Margarita and Pancho, cannot be all bad, but this Universal production certainly tried. **Variety** was less than kind with it's criticism: "Designed as a "romantic" tale of the Incas, [did that mean that the present day Peruvians were considered to be Incas?] it develops into a [sic] hidge-podge of bewildering zoological exhibits calculated to give the spectator delirium tremens without the aid of "hootch." The reviewer was apparently unaware of the hazardous wildlife that could be found in those Andes, every Anglo child knows that llama's could spit a mile. The scenario had Gringo Pete, a renegade Anglo, leading a gang of bandits high in the Andes, [the Sundance Kid thought it was a good idea.] Nearby lived the beautiful Dulce, loved by the halfbreed/halfcaste, Pancho who knew neither part of him would ever enjoy the señorita's favors, yet still he would be her protector. One day, Gringo comes by to rob and in doing so, kills Mother Alverez. Dulce vows vengeance and immediately sets out to achieve her purpose. But first she become a dancer in a local "dive," where she wears the costume of the "fire cat" to remind her of what must be done. Before she can deal with Gringo, she meets another American, this time only a "derelict," and the two fall in love. People were actually paid for writing things like this, and it's not over yet. Although the **Variety** reviewer had difficulty believing that there actually were active volcanos in the Andes, Cotopaxi exploded and burned Gringo and his boys right out of the picture. With Dulce's problem resolved, she now turned to rehabilitating the derelict she loved. Throw in a few jungle scenes, shots of giant anteaters, lizards and jungle cats and what more could you want from a film set in the rarified atmosphere of the Andes ... maybe just out of curiosity, one might want to know what kind of weed the scripter was smoking.] **V**:2.25.21, afic.

[862] **FOOLS PARADISE**, Lasky/P: [This DeMille extravaganza commanded the top price of $2.20 for a saturday showing, an extraordinary price for that time, the film still drew large crowds. **Variety** was enthusiastic about the director's "realistic recreation" and atmospheric touches which described life in the border oil fields. These included a "bootblack", his wife and the "two picks" who until recently had worked their trade when oil riches provided them with the huge

touring car they now possessed. It was the same for the "Injun" who had recently moved a "player piano" into his tent. But things were not going so well for the recently returned war hero, his vision diminished by poison gas even his wells had gone dry. Poll Patchouli, the "principle vamp" danced seductively into this ethnic paradise and commanded the attention of our hero, to say nothing of all the locals. As the number one attraction in Roderiguez's Mexican cantina, the only place to go in the bustling boom town, she was the smash attraction. Roderiguez, "adept at knife throwing" loved his star, but apparently his business even more. He became very angered when she prevented "a wise guy" from having his way with one of the other gals. Forced to escape, she finds herself in our hero's cabin, and falls in love immediately. But Roderiguez could not let that happen. The "greasers" he sent to retrieve her were apparently not the same killer breed as our hero's "little Boston Terrier" who's canine prowess drives the other dirty dogs away. Although Poll loves the Anglo, he has an affection for a French "danseuses who she instinctively hates. After a lot of stuff, Poll is responsible for blinding him completely, but becomes his woman by impersonating the French accent of the woman he thinks she is. Self sacrificing to a fault, she works for the dineros to get him that operation which when he opens his eyes causes him to spun her. Now oil rich, he travels to Siam [I'm not making this up] and while commiserating there, he realizes he really loves the cantina cutie, but she, "the eternal woman" spurns his advances and goes to back to her "Castillian lover" who threatens the boy to stay away. In the knife fight that develops, between the Mexican and the Anglo, the repentant Poll takes the blade intended for the Anglo's back in her breast and dies in his arms. And according to **Variety**, "this [led] to the natural happy ending of the picture."]
V:12.16.21.

[863] **FOUR HORSEMEN OF THE APOCALYPSE**, Metro: [With Rudolofo Valentino as the star attraction, this adaptation of Vicente Belasco Ibanez's novel was the super spectacular of the year, ranked with **Intolerance** and **Birth of a Nation**. The "magnitude" of the film was "staggering", costing over $800,000 and utilizing more than 12,000 extras it was a triumph in every way. Basically a film describing the horrors of war, much of the action concerns the loves and intrigues of a wealthy Argentine family with French and German roots. Its focus was the patriarch's pride and joy, Julio, his loves and hates, his eventual involvement in the war, and the tragic consequences of having members of the same family fighting on opposite sides in the same conflict. The scene in the Argentine dance hall, was an artistic triumph that still plays well today. Valentino's "electrifying" performance repopularized the tango and gave birth to a generation of "Latin lover" lookalikes that lasted well into the thirties. Because of the film's great popularity, making over three million dollars, its influence, in reaffirming Latin stereotypes would be difficult to overestimate [1183].]
V:2.18.21, **NYT**:2.28.21, **MPG**.

[864] **GENERAL JOHN REGAN**, Br: [A comedy in which the chief character is an Irishman who, as a lark, tries to convince a rich North American visitor that Bolivia as a nation, was actually liberated and created by a local villager. In as much as Bernado O'Higgins was actually one of those responsible for the liberation of Chile, the humor involved more ignorance than wit. It is possible that the scripter was unaware of this fact, no, there is little doubt that he had no historical knowledge about the liberation of the South American nations.] **MPG.**

[865] **GYPSY BLOOD**, FN: [Ernst Lubitsch was criticized for his lack of technical expertise in directing this version of the Prosper Merimee classic. But "Carmen" [it's original title] by any other name or direction would always require the star, the Polish Pola Negri in this case, to be as she was perceived and had been solidified by the silver screen in the audience's mind. The Spanish coquette/vamp/badlady was portrayed by Pola with "uncompromising realism" as a "heartless, ignorant, unmoral, basely reared Spanish gypsy, without one redeeming trait; a beautiful animal whose friendship [was] a curse and whose death at the hands of Navarro [was] richly deserved." So much for the character of naughty Spanish señoritas. The more often staid **New York Times** applauded the production, and the work of the director and his star in capturing the essential character of the Hispanic vamp: "Miss Negri's Carmen is not studio puppet; she is no grand operatic queen without a vivifying voice. She is a tempestuous, intemperate, gypsy girl; a magnetic, unmoral animal, a free living, freeloving savage of capricious appetites and a consuming zest for satisfying them. Nothing is precious in her eyes. She does not seek to have and to hold; the sport is to capture and destroy, for to destroy the captured is to carry the conquest to its natural completion. She hunts and kills in disregard or ignorance of posted fields and closed seasons. She possesses all of the natural artfulness of the female of the species without the protective finesse of the civilized variety." One must assume that was so, because she is Spanish. Certainly not a little flapper to bring home to meet mamacita in the suburbs, but if you could just get a chain around her neck and tie her to the bed, OH! You Kid.! The characterization of silver screen Carmens and most of the other chiquitas remained basically unchanged as they wiggled their was down to present days.] **MPW**:5.21.21, p321, **NYT**:5.9.21

[866] **IN BARCELONA**, Burton Holmes: [The producer of this film felt that North Americans new about as much of Spain as they did of "Greenland, [and] Iceland," and so he affixed his camera to a "Spanish city's trolley car" for a few days and let the film run out. Although not "exceptionally beautiful, nor remarkably absorbing" apparently it was something to watch that could provide the theater seat traveler with some insights to daily life in Spain.] **MPW**:8.20.21, p831.

[867] **THE KILLER**, Pathe: [Certainly atypical for the times, the story outlines the activities of an always polite music lover who hates, birds, children and anything that aggravates

him. The scene is set on the Arizona-Mexican border where Henry Hooper has established himself in this western community as a respectable gentleman, while secretly he may have been the screen's first serial killer. Over the years he had dispatched a number of individuals because of his cattle smuggling across the border. His accomplis was Ramon, a "greaser", who he uses to effect accidents like having his partner's horse, bumped over a 500 foot cliff. Another of his victims was the father of the ranch next door. In this case there was a purpose to the crime, the "machiavellian villain", wanted to gain control over the daughter so that he could acquire the wealthy property. She refuses his advances, but finally acquiesces because he threatens to give her to "his lecherous Mexican as a victim of his lustful desires" if she refuses to hand over the keys to the ranch. In time, before she could suffer a fate worse than the depraved passions of the greaser, the neighboring ranch owner rescues the little lady. It is significant that the real villain in this film was an Anglo and that the Hispanic was only his willing dupe. There are very few such films, even today which include both Mexican and Anglo characterizations in which the later is more malevolent than the Hispanic.] **MPW**:1.29.21, **V**:2.11.21.

[868] **THE KISS**, U: [Love in Spanish California was never easy, but if you had a Hollywood score card, by 1920 you could predict the outcome, you could have five years earlier. When two Dons arrange a marriage for their children, you must know by now that that wedding will never happen. He, the son, usually the pride of the hacienda, will fall for a peon lady who of course returns his love. The fathers will be upset, rich and poor alike, having their honors offended. The señorita's father, usually a poor shot, will shoot the young Don to be, but miss or only wound him. The lovely darkskinned still a maiden will then save him from further abuse and prevent the hacienda vaqueros from killing her father. The two old Dons will realize the error of their ancient ways and usually discover that the left out lady already had a substitute to bed down with for some time. All's well that was advertised as, "Fascinating Story of the Days of the Dons in California Where the Languor of Life Was oft Interrupted by the Appearance of Adventure," or "The Love of a Dashing Caballero for the Daughter of a Peon in Old California Which Culminates in an Exciting Romance."] **V**:7.8.21.

[869] **LAST TRAIL**, F: [The hero in this little western was known as the "Night Hawk" and everyone thought he was really the bandit, but the real baddie was Wallace Beery, an Anglo who steals the payroll and blows up the dam. The Hawk was really an undercover agent who during this adventure gets to play with Chiquita, the cantina girl.] **MPG**.

[870] **LOVE'S REDEMPTION**, Norma Talmadge Film Co: [Having grown up on the beautiful island of Jamaica when England was still the suzerain of that tropical paradise, Jennie Dobson, an orphan, matured beautifully into womanhood. When she met the aristocratic Clifford Standish, she knew he was the one for her forever, but Cliff liked the taste of the grape a bit too

much. In time she reformed him and he even took charge of all the blacks that worked his plantation. Life was good and things really looked up when the brother from England came with the news that the West Indian planter had inherited the ancestral estates. He was not pleased though to discover that his brother has married Jennie without lineage in her life. Of course they go to England where everyone is not nice to the wife. In the end she decides to return back her home in Jamaica, and Cliff, realizing that she is everything to him, leaves with her.] **V**:1.13.22, <u>afic</u>.

[871] <u>**THE MONEY MANIAC**</u>, Pathe: [Filmed in four countries including Spain, the story concerns an avaricious promoter who seeks to obtain all the titles to the now rich oil land, that he had sold long before. At that time, the land had been worthless, but oil was discovered, and the immigrant promoter-conman wanted the titles back from all those he had convinced to buy into the then worthless deal. His efforts eventually take him to sunny Spain, but in the end, he fails.] <u>**MPW**</u>:7.30,21, p540.

[872] <u>**ON THE HIGH CARD**</u>, Arrow Film Corp: [This western melodrama finds pretty Polly Updike learning of the death of her father upon her arrival at Rim Rock. There, Pecos Bill, Ben Stiles and Conchita run the saloon and much of the town. Harry Holt and his friend, Hank Saunders represent the law in that wild west town. Realizing that without her father, the little Anglo lady will need protection, it is decided to draw lots to see who will marry her. Harry wins, but the lady refuses to be won. The real baddie, Pecos Bill tells Polly that the law man killed her father and he tries his best to win her affection. Failing to do so, he gives her up to the Mexican bandits. In the last reel, Harry and friend save her from the Mexicans and Pecos is discovered to be the real killer of the father. As a reward, the lady gives herself to the lawman as his bride. Nice simple stuff with easily identifiable villains.] <u>afic.</u>

[873] <u>**THE OUTSIDE WOMAN**</u>, REA: [A script that never quite makes any sense, has a wife trading her husband's priceless Aztec idol for a silken shawl, which results in a flurry of activity in a vain attempt to retrieve it. After the husband has discovered the real worth of the pirated relic, the new owner who has acquired it refuses to give it back.] <u>**V**</u>:8.4.21, **MPG**.

[874] <u>**THE PASSION FLOWER**</u>, Herbert Brenon: [Anglo perceptions of Hispanic passion during love making have probably caused more insecurities and misunderstandings than even the fear of the assumed vengeful character of the Spanish personality. The reviewer for this film exhibited what may well have been the commonly accepted belief that there was a significant difference between the heated blood generated passion of Latin love and the more genteel, affectionate feelings exchanged by Anglo lover and loveress. For Anglos, passion had to be held in check, for uninhibited Latins, it was to be graphically expressed in love making. Films still project that attitude today. Not five minutes into **Wild Orchids**, 1991, one could

watch, as the apparently innocent little Anglo model did, two beautiful black skinned Brazilians in an abandoned Rio building, ripping off their clothes to be at each other in what certainly looked like a lot of fun. Fun for them, but not necessarily typical of Anglo behavior. The opening line of this review expresses the point and was essentially incorrect. Spanish passion had been a popular theme for film since the very beginning. "Any attempt to transplant the Italian and Spanish drama of primitive passion to this country has not met with success. Over here we have never manifested a liking for human nature stripped of all refinement and showing only the animal passion of a dumb brute." The reviewer's main objection to this film was the "lust of a stepfather for the young daughter of the woman he has promised to love and protect." From the first, "Acacia" had hated the stepfather "with all the intensity of her Spanish blood," reserving her feelings for the poet, Norbet. In no time at all, Esteban the brute, brings an end to that relationship by having the boy blamed for killing the son he himself has shot, thereby eliminating all rivals for his "unholy desires". In the final reel the wife shoots her depraved husband and the young lovers are reunited. It was suggested to exhibitors that they advertise this production as: "Spanish story of Lust and Murder." "Tense Drama is Found in Every Foot of **The Passion Flower**", a Spanish Story Starring Norma Talmadge [1432].] **MPW**:4.16.21, p758, **V**:4.8.21.

[875] **PLAYTHINGS OF DESTINY**, FN: [Julie living in Canada is very happy with Geoffrey, her husband until the evil Claire convinces her that he is really her husband. Shattered she heads out into a storm, a real Canadian blizzard and would have died had it not been for Hubert who happened to find her in the snow. He offers to marry her and give her child a name if she will follow him to Jamaica, gratefully she accepts the generous offer. In time another storm intervenes to change the lady's life. During a serious tropical storm Geoffrey happens to visit the island and when he is injured by falling palms, she discovers that she still loves him. Seeing this and being happy with his governorship of the island, Hubert graciously gives back the wife and child.] **V**:11.18.21, afic.

[876] **ROGUES AND ROMANCE**, George B. Seitz: [Exhibitors were encouraged to exploit the fact that this production was "A Picture About Spain That Was Actually Taken in Spain" with scenes shot in and about Seville, Cadiz, Granada and Malaga. This "Bright Story of Sunny Spain" found Sylvia Lee, leaving her lover state side and heading for those warm climes looking for adventure and finding it quickly in the arms of revolutionary leader Pedro Pezet. Aside from all of the scenic beauty included in this effort, a definite message was also provided for the price of admission. Simply stated, if you're going to start a revolution in Spain, and you have a hot blooded temptress named Carmelita in your pocket, make sure you wear a different pair of pants when you go out to be with the extra added attraction. Pedro did not listen and when the fiery Carmelita found out that some Anglo was lighting her lover's matches, she threw a definite damper on

the flames of both passion and revolution. Responsible for preventing the success of the governmental overthrow she then provoked Reggie, Sylvia's amore who had just arrived, into a fight for his woman. Despite "great personal risk" the Anglo confronts the unhappy and unsuccessful insurrecto reclaims his lady which allows Carmelita to renew her claim on the overall loser. All in all, just another tale of "High Life and Low in Spain" that one assumes did not necessarily play well in downtown Madrid.] **MPW**:1.1.21, p97.

[877] **ROUGH DIAMOND**, Fox: [Tom Mix was featured in so many western films at this time that it was difficult to find a scenario that he had not fought his way through. Here the scripters placed him in the company of the lovely Gloria Gomez, who's father, a deposed South American dictator/president was traveling out west, apparently for his health. After working on the farm where the two were staying along with the sinister and scheming Pedro, an officer traveling with them, Tom took a job as a trick rider for a passing circus. There he once more meets the lady and her father who had been searching for the right man to lead him back to power. All now head for Bargravia, somewhere south of the border, where Tom's Anglo heroics reinstate the Latin leader, foil the evil designs of the faithless Pedro and win the heart of the girl. A good days work for any cowhand, south of the Rio Grand, and a tribute to the scripters ability to steal from Richard Harding Davis.] **FD**:10.30.21, **V**:11.25.21.

[878] **SERENADE**, FN: [Raoul Walsh received rave reviews for his first First National production which employed two members of his immediate family, but only one Hispanic, Adita Milano, as the Spanish dancer. His brother was acclaimed by the same notice as "a corking Spanish lover." Walsh's wife was cast as the pretty young señorita that attracts the attention of two young aristocratic Spaniards. She loves but one and rejects the Governor's son which of course causes complications, a duel, a defeat, and escape and eventually prison for the chosen one. It all works out in the last reel with the señorita saving her true love from death and they together save the town from the bandits who are seeking to capture it. Raoul could never escape those early days with Villa.] **V**:9.9.21

[879] **THE SILVER LINING**, Iroquois Film Corp/Metro: [Some of the action for this socially conscious film which attempted to indicate that heredity did not always predetermine the future of the children, took place in Havana. There the girl with good parents goes bad, (they failed to factor in the location in this equation) and back in the states, the less fortunate girl of less fortunate parents, goes good.] **V**:1.28.21.

[880] **A SMALL TOWN IDOL**, Associated Producers: [This was Roman Navarro's first credited film part. From 1917 to 1921 he had worked as an extra in almost a hundred films without credits. In this Max Sennett seven reeler riot about a small town hick, Navarro did an exotic dance number and was billed under his real name, Ramon Samaniegos] **V**:4.15.21.

Feature Film List 1921   241

[881] **STOLEN MOMENTS**, Pioneer Film Corp: [An honorable heroine becomes infatuated with a suave South American novelist. With some foresight, he has her pledge her love in writing on the inside cover of one of his works. Completely taken with his Latin charm, the dazzled daughter defies her family and accepts his offer to return with him to the land of eternal sunshine and love, leaving behind her guardian who has always held her close to his heart. But, as was frequently the case with such hot blooded affairs, the Latin, was interested only in a little friendly frivolity, or maybe even a some dirty sex, but which ever, he laughs out loud, when he discovers that the lady assumed he wanted to marry her. The cad rejects her immediately, which forces her back north into the arms of the one who had been left behind. Pleasantly, true love blossoms. And all was well until the South American slime returned and tries to use the wife's written pledge to have his way with her once more. To save her husband's honor, now a well known prosecutor, she agrees, but at the last moment finds a chance to stab the cad. Thinking she had killed him, all were happy to discover that it was really the brother of a misused South American señorita, that had finished the womanizer.] **MPW**:6.11.21, p639.

[882] **THUNDER ISLAND**, U: [The characters in this pot boiler included, Isola Garcia, and Juan Garcia, played by the same Anglo lady, Pio Mendoza, and Sanchez the Loco, with a cast like that all trapped onboard ship, one might imagine any of several hundred scenarios. But the scenarist was apparently stuck in the all to familiar standard form. More significant than one more señorita falling for the Anglo hero and each saving the other's lives were **Variety's** comments concerning the Mexican characterizations: "the make up of the white folks impersonating Mexicans [was] atrocious." It was apparently still impossible to find those Hispanic actors and actresses. The ad copy to sell this low cost production was to read: "A revolution a Day Keeps Inertia Away." "That was the System in Lower California."] **MPW**:6.25.21, p845, **V**:6.17.21.

[883] **TROPICAL LOVE**, Playgoers Pictures: ["Love [was] born in a glance under the spell of the tropics and Adventure walk[ed] in hand with romance." Staging scenarios south of the border or anywhere in the Caribbean always drew a good audience. Things happened there that could not be allowed in the safe and secure north. Because it was "as fascinating as the lure of the tropics, as rugged as the rugged lives of the adventurers who brave it's fatal spell, as passionate as the moon flooded nights--that's why this tale of the tropics had the lure which leads to the box office." This tropical magnet was filmed in "Porto Rico."] **MPW**:12.24.21.

[884] **WEST OF THE RIO GRANDE**, Bert Lublin: [Somewhere just west of the Rio Grande, near the Mexican border, "the law is just beginning to be felt." There, Anglo "cowpuchers" duke it out with the new settlers who are beginning to fence in their open range. This screen struggle would continue for the next seventy years, frequently involving some kid named Billy who has a taste for Mexican señoritas.] **MPW**:3.26.21, p410.

[885] **WET GOLD**, Ince: [The prototype for scores of remakes which through the decades might be used to chronicle the history and evolution of SCUBA technology, this film is set somewhere in Cuban waters where two rival gangs of goods and bads struggling with their different submarines to capture the prize. Innovative advertising claimed that the film, first viewed by Senator Knox, who was so impressed with the technical aspects of the underwater photography and use of submarines he recommended it for the President's diversion. The Chief Executive, according to the copy, had "about as enjoyable an hour of entertainment as he ever spent in a theater."] **MPW**: 6.18.21, p67, **V**:9.9.21, **MPG**.

[886] **WHAT HAPPENED TO ROSA?** Goldwyn: [The very popular Mable Norman starred in this entry. She appeared as a hard working shop girl whose mother was a Spanish dancer. In time she is told by a gypsy fortune teller that she is in reality the reincarnation of a noble Spanish lady and that she will meet the man of her dreams. He turns out to be Dr. Drew and when she goes to the same masquerade ball he is attending, a fight breaks out. Being on a steam boat, she sheds the high caste Spanish lady outfit she was wearing and jumps ship. All think her drowned, but in the last scene, after having been hit by a pushcart and brought to the doctor, she finds her clothes and the doctor who is more than willing to be hers forever.] **afic**.

[887] **WHEN DAWN CAME**, State Rights: [Some Hispanic influences could be positive. Those concerned with the church could exert a powerful influence, even on Anglos. This was the story of "man's regeneration through the power of love" and the help of the good padre at the Mission of San Juan Capistrano. After discovering that his best friend had done his girl upon request, the hero of this piece fell into the pit filled with drugs and alcohol. It took a warm willing body to start his climb back to the surface. He met the lady in the old Spanish church and although blind, she was able with the help of a kindly padre, to provide him with a new out look on life and a new reason to live.] **MPW**:1.1.21

[888] **WINNERS OF THE WEST**, U: {Serial, 18 chapters} [The main theme for this silent serial concerned the valiant efforts of Captain John C. Fremont and his small troop of above average men as they continuously battled the forces trying to prevent the United States from acquiring control of California from the Mexicans in 1848-49.]

[889] **A WISE FOOL**, FP/P: [A Spanish adventurer was the cause for all the problems faced by a Canadian family, unfortunately created for them when he married into their family.] **MPG**.

1922

[890] **ACROSS THE BORDER**, Ayson: ["Big Boy" Williams starred in this western "full of snap and vim, good riding and hard fighting." The fighting was against a band of desperados which included the necessary Mexican baddies who "preyed on the surrounding ranchers." But the bandits in this story were led by an Anglo sheriff, an unusual characterization for the time.] **MPW**:4.1.22, p550, **EXD**:2.11.22, **FD**:1.29.22.

[891] **THE ADVENTURES OF CAPTAIN KETTLE**, Brit: [Soldiers of fortune were part of the British imperial tradition before others no less bold crossed the big pond to settle in the confines of Los Estado Unidos. In this film it was still an Anglo, but an English Anglo, who traveled to South America to be crowned "King" of a South American plantation and allows himself to be saved by the pretty Pacquita.] **MPG**.

[892] **THE AMERICAN TOREADOR**, Anchor: [There was a wonderful naivete about a Hollywood projection like this. The scenario cannot help but make one smile, but it also has a bit of a dark side. It was filled with the exuberance of believing that North Americans could excel at absolutely anything, anywhere in the world at anytime, but it also reflected a racial superiority that projected more than a condescending attitude toward the assumed inferiority of Hispanics in general, and more specifically in this case, that of Spaniards. Certainly 1922 was not a big year for racial harmony in the United States. Terms likes like "darkie" and "greaser" were part of daily vocabulary. The following review speaks for itself, and is reprinted here to indicate to how blithely such terms could be used with absolutely no intention to offend. It should be noted that the term "greaser" originally referred to Mexican's alone. Only later did the public, and the silver screen generalize it to all Hispanics. This reviewer for **Moving Picture World** in 1922 had already applied it to Spaniards. The scene for this North American triumph over local customs was set in the "romantic land of Spain". The femme star, Virginia Warwick was considered "as beautiful a brunette as there [was] on the screen" then and "particularly suitable to the Spanish señorita role." The over all forecast for the film's success was very favorable. The brief story outline that the trade journal provided at this time reads as follows: "Bill, a husky Western cowboy, determines to visit the land of romance and bull throwing and vamping señoritas--Spain. Bill finds the wild and woolly west tame in comparison with the Spanish everyday life, but he finds no hardship in acclimating himself. He runs into Mose, a high brown from the home of prohibition, who was a member of his regiment during the recent war. Mose elects himself Bill's valet, more for protection than anything else. So Bill finds himself given every attention, but unconsciously assuming the role of bouncer for the darkie. Bill falls in love with a señorita who spends most of her time trying to

persuade a greaser, who admits he's the champion bull thrower of Spain, that the place for bull throwing is inside the ring. But then bull throwers are bull throwers, and Bill has the time of his life trying to propose to the señorita. But toreadors are not to be cast off and in time Bill finds himself fighting the greaser. Of course he wins. But the climax is staged at the arena, where the supposed champion is pinned to the ground by a rushing bull. Bill rushes into the fray and shows the greaseball how cows, bulls and such are tossed in America--and he does and saves the champion himself. That's the beginning of the end for the champion, who is licked at a duel, kicked around like Jim Casey's dog, and otherwise made to understand that his business is bulling the bull." Anyone seeing this film or reading this review could not help but feel that it was gracious and heroic of this "American" cowboy to save the lying braggart and to show the obviously inept greaser just how to do what he had been trained for all his life.] **MPW**:9.2.22, p63.

[893] **BACHELOR DADDY**, P: [Some have written on what has been described as the first official Mexican protests directed against specific Hollywood films and production companies made in 1922. There is no doubt that Mexico was concerned and that the first real business of the newly created Hays office was focused on these protests, but in 1922, the United States had not granted de jure recognition to Mexico, they would not until the following year. What the Mexican government wanted was simply respect for its people, and although the newly created MPPDA, the Hays office sent emissaries south to sooth ruffled feelings, and promised that they would exert pressure to prevent the defaming of foreign nationals, the real impact of this organization would not be felt until WWII. In reality, no branch of the national government, State Department or other, ever officially directed the production companies to clean up their Hispanic characterizations until the creation of the Office of the Coordinator of Inter-American Affairs in 1941. Government regulation was feared by the production companies and that was the driving force behind the establishment of the MPPDA, the concept was self-regulation, not government regulation. It is true that Will Hays traveled to Mexico in 1922 and promised that the production companies that had given him his million dollar a year job would be good, and to try to do better, but in reality he did not as of yet have the power to enforce his promises with the producers. Mexico's protest of the above film is discussed briefly in the following: Helen Delpar, "Mexico, the MPPDA, and Derogatory Films, 1922-1926," "Goodbye to the "Greaser", Journal of Popular Film and Television, Spring 1984, pp34-41.

In 1922 Mexico announced an official ban on all films produced by two production companies, Famous Players and Metro. It is very doubtful that the Mexican government could have in any way made good on this threat. But no one really knew that then. One of the four films specifically mentioned as objectionable was **Bachelor Daddy**. Most of the action in this film takes place north of the border, but some significant events occur in Mexico. Daddy was very well to do and among his many properties there were some mines in Mexico which were "in danger of being ruined through the operations of a band of guerrillas." Having been advised of such, the northerner travelled south. Upon his arrival, the bandits attack and kill his apparently healthy partner who had fathered five children. Once the problem was cleared up and the bodies buried, Daddy "on his trip back to civilization" with the kiddies, promised that he would care for them forever. The Mexicans were characterized as bloody bandits who could operate in that barbarous place without fear of reprisal.] **V**:4.28.22.

[894] **THE BEARCAT**, U: [Hoot Gibson was the "Singing Kid" in this one. Cast as a likeable, if not melodious villain, a bandit from across the border, who when he comes north does so "singing bloodthirsty verses." After at first fighting with the local sheriff, they soon become fast friends. There's a girl, an eastern rival, an act of sacrifice and a happy ending.] **MPW**:4.8.22, p664.

[895] **THE BELLS OF SAN JUAN**, F: [The setting for this film was "a village on the Mexican border", but reviewer's thought that the "backgrounds [were] somewhat lacking in realism." Broderick Norton, the sheriff of San Juan, kept his town clean and vowed to run down the man who had murdered his father. He did and discovered that it was not a Mexican who had been the culprit, but an Anglo named, Garson.] **MPW**:11.4.22, p85.

[896] **BIG STAKES**, East Coast Productions: [J. B. Warner was credited with playing the role of the "Señor Americano with [a] pleasing style and a sense of humor instead of the swashbuckling" more characteristic of others, in this story of the Mexican border. The big stakes to be won were the lasting affections of Señorita Mercedes Aloyes, Elinor Fair, who was in love with El Captain Montaya, Robert Gary, until the Americano showed up. Shortly after the Mexican miss met him, his natural boyish charm made her question her love for the Captain. This of course provokes him into seeking vengeance. After having witnessed the two in a secret rendezvous, he lured them to a mountain retreat where he planned to introduce the gringo to a deadly viper. He was dissuaded from his intent by the North American's appeal to fair play. Warner challenged the officer to a game of chance involving the Mexican jumping bean called the "brincadore." That would decide who should be pressed against the killer snake. Jim wins, but allows the señorita to choose who she would be with. Meanwhile, Mary, a pretty local lady has sent for Jim to help her with her distress. In one of the few films of this era, the darkskinned lady decided to choose the Mexican over the Anglo suitor. But with some foresight, the scenarist had provided Jim with lovely solace of his own kind, Mary would be his.] **MPW**: 9.30.22, p397.

[897] **BLOOD AND SAND**, FPL: [There is some irony in the fact that Valentino, the great silver screen Latin lover, was being sued by his apparently unsatisfied ex-wife who claimed that

their marriage had never been consummated, while at the same time Lasky was fighting to provide him with the part of Juan Gallardo. But the producer wanted Rudolf Valentino to play the irresistible matador and hot blooded ladies man in Balasco Ibenez epic of the corrida's fleeting fame and tragic consequences. Bells must ring somewhere in the far reaches of the Hollywood hills when reviewers agree. All three mentioned here made reference to the same audience reaction, "gaufaws", when the former Shiek did his very best to resist, to even hold at arms length, the sexy vampire that was wanting her way with him because he looked so cute in his tight little outfit that clung so closely to his masculine frame. Audiences wanted their Spanish lovers to act the part, resist till propriety closed the shades, but submit to sweet the temptation of sin all the same. Certainly, this was behavior unbecoming to a Spaniard. Despite such criticism, the film played to packed houses and would be remade several times. Every cliche known to the aficionado and included in Hemingway's prescribed guide to death in the afternoon, appears in this production projected across the screen in broad strokes. Poor, ignorant, Spanish peasant achieves fame and fortune in the corrida, buys madre a house to take her off her knees [but she keeps the floor washing bucket just in case], is loved by the sweet clean señorita of his youth, and later vamped by the hot blooded seductress while the esposa suffers, losing his ability with the bulls, he does also with the ladies, dejected, but offered one moment for regeneration, he is magnificent one last time before dying in the arms of his faithful wife. A timeless scenario just waiting for Tyrone to grow into it.] **MPW**:5.20.22, p275, 8.19.22, p607, **EXH**:5.27.22, **V**:8.11.22, **NYT**:4.7.22, FD:8.13.22, **MPG**.

[898] **THE BORDER SCOUTS**, Distributed by Bert Hall. [No further information yet found.]

[899] **BORDER TOWN**, U: [By 1922 Hoot Gibson had shot up enough bodies to have his name added to the legendary list of those stalwarts that Hollywood history would have us believe, conquered and tamed the more uncivilized agents of the wild west, Mexican bandits and indians in general. This brief piece was more a Horatio Alger script than anything else. As a reformed gunman, Hoot was provided the opportunity of saving the rich ranch man's daughter which he did with required dispatch. For this he was made the top hand and continued to work for the best outfit around, as its protector. The Hispanic characterizations were incidental and included merely to identify the border location.]

[900] **A CALIFORNIA ROMANCE**, Fox: [Hollywood could poke fun at itself and did so with this burlesque featuring John Gilbert, still safe in silents, and sometimes swashbuckler. **Variety** suspected that this film had been shot as a straight production and, that only after it was previewed, was it considered better to play it for laughs as a parody. Gilbert played a young Spanish guitar player, appropriately named, Don Patricio Fernando, who has problems with his true love because he will not take up arms against those Anglo elements that

want to deliver California into the hands of the United States. His lady, Donna Dolores, led an active and aggressive band of local women who joined with an apparently patriotic officer to fight the merger. But when it is revealed that her countryman, a Mexican, Don Juan Diego, by nombre, was more nefarious than the prospective new landlords, that his swashbuckling sons of liberty were merely out for themselves, she sees the light and makes her Spanish/Mexican stalwart shine as he proudly helps to turn over one of the richer parts of his country to the United States. In the final scenes both join hands in their support for the red, white and blue.] **V**:5.17.23, afic.

[901] **THE CALL OF HOME**, R-C Pictures: [The scenarist for this production certainly created a nice tight little package of problems and with the help of a natural disaster had it all worked out in the last reel. Gerry Lansing loved his lady, but suspected her of having an affair with his best friend, Alan. Despondent, Gerry headed for one of two traditional areas of refuge that Hollywood provided for those who wanted to forget their past. With little military training or desire to enjoy the rigors of the French Foreign Legion, the wealthy young aristocrat headed for the wilderness of South America. There, in no time at all he acquired a plantation and an affection for Margarita, "a Spanish girl who he marries." All was well until a great flood destroyed the plantation and drowned the newly wed señora. To make matters worse, the scripter gave Jerry a nearly deadly touch of "jungle fever." When all looked darkest, Alan happened onto the scene and explained to Gerry that his little wife was at home wondering where he had disappeared to without a trace so than no one would ever find him. Better yet, she was with child and waiting for dad to return to her open arms. Never had she been unfaithful. Only in that dream factory by the sea could it all be so neat and tidy. South America and the Spanish lady had once more served their function.] afic.

[902] **CAPTAIN FLY-BY-NIGHT**, FBO: [It is apparent from reading the script for this fantasy set in Spanish California, that the scenarist had no idea that Mexico had achieved its independence from Spain in 1821. The story takes place some time around 1824, when a notorious bandit, Captain Fly-By-Night was causing the inhabitants of Spanish California a lot of trouble by indiscriminately robbing everyone he could. Most of the action takes place in an inn where two strangers play cards for each other's horse. When one wins, he is discovered to be the bandit. The other was apparently a "representative", a spy, for the Spanish government who with the help of a local señorita, was responsible for having the baddie "justly punished."] **MPW**:12.20.22.

[903] **CHASING THE MOON**, Fox: [This comedy melodrama starring Tom Mix had him playing a bit of a philanderer. When his lady discovers him dallying with a delightful little damsel, she "upbraids him", not for his indiscretion, but, frugal little flapper that she is, for not being as hard a worker as her father and brother. A little later, Tom wanders into a shop

and while looking around breaks the retort he happened to pick up. To his horror he learns that the glass vile he had cut himself upon contained a deadly poison that would kill him in thirty days unless an antidote was administered and worse, the only one with that saving drug was someone on a world tour. Luckily Tom found him somewhere in Spain, it's not that big. Even luckier, his girl and her brother found him before he could take the saving solution because it was discovered that the retort had not contained the poison and had he taken the antidote, he would have died in another thirty days. With Tom safe, the lovers enjoyed their romantic surroundings for a bit. We can only wonder what was done with the writer.] **V**:3.03.22, <u>afic</u>.

[904] <u>COCAINE</u>, Br: [Concern over cocaine use continued from its earliest appearance in film to this present day. Crusades against its use were no novel thing in 1914 or in 1922. This film was inspired by the then attempt to provide the public with more information on the evil effects of that insidious narcotic. The only difference between Hollywood's version of then and now was the supply route and the supplier. The Chinese were universally accepted as the suppliers and the route usually involved Mexico. As it is at this present time, the projected implication was established, that if there were no supply, there would be no problem. No one made films that said the supply would dry up, if the users stopped demanding the importation of the drug. Cocaine had been grown in the Andean countries for more than four thousand years. The business of North America has always been business, whatever the demand, be it booze or drugs, some entrepreneur will supply it.] **V**:5.19.22.

[905] <u>CROSSROADS</u>, William Smith: [This simple scenario belonged in films that had been made ten years before, but it still played well enough for another effort. A young Anglo who all knew would be perfect for the job, was prevented from being made sheriff of the border town by a sly and cunning Mexican named, Onate. He wanted the job for himself so that he could continue his nefarious doings on either side of the border. By deviously forging the correct papers, he has himself installed as the law and then made one of his henchman assault the young westerner who was forced to kill the renegade. With just cause, the Mex sheriff now pursues the lad who manages to escape through the intercession of a young girl no one would mess with because she was thought to be cursed. She somehow manages to obtain a pardon for her new love which forces the Mexican to plan outright murder, but he is prevented from doing this foul deed by that most favorite of scripters fantasies. Onate's own apparently not so faithful, Yaqui servant turns against him when he discovers the plot to actually kill the Anglo. The Mex is then properly punished. Now, with the border secure and the curse removed, the lady and lawman sneak off into the sunset, together.] **MPW**:1.6.23, p61.

[906] <u>THE CROW'S NEST</u>, Sunset Productions: [Augustina Lopez played the "squaw" woman in this racist confusion of mixed

breeds. It would seem that "Esteban" had been raised by the squaw which he believes to be his mother, a Mexican Indian, but in reality she is not. He happened to be the happy by-product of a night of pleasure his Anglo father, owner of the ranch, had enjoyed some time ago. As all grew older, he came to love Patty Benson but her beau, Beaugard, knew the truth and had to prevent it from surfacing, because, if it did, Esteban would legally inherit all the property. This proves impossible, because the scripter has the plot uncovered and the two young lovers joined together, after it is discovered that the little Mex/indio half breed was really "white." There were frequently rewards for racial purity in the early days of Hollywood.] **V**:11.17.22.

[907] **DAUGHTERS OF THE DON**, Arrow: ["An immense cast" was used for this production which focused on Mexican California in 1847. Careful attention was paid to the "Spanish and Indian costumes." Elaborate staging was planned for the huge battle scenes which highlighted the political intrigues present in the small valley that was Los Angles then. Included in all this historical drama, there was the ever necessary love story of the Mexican Señorita who falls for the North American soldier, falsely accused and facing serious problems. Separated by war, a British spy was exposed as the real culprit, and the two lovers are rejoined as the rival factions are reunited into a greater whole.] **MPW**:4.15.22, p764.

[908] **DIAMOND CARLISE**, Milburn Morante: [Somehow the screenwriter for this effort found himself sending a character named Lopez, to the tall pines of the Canadian northwest. Actually he was merely going along with his boss, the mastermind of the operations, "daring" [if you're Anglo, you can be daring] "Diamond Carlisle" the accomplished Anglo bandit. Once there he is employed by Black Meyer to use his talents at card manipulation to cheat Dick Boyd out of a lot of money. This he does with dispatch and was in the process of winning all of the remaining trees the Canadian lad owned when he saw the sister, little Mae. (On the screen, Hollywood prescribed that all girls named Mae, had to be referred to as "little Mae", even if they were a size sixteen. It was just one of those things.) Anyway, Diamond was immediately smitten by little Mae and quickly gives Dick back all of his trees and the money to boot. This is too much for the Mexican and so he tries kill his friend, but is himself done in by the RCMP, almost always in red and ready on the job. The man they got this time was a Mexican, after which Mae wrapped Diamond around her little finger.] **afic**.

[909] **THE DICTATOR**, FP/P: [This was the second official filming of the Richard Harding Davis novel **The Dictator** [559], and followed closely its success as a Broadway play. For the public it was a reaffirmation of what they felt to be typical of Latin American politics and revolutions, a reflection of the condescending treatment much of daily press afforded events which transpired to the south. "The pomp of South American officialdom in its settings of tropical loveliness makes a perfect background for the harum-scarum exploits of

the matter-of fact American hero." "The building up of political magnificence" is properly burlesqued. The story involves a New York taxi driver who follows his fare to the "trick republic of San Manana" to collect the money he is owed. There, he becomes involved in one of that nation's weekly revolutions and because he cannot speak their language, and they cannot understand good ole American, no matter how slow he speaks it, he is almost shot by a firing squad. Once he is aware of the situation, he of course takes over and controls the situation, ending the revolutionary activity and assuming power, winning the girl and righting the wrongs. It remains a scenario that is popularly believed and continues to play well to this date as the success **Moon Over Parador** well exhibited.] **MPW**:5.20.22, p277, 7.15.22, p240, **EXH**: 5.27.22, **V**:7.7.22, **NYT**:7.3.22.

[910] **DO AND DARE**, F: [Tom Mix was a top star in 1922, he was a western hero, but his success transcended the genre. This entry was somewhat out of the ordinary for him, while still keeping him essentially in character, as the flamboyant hero, true to the cause of those in need but humble still. Finding himself in a day dream about his illustrious ancestors, Kit Carson Boon, Tom, the town's resident fool, was transported back to those glory days where he lampoons his character with comedic skill. Back in the present, the scripters transport him by air plane into the very thick of a South American revolution. If ever there was a need for a Anglo! Leaving his clod like behavior, he assumes heroic stature, and singlehandedly subdues the rebels, saves the republic and wins the kisses of the fair señorita. An easy day's work for a North American, even a boob. All it required was pluck, a quality found in abundance north of the border, especially at the tip of an Anglo scripters pen.] **V**:10.27.22, **MPG**, **afic**.

[911] **THE DOUBLE O**, Arrow/Ben Wilson: [This film was advertised as a "typical story of the Mexican border ... with "greaser" intrigue and cattle-rustling, a love affair ... and the conventional balance of thrills and romance." The Double O was just this side of the Mexican border and run by a desperate character who's best friend was a Mexican, Cholo Pete, both were in league with the cattle rustlers just over the line. When the very pretty new owner of the ranch arrives, she refuses the advances of the manager. He has Cholo kidnap her, but not for long. The Anglo hero, Jack Hoxie as Happy Hanes, soon rescues her, but is himself captured by the Mex bandits. Although he has been forward enough to kiss the lovely little lady, she forgives him and comes to his rescue. Together the two of them defeat all the Mexican baddies, just before the marriage ceremony. Things happened fast on Hollywood's Rio Grande border back then.] **MPW**:12.9.22, p576.

[912] **FASCINATION**, Tiffany/Metro: [Mae Murry was one of the bright stars of the silents. In this work she portrayed, Dolores de Lisa, a special kind of a "flapper" whose creed was to live only by "impulse." This philosophy was attributed to her "hot blooded" heritage, as she was the daughter of a

Spanish father and an "American" mother. To calm these hedonistic desires it was decided to send her to Spain, under the care of a watchful tia who would curb these impulses to live only for the moment and not plan for the future as most good North American girls did. Unable to restrain her little sobrina, the aunt really becomes troubled when the flirtatious fun loving flapper attracts the attention of the great bullfighter, Carrita, who was moved by watching her interpretation of "La Danza del Toro" at a party given in his honor. All this was great fun for Dolores, but the aunt knew that the girl had no idea how "serious" such affairs were in Spain. After a series of complications, including another interlude with a cabaret dancer named Parola, a really bad sort, and at the very last moment, her father and Anglo fiance arrive in Madrid. Somewhat relieved she agrees to marry her former beau, realizing that a mixture of seriousness and gaiety was the best combination for a happy life. Apparently the more practical North American side had taken control.] **MPW**:3.11.22, p160, 4.29.22, p968, **V**:4.21.22.

The **Moving Picture World** in order to help some of the exhibitors increase their attendance figures for this film devoted a five page article filled with suggestions on how to take advantage of its Spanish setting. A masked Mae Murry was pictured in a revealing form fitted dress, wearing the horns of a bull, all of which was superimposed on a huge fan which was to be displayed over the marquee. Some of the provocative "Teasers" suggested to be employed to promote this racy Spanish story included: "Have Good Girls got **FASCINATION?** ... Is Love the Same as **FASCINATION?** [and] Can Men Resist **FASCINATION?**" Costumes for personnel were suggested. They could be simple and inexpensive. "For the girl in the ticket booth, nothing is needed save a brilliant shawl, a big comb in the back of [the] hair which should be done high, in Spanish fashion. For the men employees, the doormen, and ushers, a distinctive note [was] the hat. The usual Spanish hat ... wide brimmed, stiff felt of black ... A red handkerchief tied about the head so that a bit of it showed slanted across the forehead [would] complete the headgear. The short jacket, a white shirt, with soft collar attached and a long thin black fore-in-hand tie hanging straight, a red sash bound about the waist in a wide band, black trousers and black shoes." That was all that was needed to create Hollywood's version of a Spaniard. **MPW**:3.25.22, pp352-356.

[913] **FORTUNE'S MASK**, Vitagraph: [This O'Henry adaptation told the story of a "typical" "Dictator" "with a lot of Latin-American intrigue, revolutions and "shot at sunrise" stuff in it." It would seem that after the dictator was killed by rival politicians, his son was sent to the United States by his father's supporters with a long range plan. As the years passed, he was instilled with the idea of returning to overthrow those who had killed his parent. Apparently they had managed to retain power until he reached his majority and just at that moment they made the fatal mistake of charging the United States banana exporters an extra ten cents a bunch tax to continue operating in the Republic. Infuriated that

these crooked politicians could take such advantage of them, the company provided the young man with the necessary funds to overthrow these impediments to capitalism by "rousing the populace." He does and in so doing, becomes the new savior of the nation, with the pretty señorita at his side that he had met during the counter revolution. "Ruth Miller [was] cute and managed to make much of the role of the little Spanish girl." This slick screen justification for "Dollar Diplomacy" may have played well with audiences in the north, but it was another of the specific films mentioned by the Mexican consul that was considered seriously offensive to that nation's officials. Although the protest caused a bit of a stir, it produced no lasting results. If Hispanics south of the border wanted to see films, and they certainly did, they had to purchase them from Hollywood, and they did that in ever increasing amounts.] **V**:10.6.22.

[914] **THE GAME CHICKEN**, Realart: [Bebe Daniels, super silent screen star provided the female charm in this film of Cuban life. Always essential to Hollywood's Cuban characterization, the cockfight was featured and emphasized that its attraction transcended gender. The perky Inez, an addicted enthusiast although forbidden to attend such competitions, does so by simply wearing boy's clothing and sneaking out to see the foul competitions whenever possible. In this film, because of the ASPCA, the actual combat was only suggested. Having satisfied her blood lust for the day, she later on meets a young United States revenue agent responsible for stopping the illegal production of rum in that protectorate under United States control. [The fiasco of trying to enforce the Volstead Act in Latin territories under United States occupation in the Caribbean was considered madness, but was suggested and actual attempted.] The two immediately fall in love, but serious conflicts arise when it is discovered that either her father or the señor he wanted Bebe to marry, was a possible bootlegger. Although, the troubled lover can do little in Cuba, he is waiting on the dock in the good ole U S of A to nab the rum runners. There he meets Bebe again, but both are in great danger. Working together as lovers should, they overcome it. Thankfully, dad was not involved. But the rum never stopped flowing. A lesson present day narcotics agents have yet to learn. The supply will continue so long as North Americans demand it and have the ready cash to make the suppliers multimillionaires.] **MPW**:3.18.22, p299.

[915] **GAS OIL AND WATER**, Indy: [Many of the trade journals, especially in the previous two decades, whether consciously or not, promoted anything that was on film. Like the proverbial indiscriminate seducer, they favored anything that moved. But, by 1922 **Variety** exercised it's critical license with increasing frequency. As such, they could see no reason why this film had ever been made. What story line there was, made no sense at all. The hero seemed to be something like a secret service man, and he did establish a gas station on the Mexican border to watch for smugglers operating out of Mexico. Apparently he did not watch closely enough, because there were no arrests, and according to the reviewer, there was no ending

to this film either. Exhibitors were advised to stay away.]
V:7.7.22.

[916] GHOST BREAKER, Lasky/P: [When the beautiful Maria Theresa inherits a Spanish Castle from her aristocratic father, she soon learns that somewhere on the grounds or within the premises, there is a treasure. Other members of the family, who were not in the will knew that before, so in an effort to discourage the heiress from staying around to find it, they try to scare her out. Wallace Reid, who had been smuggled to Spain by the sympathetic señorita in a truck so he could avoid capture by the police, was the Anglo hero who came to the lady's aid. Seeing through the family's plan almost at once, he shoots her cousin the Duke and immediately dispatches all of the other psuedospooks. Although they do not find the monetary treasure all thought to be in the castle, they find a more important one in their love for one another.] MPW:9.23.22, p296, V: 9.15.22, NYT:9.11.22.

[917] GOLDEN DREAMS, Goldwyn: [All seven of the Hispanic characters in this oft told tale were Anglo actors. It included another Spanish Grandee wants to marry his daughter off to a wealthier nobleman, but she loves a less affluent engineer. As usual, the complications cause consternation with the parents, but this production featured a little variation. When pressure by the Don failed to convince his daughter, he tried force and hires a few unsavory Spaniards for the task. Luckily for the lovers there was a small circus in town and when the baddies come to harm the boy, he manages to release the lions, which frightens them away.] V:6.16.22.

[918] THE GOLDEN GIFT, Metro: [A husband looking for an easy life married Nita Gordon because he believed she would make a fortune with her singing career. After she bears him a child, she loses her voice and her job. When he leaves her, she is forced to take work as a cantina girl in a Mexican town. Provided with an opportunity to regain her voice, she leaves the child, and when the miracle happens, she becomes a renowned opera star in Europe. The deserted child had in the meanwhile, been adopted by an oil rich millionaire who left the sleazy confines of the border town for the lights of the big city. There he falls in love with a touring opera star. Yup, you guessed it, one and the same. After overcoming the explanation provided for having left the child, all were reunited.] V:3.3.22, MPG.

[919] GOLD GRABBERS, W. M. Smith: [Variety could not say enough that was bad about every aspect of this 'quicky' production which appears to be one of several the company shot in the same few days. Set on the border it dealt with the activities of claim jumpers who were trying to steal every profitable mine around. For some unknown reason, in the final reel, the head baddie gets religion and signs off a half ownership in one of the properties to the heroine of the film, a Mexican lady named Chiquita. She and the hero are then free to marry, for another unknown reason.] V:11.24.22.

[920] **GYPSY PASSION**, Fr/Indy: [A French interpretation of the classic desire expressed by all gypsy mother's that their daughter is destined to marry the King of the Gypsies. After a great deal of melodrama, and by now, very familiar characterizations, of course, she does.] **NYT**:3.27.22.

[921] **THE HALF BREED**, FN: [The reviewer for this film postulated that, at this point in time, there still existed "an almost insurmountable blood barrier against which the half-breed Indian ha[d] to fight, regardless of the advantages given him by education and civilization." Neither in society nor on the silver screen, was the halfbreed accepted as a whole person. Given this sanguine premise, he explained further that, this film explored the reasons that might allow the negative traits of "his indian blood" to "surface". The reasons were multiracial and timeless, a woman. After a lot of heartache, disappointment and adventure, he finally meets a willing white lady who would share a life with him. Luckily for both of them, she was all French, and together they decided to go to Mexico where they could be safe from the those who would condemn their union north of the border [657].] **MPW**:7.1.22, p11, p57, **V**:7.21.22.

[922] **HER HUSBANDS TRADEMARK**, P: [This society drama/western tied together by all the charms of a youthful Gloria Swanson, has her married to a materialistic man who merely uses her for his own personal gain. For a while it works well, but when he overextends his lavish life style, he needs a new business success. A mining engineer from Mexico provides an opportunity with the promise of rich oil land. Using Swanson's seductive allure's to entice the prospect, they come to a preliminary agreement which requires a trip to the land of bandits and oil. Soon seduced by the heat of the tropics, the lovely lady finds herself falling in love with the engineer. He had loved her from the first, but there was the husband. Luckily for the pair of tropical love birds the scripters provided a lustful General who chances to see the swan and desires her for himself. With his troops he attacks the oil camp, but manages only to perform the service of shooting the impediment. The two now high tail it for the Rio Grande where the Calvary come to their rescue and all is well on the border. This was the third film mentioned in the Mexican protest of 1922. They may well have felt that violating international borders was hardly a subject for screen glorification.] **MPW**:3.4.22, p81, **V**:2.24.22.

[923] **HILLS OF MISSING MEN**, Playgoers Pictures: [Unhappy with life, and "a half-crazed dreamer," Crando organizes an army of like minded men, mostly wanted outlaws and plans to take over lower California, resting it from United States control, and establishing it as the refuge for bandits it once was. With that accomplished, he would easily have himself proclaimed king. To help him in this exercise in empire building, he enlists the aid of "the Dragon" alleged to be the fiercest fugitive in five states, and wanted by the North American law everywhere. Yet, as with many of the best laid plans of Hollywood writers, it turns out that the fire breather was not

really a Mexican gringo hater, but really a United States secret service man who was out to thwart his rebellious plot. He does and California was once more saved for the union.] **V**:3.31.22, **EXH**: 3.4.22, p5, **MPG**.

[924] **I CAN EXPLAIN**, Metro: [Another of the four films that Mexican secretary of foreign relations, Alberto J. Pani, specifically complained about in the 1922 protest. Again, most of the action takes place in the north where a successful business man becomes jealous of the attention that his younger partner is paying to his wife. He suspects no good, but is convinced that all is well. Shortly thereafter, his jealousy is once more activated and this time he elects to remove the problem. Deciding not to use the weapon he wanted to employ, he plans to send the youth to be the head of the South American branch of his operation. There the youth gains confidence. Faced with a bandit named "El Pavor" he becomes involved in a number of comedy situations finally returning home to seek his true love who is at that moment being married. With his new personality and experience he plays the last scene of **The Graduate** and "walks away with all the honors." Juan Pedro and Carmencita Gardez, were played by Anglos. The Mexican government did not like the film and told the production company that all it's films would be banned in Mexico. But there is no evidence that this was ever implemented, exhibitors needed these films for their audiences.] **V**:4.7.22.

[925] **JUST TONY**, F: [Considered by **Variety**, "Hollywood's only absolutely natural actor," [the fickled reviewers said the same thing about Rin Tin Tin] Tony the most talented horse before Trigger, was truly Tom Mix's pride and joy. Here he is the featured star, with Mix playing second banana but slippery enough to save the animal from a terrible, "brutal" Mexican, Manuel Cordoval, his owner who constantly beat him to break his spirit. Actually the killing of the Mexican was left to Tony himself, who justifiably tramples him to death just as he appears with the whip once too often. Then, he and Tom, who played Jim in this hos opry, get it together and head north.] **V**:8.11.22, **NYT**:8.7.22.

[926] **THE KICK-BACK**, FBO: [By 1922 Harry Carey had ridden back and forth across the border more than any other western star, he was a favorite with devotees of the western but his popularity transcended that of the oater genre. In this his first personal production, he chose to cross the border once more. It was good boxoffice. White Horse Harry, Anglo hero and very much taken with Mignonne, a sweet Mexican girl accepted an assignment from some baddies he was told just wanted to push a few horses across the border. In reality the bandits wanted his ranch, which possessed the only water hole in the county. The complex plan has him unknowingly crossing the line with the cargo and some forged papers, with the Mexican official prewarned. When they stop old White Horse and try to arrest him, he kills one of the "Mexes", is captured and sentenced to be shot. He of course escapes, crosses back over the Rio Grande and quickly discovers that

the schemers have taken over his ranch and poisoned his lady's mind against him. Real men, who knew the meaning of the word, did not take such perfidy without retaliation. Once he finds the head heavy he shoots him and disposes of the rest of the gang, but the local sheriff takes him to jail. Just as he is about to be lynched, the Texas Rangers come to his rescue and restore order. The final shot shows the lovers reunited, about to be wed, which was apparently considered punishment enough for having "murdered" two men, one on either side of the border. "Mignonne" a French import, was applauded for her role as "the little Mexican girl."] **V**:7.28.22.

[927] **THE KINGFISHER'S ROOST**, Pinnacle: [The other Hart, Neal also had a following, though not as large as his namesakes. In this typical, what could now be called "B" western, he clears his name, by proving that he had been framed. Working with the chief of the Mexican rurales, he breaks up the gang that was responsible for giving him his bad reputation. He also gets the girl, it was still required. The industry had grown sufficiently by this time to enjoy a significant amount of class stratification of its own. Nickel houses still existed and provided those not so affluent members of society with a significant amount of entertainment. Films not considered top of the line, frequently found themselves making the rounds of such establishments.] **V**:4.28.22, **MPG**.

[928] **THE LOADED DOOR**, U: [This time Hoot Gibson returns to his home ground and finds that his former employer has been killed by a bunch of baddies who are running a drug smuggling operation on the border. Blackie Lopez was the Texican who headed the dirty dealings. When Hoot begins to interfere with the established order, Blackie quickly responds, he captures Hoot's woman and threaten him with taking her life if he refused to lay off. To no avail, Hoot had more than enough to clean up the baddies, stop the drug flow and get the girl back, it was still required.] **V**:8.11.22, **MPG**.

[929] **A LOT OF BULL**, U: [This Universal one reel comedy featured Carles Molina as an auto salesman in Mexico whose adventures there included chasing four bulls out of the corrida with a broom, escaping from a bandit by donning a little drag and wearing a beard. In the last scene he is being shaved by a barber who turns out to be the individual he was trying to avoid.] **MPW**:12.9.22, p578.

[930] **LURE OF GOLD**, Steiner: [A low budget western starring Neal Hart who becomes rich by discovering gold and winning the favors of a lady opera singer he happens to save from rampaging wild bulls. His fortune though, draws the attention of the bandit breed, including Latigo Bob. Together with his baddies, the halfbreed robs Hart, but they in turn are thwarted by the brave female who, as many a screen woman was in the twenties, strong, silent and willing to fight for the man she loved.] **MPG**.

[931] **MAN OF COURAGE**, Aywon: [By this time **Variety** seemed to enjoy the opportunity to be highly critical, and they showed

little mercy for this production, which in their analysis, was in every way bad. Basically this was a quicky which made no pretense at reaching for the stars, or even as high as the Hills out in Beverly. Part of the scenario had been used several times before and would be again, a rich father's son was more than a disappointment to the family. Sent on his own, in tie and tails, he wakes up in a box car that has taken him to border country. [See **Border Cafe**, 1937] There he discovers that his true love has been taken from an international train by Mexican bandits, Aquila, El Cholo and friends, and is being held for the prescribed dineros. Provided with the opportunity to prove his manhood, he does and rescues the girl sending the Mexicans scurrying for the deep badlands.] **V**:4.21.22.

[932] **MIDNIGHT**, Realart Pictures: [Talk about close ...! Edna Morris, the daughter of a North American Ambassador to a South American republic falls in love with Potter an embassy attache, but not a real nice guy. Immediately after they wed, it is discovered that the spouse would be arrested for embezzlement. To escape this Potter, jumps into the bay and all think him drowned. Now back in the states, Edna falls for Jack Dart and they plan to marry. No sooner are the bans posted, then Potter resurfaces and demands blackmail. The two lovers ignore his letters and marry anyway, but when they return from the ceremony, they find the louse in the library. Luckily he was dead or had at least ceased breathing, a mere ten minutes before the two had become one.] **afic**.

[933] **MORAN OF THE LADY LETTY**, FP/P: [Ramon Laredo, a society idler, much sought after by the San Francisco debs, was played by Rudy Valentino, the "tango idol," in this top line production which attempted to make proper use of the "Latin Lover's" charm and for some, his surprising athletic ability. During a night of frivolity on his yacht, he is drugged and shanghaied aboard a pirate ship where he proves his manhood by hard work and stuff and achieves the position of first mate. While at sea the pirates chance across the **Lady Letty's** burning hulk. Only lovely Moran, the captain's daughter has survived the fire and she is taken on board to become the object of the lecherous chief pirate's lust. When Ramon learns of this, and that she will be sold into slavery to the slimy natives when they reach their next port some where in Mexico or Central America [the reviewers disagreed], he determines to prevent it. Once in port the native bandits are invited aboard to see the wares and are 'wowed' by Moran's marvelous frame. Quickly Ramon organizes the crew and together they beat the bandidos into submission with belaying pins. Even the captain is forced into hiding. Returning home with his prize, the Latin hero scorns the advances of all the ladies who have been waiting dock side for him and after a battle royal with the former captain, finds happiness in the arms of his true love, Moran, who proved she could love him best of all.] **EXH**:2.18.22, p51, **V**:2.10.22, **MPG**.

[934] **MR BARNES OF NEW YORK**, Goldwyn: [Roman still credited as Samaniegos, Navarro in his second credited role played,

Antonio in this early Maffia movie which involved, what else, a vendetta. Latin blood was hot in Corsica also.] **V**:6.2.22.

[935] **MY AMERICAN WIFE**, FP/PAR: [Gloria Swanson at her most seductive best portrayed a Kentucky horse woman in this film. At a local race, she meets and falls for Manuel La Tassa, Antonio Moreno, handsome Latin lover that he was. This time he was an Argentine sportsman who's life was simple, he raced horses and loved his lady. She unfortunately, attracted a lot of attention and many admirers, so poor Antonio was kept busy defending his lands and trying to get her honor back, to say little of his own. But the Latin temptress loved it all, he always won and so did his horses. Being macho, it was a toss up as to which pleased him more. But in the final scene, after having been wounded one more time, Gloria saves him from the further evil intent of Don Fernando De Contas, and convinces her man to enter the more secure profession of serving his country as a member of the government. Gloria had apparently not seen any movies dealing with Latin Revolutions.] **V**:1.5.23, **MPG**, afic.

[936] **NORTH OF THE RIO GRANDE**, Lasky: [Lasky promoted his star Bebe Daniels in this change of pace western which offers little new in story line. She loved her man and had no real problem with her chief competition, the dark skinned and beautiful, Lola Sanchez, who had once stimulated the hero's ardor. He is so taken with the Anglo gal that it does not even bother him, when it is discovered that her dad turns out to be the chief heavy.] **MPW**:4.27.22, p416, 6.24.22, p732, **V**:5.19.22.

[937] **OLD SPAIN**, F/Educational: [This travelogue took audiences to Spain and displayed "the abundance of beauty" easily found in that romantic country. "The Alhambra, the celebrated edifice which date[d] back to the Moorish occupation [was] minutely described. ... Most attractive of the various native features included a selection of the typical Spanish beauties. An informal dance given out-doors by some of the younger girls. The close-ups of two or three of the women are lovely enough in themselves to make the film worth-while." One assumes the reviewer may well have been a male.] **MPW**:12.2.22, p462.

[938] **ONE WEEK OF LOVE**, Selznick: [Mexico was used in this film chiefly to provided a properly malevolent place to crash the madcap heroine's airplane so that she could be saved by the more down to earth renegade Anglo who was the only one that could tame her wilder side. Actually she crashes the plane into a mountain hut, but the three men who come to the rescue claim her as a prize and cut cards to determine sole proprietary interest. One of the more nasty Mexicans wins the draw, but the Anglo convinces him to sell her to him. She of course loathes him from the start, but he manages to turn her disgust into love right after they survive the train wreck and flood which were included to provide a few added obstacles to overcome. They cause a couple of hitches, but no real problems, and by the last real, the once haughty lady was

properly submissive and anxious to wed. Not even in Mexico, only in Hollywood.] **V**:11.17.22.

PATHE REVIEW:

[939] **#185:** "Some beautifully colored effects [were] obtained in this picture ... of the Pyrenees along the Franco-Spanish border." **MPW**:12.9.22, p576.

[940] **PRIDE OF PALOMAR**, P: [The dark shades of anti-Japanese racism cast by the Hearst's invasionary nightmare in **Patria** [684] were still evident in this blatantly racist production. **Variety** claimed that it would not be surprised to hear some form of protest from the State Department because of it's offensiveness to the oriental character. Filmed amidst the beautiful scenery of lower Spanish California, with ancient mission churches and impressive [North Americanized] haciendas, the story had Don Miguel, Don Mike, to his friends, returning home from the recent trouble in Europe, a hero with the A. E. F. Arriving home, he discovered his father dead and an eastern capitalist trying to sell, his inheritance to a consortium of Japanese who want to start a colony of settlers in that region on his very rancho and other contiguous properties purchased for that purpose. Quick to react, and in no subtle manner he informs the "Jap", that no one with his peculiar ocular aberration is going to sleep in his bed. Quicker still to be offended, the oriental announces that if he cannot buy the property at that time, "one day" he will return with the Japanese army "and take [his] damned ranch." In defiance, he strikes a match across the face of the bust of George Washington that just happens to adorn the atrium. Audiences shuddered at such contempt. Needing $300,000, Mike disguises himself as a Mexican, apparently admitting his ancestry, and goes to the track with his favorite horse which is entered in the big race at 200 to 1 and wins enough to prevent the tragic first wave of the sons of the rising sun from establishing their beachhead. The screen divinity was always on the side of the Anglo Saxon right. It all ends with the old family retainer, Pablo, roping the invader and dragging him across the desert. Well, Don Mike does get the capitalist's daughter, also, there should be some reward for saving the nation from the "yellow peril." Actually a one armed Spencer Tracy ends the final chapter of such screen reinforced racism out west with his performance in **Bad Day At Black Rock**. Somewhat more sedate, the **NYT** quipped somewhat sardonically: "Cheers--if you like that sort of stuff." The Hays Office was made aware that Hearst planned this production and Will penned a letter explaining that such a film would certainly prove offensive to the Japanese government. He asked for five specific deletions to be made, but no response appears in the **Hays Papers** and the film's production was not interrupted. Neither were the deletions made, George still had to suffer the indignation of being struck in the face with searing magnesium.] **MPW**:12.2.22, P456, **V**:11.24.22, **NYT**:11.20.22, **MPG**. W. Hays to W.R Hearst, 11.18.22.

[941] **THE PRISONER OF ZENDA**, Metro: [Roman (Samaniegos) Navarro played the role of Rupert of Hentzau in this classic adventure. Ever innovative, Rex Ingram the director shot both a happy and unhappy ending to this film and allowed the exhibitors to choose the one that pleased them.] **V**:8.4.22.

[942] **RED HOT ROMANCE**, John Emerson and Anita Loos/FN: [This attempt at satire aimed its barbs at films like **Soldier of Fortune** [509] and **A Man's Man** [990]. The hero was named Washingtonian Rowland Stone, son of a recently deceased father who's legacy left him wanting more than a low paying job with the family insurance company with prospects of inheriting all, if he did not lose a penny of the established assets. Certainly a problem for southern theaters at this time, the hero's friend and side kick was a black man, named Thomas Snow who, although he takes good care of his masser, has more significant responsibilities later in the film. The boy is in love with Anna Mae Byrd, but things look bleak until one Enrico de Castanet arrives on the scene as the minister/representative of Bunkonia, a besieged kingdom somewhere in the "Pyranees." He is traveling with an international spy, the Countess de Plotz and planned to use her to attract an American consul that he could manipulate, one that will do his bidding and not interfere with the revolutionary activity in his kingdom. When Colonel Byrd is appointed to the post and takes his daughter with him, the hero follows. There he is persuaded by the enterprising Castanet to insure the life of King Caramba XIII, whose luck is about to run out. When the stalwart lad discovers the plot, he realizes that all will be lost if the monarch dies. Employing his Anglo ingenuity, he manages to save the King through his heroic efforts and by using a troop of "colored" American soldiers led by his friend. With the company and country saved, he inherits all of the dad's wealth and the little lady's favors. For southern audiences, the concern was not the ridiculous characterization of the buffoon like Hispanics, but that black men in bluejacket uniforms were prodding white men with bayonets, and that Snow was actually made a bailiff in the courtroom scene. The film did not play well south of the Mason Dixon line.] **V**:1.27.22.

[943] **REJUVENATED MEXICO**, Kineto: [A travelogue presenting "the great possibilities of that country ... the industrial and mining centers of Pachuca, near Mexico City" and some hope for the future.]   **MPW**:1.14.22, p205.

[944] **ROLLING DOWN TO RIO**, U. S. Navy: [This film made by the Navy Department, was shown in theaters under the title: **Rolling Down to Rio With Secretary of State Charles E. Hughes"**. It featured the hundredth anniversary celebration of Brazilian independence with "points of interest in that city, warships and delegations from various countries, a parade with U. S. Marines and gobs in a boat race won by boys from the U.S.S. Maryland notwithstanding a bad start. There is also a full chronicle of the daily life of the sailors on Uncle Sam's warship, from reveille to taps, showing battle drill with the big guns's various sports and amusements ... which are so

attractive as to make you wish you were one of the sailors."
Did you forget that you were reading a review about rolling
down to Rio? Apparently this thinly disguised recruitment
film had one of the loveliest back drops any such two reeler
could want.] **MPW:11.25.22, p363.**

[945] <u>SILVER SPURS</u>, Doubleday Productions: [When a well liked
and general all around good guy was honored by his friends
with a going away party at one of New York's finest niterys,
the boys decided to give the stalwart fellow a set of silver
spurs. It would seem that this Anglo adventurer had decided
to go west to seek adventure, what else? In as much as such
starred spikes were considered standard western attire, how
could they let him go questing naked? Almost immediately upon
arriving in the wild and wooly he met a lovely señorita lady,
a Spanish one and they of course fell in love ... boy when
things are right under Hollywood's western skies. Events now
began to move even more quickly, after a few essentials were
tended to, the erstwhile hero discovers that his lady has been
defrauded out of her inheritance by an unscrupulous half breed
Mexican/Indian and now her very life was threatened. The Anglo
was amazed, just two weeks before he had been with the boys
back at Delmonicos just hoping for such a chance and here it
was handed to him on his silver spurs. In no time at all he
calls out the culprit, fights several battles with him and his
bandit band and wins the day and the dineros for what was now
his woman. With the adventure just beginning, he put those
shinny spurs right under the bed in the sleeper he had hired
to head them back to civilization, where the boys were waiting
to inspect his prize and listen to all the tall tales of
glory. No one would be disappointed.] **afic**.

[946] <u>SKY HIGH</u>, F: [Certainly one of the most spectacular Tom
Mix films in terms of the super stunts the star performed, he
also manages to secure the nation against the illegal influx
of Chinese immigrants who were being smuggled across the
Mexican border. When Tom discovered that there was a
veritable army of the 'little yellow men' holed up in the
grand canyon being readied for transshipment to all parts of
these United States, he uncovers their leader, breaks up the
operation and wins the little lady, all this while performing
some of the "most breathtaking stunts yet filmed" for the
silver screen.] **V:1.27.22, MPG.**

[947] <u>THE SPANISH JADE</u>, P: [This dramatic romance set in sunny
Spain told the story of a "good and beautiful señorita, who
[was] sold to a young dilettante by an unscrupulous an brutal
father." The struggle of this "soft-eyed" Spanish heroine,
Manuela, with her purchaser, results in his death and forms
the basis "for a series of murders, with "blood for blood" as
the battle-cry". "Relentless vendetta always follow[s] such a
mysterious death in Spain." The North American in this, Gil
Perez, manages to extricate the madonna in distress and win
her heart in the process. Exhibitors were generally pleased:
"Here is something different. An entertaining picture staged
in Spain with a wealth of attractive exteriors which are a

decided relief from our own California locations [616].] **MPW**: 4.27.22, p416, 6.24.22, p734, **EXH**: 5.13.22, p59.

[948] **THORNS AND ORANGE BLOSSOMS**, Preferred: [When a New Orleans business man finds himself with a little time on his hands in Spain, he falls in love with a Spanish opera singer, Rosita Mendez. What else would you do? As warm as the affair was, he cannot forget the girl he had been engaged to back home. Unwilling to let him go, the fatally attracted and hot blooded Hispanic, follows him back to the mouth of the Mississippi and discovers that her loverboy was secretly going to be married to his lady. When she confronts her former lover, they struggle and she manages to shoot herself with a single shot. For this the Alan Randolph, is accused of attempted murder and sent to prison. Once the bad lady discovers his wife is pregnant, her heart softens and she tells the truth. Little Anglo boys should never play with hot Hispanic matches, luckily for Hollywood, they never listened to their mother's advice, and they made a lot of movies.] **MPW**:11.25.22, p361, **V**:1.5.23.

[949] **TILL WE MEET AGAIN**, Cabanne/Associated Exhibitors: [A melodrama which has the heroine placed into an institution so that the not so nice family members can acquire her dollars. Somewhere in all their collusion with a gang of crooks there was included an "attractive cabaret scene" featuring a "Spanish dance" which served to enhance the entire production.] **MPW**:11.4.22, p82.

[950] **TIS THE BULL**, Educational: "Mexico, the land of love, romance and chili beans," was the title of this Christe Comedy. Acknowledging its offensiveness, the reviewer projected that, "it [would] seem almost certain that everybody but Mexicans will like it." Bobby Vernon, to win the hand of a "Mex" maiden posses as "Americas's greatest bull fighter." To allow him to demonstrate his skill, the Mexican matador arranges a real fight. Frightened, Bobby bounds for the border only to be stopped by Mexican and American soldiers facing each other. In the corrida he expects a fake bull, but a real one is used which chases him in ever tightening circles. Finally knocked out of the arena, his "Mex" miss falls into the arms of the real thing. Bobby vows to swear off señoritas and settle down with one of his own kind.] **MPW**:4.1.22, p551.

[In 1924 the acting secretary of the navy, Colonel Roosevelt asked the Hays office for films to be used in Haiti "to assist in the general civilizing process of the islands." Honored that they could attend to such a high purpose, bringing light into the dark recesses of the Caribbean, they responded by sending to Major General D. C. MacDougal, the commandant of the Gendarmerie D'Haiti a number of these Christie Comedies, including the above entry. Aside from insulting foreign nationals, the few blacks which were included in these comedies certainly reflected the racial prejudice of that time. Not necessarily the most tactful selection they might have made, the films apparently accomplished some purpose.

Certainly few of the islands inhabitants had seen any moving pictures at all and to watch the parade of beautiful young starlets, who were forced to pay their dues by displaying their natural attributes as they worked their way through one silly situation after another, may have accomplished some pacifying purpose. Responding to the Hays office, Commandant C. B. Matthews, who headed the touring parties of Marine officers that brought these films to the "outlying native districts of the islands," wrote: "You have no idea of the success of our picture shows ... When it is considered that in the localities where these pictures [were] shown, less that [sic] 1 per cent of the population can read and write. The showing of pictures leaves the audience happy and contented for weeks at a time." Apparently happy and contented natives did not cause problems. But certainly some others did. Possibly they were not fortunate enough to be exposed to the films as a civilizing agent in the general pacification of peoples considered too primitive.] See: **Soldiers and Women** [1450], **MPW**:9.20.24, p209.

[951] **TRIFLING WOMEN**, Metro: [This was the first film in which Roman Navarro was billed under his new Hollywood name. It was a sexy tale of a super vamp who causes the death of three young men was first filmed in 1917, as the **Black Orchid**. Roman was one of the easily led down the garden path to sniff the deadly flower. He dies, but she is punished by winding down in the depths of a dark dungeon where she goes mad. The writers allowed her her fun, but she had to pay the price for such scarlet behavior.] **V**:10.6.22.

[952] **THE UNCONQUERED WOMAN**, Indy: [The only interest here is that Ruby De Remer found herself in the far north woods trying to pay off a family debt and knew that the only way she could obtain any real money was to sell herself in marriage to anyone who had the price. Antonio, the half breed did and Hollywood made him jump at the chance to get his hands on a white woman. But they also provided for her salvation. They could not allow her to suffer "such a miserable marriage" and so they gave Bruce Devereaus, a handsome young woodsman, the task of defeating the lascivious brute. He does.] **MPW**:9.9.22, p140.

[953] **WHEN DANGER SMILES**, Vitagraph: [The locale for this western melodrama was "New Mexico or some such part of the Southwest, where there is a Spanish population." This reviewers demographic inexpertise was only matched by his lack of ethnic savvy: "The romantic element in this story gets "some pictorial quality from the Spanish [or maybe it's Mexican] heroine played splendidly" by an Anglo gal. She is the daughter of an aristocratic Spanish rancher who is not permitted to play with the boys, but is promised to a rich North American cowman who she does not like. She prefers the poor lad she chanced to meet in the woods. He is the "super hero" of the "impossible type" who can singlehandedly vanquish any number of bandidos, but seems, to get into a lot of trouble. When the two happen to meet again, he fails to recognize her. Vengeful daughter of Spain [or Mexico] that

she was, she plans his demise, but succeeds only in killing another. He is blamed for the killing and just the second before they are about to swing him from the nearest cactus, she saves him.] **V**:11.17.22.

[954] **WITH DAVY CROCKETT AT THE FALL OF THE ALAMO**: [If only it had been left up to Davy, them darn Mexicans would never have taken that little cradle of Texas independence. They only out numbered the "immortal" a hundred to one. The Mexicans were portrayed as brutal invaders bent on slaughtering the almost defenseless Pueblo of San Antonio, inhabited by North Americans that just wanted to mind their own business had the Mexican government left them alone to live in their country as citizens of the United States.]

[955] **WITH WINGS OUTSPREAD**, Camus Productions: [Some of those Hispanic bandits were truly brazen. Even as Cuba was still enjoying the beneficence of the United States guardianship, even while some few of that nation's defenders of the status quo were protecting the very island they had freed from the yoke of Spanish oppression, so called "bandits" were operating just outside the immediate environs of Havana itself. This particular group of bold bandits were so enterprising and elusive, that the Cuban Government had to ask the commander of the forces stationed [not so specified in the film] on Guantanamo for the service of two North American flyers and their aeroplane. Flying over their hideout, a lucky chance rifle shot wounds the mechanic and the pair are forced to land. After they have hidden the plane, and find a nurse for the wounded aviator, the bandits capture them, but being the happy go lucky Yankees that they are, beloved by all, they win the confidence of the bandit chief. Yet true to his character, the head bandido openly covets the Anglo nurse which forces the trio to escape and hide in a cave. Having fooled their pursuers they now use the plane to make it back to the base and identify the bandit band's hide out.] **afic**

[956] **WOMAN WHO FOOLED HERSELF**, Pathe: [This was the first of a series of productions made by Edward A. MacManus in Puerto Rico using the lush tropical locale so readily available on the beautiful island. In a small way, it registers an implied protest to the commonly accepted North American business practice then current in Central America. To obtain a valuable piece of land in one of the regions unidentified republics [of little consequence, United Fruit was everywhere], an out of work show girl agrees to work for a North American exporting company, as a seductive vamp. Her task was to woo the unsuspecting son of the great hacendado who controlled thousands of hectares of land. The Anglo firm wanted to obtain the title to these vast holdings so that they could properly exploit them. But, alas, love interferes. Just as the romantic Latin was signing the papers, she discovers that she wants him for her own forever and spends the last reel gaining back the lost property for him and the family.] **MPW**:11.25.22, p361, **V**:11.17.22.

[957] **WONDERS OF THE SEA**, Williamson-Submarine: [An "out of the ordinary and intensely interesting" picture filmed under the lovely waters of the blue caribbean. The new technology and the clarity of the West Indian waters allowed audiences to see two men "walking along the ocean be with strange deep-sea plants growing around them and numerous fish swimming about." There was "an encounter with a large poisonous moray and also an attack on an octopus that sent out an inky fluid coloring the water which prevented a view of the fish itself." Few things ever changed from the very beginning in underwater film, there was always something mysterious and threatening in those lovely unpolluted waters.] **MPW**:11.2.22, p82.

[958] **YANKEE DOODLE JR**, Burnside: [As an expression of felt and projected superiority reinforced by a critic, this reviewer's comments said it all: "Call it "Hoakum" if you will, but this production, is a thrill in every way ... it has everything and then some." "It is an all-American wonder for all-American theaters catering to any class." Continuing in this vein for several paragraphs, the writer claimed that the film was pure box office for it "out-Cohanesques" George M. in flag waving. That it certainly did. Sent to the mythical South American country of "Santa Maria", the Anglo hero was there to find what kindastuff he was made of and sell a lot of fireworks for dad and the family business. He arrives just in time to see the president of the alleged republic deposed and a new dictator installed. By accident he ignites some of his product and the pyrotechnical display so frightens the apparently stupid natives, including the hardened revolutionaries, that they disperse and hide [of course they have never seen fireworks in Central America, legal everywhere and always used in celebrations south of the border.] Thinking, he is onto something, he approaches the dictator on a personal basis and cuts a deal to use his stuff in a fiesta. It is at that crucial moment that he meets the lovely señorita, falling in love in a Latin instant, he promises to reinstate her deposed father and kiss every nino in the ciudad. Of course he does, after which the "startled natives" look upon him with awe, and the little lady lies at his feet. One can see why this might have played well up north.] **MPW**:3.18.22, p299.

[959] **YELLOW MEN AND GOLD**, Goldwyn: [Richard Dix was the hero for this film with a catchy title which did little to abate the development of the other favorite North American "bogey-men". The action here actually took place in the south seas, but the search was for lost Spanish treasure. The heroine's nemesis was the usual darkskinned, [you can lose yourself in my brown eyes and do things with me that pale skinned white woman never ever dreamed of], Hispanic named, Carmen. But be sure that though he might have toyed ever so briefly with that fantasy, Richard Dix always did the right thing.] **V**:6.2.22.

[960] **YOU NEVER KNOW**, Vitagraph: [Eddie Manning appears to be a man without "any definite purpose and always without funds." When he befriends a street urchin that has been knocked down by Miriam Folansbee's auto, the reckless driver offers him a

job as her chauffeur. Because he frequents a "Spanish cafe" he happens to learn about a plot to start a South American revolution. It could happen! Not only that, he is further informed by the dancer, Inez that the man responsible for the plot, Medina was a friend of the lady he works for. Lucky for Eddie, he has a dumb but strong friend name Muggsy who manages to save him so he can prevent the revolutionary upheaval from taking place. The **Moving Picture World** in commenting on this film indicated how popular such south of the border scenarios were to Hollywood scripters. They also commented on the possible effects this might have had on the general public: "South American politics [have] probably been more abused by frequent use in screen melodramas than any other factor. It seems to be regarded as the quickest and most effective route to thrills. The average theater-goer is probably too familiar with such plots to be much moved by them." Apparently it was recognized by some that the constant reinforcement on film that South American politics were not characterized by the peaceful transference of political power, and that the Latins needed Anglo saviors, had been firmly ingrained in the viewing public well before this date.] **MPW**:12.2.22, p456.

1923

[961] **ADAM AND EVA**, Cosmopolitan Productions: [James King, a successful business man, has an extravagant daughter that is constantly pursued by parasitic suitors. Having devoted his life to family and firm and not knowing what more to do, he decides to run to where he can lose himself and escape all, South America. After turning over the business to an employee, he heads south and when, after some time he returns, he discovers that all have learned their lesson. The young man in charge has even made the daughter work for a living. And she loved it, and him too.] afic.

[962] **THE BAD MAN**, FN: [Destined to be remade numerous times, this film, and the character it projected on the silver screen, would in 1927 produce the first significant protests from the Mexican government because of the severely negative stereotypes it perpetuated. The revolutionary upheaval that Mexico experienced in the prior decade, had achieved some stability by 1923. By the end of the year a recognized and established government conducted business in an orderly fashion. Whereas before 1920, there was little enough centralized authority in the Capital to issue formal protests over such negative characterization, by this time the situation had changed. More important, the central government appeared to possess the power to be able to affect the importation of North American films and could threaten the various production companies with banning their films. [See: **The Pilgrim** [999]] First National, was the first to experience such a threat because of this film. The **Bad Man** came to Hollywood from the broadway stage along with Holbrook Blinn, the star, who made it "a work of art." "There were moments in witnessing the picture when one could almost hear Blinn hiss words through his teeth, words that would have the Mex dialect, instead of the half French Canuck, that appeared in the written titles." The production's success was phenomenal breaking records from coast to coast, it was considered a "fortune maker." The public loved the concept of a good badman, "a genial border bandit", "a very bad hombre," but under the dark skin, not so bad "when he gives a white man a wife, a fortune and a diamond-studded future." This film would be remade twice in a very similar format, but the characterization of the good Mexican bandido, would continue to appear in modified forms in dozens of other productions through the century to present times.] **MPW**:6.2.23, p361, 6.16.23, p595, 8.18.23, frontpiece, **V**:10.11.23, **NYT**:10.9.23.

[963] **BELOW THE RIO**, Steiner: [Very few westerns ever have the police forces of three nations actively pursuing the baddie, but in this film the Royal Canadian Mounted Police, a United States Sheriff and the Mexican rurales were all after a desperate French Canadian hiding out in a small, remote Mexican town. The riding was rough, the fighting tough, and

communication, had it not been a silent film, would have been impossible.] MPW:1.20.23, p194, V:10.18.23, afic.

[964] **BLINKY**, U: [Hollywood more frequently than not came to the aid of the underdog in this case, the scripters were helping "Blinky, the bespectacled son of Col. "Raw Meat" Islip" stationed on the Mexican border. Blinky was forced to endure the scowls of his fellow cavalry mates, as a result of his 'four eyed' condition, but more so because the only previous military experience he had enjoyed, had come from the Boy Scouts. In the final reel the writers allow him to show up the entire troop by employing the training he had received while a Scout to track and rescue the daughter of Major Kileen from the baddies across the line.] afic.

[965] **THE BRIGHT SHAWL**, FN: [Shooting much of this film on location for three months in Cuba provided a most convincing backdrop for this story of early insurrectionist activity in the first stages of that colony's separation from Spain. "The atmosphere [was] conspicuously convincing ... scenes in the country have the tropic landscape and vegetation and the mob scenes have authentic people." Dorothy Gish, the heroine, played, the vivacious, "La Cavel", an "Andalusian dancer" or, "a dark eyed Cuban dancing girl," who risked her life obtaining information from "arrogant Spanish officials", the oppressive tyrants who were crushing the native Cubanos. Working with Richard Barthelmess, a young Americano sympathizer, whom she loved, the information was passed to the first group of revolutionaries that fought in the 1870's to make Cuba Libre. As almost all films dealing with United States involvement with the Spanish American War were, this film was a big success and received significant praise.] MPW:5.5.23, p17, p76, 5.12.23, p110, 6.16.23, p555, 7.7.23, p89, V:4.26.23.

[966] **THE BROKEN WING**, Preferred Pic: [Apparently it was essential for the North American movie goer's to have their Mexican women appear darkskinned, that certainly was the case for this **New York Times** reviewer who voiced but one criticism of the Anglo star: "It might have been more convincing if Miss Cooper had used a darker make-up on her face, but there is no gainsaying that she is an appealing Mexican girl, even if her skin is unusually fair." The scenario involved a North American flyer who's plane crashes in Mexico. Immediately, he is arrested on suspicion of being just what he is, from up north. It is not too much to use one incident to characterize the Anglo scripter's felt superiority for all those south of the border. It happens that when the Mexican guard, assigned to make sure the Anglo did not leave without permission thinks that there is a possibility he has fixed his plane, he does so just at the same time he needs his siesta. So to ensure that the plane will not take off, he ties one end of a long rope to one of the wheels and the other to the leg of the chair that he is going to sleep in. This film was not a comedy, the scene was intended to point to the felt stupidity of the Mexicans. The title card read: "I guess you no fly now." Such dialect would cause more serious problems

with the arrival of the talkers and continues to the present time as the most immediate of the identifiers of Hispanic characters [1563].] **V**:10.11.23. **NYT**:10.9.23.

[967] **CANYON OF FOOLS**, R-C, Pictures: [When former lovers find themselves on a train out west in desperado country very near the border, Bob learns that May and her new fiancee, Jim, are foolishly heading for the Canyon of Fools, a place well known to be dangerous. A little later Bob offers to help the sheriff find the bandit gang responsible for all the gold robberies. While inspecting a cave in the dreaded canyon, he discovers that Jim leads the gang they are looking for. After a bit of trouble, he and May capture them all. Included in Jim's gang were some Mexicans named, Terazaz, and Maricopia. Incarnacion was a local cantina gal with a halo hovering above her head.] **V**:3.15.23, afic.

[968] **THE CHEAT**, Indy: [In this production the Polish superstar, Pola Negri, as the Spanish Carmelita, was provided with the opportunity to show off her many talents and a wardrobe that might have made Diana Ross sell her soul. She was cast as a South American heiress accustomed to the very good life and now required to choose between a rich Hindu "faker" conman, and an aspiring young North American entrepreneur, trying to sell the French government on a big deal. The scripters have her faithful to either her ethnic background or her sex, playing both ends against the possibility she will not be caught. She is, but refuses the prescribed punishment from the third world cuckold. Her hot blooded Spanish temperament could not stand still for having her "shoulder branded" by the "Hindu" who was trying to break her, so she shot him. This allows her true blue Anglo lover to save her from the chair in the court room scene.] **MPW**:7.14.23, p111, **NYT**:8.31.23.

[969] **CHILDREN OF JAZZ**, Famous Player/Lasky: [Films had become a significant international force by twenties. Not only could a domestic product insult a foreign government, it was more often than not the agent of capitalism. Shortly after a certain brand of automobile appeared on the screen of a film house in Rio de Janeiro, that company's agency sales rose a dramatic thirty-five percent, much more would be made of this in the next decade. Films might sell swimming pools and refrigerators, but there were those who were well aware that film also projected and promoted a way of life, even if that just happened to be some imaginative scripter fantasy. Will Hays and the newly formed MPPDA were very conscious of this fact. In 1922, Hays wrote to a friend in Boston that: "the producers have taken definite steps to make the fullest possible use of the motion picture as an instrument of international good will. They are making certain that all films which are sent abroad, wherever they may go, shall correctly portray American life, ideals and opportunities. <u>We will sell America to the world with motion pictures</u>. American producers furnish the majority of all pictures shown in the world and this correct depiction of the life and habits of our own and foreign people each to the other, will go far toward

bringing the international understanding and appreciation which will move us in the direction of a world peace." Certainly a most lofty and worthy aspiration, but one that the producers achieved only on rare occasions, especially in these early days.

Ricardo Cortez was included in this little moralistic lesson about the negative influences of "Jazz". The captivating rhythms of that new musical craze were apparently intoxicating enough to increase even further the established Hollywood formula which so frequently portrayed the dissipation's of the rich, especially the youthful "American rich". Ricardo Cortez was in attendance at a party for these gay revelers that lasted pretty much from Christmas to New Years along with a cad, a bully, a soldier of fortune type, the hero and a cast of perky, devil may care, free with their affections, flappers. "The heroine [was] worse yet, a half-naked young fool who [went] from one affair to another with the sweethearts and husbands of her intimate friends." She spent her time accumulating engagement rings and consuming synthetic gin. At one point she was engaged to three men, one of which was still married. At this point **Variety's** film criticism took on a more moralistic tone: "It is a sweet picture of American life to go abroad." When the hero discovered that he was in a line of three, even as he realized that he was leading the parade, he decided that it was time ply his trade and he sets out to organize an expedition designed to help the rebels in the revolution that was brewing in San Sebastian, apparently somewhere in the Caribbean. The revelers hardly notice his absence and themselves decide to "fly to Havana" for breakfast. Why not? On the way the plane goes down right about where the hero's ship is, (it could happen) so he saves them and brings all to his father's island, also in the blue Carib. There he takes charge and puts everyone to work, washing dishes, doing the same house work required of the natives, and other menial tasks the wastrels were completely unfamiliar with. After all have learned their new social values, and having fought for his lady with fists and a lot of attention, he again decides to go fight. Two in the company, apparently having learned that filibustering was required of North Americans, want to join him. But just as the last moment, the sexy lady, possibly in just a cute little apron, wiggles herself into his arms and offers to be his maid forever. He of course accepts. San Sebastian could wait. One can only wonder what the reaction to such presentations might have been. It will make a good sequel to these volumes.] **V**:7.12.23. **Hays Papers** on microfilm: Letter from Will Hays to General Charles Cole, 10.11.22. "Trade Follows the Film (How American Movies Sell American Goods)" **Congressional Digest**, November 1928, pp.298-99.

[970] **COLUMBUS**, Chronicles of America Series, Yale. Pathe release: [Yale's attempt to sell history to the public through the new medium of film continued with this thirty five minute featurette on Columbus. The cast of characters was certainly a regal one, King John II of Portugal, Queen Isabella and King Ferdinand, and the Bishop of Ceuta [the first piece of North

Africa recaptured from the Moors], but the old established scenario remained the same. Poor old Columbus was seen wandering from royal court to royal court looking for support, even suffering the intrigues of King John of Portugal, trying to convince people that the world was really round. It was not until he finally convinced Juan Perez, the Prior of La Rabida and the Queen's former confessor, that he was able to attract the monarch's interest. She then, because her husband would not finance the adventurer, sold her very own jewels to provide the brave sailor with the money to purchase three ships so that he could go discover peoples that had been living on their own land for more than four thousand years. One can almost be certain that most children know the date 1492, some others, a great many more a few decades ago, also knew also the apocryphal story about the jewels. All film versions including the 1949 British version starring Fredric March use that bit of fluff, it's the stuff little legends are made of and easily perpetuated on film. It is somewhat surprising that the folks at Yale continued the tradition, but historians are also human beings. It is a nice little story, we would all like to believe it were so. At one time, most of the people in the audience were romantics, unconsciously, that's why we went to the movies, to see life as it might be.]
See: **Chronicles of America**, [1033].

[971] **THE COMMON LAW**, Selznick: [Eliot Dexter played Jose Quirida in this remake. He's was still the Hispanic heavy.]
LCFL:Clippings file.

[972] **CRASHIN' THRU**, FBO: [Harry Carey, by now well established as one of Hollywood's most identifiable character actors, as well as a western star, was the hero in this sagebrush love drama. Indebted to his partner, who was crippled when saving his spouse, Carey attempts to find his now handicapped friend a wife. He also saves his son from the clutches of the Mexican rustlers, Morelos and Garcia. It was too late for the boy who was killed by the banditos, but the two men acquired new wives by taking out a little advertising, a solution not infrequently used in later westerns.] **V**4.19.23.

[973] **THE DEVIL'S BOWL**, William Steiner: [The reviewers were especially harsh on this production which they felt was not good enough even for the nickel houses, "if there were any of them left." Their criticism indicated that they felt audiences were becoming more sophisticated, that the more critical needed something other than western locations, and a lot of action to generate a degree of approval. This may not have been an accurate assessment. Evidence indicates that so long as there was a nemesis, a Mexican, Hispanic or other ethnic enjoying a negative vogue, the film would probably play well in North American theaters to a people who were/are essentially provincial at best. This script had Neal Hart as a foreman engaged to a jealous lady who was angered when he receives a letter from another woman. She leaves and so does he, but he in answer to his sister's plea for help. She was being held in the "Mexican Badlands" by her horse thief husband who after getting the drop on Hart has him blamed for

his own dirty deeds. Worse he kills the wife and the Mexican authorities, hold the brother for that also. After a lot of confusion in trying to communicate with one another, Spanish and English "I don't understand" and "you don't understand" titles were flashed, Hart breaks away and captures the culprit. The Mexican officials were cast as semi-illiterate buffoons who did not have the ability to grasp the situation and required an Anglo to resolve the situation for all concerned.] **V**:4.26.23, **afic**.

[974] **DON QUICKSHOT OF THE RIO GRANDE**, U: [This humorous western served to introduce Universal's new western star, Jack Hoxie as "Pep" Pepper, an apparently literate cowboy dreamer who pictured himself as Cervantes's "Don Quixote," doing good deeds and saving maidens and the like. After a series of adventures which involved not windmills, but inept Mexicans throwing a lot of knives in his direction, he succeeds in winning the hand of the fair Tulip Hellier. Esmeralda was not cast.] **MPW**:6.9.23, p492, **FD**:6.3.23.

[975] **DON QUIXOTE**, Br: [An early British import that squeezed through Hollywood's fear that foreign films were any competition at all. It was played mainly for laughs, and indicated that very similar stereotypes were accepted on the other side of the Atlantic in heart of Anglo Saxon purity. The last Hollywood version had been made in 1916 [**44, 646**].]

[976] **THE DRUG TRAFFIC**, [One of two films produced by Irving Cummings, both of which were attempts to exploit the latest in this nation's attempts to point out the evil of drugs. In the first it was the Chinese, the traditional opium providers, that were emphasized, but in the second, an Anglo doctor succumbed to the evils of burning the candle at both ends, which was provided as the justification for his addiction.] **V**:4.26.23, **MPG**.

[977] **THE ENEMIES OF WOMEN**, Goldwyn: [In Monte Carlo, Pedro De Cordoba, as Atilio Castro, was scripted to enjoy a wild debauch staged by a group of woman hating misogynists trying to even the score in the battles of the sexes. At least popular with some males, it broke all attendance records at the Imperial Theater in San Francisco.] **MPW**: 6.2.23, p359, 8.4.23, p335, **MPG**.

[978] **THE ETERNAL THREE**, Goldwyn: [The action for this sordid love triangle between the wife of a wealthy man, visiting an even wealthier North American hacienda owner in Mexico, was made easier because much of it took place south of the border. The husband loves his young wife, but is too busy with business. Ignored, she contemplates an affair with her step son. The latter has some difficulty with that and ends up doing her secretary instead, after which he has a near fatal accident. Once recovered, he is punished by being sent to Europe and the husband begs his wife for forgiveness for ignoring her. The director for the film, Marshall Neilan, did some extensive location shooting in northern Mexico which certainly added a pleasant atmosphere to all the rather sordid

happenings. Possibly as a promotional stunt, he sent a copy of the film to the then President Obregon, the one armed revolutionary leader of Mexico. Obregon graciously accepted the gift and acknowledged that it would become part of his "official library--the first time such an honor [had been] bestowed upon an American production."] **MPW**:5.12.23, p170.

[979] **THE EXCITERS**, FP: [Stepping out from his Hispanic cast, Antonio Moreno was allowed to play a suave gangster, who's still hot temper had him even hotter on the trail of his wealthy socialite flapper wife, Bebe Daniels. Not a nice lady, she gets her's in the end.] **MPW**, 5.26.23, p295, **MPG**.

[980] **THE GENTLEMEN FROM AMERICA**, U: [Hoot Gibson was finally allowed to leave the wild west in this production, but he still has to deal with Hispanics, this time in Spain as a visiting doughboy. There he becomes involved in the volatility of local politics and meets a "dashing Spanish Señorita." It was all played for laughs as Gibson and his buddy were made to impersonate a notorious bandit and friend. Successful in his duplicity, he was elected the ruler of a local principality, all this on two weeks furlough. The fantasy abruptly ends when the hero finds himself in the lockup for being AWOL. In the last scene he promises to return as soon as he can to his little señorita. Oh! those doughboys, after they've visited Spain, never mind Paree!] **MPW**: 2.17.23, p691.

[981] **GIRL FROM THE WEST**, W: [Once more the Hollywood scripters sent the young easterner, scorned by his fair lady, out west to prove his manhood. He does and quite easily, with the lovely Juanita Hansen.] **MPW**: 7.7.23, p60, **MPG**.

[982] **GIRL OF THE GOLDEN WEST**, FN: [The **New York Times** critic [there were no credits yet], possibly looking for a job in First National's casting office, was highly critical of this second filming of the Belasco play, he objected seriously to the star, whose part would have been better handled by the little Irish/Anglo combo playing the role of Nina Micheltorena, the hotblooded chiquita. More interesting though were his comments on the characterization of Ramerez, the bandit, which provides us with what at least this newspaperman's idea was of what such an individual should look like: "In those golden days of '49 there may have been Beau Brummell bandits, but Mr. Kerrigan outdoes the usual conception of a handsome beguiling bandit His face is too smooth, his eyebrows too straight and neat and his hair too wavy, for anyone who runs a band of highwayman [Frank Sinatra take note]. When garbed as a Mexican, he has slashes in the lower extremities of his trousers through which protrude fine lace. When he is wounded by the Sheriff and kept in bed by the girl, his chin is wonderfully free from any sign of a beard. Mr. Kerrigan is a most unusual Mexican." What this film needed then was a dirty, beard infested with little friends, ugly and unkept Mexican bandit, was nothing sacred? [566, 1405].] **MPW**, 5.26.23, p291, 293, 6.2.23, p399, 6.23.23., p628, 8.11.23, p481, **V**:5.24.23, **NYT**:5.21.23, **MPG**

[983] __GOLD DIGGERS__, W: [Warner's had merely to employ this title to insure a large female audience and a success. They did numerous times. It would be interesting to know how many home town girls it brought to the big city looking for the allure and mystique of the Broadway stage. This one included a Spanish dance number that the critics were a bit snide with. They apparently wanted their Carmen's as hotblooded and tempestuous in their dancing as they wished their Mexicans dirty. "Miss Hampton's Spanish "Carmen" dance ... wasn't exactly as wild as she may have thought it was." To which she may well have replied, "let's see you out there humping and grinding your cupcakes off big feller."] __V__:9.13.23.

[984] __GOOD MEN AND BAD__, F. W. Kraemer: [While visiting in Argentina, North American cowboy, Steve Kinnard falls in love with the beautiful Felicia, daughter of Don Pedro Martinez. She likes him a lot too. The writers of course had to create a problem for all these pleasant palpitations on the Pampas and their choice was already quite old back in 1911. It would seem that Hollywood Don's could not keep out of debt, especially when they had a daughter. This one was no different than any of the others, he was willing to trade his desired offspring for enough dineros to clear his obligation. She of course objected and at a fiesta, told all present that she would marry the señor that could tame the wildest horse. A tempting invitation, but not for the cowardly Don Esteban Valdeo who refused. With a grin as wide as the open plain, Steve mounted that mare and rode into a smiling submission, winning the señorita's hand, and the rest of her forever. Long before 1923, it should have been clear to these poor chumps that the writers would allow North American men to take their women at any time and any where in the world they happened to be, but especially so south of the border.] __afic__.

[985] __HELL'S HOLE__, F: [Apparently located out west because of the robberies, bar room brawls and gun fighting, it included the necessary Mexican, Pablo, whose only function was to die. Actually the film was filled with a great deal of dramatic action including an avalanche, but most of the story takes place within the squalid confines of a border prison, with the highlight being the "revolution" by the prisoners. The Hispanics were as much the victims of misused authority in this prison, as the Anglos.] __MPW__: 7.28.23, p314, __V__:11.23.23.

[986] __HER REPUTATION__, Thomas H. Ince/FN: [This simple story of a former convent girl who is pure as the driven snow and sweeter than the essence of saccharine, has her falling in love with the son of a rich newspaper publisher who objects to the union and seeks to use his sometime scandal sheet to ruin her reputation. As she lives with a family of cabaret performers, the task proves simple and she is forced to leave town when a story appears indicating her lack of virtue. In a new city, San Francisco, she assumes the guise afforded her by the newspaper and becomes, the really naughty, "Conchita" in the "El Toro" nightclub. Pursued by a reporter who wants to print more dirt, she discovers his intent and pleads with the editor father not to do it. Mercilessly he ignores her

cries, but the son now comes to his lady's rescue. All is worked out in the last reel and the lad likes her as Conchita, but insists that all future performances be for him alone.] **MPW**:6.2.23, **V**:9.13.23, 9.27.23.

[987] **IN THE PALACE OF THE KING**, Goldwyn: [An excellent example of la leyenda negra alive and well perpetuated by Hollywood in another stereotypical production. This costume epic, was produced on a large budget for 1923. It purported to be a story of love at its intriguing best in the court of Philip II of Spain, "well known to be a murderer and a religious fanatic." His brother Don John of Austria and a Lady name Dolores Mendoza were hero and heroine. As portrayed by Hollywood, courtly love and romance, from the very first flickers, differed significantly in the palaces of Madrid and London. There was always something charming and alluring about the aristocratic trysts of the English monarchs and their loyal retainers, but those which took place at the Spanish court, and were generated by the King himself, were of a much more sinister nature. This of course excludes the greatest of the mythical romantic lovers, Don Juan. He was a citizen of Sevilla, and not a member of the court family. This intrigue which focuses on the villainous happenings at Philip II's court was first filmed in 1915, under the same title, it had by then already been part of the scenario of two other one reelers: **Don Carlos** [84] and **Don Juan and Charles V** [246]. It would seem that King Philip of Spain, then the most powerful man in the Christian world, was jealous of the popularity of his brother, Don John. In hopes of having him killed without incurring the onus of such malevolent action, the original author (**Marion Crawford**, **In the Palace of the King, A Love Story of Old Madrid**, 1900), and the scripter have Philip send Don John to fight the handy Moors, apparently without remembering that they had been driven from Spanish soil more than a hundred years prior to that time. Don John loved the beautiful Dolores, and she he, but her father knew that even if the prince returned from the suicide mission he had been sent to accomplish, he would be forced by Philip to marry the sister of the Queen Elizabeth of England. One could only wonder who that might have been. Don John, after having located what must have been the very last remaining contingent of Moors still unaware that the fighting between the two powers had ended, (it would happen to Hollywood's Japanese in WWII) was affected this time, not by the scribe's lack of historical knowledge, but more by what must have been his perception of current racial discord in the states. The irony of providing the religious crusader with "original K.K.K. methods" to drive the remaining Moors out of Spain, may well have been lost on all but the most intellectual Catholics in the audience. The crusading Don John used a "fiery cross" as a mountain top warning and to set the enemy tents, filled with "cooch dancers" aflame in his campaign against the infidel. The ploy worked well and he returned victorious, was given his proper hero's welcome not in public, but in private, Philip stabbed him with his sword and left him for dead. Luckily, Dolores had seen all. Her father, Mendoza was blamed, but the enterprising lady threatened to tell all of Spain the truth if

Philip did not pardon her padre and allow the two to wed. What could the old devil do? Aside from his problems with maintaining the purity of the faith in his own country and throughout all of Europe, the ramifications of Reformation, Elizabeth's marriage refusals and the failure of the great Armada, the most powerful monarch in all of Christendom was now faced with being backed down by a an angry little señorita, albeit, of high station. He was forced to submit. Even in Hollywood's Spain of Philip II, the love of an honest woman might conquer all.] **V**:12.6.23.

[988] **ISLE OF LOST SHIPS**, FN: [Some of us, somewhere in childhood, learned that there was a mysterious corner of the Caribbean that had to be avoided at all cost, for once trapped therein, there was no escape for man or vessel of any kind. That place was the Sargasso sea. Spanish sailors knew of its existence somewhere in the southern latitudes, ships were becalmed, rendered motionless, choked by the thick growth of seaweed that kept the swiftest of hulls still, dead in the water and lost to the real world forever. Unlike most of childhoods many myths that sadly fade away as years move us into the absurdities of adulthood, the Sargossa sea maintained its mystique. Some, who are a good deal more gullible, have expanded it into an imaginary triangle that proves deadly to anything that intersects its path. But for those of us who know, it's a much smaller area than that, and its out there somewhere between the Dry Tortugas and the northwest coast of Cuba. Several feature films have focused on this myth, the first was this truly atmospheric entry, with eerie sets and all the mystery an audience could enjoy. A remarkable production for the time, it placed a wrongly accused man, being transshipped from Central America and a young female tourist, in the clutches of the brutal leader who ruled the fifty or so ships trapped therein. The lecherous lout immediately goes for the girl, there being few in the colony that was first formed in the days of the Spanish Conquistadors, but her man protects her. After many adventures the two escape to the safety of the United States navy and the colony mysteriously sinks back into the fog which hides it from those searching to prove its existence. The film was a resounding money maker. "The goods are there", reported one exhibitor, for others to make "a million." Many submitted examples of the "ballyhoo" they used to promote it to the **MPW**, almost all used some outline of a disabled ship to advertise the production outside their theaters. The remake will appear in 1929 as a sound production. [1340].] **MPW**:5.12.23, p109, 7.14.23, p143, 7.21.23, p235, **V**:5.17.23, 6.23.23, p408. **MPG**.

[989] **LOST AND FOUND**, Goldwyn: [Raoul Walsh sent Antonio Moreno out to the south seas in this one to provide a little love interest for one of the scantly clad, skin shimmering in the sunlight, lovelies that inhabit such exotic places. Usually it was the Hispanic darkskinned ladies that had to make such journeys, but Antonio did not complain. He did what he had to as Lloyd Warren, Anglo, he loved and left the lady to swim away her days dishabille thinking about what might

have been had those of his kind been allowed to stay and play a little longer by a silent Hollywood which could not promote the mixing of the races at that time.] **V**:3.22.23.

[990] **A MAN'S MAN**, FBO: [This simple reworking of the 1918 version [800] used the very same cast and director although some of the scenario was slightly changed. The original film was created from a story that appeared in **Redbook** in 1916. The main character John Stuart, was something of a romantic returning to his native Denver having been unsuccessful in his search for adventure. Yet once in his own back yard, he meets the delightful Dolores Ruey, who just happened to be fighting off the fast moving hands of a masher. He, of course, saves the Hispanic lady and a close friendship develops bonding the two into a pleasant romance. At that moment the hero receives a cry for help from his friend Billy who was having some difficulty fighting off the South American natives that wanted the property he had developed in that uncivilized region of the world. Without a word the Anglo headed for Buenaventura to provide assistance to his beleaguered friend. As it often was for soldiers of fortune, fate intervened and on the way he chanced to meet Ricardo Ruey, the hunted son of the former president of the very republic they were headed for. And to everyone's surprise, when they arrive in the midst of the fray, Dolores was there waiting; Billy had actually fallen in love with her. Not only a fighting fool, but gracious and a good friend, John tries to hide his love for the lady from his friend. After some whirlwind fighting, John and Ricardo successfully effect the revolution which establishes Ricardo as the new President who promises to be the savior of the people, but more important, the two lovers are reunited and John is most happy to discover, that the sweet señorita is really Ricardo's sister.] **afic**.

[991] **THE MAN WHO WAITED**, Playergoers: ["The dark plottings of two Mexicans" who have held the daughter of an old enemy captive since childhood now include a plan to acquire the rights to her mine. The hero overcomes "considerable intrigue," to save the little lady and her property. They had wronged him also.] **MPW**:5.12.23, p159.

[992] **THE MASK OF LOPEZ**, Indy/Monogram release: [A warden's daughter continues her deceased father's work which helped former convicts achieve some dignity and decent employment after they have been released. Lopez was one of the many who profited by the young woman's self sacrifice [1235].] **V**:11.15.23

[993] **MASTERS OF MEN**, Vitagraph: [In this melodrama with the Spanish American war as a backdrop, Dick Halpin loves Mabel. Her not so nice brother steals a lot of money and has Dick blamed for the theft. To save his sweetheart pain, Dick signs on with the Navy, and in no time at all is shanghaied along with his best buddy, Lieutenant Breen. Cruely treated by their captors, they suffer some before escaping, but fortunately find themselves in Cuba just before the battle of Santiago Harbor. Dick and friend exhibit distinguished

behavior as they aid in the total destruction of the remainder of Spain's wooden armada and are duly decorated. Complications over love interests are resolved and Mabel's brother even confesses his crimes allowing the two reunited lovers to bask in the wonder of having made Cuba safe for democracy.] **V**:5.17.23, **afic**.

[994] **MR. BILLINGS SPENDS HIS DIME**, FP/P: [He spends his dime on a cigar which changes his life completely, because on the cigar band there was the picture of a girl he falls in love with immediately. The problem was that the smoke came from way south of the border. No matter, our young Anglo adventurer journeys to that undisclosed Latin republic where he actually finds the pretty señorita and then to his amazement [imagine that of the audience] discovers that the beauty was the daughter of the President of that besieged nation. Grateful at his good fortune, what could he do but help the president out. With very little effort, the Anglo, puts down a few revolutions and the thankful dad consents to the marriage.] **V**:3.8.23, **MPG**.

[995] **MYSTERIES OF YUCATAN**, F: [The aura and mystery surrounding the discovery of the burial chamber of King Tut captivated North America's imagination for months in 1923. Many were also amazed to discover that there were pyramids that rivaled those of old Egypt, right here in this hemisphere, almost in their own back yard, just across the border in the Mexican Yucatan. Even more amazing to some, were the Mayan, a civilization of the highest order that apparently had been responsible for these incredible structures at "the beginning of the Christian era."] **MPW**:8.25.23, p671.

[996] **THE NE'ER-DO-WELL**, P: [This Rex Beach novel was first translated to film in 1915 [594] in what was considered then a Selig "super production." A decade later, Paramount considered that it has sufficient potential to be remade. The scenario describes a young, irresponsible, playboy type who while hosting another of his famous debaucheries, was shanghaied to Panama, where he finds himself penniless and disinherited. Forced to make it on his own, he takes job a with the Panama Railroad and falls in love with "Chiquita", of course, a lovely local señorita, not your usual cantina cutie. But before they can happily ever after it together, he has to clear the debris of his involvement with a suicidal married woman who also wanted his favors. He does and regains the love of his Chiquita and the respect of his father. The film footage of Panama, the railroad and the Canal provided a good indication of what a decade of North American involvement, occupation and business enterprise had accomplished.] **MPW**:5.12.24, p158.

[997] **THE OLD FOOL**, Hodkinson: [A rejected old Civil War veteran leaves his southern home and travels to the Tex/Mex border with his faithful young grandson. There he find a new reason for being and even manages to prevent the gun smugglers working the border from continuing their operation.]

[998] **ONE MILLION IN JEWELS**, William B. Bush: [United States Secret Service man, Burke, was assigned to stop a group of jewel smugglers operating out of the sin capital of Caribbean, Havana, Cuba. The leader of this gang, out of reverence to the 19th Amendment, was Helen Morgan. Her problem was that she secretly loved that big lug who was trying his best to do his duty and put her behind bars. Burke had befriended Sylvia, she liked him too, but unknown to both, Helen was using the lady as her agent to bring the hot goods into the country. In the final scene, Helen gives up her life for the undercover policeman and Sylvia helps him round up the remainder of that desperate group.] afic.

[999] **THE PILGRIM**, FN: [Charlie Chaplin's last picture for First National has him leaving prison and finding clerical garb which when he puts it on, makes the townspeople think that he is their new minister. He performs well at the task giving sermons in pantomime and saving the poor widow's mortgage money from a former fellow inmate. When he is discovered, the sheriff takes him to the border and kicks him across to the Mexican side. There he has an encounter with two bandits having a ridiculous shoot out with each other. He is pictured in the final scene walking in his typical manner toward the horizon with one foot on either side of the border line heading for a new and greater destiny, possibly to form a new production company. More significant than his departure was the effect this film and **The Bad Man** had on the Mexican government. In a brief blurb the **MPW** announced: "MEXICO BARS ANY FILM OF CHARLIE'S OR DOUG'S", Punishing for Kidding Country in Past Pictures--Spanish Paper Gives Information." The paper gave "the information by way of comment and not as a startling news item." Probably with good reason, because the films of both stars continued to play to large audiences in Mexico. Neither was there a significant change in the characterizations used by the production companies at that time.] **V**:3.1.23, **MPW**:1.27.23, 3.15.23, **MPG**, afic.

[1000] **THE PRISONER**, U: [A home town lad traveling in Europe, with apparently world wide knowledge of the criminal element, happens to run across his former sweetheart and saves her from the evil designs of a Brazilian who was wanted for murder his native land.] **V**:3.8.23, **MPG**.

[1001] **QUICKSANDS**, H. Hawks: [This production was one of 1923's biggest box office draws, featuring a cast of 18 known and established players. **Variety** considered it "timely" "inasmuch as it deal[t] with the smuggling of narcotics into this country across the Mexican line." The film went to great lengths to show how the government troops were waging an incessant battle against the insidious traffic. Sound familiar, this was 1923?! Richard Dix was the handsome lad who foiled the evil drug dealer and his only bad moment came when he was watching the Mexican cantina which housed the "headquarters" of the "viciously active ring of narcotics smugglers." While there, he thought he spied his lady dressed as a local Chiquita consorting with the baddies. Upon investigation, she made suggestive advances toward him, but he resisted her seductive ways. Somewhat dejected, he realized that it had been his true love. Could she really have been part of the gang? He worried needlessly, she was on the right side when she crossed back over the border. Actually she had been trying to help him out. Aside from considering this a "box office magnet," the reviewers and exhibitors praised the film for its production values: "Mexican border pictures, frequent as they have been, seldom had the effect of an authentic military background"; this one did [502].] **V**:3.29.23, **MPW**:3.17.23, p299, 4.7.23, p664.

[1002] **RIDERS OF THE RANGE**, Truant: [Despite the fact that this western was afforded rave reviews, it is significant here only to mention that the immortal Helen Hayes received some notice playing a small part as the sexy Spanish chiquita. Even the greats had to begin somewhere, for not a few, it was south of the border.] **MPW**:5.12.23, p159.

[1003] **ROSITA**, UA: ["**Rosita**" was described on the program as a "Spanish Romance", in which the much loved, Mary Pickford, played a sweet street singer. This was one of the two productions shown in 1923, based on the play written by Don Cesar de Bazan. The other featured Pola Negri as the **Spanish Dancer** [1007]. In this production the sweet young thing attracts the attentions of the Spanish King who, although married, (what did that matter in Spain anyway,) was immediately smitten. Mary the Anglo señorita, of course refuses such advances, preferring to love the penniless noble Don Diego. This understandably angers the king and hurts his pride and when the song bird was accused of singing a lyric offensive to the monarch, she was arrested, and so was her man. Don Diego was sentenced to death, and she was subjected to the kings advances. Cruelly and insidiously, the king arranges a blindfolded marriage between the two, not as their last wish, but to serve his own ends. The wedding would make her a noblewoman after which it would be a simple thing to have the Don executed. But the queen intercedes in this complex intrigue, and saves the latter's life. It was in her best interest, she wanted to remain the monarch's only wife. In the final reel, just as Mary was about to save her honor by stabbing the king in the back, the Don saves his life. He is pardoned into Mary's arms leaving the lecherous king to face the queen's wrath. The price for seeing this complex feature at prime time was as much as the traffic could then bare $2.00, a good days wage for almost anyone working then.] **V**:9.6.23, **NYT**:9.3.23, **MPG**.

[1004] **THE RUM RUNNERS**, C. B. Hurtt/Aywon Film Corp: [A western melodrama which dealt "with the troubles of the Mexican border patrol in suppressing the shipment of liquor across the border." These were very dry times in Los Estados Unidos del Norte. The world may have laughed, certainly the Mexicans did, at the 'nobel experiment', but most people who found themselves without their particular hair of the dog, did not think it too funny. Liquor was transported across both borders north and south, almost without interruption, throughout that peculiar time. It was landed on both shores in even larger amounts. Just a reminder for those who think that "drying up the source" is the answer to North America's drug problem. In this film the border agent is successful in stopping the flow of demon rum into the United States. For his services he was awarded a lovely "Mexican heiress." Drug enforcement agencies throughout the land might well use this as a training film, to provide a little inspiration.] **afic**.

[1005] **SCARAMOUCHE**, Metro: [Roman Navarro had now achieved recognition for his athletic ability and was provided an opportunity to exhibit it as the romantic swordsman and hero of the early French Revolution, on the side of right, but more so the lovely ladies.] **V**:9.20.23,10.4.23.

[1006] **THE SILENT COMMAND**, F: [The broad strokes of this scenario should be easily recognized in Bogart's **Across the Pacific**, where his task and the manner in which it was accomplished were quite the same as the hero in this production. Both appeared to be dishonored by their service records, while having as their important undercover assignments, the task of protecting the Panama Canal from destruction. The reviewers agreed that this work would have made a great promotional film for the navy, it's over all patriotism and extolling of North American virtues were not applied in small doses. An indication that by this time, the Latin American market for North American films was a concern for Hollywood producers was provided by the inclusion of "a love interest carefully designed to make an impression in the Latin American territories." An Annapolis graduate woos and weds the daughter of the representative of a Central American republic as a very nonessential part of the story. Some of the ads used to promote this film were much more self glorifications describing United States technological achievement, French failure and the benefits the Canal had brought the world, than descriptions of the movie itself.] **MPW**:8.4.23, p342, **V**:9.6.23, **NYT**: 9.5.23, **MPG**.

[1007] **THE SPANISH DANCER**, Indy: [This version of Don Cesar de Bazan's play featured Pola Negri as, Rosita the Spanish gypsy dancer, not the singer of its rival production which was generally considered far superior. The directorial approach for this production was more historical than romantic, but with the dashing Antonio Moreno as Don Cesar, the ladies in the audience still swooned over the handsome Latin who many thought as good as Douglas in his athletic performance. Exhibitors were encouraged to show this film along with **Rosita** [1003] in a conjunctive rivalry to promote both of the very similar works. Some of their reactions indicate that "where audiences were well read on foreign customs and history ... it pleased highly." But in the more bucolic backwoods ... "in the farming communities where patrons like action in its wild state, without straining the mind, it fell flat."] **MPW**:2.2.23, p902, **V**:10.11.23, **NYT**:10.8.23.

[1008] **THE SPIDER AND THE ROSE**, Principal: [Once more audiences found themselves in sunny Southern California under

Mexican rule in the days of the Dons before the United States took control. The problem was that they also found themselves watching an inferior version of the **Mark of Zorro** [846]. The young Don who returns from the wars finds that his father's secretary has usurped control and is ruling the province like a tyrant. Not having been there to prevent it, what else could he expect? In any case, with the help of the local population, in proper garb for swashbuckling, he overthrows the nefarious Mendozza, [Noah Beery] and reestablishes justice. **Variety** suggested that it be cut from seven to two reels to make a better production.] **V**:7.26.23, **MPG**.

[1009] **STORMY SEAS**: Continental Pictures: [The only connection here is that a seaman, actually a Captain who promised never to drink again, does so and as a consequence of his insobriety, causes his ship to be wrecked. For this he is punished by the scripters to be exiled in a sleazy Central American port city to suffer it out until his rescue is finally effected by the very man who was his rival for the girl. Thankful to be freed from his confinement, [one might wonder why he did not book passage on a banana boat bound for Boston], he realizes how worthless he really was and gives up any claim to the lady, at least happy to be back in the good old U. S. of A.] **V**:7.19.23.

[1010] **SUNNY SPAIN**, Pathe: [A simple one reel filler which attempted to be "too hilarious" about customs unfamiliar to people in the states. Paul Parrott was a soldier of fortune operating out of Spain. There his Anglo prowess allows him to dodge "huge cannon projectiles" fired at him by inept Spanish gunners with great ease. The bull fight sequences would have been, at best, insulting to any, but especially the Spanish audiences.] **MPW**:5.5.23, p82.

[1011] **SUZANNA**, Mack Sennett/Allied Producers: [Mable Norman was highly praised for her performance in this costumer of old Mexico. The story revolved around the complications created by the desires of two great Dons who want to unite their vast estates by the marriage of their respective son and daughter. Problems arise when Dolores was expelled from boarding school for having an illicit affair with Pancho the toreador. When she returns home, he follows and upsets all the arrangements. Meanwhile, Suzanna has not been inactive. Supposedly the daughter of a peon on one of the haciendas, she has attracted the attention of Ramon, the other party of the first part. As tradition required, she was sent far away. But, letting the writers once more have their way, is was discovered that the now exiled beauty, was in reality, the daughter of one of the Dons who apparently had had some trouble keeping his extra curricular activity straight. As such, she was allowed to return to marry the randy Ramon, which of course, left Dee free to marry the matador. If only life could be so easy, alas, it would be so dull.] **MPW**:3.3.23, p68, **V**:9.29.23.

[1012] **TANGO CAVALIER**, Aywon: [George Larkin and Ollie Kirby were the experts who danced their way in to the hearts of many señoritas while enjoying the adventure always available south of the border.] **MPW**:8.4.23, p375, **afic**.

[1013] **WEB OF THE LAW**, Indy: [This small time western has a gang of baddies heading for the Mexican border to safety with an undercover Ranger in their company who does his job. Among those taken in was "Squint" Castile, a Mexican halfbreed with serious vision problems.] **MPG**.

[1014] **WHY WORRY**, Hal Roach/Pathe: [Harold Lloyd had become a star of the first magnitude when this film finished production, it would be his last effort with Hal Roach and a four star film. Lloyd played a millionaire hypochondriac who goes to a "South American paradise island" to regain his health. When he arrives there, he finds himself in the middle of a revolution which results in his being jailed. The giant in the cell with him is really sick with a very bad tooth ache, but once that pain has been removed, the two escape. Together they free Lloyd's nurse, quell the revolution and bring justice to the lout that began all the trouble. That settled, the comedian and his angel of mercy return home to marry.] **V**:9.6.23, **MPG**.

[1015] **A WIFE'S ROMANCE**, Harry Garson Productions: [In another neatly packaged formula piece with a Spanish setting, Joyce Addison played an artist-housewife who uses a local Spanish crook as her model and becomes attracted to his good looks as she paints his portrait. Her husband, a hard working diplomat, has unintentionally been neglecting her because of his heavy work schedule. Joyce is really drawn to the young man, but understands the damage that could be done to her marriage if she were to consummate the relationship. As she explains the impossibility of the liaison to her model, the husband happens to overhear everything and he determines to make things better for both of them. The characters included Isabel de Castellar, friend of the family and the properly subservient help, Pablo. Josefa was the attractive señorita friend of the thief who was pleased the Anglo lady took her self out of the competition.] **V**:9.20.23.

[1016] **THE WOMAN IN CHAINS**, Amalgamated Producing Corp: [Boy this lady, a French one, was a real beauty. First she deserts her loving husband to become a cabaret dancer where she snuggles up with another character who takes the rap for her and does time in jail so that she will not have to. She then marries an artist who was apparently unaware of her activities. When her jailed lover is released, she returns to him. The second husband realizing the futility of waiting around for the guy to do a little more time, decides to leave it all behind and seeks refuge painting pictures on the beautiful tropical island of Martinique, a Caribbean refuge for broken hearts.] **afic**.

1924

[1017] **THE AIR HAWK**, FBO: [A western set in the days when some cowboy hero's could leave their saddles for the seat of a Spad, Sopwith Camel, or more likely a Curtiss Flying Jenny to help them catch the baddies. On the Mexico/Arizona border there were bad men involved in stealing, not gold, but platinum and with the help of his faithful flying machine, after a little demonstration in stunt flying, the Mexican thieves were brought to justice.] **MPW**:12.20.24, 737, afic.

[1018] **ANOTHER MAN'S WIFE**, Regal Pictures: [A husband filled with vengeance for the abductors of his wife pursues the culprits to the Pacific coast of Mexico. There, somewhere off shore near Mazatlan, Helen Brand was kept captive. Following the rum runners too closely in the dark and fog, the husband's craft collides with the busy bootleggers and he is taken on board the very ship his wife is on. When he recovers, he overpowers the crew and is reconciled with the happy wife. It was that simple.] **V**:1.21.25, afic.

[1019] **THE ARAB**, Metro/Goldywn: [The first big, successful superstar from just south of the border was Roman Navarro, at one time considered a real rival for Valentino's loyal following of ladies. Here he was placed out on the desert in a feature that has this Moslem son of a Bedouin tribal leader falling in love with a Christian missionary's daughter and she with he. Many Latin stars throughout the twenties and thirties would be required to portray other ethnic nationals whose skin was somewhat darker than the average Anglo who has not summered in the Bahamas] **V**:7.16.24, **MPG**. "Coogan, Keaton and Novarro Are New Metro Stars," **MPW**, 1.27.23, p317.

[1020] **ARGENTINE LOVE**, FP/P: [All who reviewed this film commented on the "army of Valentino" lookalikes that Bebe Daniels was cast against. Most things have a beginning, but once duplicated, the change they experience is only slight until they fall into disuse. This was more often the case in Hollywood. Hollywood may well lead/have led the world in its slavish susceptibility to various fads. One thing in this film was new, certainly not the story, that concerned Ricardo Cortez as an Argentine strong man who becomes angered because his love, "Consuelo Garcia", prefers the bridge building American engineer. What was an innovation was the announcement that Miss Daniels had hired an Argentine expert to tutor her in the various ways of the residents in the port city and on the pampas. The problems that First National had experienced with the Mexican government over the **Badman**'s [962] negative characterizations jolted some of the executives into the realization that it might not be wise to offend foreign nationals if they expected to sell their film in that particular country. Competition for the Latin American market was intensifying all of the time. It was responsible for significant "coin" and Argentina was second only to Mexico in importance in total sales. It is no wonder that the lights went on and that it was at least announced that an "expert" was to be hired. That it made little difference to the characterizations, was of less consequence. More often than not, it was the government that was offended, the people still wanted the product of the worlds leading producer.] **MPW:** 1.3.25, **V:**12.24.24, **NYT:** 12.23.24, **MPG.**

[1021] **THE BANDOLERO**, Metro/Goldwyn: [Sunny Spain provided the background for 1924's entry depicting the "hatred, romances" and various problems of being a bullfighter. In this case they involve Dorando Bandolero, played by Pedro De Cordoba, who has been driven to banditry to "visit revenge" upon a Spanish Marquis who attempted to have his way with his wife. To punish the offense, the bandit abducts the aristocrat's son, Ramon and keeps him a captive in the outlaw camp. Problems arise when Bandolero's own daughter falls in love with the young man. They become a lot worse when another señorita also wants to run her finger through his hair. Perplexed, and unable to understand the wiles of women, he turns to the corrida and there becomes the matador idol, "Caneroa." Concha, the other woman also decides to venture to the city where she becomes the enticing dancer that all men desire, including the Marquis. The writer now makes both the father and son fall in love with the lady and arranges that the two come into conflict for her affection. Ramon runs once more to the corrida where he is seriously injured. The Marquis then discovers that the matador is really his son which causes him grief and makes the bandit happy. With his vengeance satisfied, he then allows his daughter, Petra to nurse the innocent victim back to health. Reviewers claimed that the producer, Tom Terries took his cast to Cuba and Spain to obtain some of the beautiful background shots that grace this production.] **MPW:** 10.11.24, pp520-21, 12.6.24, pp480-1, **V:**10.29.24.

[1022] **THE BEDROOM WINDOW**, FP/P: [Ricardo Cortez would many times later be cast as a heavy, usually some sleazy Italian, or darkskinned ethnic, a Chicago mobster, but in this case he was the wrongly accused. Lucky for this "Latin from Manhattan" his lady had an aunt that wrote mysteries and after a series of adventures, the clever lady used her sleuthing skills to uncovers the real criminal.] **V:**6.11.24, **MPG.**

[1023] **THE BORDER LEGION**, FP/Lasky: [Antonio Moreno was being given a lot of playing time on the screen by 1924, his manly appearance could be adapted to either side of the border. In this case he's north of, but still on the edge of the law. He had a job tending cattle, but lost it, so he decided to join a bunch of the boys and that involved other peoples cattle, the baddies of the Border Legion. Problem was, the renegade head of these hombres, a halfbreed Mex had it hot for Jim's girl, so when he joined up, he was forced to do a little fast work with his shootniron to save the little lady's honor. Exhibitors all claimed that the name Moreno was a drawing card and "Should make anybody lots of money ...[it was a] good picture."] **V**:10.22.24, **FD**:11.9.24. **MPN**:10.1.24.

[1024] **THE BORDER MAID**, U: [The Mexican character in this brief two reeler was cast as a sympathetic hero. To save the man that he thinks his girl loves, he makes it appear that he is going to take him across the Rio Grande and turn him over to a gang of smugglers. When the baddies are caught, it is discovered that the man who was saved was in reality a revenue officer and the half-brother of the girl. For this the writers gave the Mexican the lady and her gratitude.] **MPW**:12.14.24

[1025] **THE BORDER RIDER**, Essanay Film Co: [No other information found.]

[1026] **BORDER WOMEN**, Goldstone: [All of the action in this western melodrama takes place on and just over the Mexican line. Star Texas Ranger, Big Boy Meritt had long pursued the Cocas Kid and his notorious gang of outlaws. Gentleman Jack had been the Kid's first henchman for just as long, but after his capture and escape the two quarrel and Cocas shoots Jim. Big Boy finds Jim dying in the desert sun and promises to care for his sister till the end. In time he captures the Kid and wins the love of the little lady.] **V**:8.27.24, **FD**:10.12.24, **MPG**. afic.

[1027] **BORROWED HUSBANDS**, Vitagraph: [Typed as a "society comedy-drama", this old formula of hard working husband and flirtatious wife had Nancy Burrd playing around with almost anything that moved while her husband was off in the wilds of South America on an archeological expedition. The "vivacious" Nancy filled her boredom with many suitors but two were more important than the others. Major Desmond who believed her to be a widow and Dr. Langwell, who wanted her for his wife. When the honorable soldier, happens to meet her husband in an undetermined part of the southern hemisphere, he was at first horrified to discover that Gerald and he had shared the very same bed. Gerald himself, thought he might have a few words for his wife and headed home. Once there, somehow all was resolved. There was even the possibility they would go searching for the Inca ruins together. To remove the military man, the writers had him commit suicide when he learned about the reconciliation. For good measure he shot his nurse just before ending his own life. Going too far south could be tough on all concerned.]

[1028] **BUCKING THE WEST**, William Steiner: [Xyethia Tomkin an intrepid archeologist passionately interested in Aztec treasure, happens to meet Cal Edwards who along with a couple of cowboy friends had purchased the ranch belonging to Xyethia's brother. The brother had died under semisuspicious conditions of snakebite, leaving a lot of talk going around about a secret treasure map, possibly Aztec treasure. International crook, Jacques Ledoux had heard of the rough map and wanted a piece of the action. He discovers that Xyethia held the prize and made an unsuccessful attempt to take it from her. To keep the map safe, the lady archeologist gives the map to her French maid. Of course the French crooks first kidnaps her and then her mistress, requiring her services to interpret the directions. Cal rescues both, apprehends le voleur, throws him in jail and then falls in love with the lady. They then planned to spend the rest of their lives in a pleasant search for the Aztec treasure in Mexico.] **afic**

[1029] **THE BULL FIGHT**, Fox Educational: [This one reeler scans the entire career of the bullfighter, "the idol of the Spanish populace." From the first beginnings as a young boy on the farm imitating the matador and later, learning the tricks of the trade. Fighting his first bull at the home town fiesta, a young man if he triumphs, continues to greater glories until he becomes the most noted bull fighter in Sevilla, well, at least it was that way in this documentary.] **MPW**:11.9.24

[1030] **CALIFORNIA IN 49**, Arrow Film Corp: [This fairly involved scenario touched on some of Captain John Sutter's initial success at establishing an empire in California and added a few embellishments of its own. Sutter was shown acquiring the huge land grant given him by the Mexican governor of still then California and the plan for his grand scheme was outlined from the beginning. He had with him an unscrupulous soldier of fortune named Marsdon and an attractive lady, Arabella Ryan. All was well until Sutter's daughter, Sierra discovered her father's affection for the lady. This causes her to lose control because it was strongly implied that dad was forgetting the memory of the deceased mom. Those things were important then. Apparently Sutter was shamed into remorse and ordered Ryan and Marsden out of his thriving empire. At that point Cal, a guide for the Donner party heading across the mountains, appears. The wagon train he had been leading had become snow bound, but he managed to reach Sutter's fort seeking assistance. There, pretty little Sierra nurses him back to health and when the Mexican-American settlers decide to revolt against Mexico, Cal is elected to lead the assault against Fort Sonoma. Success brings happiness to the lovers, but eventual tragedy for the dad. His lands are overrun by the gold hungry mob. Marsdon is killed in a duel, still permitted in Hispanic areas, and Arabella commits suicide. And that's how Hollywood brought California into the Union in 1924 folks. With some small changes the film would be rereleased in 1927 under the same title, [1215].] **afic**

[1031] **CAPTAIN BLOOD**, Vitagraph: [The first real attempt to adapt Sabatini's work to the screen, the story concerns Peter Blood, falsely accused in England and transported to Barbados to work as a field hand. There his medical skills are discovered and he is moved to the villainous Governor's home to be his personal physician. Provided with the opportunity to escape when the Spanish raid the capital, he and the boys take over their ship while they sleep off their drunken celebration. After having signed the articles, they become among the most feared pirates on the Spanish Main, but are always careful with Anglo ships. The prize most sought after was Spanish gold, and whatever else might be on the Spanish ships which were the primary targets. Blood may well have been the best dressed, the most dapper pirate sporting the Jolly Roger. When James the second finally runs to France in 1689, his successor, William III offers Blood a pardon for the injustice done him and because with his crew he had destroyed a significant portion of the French fleet. He accepts and wins the hand of the fair Arabella, daughter of the former governor. A dashing Errol Flynn will have that privilege in the 1935 remake [1726].] **V**:9.10.24, **NYT**:9.9.24, **FD**: 9.14.24.

[1032] **CARLOS AND ELIZABETH**, Ger: [This Spanish costumer was an early German import, an attempt to break into the lucrative North American market. It was a poor choice. The credits identify it as a bit of Spanish history, but in reality it was taken from Schiller's **Don Carlos**, and proved to be a little heavy going for North American audiences. Spanish history interpreted by a German script writer did not play well in Peoria.] **V**:4.16.24.

[1033] **THE CHRONICLES OF AMERICA**, Pathe: [This series produced in conjunction with Yale University which holds most of the file material on these productions, promised "one three reel picture every four weeks," putting to film the fifty volume series of historical works edited by Alan Johnson. Three of the volumes should be considered here: Columbus and the discovery of America, Spain in the Americas and the Elizabethan Sea Dogs. The written text of the latter two were especially important in maintaining la leyenda negra, or the black legend of Hispanic tyranny and Anglo Saxon superiority.] **MPW**:8.2.24, p364.

[1034] **CLASSMATES**, Inspiration Pictures: [Sometimes those South American jungles could have far reaching affects. Duncan, a cropper who manages to rise above his station in life, loves Sylvia and becomes a cadet at the Point. Duncan, her cousin and his social better decides to attend that military academy also. Once there he refuses to take orders from Duncan and later is responsible for his dismal from the Army. Forced to leave West Point in disgrace, Duncan retreats and successfully separates himself from an unfair civilized world, by seeking refuge in the jungles of South America. In time he learns that his true love's nasty cousin has somehow become lost in the same patch of tropical rain forest. Now true colors come into play and good southern Christian that he is, Duncan leads an expedition to find the his enemy and does. This removes the snob's social crust and he later tells the truth which allows Duncan to graduate from West Point after all. Now that he was good enough to marry the southern belle, he does. There's no telling what spending a little time under the tropical rain forest canopy can do for your social standing sometimes. Originally brought to the screen by Biograph in 1914, [440] the updated version was simply somewhat longer with slightly better jungle footage.] **MPW**:11.29.24, p450.

[1035] **CYTHEREA**, FN: [He loved his wife, but Oh you kid! After some years of marriage, Lewis Stone became bored with his wife and children, so when a beautiful little vamp makes him an offer he cannot refuse, they are off to sun and sin a little in Cuba together. All goes well for a while in their tropical haven, some of which was photographed in color, but this was 1924. Will Hays had been placed in charge of cleaning up Hollywood's act, and this gave him enough power to make a lot of trouble in paradise. The husband's cutie, the little extramarital affair, was ordered to die of a tropical disease, thereby being punished for behavior unbecoming a lady, at least according to the Hays office.] **MPG**.

[1036] **THE DANCING CHEAT**, U: [As a great many early film adaptations were, this story was taken from the pages of the **Saturday Evening Post** where it first appeared as "Clay of Calina." There were no major Hispanics characterizations in this film, although it was set in an unidentified, tropical Spanish local, where one bunch of Anglos were working the old badger game out against another group with a pretty lady as bait. That routine seemed to work better for Hollywood when the action was staged in the uninhibited tropics.] **V:4.16.24**.

[1037] **DANGEROUS COWARD**, Andrew Calleghan: [A well received western with the hero falling for one more lovely little señorita named, Conchita. She had the cutest tortillas in town, but he first had to fight the big fight if he had any hope of ever tasting them. That involved a real problem, somehow he had to overcome the fact that he felt responsible for having crippled his last opponent, before stepping in the ring again. As it turns out there was a great deal of the **Quiet Man** in that **Dangerous Coward**, and he beats the guy to get the gal.] **V:10.8.24**.

[1038] **THE DANGEROUS FLIRT**, Gothic: [At times, the mere association with a Hispanic could cause dire consequences. Julie Herne, the main character in this romantic melodrama had been raised by a puritanical spinster aunt. She was apparently so modest that her own semi-clad reflection in the mirror might have caused her to blush. **Variety** called this film a "dirty picture" from the first, classifying it unfit to be shown in family theaters. The reason for this was that somehow she finds herself involved in an "all night escapade" with a seedy character named "Jose Gonzales. Nothing happened, but the mere association with Jose has ruined her reputation. Despite this, Dick Morris, a mining engineer marries her, but on their wedding night, the prudish girl is so frightened that she curls up in a closet cowering at her husband tender embraces. That Hispanic had really ruined it for her. Dick, blaming himself and feeling unloved, runs to South America where he meets Don Alfonso. Julie realizing that she loves him and does want to rub noses together, runs after him. By a strange coincidence, it is discovered that Jose Gonzales was really the nephew of Don Alfonso. When Julie arrives, both of their lecherous natures surface and the two Spaniards fight over the girl. Jose is killed by the Don who quickly convinces the local authorities that the Anglo was responsible for the crime. Dick is sentenced to the face the squad in front of the white wall at dawn, but now the true character of the little lady surfaces and by a clever ruse, she saves her swain and they head back to redo their wedding night.] **V**:12.17.24.

[1039] **THE DIAMOND BANDIT**, Ben Wilson Production: [Somewhere high in the mountains of South America, there was a village called, Pala that was looked after by the selfsacrificing padre, Father Cantos. He provided the spiritual assistance which made life barely tolerable and frequently tried to intercede between members of his flock and the tax greedy comandnate, Jaspaz Lorenzo, who ruled the region with a cruel iron fist. One day a savior appeared in the guise of a masked man, whose ability to weald his whip would have made the later Whip Wilson envious. Formerly the village idler, he now becomes the avenger of the community and attacks Lorenzo's forces with reckless abandon. In the fierce battle, the good father is killed, but not before sending one of the lovely orphan waif's with a plea that Pinto forever take care of his mission. Pinto is captured, but quickly escapes and routs the evil tyrants troops once and for all. In time he is proclaimed Governor of the province and the waif provides him with a wife. A paternalistic tranquility now settled over the mountains broken only by the soft sounds of lovers in love.]

[1040] **DOWN BY THE RIO GRANDE**, Goldstone: [**Variety** considered this production a "complete bust", at best for the smallest of houses. What story there was revolved around a villainous member of a Spanish family who knows where the missing deed is to the giant hacienda and its vast properties. This distant cousin tries to force the daughter señorita to marry him in exchange for the information that will save the rancho. She says "no," and the Ranger enforces her negative. What action there was involved a car chase in which the hero and heroine end up swimming for it in the Rio Grande.] **V**:6.18.24, **MPG**, **afic**.

[1041] **FAST AND FEARLESS**, Artclass: [A bit of a contradiction in characterizations, there are both good and bad Mexicans in this one, but the bad ones are really, really dumb. The smarter ones are members of the Mexican Rurales who actually aid in the capture of the not so smart ones. Actually the hero's horse was depicted as much brighter than any of them. It would seem that at a crucial juncture in this tale, the hero was far outnumbered by the bandidos. Happening to have more than several extra pistols, he lines them all up and attaches strings to their triggers so that he and the horse can make it seem as if they comprise a much larger force than they appear to. This of course fools them and later with the help of the Rurales, the baddies are captured. There might have been a few more oats in the old feedbag that evening, but it was behind the bars for the bandidos.] **LCFL:Clipping file**.

[1042] **FIGHTING AMERICAN**, U: [Reviewers for this soldier of fortune swashbuckler in which the young American hero, a former fullback, goes in to save the lady from the revolution that he quashes as easily as he had Harvard's best, noted: "Only one or two twists are the highlights of an otherwise conventional plot, with China the locale instead of the usual Central American dive ...." It had firmly been set in the viewing publics mind that such going's on happened mainly south of the border. But it was no more difficult to believe that little yellow men would want to "paw" "with lustful hands" at the heroine's dress than would brownskinned ones with thin mustaches and gleaming smiles, they just had to reach higher.] **V:6.4.24**.

[1043] **FIGHTING COWARD**, P: [This James Cruze satire of life in the old south where "honah" was everything and if you did not defend it you were no better than "Mexico", the octoroon. Which was saying that you were at least one eighth black and, worse, some of your parentage might have been from south of the border.] **V:3.19.24**, **MPG**.

[1044] **FIGHTING FURY**, U: [Another of the legendary western stars of the silent era, Jack Hoxie, was cast as a Mexican with a grudge against a crooked ranch owner in this film. Far from being the heavy, few, if any, western stars would have allowed such casting at that time, Jack and his amigo were treated sympathetically, and brought the Anglo baddie to justice. Such scripts were quite uncommon.] **V:10.8.24**.

[1045] **THE GREAT DIVIDE**, MGM:[Very often in these still early days of film, the popular journals, weekly's and monthly's provided the material for scripts. If a story was featured in the **Saturday Evening Post**, many producers considered it potential movie material. The **Post** itself did a significant amount of popularizing the industry with frequent articles glamorizing various aspects of motion picture production and Hollywood life. This tale of how a woman could regenerate even the worst of men is one such example. "Three grim unbroken centuries of Puritan ancestry had made Ruth Jordan what she was, a girl uncompromising in her standards, high principle, intellectual and deeply religious." Certainly enough character to face the problems that the west provided, once she journeyed out there. But, the peaceful, patrician life style she left back east, was nothing like what she encountered. In time she finds the man she must change and begins the process, a tiring one at best and during one afternoon's respite from her trial she slept by an open window as two brutish men watched. One, a burly Wallace Beery, named "Dutch," the other "was a short dirty and viperous" man, "a Mexican of low order, contemptuously dubbed, "Greaser". "Even in the free and easy cowcountry, seldom was a half cast of Shorty's type found in the company of white men." Ruth of course "shrieks" as she sees his sleazy face framed in the window, a scene that had been overused as early as 1912, yet still effective enough to stir audiences ten years later. Newspaper clippings featured this scene, with the Mexican's leering at the reclining Zazu Pits. In time her man gives the culprits their due. The Lincoln Center Film Library has a significant number of scrapbooks collected from film fans devoted to these early silents and some to specific stars of that era. There are some few citations penciled into corners of the gathered material which varies greatly. Included are newspapers from widely different areas, fan magazine clippings, reviews and studio press releases in different forms, which include partial scenarios, highlights and stories on the various stars. Sadly, many of the early volumes have lost pages because of long use and age, but the collection is valuable for film historians and fans alike. This film was re made in 1930, [1406].] LCFL: Scrapbook: Broken Barrier [Includes, Great Divide.] V:2.11.25.

[1046] THE HEART BANDIT, Metro: [A not very well received comedy/melodrama with a lot of action and characters named "Angel Face Molly", "Spike" and "Monk" looking out for the little orphan who finds herself adopted by a rich little old lady. She reforms but has to "crack one more safe" to save the hero's chestnuts. One of the real baddies was named Ramon Orestes Cordova.] V:1.31.24.

[1047] HE WHO GETS SLAPPED, MGM: [Apparently never forgets. [This production featured an all star cast, Lon Chaney, the slapee, Norma Shearer and John Gilbert. In the first reel, Lon loses everything to Baron Regnard, his invention, his wife and his fame. Regnard laughs. With little else to do, Lon joins a circus and falls for Consuelo, the bare back rideress. She also rejects him. Shortly thereafter, he learns that she will marry the Baron. Seeing, Consuelo's father and the Baron together, he releases the lions who feel privileged to dine on aristocracy. Lon himself dies in the little señorita's arms, happy now that she can marry some other clown.] afic.

[1048] HIS MAJESTY THE OUTLAW, Ben Wilson: [King Carson, was a small but honest rancher in Cochise City, Arizona Territory, near the Mexican border. Jeff Williams, prospective empire builder, owned the town and everything else. He wanted Carson's land too and turns the people against him. He had no compassion for anyone and was very bitter because his wife had some time past run off with a cowpoke, taking his beloved infant daughter with her. While attending a play production in the western town, Carson saves a young actress from the vegetable bath the friendly's were providing her with. The two run to a cave just outside of town, but the little lady was in need of a doctor's care. When he tries to obtain it, the townies chase him back to the cave with Jeff leading the lynch mob. Had it not been for a young Mexican girl, the lad would have been killed. Then to no one's surprise, it is discovered that the actress lady the sheriff had saved was the long lost daughter. In the last scene Jeff not only regains his little girl, he also acquires a son.] afic.

[1049] HIS OWN LAW, Sable Productions: [This western melodrama set on the Mexican border involved Dad Emerson a sheep rancher and his children. The hero was an eastern photographer who helped Dad prevent Blackie Duncan from stealing his property. Blackie was the real heavy, but he employed some Mexican assistants to help him do his dirty work. afic.

[1050] **HUTCH OF THE USA**, William Steiner: [There's a lot in a name. If you want your child to be a concert pianist, don't name him "Brick" or "Hutch", Hutch connotes action of a different kind, and in this film "laid in a turbulent Latin American Republic," a "Leonard" might not have proved to be the right kind of a "go-getter type of American" to do the job. In the Latin American Republic of Guadala, General Moreno ran the government and was the personal guardian of Marquita Flores who he planned to marry against her wishes. The people were unhappy and oppressed. Revolution was in the air. What better situation could a young Anglo be sent to investigate for his metropolitan newspaper. Compound this with the fact that he happens to look exactly like the señorita's señor, Juan who has been eliminated by the General, then, certainly things must happen. They do. Hutch and the lady fall in love. The general tries to eliminate him, but fails which allows the Anglo to join the revolutionist and save his señorita from the tower where she is about to be forced into connubial bliss. Moreno is defeated, a new government established, justice restored and the North American way proven best. Happily, the two lovers leave Guadala for the land of the freer and braver, soft hand in strong arm.] **MPW**:5.31.24, **p495**.

[1051] **HYSTERICAL HISTORY COMEDIES: [IT'S TO LAUGH] WHEN COLUMBUS DISCOVERS AMERICA**,U: Nationally advertised in the **Saturday Evening Post** this "big new idea in comedy," attempted to treat certain historical events with tongue in cheek humor. One of the first of the series asked the question. "How could Columbus prove the earth was round if he was not on the level?" The series promised "wholesome, side-splitting" humor throughout the ages."] **MPW**:7.12.24, **p78**.

[1052] **INEZ FROM HOLLYWOOD**, FN: [Inez Laranetta, "The Worst Woman in Hollywood" was a successful silver screen vamp who loved to play the hot Latin chiquita on film, but in real life she was simply every little boy's nightmare, a gold digger with an announced philosophy: "In life it is the man that shall pay and pay and pay." She stages wild parties to enhance her reputation and tries her best to instil her [temporarily] winning ways in Mary Astor, [If one is to believe the reports that the Legion of Decency kept on Mary, she apparently learned her lessons well.] In the end Inez realizes that her image was actually jeopardizing her little sister's future and so, just like that, scripted woman that she was, she reforms.] **V**:12.17.24, **NYT**:12.16.24.

[1053] **A JUMBLE IN THE JUNGLE**, Educational: [Reviewed as the "usual" Lyman H. Howe "hodge-podge" which included a mixture of interesting and instructive scenes and comedy cartoon, "the mountains and volcanos of Mexico and a trip through the Panama Canal."] **MPW**:7.12.24.

[1054] **THE LIGHTNING RIDER**, Stellar Productions: [Another western melodrama played straight and not for laughs had the durable Harry Carey in the lead as the deputy sheriff of a town called, Caliboro which was menaced by a bandit known as the Black Mask. The town was filled with Mexican characters, the most attractive of which was Patricia Alvarez, but her father was actually Harry's boss. Certainly uncommon for this time to have a Mexican sheriff, he apparently did a good job. The real problem in the town though was, Ramon Gonzales and his helper Manuel. Ramon has Harry blamed for his misdeeds, which forces the deputy to go underground and in the end rip the mask right off Ramon's face. As always, for such services, the reward was the willing and waiting señorita.] **afic**.

[1055] **THE LONE WAGON**, Indy/Sanford: [In one sense this film was merely an attempt to capitalize on the popularity of the great success the **Covered Wagon** enjoyed, but it had a unique feature for it's time. The hero was a Spaniard, [Matty Mattison] who suffers the taunts and abuses of the southern family he is leading out west until they realize his worth when he saves them from a series of attacks by the savage indians. In fact they like him so much, they offer their daughter as payment, which of course, he was honored to accept. Certainly, not a typical scenario for this point in Hollywood history.] **V**:3.12.24, **MPG**.

[1056] **THE LOSER'S END**, Steiner: [In the twenty's Mexico became Hollywood's favored route for transferring all manner of illicit stuff into the United States. In this fast moving western the Anglo hero captures the drug smugglers just as they are about to bring the stuff across the border.] **V**:1.21.23, **MPG**.

[1057] **LOVE'S WILDERNESS**, FN: [In this film love's self sacrificing soul stretches from the shores of a southern plantation, into the African jungle and eventually finds itself in the close confines of Devil's island. There, the lady finally finds both her true love and the lout she married, the former was a doctor administering to the unfortunates in the care of the French penal system, the latter, an inmate. Fortunately, fate was once more on the side of romance, when the husband was killed by some of his fellow prisoners, the belle was free to marry the man she always loved. The French government would make sure not to let this one be shown in downtown Saint Germane. Serious protests will be lodged with the industry and the State Department concerning later Hollywood versions of life in that most dreaded of colonial empire prisons.] **V**:12.24.24, **MPG**.

[1058] **MADEMOISELLE MIDNIGHT**, Metro: [For some film historians who have given a cursory glance to the significance of Hispanic's in Hollywood productions, 1939 stands out as a year of change. From that time on their claim is that the Latin image on the silver screen began to improve significantly. These pages should help the reader determine the validity of that assumption which hinges mainly on the dramatization of the life and times of Benito Juarez and the French intervention in Mexico. **Mademoiselle** was the first Hollywood production to touch on that topic in anyway at all with this semi-historical-fantasy which made reference to those circumstances. As the film begins, the scene is set in the court of Napoleon [the small], III as it will be in **Juarez**, but all similarities between this and the other film end there. Although the French intervention provided the backdrop, this production was simply another variation on an existing theme, one that would continue to be used. It included some good Mexicans trying to prevent a lot of other bad Mexicans from taking over the government and abusing the people even further than they had been already. When one includes the inevitable Americano "who of course wins the girl" and who straightens out all the problems for the helpless Mexicans, we have a scenario that Richard Harding Davis would have easily understood. A more elaborate version of this story line will allow Burt Lancaster and Gary Cooper to do exactly that. Their Anglo intercession will result in the defeat of Maximilian in 1954's **Vera Cruz**. The **Moving Picture World** certainly recognized an existing problem when they claimed that this was a very different type of Hispanic film, a film "that differ[ed] from the usual Mexican story." But they may have been somewhat premature in assuming that "it [would] not give offense to the Mexicans themselves. The tenor of the story [was] thoroughly pro-Mexican." Although there was some substance to this evaluation, the film included many good, loyal and patriotic Mexicans, it also featured, the usual array of sleazy types in large numbers, all dirty, malevolent and sinister. **Variety** claimed that de Ruiz, "was the perfect type as a Spanish dirty dog," "a greaser." The scenario had the very lovely Mae Murry, half French and Spanish/Mexican, haunted every night by the ghostly gliding spirit of her departed mother. To rid herself of the vision she apparently "had to dance" out her dream for all to see, mainly the audience. When the Anglo star Monte Blue falls for the midnight danseuse and becomes involved in her nightly entertainment, he protects the lady from those dirty "greasers" who consider her to be a "maniac." These baddies want to steal her fortune, but they also want to overthrow the Mexican government. The two events were not necessarily connected. Blue, as the North American agent of the Monroe Doctrine, prevents all this from happening. Had it not been for his intercession, Mae would have been penniless, dead and the Mexicans might have been singing "La Cucaracha" in French in their next revolution. See: **La Poloma** [2078]] Allen L. Woll's, **The Latin Image in American Film**, [Los Angles: UCLA] 1977, based on fewer than fifty film was one of the first works which evaluated Hollywood's role in creating Hispanic stereotypes. **MPW**:5.17.24, p318, **V**:5.28.24, **NYT**:5.27.24.

[1059] **MAN FROM GOD'S COUNTRY**, Renown: [By this time almost every conceivable western formula had been long established, the success of a particular low budget production often hinged on the ability to find a slight variation from the established norm. Two suitors for Carmencita's affection had been overdone before 1914, the twist here was not that the rivals were antagonists, but fast friends, "with the Mexican gracefully making his exit when he realizes he has been fairly licked in the great pastime of two fellows for a girl." Also the chief heavy, who loved to brutalize his Hispanic help was a not so nice Anglo. Fairly unique for its time.] **V**:10.22.24, **afic**.

[1060] **THE MILLIONAIRE COWBOY**, FBO: [An eastern youth is spirited away from the gay white way to an almost deserted desert town filled with Mexican bandits. Fearless Anglo that he was, he invades their den singlehandedly, and destroys most of them with but a little trouble. There was an Anglo girl to rescue from their lecherous clutches. Actually he did have some help from the State Police, but he could have done it alone. Ever enterprising, he makes the town famous by placing a chemical discovery he has made in his spare time on the market. It proves to be a great success. Everybody in town loves him, especially the lady.] **Motion Picture News**, 11.1.24, p2232.

[1061] **THE NEXT CORNER**, P: [The problems of the neglected wife which cause her temporary infidelity, a momentary indiscretion, have been the theme for many Hollywood productions. In these silent era days, the temptation or the justification for such behavior usually had a Hispanic cast. In this case it was a suave and handsome Spaniard, Ricardo Cortez, who steals the wife's affection while the hard working husband was in the Argentine slaving away. The affair is brief, because the equally Hispanic father of a wronged daughter, kills the cad while the lady is foolishly being entertained at Ricardo's sex palace. There, before anything was consummated, she has pledged her love to him. To affirm her resolve, she had foolishly done so in writing a note to her husband informing him she wanted her freedom, a romantic indulgence all in the audience knew she would soon regret. The Spanish servant had also been witness to all these events and although he helps the lady escape, he had his own plan. Remorseful, or at least forced by circumstance to be, she joins her husband in the Argentine. He notices the change, but is kind and lovingly understanding. Later when the servant shows up with the incriminating note, which he had not mailed and kept for just this nasty purpose, he threatens to blackmail her if she will not do his evil bidding. She refuses his advances and he is forced to leave. She gives her husband the letter, but the pages are blank. He gives her no chance to confess and forgives her. This exact scenario, save that the location for the filthy fun was Spain, will be produced by RKO, in 1931 as **Transgression** [1548], with Kay Francis as the bad lady.] **MPW**:2.23.24, pp670-1.

[1062] **THE NIGHT HAWK**, Stromberg: ["Strictly for the smaller houses where the clientele's conception of the west is Elizabeth, N.J." **Variety** frequently employed such caustic quips when they could see no conceivable reason for a particular western to have been made. This one starred a not frequently cast as vengeful, Harry Carey, who with a gang that included Mexicans, were out to kill a local sheriff for some violation of Hollywood's western code.] **V**:4.16.24, **afic**.

[1063] **NORTH OF 36**, FP/Lasky: [What the **Covered Wagon** did as a first historical epic, outlining the problems of trekking to the California gold fields of 1849, this film accomplished as the equally epic first to picture the problems of driving cattle north to the rail head from Texas. Among the colorful characters in the drive was one, "Cinquo Centavos", invited along for comedy relief.] **V**:12.10.24.

[1064] **PASSION'S PATHWAY**, Lee-Bradford: [Scenes shift dramatically in this film, from the city, to a Mexican local, where an enterprising superintendent for the home office saves the owner's son from the clutches of Mexican bandits. They were included as the only action in what was considered "an otherwise dull programmer."] **V**:9.17.24.

[1065] **PURE GRIT**, U: [In this average western, a true blue Texas Ranger chases a real bad hombre to the Mexican border where he is working with other rustlers and places him behind bars. He was also required to save the little lady from the baddies lecherous intentions, [by now it must be obvious that they never had any other, intentions that is.] As he rode off into the sunset, he knew what a good days work he had done and how tough, but adventurous it was to patrol so lawless a place.] **V**:1.10.24, **MPG**.

[1066] **QUEMADO**, FBO: [Fred Thompson and Silver King, in the "greatest Western to date." An adaptation of the Marvin Wilhite story published in **Popular Magazine**.] **MPW**:12.13.24, p588.

[1067] **RAINBOW RANGERS**, Steiner: [Described as a western comedy in which the Texas Rangers save the girl from the clutches of Mexican bandits, one of them named Manuel Lopez.] **V**:8.20.24, **MPG**.

[1068] **RECOIL**, Goldwyn: [This Rex Beach short story has Gordon Kent returning from twenty years in his South American mines to Paris for a little cherche la femme, which takes the form of the lovely Betty Blythe, when he stops looking around. She does not love him, but agrees to marry him anyway, what else could a scripter expect from a woman, especially a French one in 1924?. Soon she is in someone else's bed and the apparently extremely optimistic Gordon is really put out. It gets worse when he discovers the wife is sharing it with a crook [don't be harsh, she was only seeking a little adventure.] As his anger grows, he devised a proper punishment. Because of his fortune, he makes the two strays stay together, even after the new toy has acquired a few other play things. Gordon now revels in their hate for one another, but repents when his wife saves his life. With forgiveness all around, they are rejoined and head back to the mines in South America to work there forever.] **MPW**:7.12.24, p139.

[1069] **THE RED LILY**, Metro/Goldwyn: [Something of an early antihero, Roman Navarro was cast as a likeable Montmattre thief who had once, as a younger man, fallen in love with a little lady back in the friendly provinces. Now fallen on hard times, he discovers the girl in Paris in equally unhappy circumstances. After she saves his life, they both decide to return to more bucolic surroundings where they had once known true happiness.] **V**:10.1.24.

[1070] **ROMANCE RANCH**, F: [The similarities in scenarios between this film and **Down By The Rio Grande** [1040] are so striking that if the titles were removed, it would be difficult to know which belonged to which. A pony express rider is killed and his letter is delayed by some fifty years. When it finally arrives, the young Mexican lad who thought that his father had never forgiven him, discovers that he had and not only that, he had actually left the rancho to him and not his evil brother who had been abusing him throughout that entire miserable time. Those scripter's could really make life unfair, if you happened to exist just a bit north of that border. But there were compensations, to gain rightful ownership of his rancho, John Gilbert, as Carlos the great grandson, marries the granddaughter of the evil one and thus solves the problem by becoming the legal owner of the property that should have been his parent's long ago.] **V**:7.16.24.

[1071] **THE SAINTED DEVIL**, FP/P: [With some hope of reestablishing the stature Valentino achieved in the **Four Horsemen** [863], he was cast in this production as an Argentine aristocrat who has his wife taken by "el Tigre" the bandit, on the very night of his wedding. Following closely on the heels of the abductor, Rudolpho locates his gang in a deserted church where, horrified, he witnesses what he thinks is his wife dressed in her wedding mantilla in the arms of the tiger. Totally disillusioned, in despair, destroyed, he leaves forever to be free from the wicked whiles of women. Later, the two men meet once more and fight, but not to the death. When the bandit attempts to leave the scene, he is killed by another of his many enemies, which does not make the still virgin bridegroom unhappy. What pleases Don Alonzo Castro, even more is the discovery that his Carlotta, did not dishonor him at all, she had been forced to part only with her wedding dress, a gift for the 'Tigers's' woman. All that worry proved unnecessary, for as it turns out, the bride was safely hiding in a convent, just waiting for when her manly hombre would come to take her safely back home. The film failed in its purpose and was not a great commercial success. Ironically, the greatest of the so called "Latin Lovers" had come under the control of his shrewish second wife, whose desire to have him portrayed more sensitively, probably resulted in the above inane script and certainly was the reason for his being called a "painted, perfumed pansy," by a none to kind critic in the Windy City.] **MPW**:11.29.24, p548, **V**:11.26.24, **NYT**:11.24.24, **MPG**.

[1072] **THE SEA HAWK**, FN: [**Variety** predicted accurately that this production would forever be considered a masterpiece of film making, it remains so today. Despite its $800,000 price tag, it returned a significantly greater sum than that to First National, and could have remained at the "Astor" as long as they wanted to keep it there. The story, taken from another Sabitini novel, reinforced what audiences unknowingly believed, that everything English was good, and all that was

Spanish was evil, in essence, what historians refer to as the "Black Legend" of Hispanic villainy, "la leyenda negra". The action begins in England where the hero, Sir Oliver is to be sold into slavery to the Moors, so that by his absence, all will think that he is guilty of a crime committed by his brother, the salesman. Before this can be done, a Spanish galleon takes the English ship captive and makes a bound galley slave of the hero. The evil treatment of the Spaniards convinces Sir Oliver that there is nothing good in their brand of Christianity and he becomes close to a fellow Moorish captive. Provided with the opportunity to escape together, the Spaniards kill the Moor, but Sir Oliver escapes and from that point on he devotes his life to revenging himself on the Spaniards in a just war that had audiences cheering in movie houses throughout the United States. Still an Englishman at heart, for the next three years he sinks as many of the hated enemy's ships as is possible. During that time he has also abducted his former bride to be and his nefarious brother. Both had been sold into slavery, he had purchased them. In the last reel he is faced with the choice of having his true love taken prisoner by the English or killed by the Moors, the Moorish prince wanting his woman, he gives up to the former. Recognizing the service he has performed, the authorities must still hang him for murder, but when his brother confesses, he is saved, for future use against the Spaniards no doubt. The Vitagraph company took out a series of two page spreads in many of the trades and daily newspapers which were designed to look like the front page of a special edition announcing some fast breaking story, the bold face captions read: **SPANISH BUCCANEERS SACK CITY/PETER BLOOD SAVES GIRL'S LIFE/PETER BLOOD CROSSES SWORDS WITH SPANISH RUFFIAN! CONVICT SLAVE BESTS ENEMY IN SWORD DUEL.** The accompanying pictures showed a dashing looking Blood dueling against a iron helmeted and vested Spaniard. The film played to capacity audiences at one of New York's premier houses throughout the summer.] **MPW**:7.12.24, p139, 9.27.24, pp268-9, 10.4.24, pp360-1, **V**:6.11.24, **NYT**:6.2.24, **FD**:6.8.24, **MPG**.

[1073] **THE SHOOTING OF DAN MCGREW**, MGM: [The "lovely Lou" of Robert W. Service's narrative poem provided the broad outlines of this production which placed the tempestuous lovers performing in a South American cabaret and enjoying great success. The problem for Lou was that the "squalor of the surrounding" so "nauseated her" that she was afraid her boy would be marked for life, and as such demanded to leave the unpleasant atmosphere for cleaner and more prosperous climes. Jim refuses, but she leaves anyway, having made a business arrangement only, with the dangerous Dan McGrew. The rest is a poem.] **MPW**:4.12.24, p585, **V**:6.11.24.

[1074] **SIREN OF SEVILLE**, Producers Dist Corp: [**Variety** thought this such a "corking picture for almost any audience," that it certainly should "have a tremendous vogue in the Latin American countries as well as in Spain." This despite the fact that Dolores, Calito, and Cavallo, the stars, and everyone else, were played by Anglos. Dolores the pretty peasant girl, loves Calito who she helps become the idol of Seville's aficionados. The baddie, Cavallo, President of the Corrida, wants the lady too and plans to drug the hero so he will be killed by the bulls. Ignoring the fact that she has been momentarily forgotten by her matador, now enjoying the ardor of all the ladies of Sevilla including one special 'vampacita,' she rushes to the arena to save her man. She does, he realizes his mistake, scorns Ardita and takes Dolores in his arms for the everlasting clinch.] **MPW:9.20,24, p211 11.29.24, p451-50, V:11.19.24**.

[1075] **SOUTH OF THE EQUATOR**, I. J. Barsky: [The producer of this film was accused of taking a little too much license from Fairbanks and the **Americano** [632]. A "little too much" was kind, in effect, it was a direct steal from the R. H. Davis character, but who is to say, Latin American republics being "addicted to revolutions," as they were and are. Another time and another republic, that makes a different motion picture, correct? The heroics in this film, to add a little variation, were shared by the daughter of the deposed president who makes her way north to buy guns and discovers that she loves the handsome young man from the "Estados Unidos." The Spanish helped make it different. The inclusion of the "colored pal" for comic relief, as if these Latin's weren't funny enough, merely added more variety to the ethnic characterizations and heavy Hispanic parody. The Anglo hero "down in the old South American country" earned his pay. He staged a few battles, waved a few flags, easily destroyed the villainous force and wound up with the heroine. Different or not, R. H. would have loved it and probably quipped that "imitation was the sincerest from of flattery".] **V:1.7.25**.

[1076] **SOUTH SEA LOVE**, F: [Wherever the undisclosed location for this "South Sea" adventure was, it was filled with Hispanic characters, Dolores Medina, the heroine who has to fight for her honor, Manuel Salarno who almost takes her most prized possession from her, Maria and Captain Medina, along for the adventurous ride and all of them, were Anglo's trying their best to act in ethnic character.] **V:1.17.24**

[1077] **SUNDOWN**, FN: [One of Hollywood's many attempts to describe the struggle between the cattlemen and the new homesteaders. The latter need the land to make new settlements, the former needed open range to provide the nation with beef. To satisfy the cowmen, an arrangement was made between the governments of Mexico and the United States to provide grazing rights across the border. Unique for its time, it was one of Hollywood's more practical scenarios, but never a reality.] **V:12.3.23**.

[1078] **THE SWORD OF VALOR**, Goldstone: [So many daughters of so many Spanish Dons fell in love with so many North American soldiers in Hollywood, it is a wonder that the ethnic blurring did not wipe out all traces of the racial purity some so seem to covet. Once the wealthy Don Guzman de Ruis y Montejo [Otto Lederer] discovers that his daughter, Ynez, loves the North American captain, he takes her to the Riveria and tries to sell her to an even wealthier than he is, cad, [according to

Variety, Ismid Matrouli, "a Levantine of mongrel origins."] The captain arrives in time to save his lady, but is forced to fight a duel with swords to win her. His success is made easier when a former gypsy lover of the apparently active, but discreet, Ynez, shoots at the soldier and hits his opponent. Undeterred by his lack of marksmanship, he later kidnaps the señorita and takes her to his Spanish mountain hideaway where our hero rescues her once more. Possibly, with some reluctance.] **V:5.14.24**.

[1079] **THREE MILES OUT**, Kenma Corp: [... and on the way to South America. Molly, just a half hour before she is to be wed, is told by a friend, Captain John Locke, that the man she was to marry, Luis Riccardi, was in reality a thief and a smuggler. Locke, who also loves the girl, manages to persuade her to sail to South America with him, but on the way, Riccardi's boys take over the ship and throw the captain to the sharks. The leader of the cutthroats, Jordon, was just about to make her his victim, when the captain, who somehow has saved himself, returns and ends the mutiny. Riccardi and Jordon, who it turns out has actually murdered a man in the captain's home town, are sent to prison. The two new lovers now continue on to the land of love and eternal sunshine.]

[1080] **THUNDERING HOOFS**, FBO: [Reviewers praised this production which included a bullfighting sequence that was "staged with [such] a fidelity to the real thing that [it would] make you want to go across the border and swap hisses and bravos with the natives." The story itself concerns a highwayman who attempts to rob a stagecoach on which is riding the Governor of a Mexican province and his pretty daughter. He is foiled in his efforts by the North American hero whose gymnastic ability rivaled Fairbanks, but even more significant, whose appeal was so strong that not only does the daughter fall immediately in love with him, so does the bandit's horse. When given the opportunity to chose, Silver King, the steed, "stalks deliberately" to the new owner of his choice. Hollywood's message remained consistent. Anything Mexican preferred to be on the other side of the Rio Grande.] **V:1.14.25, afic**.

[1081] **THY NAME IS WOMAN**, L. B. Mayer: [Set in the Pyrenees, this Spanish tragedy of an aging smuggler and his youthful wife, Barbara La Marr, had the rising star, Roman Navarro, a Spanish, soldier sent to ensnare "the fox," as the bandit was called. Informed by his captain that he might play upon the young wife's affection to capture the smuggler, the "fox" counters by asking his loving lady to see what she can do about using her feminine wiles against Navarro. Ever proud, as were all Hollywood Spaniards, Navarro, was even more so, his mother spit shined his boots every day. Knowing this, the outlaw's lady played with his manly pride, complementing his physical features, while secretly planning his demise. Still, a film writer was responsible for all this and so the expected happens. The two youths fall in love. Although she wishes no harm to come to her older amigo, she informs him that it is the other she must now follow. The sad news proves to be too much for old Pedro and as the two youths depart, he leaves his hiding place to fatally plunge a knife in the lady's bosom. You had to be careful if you were a wife fooling around in those days, and certainly so in Spain. Navarro then shoots the old "fox" and deals severely with the real villain, another soldier sent to spy on everyone who had actually sold out to the bandit. Brought to trial, Navarro has his life hang in the balance of the commandants's daughter's plea that he acted chivalrously and should not be executed. The audience was left unaware of the hero's ultimate fate. All in all, a simple story of Spanish love and business in the far reaches of the beautiful and mysterious Pyrenees.] **MPW**:3.1.24, **p69**, **NYT**:3.4.24.

[1082] **TIGER LOVE**, P: [Taken from a popular light opera, **"The Wild Cat"**, **Tiger Love** was one more variation on the many "dashing bandit of the Robin Hood," variety, who wins "a proud daughter of the Spanish aristocracy." Set in Spain and starring Antonio Moreno, as the Wildcat, a "notorious" but "gentlemanly" bandit, he as tradition required, robs from the rich and gives to the poor, peons in this case. One day, he and his band of happy brigands happen to capture the lovely "dark-eyed beauty", Marcheta, as part of their loot. She and he immediately fall all over each other, tripping into deep love. She, as was almost always necessary in such cases, was scripted to marry the son of the Mayor to save her father from financial ruin, those Grandees never could keep their dineros. Because he is honorable, he must sadly give up his prize. Returning her to her family, and possibly, thinking he had been a bit too much the gentleman, the Wildcat waits for the day of the wedding and then abducts both prospective bride and groom. In camp the latter is challenged for the bride's favors, but he proves himself a coward. When soldiers come to save the kidnapees and take the Cat, it is discovered that he also is a son of the Mayor, who has simply been exercising his Hollywood given, Spanish birthright to play at banditry. As the lovers kiss, they may well have fantasized about procreating a whole new generation of loveable little bandidos, for future film productions.] **MPW**:6.28.24, **p837**, **V**:6.11.24.

[1083] **THE VIRGIN**, Goldstone: "Splendidly cast" Miss Dorothy Revier, plays Maria Valdez, the Virgin of San Blas, and according to the critic, her performance was "exquisite and convincing" providing a "sense of credulity" to the role. Set in the Spanish town of San Blas, Maria, known as the "Virgin," was popular despite her appellation, possibly because of the wealth she stood to inherit. This attracted at least one suitor who was seeking to reestablish his lost fortune by wedding her. His plans were foiled with the arrival of the young North American who was seeking to discover who had killed his father some time ago. He falls for her and she him, but he is unaware of this until just before she asks him not to leave. Although strong in every way, such stalwarts were frequently scripted with naivety. Realizing all of this, the evil Ricardo Ruiz, now arranges to have the widow Montez tell the Virgin that Kent's father had killed her dad.

"Maria learns the truth at a [sic] siesta in honor of her approaching wedding". Torn between love and the Latin desire for revenge, she now offers to marry Ricardo, but "in name only." Enough. She still loves Kent. He and Ricardo fight a duel which the nefarious Spaniard has had arranged to insure the North American's death, but the ploy backfires and kills it's designer instead. Having over come all this adversity, Kent is now free to help the Virgin loose her disability.] **V**:10.22.24.

[1084] **VIRTUOUS LIARS**, Vitagraph: [A rising young artist has a cad for a husband, he womanizes while she works at her painting. After a stormy scene, he deserts his wife to go to Cuba where "he engages in dissipation" and has an affair with the hot blooded Juanita. The Cuban cutie was played by Dagmar Godowsky, of course, and lives only into the third scene, when she is shot by her enraged local suitor, (for being a German Pole impersonating a Hispanic, well ... that could have been one of the reasons, aside from her passion for infidelity.) Meanwhile, the wife, claiming to be a widow gains recognition and becomes very successful. Her art has attracted many, one in particular loves her, much too much in fact for when he discovers that she is married, he dies of a heart attack, but not before leaving her with lot of money. Learning this, the husband returns to claim his prize, not anticipating the vengeful character of those Cubans. The jealous lover who had taken care of Dagmar, now finishes the business and kills the nogoodnik. All of this activity leaves the lady well off and ready to marry the man of her choice, which prompted **Variety** to do a little moralizing: "White lies breed sorrow. Love cures all pain." One assumes, no matter what one's nationality might be.] **MPW**:4.19.24, p664, **V**:4.2.24.

[1085] **WESTERN WALLOP**, U: [Considered an inferior Jack Hoxie western feature, it was not all his fault, he was not responsible for the writing. We could search out and shoot at the scripter, if for no other reason than considering it necessary to include a Mexican named, Pedro, just because some of the action took place somewhat near the border.] **V**:10.15.24, **FD**:10.5.24.

[1086] **A WOMAN'S SECRET**, Br: [A British film company went to Spain to create the proper atmosphere for this story about a Spanish gypsy who is placed in jail because her lover killed the aristocrat that attempted to have his way with her. Most of the film's action features the loyal members of her "tribe" and the various attempts they make to free the beautiful dancer from what they consider a most unfair sentence of life behind bars.] **V**:4.16.24.

[1087] **YANKEE CONSUL**, MacLean: [The hero in this one, whose family has not worked for seven generations, takes a job in the diplomatic service, but only on a bet. This provides the action for what is termed a "rockling comedy" as he interacts with Margarita, Donna Teresa and Don Rafael Deachado in situations created to play humorously on their ethnic characterizations. Never having had any responsibility at all, he now travels south to help solve South American problems, and he does, little has changed since 1924.] **V:2.14.24**.

[1088] **YANKEE MADNESS**, Sceling: [Placing a south of the border revolution within the narrow confines of a silent screen musical comedy may seem humorous enough, but it had obvious limitations. Regardless, Walter Long played the Hispanic drunk who threatened the Anglo hero in the cantina scene where the lad was attempting to demonstrate his tango abilities. Also included was the grand fiesta with all of the native extras acting "notoriously bad," and a character called, "Cicero" who played a "scared darky," to provide a little ethnic variety. It was advertised as "The whirlwind action of the one-man-conqueror" our Anglo hero who bowled over "bandits and rabid revolutionist in a Central American country" "three or four at a time" with his "mighty fits" only. What else, all Anglo heros take notice.] **V:4.23.24**.

[1089] **YANKEE SPEED**, Sunset: [This scenario was by now so familiar, that **Variety** claimed that it was no different than "100 that had gone before it." "A typical moment" in the film came when the Mexican villain "after glancing carefully around the empty room, "hisse[d] to the villainess" [equally Hispanic], "Are we alone?" The Spanish beauty gave a knowing look. The North American hero was typical of "roof-climbing athletes" and indulged in "the usual quota of chases and fights, with the brawn of one Americano superior to that of an army of gringos." [Quite surely the reviewer meant, "greasers", not "gringos."] **V:7.17.24**], **afic**.

1925

[1090] **THE AIR MAIL**, Willat: [This production could easily have been used as an advertisement for the U. S. Post Office's Air Mail service. A high flying drama, it featured bandits using their own plane to rob the United States mails by forcing the government pilots to land in a deserted desert ghost town near the border so that the crooks could cross over easily and escape capture with the bags full of loot. Douglas Fairbanks Jr. had a minor role.] **MPW**:5.30.26, p547, **V**:3.25.25, afic.

[1091] **BEAUTY AND THE BAD MAN**, Frank Woods: [The enduring permanence of certain Hispanic characterizations is still even today, sometimes surprising. Certainly Hollywood has helped these images become part of an accepted folk mythology which merely readapts itself to peculiar fears and aspirations of every new generation. This particular 'wicked Felina' was another of a long line of beautiful darkskinned dance hall girls, that "whirled" across the silver screen sets and stages as her man watched with scripted lust in his eyes. The writers always made lust, especially Hispanic lust, a negative quality. One might assume from the implication, that most North Americans were conceived, with what, luck? Some time ago, Thomas Jefferson drew a similar parallel when comparing the romantic involvements of Blacks and Whites. For the latter, love, with all its tender applications characterized their relations, but for Blacks, the more primal lust was the moving force. All of this is easily applied to the North American views held by certainly not a few in this nation. Such a simple film to provoke all this. Meanwhile, he, her Mexican man, watched as she whirled devouring her every sensuous movement. He twirled his long silky mustache, as she drew nearer. The brim of his huge sombrero gathered the lazy upward curling smoke of the cigarette he held securely in the corner of his mouth, his thin lips making love to the [for today's viewers] foul weed as his dying lungs exhaled the deadly vapors. Felina's reflection glitters in his lusty eyes and single golden earring ... Enough. Audiences have bought it from beginning to end. And more than likely, will continue to till the big projectionist in the sky shows the last reel.] **MPW**:3,28,25, pp321-2.

[1092] **BEN HUR**, MGM: [This first major filming of the Wallace epic cost four million dollars to produce, but it grossed over nine million. For our purposes here it may be considered a high point of the Mexican, Roman Navarro's career. There is a certain tragic irony in the **New York Times**'s glowing praise, it would not be repeated: "Then as to Roman Navarro, he may never have appeared in former productions, but anyone who sees him will have to admit that he is without doubt, a man's man, and 100% at that. Navarro is made for all time with his performance here."] **NYT**:1.6.26.

[1093] **BEYOND THE BORDER**, Indy: [Harry Carey, who crossed back and forth over that line more than any other early western actor, starred in this feature.] **MPW**:5.30.25, p541.

[1094] **BORDER INTRIGUE**, Goldberg: [Although it claimed to be a new kind of western, because of its emphasis on the love interest, this production was panned by the reviewers who claimed to have seen nothing new in the genre for the past ten years. What Goldberg did in this border tale was to increase the numbers and the complications. Two brothers, a North American girl, two señoritas of very dubious morality and two villains named Juan Vertigo and Pedro Gonzales all were thrown into the pot boiling western cauldron. Much of the stew concerned one brother's attempt to prove to the other how bad the señoritas would taste to any but their own. "At the point of a gun", the one forces the other to go with Edith, the good Anglo girl and leave the Mexican tramp to her own kind.] **MPW**:5.30.25, p537, **V**:5.13.25, **FD**:5.17.25.

[1095] **BORDER VENGEANCE**, indy: [Although the film's title attempted to capture some of the notoriety of the region, there are only incidental Hispanic characterizations. This very low budget feature served mainly to introduce the newest of the "glorified gallopers," Jack Perrin to audiences addicted to the western genre.] **V**:8.12.25, **FD**:8.2.25.

[1096] **BRAND OF COWARDICE**, Goldstone: [First made in 1916 [635] with a young Lionel Barrymore, this better than average western by Goldstone added new variations to the original. Still strictly a formula script, the hero poses as bandit to trap bandidos who are trying to rob a rich Mexican ranchero. To do so he enlists the help of the daughter who quickly falls in love with him despite the fact that "she is kept in doubt as to his moral worthiness" until the last reel. But then again, he was a North Americano, that was all the little señorita had to know to give her heart away.] **V**:7.29.25.

[1097] **BREED OF THE BORDER**, FBO: [One more superhero sanitizing the riffraff on the Mexican border. Singlehandedly he, Circus Lacy, "cleans out a nest of bad men and frightens them to such an extent with his lightning like twirling of forty-fives that they seem to be rendered dumb when he appears." One of the dummies is a Mexican, Pablo the bandit [1597].] **MPW**:3.14.25, p149.

[1098] **THE CHARMER**, P: [Pola Negri left her usual vamping roles to play this more sympathetic Spanish dancer, Mariposa, transplanted to the United States and achieving fame on Broadway, she is afforded scores of admirers and two suitors, one wealthy, the other, his chauffeur. She of course chooses the later to struggle through life with, these were not yuppie times. There was always some romance in the air, if only hovering over the Hollywood hills. Much of the comedy in this backstage melodrama was provided by "Mama", played by Trixie Friganza. Most of the reviewers praised the Polish Pola for her characterization of yet another **Spanish Dancer**. [1007]] **MPW**:4.18.25, p677, **V**:4.8.25.

[1099] **CLOTHES MAKE THE PIRATE**, [In this fantasy Leon Errol played a revolutionary era henpecked husband named, "Tremble-at-Evil Tidd, that was transformed by his dream and mistaken costume into a member of a pirate crew that plied its trade on the Spanish Main. One of his adventures even allowed him to capture his wife and threaten her with the walking the plank.] **V**:12.2.25 **FD**:11.29.25, LCFL: Press Sheet.

[1100] **THE COMING OF AMOS**, Cinema Corp of America: [Rod La Roque starred in this feature with Noah Beery playing the heavy, Ramon Garcia, "a dirty dog whose villainy is trumped only by his manners." Amos, an Australian Anglo, had promised his dying mother that he would visit an uncle on the Riviera. After her death he does and despite his rough exterior excites the interest of an exiled Russian Princess. Before his arrival, she had been the quarry of an insidious Spaniard, Ramon Garcia, whose only interest in her was transitory pleasure. Seeing that his prey is being taken from him, Ramon has his equally nefarious henchmen, Pedro Valdez assault the Assuie, but the down under Anglo, proves to be too tough for the sneaky Spaniard. As a last resort, Ramon kidnaps the sophisticated and beautiful exile and places her in the dungeon of his island retreat. There he "begins a gentle torture system to make her acquiesce to those dirty ideas only [Hispanic] villains have." In time, Amos brings Ramon "a message to Garcia," and throws him in his own pit where he drowns. He and the lady make plans and Trixie Friganza, as a dowager duchess, makes them laugh.] **V**:9.16.25.

[1101] **THE CRACKERJACK**, East Coast Films: [An eastern college student works energetically for his tuition, but is mainly supported by uncle's pickle factory. Problems arise when the natural indolence of the southern worker makes the company go "smash," [note that the further south you travel in the hemisphere, the less assumed proclivity to manual labor there is.] Forced to return home, the natural eastern pep the boy possesses revitalizes the company. One of his promotional ideas features pickles stuffed with cheese. To increase sales he travels to a border town where the local grocer apparently has a taste for filibustering. His establishment is merely a front for transferring ammunition to the "neighboring Esquasado," where a rival party is attempting to foment a revolution. How to get the bullets across? Inside the stuffed pickles. Yes! But the daughter of the arms dealing dad is afeared that his trade will be his end. So our young hero goes to the neighboring republic, wards off the advances of a "Central American vamp", ends the revolution and wins the girl. Just another's days work for the average Hollywood hero.] **V**:5.13.25, afic.

[1102] **CUBA STEPS OUT**, F: [Part of the Fox Variety series: "The World We Live In," this one reel travelogue began at Morro Castle overlooking Havana harbor and traveled to the source of the islands major export income, sugar and tobacco. There audience were treated to the new technological innovations the North American producers and owners had introduced to improve production.] **MPW**:9.26.25, p334.

[1103] **CYCLONE CAVALIER**, Rayart Picture Corporation: [Reed Howes, an athletic and agile young buck, was chosen to revive the specter of Richard Harding Davis for the 1925 version of Anglo lad saves South America. As Ted Clayton, a restless youth and "live wire" he was sent by his dad south of the border to the Republic of Costa Blanca where in route he meets up with Rita Gonzales, the daughter of that nation's president. Complications arise when the soon to be hero inadvertently offends an old señor, her father, by cutting off his beard. It was an accident. But all is well when they arrive in the war torn republic and Reed manages to save El Presidente's office. No rabble of Hollywood revolutionaries could ever withstand the onslaught of a determined and righteous young Anglo. In no time at all he has repelled all invaders and established himself as the dictator which allows him to send for the lady, who willingly runs to his embrace. In the end the dad was satisfied with being figure head for the real source of power, his new son to be.] **MPW**:9.26.25, p334.

[1104] **THE DANCERS**, F: [Tony and Una, childhood sweethearts vow to marry when old enough to do so. Forced to go to the Argentine for family reasons, Tony remains true to his pledge. Una, on the other hand [apparently unaware the Hays office was clamping down on such behavior] "becomes a devotee of jazz, mad parties and forgets Tony." After his uncle dies, Tony inherits the Argentine nightclub and property. Wealthy enough to return home to claim his lady, she is at first glad, but then cannot live with the fact that she has allowed someone, actually teased him, to take advantage of her. So displeased with her now sordid past, she takes poison and dies on what would have been her wedding day. The Code was tough, but it was equally hard on Tony, who was now forced to find solace in the arms of another, an honest woman, if there could be such a thing.] **MPW**:1.24.25, p350, **V**:1.7.25.

[1105] **THE DESERT FLOWER**, FN: [**Variety** devoted a paragraph explaining that everyone under the sun not only panned this production, but "hammered" it, first as a play then as a film, but when the audience viewed it they did so with applause. Apparently they were making a point that there's no accounting for artistic appreciation, taste, or maybe that at least this audience was pretty dumb. The scenario sent a poor little orphan girl to live with her stepfather out west where she took care of her baby half sister who "was allowed to run around like a wild [sic] arab." He worked for the railroad and they lived in a boxcar. There was little running water or education until a young bum staggers onto the scene. Apparently his "proficiency at drinking was the result of honest practice", but he gives up his vocation when he meets the miss. Sober he was no longer a philosopher, but something of a scholar and shares some of his book learning with the lady. Recidivist that he was, he soon finds his way to a saloon leaving her to the evil intention of her father. She quickly follows whirling the little dervish along with her to escape a fate worse than death, but her parent follows. A sympathetic Mexican sees the situation right away and "shoots him sufficiently to make him drop." Everyone tries to take the blame in front of the sheriff, but finally the Mexican admits to it himself. The tobacco chewing sheriff with the soul of Solomon apprises the situation, bites off another chaw and concludes that "it looked to him like a clear case of suicide." This was one of the few times that a silver screen Hispanic was allowed to go free for having shot an Anglo, no matter how deserving the deed might have been.] V:6.3.25.

[1106] **THE DEVIL'S CARGO**, FP: [When a transplanted Eastern newspaper man crusades against corruption in Sacramento, in the days of the forty-niner gold strike, he gets results, but also suffers the consequences of falling in love with the wrong kind of saloon girl singer.] V:2.4.25.

[1107] **DON DARE DEVIL**, U: [Universal's star Jack Hoxie was reaching the very height of his popularity when he made his version of Anglo cowboy goes way south to help the folks back home get it straight, the film was quite successful and appealed to those beyond his usual audience. Jack had been riding the range in Wyoming when he developed a hankering to return to his South American home for a while. For company he decided to take a few of the boys with him. Once there, [it was impossible to determine where that was save that it was south of the border], he and the guys attend a fiesta where he meets his old friend Menocal. Mere moments later, Menocal is slain by a North American bandit under the protection of the local jefe, a despicable sheriff named, Berengo. Thus we had the best of bad from both sides of the border as the evil characters, no one could complain about that. Jack must, of course, avenge the death of his amigo and so he pursues Latham and in a brutal fight, beats the living hell right out of him. It turns out that Latham was actually chasing down a local named Remado who knew that Berengo was doing his fellow peasants wrong, so when Latham returns to tell all, the sheriff captures Remado an puts him in jail. His daughter now enlist Jack's help to free her father, which he does with the help of his Wyoming wild men. In the final scene there is one heck of a pistol shootout which disperses all of the desperados. Jack rescues the lovely Ynez and leaves Latham in his cave for good. With peace restored all return to the fiesta and happy señoritas are provided for all the guys, a grateful reward from a simple people.]

[1108] **DON Q, SON OF ZORRO**, UA: [In this successful sequel to **Mark of Zorro** [847], Douglas Fairbanks was at his athletic best playing the dual role of Don Cesar de Vega, the son, and Zorro, the father. As a team, the **New York Times** considered them unbeatable, twenty Spanish soldiers might have been too much, but "fifteen were no match for the pair." The fair Doug forswore his sword for this adventure demonstrating a learned skill with a bull whip that still amazes audiences. The enemy remained the evil Spanish governor of lower California who desired to squeeze every dinero out of the peasant population and reduce each peon to being his slave, but, the two, Don Q and the dad of course prevented this. When the former was not wearing his fantastic fighting costume, black mask and flowing cape, Hollywood presented the audience with their conception of what was every day attire for the aristocratic Spaniard, "the ilk that settled in California." He wore bell-bottomed trousers that fit tightly around the waist, a bolero jacket and a wide flat-brimmed hat. This was touched off with the "small mustache waxed at the ends and Spanish whiskers." Not much has changed since then.] **MPW**:1.27.25, p987, p961, 8.15.25, p737, **V**:6.17.25, **NYT**:6.16.25, **FD**:6.21.25.

[1109] **DON X**, Steen/Goodman: [Costumes and disguises were popular in 1925, for obvious reasons. This variation of the Hispanic savior has a wealthy Mexican beef buyer assuming the role so that he can bring to justice, Perez Blake, a half Anglo rancher who was responsible for all the stolen cattle on the range.] **MPG, afic**.

[1110] **DURAND OF THE BAD LANDS**, F: [First made in 1917, this version has newcomer and destined to be very popular with kids and adults alike, Buck Jones fighting for law and order in Mexico and on the border, where he has to clear his name of every possibly western offense every committed, all of which occurred while he was across the border in Mexico. The Mexican characterizations were simply for atmosphere, the story was all Buck Jones.] **MPW**:10.24.25, p650, **FD**:10.25.25.

[1111] **FIGHTING DEMON**, FBO: [In an attempt to vary an already overly familiar scenario, the scripters sent this "stunt-man" hero to an undisclosed location in South America where he has to open a safe in Señor D'Arcy's bank. Jim is unaware that crooks have hired him for the task. Traveling by ocean liner, he meets the bankers pretty daughter, but is also the object of Dynamite Diaz's new, somewhat flirtatious wife which causes the Latin pugilist no small concern. Once they arrive, the hero outwits the crooks by locking them in the safe and calling the policia. He also K.O.'s Diaz, which makes him popular with the locals and is rewarded with, Dolores, the lovely señorita. A neat little package indeed.] **MPW**:6.6.25, p628, **V**:7.29.25.

[1112] **FLOWER OF THE NIGHT**, FL/Lasky: [More frequently than not Hollywood's Hispanics had to pay the biblical price for maintaining their pride and honor, this was especially true for the Villalon family of Southern California in 1856. There Don Geraldo y Villalon a descendant of the once proud Spanish grandees, had his gold mine, the Flor de Noche, taken from him by dishonest North Americans. The problem was intensified because the old Don's beautiful and virginal daughter, Carlota Y Villalon, played by the sometimes vampish, Pola Negri, was attracted to those cute little gringo rascals. One especially, John Basset, the new mine superintendent caught her fancy. He liked her too and secretly took her to the company dance, where, when he was off getting refreshments, Derck Bylandt tries to force his attentions on the sweet señorita. Having had too much to drink and rejected because the lady said, "no," he drops dead on the dance floor in front of John who almost dropped the drinks he had in his hand because he was so disgusted with what he thought had been his dates behavior.

Now it really gets heavy. Carlotta returns home and has to tell the proud old Don that had forbidden her to even talk to one of the foreigners, what had transpired. Her confession causes him to commit suicide which forces her to leave for San Francisco. There Paula quickly degenerates into the role she liked best and becomes a vampish dance hall queen who easily infatuates Luke Rand, the sinister head of the Vigilance Committee formed to rid the region of all those who would challenge Anglo authority. In no time at all she has him eating out of her hand and tells him she wants her gold mine back. Realizing that that would cost John his life, she recants and goes to warn him. He kills Rand and the two rekindle the fires that set this conflagration off in the first place. Falling for a señorita could provide the screen with a complicated scenario in the silents, and also leave a lot of bodies around.] V:10.21.25.

[1113] **FORBIDDEN CARGO**, FBO: [In 1925 that forbidden cargo was rum, today drugs, yet one of the transit points remained the same, Bimini in the Bahamas. This was a simple story of secret service men trying to stop the illegal entry of demon rum and the men who would eventually get rich doing so because it was impossible to stop suppliers so long as the demand was there. Boris Karlof was one of the baddies, who loved the lady captain that falls for the G-man. In such films the government had the help of the Hays office which gave orders that not one drop of that demonic stuff was to reach the sacred shores of the land of prohibition. Such movies were comforting to those who were charged with enforcing the Volstead Act, and despite all evidence to the contrary, they may have reassured some in the audience and a few G-Men that the job was being done. A cynic might think that there could be a real lesson in all this.] V:5.13.25.

[1114] **THE FUGITIVE**, Arrow Pictures: [Heading west, a man is taking with him a reformed lady who had given up her fast life for the possibility of a good future out the great wide open. Having to leave the wagon for a moment, the man returns to find that the young regenerate has given up her life to desperados who would have had their way with her. Heart broken but determined, the man sets out after the bad guys. In a violent sandstorm, he tracks them down and kills all three of them. Drowning his sorrows in what one must assume was a desert oasis cantina, he meets Lolita Mendez and they hit it off right away. Now apparently pursued by the local law, the two make their escape and continue heading west to make a new life. It could be that simple sometimes out there, it was all up to the screen writer.] **afic**.

[1115] **GIRL ON THE STAIRS**, Peninsula Studios: [This is an excellent example of Hollywood's employing the easily activated prejudice or fear that many felt for Hispanics in general. Anyone could have been the heavy in this film, ethnic origin was absolutely unessential for the plot development. In times of national crisis, understandably, it has always been easy for Hollywood to use whatever enemy as the negative focus. But since the first days of film

Hispanics were the most consistent ethnic preference for such implementation, despite the fact that they never really posed any real external threat to the national security. Using them has also always made it easier to displace blame in affairs that involved drugs or the heart, Latin lovers and Hispanic drug pushers allowed Anglo's to be victims and avoid responsibility for their actions. To really enjoy this untypical mystery the audiences were asked to accept the premiss that the subconscious mind directed the activities of the sleep walker and that "the somnambulists do not remember anything they do while in the coma," but if hypnotized, all could be brought back. It would seem that the pretty young thing had been a bit indiscreet. She had written a number of letters to an attractive married cad who offered to return the naughty correspondence for certain favors beginning with a kiss for each note. At a "wild party", in the process of paying off, the wife witnesses the girl retrieving her mail. She immediately leaves and later that evening, the cad is found dead on the floor of his library. Of course the pretty young thing [pyt] is accused of the crime and brought to trial. She maintains her innocence and one who loves and believes in her suggests that she be put in a trance. All agree to the experiment and as a results she clearly relates what transpired that fatal evening as she walked about in her sleep. The murder scene she describes involved Jose Sarmento, a rich South American, whose wife had been "keeping an amour" with the cocky cad. As the scripters would have it, the Spaniard was right there in court with his errant wife and after the testimony, he confessed all. The pyt was then freed.] **V**:3.4.25.

[1116] **THE HAPPY WARRIOR**, Vitagraph: [The English were almost always nobel on the screen, but hardly ever this romantic. Lord Gordon dies while traveling abroad. He was married and that lady dies before she can get the keys to the manor. Her child survives and is raised to manhood by a sister. As a man he joins the circus and lives for a while in Argentina where he makes a life long friend of Jose. There was a lady in the circus he loved an never forgot and upon reaching his majority, the step mom tells him who he really is. Instead of leaving for England to claim the huge estates, he and Jose elect to go find his lady love and leave all the land to the greedy family members who needed it more than he.] **V**:7.8.25, **afic.**

[1117] **HEADS UP**, FBO: [Being a Hollywood millionaire in the twenties was sometimes boring, who would doubt a premiss like that? Well, anyway "Lefty" Flynn, as Breckenridge Gamble, was bored and he was also rich. To break up one of his days he decides to deliver a secret message from a North American tycoon to President Losada in the South American republic, of Centralia, [one reviewer called it, "Costa Casaba or somewhere".] It was his intention to purchase that nation's entire oil deposits. But the deal goes bad. Once there, he is arrested, imprisoned and escapes. Having freed all of political prisoners in the effort, he forms an army and "breaks up a revolution, rescues the president" and wins the heart of his lovely daughter. Any North American could have done it, you simply had to be rich or have some copycat Hollywood writer with little imagination to trace over a Richard Harding Davis script. **Variety** indicated a little incredulity by snidely commenting: "Here comes the Americano now. Whereupon a group of Latin generals grab their swords and run."] **V**:4.21.25.

[1118] **HEART OF A SIREN**, FN: [The Carmen character was never a really nice little lady in the first films, but she certainly became more salacious as she swiveled her hips into present times. Of the four or five oldest and most enduring stereotypes established from the earliest flickers, that of the Hispanic whore, by lots of other nicer names, was one which remained consistently negative. Actually the lady lost whatever positive qualities she once possessed becoming even more nasty in recent decades walking the streets of the Big Apple almost naked to the core. In this Parisian panache, Barbara La Marr played a naughty lady named Isabella Echevaria, who danced for all to enjoy, but earned her real dollars by a means undisclosed to but to a few. She was the cause of much male palpitation with the camera trained on her "during a series of poses with heaving chest" and flashing eyes. In the story itself she was somewhat more deadly, as the leading vamp in Paris, she was pursued by an American millionaire, an aristocratic Englishman and another who commits suicide. The ad copy might well have read: When her hot Hispanic heart heaved the bounty of her bosom, all the men in Paris dreamed of seeking solace in the Spanish siren's soul, to say little of her clevage.] **V**:4.8.25, **NYT**:4.8.25.

[1119] **HIS SUPREME MOMENT**, Goldwyn: [John Douglas, dedicated mine engineer has returned from South America to seek financing for an important gold mining project. While in the big city he meets Sara Deeping and they attend the theater together, but with a little nerve, he falls deeply in love with the star of the show, Carla King. Understandably, Sara is a bit miffed and jealous, but she still secretly arranges financing for the venture. John proposes to the Carla and she accepts providing he concedes to the scripters ridiculous codicil. She will go with him to the wilds of South America if he agrees to live a year with her, without passion, to say nothing of consummating their love. The fool accepts, Sara does a lot of chuckling and the two leave. There in the rough, dreary, dirty and isolated romantic surrounding they inhabit while John tries to squeeze a little gold out of the Andes, Carla becomes severely depressed. Reacting a bit like a male, he thinks a little passion will provide the answer to the lady's problem. It does not and the gulf between them becomes wider. In time, Carla saves John from the wrath of a miner's dispute after which they return to the city. Now John, probably a bit on the edgy side, after a year of scripted abstinence, makes a few moves on Sara. Carla, not forgetting her duty, agrees to divorce John and marry a rich millionaire so that she can provide him with his own money to finance mining operations. But John decides at the last moment he would rather be with Carla than anyone else and stops the marriage. Bowing to true love, Sara gives him the money to dig to his hearts content, and the two lovers, head for the South American Andes to try it again, but this time with no prohibitions. People actually paid money for scripts like this.] **V**:4.15.25.

[1120] **HURRICANE HAL**, Ermine Productions: [This western melodrama opens up with Buck Anderson, a young Texan saving the life of Bill Adams who has been captured by Mexican bandits. In gratitude, Bill gives Buck a job on his prosperous ranch. After a series of adventures, involving Lacey, the crooked ranch foreman who tries to get Buck into trouble, the Anglo hero and a lady he likes, Virginia are trapped by the baddies. For one of the few times in silver screen history, the Mexican federales come to the rescue and save the pair, capture Lacy and bring him to justice. There must have been a reason, but it's a bit tough trying to understand where the title of this film comes from. There are neither Hals nor strong winds in this one, maybe it was the shock of having the federales help the Anglo heros that affected the scripter.] **afic**

[1121] **IN THE NAME OF LOVE**, P: [Ricardo Cortez as a very poor peasant Latin lover, Raoul, plays his role well in this romantic melodrama that has an even poorer young lady acquiring wealth and riches, only to find that they rarely, if ever in Hollywood, bring happiness. Because of the attention paid her by the Count and the Marquis, she forgets Raoul, for a brief tryst, only to discover in the last reel, that his love was worth more than gold. Many in the audience bought it completely, they were only the great grand parents of that yuppie generation.] **V**:8.26.25.

[1122] **THE ISLE OF HOPE**, Richard Talmadge/FBO: [A simple story of looking for and finding buried pirate (Spanish) treasure in the Caribbean. As a little extra the captain's daughter also discovers true love in those tropical climes.] **afic**

[1123] **JOANNA**, FNP: [This was Dolores Del Rio's first Hollywood feature. She played Carlotta de Silva and was not mentioned in the review.] **V**:12.16.25.

[1124] **A KISS IN THE DARK**, FP/Lasky: [Adolphe Menjou had a wonderful life. He was young and handsome and he owned a sugar plantation in Cuba. Best of all for him because he loved the ladies, the señoritas loved him back, a great many of them. Things get even better for the healthy little swain when the Kings, who yearly wintered in Cuba arrive for the season. This year they have brought the new son-in-law along and he seems to be quite understanding of his wife's desire to fool around a bit. She does, but it's all harmless. After all they were under tropical skies. When it comes time for all to return to New York, Betty misses the boat and she and Adolphe share a kiss in the dark, at his plantation, but no more than that. When she does make it back to the mainland, the little tryster discovers her husband in the arms of a willing chorus girl. With a great deal of understanding the lady gives the naughty guy another chance, while omitting her own Cuban adventure. Those things were allowed there anyway.] **V:4.8.25**.

[1125] **LADY ROBIN HOOD**, FBO: [The influence of Zorro and Don Q transcended the bounds of gender with this production. There was little if any difference in the scripts save that it was a Lady Robin Hood, a Spanish aristocrat's daughter who took up the cause of justice in Spanish California and fought against the forces of the evil, Cabraza, the power behind the weak willed provincial governor. With as much zest but not quite the athletic ability of her male counterpart, she roamed the countryside avenging the injustices of the tyrannical government and protecting her peasant peoples.] **V:8.26.25**.

[1126] **THE LIGHT OF WESTERN STARS**, P: [Another of the many Zane Grey adaptations for the movie screen, this one pits two solid character actors recognized for their realistic portrayals, Noah Beery and Jack Holt against each other, [later, both produced progeny that would ride the same western range.] The former plays a good guy gone wrong but, set straight by the sweet fidelity and faith of an honest woman, a tough commodity to find anywhere, but especially on the border. There women were more like the beautiful, but deadly little Bonita, one of the bandit Beery's many tarnished but attractive angels of the evening. The bandits do what is required of them, they take over the town, set up headquarters in the "adobe" city hall, rape the women and generally terrorize the male population. Holt, with his new found inspiration, rides in and cleans up the nest of bandidos, without much trouble.] **V:6.24.25**, **afic**.

[1127] **THE LOST WORLD**, FN: [One of the truly unique productions of the twenties, especially for the remarkable animation. Willis O'Brien was the creative genius responsible for the introduction of the stop motion photography this film employed. It astounded audiences everywhere stock footage from this film continued to be used for years after the original work in a number of copycat releases. The story was an adaptation of Arthur Conan Doyle's "fantastical novel" which dealt with the myth "that there still exist[ed] in this world a plateau, somewhere in the unexplored wilds of South America upon which the animals of prehistoric times still live[d]." These animals according to modern science, had been extinct for more than 10,000,000 years. But whereas, time almost stood still south of the border, these great and fantastic creatures survived and inhabited the high reaches of the altiplano. It would take an expedition of Anglos from London to uncover their hiding place. Either the native were too stupid to realize what lived in their back yard or they had learned to live with them as part of the every day and saw little need for such excitement. In 1931 Marion Cooper convinced RKO and O'Brien to work on another land that time forgot somewhere off the coast of South America for a film called, **Creation**, but the production proved too expensive [consider the times] to complete and it was never released. It too would have featured other fantastic animals and creatures still living in yet unexplored parts of the southern hemisphere. The two would collaborate on a little thing called **King Kong** in 1933, but **Lost World**, was the first real production of what will be called in future volumes, "it came from south of the border," featuring piranhas, creatures from the black lagoon and killer bees. Along with a lot of big snakes and reptiles, they were Hollywood's favorite threat aimed at North America until audiences became sophisticated enough to understand the meaning of the word ideology.] **V**:2.1.25.

[1128] **LOVE ON THE RIO GRANDE**, Independent Pictures: [Aside from knowing that Bill Cody was in this film, no other information could be found. But even if we allow our imaginations to run toward the warm side because of the title, wild thoughts should be tempered by the nature of the genre and the rather nebbish character of the star.]

[1129] **A LOVER'S OATH**, Astor: [Roman Navarro, as Ben Ali, in this spin off of a **Thief of Baghdad** provided the attraction that all the ladies lusted after, a manly physique covered by a darkskinned exterior. Originally lensed two years before, he along with the terrific sets were the movie's only assets. Navarro was not allowed to adequately demonstrate his athletic agility, rather, the director focused on his sparkling good looks and the reaction of the ladies. The sets were terrific. Still silent, the title cards were a humorous disaster: 'Oh moon of a thousand delights ....']. **V**:10.7.25.

[1130] **THE LUCKY HORSESHOE**, Fox: [Finding new scripts for the great Fox star Tom Mix was apparently getting to be problem for the writers, so for this feature they simply borrowed a page from the swashbuckling success of the great Douglas and wrote a dream sequence which placed Tom somewhere in sunny Spain. The **New York Times** loved the idea and kidded the popular western and very wealthy star by accusing him of buying one of the smaller Spanish provinces simply so he could play the part of the great lover. There, as Don Juan, he outwitted numerous body guards, swordsmen and other protectors of the fair lady. And after exchanging great lines like: "Fairest of all Spain, I award you the crown of beauty" "Oh Don Juan, you are a man, but will they take me from you," the two of them rode off into the Spanish sunset, together. It proved a great success to audiences all over and may well have indicated that almost any virile Anglo could be Spain's greatest lover, at least in Hollywood.] **V**:8.19.25, **NYT**:8.18.25.

[1131] **MAN WITHOUT A COUNTRY**, Fox: [This was the second production of the Hale story in which a promising young officer becomes involved in Aaron Burr's conspiracy to carve a great personal empire, out of Spain's territory in the Southwest. Nolan's famous lines after Burr had been acquitted, but cashiered out of military service, "Damn the United States. I hope that I may never hear of the United States again," prove to be his punishment. Placed on a ship for years, no one was allowed to tell him anything of the nations growth, expansion or any other news concerning his country until the few moments just prior to his death. A patriot's dream [761].] **V**:2.18.25.

[1132] **THE MIDSHIPMAN**, Metro Goldwyn: [This was Roman Navarro's first starring role as an Anglo and he made the most of it by becoming an immediate hero at the academy and earning his degree, which was placed in his hands by none other than President Coolidge. Gilbert Roland, a new hire from across the river, also made an appearance.] **V**:10.14.25.

[1133] **MIXING IN MEXICO**, Short Films: [These newspaper cartoon characters had frequently crossed the border during the troubled times in the teens, but now Mutt and Jeff, the two very popular comic strip heros were fighting bulls and chasing señoritas all over Mexico on the silver screen with expected results. They appeared only slightly less ridiculous than the characters they encountered [1775].] **MPW**:10.17.25, p567.

[1134] **MY SON**, FN: [A lot of interesting stuff can happen in a small New England town inhabited by Portuguese fisherman. In this story of maternal love, the fantastic Nazimova played a simple store keeper whose entire life was wrapped up with her son and his future. All was serene until one of those city wise, hip wiggling flappers came to town for a change of pace visit. In no time at all she has twisted Tony around her every little desire and made him completely forget Rosa Pina his Portuguese sweetheart. Worse, Tony steals a bracelet from the well to do flapper's mom so that the two of them can head for the big city for a little fun. That was never going to happen. Hispanic mother's, especially those from Hollywood, fight fiercely to protect their children. Ana, confronts her son and reminds him of his lady, but his lust for the blonde baddie has blinded him to his duty. Things became even darker when his mother hit him over the head with a shovel to prevent him from leaving. With the help of Felipe Vargas, a local fisherman that has been warm for Ana for years, she loads him onto Bamby's boat, another "portagee" who is just leaving for a long battle with the fish. Rosa is sent along with the basically good but momentarily errant lad so that she can be the first thing he sees when he wakes up. The sheriff agrees to the idea and Ana and Felipe head home to share the pleasure of a deed well done. There was hot blood where ever those Hispanics were even in cooler climes of Cape Cod, especially when a little white stuff was available.] **V**:4.22.25.

[1135] **THE NIGHT SHIP**, Gortham: [Basically a strange love story which has a seaman returning home to Maine after six years and discovering that his mother has died and his sweetheart has married a local villain. He gets rid of the baddie, marries his widow and the becomes involved in a gun running operation for Central American rebels. Why not, he was only several thousand miles from that particular border.] **V**:4.8.25.

[1136] **PATHS TO PARADISE**, FP/P: [Considered one of the great comedies of any time, the script has two great rival thieves agreeing to work together on a big job to heist a fabulous necklace. They do and there follows one of the great chase scenes of film history as the pair head for the Mexican border. Overcoming one obstacle after another, they cross the border and fall in love with those salubrious climes where there was lots of time for love, but very little for industrial development. Of course they return the stolen stuff and are rewarded with happy honest lives in the warm sun, at least for a while.] **MPG, afic**.

[1137] **PERCY**, Pathe: [Simply another case of the border making a man out of a "sissy." Much to the disgust of his father, a politician, his son was raised by his mother in an unmanly fashion. When the father's friend offers to help make a man out of the pansy, dad is deelighted. Percival was now introduced to demon rum, despite the Volstead Act, but finds that one of its side affects caused him to wake up in an empty boxcar just out side some Mexican border town. There he discovers what can really make a man of him, Lolita, the lovely Mexican cantina dancer, who, as with most women of her kind, was more than willing. In no time at all, she has given him the strength to challenge the local land grabbing tyrant who is mistreating the peasantry. When Percy's father arrives to witness the manly transformation, he is so pleased, that without concern for his own political future, he allows his son, the man, to marry this Mexican Lolita, despite her past. With only slight variation, **Border Cafe** in 1937 will tell the same story,] **MPW:3.14.25, 150**.

[1138] **THE PONY EXPRESS**, FP/Lasky/P: [Not the planned epic it proved to be, this major production concerned the efforts of a corrupt United States Senator who was attempting to create his own kingdom by annexing California and other Mexican territory's with the help of characters like "Ascension" Jones and Wallace Beery as "Rhode Island" Red. It was left to Ricardo Cortez, a reformed gambler turned pony express rider, to foil the evil designs of empire building, and save that Hispanic territory for the United States's manifest destiny.] **V:916.25, MPG**.

[1139] **PRAIRIE PIRATE**, Producers Distributing Corp: [Brother turned bandit seeks killer of sister and is befriended by Don Esteban a loyal Mexican who helps him resolve the problem in an acceptable manner. His character was not unlike that of Holbrook Blinn's **Bad Man** [962], a "suave Mexican bandit who would always attend to things, personal." The killer was brought to justice, and another señorita was saved from his evil designs. Not that the tide had yet turned, but there were many more good Mexicans in this one than bad ones.] **FD:11.15.25**.

[1140] **PROUD FLESH**, Metro/Goldywn [Fernanda, born during the San Francisco earthquake and raised in Spain, was the object of Don Jamie's affection, but so were several hundred other señoritas. Harrison Ford's, tongue in cheek portrayal of the Latin Lover, provided an entertaining and satirical interpretation of a proud Spaniard actively pursuing his hearts desire. In Spain Don Jamie travels about with a troop of acrobatic troubadours at his disposal, ready to furnish music for the lady on the balcony and to form a human pyramid allowing him access to her tender kisses. Once back in San Francisco, Fernanda, whose fetish for bathtubs was well known, brags that there are twenty four of them in the family home. She soon requires the services of a plumber who immediately falls in love with the sophisticated Spanish belle. The remainder of the script has the two suitors vying for her affection. At a grand ball, the proud pair, try to out tango each other while viewing themselves in the mirror. In the last reel, despite the fact that the plummer's mother does not think the lady is "quite good enough for her boy," he wins her promise of marriage. Undaunted, Don Jamie thumbs through his little black book and the audience is provided with a glimpse of the lady he has next on his list. It may well be a cynicism generated by having seen too many movies or at least, movie stereotypes, especially those Hispanic, that makes one tempted to wonder a bit about the title: Just what flesh was it that the producers intended their actor to be proud of?] V:4.15.25, NYT:4.13.25, MPG, LCFL: Clippings, half tones.

[1141] **QUICKER'N LIGHTNIN'**, Action/Weiss Brothers/Artclass: [Although the local is imprecise, they were out west in Indian country, where Buffalo Bill Jr. was afforded plenty of room to demonstrate his riding ability. He was also provided with the opportunity of saving a girl from being the victim of human sacrifice as practiced by indians, the ancestors of ancient Aztec tribes, who had apparently revived the practice to regain their once great power and reclaim their land from the hated white man. It might have worked, had there not been just one Anglo to prevent it.] **MPG**.

[1142] **THE RECKLESS SEX**, Goldstone: [A young Bostonian is sent to New Mexico to check on the family estate and discovers that there are some real baddies on the place running guns into Mexico. He quickly ends the operation and at the same time discovers a stranded young actress who brings him love and happiness.] V:4.1.25, afic.

[1143] **SADDLE HAWK**, U: [Considered a nice little western with Hoot Gibson as the peace maker between the cattlemen and the sheepmen, this was strictly a formula production. The riding was hard and the action fast. One of the not so nice guys was the ubiquitous Mexican, Vasquez. Little fear, when Hoot rescued the kidnapped little lady, and she had been untouched by foreign hands, all was well amidst the moo's and baa's and serenity returned to the range.] V:4.22.25, FD:3.8.25.

[1144] **THE SCARLET HONEYMOON**, F: [Pedro Fernando was the son of a wealthy Argentine businessman who wanted his boy to experience life and see how they ran a big business in North America. He was sent to a company branch in New York where within the week he had fallen in love with a girl at the Automat. She, a poor hard working stenographer, had an avaricious family who object to the relationship when they think that Pedro makes only thirty a week and change. They wanted a lot more for their little Kay, to say nothing about themselves. Not long thereafter, Pedro returns with cars and presents for the family which makes the parents jubilant. This in turn makes the dad back home in Argentina very suspicious. As a test, he has his son arrested to see what will happen. All but Kay scorn him, she pleads with the manager not to press charges. Still not satisfied that the little gal would be right for his beloved son, father, has one of the good looking office boys make advances, but our heroine nearly beats the frail Latin to death. That was enough for the Señor and Señora Fernando. They now invite the happy couple to come live the good life back home in Argentina where neither will ever have to work again.] **MPW**:3.14.25, p168.

[1145] **SCARLET WEST**, FN: [Although there are no Hispanic characterizations in this production, it is included because the indians "as a race" were portrayed as villains and the producers were using film to promote their message. Supposedly, it was extensively researched and filmed under the guidance of the Colorado Historical Society. Reviewers believed that "any Yankee kid" who saw this film and did not receive a big thrill had "the wrong color of blood." "Every school with a projection machine should get a hold of it, as it will do more to instill patriotic spirit [and the knowledge that the only good indian, was a dead one,] than months of lecturing." Certainly a good indication of the felt impact that film could have on its viewers instilling what might be considered a little race hatred. Remembering that most Mexicans were indians anyway, there must have been some stereotypical overlap.] **V**:9.25.25.

[1146] **SON OF HIS FATHER**, FP: [Typical handsome anglo, pitted against a dirty evil Mexican villain stuff. "The villain in this is a smuggler over the Mexican border, his business being to supply guns to rebels". He also wants the keys to the hero's ranch. There was not much chance that he would succeed in either of his enterprises, because the Anglo hero was a slim, trim, approaching the peak of his career, Warner Baxter, who not only thwarts all the plans, but wins the heart of Dolores, the baddie's favorite chiquita. The west was scripted that way in 1926, but Baxter himself would help change that characterization significantly by transforming the Mexican bandit into a lovable good badman in just a few years, at least in **Old Arizona**, [1338].] **V**:9.30.25.

[1147] **THE SPANIARD**, P: [Directed by Raoul Walsh, Ricardo Cortez played in this version of the Spanish bullfighter's problems in and out of the corrida. His lovely señorita was Jetta Goudal and his nemesis, Noah Beery. All the accepted cliches played through the last reel. **Moving Picture World** to help other exhibitors with their sales ran an article showing how the enterprising owner of a small film house in Jacksonville, Florida promoted this movie. He commissioned a local to do a poster of Ricardo in his matador outfit with the copy written in Spanish and aimed directly at the thousands of cigar makers in his town. The translation was done by the orchestra's flute player. A woman tango dancer, another Juanita, and a singer were also hired to perform in the lobby.

The film proved a big success securing these stereotypes for another season. In fairness, Jacksonville's substantial Cuban population loved it.] **MPW**:7.11.25, p159.

[1148] **SPOOK RANCH**, U: [This Hoot Gibson western managed to take advantage and get its licks in at the three most negatively stereotyped groups of early Hollywood, all in one film. With the action set in a haunted house out west, the animated Chinese cook had a dish broken over his queued head which caused him to spout a very animated gibberish until the scene changed. The Mexican Don Ramies was properly villainous and evil, and Gibson's personal black servant, was able to do, what every black with bulging eyes did so well, his "feet's git moving" routine. All of this in under sixty minutes.] V:9.23.25, **MPG**.

[1149] **THAT DEVIL QUEMADO**, FBO: [From the very beginning of the industry through the recent production of the **Old Gringo** Hollywood consistently projected the idea, that to help Mexico, to right wrongs, to remove injustice, you had to use extralegal means. It was impossible to work with a corrupt system. Aside from using North American help, relying on local talent, only a bandit, a Zorro or a revolutionary, some single factor savoir, a Villa or Zapata, employing revolutionary means, could really fix Mexico's internal or external problems. Quemado was fashioned from that same mold a "bold bad bandit of the Robin Hood order, who helped the oppressed of Mexico in their struggle against the richer folk." But there was more to it than that for the North American audiences to cheer at. Quemado was introduced being "cussed and discussed" by the daughter of a wealthy visitor from the north. Having rejected his advances as distasteful, he continued to pursue her and manages to win favor with her father for being able to shake her dyspeptic brother out of his depression. Then, to everyone's surprise and elation, it is discovered that hero was really, Jim Fairfax, a Yalie no less, who was merely "letting the steam of the ancient Dons from his veins." A perfect combination to solve Mexico's problems. In the final scene the two are seen galloping away into the Mexican sunset. The Motion Picture Commission of the State of New York reviewed this film and asked for various eliminations. They objected to the gun being fired directly at the camera and the use of "book in hands of the minister." What was considered too violent was always a problem and foreign censors usually removed scenes which used specific prayer books or the bible. There were no comments on the characterizations.] MPW:4.18.25, p678. V:7.8.25, FD:4.26.25, afic. NYMPAA, That Devil Quemado.

[1150] **TOO MANY KISSES**, P: [Richard Dix was being groomed for superstardom in this role as the son of a wealthy North American who sends the boy for the grand tour throughout Europe accompanied by a watchdog to keep him away from the ladies. Everything was fine until they arrived in the land of love where the silver/blond haired Dix falls for the darkskinned señorita who was engaged to Juilo, a Spanish Captain fire eater "and expert knife thrower." The necessary struggle takes place, with the outcome a foregone conclusion. The Anglo bests the Spaniard and takes his señorita back home with him to the land of milk, honey, Madison Avenue and mayonnaise. A brief footnote would mention that Harpo Marx played the Spanish village idiot, in his first silent role. A more significant one would quote an outraged "Spaniard Protest" in a letter to the editor of the **NYT**:"Any one who knows Spain a little also knows that in the Basque provinces nor any other province for that matter, people do not sleep in the streets nor do men carry knives by the dozens in their sashes [Basques do not wear sashes as a rule], and that on the contrary, they are a hard-working gentlemanly and courageous people, with enough physical strength to use face to face against any man, American or otherwise, when the necessity arrives. ... You might as well imagine the New Yorkers going to their offices with a gun on each hip, a bandanna around their necks, to shoot their stenographers because of a mistake they made while taking dictation! The "atmosphere" would be just as true."] **V**:3.4.25. **NYT**:3.25.25

[1151] **THOSE WHO DARE**, Creative Pictures: [Marguerite De La Motte was the femme lead in this tale of sea faring men who come under the influence of an evil voodoo practitioner.] **V**:3.11.25.

[1152] **TRIPLE ACTION**, U: [As part of some felt cultural superiority from the very earliest days, literature and later film, always presumed that everything south of the border was hygienically inferior to that in the north. It may be just a bit unfair to postulate that the vast majority of North Americans traditionally assumed that excluding tequila, and that came with a worm, things from south of the border were/are always dirtier than they are here at home. That was unquestionably the case when it came to water and cattle. The border states have lived in fear of anthrax and the dreaded hoof and mouth disease from earliest times. Of course it was always assumed that all such curses had to originate in Mexico. This "Blue Streak" western was based on just that assumption. Ranger Dave lost his badge for allowing a notorious band of bandits to drive such diseased cattle past his border patrol point. In an attempt to vindicate himself he is shot by one of the gang members but is saved from death by the daughter of Don Pio Mendez, Donna Mendez. Dave sends Donna for the rangers, while the bandit chief brings the sick cows to her hacienda along with the hero's Anglo girl, Doris, where she is held captive along with the cows. When Dave learns this he enlists Dick's aid, Doris's brother. Dick happened to be an aviator, a sky Ranger, and so with his help, Dave parachutes onto the Hacienda's grounds and singlehandedly defeats the bandits freeing, Doris, Donna, the Don. The diseased cows were destroyed. Dave then proudly displayed his new badge, the reward he justly deserved for having distinguished himself against such depraved desperados.] **afic**.

[1153] **THE VANISHING AMERICAN**, P: [One of the first seriously sympathetic portrayals of the plight of the North American Indians includes a beginning scene which has become part of many first lectures in various history classes, answering on film what is frequently asked in the classroom: How was it possible for the Spanish Conquistadors, so few in number, to overcome the massive hordes, the millions of Indian opponents, they first encountered. Cortes had fewer than 600 armed soldiers and sailors when he first took Montezuma's Capital in 1519. There were literally hundreds of thousands of trained and disciplined native warriors who might have faced him. In the film, it is shown and explained that the locals, who had never seen horses before, thought them to be monsters, and considered the white men to be gods and as such ran before the conquering few. Some of that is accurate, the Aztecs even thought man and horse to be one, but it reality, Cortes succeed because of dissension in the Aztec confederation. He had hordes of indian allies himself. Possibly of more interest for what would eventually become the film capital of the world a bit further north, were the horses themselves. It is difficult to imagine the film industry without its westerns and even more difficult to imagine westerns without horses, without them an entire genre might have been lost. But native North American horses did not exist before the Conquest. There were no families of equidae larger than a dog even in prehistoric times, so we have all those apparently very healthy little mares and stallions that the Spanish introduced into this hemisphere who eventually journeyed north, to thank for those happy Saturday afternoons at the Pastime theater watching all those westerns and learning our indian and Hispanic stereotypes.] **MPW**:10.24.25, p652.

[1154] **WAS IT BIGAMY?**, Steiner: [The most valuable **Motion Picture Guide** considered this film, "Horrible hokum" in which a lady marries one man because she loves him and the other to provide him with support. The low budget production was substandard in all ways, "including the South American set ... used as an excuse to have a jealous native kill" the so called lady's second husband. Equally valuable, the **American Film Institute Catalogue**, identified the region more specifically as Central America. But in reality what difference did it make, they were all "spics" down there anyway wherever they were, and the guy would have been just as dead in Santiago, Chile as he certainly was in Tegucigalpa, Honduras. What was essential to this script was the necessary hot Latin temper to kill the extra husband.] **MPG**, **afic**.

[1155] **WITHOUT MERCY**, Metropolitan Pictures: [In the 19th century, British economic influence throughout South America was significant, far outweighing that of the United States. The Bank of England was in effect, a world bank, with interests in each of the Latin nations. In Argentina, it had financed the building of the best railroad system anywhere in the southern hemisphere. The English population in Buenos Aries and in the outer provinces was significant. This film described one such English family "living in the Argentine", and the influence that that place had on the Anglo character. When Enid Garth's family was fortunate enough to discover a valuable mine on their holdings, a fellow countryman properly named, Sir Melmoth Craven became jealous and greedy. He wanted the mine and to obtain the information of its whereabouts, he whips Enid "into insensibility". Years later, Enid has become the head of a leading London bank and when she discovers that the institution is holding Melmoth's note for a huge sum of money, and that he needs funds to hold his seat in Parliament, and apparently having picked up a little vengeance training in the land of the gaucho's, she "revengefully" calls in his note. This provokes him to criminal behavior which ends his career. Enid finds a man and they marry.] **V**:9.30.25.

[1156] **WITH THIS RING**, Schulberg Productions: [The only connection in this melodrama of a wife stranded on a desert isle is that her husband is knocked unconscious while being attacked by a mad Portuguese which make her think that he is dead. They leave him behind when they come to rescue the woman and you can take it from there.] **V**:9.23.25, 6.23.26.

[1157] **WOMEN AND GOLD**, Renown: [A "meller" thought too good to be exhibited on a double feature bill. After a bit of action between husband, wife and child, Frank Mayo had to go to jail. Once there, he pals it up with an inmate who's jus gitin ready ta bust outa de place. There's an urgency to the plan because a "Spaniard" has ("copped") wronged the prospective escapee's little girl and for some unknown reason, his new cell mate thinks he might be doing his lady also. It turns out that the wife was safe enough, but the Spaniard was killed with his own knife on the very night he was to be wed. Apparently the title was intended to make something of a moral statement. Something like, men would disregard all laws for either women or gold. **Variety** added with a bit of cynicism that at least gold was "always pure." They might well have further thought that Hollywood was justified enough in allowing the break to rid the streets of another immoral "spic."] **V**:1.21.25.

[1158] **WONDERS OF THE WILD**, indy: [This travelogue was produced by Burr Nickel, simply a tourist who wanted to find the out of the way places and avoid the tourist traps that were already established by that time. The film begins with a map showing the route that Burr took from Mexico City by burro to the land of the Yaqui. There with a few friends, the journey continued to the west coast snow covered mountains and down to the sea. For the audience it must have proved an enormously exciting and enviable adventure.] **V**:4.1.25, **afic.**

1926

[1159] **ACROSS THE PACIFIC**, WB: [More frequently in westerns, Monte Blue found himself in this film fighting the heroic Philippine guerrilla leader Aguinaldo, a patriot who had pledged his life to end the oppression of the United States occupation of his homeland. In 1926 he was still portrayed as a savage barbarian, a butcher of "American" boys. Only later would his silver screen persona be completely reversed and that happened simply because the Japanese attacked Pearl Harbor and the United States need every ally it could find. Then Hollywood's historical interpretation would picture the Filipino as the hero of his people, a champion of democracy. [See: **Real Glory**, 1939] But in this film he was still very much the enemy. To capture him Blue had the not so difficult task of making love to an orientalized, young and beautiful, Myrna Loy. As the rebel leader's lady she had information about guerrilla troop displacement, and he had to get it out of her. Difficult duty, but someone had to do it, yet his Anglo girl, was offended. She had recently arrived at this far out post of North America's civilizing efforts, and was disgusted at Blue's personal implementation of the policy. What bothered her most was that the creature he was snuggling was a halfbreed. Eventually her patriotic ardor allows for his forgiveness, when she convinces herself he had merely been following orders. It all ended well, Blue, lost his colorblinded love/lust, decided on the white girl, and eventually even captured the rebel chief. In reality, during the campaign against him, Aguinaldo's was so successful against United States forces was, that newspaper reports, especially those in the Hearst press, were at best covered up until his eventual capture which took years. Shades of similar practices during a more recent conflict in the Asian theater.] **MPW**:6.4.27, p370, **V**:11.10.26, **MPG**.

[1160] **ALOMA OF THE SOUTH SEAS**, FP/Lasky: [Much of this very successful tale of South Sea love was filmed on the beautiful island of Puerto Rico.] **V**:5.19.26.

[1161] **THE BLACK PIRATE**, UA: [Certainly the most successful of the silent screen swashbuckling pirate films with Fairbanks at his usual best, it included, what can be considered, the greatest sword fighting sequence until Flynn battled Rathbone in **Robin Hood**. The locations are those of the sea, the only direct Hispanic connection is the Spanish Princess, a darkskinned lovely, who was traveling with her duenna, the traditional nanny-chaperon. The film was simply all Fairbanks, an Anglo superhero who captures a ship singlehandedly and seeks vengeance for the death of his father. The censors for the State of New York, Motion Picture Commission, requested that some of the bloodier sequences be removed by United Artist. They complained that the violence was too graphic.] Letter to John F. Donnelly, 2.26.26, **New York Film Archives**,

Albany, NY. **V**:3.10.26, **NYT**:3.9.26, 3.14.26, Literary Digest: 4.10.26, pp37-38,42, Outlook, 4.14.26, pp560-562.

[1162] **BLUEBEARD'S SEVEN WIVES**, FN: [This example of Hollywood's satirical lampooning of its early self, featured Ben Lyon and his distinctive eyes. Hired on as an extra who eventually takes over for the star, the promotion department decided that he must undergo an image change. Cast as the most unlikely Latin Lover of all time, the writers place him aboard a ship arriving from Spain. Upon debarking, he must face the press and answer questions about his love plans. Being what he is, his magnetism attracts the females immediately and in quick succession he is married and divorced to seven women, including one Hispanic vamp that he easily has eating out of the palm of his greasy hand. All of these women have allegedly been captivated by the Latin love making ability that the writers have given him. A clever, even if unconscious at times, critical view of Hollywood stereotyping as practiced by all of the production companies.] **V**:1.13.26.

[1163] **THE BLUE STREAK**, FBO: [Richard Talmadge, who had stunted for Douglas Fairbanks in earlier days, was featured in this western which had him traveling to Mexico for his father to check on the problems at the old gold mine. While there, he demonstrated the agility that had him considered one of the best stunt men in Hollywood. In the process, he uncovered the Mexican baddies, brought them to justice and fell in love with Inez Del Rio, a lovely local señorita who responded to him immediately, it was so written.] **V**:3.3.26, **FD**:3.10.26, afic.

[1164] **BORDER JUSTICE**, Independent Pictures: [In this western melodrama Bill Cody played Joe Welland, a Texas Ranger ordered to bring in a baddie that has killed and indian. When he catches up with him, he discovers, much to his displeasure, that the youthful killer, was really his brother. On the way back to the post, the boy conveniently falls off a cliff and all think him dead. Mary, the necessary little lady, tries to help Joe with his pain and succeeds, but sustained happiness was not to be Joe's good fortune. He now discovers that his girls dad, the Captain of the troop, has been allowing Angus Bland to smuggle all manner of goods back and forth across the Mexican border. The father did not want to be bad but he simply could not repay the debt he owed the crook for the his daughter's education. Joe now resigns his commission and determines to capture Angus. Pursued into his cabin retreat, Angus accidently sets off the dynamite which kills everyone of the baddies, but one. The survivor turns out to be a hopeless maniac who raves insensibly and turns out to be the battered brother. After he dies in Joe's arms, Mary has a lifetime of work ahead of her trying to help her man recover from his scripted grief. That Mexican border could really be hell on an individual.] **V**:4.21.26.

[1165] **THE BORDER SHERIFF**, U: [Considered by the reviewers a "very good little western", this entry continued the almost yearly production of at least one film in which the Mexican border was used to smuggle drugs into the United States. This time it was Jack Hoxie's duty, as the dedicated border Ranger, to stop the illegal traffic which was flowing out of Mexico into the bodies of those poor Anglo wretches who suffered the affliction. As Cultus Collins, sheriff of Cayuse County, he began his fight after having briefed at Washington conference on narcotics smuggling. From there he travelled to San Francisco's Chinatown where he breaks up the gang. For his trouble, he managed to handcuff himself to the lovely little [an adjective required in all westerns] lady. She thinks, because of her innocent involvement with the baddies that, she is heading for jail, but discovers to her pleasure that her life sentence would be shared on the border with Jack instead.] **MPW**:3.27.26, p286, **V**:4.21.26.

[1166] **BORDER WHIRLWIND**, FBO: [Bob Custer played Tom Blake Jr. in another western melodrama filled with Hispanic characters. Julian Rivero, who would spend long time in both silents and sound films, was Captain Gonzales of the Mexican police in this one. As it turns out, Tom's dad was well to do, but more importantly, he had a Mexican friend, Señor Jose Cordova who was being threatened by "the Scorpion, a mysterious desperado on the Mexican border." In an attempt to help uncover who the masked bandit really was, the father was killed and young Tom sets out to avenge his padre's death. While in pursuit of the killer, Tom is falsely accused of being the bandit himself, but manages to escape and prove that Palo, possessed the deadly stinger. In the final reel, Tom finds loving comfort in the arms of Isabella Cordova, played by an Anglo gal. The two manage to spend a lot of time together trying to evade the watchful eye of her duenna, a custom Hollywood kept alive long after it had ceased to be an part of Hispanic family life, even among the aristocratic rich.] **MPW**:4.9.27, p594, afic.

[1167] **BUTTERFLIES IN THE RAIN**, Universal/Jewel: [A supposedly ultra-modern aristocratic English woman who loves the company of the pseudo bohemians she hangs with, falls for a less sophisticated English lord. They agree to the twenties' version of an open marriage, but the little lady is apparently too shy to consummate her union even a month after the wedding. Unhappy, she goes on a Spanish holiday with her friends who have her do things in romantic Spain she would not at home, but there was a price. After the coy little bride has been sufficiently naughty, the former friends want to be bought off or they threaten to tell all. Now class tells. Although the Lord is not well to do, he rescues his lady and she promises never to go to Spain again, unless he is with her. Hollywood had decided long before that if Spain's warm sun heated Hispanic libido's it would work just as well on uptight white Anglo's. Not unlike in the tropics, things could be done there that could not back in cooler climes.] **V**:12.29.26.

[1168] **THE CANYON OF LIGHT**, F: [Very much a Tom Mix formula action film in which he discovers that his sister, Carmencita Geraghty, is married to a villain and he is forced to take action to save her. His reward was eagerly given to him by,

Dorothy Duan, known lovingly in Hollywood as, "the Lady of the clinch finish."] **FD**:12.19.26.

[1169] **THE DANCER OF PARIS**, FN: [To be a dancer in Paris was one thing, but to be a Spanish dancer named Consuelo, was really bad. The main concern of the reviewer in his critical analysis of this film was that First National was "making several attempts to introduce obscenity" into the film. To make things acceptable, and guard against the increasing influence the censors were trying to exercise, the production company had actually recast the Latin lady as an innocent, still virginal in heart, having suffered the abuses of men throughout her life, in effect, a sympathetic character. For obvious economic reasons, long before 1926 producers wanted their films to open or at least be shown in New York City. Success in that movie Mecca almost always insured success throughout the nation. Although most film makers worked at producing acceptable versions for the New York market, frequently adjustments had to be made. One of the more positive consequences of this censorial activity was that, every film shown in that state from 1924 until the early 1970's, no matter where it was produced, was previewed by the New York State Board of Regents, [after 1927 the official state censor.] This required producers to send the film scripts, and the films to be read and reviewed, before the movies could be exhibited to the public. Although the films were returned, the great majority of all of the scripts were kept and are presently housed in the state archives at Albany intrusted to the capable custodial care of Bill Evans who provides pleasant and willing assistance to interested researchers. These more than 70,000 scripts represent the largest single repository in the United States and are made available for study. This film was one of the many which experienced the censorial shears, as the sexy Consuelo had the scene cut in which she lost everything but her purity.] **V**:3.31.26.

[1170] **DESERT GOLD**, FP: [Famous Players, more than any other production company adapted the novels of Zane Grey for screen presentation. Often, they simply reused the same basic story with different character names. Using stock players they were able to do this often, the public was in love with movies, and seemed not to notice. Here was one more daughter of the west falling in love with the handsome young calvary officer. He is looking for "Snake" Landree and other desperados who were terrorizing the border. When the young soldiers's "friend from the east", comes to visit, Gale thinks he is handsome. But before they can really get acquainted, she is captured by the across the river baddies. Quick to react, the officer rescues the girl, but not without the self sacrifice of his loyal 'tonto', a yaqui indian, who had for some time been his loyal companion. With some sloppy sentiment, properly obsequious of course, he was required by the writers to willing give up his useless Mexican/Indian life for the greater good of his Anglo race. Safely back at the fort, Gale herself had to choose between the two young men she loved. The **Variety** reviewer may not have been much of a romantic, for he objected to the lady's choice. Having known the officer for a much longer time, a man of "exemplary character and outstanding bravery," she selected the friend who she has just met. He obviously did not know much about women, what man does? [823]] **V**:3.24.26. **NYT**: 3.23.26, afic.

[1171] **THE DESERT'S TOLL**, AKA **THE DEVIL'S TOLL**, MGM: [Interesting because, another oriental, destined for stardom, at least in the "B's", Anna May Wong, was chosen to play, Oneta, the villain Santschi's border indian lady. When Hollywood could not find Hispanic ladies that looked indian or Mexican enough for the audience, a lovely oriental was close enough, it had worked for males like Sesue Hayakawa. See also: **Brand of Lopez**: [840] **MPG**.

[1172] **DEVIL'S ISLAND**, Chadwick: [Hollywood made more than a dozen films which featured the world's most notorious penal colony, Devil's Island. In many others writers merely used its imagery by alluding to it in some negative way. TNT's made for cable, **Prisoner of Honor** 1991, provides the most recent example of this use. The remnants of colonialism's tribute to incarceration can still be viewed today by traveler's looking for an out of the way experience, or maybe a Steve MacQueen souvenir. But until it's closing, the French Government was very touchy about films which focused on it's brutal image. This production was straight forward in presenting daily life in the prison, as it functioned through the eyes of a wrongly accused surgeon. Working as a doctor he eventually gains parole to the mainland Cayenne, where he was permitted to stay and practice. But where as Hollywood was helping to make up the rules, neither he nor any family member who traveled there could ever go back to France. In time he was joined by his wife and son, a brilliant surgeon in the making, but soon after they arrive, the father dies. The focus of the plot then shifted to the mother's efforts to have her son freed so that he might return to France and benefit the people there. But in meanwhile the scenario is further complicated by having her become the island commandante's major attraction. Luckily, she likes him too, but is loyal to the husband's memory and her son avocation. Not so strangely, it all works out. The writers balance the ledger by allowing French justice to prevail. When it is finally learned that the father had suffered unjustly, the son and his family are allowed to leave the tropical hell hole and walk once more the wide boulevards of Paris.] **V**:8.4.26.

[1173] **DON JUAN**, W: [The "Great Profile" John Barrymore, had his fun starring in this production featuring an incident in the life of the greatest of the Latin Lovers, immortalized in fiction, Don Juan. His overly active libido may have belied an essential romantic character, but he did not let that stand in the way of his trysts. This production has him operating mainly at the Borgia court, trying to stay in the good graces of Lucretia and Caesar, while he persued the object of his current affection, Adriana. It was strictly designed for the flappers and "juves" but, even back then it was considered hot stuff for everyone. **Film Daily** called it the "Greatest romance of impassioned love ever screened." For our purposes, there is one title card on which the great lover expresses a fear that his lady has been having it on with either a "dangerous looking Turk or Mex." Aside from the fact that there may not have been too many "Mex's" at that time, the naughty lady referred to in the film was a hot blooded Mary Astor. Apparently very well cast, if one considers that she would later be a favorite target of the Legion of Decency because of her off screen activities. The film was premiered as Grauman's Egyptian before an ultra stellar cast of Hollywood's best: "Practically every star, director and motion picture executive" attended and cheered.] **MPW**: 4.21.26, p485, 9.4.26, **V**:8.11.26. **FD**:1.17.27.

[1174] **THE EAGLE OF THE SEA**, FP/Lasky: [This version of the relationship between the notorious French pirate who operated out of New Orleans and was so helpful to Andy Jackson at a later time, included an attempt by a French patriot to enlist the famous buccaneer's help in rescuing Napoleon from his captivity on St. Helena. It also pictured a number of sea battles with Spanish man-o-wars which the patriotic pirate of course won. Don Robeldo was one of the lesser, but just as sinister, Spanish bad guys.] **V**:11.17.26.

[1175] **EN LA TIERRA DEL SOL = IN THE LAND OF THE SUN**, Sp: [This was Antonio Moreno's 84th film, made during a trip to his homeland for a little r-n-r. He was without question the star of this very early Spanish production which was only seen in the United States at a much later time. The Spanish film industry still very young and only beginning to think about exporting its product, this one played throughout Latin America.]

[1176] **THE FIGHTING BOOB**, FBO: [In this entry Bob Custer played a character with a Hispanic cast called, "El Tigre," an avenger of Hollywood's oppressed who could never quite seem to care for them selves without some kind of Anglo help often disguised as a avenging bandit. Bob did this for his friend, with whom he had served in the Great War, but who had been killed in a poison gas attack. More fortunate, Bob lived and managed to save his friend's father's ranch from the desperados who were trying to take it. Artie Ortega, as Ortega, destined to appear in almost a hundred westerns films, almost always in the same role, was one of the baddies, a necessary ingredient to make Saturday afternoon's film fare successful. He was one of the many nameless Hispanic villains we loved to hate at a time not so long ago.] **FD**:6.23.26, **MPG**.

[1177] **FIGHTING EDGE**: [Juan de Dios O'Rourke, United States government agent, was assigned to free his friend who had been captured by Mexican smugglers and was being held somewhere south of the border. Fearlessly, the hero crossed into Mexico disguised as a halfbreed to save his compatriot. Once there, and merely by chance he happened to meet the captured man's daughter and they working together, effect his freedom, but not without a little luck. Just as they were trapped and running out of ammo, about to be killed, wondering if they should share just one kiss before dying, the United States calvary crossed the border and came to the rescue. Scripters, at almost any time in Hollywood history were allowed to violate international law and boundaries to save the endangered lives of "Americans" where ever they were, just as easily as some Presidents of the United States, especially when nations south of the border were concerned. As a beautiful but slimy dear, or was it a fawn, who might have seen too many of these movies, and suffering from a lot of misguided, so called, patriotism, once said on national television: "Sometimes you have to go above the law." Did one of those actor presidents, say that also? In any case, there was always a lot of cheering in the audience when such rescues was made. Surprised?] **FD**:4.21.26, **afic**. LCFL:Kenneth Harlan Scrapbook, Clippings.

[1178] **FLAME OF THE ARGENTINE**, FBO: [The similarities between the North American southwest and the vast Argentine pampas are many. The cattle industry and all of its accompanying accouterments provide the most striking parallel. Everything from cattlemen making war against sheepmen to the genocide practiced against the native inhabitants has a counterpart in either area. Cowboys and gaucho's share a common tradition: The gaucho is as much a North American cowboy as the cowboy is a gaucho. Any of the scenarios which were developed for the southwest could easily be transferred to the pampas, and many were. This little western is but one example. Donna Aquila was the mistress of a vast rancho and a valuable emerald mine [the scenarist added a little Brazilian flavor with this.] Her head gaucho was a bad hombre named, Tovar. He was well aware that for years, she has pined over the loss of her infant daughter and so devised a plan to use this information to take over the holdings. The writer here has another little problem with his geography for he has Tovar in New Orleans (at least 5000 miles away) discovering Inez Remirez. (He could have been on vacation?) In any event, he hires Inez, to pass herself off to the señora as the her long lost daughter. Overhearing all of this, a North American muscles in on the deal and Tovar makes him a partner. But that proves to be his big mistake. The tough guy falls in love with the lady and when Donna's great kindness and affection for Inez melts her mercenary heart, the girl tells all. It is then discovered that the lover was really an Anglo secret service who wanted to protect the old lady. (Talk about surprises!) Donna now adopts Inez and looks forward to soon having a son-in-law, and maybe a lot more as part of the bargain.] **MPW**:8.14.26.

[1179] **FLESH AND THE DEVIL**, MGM: [The divine Garbo playing Felicita von Eltz, only half Hispanic in origin, was as salacious a satanic seductress as ever slinked across the silver screen. Nothing in pants had a chance.] **V**:1.12.27.

[1180] **FOOTSTEPS OF AZTECS**, Ufa: [Produced by the state subsidized production company, Ufa, this German import was considered by critics on this side of the pond, as their best example of an educational travelogue. The comment was meant as a criticism. After it was shown to a Mexican Commission traveling through Germany in an effort to promote their films for export, **Variety** was highly critical of the German work. They pointed out that only the first 500 feet dealt specifically with the ancient indian cultures, "the remainder being a disjointed hodgepodge of scenes taken in Mexico City itself." The final sequence presented some bull fight scenes. With characteristic teutonic tact, the film's title cards referred to these as a "revolting display," while continuing to show the more brutal aspects of Mexico's National sport. The trade journal's forecast for such a product's success in the good ole U S of A was dim.] **V**:8.10.26.

[1181] **FOUR HORSEMEN OF THE APOCALYPSE**, [Reissued by Rex Ingram in this year, it was considered, despite all the technical advances made in films, to be superior. The critics wrote that it "outshines most of the pictorial offerings in the splendid clarity of its story," that 1926 produced [863].] **NYT**:10.3.26.

[1182] **HANDS ACROSS THE BORDER**, FBO: [Tyron Power [senior] starred in this early attempt to create a Hollywood Good Neighbor Policy. When, the lovely señorita, Ysabel Castro, is kidnapped from a Los Angles horse show, she is soon rescued by the stalwart Government Agent, Power. For this he is rewarded by being assigned to the border to investigate a drug smuggling operation. While there, he discovers that the gang was operating right near the beautiful, Ysabel's fathers hacienda. Rekindling the relationship and enlisting her aid to thwart their activities, he joins up with the baddies, but they uncover his identity and hold both he and the girl captive. Then, the great Silver King, left to his own diplomatic devices, has the good horse sense to bring both the United States Calvary and the Mexican Rurales to the rescue. They could have used more horses like that in Washington in those days when this nations Latin American policy was so unpopular [at least with the Latins] throughout the Hemisphere.] **MPW**:6.12.26, p564, **V**:6.30.26.

[1183] **HIGH STEPPERS**, FNP: [In her second film, Dolores Del Rio played Evelyn Iffield. For a complete listing of her screen appearances see: **Allen l. Woll, The Films of Dolores Del Rio**, Gordon Press Film Series: 1978.]

[1184] **LOOKING FOR TROUBLE**, U: [In later years this might have been called, Son of Don Quickshot or something even more imaginative like Don Quickshot II. At this time it was just Jack Hoxie once more on the Rio Grande, in another "Blue Streak western looking for trouble and finding it." But Jack was the "kind of a fellow who could always be counted upon in an emergency" even though he was frequently at odds with the local sheriff. Although most of the action took place on the Mexican border, the baddies were all Anglos as was the little lady Jack had to protect.] **MPW**:5.8.26, pp170-171.

[1185] **MARE NOSTRUM**, MGM: [Reviewed by some unfavorably after it's premier as just another "war picture", this film is presently considered by those who have seen it, (no complete prints are now known to exist), a stunning, dramatic, any superlative you can think of, production. The story described the events leading up to the death by firing squad of a female German spy who gave up her life for the Teutonic gods that were her fatherland. Filmed entirely in Europe, in Germany, France and Spain, a neutral in the world war, the plot utilized several major Spanish characters. Antonio Moreno was unsympathetically portrayed as a Spanish sea captain who deserts his loving wife and son for the beautiful German spy he considers to be the personification of Aphrodite, goddess of the sea, his only true love. After her execution, he declares his own personal war and destroys a German submarine with his boat, and is killed in the process, buried anonymously in the sea he had worshipped since childhood. This filming of the Blasco Ibenez novel was certainly unpopular with some governments and so called "patriots." The story and film were designed to point to the absurdity of war and the price nationalism charged the individual. Although aimed at Germany's aggression, it was not difficult to generalize the circumstances. There were no laugh's in this one, almost everyone dies in the end. Even the captain's son is drowned as a result of the indiscriminate German sinkings. Rosita Ramirez, part of this international cast, was Pepita. The film was well received in all but Germany and later appreciated by many not sympathetic with employing war as a means for solving national differences.] **V**:2.17.26, **LCFL**: Press sheet, 1926, Press Book, Clippings.

[1186] **MONEY TO BURN**, Gotham: [The lovely Dolores Valdez, a "Latin American heiress" was returning to her "aristocratic" estates in "South America" by ocean liner, when on board ship, she meets and falls in love with the bright young doctor, Dan Stone. Thinking he has killed the drunk that was bothering her, he jumps ship in her home port and somehow finds himself in the employ of Don Diego Valdez, her guardian and master of the mysterious estate she inhabits. A strange character himself, he was pictured forever moving about in "a sinister atmosphere of intrigue." The Anglo lad was hired to care for the person who was apparently dying in a remote wing of the casa grande. Moreover, the entire estate was guarded by an equally "huge negro," who could take orders well, but was not too bright. His function south of the border was the same as his counter parts who worked in films back up north, to provide the so called, comedy relief. It turns out that the guardian who was trying to marry the lady off to another sinister character was deeply involved in a counterfeiting scheme that was flooding the Latin republic with phoney pesos. With the help of the North American consul, and the Marines, [who Hollywood had apparently assigned to protect the entire hemisphere], the marriage was stopped at the altar of Hacienda chapel and all of the aristocratic bandidos were brought to justice. The señorita was pleased that everything turned out so well which allowed her to rejoin the Anglo hero responsible for saving her country's fragile economy.] **MPW**:11.29.26, p302, **V**:11.24.26.

[1187] **NIGHT CRY**, W: [Some film historians without too much jest like to claim that the K9 hero, Rin Tin Tin, saved the sagging film industry in the early twenties. It is difficult to discover when he might have done that, but in this film he certainly can be credited with saving a lot of sheep. Falsely accused of killing the little furry creatures at first, he is forced to uncover who was really responsible for such dirty deeds. In time he does and so justly becomes the hero of the production. Gayne Whitman playing Miguel Hernandez and Don Alvarado as Pedro provided the unnecessary Mexican characterizations.] LCFL: **Clippings**.

[1188] **THE NUT CRACKER**, Indy: [Edward Everett Horton plays a henpecked husband willing to do anything to escape his wife in this film frolic. When opportunity comes down Main street and hits him, he takes the settlement provided by the street car company and makes a killing on the stock market. Donning the appearance of a rich South American millionaire, he establishes himself as big party man whose only purpose in life was to enjoy it. His wife, anxious to meet a rich Latin, and possibly a new lover, has herself remade and pursues him. In no time the two reestablish their relationship and head for happiness. Sometimes, in Hollywood, finding love was easy as getting hit by a street car, or being a rich Latin.] **MPG**.

[1189] **OLD SPANISH CUSTOMERS**, MGM: [Leslie Fuller and Binnie Barnes, as Carmen, were featured in this formula production which had Englishman Fuller finding himself mistaken for a matador and in a lot of trouble in the corrida. It was all played for laughs, much at the expense of the locals.] **MPG**.

[1190] **THE PALACE OF PLEASURE**, Fox: [This film was an adaptation of a play that featured an incident in the life of the legendary Lola Montez, a beautiful Portuguese singer, who was "received at some of the proudest courts in Europe" and was admired by "kings, princes, artists, composers and authors." Set in contemporary Portugal, the action featured Lola's love for a royalist refugee accused of treason by the republic. After one of her most ardent [royalist] admirers used her to capture the revolutionist, Madons, she discovered that she loved the rebel. To prove her affection, just as her lover is to be executed, she takes his place and the bullet intended to kill him. Although wounded severely, the two escape and make it across the border to be married.] **MPW**:1.23.26, p343.

[1191] **PALS FIRST**, FN: [The plot outline here is incidental to the reviewers comments about del Rio's third picture: "Dolores Del Rio's, [performance was] disappointing. As the second lead, "Her Latin type for one thing does not jibe with the aristocratic southern atmosphere, in addition to which Miss Del Rio's personal accomplishments as a screen actress are negative. Her eyes of Oriental type, are an odd combination with the Spanish features. Whatever registration is essayed but mild." So much for that critical seer's slant, on what the lovely Dolores would do with those sad eyes.] **V**:8.25.26.

[1192] **SEA HORSE**, FP/Lasky: [The action for this tale of a tragic triangular love takes place in Portuguese East Africa, described by a turn of the century author as the real "heart of darkness."] **V**:2.24.26.

[1193] **SEÑOR DAREDEVIL**, Charles Rodgers: [In 1926 Tom Mix was earning about $2000 a day, he was the acknowledged "king of the western features". Many young stuntmen aspired to that title, Ken Maynard was one of them. As the Señor Daredevil, he started a climb to the top that would eventually bring him significant respect, but never the title. Continuing the mythology that at some point in Mexican history a significant influx of Irish men had infused Mexico with the presence of their manliness, the Señor had an Irish father and a Mexican mother, although Catholic, they had been separated for years because of a clash of temperaments. Because Don Luis O'Flagherty had lived with "maternal relatives most of his life, he spoke like a Latin." When his great horse, Tarzan, insisted that he ride him and "no other horse," the young Don's title card read, "You no want me to ride heem." Within just a short time, the talkers would translate such verbal identifiers of Hispanic character to sound, condemning several generations of Latins to speech patterns that made them sound like the inferior idiots most North American audiences preferred them to be. The concept, once translated to television, would be at least partly responsible for creating the most successful husband/wife situation comedy ever filmed. Taking little away from Lucy Ball's talent, Ricky Ricardo's difficulty with the 'inglis' language produced laughter that can literally still be heard, in syndication, around the world, every day of the year.]. **MPW**:7.10.26, p115 **V**:8.18.26, **NYT**:8.17.26.

[1194] **TELL IT TO THE MARINES**, George Hill: [Marines will always be Marines, those in San Diego, go to the track in Tia Juana and come back broke, they can never figure out the money exchange. When called upon to fight, they do that best, especially against bandits in the Philippines, Nicaragua or China. But there is no fighting with the local native women at first, but hot tempers invariably flair later. In this film the lady was called, Zayz, a lovely darkskinned beauty. She generates a lot of manly loving, and not much conversation until it's time for the old universal Marine exit line understood by Third World women all over the occupied world, "me no marry, me have to go, babiee." **V**:12.29.26.

[1195] **THE TEMPTRESS**, MGM: [The year 1926 was a productive one for the prolific Spanish writer Blasco Ibanez, at least four of his works appearance in New York theaters that year, **The Temptress** was the second in which the lovely Garbo starred. Playing to mixed reviews, one thought she did not possess enough fire to be the woman of "sinister passion" created by the hotblooded Spanish writer, she "might play the more anemic type." Another disagreed, the **NYT** critic thought her well suited as Ibanez's conception of the "beguiling beauty" with the "soul of a selfish siren." The story described how Robeldo, played by Antonio Moreno, an Argentine engineer, came to Paris and was vamped by the sexy Elena. Only when it's too late, does he discover that she was married and had already been responsible for the suicide of at least one other man. Returning to his native land with the raw edge of his emotions exposed, he was forced to fight "The Argentine", a bloody battle of slashing bull whips within a confined circle from which no macho ever left unscarred. Bloody himself, he beats his opponent, Manos Duros. After surviving a flood, he discovers that the wicked siren has followed him, and is in the process of seducing every male she meets just to get his attention. Robeldo remains aloof for a while, but is finally beaten and forced to tell the lady he loves her. But by then, its all too late, realizing what she is, and to save the one man she really cares for, she returns to Paris to kill herself by drinking absinthe for the next fifteen years in sleazy bistros. In the final scene the two are reunited for her death scene. Sometimes it had to be that way.] **MPW**:10.23.26, p503, **V**:10.24.26, **NYT**:10.11.26.

[1196] **3 BAD MEN**, F: [An early John Ford entry had three bad men, who were of course, basically good guys, wanted everywhere from the Canadian to the Mexican borders, by every lawman in the country and with a special price on their heads in Mexico. Most of the action for this manly piece, takes place in the Dakotas, where the three save a young woman and her true love, giving up their lives by so doing. As might be seen, this was another early version of the later Ford/Wayne production, the **Three Godfathers**, in which the child saved is younger and one of the main characters, Pedro, more Mexican.] **V**:8.18.26.

[1197] **TIN GODS**, Famous Players/Lasky: [Roger Drake, the main character in this melodrama, loved his wife enough to allow her her own career in politics, providing there was time enough for a family. Janet Stone was a bit on the self centered side, but agreed and they have a lovely child. One evening while the active mother was delivering a political speech, the little baby was allowed to fall out a window. Her parents were rich and the house a big one, the baby did not make it. Crushed, the husband leaves for South America and gets drunk in every cantina he can find on his way to the equator. There he is saved by the love of a local darkskinned woman, Carita, a dancer, with mountains of soft sympathy to sooth the broken hearted engineer. Having recovered some of his former self because of the lady's tender loving care, he agrees to build a bridge across a dangerous gorge for the locals. They, from the characterizations provided, are too stupid to do it themselves. Big John Wayne will do the same thing some time later in **Tycoon**, 1947. For a while all was well in the Andes, the bridge was terrific and the new lovers were very happy. But all this ends when old Janet lost the election back in the States. With nothing better to do, she seeks a reconciliation with her husband. Carita thinks that he still loves his former wife and before he can convince the little señorita he is hers, she flings herself off his bridge into the raging torrent. Heartbroken once more, Roger builds a memorial to her memory and every year there after returned

to place flowers on the cold stones of his broken life.]
V:9.22.26.

[1198] **THE TORRENT** aka **IBANEZ'S TORRENT**, COS/MGM: [Ibanez Belasco had more of his works adapted to the silent silver screen than any other Spanish or European writer. This production opened in New York a week after his **Mare Nostrum** [1185] premiered in the same city. **The Torrent** was not his best work, but this film served to introduce Greta Garbo to North American audiences, her presence carried the film. Playing a beautiful Spanish peasant girl who falls in love with Ricardo Cortez, she is forced into exile because his mother objects to the affair. In Paris she becomes famous as an opera star wearing glamorous and exotic furs, but can never forget Ricardo who at home has risen to great height in business and politics. One day, Leonora, now Donna Brunna decides to return to see the love of her youth, but it was all Thomas Wolfe, she should never have tried to go home again. Although Ricardo saves her from a flood, and the feelings are rekindled, the essential fires had burned out, nothing was the same and the former lovers sadly left each other and went off on ways.] **MPW**:4.3.26, **V**:2.24.26, **NYT**:2.22.26.

[1199] **VALENCIA**, MGM: [**Variety's** review for this film provides one with an insight as to what was considered the conventional morality of the audience and certainly that of the critic. He felt that, Valencia the main character, it was difficult to consider her the heroine because she subscribed to what he called, "Continental morality", could not possibly capture the sympathy of the audience. That would have been impossible because she had allowed a sailor she favored momentarily, to spend the night with her. May be not as much in the big cities, but "Yankee" audiences wanted their heroines "pure", "the general attitude [was] that the first feminine character must abound in virtue no matter what [happened] to the remainder" of the cast. And worse, this señorita seemed to have no heart, and expressed no remorse for her lewd behavior. It might be all right, maybe even accepted in those warmer climes, for a Spanish lovely, to use a man for her own physical satisfaction, but that was certainly unacceptable behavior in the good ole US of A. Worser yet, once she has had her way with Felipe, she discarded him. And more worser than that, her number one caballero accepted her momentary indulgence, her primitive desires, justifying the tryst as a mere physical need with no love involved. Few fragile Anglo male ego's anywhere, but especially in the psuedopuritanical remnants of North American culture, could accept such a view. After a lot of soul searching and being pursued by her sailor who jumps ship to try once more to make her his on a more permanent basis thereby placing himself in the clutches of her lover, the local authority, she makes a conventional bargain with the official to set the swab free. In the end her crying over his departure requires the understanding magistrate to send her to the docks where the two lovers are united. Don Fernando knew that many other pretty señoritas were easily available to him as he graciously allowed to two to leave together while speaking immortal lines like: "Your lips are a nest of kisses, do not twist them with sobs." The reviewer allowed that this production might have a chance to play well enough, but only because it would open during the Christmas season. One wonders what he might have been unconsciously implying.] **MPW**:1.8.27, p144, **V**:12.29.26, **NYT**:12.27.26.

[1200] **VOLCANO**, Zukor/Lasky: [Bebe Daniels, Ricardo Cortez and Wallace Beery are the leads in this adaptation of the play, **Martinique**, which dramatized the events in that tragic French Caribbean tropical paradise just prior to the explosion in 1902 that took the lives of all but three of the more than thirty thousand souls who perished when Mt. Pele blew the island capital, St. Pierre, out of the Caribbean. The film also provides a commentary on the then current point of view of having a pure blooded Frenchman going native. When Bebe arrives at the island, she discovers her father had died. Because he had cohabited with a local black lady, Bebe is suspected of being a mulatto and is sent to the back of the island where she barely ekes out an existence. There she also has to constantly fight off the advances of the halfbreed, mulatto villain, Wallace Beery, who wanted at least, her virtue. In time Ricardo came along and told her it was ok with him that she was not all white. This little act of compassion ends up saving the two lovers. And as an extra for apparently being so color blind, the young swain discovers, after they have sailed to mother France, that Bebe, was not a mulatto at all, but is in reality, all white. Meanwhile much of the island is blown away in a volcanic eruption that darkened skies in some portions of the world throughout much of 1902. Not having seen the real thing, one reviewer felt that the explosion was staged well enough to "send any audience out talking about the picture."] **MPW**:6.12.26, p564, **V**:5.26.26, **NYT**:5.24.26.

[1201] **WHAT PRICE GLORY**, F: [Raoul Walsh was responsible for establishing this classic cliche in which the two incredibly tough Marines with good hearts, fight the enemy fiercely, but would much rather fight each other for fun and for the affections of ready and willing women all over the world just waiting to nurse their wounds. Dolores Del Rio played the sexy Charmaine, who loved both these brawlers, Capt. Flagg and Srg. Quirk (Victory McLaglen and Edmund Lowe), but she cared for the latter a little more. The hot blooded Spanish temptress, was Elena Juarado as Carmen who provided entertainment for the big Irish lug. Del Rio certainly helped make this one of the ten best films on the **NYT**'s list for 1926, but the characters created by the two fighting fools, "Pride of the Marines" may well have been more important to the males in the audience, than that very enticing lady herself. This production was so successful that it generated three sequels. In **Women of All Nations**[1554] the two repeated their Marines in heat routine with a selection of south of the border señoritas.] **V**:12.1.26.

[1202] **WHITE MICE**, Associated Exhibitors: [This Richard Harding Davis adventure finds a North American [William Powell as a good guy this time] who is part of group of young men that are always ready to help people in distress any where in the world. Davis's world was always south of the border, this time in the mythical republic of Montebello, where the hero finds a young woman whose father is the idol of the nation, but behind bars. Of course he aids the revolutionaries that are trying to free him and when the patriot is rescued, the hero has himself a new father in law. A nice Anglo girl plays the Hispanic lovely, Inez Rojas, in an "attractive and vicarious [sic] manner."] **MPW**:3.27.26, **p286**.

[1203] **THE WHOLE TOWN'S TALKING**, Universal/Jewel: [In her fourth feature film, Dolores Del Rio played a secondary naughty lady named Rita Renault.]

[1204] **YANKEE SEÑOR**, F:[Considered one of the very best of the Tom Mix entries, Fox added a bit of technicolor in the opening scene showing the bright colors of the native costumes. The story has Tom, a soldier of fortune type, with a natural inclination for the Latin countries because of his heritage. He was the son of a "high caste [which makes it acceptable] Mexican mother" and apparently a less than inhibited, New England father. In this adventure he prevents a bunch of not so nice Mexican bandidos, from stealing the company payroll and then with time on his hands, decides to visit some of the old relatives who live across the border. Problem is that the uncle, who was a "foxy greaser" turns out to be the head of the bandits that Tom has outsmarted. With little respect for either the law or for family ties, "the greaser" decides to do in Tom and has him spread eagled in the desert sun waiting for death. What the Mexican should have done, and might have, had he seen some of Tom's other movies, was to tie the horse down right along side of the Anglo hero, because when the faithful and trusty Tony sees what has happened to his master, he saves him. For a little revenge of his own, Tom was allowed to fall for a local lovely, which just happened to be the property of the uncle. This makes him mad, but when she appears to be returning the affection with a some gusto, the bandit becomes really enraged. Employing what he is sure will work, it would have with a Mex, 'el tio' hires another Mexican "dancing dame" to vamp the Tom. The audience is led to believe that the ploy is succeeding, all that hot blood, passion and stuff, but when rejected, she becomes Tom's chief nemesis. Infierno conocer no fury like that of a señorita scorned. But it all works out in the last reel. Of all of Tom's film's, this one was most faithful to all accepted stereotypes, some more negative than others. For his not all so youthful audiences, it merely reinforced views of "ole Mehico" that they had seen elsewhere.] **MPW**:9.26.25, **pp296-297**, **V**:1.27.26, **NYT**:1.28.26.

1927

[1205] **AFLAME IN THE SKIES**, FBO: [A nice combination of the old and new west has two aviators working on their sky writing in the New Mexico desert. In time they learn that at the nearby hacienda of Inez Carillo, some dastardly goingson are taking place. Someone is trying to "slow poison" old Grandfather Carillo. The two North Americans of course discover the culprits and send for help by using their skywriting ability, the main hero does so while "making love" to the rescued señorita. Darn warm blooded those ladies, and with over active libidos high in the sky.] **V**:11.2.27, **MPG**.

[1206] **AFRAID TO LOVE**, P: [Used numerous times before with various nationalities employed as the necessary foil, in this case it's a South American adventuress who must be outwitted and is, by the pretty and virginal Anglo girl who would not stoop to the depths of the bad lady. Sir Reginald must marry to gain his inheritance, but he cannot decide until the last scene, which is to be the wife of his dreams. The comedy revolves about the conflict between the two women that want his love for far different reasons. The señorita was much more passionate, but her intentions, not as honorable, certainly a difficult choice for the reserved and proper gentleman.] **MPW**:4.23.27, p749.

[1207] **ARIZONA WHIRLWIND**, Pathe: [After Bill Cody's dad has been killed for the map that shows where a rich mine can be found, his son pursues the culprits. Hot on their trail, the baddies, including a Mexican named Gonzales, have Bill framed for something that he did not do. The enterprising hero then disguises himself as a "Spaniard" escapes from the prison, infiltrates the band of bandidos and captures them all, of course, singlehandedly.] **MPW**:3.19.27, p214.

[1208] **BELOW THE EQUATOR**, Pathe: [A Fox Variety travelogue showing Rio De Janeiro, the Brazilian capital to be "not only a thoroughly modern city in every respect, but a veritable fairyland when it comes to scenic beauty. The towering mountains and hills in and around the city offer vistas of unusual magnificence. In fact this is a regular dream city that is unique among the world capitals." Certainly fair praise and a indication that film was helping to remove the stigma of the dark ages from North American minds about some of the Latin lands south.] **MPW**:4.9.27, p574.

[1209] **BLIND ALLEYS**, FP: [Not intended to be a comedy the complications which arise when a sea captain loses his beautiful Cuban bride on their first night in the Big Apple produced a series of situations that prove more humorous than melodramatic. On his way to purchase flowers for his lady, the newly wed is knocked down by a car and brought to the hospital. Maria D'Alverez, unable to locate her husband, happens to run across a fellow Latin American, Julio Lachados, apparently an early gang leader, who involves her in a robbery and keeps her captive. In time the Captain recovers, but an Anglo nurse keeps him from his lady for a while. Eventually, after some further scripted problems, they inevitable find their way back into each other's arms.] **V**:3.2.27, **MPG**, **afic.**

[1210] **BORDER BLACKBIRDS**, Pathe Western: [An exciting western that merely uses the mystique of the term "border" to enhance its marketability. All of the main characters were Anglos and there was little action on the border. But the law in this film is enforced by the colorful RCMP, not the rurales.] **MPW**:9.19.27, p114. 10.8.27, p337, **V**:10.12.27.

[1211] **BORDER CAVALIER**, U: [The "oldest of the old stuff" placed on the border because there was always trouble there to overcome. Advertised as: "COURAGEOUS COWBOY TURNS OFF RESCUES AND FIGHTS IN MILE-A-MINUTE FASHION."] **FD**:9.25.27, **V**:10.12.27.

[1212] **BRONCHO TWISTER**, F: [Reviewed as one of the better Tom Mix entries in some time, the hero returns home from the Marine Corps to modern Arizona where he saves the pretty señorita, Paulita Brady, from an army of baddies. One exhibitor claimed that he counted at least twenty sure dead and an indeterminate number of "possibles" in the sixty minute production. Chuck Norris, eat your heart out. This unusual body count for was not accomplished by Tom's handy pistol work, but mainly by devising improvised grenades made from dynamite found in the Spanish mission, that he and the chiquita he was saving were using for refuge. For these heroics Tom was allowed to keep the dark eyed beauty, at least for a while.] **V**:3.30.27, 5.18.27.

[1213] **THE BULL FIGHTER**, Pathe: [A Mack Sennett two reeler with a pair of his brave boys yucking it up in the corrida, but being bested by the bull at every turn. A pretty Spanish lady added some typical romantic flavor to the non stop action, but it was all played for laughs.] **MPW**:11.19.27, p18.

[1214] **CALIFORNIA**, MGM: [In the summer of 1927 after having watched a special screening this Tim McCoy film, and considering it to be "hopeless," the Mexican Consul General informed Hollywood's major production companies, that if they did not change their negative projections of Mexican characters, that the entire industry would have to face the consequences of a total boycott of its product. Mexico had by then become a significant market, and every peso was important to those penny pinching producers. The objection did not attempt to claim that there were not nor ever had been, "Bad Men" in Mexico, but that there simply could not have been as many as Hollywood continuously showed there to be. More importantly, there were a lot of good men south of the border, and the Consul wanted to know why these were never featured. That it would have been possible for the Mexican government to totally ban North American feature films from being shown in Mexico, this writer seriously doubts. Hollywood's films had become too great a part of what was being shown by Mexican exhibitors on a daily basis. In some parts of the country more than 85% of all movies exhibited were North American product. The Mexican industry was sill producing less than five films a year [only thirty five between 1921 and 1932], German films were not well liked and only the French added a little spicy flavor to the Mexican filmgoers fair. Reading through some of the Production Code files it seems strange that many of the producers in Hollywood appeared to be unaware of their dominant position. It may be that they worried that a selective protest against an individual company would hurt their own particular company. All that considered, the protest did produce significant results. Will Hays planned another trip to Mexico to see what could be done to smooth things over, although there is nothing but the announcement of such in the much celebrated, but certainly overrated **Hays Papers**, at least so far as the film industry south of the border is concerned. Those who know little about the Production Code, may well believe that it's chief function was censorial, with Hays functioning as the chief censor, something of a guardian of public morality. That was essential true, but he exercised his duties so as to insure that the product, the motion picture, would be as marketable and inoffensive to any particular interest group as it could be. As such, a major foreign market could not be jeopardized. The Mexican protest could not be ignored. The United States film industry led the world, it had only marginal competition for the international market. More over, for business as a whole, Hays was convinced that trade followed film. [See: **Children of Jazz: 969**] Everything possible had to be done to maintain that leadership position. Hollywood itself took cognizance of the warning and **California** is one specific film that points this out. For a quick introduction which provides 48 specific taboos frequently censored by other governments, including the defaming of foreign nationals and their history, and the complications the introduction of sound would further create, see: Victor Volmar, "The Babel of Tongues," **Films in Review, March 1951, pp11-16.**

Basically a pictorial history of the birth of the Bear Flag Republic, with Tim McCoy as the hero battling "a foreign foe", the Mexicans were not named as the enemy in a supercilious attempt to please. **Variety** reacted as follows: [The film] "deals with California in the days of its Mexican provinceship [sic]. While the sub-titles studiously avoid mention of Mexico, alluding to it as a "foreign power" when at all, the villainy is attempted by Mexicans and thwarted by the always-efficient American hero so that the picture hardly qualifies as one that will make and hit south of the Rio. On the other hand there is still no reason why it should be offensive." If one accepts the concept that a divinely inspired manifest destiny drove our aggressive fore fathers to the Pacific across lands that the divinity ordained should be United States territory, no matter who might have owned it once, one might agree with **Variety**, that the Mexicans should not be offended by their portrayal as savages and brutal overlords who deserved to loose it anyway and would because the good lord wanted it that way.] **V:6.27.27.**

[1215] **CALIFORNIA IN 49**, Arrow: [A very poor retelling of the activities of the pioneer patriots at work in the California of 1846, with absolutely no historical sense at all. The scenario eventually made its way to the discovery of gold at Sutter's mill and again, all of the good guys were Anglos, but at least in this retelling, not all of the Anglos were good guys. The production values in this movie were so poor that it was difficult to differentiate between them in any event. According to one reviewer, it was even impossible to tell when film might have been made, and it would have been better if it had not because of the "horrible out of focus camera work." [1030]] **V**:3.30.27.

[1216] **CAMILLE**, FN: [In his biggest role to date, Gilbert Roland played the intended to suffer Armand opposite Norma Talmadge, destined to die for her naughty but fun life. Many of the critics thought that this new Mexican actor, not identified as such, had stolen the picture with his fine performance.] **V**:4.27.27.

[1217] **THE CLIMBERS**, W: [Set in nineteenth century Spain and Porto Rico, this work attempts to present a romanticized view of love and intrigue in the last days of Spain's imperial sway in the Caribbean. The action first takes place in Spain where "the Duchess of Arrogan" [sic], had been banished to the colonies because of the jealousy of another woman. Having to leave the sumptuous comforts of the indolent Spanish court for the rigors of life in Porto Rico, she becomes a hard and cruel task mistress. Without love, her bitterness grew, without provocation, she whipped her slaves and even maltreated her daughter. The señor responsible for all of this tragedy and transportation was a courtier himself. In time he decides that the only way he can win back his lady's heart is to become a non traditional bandit, one of the Robin Hood type. This pits him against, Martinez, a brigand of the more bloodthirsty type who terrorizes the island. In time the hero wins the day and the damsel, love softens her heart and improves her disposition. Now in the new world, a new life is possible with new horizons. They played this straight and not for laughs.] **MPW**:5.28.27, p291.

[1218] **CODE OF THE COW COUNTY**, Pathe: ["A bright and smart little western," with a hero, a heroine, the spineless brother of the heroine, gambling, a dance hall, the pleasing ladies of the second floor, lots of cows and Dolores, the Chiquita, played by an Anglo lady, that makes life difficult for the sissy sibling. A little better than several thousand others but not much different.] **V**:6.15.27.

[1219] **CRADLE SNATCHERS**, F: [In the twenties and thirties, Latin Lovers were found everywhere. In this case there are three wives that want to teach their erring husbands a lesson so they hire some boys to act the parts of their lovers. One of them assumes the role of a hot blooded Spaniard and plays him to the hilt for laughs. The wife is moved, the husband does not think it funny, but the desired results were achieved. Just the fear of a little Latin love will keep those inattentive husbands in line, every time.] **MPW**:6.4.27, p364.

[1220] **CYCLONE OF THE RANGE**, FBO: [When Tom MacKay's brother is killed, he gets really mad, so he goes to the area of the homicide and takes work at the ranch. Not necessarily forgetting his intent, he immediately falls for the owner's daughter, but he has to stand in line. The attractive miss has the Hispanic foreman, Don Alvarado, owner of rancho next door and several others warm and waiting. As it turns out the hotblooded Don does not want to wait for his gratification and so he kidnaps the lady. Such a foul deed leads Tom to believe that he may be the "Black Rider" that killed his brother. Wouldn'tcha know it, Tom's assumption turns out to be correct and after dealing 'proper' with the culprit, he more properly proposes to the lady. Considering he has rescued her from the lecherous Spaniard, what could she do but accept.] **V**:5.4.27.

[1221] **DON DESPERADO**, Pathe: [The title implies the use of Hispanic characters, but there are none in the cast. Apparently the writer felt it would be a drawing card, things were/are more dangerous or sinister if there are Hispanics involved. The story was basically a morality play about the problems of lynching. If you are the lynchee, its not considered a good idea.] **V**:5.11.27.

[1222] **DON MIKE**, FBO: [Considering all the films that had already been made by 1927 about the acquisition of California its a wonder that some Mexicans still seemed to resent the idea that God and Hollywood had destined those sunny climes to become a part of the United States. Further, all the problems the writers usually provided for the settlers living there, should have made the former owners grateful to have another nation take on the responsibility of solving them. But in this story the writers went one better, they had a former Spanish Grandees save California for the Union a short while after the transfer of flags, when recognizing the original Spanish land grants became a complex issue for the officials of the new government, [and a frequently used theme for film scripts.] In this movie it seems that the hero, the Don, saves a desperate character, actually an Anglo from a thirsty death in the heat of the desert. But the ungrateful lout repays him by trying to steal his hacienda and his girl. It was still not common to make the Anglo the heavy. But this character was more than just a thief, he had a grand plan. He had visions of empire. He first wanted to create an independent republic out of California and then build an empire at the expense of the United States and Mexico. Luckily for all concerned, the Don had had a Spanish father and an Irish mother, heroic blood coursed through his veins. True to his heritage, he put on the traditional costume and by the last reel he had driven the little Napoleon and his boys out of the territory. In one scene set in the great hall of his hacienda, he routed a number of Anglos by swinging two ropes that had knives tied to their extremities. In hand to hand combat with the chief baddie, he defeated him and regained possession of the woman. With all the work completed General Freemont arrived, but the hybrid son of Spain had almost singlehandedly saved California for the land of the free. Hollywood could ask little more of its Hispanics.] **MPW**:3.5.27, p58, 5.23.27, p292, **V**:2.23.27.

[1223] **THE FIGHTING HOMBRE**, FBO: [With western plots so standardized to formula by 1927 that a child could before the end of the first reel predict with certainty the outcome of the entire film, any new variation that might interest audiences was welcomed by producers. This little western was a good example of the old Hollywood switcharoo, instead of the hero being falsely accused, it was the heroine. One reviewer who liked the idea was annoyed because he could discern that the lady, while kissing the guy, "was badly sweated under the arms." Apparently those Spanish señors were truly hot stuff! Two Hispanic newcomers were introduced in this film, Carlo Schipa, who played a "sympathetic Mexican character" but still "true to type," and the Chiquita, also a "good type", Zita MaKar. Neither was destined for fame.] **V**:7.27.27.

[1224] **THE FLYING U RANCH**, R-C Pictures: [In this Tom Tyler western, he takes on the appearance of a Spanish fop, Señor Miguel Garcia, appearing to all to be incapable of doing anything right. The lady in the piece, was selfsacrificing, Sally Denson whose father owned the ranch. She likes Miguel, there was something about him, but she also considers him a supercilious Spaniard. Only the innocence of youth can see the inner strength beneath the surface of Tom's outward incompetence. Chip knows that Miguel is something else. When the heavy in the story steels the water rights to the ranch and tries to exchange them for the girls affection, she is forced to accept, but Miguel comes alive and rescues her. This makes the desperate Dunk really mad and while trying to kill the hero he manages to drown himself in the very water he had stolen. In the last scene it is revealed that Miguel's strength came from his Anglo heritage and the lady graciously and willing offers herself to the hero.] **V**:11.1.27, afic.

[1225] **FRAMED**, FN: [Not once but twice the Anglo hero was framed in this film. First he was wrongly accused of committing an error that almost loses a war for France, no small fault pas. That was bad enough but later, after he has gone to build a new life in the mosquito and snake infested jungles of an Amazon diamond mine, a jealous foreman, who fears him as a rival, also has him blamed something the unfortunate victim is not responsible for. Obviously there was a woman involved and the boss was afraid that he was no longer number one with the local lady. As the writer would have it, he wasn't. She had gone for the new man almost immediately upon his arrival. But this was not a time when Hollywood could allow too much injustice, even in the Amazon. So, all was resolved when the culprit contracts a deadly fever and the selfsacrificing hero tries vainly to save him. On his death bed the rival, moved by conscience and the fear of hell fire, clears the innocent of the offense. With his dying breath, he repents and accepts the blame and the punishment Hollywood's god has ordained. This allows the lovers to happily ever after it together slipping and sliding into each others arms in the mud slides and the diamond fields, a little dirtier but much more satisfied.] **MPW**:7.9.27, p116.

[1226] **THE GAUCHO**, UA: [In this the last of Douglas Fairbanks' great swashbucklers, he played a pagan gaucho, lord of all he surveyed and master of most women he chanced to meet. One such beauty [Lupe Velez] was a seventeen year old Mexican dancer, starring in her first major role as the hot blooded and tempestuous mountain girl, that loved to tempt the intrepid hero. Her performance earned her the plaudits of all the reviewers and made her an immediate rival of Dolores Del Rio for top female Mexican import honors. As Doug's woman, she fought for and along side of him, his agile equal. More than his equal, for in the last reel, she has won the right to lead him to the altar. The religious aura cast throughout this film forced the pagan Fairbanks to contract the dread "Black Doom", leprosy, which discolored his hand and threatened his life. Laughing at God and defying death, he was concerned with more important things. There was a mountain population to save from an evil "South American dictator' who "sends the poor to jail" and "casts dirty looks all around." For every new film, the talented superstar acquired a new skill with a new weapon, this time it was the bolas, which he employs to incapacitate the tyrant. [Leaving nothing for Latin ingenuity, **Literary Digest**, postulated that the weapon might have been developed when the Patagonian indians felt the hurt of Anglo, British "grape-shot" during the Voyage of the Beagle and developed this unique Argentine innovation from that lesson.] Having saved the people by using what one reviewer called a "thousand excellent Mexican actors", a herd of Texas longhorns which he stampedes through the "Village of Miracles" to chase Riuz's men from the scene, he is brought to a Lourdes like shrine where he spies a beautiful Spanish señorita. She urges him to ask god for a cure instead of seducing her and the appearance of the Virgin Mary Pickford, prevents his original intent. He prays and is saved. Lupe now arrives to reclaim her divinely cleansed man. Then, all was well in the "mountains of the Argentine pampas," where some Gauchos go for salvation, if they can ever find them on that flat plain.] **MPW**:9.26.27, p25, **V**:11.9.27, **NYT**:11.22.27, **MPG**.

[1227] **THE GAY DEFENDER**, P: [Doubly difficult to believe, Paramount produced yet another version of saving California for the Spaniards, but worse was trying to have the fair skinned, silver blond haired Richard Dix, portray the Hispanic. You think Quasimotto used a lot of heavy makeup, Dix required a disguise, aside from that to play the part. It helped nothing to have him cast as a Murietta type character, the audiences could not accept the sideburns and mustache. He may have experienced some discomfort trying to be made into what Hollywood thought a Mexican bandit whose family has just been slaughtered by baddies, should look like. **Moving Picture World**, which rarely panned a film, believing it was better not to review it at all if it could not promote it, was more favorable, but they managed to find something positive to say about every film they included. They liked Dix's skill with the traditional tools of the trade, the bull whip and swords, and the star's "unerring aim" with a knife. But the industry was still not looking for male Hispanic leads, which could easily have been found across the border. With continuing concern, the **Variety** reviewer recognized that there should be absolutely nothing in this film that could possibly offend either Mexico or Spain, especially since the real villain was an "American." Will Hays had no small influence over his little family.] **MPW:V**:12.28.27, **NYT**:12.26.27.

[1228] **THE GIRL FROM RIO**, Gotham: [When a young Englishman, [Walter Pidgeon] arrives in Rio de Janeiro to purchase coffee for the tea drinkers back home, he is immediately taken with the loveliness of a Brazilian coquette and falls deeply in love with her. Of course, she cannot resist his Anglo charm. But there was a slight problem. It happens that the scripters had made her the mistress of the richest man in all Brazil and her attraction to Britisher did not please him at all. That was his problem, but there was a moral question here for the critics. That she was a mistress troubled the **Motion Picture World**, and was contrary to the Production Code even before its editor, Martin Quigley, had his part in writing it in 1927. The long list of do's and don'ts, did not condone cohabitation or mutual consent unless it was perfectly understood that such lewd ladies sometime time before the end of the last reel, would be forced to accept severe punishment, loss of wealth, health, the convent, being stoned naked against a wall, branding or death, something of that order that would uphold the double standard. What was commonly referred to a "continental morality" would no longer be acceptable on North America screens, even if it was common in South American capitals and European films. Another reviewer objected to the gentleman's reaction. Apparently he felt that rich man from Rio was justified in seeking revenge, which at first he did. It was his plan to have his rival eliminated, to hire local thugs to kill him, but then something happened, either his wealth, or his love of love, being a Latin, changed his mind. **Variety's** critic explained it in simpler terms, he thought that the cuckold was the biggest boob in all Brazil not to shed a little blood. Whatever the reason, the former master wished the young lovers well and allowed the lady to sail with the buyer back to England. There the two might be damp, but happy. For the Anglo trade journals and the Production Code, that was hardly punishment enough.] **MPW**:9.24.27, p249, **V**:10.19.27.

[1229] **JEWELS OF DESIRE**, PDC: [When a young Anglo lady of Hispanic extraction [Maragarita Solano] is mentioned in the old Don's will, she finds herself the owner of a lovely Spanish estate. Traveling there with friends they soon discover that there is a map which could lead them to a buried treasure of great wealth. With the buddies, the plucky lady experienced a series of adventures battling the baddies, including Spanish Joe, whom she defeats in heroic tradition. In the end all are rewarded for their efforts with the discovery of great wealth.] **MPG**.

[1230] **LOVE MART**, FN: [A very handsome and very young Gilbert Roland romps through very early 19th century New Orleans in this one as Victor Jallot convincing all that the French accent no one could hear in this silent was just that. He looked French. Billie Dove was the object of his infection.] **V**:12.28.27.

[1231] **LOVE OF PAQUITA**, HiMark: [Using entirely Spanish locales, Paquita plays the usual lovely señorita who has the added attraction of two equine heros on who's backs she demonstrates superior riding skills. In a dramatic climax she saves her true love from being hanged.] **V**:9.21.27.

[1232] **LOVES OF CARMEN**, F: ["Plenty of hell, sex and box office in this latest film biography of a well known Spanish damsel." Raoul Walsh, never too far away from things Hispanic, directed still another version of the Bizet opera which featured Dolores Del Rio, now established as a super commodity to be marketed by Fox at every opportunity. Certainly a significant change for the better and opening the doors for others to follow. What might be considered a unique concept in casting, had a fairly young Victor McLaglen, who had once fought for the heavyweight championship of the World, playing Escamillo, the [at best] semisvelte toreador, who could have beaten the bulls to death with his fists, instead of using the customary sword. But the scenario was still the same familiar story, Jose [Don Alvarado] falls for "the woman who has the heart of a wanton, the mind of a child and the soul of a woman." Dolores Del Rio's performance was "the very personification of this conception." She was "the very embodiment of tempestuous and unrestrained youthful femininity, who scoffed at convention, sneered at the real love of Jose and to whom sex attraction was ever paramount." A real Spanish dame, Hollywood continued that characterization to present times.] **MPW**:6.4.27, p345, 10.8.27, p381, **V**:9.28.27.

[1233] **THE LOVE OF SUNYA**, UA: [Gloria Swanson gets too look into the future with a little Hindu magic and finds herself trapped by a Spanish impresario, Andres De Segurola, living the life of a demi-monde and suffering as she should for such excesses. He reaps the profits, she pays the price, as all Hollywood women who have fallen from respectability had to, even today.] **V**:3.16.27.

[1234] **LOVERS?** MGM: [Honorably resisting for as long as he can, suspicious gossip drives Roman Navarro into the arms of his best friends wife. Luckily for both parties, the scribes kill off her husband in the last reel allowing the two to be one, respectfully, but not before Ramon defends the lady's honor in a duel which also avenges his friend. To save the woman he loves further disgrace he heads for Argentina, but as it happened they just happen to have the very same idea which makes the trip to the land of the gauchos a very eventful one. John Miljan played a heavy named Alvarez and Roy D'Arcy, El Gran Galeoto.] **V**:4.20.27.

[1235] **MASK OF LOPEZ**, Monogram/Biltmore: [This was a reissue of the 1923 production intended to be used as a filler in small houses and for short runs. A Hispanic bandit is the villain who has his own involved ritual for executing his enemies. The gusano turns when the hero substitutes the villain for one of his own victims and is brought before the wall to be shot by his own men [992].] **V**:10.26.27.

[1236] **THE MILLIONAIRE**, Micheaux Film Corp: [Most certainly an uncommon film for 1927, one that it is doubtful ever played south of Washington, if it even was shown that far south. Most of the action revolves about Pelham Guitry, a Black soldier of fortune who travels to South America to improve his condition in life and do a little good. After fifteen years in an undetermined Latin location, he had accomplished both and returns to the far north to enjoy his millions. There he meets a black lady leader of the mob and helps her to reform her ways and appreciate beauty and life within the law.] **afic**.

[1237] **THE MOJAVE KID**, Joseph P. Kennedy/FBO: [The father of the future president of the Camelot mythology, presented this Bob Steele western, which served to introduce the new personality for his long ride through the western genre. Somewhere after the third grade some teacher with just a little bit extra in her background, plans a section for the kiddies on Native Americans. It is probably then, if the section deals with the southwest, that the word "Aztec" is first heard by the youngsters. Some will remember, others will not. In most North American schools, there is little emphasis given to what was truly one of the great confederated empire of city states the world ever knew. A fact that we as "Americans" all, north and south, should recognize as significant to world history. It is frequently deemphasized simply because many assume that it could not possibly be as important as things that have occurred in what in considered the more traditional, Ancient World. The "Inca", several thousand miles to the south ruled and even larger domain at a time when Europe was still struggling its way into nationhood. To have the producers of this film place the Incas somewhere in the Mojave desert, defies comprehension, even if we consider it Hollywood mentality. Many years later, James Bond will float a raft over the great falls at Igassu, and understandably survive, but how he could come up in a grotto just behind Templo II, in Tikal's jungle [several thousands of miles from that point] indicates that many scripters knew/know little history or geography and apparently cared/care much less [**Moonraker**]. So much for pontification. Here, Bob discovers that the bandits have selected an Inca temple somewhere in the far reaches of the Mojave and must be captured at all costs, especially since they are holding his girl and have killed his father. **Moving Picture World**, starting a new feature, used a two page pictorial spread of individual clips to help promote this production.] **FD**:8.7.27, **MPW**:8.6.27, p414.

[1238] **THE NIGHT OF LOVE**, UA: [As Gilbert and Garbo's **Flesh and the Devil** [1178], entered its third week of success at the

Capital in New York City, this Ronald Coleman/Vilma Banky costumer opened for its run. Coleman played the gypsy Robin Hood, Montero, who's bride was stolen from him on his wedding night by the nefarious Duke de la Garda. She, unable to bear the pain, kills herself. He was then forced to exercise what **Variety** accepted as his given birthright: "The traditional vendetta [of] the Latin races." To even the score the gypsy kidnaps the Princess Marie, the Duke's dame. With either more luck or more Hispanic sex appeal, Montero soon discovers that his captive has fallen in love with him, and he with she. The final reel has the two macho's dueling which allows for the Duke to die, clearing the way for Marie to return from the convent, eager to consummate what the Production Code prevented until it was legal.] **V**:1.26.27.

[1239] **OLD SAN FRANCISCO**, W: [Using a nine minute prologue to set the scene for the later development of the scenario, the audience was told how the King of Spain wishing to reward his loyal retainers in the New World had deeded vast estates to the loyal Vasquez family. Life for them flourished until the gold rush of 1849 when the North American influx became unstoppable. By the 1900's hard times had visited the once proud family now faced with selling off hectares to maintain a semblance of their way of life. Here the screening of scenario begins, and after the historical survey the audience may well have been more familiar with the background than they cared to be. Dolores Vasquez is forced think about doing business, actually selling part of the estate to the villainous Warner Oland, boss of the "Tenderloin", a hugh ranch contiguous to the Spanish grant. Apparently Oland had coveted the Spanish hacienda and it lands for years. Having failed in his all his efforts he finally employees an Anglo attorney to make the deal. Accompanying the lawyer, was the young and handsome Terry, who immediately leaves his ugly boss and enlists on the Vasquez side. Later it is discovered that Oland is not really an Anglo, but an Oriental, a "Chinaman", [shades of Charlie Chan] who has maltreated his people also. The sympathy in this production was cast heavily on the Hispanic side. Still uncommon enough to mention. It all ends with the Vasquez property remaining intact, but San Francisco falls apart in the big one of 1906. Critics thought it was a bang up finish.] **MPW**:6.25.27, **V**:6.29.27.

[1240] **PATHE REVIEW #15**, Pathe: [The first part of this reel featured nothing more dangerous coming out of Colombia, South America, than banana's. Film and time certainly can change images. Historian's new that the coca leaf was grown in that nation for at least three thousand years, but not for export. Banana's were a major export then and although some sixtie's hippies smoked banana peels, they did so only for laughs.] **MPW**:5.7.27, p44.

[1241] **PETER THE PIRATE**, UFA: [For a view of the Spanish Main through German eyes with acting styles "dating back to the days of the Spanish Armada," this German entry was offered to local audiences. The **NYT** aware that the Germans were trying to break into the North American market, was not worried that this movie would do much damage to this nation's world leadership in the film industry.] **NYT**:1.7.27.

[1242] **THE PHANTOM BUSTER**, Pathe: [Buddy Roosevelt played a dual role in this western feature. He was first a helpless weakling who had difficulty taking care of himself, abused by all. But in his transformation as a Texas Ranger, he was the hero responsible for bringing the Mexican border smuggles to justice in a series of adventures involving baddies from both sides of the Rio Grande.] **MPW**:8.20.27, p546, afic.

[1243] **PORTUGAL TODAY**, Fox: ["A comprehensive series of scenes picturing Portugal as it is today is offered in this Fox Variety. We are shown the old section of the Oporto in contrast with the modern part of the town ... an exceedingly beautiful ... interesting and instructive reel." **MPW**:3.5.27, p46.

[1244] **RESURRECTION**, UA: [Dolores Del Rio played the abused and seduced, Katusha Maslov, with Rod La Rocque as Prince Dimitri the offender in this Edwin Carew tale of a Russian peasant girl ruined by aristocratic lust and redeemed by the love of another in the Russia of the 1870's. Her role would be duplicated by another sultry Mexican beauty, Lupe Velez, in the 1931 remake [1534].] **V**:5.18.27.

[1245] **THE ROAD TO ROMANCE**, MGM: [After his dramatic success in **Ben Hur** [1092] Roman Navarro had been cast in even more romantic and heroic roles. In this one he became the Captain of the Spanish Dragoons who saved the lovely señorita from the swashbuckling pirates and the governor of the province who lusted after her. But his presence could not carry this lame production, even **Moving Picture World** panned it. The film was filled with other Hispanic characters, including the lovely lady, Serafina, but all of them were Anglos in darkskin make up.] **MPW**:11.19.27, p29, **V**:10.12.27.

[1246] **ROARIN BRONCS**, Action Pictures/Pathe: [If it wasn't booze or dope those smugglers were sneaking over the border, it had to be Chinese. In this one, Buffalo Bill Jr. played Bill Morris, of the United States border patrol assigned to study and prevent any further violations of the "Gentleman's Agreement" designed to keep the yellow peril in manageable numbers. Moving quickly after his assignment, Bill takes a job at the ranch he suspects is the center of the operation. Two men own the ranch, one is Rose Tracy's father, the other the head of the gang responsible for the illegals. He has a thing for the pretty daughter. When Bill first arrives, he immediately attracts her attention by saving the lady from a runaway. Later the hero learns of plans to make another crossing, but is captured on his motorcycle trying to prevent the illegal flow. Kept captive in an abandoned cabin until he could escape, he soon captures the entire gang using a tractor. Having completed his task, he rides off into the sunset on his trusty steel steed secure that he has done his best to maintain the nation's racial purity.] **FD**:12.11.27.

[1247] ROSE OF THE GOLDEN WEST, FN: [It is not too much to say that the epicenter of film making in 1927 could be found in Southern California. Hollywood was the film making capital of the world. This pleasant locale "burnished by the golden sun and drenched by the foam of the Pacific," whose weather generally allowed directors long hours for filming, certainly had producers looking for scripts that could be adapted to nearby locations. This, combined with the region's history, which had had an identity under four different flags, helps to explain why so many films dealing with Spanish California found their way to the silver screen. First National used the above quote in their advertising to present what was simply one more variation on an already old theme, the struggle for the control of Spanish California, but with a new twist. This may be considered one of the earliest of, the Russian's are coming and have always been the real enemy, films. In this production, which would be remade several times, the Russians, with a contemptuous disregard for the Monroe Doctrine, were attempting to gain control over Spanish California before the North Americans could assert themselves. Mary Astor was cast as the pretty Rosita, who loved the dashing Gilbert Roland, [a recent Mexican import, destined to please audiences well into the last decade.] He was cast as Juan, who, employed by the secret service was given the honor of uncovering the scurrilous plot to turn over the entire territory to the Russians before power could be assumed by the Union. The problem was that the culprit, the slovenly Spanish Governor, was also Rosita's father and when she discovers that Juan must kill dad to prevent the territorial transfer, she is forced to betray him, but only for a little while. In the last reel, designed to please the most ardent patriots, Rosita, realizing that only the Red, White and Blue must wave over her home land, leads a troop of United States Marines against her own father and the Russians to save her lover and California for the United States.] **MPW**:10.8.27, p384, **V**:9.28.27, **NYT**:9.26.27.

[1248] THE ROUGH RIDERS, FPL: [Reviewers were tepid in their praise for this very costly production, a million and a quarter real dollars was more than a large sum of money in pre[real]income tax days. Basically, the film was designed to describe the patriotic activities of T. Roosevelt and the organization of the Rough Rider regiment, led by Leonard Wood and their participation in the war that would take Cuba out of Spain's control and place it under the hegemony of the United States. Roosevelt is shown in his position as secretary of the Navy, after the sinking of the Maine, ordering that "water be placed under everything that can sink, swim or float" knowing full well that the end was in sight for four hundred years of Spanish imperial control in the Caribbean. The producers claimed to have checked with and been honest to historical records in their recreation of the historic battle. That may have been the problem with the film. Audiences have had a notorious difficulty with historical fact. The line between documentary and drama has never been easy to divide in terms of box office profits. Although this production tried to blend history, love and comedy into a successful production, contemporary critics felt that it failed in its intent. So far as historical accuracy was concerned, that was easy. The Spaniards were bad, the North Americans, were good, that's always proved to be solid enough with local audiences. Considering that some would be historians in 1898 could write lines like, "Once more the flag of freedom has been unfurled in the face of a foreign foe," this work did not wave the flag much too high in 1927.] **MPW**:3.19.27, p211, 7.23.27, p222, 10.1.27, p301, **V**:3.20.27, **NYT**:3.16.27.

[1249] **THE ROYAL AMERICAN**, Harry J. Brown: [After a young Coast Guard Officer has successfully completed a couple of "corking good fist fights" on shore, he is shanghaied by the evil "Hawk" onto a boat loaded to the gunnels with arms and ammunition destined for some South American port where the rebels are waiting for the supplies to start a revolution. Possibly mindful of his duty to uphold the Neutrality Act, the young hero does his very best, he singlehandedly subdues the entire crew and turns the load of contraband over to his grateful Captain. Just another day's work for any Anglo hero.] **V**:8.10.27.

[1250] **RUBBER TIRES**, Hale-DeMille: [Always ready to find some place to stick in a Mexican Bandit, the producers found one here when they sent a family on a cross country car journey. They decide to sell all they have in NYC and strike off for the other coast in a none too sound auto. There are many incidents along the way, including one with a not so terrible "Mexican," who causes them some trouble when they get to the bad lands. Of course they also encounter an available Anglo who makes the adventure more fun and a whole lot safer.] **V**:3.9.27.

[1251] **SAILORS BEWARE**, Pathe/Roach: [With significantly more to do in her second silver screen two reeler, Lupe Velez played against Laurel and Hardy in this Hal Roach comedy. Her comedic ability was quickly realized, but her seductive good looks would require her to play many naughty lady roles before finding screen immortality as the talented comedienne she truly was.]

[1252] **THE SEA TIGER**, FN: [Although the Canary Islands are some distance from the Iberian peninsula, their population originally came from that Hispanic base. This poorly reviewed production claimed to describe life on these then rather simple and isolated specks of land frequently used by early mariners as jumping off points when heading for the Nuevo Mundo. **Variety's** rather priggish comments focused on the fact that two women, obviously the reviewer did not know they were hot blooded Hispanics, have a real knock-down-drag-out-hair-pulling-biting-scratching altercation over this sea tiger that seemed to the writer to be more like a pond pussy. Even the "man struggling against the forces of the sea" stuff did not seem to improve his opinion of this production.] **V**:4.13.27.

[1253] **SEÑORITA**, P: [In this spectacular production, Bebe Daniels scored a resounding hit with her version of the **Mark of Zorro** [847]. Audiences saw her as a combination of Douglas

Fairbanks and Tom Mix. A skillful swordswoman, she was said to have made "pin cushions" out of a number of her fencing instructors. In the film itself, the real story and action started twenty years after the birth of a baby to the Don Francisco family. At that time, a confusion on the part of the old Don, had him believing that the child just born, was a boy. Pleased that the male heir would insure the continuity of the family name, he left for his home in Argentina. In reality the baby was Bebe, and very much a female. For obvious reasons the writers never allow any of the characters to clear up the confusion, and when the little lady finally journeys to Argentina to see her uncle twenty years later, she soon learns that the nasty Olivero family is besieging the old hacendado and that the uncle expected his macho nephew to save the rancho for the family. Somewhat taken aback at his shapely nephew's diminutive size, the old Don is more impressed with his skill as a swordsman. Realizing what she must do, Bebe dons the customary costume and become the Masked avengeress leading her gaucho's to battle the culprits with such force, that they are quickly overcome. For at least the third time, the future Thin Man, suave and sophisticated, William Powell, did his grub work brilliantly as a South American Bandido leader. At least in this instance he was rewarded by falling prey to the fighting señorita's charms, and after being bested in every way by Bebe, he becomes the real man of the hacienda. All of the major and secondary characters in this top production were played by Anglos [64].] **MPW**:5.14.27, p135, **V**:5.11.27, **NYT**:5.9.27.

[1254] **SHE'S A SHEIK**, Paramount/Famous/Lasky: [Possibly remembering that the original Sheik had been the off spring of a Spanish Christian father and an Arab mother, and recognizing that women were no longer essentially tied to their kitchen duties, Lasky updated that romantic tale of desert adventure with a little gender modification of his own. Bebe Daniels was every bit the hot blooded and much desired fiery damsel of the desert who would choose her own Christian company to sleep with if she so desired. And she did, warding off all Arab type with the point of her rapier.]

[1255] **SLIGHTLY USED**, W: [There was this bandit who spent a lot of time on the front pages of all the metropolitan dailies in 1927, he was simply referred to as, "Sandino." Aside from causing ole Uncle Sam significant trouble in Nicaragua, he was attempting to rid his nation of corrupt military rule, free his country from United States domination, and trying establish some kind of a democratic base which the people could use to elect their own leaders. Whatever political orientation one might hold concerning these issues, Warner Brothers obviously took advantage of what they felt was good publicity by placing their major characters in this film in the middle of that military occupation. All in all it was a silly piece of fluff in which one sister was so peaked by her younger one that she claimed to have married someone called Major John Smith in a quicky ceremony that provided only enough time for a few kisses before he had to return to Nicaragua to try to capture the notorious bandit that was doing in his boys by using sneaky unAmerican like guerilla tactics. The younger one buys it all, but is horrified when she sees the apparently married one falling for another male. Sis takes care of that by placing an obit in the paper announcing that her husband had been killed while valiantly pursuing the enemy. Yup, when the real Captain Smith reads about the premature declaration of his death, he leaves that troubled jungle and heads north. You can finish this, I'm sure. Interestingly enough there were no films made in 1927 which took either a right or left point of view on the Nicaraguan situation. The first one to mention Sandino as a character was **Flight** [1332] made in 1929, but he was incidental to the football player turned Marine in that film. The Sandinista would have to wait for a far distant decade for major film recognition with the production of **Under Fire**, **The Last Plane Out**, 1983 and **Walker**, 1986. Broadway produced a patriotic support for North American intervention in 1927, **Spread Eagle**, but it focused on Mexico, and it featured extremely negative characterizations of the locals as stupid peon's led by ridiculous and lecherous bandits. Although there were plans to bring this to the screen, the producers claimed that Will Hays considered the production too "unpatriotic" and prevented it form getting beyond the talking stage. Considering the threat of a Mexican boycott that year, it seems more likely that Hays would have been more concerned with the negative nature of the Hispanic characterizations than anything else. There is no information about this in the Hays Papers.] **V**:10.26.27, **NYT**:5.10.27.

[1256] **SOMEWHERE IN SONORA**, FN: [An above average Ken Maynard western in which he saves his buddy from joining up with a real bad bunch of hombres, some of which were from south of the border. Mexicali Burton was a product of both sides of the Rio, but Ramon Bistula, the real Mexican was pure and true in his characterization. The great Tarzan managed a few tricks for the kiddies while helping Ken save and the pretty lady. An excellent example of an established formula well done. Remade in 1933 [1638].] **V**:3.30.27, **MPG**.

[1257] **THE STUDENT PRINCE**, MGM: [In this classic cliche destined to be remade and reused numerous times, Roman Navarro played Crown Prince Carl, handsome to a fault and carefree as the devil, warm of heart and guided by the spirit of spring, who falls in love with a beer garden commoner cutie. It was Old Heidelberg where love was mixed with intellectual pursuits which allowed everyone to ignore that this good looking Mexican had joined the Hapsburg aristocracy and would do his duty when called upon to leave the lady.] **V**:9.28.27, **NYT**:9.22.27.

[1258] **THE TIGRESS**, C: [The Tigress was a Spanish gypsy who wanted to revenge herself against the Englishman she thought had killed her father, but instead found herself falling in love with the charming fellow. It all works out, she gets both the man and her revenge because it is discovered that another "villainous" gypsy was really the one who had done her dad dirty.] **FD**:12.11.27.

[1259] **WHAT WOMEN DID FOR ME**, Pathe: [This was the first feature film appearance for Lupe Velez in which she had only a "bit" part. Her career is sketched briefly in: **Alfonso Pinto**, "Lupe Velez 1909 -1944", Films in Review, November 1977, pp513-24.]

[1260] **WHITE GOLD**, PDC: [The De Mille Picture Corporation produced this much reviewed, highly publicized and controversially ending western built around the unending conflict between sheep and cow men. There are only five characters in this melodrama. One of them, the father's son, was sortaofa weak personality, but good looking enough to capture the heart of Dolores, the Mexican cantina dancer. Having done so the now proud son brings her back to the ranch as his bride. "Transformed from the bounteous feast" life in the cantina provided, she now faced the "hollow husk" that life on a torridly hot Arizona ranch presented. Part of the heat was provided by the foreman, in charge of the "white gold" that baaaed around the place all day. Worse for the son he was soon subjected to his father's vindictive plan to destroy the already strained relationship. His constant lies breed insecurity into the weak willed lad who now accused his lady of not being very nice. She had in reality remained faithful to the point of defending her honor by killing the foreman who desired her. But in the end she realizes that she cannot break the filial bond, the boy will not believe her, he will stick by dad, and in the final scene she walks off into the desert by herself, leaving the two of them to their own devices. Rarely had Hollywood allowed the development of so much sympathy for a Hispanic character.] **MPW**:3.25.27, pp25-27, 4.9.27, p584, **V**:3.2.27, afic.

[1261] **WINDS OF THE PAMPAS**, Superlative: [Bitter family feuds on the Argentine Pampas could be even deadlier than those that took place in Kentucky. This one involved two brothers, one of which for fairly understandable reasons, was still quite angry after twenty years because the other had stolen his woman. To remind him that he has not forgotten, every year he sends the offender a very poisoned "gift of hate." This makes the receiving brother slightly nervous, so when his son returns from having had the traditional European education, he enlists his aide to have this stopped. The son now seeks employment with the deadly gift giving brother who is unaware of the boy's real identity. He does know that he has two daughters. As Hollywood would have it, the one that loves the new boy is older, but he prefers them younger and is forever sneaking kisses from her in the dark halls of the old hacienda. Warned against doing this, his life is further complicated by his "lunatic" father who actually sends him a letter inquiring about the disposition of events. Trapped now as a spy, he must face the "law of the Pampas," which involved, for this writer, enduring several hundred strokes of the lash and then being sent out on horse back, hands tied behind the back, to face the winds of the Pampas. The movie makers were tough on spies in that far off place.] **V**:11.21.27.

[1262] **WOLF'S TRAIL**, U: [**Variety** was highly critical of this production, not because of the acting, but with what they considered to be an overly used theme. Strong willed Texas Ranger goes after moonshiners [only the crime varied] operating on the border and brings them in after experiencing the necessary gun play. The Mexican characterizations no longer added to the mystery or malevolence. It was expected by the audience. The trade journal predicted that if Universal continued in this fashion, that soon, they would not be able to "give away" such productions. Something new was required on and of the border. And in that very next year, it would almost be clearly audible.] **V**:1.18.28.

1928

[1263] **ACROSS TO SINGAPORE**, MGM: [Cast as the stalwart younger brother of an adventurous family of seamen, Roman Navarro saved his half crazed brother from a gang of orientals in a Singapore dive and the ship from mutineers.] **V**:5.2.28.

[1264] **THE ADVENTURER**, MGM: [The shadow Richard Harding Davis first cast in 1914 with **Soldier of Fortune** [509], has stretched well into more recent times; nineteen-twenty six's entry in the North American hero saves another Latin American republic series, was led by Tim McCoy. Such Anglo heroics had traditionally been taken for granted, but one reviewer apparently had some doubts. The cowboy hero in this production was sent to the land of the gauchos where with little effort he rescued the mine owners daughter from local marauders and returned all of her father's stolen property. In his spare time as a little extra, he also managed to restores the deposed president of that Republic to his former office. Considering that Argentina was in size the third largest nation in South America, this was a good days work even for an Anglo hero. But one reviewer was somewhat skeptical, he thought that there was "too much bravado and too many extras who toppled over like props every time McCoy tightened" his fists.] **V**:9.26.28, LCFL: Press Sheet.

[1265] **APACHE RAIDER**, Pathe: [Apache Bob, Breed Artwell, Don Felix Beinal, and other such colorful characters inhabit this film about cattle rustling on the border and lynching in the town. There were both semigood and bad Hispanics riding through this still silent western.] **V**:9.26.28, **MPG**.

[1266] **ARIZONA WILDCAT**, F: [Still riding for Fox studios, but always searching for new scenarios that would keep fan interest, Tom Mix took to selling polo ponies to the rich in this piece of fun. It would seem that the well to do, also have their troubles and when the daughter of the family is kidnapped, Tom rescues her from the Spanish mission the bandidos are hiding in. What probably made the audience most happy with this familiar story was Tom taking the faithful and agile, Tony up a set of stairs to the second floor of the mission as he knocked the culprits to the tiled floor below.] **V**:1.25.28.

[1267] **BATTLES OF FALKLAND ISLAND**, Br: [President Monroe's famous message of 1823 warning that there would be no further "colonization" in the American Hemispheres was hardly enforceable by a United States that had no navy. But at the same time British had more than 5000 ships of the line and because they could and felt the need, Her Majesty's Navy took the Falklands in 1833. The Argentines had always claimed the islands, they called them the Malvinas, but as the recent war indicates, the British would never relinquished their control. In 1982 they could have given all 2000 plus citizen sheep herders more than a million dollars apiece and transported them elsewhere, it would have been much cheaper than the total cost of the war, but they chose to fight Argentina to keep possession instead. This little film recounts a fictionalized conflict between the German and British navy off the Falklands during World War I, many years before. It was a time when men of honor still conducted war in a chivalrous manner, seemingly a contradiction in terms, but important to Hollywood and British movie makers. One of the German naval characters in this film is named Von Spee and at the dinner table, with the British in attendance, he brags that he will capture the Falklands. Interestingly enough, the **Graf Spee**, Germany's most famous World War II raider will be damaged off the coast of the Falklands and have to put into Montevideo harbor where, unable to escape, she will be sunk by her own men to prevent the British Navy from having the glory of finishing her off themselves. Had Hollywood writers put coincidences like that together for the screen, some in the audience might have been doubters.] **V**:2.19.28.

[1268] **BLOCKADE**: FBO: [This romantic melodrama involved a bunch of pirates and rumrunners who operated between Nassau and Florida doing their best to prevent the entire nation from going dry. The rumrunner capture the pretty lady pirate, but she escapes and with the help of the United States Marines is responsible for stopping that illegal traffic. For all her trouble she was allowed to keep the one she thought was really cute.] **afic**.

[1269] **BOLIBAR**, Br: [Possibly because of the Production Code's influence, at least some of **Variety's** reviewers displayed what may charitably be called a pseudopuritanical nationalistic predisposition, or in the vernacular, they seemed to think a lot of foreign products, even the British ones, were dirty. This film outlined the story of the beginning of the end for Napoleon. Traditional enemies, England and Spain combined for a while in 1808 to drive the French armies out of Spanish territory. This early version of the **Pride and the Passion** [1957], made in Britain, was at best, panned by the reviewer. But with a little irony, he seemed to attribute to the English characters, what had for a generation been accepted as normal for the Hispanics: "Whether the British board of censors is particularly simple-minded or whether it's the heat, they have done an amazing thing in passing this picture for "universal exhibition." For "the story is almost entirely concerned with the antics of half a dozen [British] officers who have the minds and habits of barn door roosters and the mentality and behavior of cads. That is doing the theme more mercy than justice." "It is hard to understand why this film was ever made. It lacks almost every essential of a motion picture." Apparently this prudish pundit had not yet learned that a little sex sells a long way. It is not unfair to postulate that if that same behavior had been exhibited by the Spaniards in this film, there might not have been the same moral condemnation, it would have been accepted as the norm. It must also be remembered that silver screen Anglos were almost always affected by the sun and heat in the tropics or Spain itself, the heat seemed to stimulate libidos apparently not as active in their cooler homelands. Being provided with affectionate and warm blooded señoritas allowed activity not possible elsewhere.] **V**:8.29.28.

[1270] **BORDER PATROL**, Charles R. Rodgers: [Once more on the Mexican border, this time at El Paso de Norte, Harry Carey, as Bill Storm, Texas Ranger was looking for some crooked counterfeiters working both sides of the Rio Grande. They made the money in El Paso and used Juarez, just over the bridge as a casa de cambio. On his way to end the practice, Bill assists Beverly Dix whose car had broken down on the road outside the city. Of course everything was connected by the scenarist and in the final scene, the baddies were behind bars while Bill and Beverly were exchanging lotsa besos.] **afic**.

[1271] **BRANDED MAN**, Trem Carr: [There were no sympathetic characters in this one save for the wife that was left. The protagonist was a bum who drifts around the country till he gets to Texas. In El Paso, he crosses over the international bridge into Juarez, Mexico and gets into the fight game, sleazy Mexican style. The characterizations on either side of the border were less than attractive.] **V**:6.6.28.

[1272] **THE BRANDED SOMBRERO**, F: [One of the real good guys, Buck Jones, did his best with little script and lots of action to make this one a success. There are few Hispanic characterizations to be found here, the sombrero was used mainly as with other border or Mexican identifiers, to add a little punch to the promotion of an unusually poor product.] **V**:3.21.28.

[1273] **BREED OF THE SUNSET**, E: [Just as good a feller as Buck Jones, Bob Steele, was chosen to play stock formula, "#444" where he tires of the Rodeo circuit, decides to go to California and gets to save a lovely señorita, Maria Dominguez, who, rewards him with her affection. That was all the code allowed in those day, the code of the west, as well as the Production one. Actually, there was a little extra in this variation, a touch of **The Graduate**. It seems that the lady had been promised to another, a local caballero and on the day of her wedding, macho Bob, abducts her and carries her away. The Hispanic father, impressed by such bravado, has no one arrested, but consented instead to their marriage. Maria was attractive and sympathetically portrayed.] **V**:6.29.28, **MPG**.

[1274] **THE BROKEN MASK**, Morris R. Schlank: [Now here was some kinda woman. Caricia, who had achieved fame in Argentina as a dancer, came to like and later love, Pertio, who could tap out a few tangos in fine style himself. The problem was that the señor was really ugly. Not so much in all his features, but his face had been scarred. His lady suggested that he see a plastic surgeon, (yes, in 1928) and so he did. All went well until the doctor who managed to remove most of the scars fell in love with the sexy dancing lady himself. So to remove his competition, he made the scars reappear. Realizing this, the very angry partner, remained true to her lover and beat the living diablo right out of the not so nice doctor with her trusty whip.] **V**:3.21.28.

[1275] **CANYON OF ADVENTURE**, Charles R. Rogers/FN: [Many of the great cowboy heros of the day eventually made their way to sunny southern California in and around 1849, this was Ken Maynard's and his terrific horse, Tarzan's turn. The formula was not varied, there were the usual very bad Spanish/Mexican heavies ready to kill or corrupt the picture of Anglo purity, the heroic Americano, but to no avail. The climax of this particular plot and counter plot focused on the Spanish land claims of a very very bad Spanish heavy who was taught the true meaning of Anglo justice at the workin end of Ken's shootin arn. This type of reinforcement simply reassured audiences that all was still right, very right in the far southwest.] **V**:3.21.28.

[1276] **CAPTAIN CARELESS**, FBO: [Hollywood's obsession with cannibalism still continues, although they seem to have moved it's location from the Philippines, the black or indian Caribbean, the Amazon, and all of Africa into the living rooms of middle class North America with **Eating Raoul**, while the **Texas Chain Saw** trilogy keeps it alive and well near the border. No one has focused on Milwaukee yet. In this film though, it could still be found in one of it's most familiar locations somewhere in one of the more remote island of the Philippines. There, in a place with an unpronounceable name, Bob Steele, careless with everything but his Anglo courage, saves a maiden from a fate, more deadly than the one usually intended by those dirty natives. The film was one long chase with the two constantly pursued by apparently hungry natives, very black ones, from start to finish.] **V**:10.17.28.

[1277] **CARMEN**, Fr: [This "French flicker" was more a faithful adaptation of Prosper Merimee's original novel than it was the Bizet opera and the reviewers all applauded the production as well as the acting. By 1929 there had been so many versions of this work that any ten year old "could recognize the plot as the basis on which most vamp stories for the screen" were founded. It's influence on Hollywood productions would be difficult to overstate. Moreover, most of the movie was shot in Spain where the author originally conceived the story of the lovely bad lady "who takes her lovers where she finds them and flings them aside whenever the gypsy in her craves freedom." Free from North American censors, one of the "high spots" in this version was the bull fight, the most realistic to date depicting the action in the corrida more graphically than it had ever been done before. Everything but the actual kill was shown. The battles between the gypsies and the Spanish soldiers were lauded as was the film itself. It is still today, considered by many the most faithfully rendered picturization of the naughty little lady to date.] **V**:5.15.28, **NYT**:5.7.28.

[1278] **THE CAVALIER**, Tiffany-Stahl: [When sound came to the silents, Hispanics were forced to speak. The title cards that had formerly implied accents, and other aberrations of 'ingleesh' usage, began to slowly disappear to be replaced by a multitude of actors who would slaughter the most simple pronunciations for audience approval for the next sixty years. **The Cavalier** was the first feature film with a Hispanic theme that employed sound. The Photophone process used synchronized records to match the actors lip movements, it may never have worked well even once. The slightest jar subjected the production to unintentional ridicule and provoked undesired humor. But this film had even more serious problems. It was the story told once too often too soon and no where near well enough. A poor imitation of Don Q, it was one more masked avenger protecting the poor while still having the time and energy to fall in love with the lady he saved from the same Spanish tyrant who was forever ruling Southern California. As silents acquired sound and approached a new decade, a somewhat more sophisticated audience required something new, something more entertaining. Although the slight application of sound and voice to this film was not sufficient to make it a success, the rapid improvements in audio technology would allow many old silents themes to talk their way into the thirties. In a very short time the masked Hispanic bandit lover, good guy and bad, would make his broken English comeback, with a characteristic vengeance that would carry him well into most recent times. See also: [1108]] **V**:11.7.28, **NYT**:10.31.28.

[1279] **A CERTAIN YOUNG MAN**, MGM: [In its first version, this film had Roman Navarro playing an aging roue looking back on his long career as a lusty and very successful lover, but in the final version his character was changed into a young gay blade who is surrounded by many willing women whom he scorns for the love of an innocent maiden. A real Hollywood switcharoo, which kept Navarro essentially in character as the desired Latin lover.] **V**:6.13.28.

[1280] **CHARGE OF GAUCHOS**, Julian Adjuria: [With the Argentine film industry still in it adolescence Adjuria, a well intentioned patriot who wanted to make the best film possible about the life of that nation's emancipator, Juan Belgrano, came to Los Angles with lotsa dineros and great expectations. He knew that Hollywood films dominated the South American market, and for that reason he trusted that the California image makers would produce a superior product. Unfortunately, he was disappointed and so were audiences in both hemispheres. History has not always been considered entertaining by the majority of audiences, and it was especially true for this production. Hollywood had never really succeeded in making the North American Revolution popular on the screen, doing that for Argentina proved impossible. Considering how much of Jane Fonda's soul and still lovely body she thought necessary to apply in an effort to make the **Old Gringo** a success, one can understand that a straight forward film biography of an unknown Argentine hero, without such lovely accouterments, had little chance at the box office. As hard as he may have tried to be heroic, the forced histrionics of Francis X. Bushman served merely to amuse. Reviewers panned the picture with unkind and unnecessary, nationalistic quips: "The whole thing impresses like Mexican rookies lined up with West Point seniors." The citizens of the great port city must have loved that one.] **V:10.17.28**.

[1281] **CHICAGO AFTER MIDNIGHT**, FBO: [Chicago in the fun days of the mobs killing each other for control of the north and south side provided the setting for this story in which Ralph Ince goes after a rival gang leader who has wronged him. In the process he meets the lovely Jola Mendez, characteristic dancer in the enemies Cabaret. There he plans to work his vengeance and implicate Jola's lover. Discovering this, the lady infiltrates the gang, but is soon found out. Before the baddies can "make it really hot for her", Ince learns that Mendez is in reality his own daughter. Talk about a surprise! Heroically he gives up his own life to save her. Hispanics were making their way north, but soon, many of them would be forced to change their nationality. The mob, the mafia and the like would require Latin blood of an other variety.] **V:3.7.28**.

[1282] **DON JUAN OF THE WEST**, Anchor Film: [No information found.]

[1283] **THE DOVE**, UA:[The threatening protest made by the Mexican government that Hollywood films would be banned for exhibition south of the border unless the more negative Hispanic characterizations were removed from productions like the **Bad Man**, [962] had definite, but mixed results, Willard Mack's good bad guy was too marketable a character to lose to the sensitivities of certain nationals. The **New York Times** expressed a halfhearted understanding of the problem, Mexico may have had reason to be offended, but, there was a bit of a " but." "Taking it by and large, Jose is perhaps a screen character to which the Mexican Government might have objected for he is greedy, sensuous, boastful, cold-blooded, irritable and quite a wine-bibber, but he does dress well. His top boots are always like a mirror, his riding breeches are spotless, and he is a good figure of a man. He hates to have his luncheon spoiled by a noisy victim of his shooting squad. He adores beauty, but is inconstant." One might add, "What was Mexico objecting about?" With only slightly more understanding, Hollywood producers moved this version, the next of many to follow, to a distant location. What could Mexico complain about if the republic of Costa Roja were located in the Mediterranean? There, Don Jose Maria y Sandoval, the country's number one bad man, still speaking Spanish, "Dios what a man I am," could ply his trade without offending the tender sensitivities of our Latin neighbor. Noah Beery was the goodie/baddie and the object of his affection [aside from his darkskinned mistress] was the lovely whiteskinned Anglo, Norma Talmadge. Gilbert Roland, the only Mexican in the film, as Hollywood would have it, played the North American boy she loves and to whom Don Jose gives the lady in the last reel. Moving the location had little affect on the public's conception that all these people were Mexican, but at least the effort had been made not to offend, at least too directly. Subsequent remakes, even 1939's **The Girl and**

the Gambler, [2160] moved the location back to Mexico.]
V:1.11.28, **NYT**:1.3.28.

[1284] **DRIFTIN' SANDS**, FBO: [Simple and straight forward, Bob Steele, played Driftin', who happened to wander onto Señor Quartaro's very big hacienda looking for work. The gentleman hires him as one of his vaqueros and all is well until, the daughter, Nita, played by Gladys Quartaro, falls for the cute little Texas tumbleweed. Immediately banished from the rancho, Bob manages to wait around long enough for the ever lurking bandidos to attack, so that he can employ his [god] [Hollywood] given North American powers to save the oppressed, even if it was the stupid old Don who threw him off his rancho. He does, and was rewarded with a very grateful Nita.] **MPG**, **afic**.

[1285] **DRUMS OF LOVE**, UA: [Considered to be one of his better efforts, it was hailed as a successful directorial comeback for D.W. Griffith. Filmed almost entirely with sets, the locale was a nineteenth century South American estate belonging to two brothers, one handsome, the other deformed, but with the deed in him name. This tragic love story of Paolo and Francesca, the brother and wife, took almost two hours to tell, but all waited for the big finish The women were enthralled by intensity of the hot blooded and illicit love affair, the men loved the silky nightwear the heroine was forever wearing. In the final scene, to save the family's honor, Spanish pride forces the hunchback brother to kiss both the lovers and then stab each one respectfully in the bosom as he tenderly places his lips to theirs. Having enjoyed the sinning, they accepted death with characteristic Latin fatalism.] **V**:2.1.28.

[1286] **FORBIDDEN HOURS**, MGM: [Being the king of a mythical kingdom can be a lonely life, it really separates you from your people, but in this one, there was a special evening during which the monarch was allowed to leave his title behind and mingle with the masses. Roman Navarro, on that night out with his officers, falls in love with the commoner daughter of his Prime Minister which creates a fairly predictable set of circumstances to follow.] **V**:7.25.28.

[1287] **THE GATEWAY OF THE MOON**, F: [Bringing the lovely Dolores Del Rio back across the border, we find her way south in the Bolivian jungle, a beautiful halfcaste, Chela Toni, the niece of the crooked foreman. Bridge building and railroad inspection required the services of an English Anglo inspector, Walter Pigeon who would do his assigned task without being corrupted, as one of the locals might have been. The foreman, angered that neither he nor his work passed inspection, and unable to bribe the stalwart, planed to kill him. By this time the delectable Dolores had fallen in love with the Anglo innocent and of course prevents his death so that they might share more intimate moments together in a different climate.] **V**:1.11.28.

[1288] **THE GIRL HE DIDN'T BUY**, Dallas M. Fitzgerald: [Havana merely provides the backdrop for this fluff about a virtuous Broadway actress who refused to submit to the advances of a philandering play backer. When she runs to that tropical capital of Anglo fantasy and free wheeling fun, she just happens to meet the right man, a rich English man who has the captain of his boat marry them, thereby preventing the scandal many had thought was taking place in the middle of Havana harbor beneath the shadow of El Moro.] <u>V</u>:6.20.28, <u>afic</u>.

[1289] **A GIRL IN EVERY PORT**, F: [The great success of **What Price Glory** [1201], in 1926 brought the battling buddies quickly back to theater screens. Victor Mclaglen and friend most certainly enjoyed playing two rough and tumble seaman who traveled the high seas and competed for the girl in almost every port. Every macho, or red blooded, as they then called it, male's fantasy, husbands and boyfriends must have had to drag their ladies to the theaters for this production. As irresistible Anglo sailors, the two fight, brawl and love their way around the world with no more care than wondering who it was they left wherever, and what was the next port of call: In Rio the lady to be loved and left, was Chiquita [Maria Casajuana], and in Panama, the Hispanic entry was played by Elena Juardo, whose little Katy would later have a somewhat longer career.] <u>V</u>:2.22.28, <u>NYT</u>:2.20.28.

[1290] **THE GUN RUNNER**, Tiffany-Stahl: [Lasting fame may well be as fleeting as a faithless lover's affection and sadly for Ricardo Cortez, although he would continue to work well through the next decade, it would never be quite the same as it had been in the **Torrent** [1198]. As Julio, in this work, his task was to capture a bandit that threatened the President of another imaginary South American republic with still another revolution. Hollywood was always quick to agree with some political scientist, that the Latin republics could not find peaceful means to settled their political problems. Ricardo, attacking his task with enthusiasm, finds the bandit strong hold, but falls in love with the revolutionary's sister. That was not political science, but frequently the case in such scenarios. Yet, his duty was clear, his Latin heart required that love should triumph and so he allows the bandit to escape. For this he is heartlessly sentenced to death by the authorities, but is saved by his lady, yup, in the last reel and at the very last moment. The cheering peasants were pleased too. Unfortunately, **Variety**, reported only "giggles and laughter," they had seen it before and done better.] <u>V</u>:1.9.29.

[1291] **HAPPINESS AHEAD**, FN: [The only connection hear is that a cardsharp who loves his wife and has to go to jail for six months, uses Buenos Aires as a mail drop to convince her that he is really in that port city on business and will soon return to her.] <u>V</u>:6.20.28.

[1292] **HOLD THEM YALE**, DeMille Pictures: [Rod La Rocque starred in this sometimes difficult to believe scenario. Rod was Jaime Emmanuel Alvarado Montez a slightly stereotypical, rich Argentinean who comes north with his valet and his pet monkey to win the big game against Princeton in the final few seconds and score as well as one could in 1928 with the favorite daughter of the favorite professor that both like the gutsy little gaucho. There's more. Some obviously halfwitted detective was forever following the hero about thinking that he had to be guilty of something because of who he was and where he came from. You could make a film like this back then, you could probably make it now.] **afic**.

[1293] **HOT HEELS**, U: [... was the kind of a title used to attract expectant males who had high hopes of seeing some hip swaying hussy's, derriere held high in the air, seductively slithering across the screen. In this film, they were disappointed, hot heels, was simply a fast horse who wins a race that allows the theatrical troop stranded in Havana to buy passage back home. Those familiar with that city's constantly reinforced screen persona, at best uninhibitedly free and fun loving, probably recognized some of the identifying shots of Havana's legendary night life and the exclusive Jockey Club at the track.] **V:5.23.28**.

[1294] **LEGION OF THE CONDEMNED**, P: [Had an enterprising producer possessed the benefit of foresight, he might have called this sequel to **Wings**, "Half a Dirty Dozen Take To The Air," to kill those even dirtier "Huns." All of the major characters in this WWI flying circus including Gary Cooper and Fay Wray had done something or had some reason to make them want to die, so why not do so killing the then enemy? One was too rich and had done everything one could possibly imagine in New York and Harlem, another had killed his girl friend in a drunken auto crash, the third had been laughed out of suicide by his lady love when he went bust in the market and the South American entry had shot some husband while running off with the presently dead señor's wife. With a little variation, the Hispanic entry in the **Dirty Dozen**, would use his hands to kill his lovely, but unfaithful lady.] **V:3.21.28**.

[1295] **LIFE**, Br: [This entirely British production indicated that there was little different in the accepted Spanish stereotypes on either Anglo side of la mar, save that it was apparently a lot easier to hire Hispanics to play themselves in England than it seemed to be in the United States. All but the lovely señorita, the star, Marie Ault were Spanish. The film was a thriller set in Spain where, Juan Jose was about to lose his job as a mason because he could not keep his libido in check when thinking of the beautiful temptress, much less lay the bricks on an even level. Unable to earn the pesos that would keep his dancing lady from whirling into another señor's arms, he takes to crime and is soon arrested. While in jail, it should have come as no surprise to him or anyone else, that his little Carmencita could care less he had been confined in an attempt to keep her happy. But, everyone has a breaking point, and when the Spanish seductress takes up with the boss, it's too much. There were bodies everywhere. When ever Hollywood employed the green eyed monster to heat

Hispanic hot blood to the boiling point, audiences knew very well that there could never be a happy ending.] **MPG**.

[1296] **THE LOVE PIRATE**, Ger/Ufa: [There was a significant amount of sarcasm in this review of Germans trying their best to be good Anglos doing what they did best on the Spanish Main. Most of the focus was on "wimmin," lotsa "wimmin" and drinkin and showing them who the boss was by dragin em about by the hair. The reviewer thought that the pirate leader was something of a nance who preferred to be with the wimmin instead of out there showing those Spaniards the business end of a sword. There was apparently so much revelry at the castle where all these Teutonic swashbucklers hung out that it looked to the reviewer like a sixteenth century nightclub with a gay crowd in costume.] **V**:7.25.28.

[1297] **MORAN OF THE MARINES**, P: [Richard Dix is a marine in China, fighting Chinese bandits, but many of the title cards make reference to Marine activity in Nicaragua against the bandits there. Sandino is not mentioned by name.] **V**:6.17.28.

[1298] **THE NEWS PARADE**, F: [This continuous comedic chase with attempts at some mild melodrama was one of the screen's first tributes to the intrepid, fearless and completely without any concern for personal safety, tributes to those daredevils who traveled the world for the "best shots" of what they considered to be news-worthy events. "Newsreel Nick" as the star was called in this fun, seemed more a precursor of the paparazzi than anything else as he hounded a wealthy family across the United States and eventually across the water to Cuba where a bunch of more modern bandido's attempted to kidnap the rich father and beautiful daughter. Of course Nick nipped the nappers and managed to get it all on film at the same time. Some ten years from this time, two other bold, brave and courageous camera-man and woman would travel way south to challenge the wilds of the Amazon for similar footage in **Too Hot To Handle**, 1938, the attempted melodrama in that one would be even more humorous.] **V**:5.30.28.

[1299] **NO OTHER WOMAN**, F: [Dolores Del Rio was getting a lot of playing time by 1928; she had achieved major star status. Don Alvarado, considered one of the leading "Latin Lovers," after his success in the **Loves of Carmen** [1233], was another Hispanic doing well, although he would never reach that same plateau, he continued to play character roles until his final appearance with another silent great, Roman Navarro in the **Big Steal**, 1949. The two had scored well with audiences throughout the nation in **Carmen** [1277], but the high hope producers had for this production did not materialize. In this film Del Rio played Carmilita Desano, a well to do Spanish aristocrat and sweetheart of Alvarado, who was this time cast as a Frenchman named, Maurice. Things look bright for the lovebirds until a suave and sophisticated South American fortune hunter appeared to darken the skies of love's horizon. He steals Carmilita away, but only stays until the money is gone. Realizing her mistake, she returns to Maurice who is happy to have her back. Hollywood's French lovers were sometimes more forgiving, but it depended on their social station. If they were rich, yes, if they were pimps, no way, Joseph!] **V:6.20.28.**

[1300] **A PERFECT GENTLEMAN**, Monty Banks Enterprise: [This farce featured the films producer as a trusted employee on his way to marry the boss's daughter. They are deeply in love but a flat tire prevents the ceremony from occurring. Attempting to fix the flat, he is knocked out and the attempt to revive him with spirits merely gets him intoxicated. When they finally arrive, Monty's rival for the lady plays upon the parents disfavor for the poorer boy and the wedding is called off. Meanwhile, some South Americans who happened to be at the festivities had plans of their own for a little celebration back in the old patria and they convince the rival to finance a revolution which will make the bank mucho dineros if it succeeds. The baddie steals the money from the dad's bank and sends dumb old Monty south with them unaware of what he is doing. But on the ship to South America, he gets wise and after some fierce and frantic fights with the Hispanic baddies, Monty saves the money, and his girl and future father-in-law, who happens to be on the same ship.] **afic**

[1301] **THE PHANTOM FLYER (Air Thriller)**, U: [A United States Border Patrol aviator comes to the assistance of a family harassed by a land baroness who controls the water for all those thirsty cows. Although the Border Patrol was shown at work on the Mexican border, no Hispanics were to be seen.] **V:5.2.28.**

[1302] **PROWLERS OF THE SEA**, Tiffany/Stahl: [This film based on a Jack London short story used the Spanish American war for a backdrop. What are referred to in the script as Cuban, not Spanish officials, know that there is going to a revolution and they want to prevent any further arms from being smuggled into the country. To do this they appoint the last incorruptible man in Cuba as head of the Coast Guard to prevent the rebels from acquiring any more fire power. Ricardo Cortez, as Carlos de Neve, accepts the position with humility. But Rebel leader Ramon Sanchez has a beautiful ace up his sleeve, his sister, that he willing will use in the cause of freedom. She is sent to vamp the young officer, but in so doing also falls in love. Surprised huh? General Hernandez, Gino Corrado, in charge of Spain's last forces on the island, it is not made clear, but certainly a Hispanic with a romantic heart, captures the rebel chief and realizes that Ricardo had left his post for other things. Unable to shoot him for desertion, and possibly realizing that revolution in Cuba was inevitable, he allows the two to go into exile until hostilities are over, first obtaining their pledge they will marry. Ricardo willing gives up his independence so Cuba can achieve her own.] **V:7.25.28.**

[1303] **RAMONA**, UA: [In 1928 Helen Hunt Jackson's classic was going through it 92nd printing. And the ballad "Ramona" was "one of the springs outstanding song hits." It did not take a public relations expert to realize that this might be a good time for the third remake of the motion picture. The popularity of Del Rio made her the perfect choice to the lead. This version differs somewhat from those before and the one that would follow with Loretta Young as Ramona, in that the heroine was depicted as being maltreated as a youngster, by her wealthy Spanish, sheepherding guardian. But the general outlines remained the same. When Ramona discovers that she is in reality a halfbreed, not a high caste señorita, she opts to marry, her childhood friend, who had grown to become the chief of his tribe. But, secretly she remains in love with the young handsome Don of the hacienda. When her husband is killed by whites and after she looses her child, she suffers from a temporary amnesia and wanders aimlessly through out the countryside until discovered by the Don. He returns her to the place of her childhood and restores her memory by reminding her of the song they loved as children. Some critics, not blaming the star, accused the directors of trying to make it more a film about Del Rio's loveliness than the classic it remained. Also: [103, 705]] **MPW**:4.2.27, P 485, **V**:5.16.26.

[1304] **THE RED DANCE**, F: [Fox was building showcases for Dolores Del Rio at this time, she was one of Hollywood's top attractions. People paid two dollars to go see her play a peasant beauty, Tasia, the Grand Duke's lady who later suffered at the hands of the Tsar's cossacks. Raoul Walsh who directed her, brought a little of his Mexican Revolution experience and influence to what must be considered an early justification for the Russian Revolution of 1917. **V**:6.27.28.

[1305] **THE RED MARK**, Pathe: [Nina Quartaro, played the lovely dark skinned native lady all the trouble was about in this story of lover about to be separated by a beheading execution on the island of New Caledonia. At the last moment the evil executioner discovers that the red mark he was about to use as a dotted line was the same as that his long lost son had at birth and spares his life.] **V**:10.31.28.

[1306] **REVENGE**, UA: [In this her first semisound film, Del Rio, plays a gypsy who's blood requires that she revenge herself against one who has wronged her. As the daughter of an animal trainer, she is called Rascha and knows the meaning of cracking a whip. She uses it a lot on the gypsy brigand, Costa, whose band of bandits have been responsible for cutting the hair off some of the female "gyps." She further seeks her revenge by plunging the even more tradition knife into him, but to little affect. The reviewers felt that only her presence made going to see this nonsense worthwhile.] **V**:12.12.28.

[1307] **THE SHOWDOWN**, P: [This was a man's story, women who attended performances took their own chances. Set in the tropics, more than likely Mexico, the plot concerns two arch globetrotting rivals. Only three things motivate them, discovering oil, women in general, preferably attractive and willing and the desire to outdo each other in all areas of endeavor, especially when a new woman or a new oil field was to be had. It mattered not which, besting each other did. The reviewer considered this premise a new innovation and a solid one artistically, but wondered about it's romantic marketability. When the hero discovers a new field in Mexico, the rival soon shows up. All of the Hispanic characterizations were incidental, save for the cantina girl, who immediately falls for the Anglo hero. He does not love her, but is willing to employ her services. The rival tries to take her away, but fails. At this point the aristocratic wife comes into the picture. Now the tropical influence really takes hold. Both men compete for the woman, not because they care for her, but to win, to best the rival. In a brutal fight, provoked by the rival's attempt to take the lady by force, the hero beats him almost to death. The wife knows the combat was not for her personally, but is willing to be taken under those circumstances. Just then the milktoast husband shows up. The Anglo now plays cards for the woman and the oil concession, but throws in the winning hand so that she can break out of that tropical hell hole and "return to civilization." Reluctantly she leaves. He gets to keep the chiquita. She knows, but is grateful.] **V**:3.7.28, **afic**.

[1308] **SIREN OF THE TROPICS**, Fr: [This is a French version of the selfsacrificing darkskinned woman who gives up her own desires for those of her white colonial master. The story begins in France where the capitalist, Severo wants to get Berval out of the way so he can have his way with Denise. As such he sends him to the French colonies in the Caribbean. Alverez, his evil Hispanic confederate, is sent along to do him in when they reach the tropics. Once there, Berval saves a beautiful negress, Papitou, from the advances of the lecherous assassin. From that time on, she is his willing slave and is instrumental in later saving his life. Upon returning to France, Berval seeks out Denise and they plan to marry. Papitou has stowed away and followed. With her natural talent for singing and dance, she becomes a star overnight. Severo uses her former relationship with Berval to break up his wedding plans, but in the final reel, the selfsacrifice of the beautiful black lady brings the two back together. She then gives up all and returns to her barren beach broken hearted.] **V**:1.18.28.

[1309] **THE SKY RANGER**, Educational: [Russ Farrel works for the United States air border patrol watching for various illegal activities that are forever taking place on the banks to the Rio Grande. This time its the smuggling of Chinese into the country from Mexico and it has to be stopped. The fearless air hawks easily locate and destroy the entire operation. Meanwhile, because it was considered necessary to add a little paprika to such mundane tasks, there's was a girl, and because the hero gets his men, he gets his gal too. Residents were assured that all was safe, secure and quite the same on Hollywood's favorite border.] **V**:11.14.28.

[1310] **SOUTH OF PANAMA**, Chesterfield: [The cast featured Carmelita Geraghty and Edouardo Raquello in this tale of an American entrepreneur's attempt to generate a little extra business for his failing arms and munitions company by sending one of his subalterns south of Panama to see what he could do about starting a revolution and thereby increasing the possibility for sales. Once there he meets a number of likely prospects, bandits, who are interested in the gun running operation, but their ineptitude prevents it from happening. It was not so much that the bandits were stupid, that was a Hollywood given, but the fact that the hero fell in love with the daughter of the president of the republic that foiled the plans to form another new government by direct action. Over all, there was enough violence in this action melodrama to have the New York State censors ask for a number of eliminations in the script. One of the scenes that was considered too graphic, pictured a baddies already wounded, lying in a river bed, clawing his way out of the water, clutching a few strands of grass. It was redone. The guardians of public morality also required that "the distinct view of Emilio sawing [the] bars of the cell window," be cut, because they felt that "such scenes tended to incite lawlessness" and apparently they did not want to give out even simple pointers on how to break out of a Panamanian jail.] Script: **South of Panama**, NYSAA.

[1311] **STAND AND DELIVER**, Pathe:[After her initial success with Fairbanks in **Gaucho** [1227], great things were expected from Lupe Velez, but the critics thought in this production she appeared "becalmed", her only real movement being a noticeable "heaving chest habit". Although interesting, the projection in its self would hardly be enough "to keep her in Hollywood for very long." So much for this scribbler's forecasting talent.] **V**:4.4.28.

[1312] **THE STRONGER WILL**, Indy: [Reviewers had not one good thing to say about this production which had a Wall Street finance king engaged to something of a brainless flirt just before he was forced to leave for Mexico on business. While there, Hollywood showed audiences not only the usual array of poverty they expected to see in the Mexican capital, but also some more modern and prosperous business establishments. Upon his return the hapless financier discovered that the lady had made plans to wed another, you can take it form there.] **V**:4.11.28. afic.

[1313] **TRAIL OF '98** MGM: [This more than million dollar production told the epic tale of the trials and tribulations of the Alaskan Gold rush. It featured Dolores Del Rio playing a more familiar character, a painted lady prostitute forced to ply her trade by the evil Locasto. Harry Carey was a real heavy in this one.] **V**:3.28.28, **FD**:3.25.28, **MPG**.

[1314] **TWO LOVERS**, Goldwyn: [A swashbuckler pictorial romance "of those good old days when they used two hands to lift a mug of ale to their lips and punctuated their thoughts by digging a dagger into an oaken table." This adventure story romanticizes the adventures of a heroic Hollander, Leatherface, who helped bring about the last days of the Spanish occupation of his country. Hollywood's Spaniards were horrible tyrants wherever they ruled in the world, but there was always someone ready to overthrow their tyrannical oppression. This time it was Ronald Coleman and Vilma Banky.] **NYT**:3,23,28, **V**:3.28.28.

[1315] **THE VALLEY OF HUNTED MEN**, Pathe: [Certainly not one of the stock formulas, this good little western was one more result of the pressure applied by the Mexican consul when he threatened to have any film with negative Mexican characterizations banned in his nation. Reviewers lauded the action and the comedy and the fact that it was different. They also recognized that the scenario was written with Mexican sensitivities in mind. There was the usual Border Patrol and hero and smuggling across the river by the baddies who have their headquarters there. The Anglo ranger's job was of course to lure the crooks back into the United States [no more cavalry charges across the Rio] where they could be arrested. The big difference focused on the baddies themselves. They ran guns into Mexico in exchange for rum which was returned for sale back in the States, but everyone of them was characterized as either a halfbreed or renegade North American, or "European, a tactful arrangement to avoid objections of the Latin American Republics." When money talks, capitalism listens.] **V**:5.2.28.

[1316] **VIRGIN LIPS**, C: [In what turned out to be a bit of support for North American business concerns operating south of the border, in this instance an oil company and a fairly reactionary Central American government that provided it with support, the producer and screen writer threw all of the sympathy in that direction. With "the Bandit Sandino" an almost daily news item at the time, that should not be surprising. This scenario described the activities of an American oil company operating in an undetermined Central American location which required the services of an aviator to help locate and destroy a gang of bandits led by an hombre named, "Carta," who was interfering with the vital flow of oil to the north. Considering that Nicaragua had no oil what little Hollywood had placed there made it a real precious commodity. Anglo flyer and hero, Barry Blake took on the responsibility and engaged the assistance of a local called "Garcia" to help him. While flying over the enemy's jungle location the plane crashed in that green hell, but the two survived. Somehow locating a convenient cantina to hide out in, they actually found an Anglo woman singer who had been brought to that infernal place under false pretenses. In no time at all Carta and his bunch (remember, this was silver screen Central America) of bandits arrive. Things look bad, especially when Garcia turns out to be a spy for the baddie, but North American ingenuity won the day. Blake manages to get a message to the national troops and with his help, they capture all the bandido's. The Anglo was thanked and rewarded for a job well done. Norma, the stranded singer, planned her own little surprise for the hero. The status quo having been maintained, it was business as usual. Hollywood once more assisted the State Department in assuring audiences that Central America was secure for the North American way.] **afic**.

[1317] **WHIP WOMAN**, FN: [In this not highly acclaimed pseudo masculine fantasy, Antonio Moreno seemed to really enjoy playing a Latin version of a Hungarian lover. The pretty peasant girl saves the depressed nobleman from suicide and then marries him. The whip was part of the ceremony.]

[1318] **WHITE SHADOW**, MGM: [Raquel Torres played the beautiful native girl in this not typical of the genre production, her dark complexion fit the current conception what of what a nicely featured south sea woman must look like. The story was more interesting for the time because its message was clear: White men corrupt and destroy native civilizations no matter how good their intentions are, not a common perception for 1928.]**V**:8.8.28.

1929

[1319] **BORDER PATROL**, Pathe: [There was always villainy on the Mexican border, but thanks to Hollywood's border patrol there were always men able to rise to the occasion. [Sergeant] "Well, there's a mighty important job to be done and it's powerful dangerous ... While you're the most dependable man in the outfit sometimes it don't seem fair that you should endanger your life so often. [Harold] It's all right, Sergeant, If anything happens to me my only regret is that I have but one life to give to the Border Patrol!"] With material like that, it's a wonder that there was ever any trouble on the ole Rio Grande.] Script: **The Border Patrol**, Reel 1, p1. **NYSAA.**

[1320] **BORDER WILDCAT**, U: [By this date there were a lot of dry throats throughout the nation. Had it not been for the constant supply of that then evil stuff, flowing fairly freely across both borders, even a revolutionist looking to be elected could have been so had he run on any kind of a wet ticket. This old time silent feature was just one more fairy tale quietly reaffirming that the government men on duty on the Mexican border were doing a great job preventing any of that "rotgut" "hootch" from finding its way across their fourteen hundred miles stretch. After being wrongly accused the border patrolman in this one was vindicated and returned home with his beaming new bride. So long a Hollywood could stop the illegal traffic on the screen, what happened on the border was secondary. There must be a message or two in there somewhere for the DEA or someone.] **V**:4.24.29, **FD**:4.21.29.

[1321] **BRIDGE OF SAN LUIS REY**, MGM: [This film, which pictured the tragedies that confronted indian peasants in their daily lives, high in the Andes, was taken from Thorton Wilder's Pulitzer Prize wining, "profoundly religious" story of their simple devotion and fatalistic acceptance of life as it more often than not, tragically, affected their daily existence. Set in the Lima, Peru of 1715, the cast included three Hispanic actors, Raquel Torres, Duncan Renaldo and Don Alvarado. Lily Damita, the French import, was featured as the vixen like Spanish dancer. The former Latin Lover, Alvardo, and the future Cisco Kid, Renaldo, played twin brothers beguiled by the seductive danseuse, Damita. She teases and tempts all the boys, but belongs to the aristocratic Viceroy. Religious resignation and the acceptance of life's little and great tragedies provide the heavy fair for this "magnificently staged," well acted, but rather somber production. First filmed as a silent, the arrival of sound and its success, had the producers add "25 percent dialogue" to the beginning and end of the movie. In the opening scene the bridge over the gorge to the town gives way and five people are killed. The townspeople become very worried, fearing that they have offended their Catholic god and that he is punishing them for some unknown offense. What wickedness had they committed?

The padre, Father Juniper, explains that god works in mysterious ways and calms the simple, but reverent believers. For many this could have hardly been a pleasant Saturday afternoon's lighthearted entertainment.] **V**:5.22.29, **FD**:[silent]4.28.29, [sound]10.27.29, **Outlook**: 6.5.29, p235.

[1322] **BROADWAY**, U: [The talkers were a mixed blessing for the studios. After the initial applause the creative innovation generated, the disturbing realization set in that the entire world did not speak either Esperanto or English. Desirous of maintaining their hold on the Latin American and domestic Hispanic market, the studios understood that their films would now have to utilize Spanish. Although the South American market was not as important as that in Europe it was meaningful enough to maintain and even expand where ever possible. In an early attempt to face the challenge and provide a product that would please south of the border audiences, studio sound men did a hasty job of preparing this loudly ballyhooed extravaganza which had met with some success in the United States. Although billed as the "first talker in Spanish" it was in reality mostly a collection of written titles instead of the spoken word. The Spanish idioms that it employed were unfamiliar to the audience in Buenos Aires and they booed the production loudly. The "best people" in the port city had paid top prices to see this premiere and their displeasure prompted Monroe Isen, Universal's man there to forecast that "This looks like the end of American Spanish Language dialogue pictures for this territory, at least as this one was made." **Variety** offered the following assessment of this first of several fiasco's to follow: "Universal's **Broadway** caused disorder and a demonstration almost hostile at its premiere at the Astral (Buenos Aires) theater. Audiences gave the bird ... the dialogue in Spanish was pretty terrible ... [the little Spanish that was spoken] was unfamiliar to the Argentines who booed the accent of the actors." It would get worse before the situation improved.] "FAKED SPANISH DIALOGUE GETS RAZZED IN S.A.", **V**:11.27.29. For an overall look at Hollywood's South American efforts which focuses mainly on the United Artist Corporation see: Gaizka S. de Usabel, **The High Noon of American Films in Latin America**, UMI Research Press, Ann Arbor, 1982. The United Artist collection is housed at the University Library in Ann Arbor.

[1323] **CAREERS**, FN: [This was Antonio Moreno's first talker and it almost cost him his life as a French diplomat in what people then referred to as French IndoChina. His wife, Billy Dove wanted him promoted and when he was not after four years of devoted service, she convinces him to speak to the Governor of Vietnam. Antonio tells all he knows about the womanizing president of the province which almost has Billy forced to give up her all to save her husband. Yet virtue triumphs in the last reel, the Spanish speaking Frenchman was promoted and his was wife satisfied.] **V**:6.12.29, **NYT**:5.10.29.

[1323a] **THE COCOANUTS**, P: [The madcap four end their first of many hysterical sound features at a costume party where all the boys but Harpo are dressed in various Spanish costumes,

Chico's the bullfighter, Harpo the natty ranchero. Zeppo appeared in flamenco attire and the very full figured, Ms. Dumont sported a sky high Mantilla. After a little punning around the entire troop gathered to sing a contorted aria from **Carmen**, which played on the words, "He has my shirt." Even Bizet would have laughed. Whatever Zeppo was smoking, and Graucho warns him about it, it made him flash his teeth, grimace and bulge his eyes in a menacing manner.] **V:5.29.29**.

[1324] **CONDEMNED**, UA: [With a voice like his, Ronald Coleman may well have looked forward to playing in this "All Dialogue" production which was the first sound film to focus on life, as Hollywood imagined it, on Devil's Island, the notorious French penal colony. But this screen fantasy was too far fetched in many of it's sequences for even the less sophisticated in the audience. As the story begins, the suave and smooth manners of the handsome thief capture the eye of the wardens wife. She immediately has him relocated to the main house where he is to be a servant, and her toy. Girls from the town [which in reality would have been on the mainland] know of the affair and look over the wall to watch the lover's embrace. Everybody knows what is going on but the cruel and vicious warden. When he begins to suspect, he orders the wife back to France, which was the prearranged signal for Coleman to escape from solitary. Although vicious dogs are loosed, he takes a little time to say good bye to friends, and somehow makes his way through the swampy snake infested jungle to the sea. Once there he finds a flat boat that happens to have a working outboard, just waiting for him. After joining the wife on board the big ship, he is captured, but at the same time, his best friend back at the penal colony kills the commandant. The wife, now free, promises to wait forever. Romantic viewers ignored inconsistencies. See also: **Devil's Island**: [1172].] **V:11.6.29**, **NYT**:11.4.29, TNT.

[1325] **DANCER OF BARCELONA**, Sp/indy: [This product from Spain was offered with synchronized sound disk, which at best, never worked well. The cast, entirely Hispanic, save for the recently arrived Lily Damita, were unfamiliar to North American audiences. Directed by a German, there was no real story other than having the lovely dark eyed Damita dancing her way from the cafes into the bedroom of the men she desired. At one point the Spanish dancer seemed to want to stay longer than play time allowed, but her essential character prevented her form doing so. According to the reviewer, the idea seemed to be that "art [could] be conquered by true domesticity" an Aryan conception that found some practical application in the coming years.] **V**:11.27.29.

[1326] **THE DELIGHTFUL ROGUE**, RKO: [Several thousand years ago someone probably quipped on a Myciean stage everyone wanted to be a comedians at one time or another. Certainly this **Variety** reviewer was giving it his best with the opening line of his criticism for this production: "Zat wun Castillian villaine-- wot a man! [Still in his pubescence the year before,he had seen **The Dove** [1283] an never recovered.] No guns he used, but just his head. And how he bragged and gagged! Money meant nothing to him, and jewels he flung away, just to prove the philosophy of love and win a maiden's hand." This scribe wanted to like this new "all dialogue" production, actually the first all talker with this particular stereotype, but he thought that it just missed being a candidate for the first run houses, and would be relegated to "grind circuit" [less expensive theaters for the everyday folk], it was perfect. As he continued his review he did provide a succinct outline of the good-badman formula that would be used and reused many times, one that certainly pleased audiences. "The story is the kind theater fans like to chew on. A handsome tall pirate of Spanish type, brave, philosophical and careless. A pretty dance hall girl who speaks with a cultivated tongue. An educated bounder and a ludicrous constabulary. Here are all the ingredients of those light serio-comedies, but it all got lost in the shuffle." The story itself was an adaptation of Wallace Smith's "A Woman Decides," which had appeared in **Cosmopolitan Magazine**. The Hispanic hero, Lastro was "a Languid Latin" who prided himself on his villainy. As a pirate this time, he takes over a yacht and heads for the south seas where adventures abound in the tropics. There are ladies aboard and a wealthy white man. In the end the good lady is his and the white lily livered well to do Anglo proves to be not so brave. Hispanic good bad guys resided mainly near the Mexican border, but later as Hollywood's stereotypes progressed, they might be found anywhere in the world.] **V**:10.23.29.

[1327] **DESERT RIDER**, MGM: [Tim McCoy, by now well established as a western star, was riding for the Pony Express in this one. In his travels, he happened onto the truly beautiful, Raquel Torres, Dolores, who had just been robbed of the deed to her hacienda by a bunch of baddies, mainly Anglos. Post haste, the gallant Tim ran down the bandits, captured them and reclaimed her deed. The padre, Quintoda, who had been waiting for just that to happen and looking for a proper spouse for the señorita, was so happy, that he offered to perform the service right away.] **V**:7.10.29, **FD**:7.7.29.

[1328] **THE DEVIL MAY CARE**, MGM: [This was Roman Navarro's first all talker. In it he portrayed a condemned rebel captivated by Napoleon's exploits and his personality. Managing to escape with his head still in place, he becomes the useful and carefree valet of the heroine's house satisfying all desires.] **V**:12.25.29.

[1329] **THE DRIFTER**, Radio: [Having severed his long association with the Fox studios, Tom Mix still continued in the tradition he had established a decade before this production was issued. For his new producers, he appeared as a two fisted government agent. His task was a serious one, discover, apprehend and arrest the dope smugglers responsible for bringing that evil stuff out of Mexico. After some investigation, it turns out that the man he was looking for was an aviator, smuggling the dope across the border by air. Luckily for all, Tom was an accomplished airman himself.

After forcing him out of the sky, he arrests him. It was as simple as that sometimes, but only on the screen.] V:3.20.29.

[1330] THE ETERNAL WOMAN, C: [Anita,"the proud daughter of an inn keeper in the hills back of Buenos Aires," returns home "from this South American metropolis" to discover that her sister has been wronged and her father murdered. It was not a good day. Unafraid, her hot blood boiling, she swears vengeance on the unknown North American guest she suspects of doing the evil deeds. She remembers his wife, Consuelo, Nina Quartaro, who in reality was responsible for the tragedy because of her loose ways and easy virtue. Learning that the woman is heading back north, she follows her onto the ship and waits her chance, but before she can use her knife, the ship is wrecked. She and the youth that saved her, Ralph, are the only two survivors. Obviously pleased to be alive, they fall in love, but a rival convinces her that, her new hombre was the real killer of her father. After some misadventures, it is discovered that another, the very one that accused the Anglo lad, was the real killer. This reunites savee and savior, and they combine forces to face life together back in the Argentine.] V:5.22.29.

[1331] EVANGELINE, UA: [Hollywood from its earliest days was prone to cast its actors and actresses, willingly or not, into certain types. Breaking out of such a mold was certainly one of the most difficult of things to accomplish in that land of fantasy and make believe. Dolores Del Rio had long been typed. She was the exquisitely beautiful, hot blooded Latin lady that made most men in her audiences dream of long nights filled with loving. Many could more than sense the smoldering seductiveness of her salacious smiles. As such, selecting her to play the sad heroine of Longfellow's epic poem, was not necessarily going to insure good box office. As one reviewer commented: "Doubtful that even the special following of Miss Del Rio will go wild about it. The paprika Latin girl has some good emotional sequences, but somehow she doesn't seem to fit with the role of the saint-like maid of Grand Pre." Critics and audiences wanted their hot property to stay warm. The production was basically a silent film, there was no dialogue, but the lady sang two of the four songs that were added so that it could be advertised as having sound.] V:7.31.29.

[1332] FLIGHT, C: [Although the Marine action against Sandino in Nicaragua provided the back drop for most of the action in this film, as a character, the revolutionary leader had only a minor role. Seen briefly in the jungle with his men, he and his so called "bandits" furnished the justification for the presence of Marine aviators who were testing their new equipment's functional practicality in jungle warfare. Outside of a few references to his being a dirty bandit and revolutionary enemy of the republic, little was made of him save that his activities required the Marines presence in Nicaragua as the paternalistic protectors of the installed government. Frank Capra directed this film for producer Harry Cohn, two personalities that would influence film for more

than a generation. Overall it was considered a great success, exploiting the North American love affair for aviation generated by the Lone Eagle's flight and the extremely successful, **Wings**, but few of the reviewers mentioned the intervention in Nicaragua or Sandino himself in any way. The Marine roll in Nicaragua was accepted as what most felt it should be, to protect against insurgents and bandits. Sandino was simply another of a long line of bandits, one that received a lot of press especially because his boys had managed to shoot down a couple of ancient aircraft that been shipped there for experimental use. **Variety** raved about this production and considered it to be a two dollar picture for the first run houses. They were also impressed that two new ideas had been introduced in the picture, one was a scene of cremation, the other involved what was described as the "novel idea" of having two good buddies love one girl, with one of the Marines so nice, that he proposed for the other. Apparently the reviewer had never heard of Captain John Smith, Pricilla and John Alden. Much of the action for this Anglo adventure took place in what was said to be Nicaragua, but the film opened with "Lefty" going the wrong way on the football field during the Harvard-Yale football game. Shamed out of school, the not to be gridiron hero, joined the Marines, but did little better there. Had it not been for Jack Holt as "Panama Williams," a veteran of many Central American campaigns, he would have been washed out of the Corps quickly. Sent on a mission to search out Sandino with Major Goodwin, the two were shot out of the sky and crashed in the dangerous jungle. There, the Major knew he was headin west, so with killer ants crawling all over him as he lay pinned to his plane and with scary jungle animal sounds all around, Lefty covered his friend with a sheet, poured a little extra gas on him and gave him a proper Viking's burial. When Sandino and his boys arrived, Lefty had already been found by Panama. The remainder of the film merely resolved the love interests. Lila Lee did not say, "Speak for yourself Panama," but that's what she was thinking. The loser had to be satisfied with having won his wings, apparently for burning up the Major. Sandino was portrayed by Jimmy De La Cruze. Most of the reviews referred to the Hispanic nemesis as "Sandino," but the **afic** called him "Lobo." He was "Sandino" in the working script.]
V:9.18.29.

[1333] **THE FLYING FLEET**, MGM: [Aviation was in the air in 1929, and so MGM put Roman Navarro right up there fighting for a place in the sky as a member of the Naval Air Corps. Only he and a friend make it, but Navarro had the added benefit of winning the girl. In films such as these, in which **Variety** wondered why he was wasted, his Latin character could be transformed into more Anglo Saxon terms. Working for his wings, he played an Anglo named "Tommy", "natural, likeable and clean cut, but at the same time unheroic". Although others, Ricardo Cortez, Antonio Moreno and Gilbert Roland could cross ethnic lines, few, in these early days, were able to portray Hollywood's conception of the innocent and well loved Anglo home boy. Navarro was one.] **V**:2.13.29.

[1334] **FROM HEADQUARTERS**, W: [The still popular Monte Blue who's start in films stretched back as far as his minor role in **Birth of a Nation**, was the featured star in one more Hollywood fantasy of Marines making Latin America safe for North American democracy, but this one had a bit of a twist. It would seem that Happy Smith, who had left the Corps under mysterious circumstances some ten years before, had elected to remain far south of the border in what he now considered his home. There, the lovable soldier of fortune spent most of his time in a state of pleasant inebriation with the pleasant Anglo loving señoritas to comfort him when that was necessary. As the story began, he accepted the job of leading a party of rugged Marines into the interior of the local jungle to search for a party of lost Americans. The screen writer, more than likely intentionally refused to identify specifically the location for the action in this film, but the implication was that it was far south of Panama where no North American Marine ever set foot while on active duty. His intention may have been to locate in either Nicaragua or Panama, but his jungle smacked much more of the Amazon's rain forest. So somewhere in South America it was all the same to Hollywood, an uncommissioned Happy led the gallant boys into a most dangerous steamy bush, where quickly the jungle took its toll. Even some of the tough guys experienced significant discomfort. Despite these privations, they pressed on and discovered a dying woman in a wagon train, no ..., just dying, but with a small child held close to her bosom, [it was a wagon train in other films [77].] Recognizing Happy, she survived just long enough to explain to the others the real reason for his having left the corps. Apparently the selfsacrificing son of a gun, loyal to the core, had done so because if he had remained he would have had to expose her husband's, a Marine officer's, malfeasance. Her dying wish was filled with thanks for the former jarhead and an expressed desire that her little daughter be kept alive to be raised by the honorable drunk. **Variety** considered this "60% dialog production" a "good picture," more than worth the price of admission, but it expressed a bit of macho incredulity about one aspect of the film. They felt that it required, "A heavy wham bang on the old imagination to believe that a tiny infant, a baby girl not long in the hectic world, could be carried through a jungle inferno, survive storms, escape fevers, endure hardships and privations that shuffle off a leatherneck of the U. S. Marines, with rebels and bandits lying in ambush--and arrive at headquarters apparently o.k." The baby makes it in fine shape, but the two surviving members of the gallant "band of Marines {who invaded?} that raging hellhole were staggering and reeling like drunken men." {There is little difference in this scene and that one in John Ford's, **The Three Godfathers**, where the big Duke staggers out of the desert barely alive with the little babe in his arms.} In the final scene of this effort Monty was invited to reenlist and be reinstated, but he decided to remain in his adopted home to father his new little nina and with a lovely Latin lady, properly named, "Innocencia," and maybe provide her with a brother or sister.] **V**:7.17.29.

[1335] **GENERAL CRACK**, W: [John Barrymore led the cast in this Austrian/Kurland costumer in which most of the aristocratic, soldier male types went crazy over a little Spanish gypsy named Fidelia, played by the very alluring Mexican import, Armida. It was all Dukes and Arch Duchesses, Christian cross's and duty to the aristocracy, but Armida stole the show. Andres De Segurola, who in the next year would be featured in many Spanish Language films, played Colonel Pons. In this film he could only dream of the sexy little gypsy dancer. Of all the members of the cast, some of which were Hollywood's top attractions, **Variety** chose to single out for notice and comment, Armida's performance. They felt she had everything that Del Rio and Velez possessed and more, if some production company chose to exploit the "fiery Mexican girl." That did not happen. This was her first Hollywood production and for a while through the war years she would become a recognizable personality, but she never achieved the status of either of her sister actresses. Her last film role would pass unnoticed in 1951. Sadly, she would make fewer than eighteen Hollywood features, for no understandably good reason.] **V**:12.11.29, afic.

[1336] **GIRL FROM HAVANA**, F: [Another film with a Hispanic cast to be voted one of the ten best for 1929 [1338], this one incorporated a few first's. Its the first talker with a female, Lola Lane, as an eager, energetic and adept private detective. Certainly not a frail, frivolous flapper, she had no fear of following the jewel thieves to Cuba where, after some pleasant dialogue and adventure, she captured them. The views of Cuba, Morro Castle and the harbor were worked into the script without the appearance of its being a travelogue filler. On the way to Cuba from Los Angeles, the ship passed through the pride and joy of North American engineering genius, the Panama Canal. As such, though quite unintentional, and with proper pride pricked just a bit at the end of the scene, the audience was provided with what was the first verbal guided tour of the great work on film. A ship's officer described the canal to two small lads as they passed through it, after which they walked away asking, "What did he say?."] **V**:9.4.29, **FD**:9.8.29, **NYT**:9.2.29.

[1337] **HUDDLE**, MGM: [Second cousin to the divine Dolores Del Rio, Roman Navarro was at Yale in this film, playing a "hot tempered" italian who has a few problems with the eli's before he wins one for the 'blue,' after which, he became just one of the boys.] **NYT**:1.13.29.

[1338] **IN OLD ARIZONA**, F: [Significant in so many ways, this motion picture which would officially begin the Cisco Kid's long ride from the silver screen in to so many North American living rooms, was the first Fox all talking feature film. Voted one of the ten best films of 1929, it featured Warner Baxter as a "jolly, romantic Mexican badman, certainly something new on the border. Fears of Mexican protest were probably lessened with the realization that Mexican exhibitors would not be able to acquire this enormous success anywhere else. O'Henry's, **"The Caballero's Way,"** by the nineteen fifties would be responsible for more than twenty variations of the basic story line in which a North American trooper chased the Robin Hood like bandido throughout the Southwest in a vain attempt to capture him. Copy cat spin-offs were just as numerous. Audiences immediately fell in love with the idea that the "Kid", a loveable bandit, was really a Robin Hood [a real Anglo Saxon] who especially selected the rich to rob and kept only enough of his take to live on, giving most of loot to the poor. If all this had been acceptable in Sherwood Forest, it certainly could be on the Rio Grande border. Raoul Walsh had to share directorial honors because of an accident, but it was his film and his characterizations. Warner Baxter as Cisco established the tradition of "broken" but "captivating" English so firmly in this talker that it would take years and all of the efforts of the Production Code's Addison Durland in the World War II era to even inhibit the practice. As a result it was almost impossible for a generation of Mexican character's to "speeek" any thing but "I theenk" English. Cisco's Chiquita, the "typical, rag and a bone and a hank of hair," was necessarily faithless and easy. Her father was from Portugal and mother resided in San Luis Obispo, but the sexy señorita was pure hotblooded Mexican, and ready for whatever took her fancy. The film was an immediate and solid success. **Variety** predicted that it could have played at the top Fox theater on Broadway which charged $2.00 a showing for weeks. The tradition is still with us today. See also: **White Vaquero** [418]] **V**:1.23.29, **NYT**:1.21.29. **FD**:1.13.29, 4.28.29.

[1339] **IN OLD CALIFORNIA**, Audible Pictures: [In this transitional year between silents and talkers, films were frequently released in both versions. It was so for this production. Because of the primitive recording techniques employed and the more precise cutting, the silent was considered a better movie. The action began on a stage coach, where Pedro Deleon, a handsome young hacendado, was attracted to the pretty Anglo lady sitting aside him. Soon bandits held up the vehicle to conduct their normal business, but all were rescued by the more equally handsome Anglo officer, who immediately captured the lady's heart. Somewhat piqued, the Spanish lad still invited all to a fiesta on his padre's hacienda. That also included the nogood gambling father of the pretty little lady. There, after a lot of melodrama which included the old Grandee's losing the rancho to the scoundrel and a fight between the two suitors with tragic results, it is revealed that the gambler had a long time ago run off with the old Don's wife and daughter. This of course meant that the young Don had fallen in love with his own sister. He had to die, it was not 1991. "Underneath a Spanish Moon", though barely discernable, was the first such theme song employed in Hispanic talker [91].] **FD**:Sound, 9.15.29, Silent, 11.24.29.

[1340] **ISLE OF LOST SHIPS**, FN: [Now there was sound in the Sargasso Sea, and if the 1923 [988] version was a great success, this film with Noah Beery as the Captain and leader of the fifty-nine lost souls who inhabited that seaweed infested prison, was even more successful. Praise was offered for the construction of the sets, "a maze of derelicts ... so great is the variety of wrecked vessels from palatial liners to pirate brigs and barkentines that the artistry of the carpentry and painting achieves its purpose." The action in this production focused on a local custom. Any woman drifting into that dead area of the Caribbean was forced to choose a mate within a day. The resultant competition and rescue provided all the action necessary to make this film a success and perpetuate the mythology that there was that mysterious region of the Caribbean in which lots of inexplicable stuff happens: One only has to pick up the latest supermarket tabloid to get the latest developments. Things may well have been quite in that enigmatic region in the past decade, at least on **The Island** that Michael Caine visited in **1980**, because in a climax well suited for the cryptic Caribbean triangle, he managed to slaughter about a hundred of the pirates who had been holding out there since the days of the Spanish Main.] **V**:10.30.29, **NYT** 10.26.29.

[1341] **LADY OF THE PAVEMENTS**, UA: [That was no lady, that was Lupe Velez whose captivating performance as a naughty cabaret singer tricked into marrying aristocracy established her as a possible threat to any of the Anglo leading lovelies that ruled Hollywood. The "entertainment [was] dominated by Lupe Velez, Joseph M. Schenck's new and interesting personality of Mexican extraction." Only her "third or fourth major picture it should definitely establish her. Of a whole flock of Spanish, Mexican and Latin señoritas she and Del Rio are practically alone in clicking importantly." For the director, D. W. Griffith, it was considered and artistic failure and tragically, did little to lessen his drinking problems.] **V**:5.13.29, **MPG**.

[1342] **THE LAWLESS LEGION**, FN: [Ken Maynard and faithful four legged friend Tarzan were the heros in this neat little western which had the pair saving a group of small cattle men form the ravages of Ramirez and his gang of Mexican cattle thieves. There was a bit of a bad moment when the Hispanic heavy doped the hero, but that horse was almost human and certainly a match for any Mexican. Licking his masters face to revive him and doing so, the two then continued their pursuit of truth, justice and the American way, and that way was to ship those Mexicans baddies all the way back over the border so that the cowmen could continue build a strong nation and eventually discover the proper hormones to put a little fat on those skinny wild longhorns. Well, you have the essentials any way, despite a little editorializing.] **FD**:3.31.29.

[1343] **LOVE PARADE**, P: [Prospects for the Latin market were not all negative after the introduction of sound. There were significant indications that if the product were solid, it would sell in any language. This film starring the incomparable Maurice Chevalier and Jeannette Macdonald as aristocratic, starcrossed lovers singing their way in every possible nook an cranny of gay Paree, played for more than two months in one of the top Buenos Aires houses and could have remained longer. The University of Maine's own **Vagabond King**,

Rudy Valle did almost as well. Laurel and Hardy were a smash in **Blotto**, "The public here is going for [them] in a big way."] Another comedian, Harold Lloyd, did far better south of the border with **Welcome Danger**, than he did in the United States, which at a much later time would be common for many North American flops. Despite these successes, producers for the next five years would go to great lengths to find a Spanish solution for the new talkers. Not a few may well have believed that it would be easier to teach the Latins English.] **"AMERICAN TALKERS BIG IN BUENOS AIRES"**, **V**:5.21.30.

[1344] **MEXICANA**, MGM: [As in any developing industry which witnessed almost daily improvements in all it's multifaceted complexities, the newest innovation has either to be copied, improved upon or otherwise duplicated, if there is any hope of retaining a market share adequate enough to continue. Experiments with sound productions had been tried through out the decade, but none were so successful as Warner's **Jazz Singer** using the Vitaphone process. When Jolson spoke those immortal word's, "You ain't heard nothing yet," little did he or anyone else know how prophetic they would be. Still in its infancy in 1929, sound searched for various vehicles to best exhibit its talents. When producers realized that to compete in the Latin market, their performers would also have to speak Spanish, the two threads were combined into a musical review featuring Hispanic artists doing their stuff as they did best. It was simple and effective. The public was in love with Latin rhythms and long legged Latin dancing ladies. One appreciative reviewer exclaimed that "the Line up of girlies [was] something to feast the eyes upon." All this plus the marvels of Technicolor and an almost totally Mexican and Hispanic cast made this feature a big success on both sides of the border. It was produced by Gus Edwards with a cast speaking in both Spanish and English, although what dialogue there was incidental to the musical production numbers. The songs included: "I'm a Terrible Toreador," "Brazilian Baby," "When I Look Into Your Spanish Eyes," "Lets Tango in the Moonlight," "Wrap Me in a Spanish Shawl" and a new discovery found somewhere in an Los Angels cabaret, Armida, who sang in both Spanish and very broken English, "I Want to be Roman Navarro's Leading Lady." Included also in this varied group was just a beginner, at that time a violinist, "Exavier [sic] Cougat." In Woody Allen's wonderfully nostalgic **Radio Days**, 1987, the aunt gives her family a living room rendition of the Mexicana.] **Scrapbook: Mexicana, LCFL**.

[1345] **MEXICALI ROSE**, C: [The sometimes cold, cautious cattle queen who ruled the **Big Valley** on television from 1965 to 1969, Barbara Stanwyck, was significantly more warm blooded as the caballero crazed chiquita who captured so many hearts only to crack them, in her first experience with the west. There, in a Mexican town on the border, she was the Mexicali Rose, adored by all and approached by many, who audiences assumed, were not refused. She loved Happy Manning, but his experience with women made him believe that there were no good ones left in the west. Angered at the rejection, Rose dallied with the likes of Loco the Halfwit and Dad the Drunk, before selecting

Happy's brother to marry out of revenge. Not satisfied with
that, she continued her trysts to bring them both to their
knees, but her love for Happy never left her and when she
realized what she had done, she flung her self off a cliff: a
proper prescribed death for any Production Code bad lady. It
had first been intended that the crazed Loco kill her, but it
was more fitting to have her realize the errors of her ways
and punish herself. She had known that in the opening reel:
"It's too late to pray for me I'm too far gone." As a talker,
audiences were treated to some of their first spoken Spanish,
Manuela the dutiful, responded to the handsome hero with "O
gracias mi patron," as he gives her a drink. Erensto also
spoke Spanish, but was more comfortable with his 'ingleesh':
"You want gold mine, you take my gold mine give her to you.
You take my house. That's great place in all the world to
make moonshine." There would be little change in Hollywood's
western vernacular until the next war, when the nation needed
to offend their little brown brothers a little less.]
V:1.29.30. Script: **Mexicali Rose**, 18pages. NYSAA.

[1346] **MOTORING THRU SPAIN**, Burton Holmes Lectures: [A four
reel travelogue usually accompanied with descriptive
dialogue.]

[1347] **MYSTERIOUS ISLAND**, MGM: [A Jules Verne fantasy with all
of its underwater sequences filmed in the azure blue, crystal
clear waters which grace the beautiful Bahamas. **NYT**:12.21.29.

[1348] **THE PAGAN**, MGM: [To the salacious strains of the **"Pagan
Love Song,"** as the palms swayed seductively above their
glistening brown bodies, Roman Navarro and his equally dark
skinned beauty, simply "a native boy and girl [in] love with
one another" were aided and abetted in their romantic but
primitive desires, by a Sadie Thompson type bad lady. All
three struggled against the forces of hypocritical
Christianity to achieve happiness doing nothing but pleasing
one another as the surf teased their little brown toes while
loving each other in the sand. This may sound like heaven to
some, but it was pure hell for those Christian missionaries
Hollywood always sent to destroy their little piece of
paradise.] **V**:5.19.29.

[1349] **PALS OF THE PRAIRIE**, FBO: [At this time it only took
one Anglo hero to do what it would take seven magnificent
sociopaths to accomplish about thirty years later. Buzz
Barton rode into town as Red Hepner and cleaned out the
Mexican tyrant that was terrorizing the citizens of that once
peaceful pueblo. This film is more significant for bringing
Duncan Renaldo, a future Cisco Kid, into the western genre,
where he would spend most of his career playing one Hispanic
character after another, none of which ever mastered his
adopted tongue. More than likely born in Spain around 1904 he
was a foundling that came to the States from Brazil in 1927
working for his passage on the boat that brought him. Rarely
a malevolent character, his broken English was copied by
countless numbers of youngsters who chose to be the good bad

guy playing the games of ones childhood.] **V**:7.31.29, **MPG**, **afic**.

[1350] **RED MAJESTY**, Harold Noice: [Of all of the mysterious regions of South America which have produced volumes of misinformed mythology created by three or four generations of Hollywood scenarists, none has been more fertile for their imaginations than the Amazon. All manner of dangerous stuff was thought to come out of that distant and foreboding jungle. Among its 'most scariest' denizens, the head hunters stood at the top of the list. Not only were the head hunters [358], in the Amazon, there were also head shrinkers. Luckily for this film crew, the Tariano were neither. Basically a documentary, the title referred to the pigmentation that the Tariano indians of the north central Amazon used to color their skins. In 1929 making a motion picture record of their activities was no small task. It proved to be a real life adventure. Producer Noice trekked and canoed to regions very few Anglos had ever seen, much less filmed. In so doing he brought back a superior documentary depicting the daily life of this simple folk "who existe[d] in a communal state. All their worldly goods ... pooled." It was a far different view of the Amazon than had yet been produced [783], in some ways an idyllic society where older men were given light duties, while the younger ones hunted. The women cooked and were responsible for the very primitive agriculture, actually food gathering. The women appeared as they lived, bare breasted. [As had traditionally been the case in **National Geographic Magazine**, where a generation of young men saw their first partially naked woman, it was usually considered permissible to show brown or black breasts on the silver screen, only the white ones caused problems for a while. [See: **Forbidden Village**, 1941 for the New York State Supreme Court ruling of the showing of little brown breasts as opposed to the white ones.] Over all, this documentary provided audiences with their first views of this remote Brazilian tribe. Although not menacing, the film may well have served to reinforce viewer belief in the backwardness of that South American giant.] **V**:5.8.29. **NYT**:5.6.29.

[1351] **RIDERS OF THE RIO GRANDE**, Indy: [This was one of a score of Bob Custer "quickies" set on the border, all of which were so similar, that the star himself might have had trouble differentiating between them. A girl is captured by border bandits, he rescues her. And that's about how much action there was in the fifty minutes it took to accomplish all that. But it served its function. So much is made out of audiences wanting something new, at times that is and was certainly necessary. But the syndication of so much inane television material should just as certainly indicate that for some, the same old stuff is still is always in demand, it's comfortable and secure. It was and presently remains the same for film today as the multitude of Son's of, various swashbuckling heros in the forties and fifties, and Roman numeralized, 1's, 2's and 3's should indicate today.] **V**:10.2.29.

[1352] **RIO RITA**, RKO: [By the fall of 1929 it was obvious to everyone that silence on the screen would not be heard for long. Films were advertized for their sound, as "All Dialogue," and "All Talking." Aside from jeopardizing the jobs of thousands of musicians, the major problem this created involved the conversion of theaters to sound, a process that would still not be completed by the mid thirties. **Rio Rita** was not only "all dialogue," [the shooting script was 85 pages] but as an import from Broadway, a Ziegfeld show, it featured "songs." As such, it was the first musical western. With Texas Rangers singing in unison as they rode their horses across the screen, **Variety** "was forced to comment" that the talkers presented so many possibilities, "the stage could never commence to catch up." Bebe Daniels played Rita, a loving Mexican señorita full of song and affection for those she cared for. The cast was filled with colorful characters, Mexican generals and lesser goodguy baddies, a "malignant" Russian and the Texas Rangers. The **New York Times** reviewer was never certain as to on which side of the border the action occurred, but it mattered not, the search to uncover who the mysterious bandit called the "Kinkajou" was wonderful film making. So notorious was this bandido that he was honored with song: "They have a dance in Mexicola / It's all the natives do, You'll have it on your pianola / Its called the Kinkajou. / They dance every night, / It is dynamite, Yea! Paprika! / It has a bit of Espanola / A bit of Chile too, Señor." The production played in the feature houses and was a great success. When remade in 1941 it would create numerous problems for the individual who was trying to remove it's offensive stereotyping.] **V**:10.9.29, **NYT**:10.7.29, **FD**:10.13.29.

[1353] **RIVER OF ROMANCE**, P: [A Mississippi River "ripsnorting" fighting romance which has a minor role for the señorita dancer named "Mexico." She crossed the border to find love, but all she could do was twist and twirl for the second lead in this "all dialogue" production.] **V**:7.31.29.

[1354] **ROMANCE OF THE RIO GRANDE**, F: [So pleased with the great success of **In Old Arizona** [1338], Fox returned Warner Baxter to the old hacienda as Pablo Wharton Cameron, the long lost and favorite grandson of Don Fernando. Antonio Moreno, played the undesirable nephew who was to inherit the vast estate if Pablo had not returned. Although Dolores Del Rio and Lupe Velez controlled the franchise in then Hollywood, there was a new Mexican lady in town, Mona Maris, Manuelita in this lavish drama of old Mexico. All of these characters, as the **New York Times** pointed out, spoke "broken English" continuing the now well established tradition. The simple plot focuses on the rivalry between the two heirs for the hacienda and the señorita. Sound, now firmly established, and the beautifully photographed scenery of Mexico, added to the production values of this second successful Fox western for 1929.] **V**:11.13.29, **NYT**: 11.9.29, **FD**:11.10.29.

[1355] **SEÑOR AMERICANO**, U: [Originally intended to be, the **Golden Bridle**, Universal scratched it to make Ken Maynard the Señor Americano instead. It was a transitional title for bringing California into the union. The first of numerous talkers with this basic theme provided the audience with "85 % dialogue" [the first reel was silent and included the justification for the action on title cards:] "California belongs to us by the right of conquest!" "The people of California right now are eager to become Americana" "What right has the Spanish King to give land he ain't never seen? If we're going to make this a God fearing country ... Our Government knows best." With lines like that from the locals, the Señor had no trouble overcoming those Mexicans in opposition. But the talkers presented Hollywood scripters with a new problem. Just how much Spanish should be used to provide the proper atmosphere? Should it be translated or used in a manner which would make it obvious what was being said? The next decade would provide a series of experimental variations that even included a great deal of untranslated Spanish, but that proved uncommercial, see **Santa Fe Trail**: [1443]. Eventually it became apparent that there was little substitute for the broken English interspersed with the most common of translatable phrases. Although the Production Code office, as well as all other censorial agencies, self appointed or legislated by various cities and states, required Spanish translations of the Spanish used in the scripts, the main purpose for this was to prevent the use of profanity, or lewd or lascivious remarks. If the Production Code office felt that the characterization would hurt the product's sale potential in the Latin market, offensive remarks would be censored. The translated lyrics to Spanish songs were also required and this film was the first of many to included the familiar refrain to Villa's marching song: "La Cucaracha", "The cockroach, the cockroach, he can't walk anymore / Because he has not any marijuana." Before the decade was over, the PCA would not allow the words to the song to be sung or spoken in either Spanish or English.] **V**:1.1.30, Script: **The Señor Americano**, NYSAA, 15pages, 3pages of Spanish translation.

[1356] **THE SHADY LADY**, Pathe: [The first talker set in Cuba sent a New York reporter to Havana looking for the gunrunners that were supplying the Central American rebels with arms. The trouble came because there were rival gangs vying for the lucrative trade, rebels there were always looking to purchase arms to foment another meaningless revolution, and they were forced to buy from the United States because Hollywood would not provide them with another distributor. While in Havana, our hero was vamped by "a knockout blonde," a lady from the rival gang who was to do him dirty, but ended up enjoying his Anglo charms so much, she joined forces with him. Having overcome all obstacles, and after he exposed the gangs and cleared the lady's name, they sailed for the real big city up north to be married, never mind that honeymoon in Havana stuff, they were heading for the gud ole U S of A.] **V**:3.27.29.

[1357] **THE SHOW OF SHOWS**, W/FN, [Two of Hollywood's most successful production companies chose precisely the same path to walk almost all of their major stars onto the silver screen to show the viewing public just how well they could all talk and sing and take advantage of the newest technological advance the movies had made. Both created segmented musical reviews. This was Warner's production, **Paramount on Parade** **[1404]**, was the other. Almost the entire Warner Brother's lot found themselves in this really big show including some of their newly acquired Hispanic stars. Paramount had a few of their top stars in their Spanish Language version speaking a few words of Spanish, but not so in this Warner extravaganza. What this gala musical did feature was a Hispanic production number, one that so caught the attention of the Mexican government that they protested its insulting implications. Remembering now that this was basically a musical, and its purpose was to spread good will, the writers put together a little sequence for Douglas Fairbanks and friends which was supposed to be a satire of the times around 1900. It's highlight was a line em up against the wall "Execution Number, laid in the badlands of Mexico" which also included western star, Monte Blue, and some of the screen's "leading heavies, headed by Noah Beery" as Mexican bandits. Had the Academy given an Oscar lack of tact and good taste in promoting neighborly good will in 1929, these simple minded scribes certainly would have been nominated.] **V**:11.27.29, **NYT**:11.21.29.

[1358] **THE SINGING FOOL**, W: [In the summer of 1929 **El Universal**, one of the leading Mexico City dailies, attempted to start a campaign against Hollywood's talking films. A front page editorial labeled "For The National Language" was really an open letter to President Portes Gil asking to prohibit the exhibition of talking films with dialogue in English. It claimed the showing of English speaking films [would] damage the Spanish language and [would] tend to make it disappear in the future." They professed to be in favor of "Dialogue" films, but objected to the use of English in Mexico. They were in effect advocating Spanish language versions of such films or over dubbing with Spanish dialogue in place. Hollywood would try both techniques as experiments throughout the thirties. As would usually be the case when a film was publicly protested, it enjoyed a significant amount of extra publicity. Although the paper objected to the English, they made no reference to the songs sung by Al Jolson. Of course "**Sonny Boy**", was the big one, but the other was entitled, "**The Spaniard Who Blighted My Life**". **V**:9.26.28. Responding to the problem Joseph M. Schenck of United Artist entered into negotiations "with a Spanish playwright, name unrevealed, to supervise those [dubbed] in the Hispanic tongue." Although dubbing would become more seriously considered and used in the fifties, most of the studios opted to make Spanish versions at this time,] **"Screen Credit for Dubbed Foreign Voices by UA"**, **V**, 11.27.29. See also: **"Must Talkies Stay at Home?"**, **Literary Digest**, 12.29.30. p21.

[1359] **THE SQUALL**, FN: [Advertized as "all dialogue", Myrna Loy played "Giggles" a gypsy who vamped all the males in the script. The reviewer felt that her "overconfidence" as to "her gypsy sex prowess" was likely the fault of the writer. He concludes "Nubi as a gypsy was a gyp out for jewelry, etc.

[and] probably the queen of the dirty skinned gold diggers."]
V:5.15.29.

[1360] **STARK MAD**, W: [Not all Hollywood film titles offer a good indication of a particular product's content, but this one could not have been named any better. Not only did it properly indicated the content of the film, it may have given some slight insight as to the mental balance of the scripter. The action for this movie took place either on the Venezuelan or Central American coast. Being charitable and assuming with a great deal of trepidation that the screen writer knew a little something about Meso-America, one might guess that the latter was the better bet. But for the **Variety** reviewer it was, "a yacht at anchor off the Caracas Jungle in South America," which speaks for itself, the capital of Venezuela being a few thousand feet high and inland thirty miles from the coast. The script tells one nothing of the location. Where ever it was, the place enjoyed the grace of a Mayan temple. The idea of the story is more simple. James Rutherford has organized an expedition to go to the "jungles of Central America" to look for his missing son. Bob has not been heard from for more than a year, and apparently someone must have thought it was time to start looking. On the way there the party encounters a Professor Dangerfield who is travelling with a raving maniac driven to that condition by his jungle experience which is not elaborated upon. Pressing on to their anchorage, they decide to go ashore and spend their first evening in the Mayan temple. Events moved very quickly then. Bob's fiancee disappears, they discover a very large gorilla chained to the floor of the temple, the captain of the yacht is kidnapped away by some giant beast of imprecise zoological origin sporting a lot of hair and huge claws or talons, messages warning of impending doom are found, one of the explorers in the party is killed by a mysterious arrow and all thorough out, the maniac has continued raving incomprehensible gibberish. Talk about **The Curse of the Mayan Temple** 1977, that jungle was an unreal nightmare. When things look darkest, [just before the dawn] the raving maniac comes out of whatever fantasy land he had been inhabiting, only to discover that he has left the frying pan for the fire. But then he remembers all of the problems were the responsibility of some hermit who just wanted to be left alone in his temple. He had fed the explorer some kinda jungle juice to drive him mad and had also killed Bob. With the enemy in sight, the demented hermit is dispatched to the nether lands and all are saved. Remember Hollywood's conception of the Yucatan before you sign up for that discounted tour to visit the pyramids.]
V:6.3.29.

[1361] **UNTAMED**, MGM: [Although Hollywood knew very well what the tropics could to women, Joan Crawford as "Bingo" seemed to require little help from the heat when she sang the "Song of the Jungle." She had been raised in the uninhibited atmosphere of the steamy tropics by her father and when she inherited all the dollars she went after the man she wanted. Having been brought to New York by her guardian in hopes of civilizing her, the task proves to be much more difficult than first thought. Apparently you could take the girl out of the jungle, but it was impossible to take the jungle out of the girl. In time she acquired some culture and savoir fair, but preferred to take her new love back to South America where life and love were more free and unrestrained [816].] **V**:12.4.29.

[1362] **WEST OF THE ROCKIES**, Charles David Productions: [Looking for rustlers Bob finds love instead in the presence of the lovely Celia de la Costa, she is played by an Angloress, but her friend, Rosita was Inez Gomez who likes Pedro, played by Antone Sanchez. All other characters were Anglos including Juan Escobar, the prime suspect for being the cow thief. After a lot of stuff, it turns out that the most natural suspect was the guilty party, but Bob was allowed to make the relationship with Celia more permanent even if his father did not trust the Spanish.]

[1363] **WHERE EAST IS EAST**, MGM: [In this silent entry Lon Chaney was somewhere in Indo China along with Lupe Velez, "in form revealing costumes." There she learned the real meaning of vamping from her on screen mom, Estelle Taylor. Mother and daughter were forced to fight love duel for Lupe's beau, which the latter wins. "By some ingenious trick of make up [Lupe's] eyes are shaped almond Chinese-fashion ... Theda Bara stuff brought up to date." Her eyes might have been orientalized, but the rest of her remained pure Latin temptress.] **V**:5.29.29.

[1364] **THE WITCHING EYE**, Ernest Stern: [Voodoo worked real well in Haiti, but in the north there could be problems. Val Napolo was a Haitian with an evil eye who possessed the secrets of that deadly mystical power. Cortex, his friend tells him that with such gifts he could do real well in the United States. Persuaded that this was true, Val heads for that Christian stronghold where demonstrating his magical ability he quickly develops a large group of followers. All seems well until Val meets Sylvia who he immediately wants for his own, but she belongs to a simple poet named Ralph, and will have nothing to do with him. Using his powers he breaks up the relationship, but Ralph employs the stronger power of love to defeat and discredit the voodoo priest.] **afic**.

[1365] **WITH CAR AND CAMERA AROUND THE WORLD**, Aloha and Walter Wanderwell: [Well named for such a journey this couple certainly lived what many must have considered a wondrous experience. They took seven years to circumnavigate the globe taking their trusty Filmo along with them every where the went, which for our purposes included time and film spent in Cuba, Portugal, Spain, and a side trip to PickFair to visit friends. Also included in their epic journey was the Caribbean hurricane of 1926 shot while in Cuba which may have been a first even for professionals, that is, shooting such a storm before, during and after, there was no weather channel at that time, they just happened to be there. The tens of thousands of feet of film they exposed was cut into some six reels [5500 feet] and was shown in first line houses to rave reviews.] **V**:12.25.29.

[1366] **WOLF SONG**, P: [This film was billed as Paramount's first "musical film romance," sound had arrived and Hispanic characterizations took on a new dimension, the actors were forced by the writers to speak like everyone expected Hispanics too, in their best broken English. Destined to be a major contributor to this enshrined sound stereotype the female lead, Lupe Velez, was never scripted to speak in any other manner. Her added "fiery nature" would later have her billed as the "Mexican Spitfire", but in this film she played opposite a real long drink of water, Gary Cooper. As some may have said before, he was knocked for a loop over Lupe, he married her. She loved him, "Yo te Amo" was frequently heard, usually in song, and translated for the audience. It was also noted that it was, "an old Spanish custom for the characters to sing at each other with guitar accompaniment at the slightest provocation." This was intended to explain to audiences that may have wondered, why Cooper was forever carrying one around. Though loved, the young swain deserted his bride and experienced a number of adventures with indians in the 1840 time frame before the two were reunited in the final reel. Lupe Velez, until her tragic suicide in the forties, an affair of the romantic's broken heart, remained one of the two most influential of female Mexican stars, although she, more than Del Rio, was rarely cast out of the Hispanic mold scripters had fitted her into.] **V**:2.27.29.

1930

[1367] **AFTER MANY YEARS**, Metro/Goldwyn: [This film is significant in that it is the first to move the drug traffic from the Mexican border down to the South American mainland. The action involves the son of a murdered policeman who while searching for the reasons his father was murdered, uncovers the killers and the drug smuggling operation.] **MPG**.

[1368] **ALMA DE GAUCHO** aka **ALMA GAUCHA**, Chris Phillis Prods: [Spanish Language feature with a story by Benjamin Ingenito aka Paul Ellis. The scenario was really simple stuff. On a Buenos Aires golf course, Antonio retrieves Elsa's golf ball. When she flashed those eyes, the suave gaucho surrendered. Later he overhears her tell friends that she was simply trifling with his affections, so he abducts her to sooth his hurt feelings. He then decides to leave the country but is prevented from doing so at dock side, by this plaintiff little voice calling his name and expressing true love for him. That was about it. The cast included: Manuel Granada, Monna Rico, Francisco Amerise, Christina Montt, Humberto Bonavi, and George Rigas.] These Spanish language versions generated an interesting series of enterprising side affects. Apparently so many of the Latin American, or Spanish speaking consular offices besieged the Hollywood production companies seeking employment as "advisory experts" at "fat fees" that the producers sought help from Will Hays to help solve the problem. **"Consular Agents Want Hollywood Film Jobs ..."**, **V**:5.14.30. Even the exiled leader of the revolution against Obregon, who claimed to have been president of Mexico, took a position with the studios as an advisor for some of these productions. **"Huerta Now Spanish Supervisor For Pics"**, **V**:5.21.30. This was not the President Huerta in power in 1914 when the United States took the port of Vera Cruz.]

[1369] **AMOR AUDAZ** SV **SLIGHTLY SCARLET**, P: [A simple story of two jewel thieves and a lovely lady who provides redemption for one of the nice baddies. Paramount used Adolphe Menjou in this Spanish language production and had him speaking a few Spanish phrases, in hopes that one of their top attractions would increase this film's box office take. The Hispanics in the cast were: Rosita Moreno, Ramon Pereda, Carmen Guerrero, Carlos Villarias, and Vicente Padula. Guess who ended up with the alluring Rosita.] English review, **V**:3.5.30.

[1370] **THE ARIZONA KID**, F: [Heavily promoted by Fox as the further adventures of the Cisco Kid, this time he was called "Arizona" and was hiding out further north in Utah, where he had his own little gold mine. He also had two ladies, the recent Mexican import, Mona Maris as Lorita, that he abandoned and the Anglo vamp, Carol Lombard, that he was willing to sell his soul for. When it was discovered that she was merely after his mine, Lorita began to look a lot better. In this adventure Arizona was graced with a "smooth Spanish accent" but audiences had difficulty understanding his Mexican girl friend and some of the other characters. Although this film was nominated by the Academy, it was simply an inferior sequel to **In Old Arizona** [1338]. It grossed very well at the box office and ensured that Cisco and later friends, would enjoy a long ride across the silver screen even though they might never quite master that "ingleesh" talk.] **V**:5.21.30, **NYT**: 3.17.30, FD:5.18.30, afic.

[1371] **ASI ES LA VIDA SV WHAT A MAN**, Sono Art - World Wide: [Based on a novel by David Belasco, the cast included: Jose Bohr, Lolita Vendrell, Delia Magana, Enrique Acosta, Cesar Vanoni, Julian Rivero, and Marcela Nivon. Of these players, only Julian Rivero would make a permanent transition to English productions, with his own particular pronunciations of that language.]

[1372] **THE BAD MAN**, FN. [This Bad Man would just not go away. He brought too much "coin", as Hollywood liked to say, into theater cash registers and producer's pockets. As much as the 1923 **[962]** audiences loved the "jolly bandit who was a law unto himself ... about the Rio Grande," they liked even better Walter Houston "in make up featured by plastered hair, black mustache and darkened face", "a swaggering, gleaming-toothed, flashing-eyed Pancho Lopez the Robin Hood of the border. Reviewers especially enjoyed his most enduring quality: "He speaks his lines in broken English tinged with a strong flavor of Spanish, which is done without a single slip and is distinctly humorous." Lopez on progress in Mexican law and order: "Oh, but Mexico ees no good place for me no more--ees too civilize. Everywhere is law and order. Soldiers, policemen, they hunt me like blazes and when they find ... one - two - time.... Lopez is not more dead like he pretend. They chase me out of Mexico ... [swish] ... like that. Then no go back. Ees much better United States." Women were responsible for his being a bandit: "Firs' time - I fight for wooman ... ever seence, I fight over wooman, run away from wooman ... run after wooman ... wan wooman, I lose to race track man in Mexico - it's too bad! I still 'ave to kill heem -- las' wooman run away with bes' frand - I fix that last night myself ... personale! Now I 'ave no wooman ... sometimes ess lonely!" And the **Motion Picture Guide** wondered why this film, characterized as the worst made that year was so popular. It would be remade using a Chinese bandit in 1937 [**West of Shanghai**] and again in 1941, with Wallace Beery immortalizing, the 'best damn caballero in Mehico." Casting the film proved to be no problem as the **Film Spectator** reported: "Hundreds of handsome, swarthy Mexicans" were undergoing tests for ... the **Bad Man**, and "how they fight among themselves" for the honor of playing even the smallest role. It would seem that some Hispanics then found the material less offensive than losing the opportunity to be discovered in films. The film was so popular that a Spanish Language production of this movie was produced in the same year, but with a rewritten script, **El Hombre Malo** [1412].] **EHW**:10.4.30, pp29-30, **V**:10.1.30, **FD**:9.28.30, **NYT**:9.27.30, **The**

Film Spectator, 4.26.30, p22, MPG. Script: The Bad Man, NYSAA: Reel Two, Page Two, 85 pages.

[1373] THE BAD ONE, UA: [Two established Hispanic stars were featured in this French bawdy house production where Dolores Del Rio, Lita, who speaks the right words for the first time on screen, and says "no" to many of the patrons. Don Alvarado, the Spaniard, is one of those who hears the refusal and is angered by it to the point of implicating the Anglo Lita loves in lots of trouble. He has him sentenced to France's favorite rehabilitation center, Devils Island. Lita follows and attempts to give herself to the treacherous head guard to have her man saved, but her Anglo manages to save her from a fate worse than. It seems that the writer gave him the lead role in quelling a prison uprising and for this he is cleared of all charges. Life in film was simpler then.] V:6.18.30, NYT:6.13.30, FD:5.18.30.

[1374] EL BARBERO DE NAPOLEON SV NAPOLEON'S BARBER, F: [This Fox featurette, focused on an anarchist barber's satiric conversation with the little emperor who runs madly from his shop shouting that he can stand a bad barber and revolution, but he can not tolerate bad poetry. The Hispanic cast included: Juan Aristi Eulate, Manuel Paris, and Nellie Fernandez. John Ford directed the English version.]

[1375] BEAU BANDIT, Indy: [Rod La Rocque as Montero, played yet another loveable bandit from south of the border who had difficulty speaking English in this tale of romance on the range, made possible by still another Mexican Robin Hood. The fact that he is a wanted hombre with a price on his head merely makes life more alive for him. For once, the desperado has no lecherous designs, but merely a platonic admiration for the adorable Anglo angel. She has it bad for a poor dirt farmer that is about to be foreclosed on by the Anglo banker, the real villain in the piece. [A little depression influence.] When he offers Montero $1250 to get rid of the farmer, cupid's little bandit tells the capitalist that he will not kill him, the banker, for $5000. The "killer" is merely having his little joke. After he had taken the money, he leaves no trace of the evil miser and with warmth in his dirty little bandit heart, gives it to the loving couple. A good days work for the Hollywood Mehicano. An indication that some critics were becoming a bit tired with the number of these characters Hollywood was turning out was furnished by Mordaunt Hall, one of two successive New York Times film critics, who had little bits of stuffed shirts in their turtle necks: "La Rocque does his best through charm and a carefully distorted accent to make his role sympathetic, although the ease with which he outwits the minions of the law becomes a bit annoying as the film wears on." This might be considered an early request for tougher silver screen judges in hopes of keeping that element off the range. If it was, it proved quite unsuccessful.] NYT:6.14.30. AMC.

[1376] BEYOND THE RIO GRANDE, Biltmore: [If the Mexican western could not be at least as good as the above, actually any horse opry at all, **Variety** seemed to enjoy bashing it: "Production sloppy", "story weak," "no commercial b. o." "dialogue no help," "incredible yarn". Basically it was the story of another Anglo hero who singlehandedly over powered numerous opponents, many of which were Mexican.] **V**:5.28.30, **FD**:5.4.30, afic.

[1377] **THE BIG TRAIL**, F: [Considered by some critics "a noisy **Covered Wagon**," because it was a sound western, it serves to introduce a "juvenile lead" in his first million dollar production. Some said of him that he was "inexperienced" but "shows he can be built up." John Wayne would star with more Hispanic sidekicks, friends, enemies and lesser types than any other top western star in Hollywood lending the weight of his ever increasing stature to those characterizations, both good and bad. This film includes a minor player named, Lopez, an outrider scout for the train. See: **Horizontes Nuevos**, [1507.] **V**:10.29.30.

[1378] **BILLY THE KID**, MGM: [This film is notable as the first sound Hollywood dramatization of the William Bonny myth, who was to some familiar with his history, a paranoid psychopath that followed Horace Greeley's instruction, left Brooklyn for the wide open spaces and made a few of his own in a number of western types. Almost all subsequent retellings of the tale, especially the latest version, **The Young Guns**, [hopefully they'll stop at two], have significant Hispanic characterizations, usually a female friend of the early serial killer is cast as a willing Hispanic señorita of dubious character, with at least a very big heart. In most of the remakes Mexico will provide Billy with a place to hide. This early piece launched the career of Johnny Mack Brown and included only a minor character named, Santiago, played by the Mexican Cris Pin Martin.] **EHW**:10.25.30, p41, 12.13.30, p43, **V**:10.22.30, **FD**:10.19.30, **NYT**:10.18.30.

[1379] **BORDER LEGION**, P: [This version of the Zane Grey novel, using some stock footage from the 1924 edition, was set in Idaho and starred Fay Wray as the female lead. Basically a story of love's sacrifice, it differed significantly from the earlier film [1023]. Two more versions would be made in 1938 and 1940 which both utilized undercover rangers joining up with the bad guys across the border to eventually bring them to justice on this side of the Rio Grande.] **V**:7.2.30, **NYT**:6.30.30, **FD**:6.29.30. Script, **Border Legion**, NYSAA.

[1380] **BORDER ROMANCE**, Tiffany: [The newest of the Mexican imports, Armida, soon found herself in demand for these Mexican westerns. In this production she played a "dainty little Mexican maiden", Conchita Cortez. More musically inclined than her sister señoritas, she did a lot of singing for her "Americano" on the run as they hid out from the federalies in her little hacienda. In disguise as a caballero, the Anglo hero sings her favorite refrain, which immediately wins her heart and induces the lovely señorita to go to the fiesta with him. There the Anglo has to kill a big Mexican feller who objected to his dancing with Conchita, but all was not so grim. There were touches of humor in this film, one of which involved "Ladies day" at the river and six or so semi nude ladies who make a bit of a fuss over nothing. But in another scene, a very aggressive Mexican women, who desires some immediate affection from her unresponsive señor, gives him a very difficult time. The screen's Mexican woman were not frequently allowed such latitude with their men, it was all right for them to be strong and selfsacrificing, but they were required to be obedient. In the final scene, the Anglo hero and Armida hold off the rustlers until the troops arrive in a typical Hollywood finish.] **V**:5.28.30, **FD**:5.25.30, **NYT**:5.26.30, afic.

[1381] **BRIGHT LIGHTS**, FN: [When Louanne, a sparkling Broadway star, gives the reporters an interview detailing her struggle to stardom, she begins her tale in Kohinoor, Africa, where in that desolate place, she had been a cafe dancer entertaining local scum. Stranded in that out post of civilization, she had been forced to endure the advances of Miguel Parada, a Portuguese smuggler who would not let her alone, but from whom she was able to keep her most precious possession. Escaping with her virtue and a small traveling carnival she had managed to make it back to the land of free where she started her meteoric rise to the top. All were impressed, but none could possible know that waiting, more like lurking in her dressing room was that same Miguel, still desirous of making what he now considered his most important conquest. Luckily for the little lady, her Anglo protector was at her side and after a bit of trouble, he did the blaggard in for the last time ensuring that the show would go on.]

[1382] **THE CABALLERO**, MGM: [With the South American market for North Americans films firmly established, some of the production companies wanting to increase their market share, produced films specifically aimed in that direction, but which could also be shown in the home market. **Caballero** was one such effort, not a Spanish language film, it was produced in both English and Spanish and featured a musical score specifically written for it by the renowned Anton Rubenstein. The scenario was incidental to the production numbers, but provided audiences on both sides of the border sufficient smiles to make it successful. Benny Rubin played a tailor who decides to try the hazards of bullfighting to win the heart of a Spanish señorita. Rubenstein's musical score was one of the first to be brought "to the audible screen." Gino Corrado, and Conchita Montenegro were also featured in the cast.] **Mexicana**, Scrapbook, LCFL. **Exhibitors Daily Reviews**, 10.17.30.

[1383] **CALL OF THE FLESH**, MGM: [Roman Navarro starred as Juan, in this romantic musical, critics called his performance, "flawless." Romantic that he was, he falls in love with a convent girl, and tries to woo her out of her habit. Apparently responding to the call of the flesh or at least his advances, she leaves the cloister for the real world and they spend a lot of screen time singing songs together. All of the characters were Hispanic, but Navarro was the only Mexican. One of the production numbers involved an attempt to create a new dance craze called "La Rumbarita." It was fun for the on screen dancers, but never made it big in the local dance halls.] **V**:9.17.30, **FD**:9.14.30, **NYT**:9.13.30.

[1384] **LAS CAMPANAS DE CAPISTRANO**, Leon de la Mothe: [A Spanish language production based on the director's own life story. The cast included: Cora Montez, Luis de Ibarguren, Ricardo Bell Jr., Carmen LaRoux, Roberto Saa Silva, Ignacio Sotomayor, Salvador Villasenor, Ernesto Zambrano, and Elias Guevara.]

[1385] **THE CANYON OF MISSING MEN**, Syndicate Pictures: [Just another western in which the Anglo hero falls for a pretty Inez Sepulveda [Sheila LeGay] daughter of rich rancho owner, Juan Sepulveda. The padre does not object to the union in this one.]

[1386] **LA CARTA** SV **THE LETTER**, P, Joinville: [This steamy Spanish version of Somerset Maugham's novel includes scenes set in a Shanghai whore house where a good hearted white naughty lady is in charge of the sleazy place. But the focus of this film centers about the courtroom, in which Carmen Larrabeiti in the lead as the not so very bad lady who shot her unfaithful lover, is on trial. Included in Hispanic cast were: Carlos Diaz de Mendoza, Luis Pena, and Cecilio Rodriquez de la Vega.] **V**:3.19.29.

[1387] **CASCARRABIAS** = **GRUMPY**, P: [The transition to sound created a series of technical problems that were quickly over come by the vast fund of intellectual resources the industry in Hollywood had to offer. But some of the other complications created by such films were not so easily dispatched, one of the most difficult to deal with was language. With the foreign market, especially south of the border and in Spain, increasing in importance yearly, Hollywood had to respond. One such response was producing a Spanish language version of an already issued film. Many studios worked with this concept before it was completely abandoned by the decades end, but Paramount and Warners gave it a real try. This attempt was headed the Spain's leading actor Ernesto Vilches, playing one of New York's upper class rich, a member of the social set who sported a rather large diamond stick pin. **Variety** thought his performance solid and praised the remainder of the cast: "as strong a Spanish combination as has yet been seen on the local screen." Betraying more than a strong bias for Castilian Spanish, this trade journal was not a little condescending about the Spanish spoken south of the border: "Local audiences have been quick to respond to what constitutes a laudable effort on behalf of Spanish-American people. Little by little, American producers are learning to avoid the pitfall into which they fell when making their initial foreign versions.. We must be thankful that Mexicans and Central Americans no longer offend our ears, however lucid their offerings may be in their own countries." Clearly this critic considered Spanish spoken in this hemisphere an inferior product. The cast included: Carmen Guerrero, Barry Norton (Alfredo Biraben), Delia Magna, Andres de Segurola, and Juan

Duval.] **V**:10.22.30, **NYT**:10.30.30. Advocates of South American Spanish were quick to respond pointing out that "some 85,000,000 Spanish-speaking people [would] take about 90 percent of future [film] output, it would be poor business to offend their ears for the sake of a standard [Castilian Spanish] imposed upon the producers by "improvised purists of the language from Hollywood." **Variety**, not withstanding, south of the border Latins, wanted to have screen Spanish spoken their way. **NYT**:5.25.30, **Commonwealth**:8.13.30, p386. See also: **Sombras de Gloria**: [1450].

[1388] **CHARROS, GAUCHOS Y MANOLAS**, Hollywood Spanish Picture Co: [This musical review featuring some of the best Latin talent then available was written, produced and directed by Xavier Cugat. The cast included: Maria Alba, Martin Garralaga, Delia Magana, Carlos Gomez, Paul Ellis, and Vicente Padula.]

[1389] **COCK O' THE WALK**, Sono-Art World Wide: [**Variety** had a definite view about the North American character, especially as it related to matters of sex and marital relations. In some instances, it was almost naive, a longing for social graces that may very well have only survived in fond remembrances of a past that never really existed, or did so only in romantic perceptions or the imagination of how interpersonal relationships were or should have been. Or maybe their scribes simply were not overly fond of the 19th amendment and the new freedom women enjoyed in the decade of the twenties. They certainly felt that there was a difference between what has been called in these pages, "continental morality" [1199, 1228] and that which they considered most North Americans subscribed to. The reviewer thought this film exhibited "a vaguely disquieting foreign flavor" and that "American audiences" would not make a success of it. The hero, in a day when all films had to have one, unless it was a documentary, and at a time when no one had heard the term "antihero", was perceived as "a bizarre character that came from abroad ... an out and out gigolo candidly living off foolish women [he was the] masculine side of sweet scented romance." It seemed to move film in a new direction, a "revolt by certain over-pictured film makers against what they regard[ed] as sugary sentimental romance formulas." That might have been ok of itself, but the "cynical attitude toward romance here revealed [was] strictly Continental." Apparently speaking for the nation, the reviewer postulated: "Americans don't understand it and it offends them." One wonders how extensive his survey might have been. The film did very well throughout the country.

The main character in this apparently revolutionary new outlook was a gigolo named, Carlos, what else. He played violin in a cafe where women came in and apparently crawled at his feet and begged him to take their money, money that their foolish husbands had earned for them. He did. In the course of some fifty minutes he enjoys the favors of four or five such females, caused one to commit suicide, but not before she has insured herself and named him the beneficiary. He does manage to save another, but by purely accidental means, it had not been his intention. Narita, played by Myrna Loy, was going to kill herself because of her brutal husband, but Carlos takes her home as his house pet, she seemed to purr a lot after that. He was fond of her, but tells her that if she's really set on killing herself that she should take out a little insurance first, wait a while until it went into effect and then do as she pleases. Suicide was a very personal thing. In the meanwhile, Narita's husband shows up and starts to beat her. Surprisingly, Carlos prevents the brute from hurting her and ends up killing him for which he goes to jail. There he learns that the señorita was out earning the pesos for his defense. Knowing what that entailed, he breaks out and stops her from doing so, explaining that absence has made his heart grow fonder, and that he now loves her. It was all too much for the trade journal, and understandable only because it had happened among Hispanics.] **V**:4.16, 30, **NYT**:4.12.30.

[1390] **THE CUCKOOS**, Radio: [Basically a comedy with a continuing story line in which two tramps pose as various characters and win ladies in the final reel. The film was made up of a series of black-outs which include a bit where one of the male leads dresses in drag to attract a large group of apparently excited, but dumb Mexican toughs who are lured into a room where the other character hits them on the head from behind a curtain. Critics thought it a was howl and so did audiences.] **V**:4.30.30, **FD**:4.30.30, **NYT**:4.26.30.

[1391] **EL CUERPO DEL DELITO** SV **THE BENSON MURDER CASE**, P: [In this Spanish language version of the popular Van Dine mystery, Ramon Pereda played the popular Philo Vance, in the role made famous by William Powell. Antonio Moreno was the foil, Maria Alba, the mysterious lady. The other Hispanics in the cast were: Barry Norton (Alfredo Biraben), Andres de Segurola, Martia Calvo, Carlos Villarias and Vicente Padula.] **V**:4.16.30.

[1392] **DANGEROUS PARADISE**, [This adaptation of a bit of Joseph Conrads's novel, **Victory**, was well received. Although the action takes place in the South Seas, the two most malevolent characters in the story are Hispanics of undetermined nationality employed by both the novelist and the screen writer to do their dirty work. Pedro was depicted as an "addle-brained strong man who stands threateningly" in corners showing off his enormous biceps and listening to his mentor, Ricardo, graced with black mustache and thin lips, tell frightened individuals that he can have the brute "crush the life" out of their bodies. The two are seeking lots of gold they think is being hidden on the island. Interestingly enough, a Japanese servant, a friend of the hero, is responsible for making the nefarious pair wish they had never set foot on the island.] **NYT**:3.2.30, **V**:2.19.30.

[1393] **DEL MISMO BARRO** SV **THE COMMON CLAY**, F: [This Hispanic version of romance gone wrong, which forces the ruined girl to go out on her own and defy the world, was somewhat more spicy than the one Constance Bennett starred in. Mona Maris led this mainly Mexican cast which included: Juan Torena, Luana Alcaniz, Rene Cardona, Carlos Villarias, Vicente Padula, Roberto Guzman and Maria Calvo.] English review: **V**:8.6.30.

[1394] **DERELICT**, Paramount-Publix: [Two seamen develop an interest in the same cafe singer that they see performing in Havana, Cuba. She likes them both but one of the officers offers to take her to Rio and she accepts. When he is made Captain on a different ship, he heartlessly tells her to forget it. Quite angry, she turns to the other and he sneaks her on ship. A lot of complications follow including a ship collision in the fog near Rio, a tropical storm at sea and a final reuniting of the lovers. There are identification shots used of both Havana and Rio.] **NYT**:11.22.30.

[1395] **A DEVIL WITH WOMEN**, F: [Victor Mclaglen finds himself in this film a big deal in some small mythical Central/South American country where the women flock to the big Anglo/Irish clod like files to punch drunk cabbage. The created locale for these amorous adventures provides us with what Hollywood considered to be the typical south of the border Banana Republic setting: There, the ladies were looser than in a wet dream fantasy, the bandits were bad bad revolutionaries, the army completely incompetent and the dictator, a drunk dummy. On the other hand, the gun runner was the lovely Mona Maris as, Rosita Fernandez. When the former big boxer comes into this pastoral tropical setting, he immediately gets himself mixed up with the nephew of the nation's richest man, and in silver screen Central America, that meant really rich! The confused complexities of Hollywood's Hispanic revolutionary intrigue, interspiced with the more important competition for the sexy señorita take it from there. Humphrey Bogart, in his first major part, was a stands out as the rich nephew rival to the soldier of fortune, Mclaglen. Other Hispanics were used in this unintentional attempt at poking a just little fun at our Latin friends: Luana Alcaniz, Soledad Jiminez, Mona Rico and Joe De La Cruz.] **EHW**:11.1.30, **V**:10.22.30, **NYT**:10.20.30.

[1396] **EL DIOS DEL MAR SV THE SEA GOD**, MGM: [Rosita Moreno was one of the real Mexican beauties given an opportunity to display her talents when the studios attempted to make Spanish versions of existing Hollywood films. In this piece she took Fay Wray's part as the lovely sought after by two rival leaders, Ramon Pereda and Julio Villarreal who lived on an island filled with savages. Others included were: Manuel Arbo, Jose Pena "Pepet", and Movita Castaneda, who in a while, would find her way into other Hollywood productions as an English speaking Hispanic.] English review, **V**:9.10.30.

[1397] **DONA MENTRIAS SV THE LADY LIES**, P: [Carmen Larrabeiti played Claudette Colberts part in this Spanish version made in Joinville, France. A wealthy, widowed attorney, has to deal with the domestic complications provided by his two children. Everything turns out well when it is discovered that the lady did not lie. The Hispanics in the cast included: Carmen Ruiz Moragas, Julio Pena, and Carmelita P. Garcia.] **V**:9.11.29.

[1398] **EAST IS WEST**, U: [Hollywood's stereotypes more often than not assumed that all people looked alike except for white Anglo Saxon Christians. In **Patria** [699] Mexicans passed for Japanese and the Japanese for Mexicans. For Hollywood the best of these cross cultural interchanges occurred with beautiful Mexican girls who easily could pass for Chinese. In this madness the lovely Lupe Velez became the "Chinese daughter of a hunky whose pride [was] pigs." **Variety** praised the choice: "Ming Toy as done by Lupe Velez is a prodigy." "She looks Chinese." In Hollywood's image factory, any nationality was subject to creation. Lupe played the same sexy role in the Spanish version, **Oriente Y Occidente**, [1431]. **V**:11.5.30, **NYT**:11.1.30

[1399] **THE EBONY SHRINE** [**VAGABOND ADVENTURE SERIES**], Pathe: [Possibly prompted by recent work which had uncovered new marvels of the ancient Mayan world, Tom Terris took his cameras to Guatemala to film the wonders, "temples, palaces and market places." It "featured people, buildings and manners totally unfamiliar to the inhabitants of North America." Audiences were promised the fascinating "majesty of ancient and crumbling temples which date from the day of Cortez, the explorer of Spain's great age of discovery." Assuming that the commentary was a bit more accurate in its description than the advertising, the film was certainly valuable in showing most North Americans who did not receive the **National Geographic Magazine** their first views of the fantastic discoveries made somewhat earlier at Tikal.] **EHW**:11.1.30, p42.

[1400] **EN NOMBRE DE LA AMISTAD** SV **FRIENDSHIP**, F: [The cast included Luana Alcaniz, Andres de Segurola, Ralph Navarro, and Manuel Paris.]

[1401] **ESTRELLADOS**, SV **FREE AND EASY**, MGM: [This Buster Keaton vehicle was also poorly made into a French version which so displeased the Parisian audience that the riot they started in the theater required the police to quell it. The Spanish version utilized clips from the original with an additional Hispanic cast. The story line had Buster breaking up a number of in production sets and completely disrupting the MGM shooting schedule. Lionel Barrymore and Cecil B. De Mille were specially targeted in this slap stick comedy. The Hispanic players included: Raquel Torres, Don Alvarado, Maria Calvo, Juan de Homs, Carlos Villarias, Emile Chautard, and Enrique Acosta. Aside from the Anglo stars, Fred Niblo, was the only entry from the English version. In that version, Trixie Friganza appeared as the mother and foil for the popular comedian.] **V**:4.23.30, 1.28.31.

[1402] **FIGHTING LEGION**, U: [Continuing in the proud tradition of so many others who had gone before him, Ken Maynard played a Texas Ranger keeping the peace on the Mexican border.] **V**:4.9.30, **FD**:3.16.30.

[1403] **LA FUERZA DEL QUERER** SV **THE BIG FIGHT**, James Cruze: [Spanish language film based on the play by David Belasco and

Sam H. Harris. The cast included: Maria Alba, Andres de Segurola, Carlos Barbe, Vicente Padula, Tito Davison, Manuel Conesa and Rafael Valverde.]

[1404] **GALAS DE LA PARAMOUNT** SV **PARAMOUNT ON PARAMOUNT**, P: [Very much like Warner Brother's **Show of Shows** [1357], this Spanish language musical spectacular was devised to show off all of Paramount's star attractions. It featured all of the original cast including the studios more recent Hispanic additions: La Argentina, Ernesto Vilches, Juan Pulido, Rosita Moreno. Jeanette MacDonald, Barry Norton (Alfredo Biraben) and Ramon Pereda acted as masters of ceremony. Eduardo D. Venturini directed the Spanish segments of this production in the United States. The French and other foreign versions were made at the studio in Joinville. For a complete list of the more than forty stars featured aside from the Hispanic cast, see the **Variety** review.] **V**:4.23.30, 12.24.30, **NYT**:4.21.30.

[1405] **GIRL OF THE GOLDEN WEST**, FN: [Ann Harding was Minnie in this talking remake of the David Belasco play first produced in 1904 and subsequently made into an operetta and then a silent film in 1923 [982]. Minnie runs the gambling house on the border and she loves a baddie. The trouble is that he likes her well enough to kiss her now and then, but his major squeeze is a señorita, a Mexican girl who lives in a town just to the south, where he has overnight permissions that make Minnie real mad. Angry maybe, but she loves her highway man and is willing to fight for his life after he has been captured. She does this in the only way she knows how by putting up stakes against his life and gambling with the sheriff. It was to be two out of the best three hands in poker, and in the final decisive play, she realizes that she must cheat to win. She does, and win her man's release. Border justice was funny that way sometimes, especially when Mexicans were involved.] **EXH**:11.1.30, p40, **V**:10.29.30, **NYT**:10.27.30, **FD**:10.26.30.

[1406] **THE GREAT DIVIDE**, FN: [Advertised as containing all dialogue, and with songs, reviewers were disappointed with the faked scenery and sets and generally panned this remake of the 1924 [1045] production set on the Mexican border. There is a fiesta scene in Mexico in which the Anglo star affects a Mexican accent while the strains of "Si Si Señor" are being sung. Myrna Loy as Manuella, also speaks in broken English, and plays the typical dancing chiquita enticing all the men, and especially the Anglo's. Nothing really new in this one, all those Mexicans girls loved that white skin. The leering Mexican present in the first issue, was not included.] **V**:2.19.30.

[1407] **GYPSY CODE**, Hollywood Pictures: [This nineteen minute short subject featured handsome "headliner" Roy D'Arcy and his very thin mustache designed by make up men to increase his Hispanic appearance. This brief piece was considered to be a "heavy drama, sometimes a little too heavy", but all right in the "not-too-particular neighborhoods." Roy was in character in this film playing the King of the gypsies who knocks out his friend's eyesight when he discovers him doing his wife. She is so afraid of having been discovered that she poisons herself which allows "the head of the tribe" to select another lovely señorita to be his queen. Life and love among Hispanic gypsies had it's own set of Hollywood assigned rules and procedures and those continued in force well into recent times.] **FD**:9.14.30.

[1408] **HELL HARBOR**, UA: [Hollywood's tropics were either heaven or hell. Either way, Anglos frequently found themselves in significant trouble when traveling south. One thing was for sure, it was always hot enough to affect ones personality and provoke behavior almost unknown in the cooler climes up north. This fantasy focused on swarthy men suffering the heat of a tropical island, forced to work a thankless job under an unforgiving sun that made white men sweat like pigs roasting on a spit. Even Anglo men could lose their humanity under such circumstances and Jean Hersholt as Joseph was one case in point. He had become so "odious that the very smell of him [could be] felt. His greasy, sweaty, sloppy-waisted shirt" became the mark of his Caribbean character. Of course it was a woman, well a woman in the tropics, the lovely Lupe Velez, object of his gone native desire, that had brought him to this low station and one that would in the end bring him to his final judgement. Apparently, this was not the place for another Club Med.] **V**:4.9.30.

[1409] **HELL'S HEROES**, U: [This was the first sound version of **Three Godfathers**. It included, Maria Alba as Carmelita, the typical cantina chiquita and Jose de la Cruz as Jose, a good hijo, but a Mexican.]

[1410] **HELL'S ISLAND**, C: [By a circuitous route, which first begins while he is fighting the Riff in the North African desert, a French Legionnaire finds himself, on his way to prison, convicted of insubordination and striking a superior officer. Men were real tough then. When his sentence is commuted to 10 years of hard labor, he knows he's heading for Devil's Island. His lady follows, sent by the scripter, to help effect his escape and with a friend who is shot in the process, they do, and in a "motor launch" no less.] **V**:7.23.30, **NYT**:7.19.30.

[1411] **HER MAN**, Pathe: [Ricardo Cortez and Helen Twelvetrees were Frankie and Johnny in a Havana water front cafe, he was her hombre, but he was also, being a Cuban, her pimp, and an expert knife thrower. To prove the point he delivers one of his lethal projectiles into an enemies back at the very start of the film, this quickly established his proficiency and his character. Satisfied with her life because she knows none better, the misused lady is amazed to discover that she can love a sailor who offers her a different kind of affection. This forces the two rivals to have a very realistically staged battle to determine who will keep the prize for his own. The struggle results in the death of Cortez. The reviewer for the **Exhibitors Herald** was very impressed with the

scene and the innovative way in Johnny was dispatched. At one
point in the fierce fight, Johnny throws a knife at the sailor
that misses him, but it was thrown with such force that, it
penetrated deeply through the door that it struck. Moments
later, when the boy hits the pimp right on the jaw with such
a force that it knocks him back, he falls against the blade
and stabs himself. It was that simple and reused once or twice
again to dispatch a despicable character.] **EHW**:10.4.30, p30.

[1412] **EL HOMBRE MALO**, SV **THE BAD MAN**,   FN: [The silents had
allowed Anglo actors to represent any of a wide variety of
foreign nationals by merely indicating with his title card,
that he was what ever Hollywood wanted him to be. Such an
actor obviously required no knowledge of that county's
language. When the first talkers arrived, they brought with
them a complex series of language related problems for the
industry's producers. As more and more theaters were wired
for sound, including those south of the border, producers
anxious about the affect this would have on foreign markets,
explored what they considered to be two possible solutions.
The concept of "dubbing" by employing either titles or
superimposed voices could be used, or a new film could be
remade using an entirely Spanish cast speaking Spanish with a
script adapted for the purpose. The possibilities seemed
boundless, but in reality they were severely limited by an
abysmal lack of information about the language, customs and
mores of almost all foreign nationals. As it came to be,
Hollywood conceived of Spanish as Spanish, without taking into
consideration various national or international differences.
Simply using a variety of Hispanic actors frequently caused
comic and insulting confusion among the cast itself. Latin
tempers flared. The results for the audience was serious
discomfort and even protest. More than a hundred Spanish
Language films were produced by Hollywood before the idea was
abandoned by all the major studios. By the end of the decade,
the idea was considered unworkable and unnecessary. In this
production, **El Hombre Malo** [1412], the problem was not so
acute, there were many Mexican actors that could be employed
and were. And in this case, the script was rewritten to make
the main character more palatable, more generous in his
intent, and without any unacceptable negative characteristics.
This script differs significantly from its English version,
The Bad Man [1372]. The fact that he, the 'anti-hero,' is
solely responsible for regaining the ranch, rejoining
starcrossed lovers and removing the undesirable husband so
that the two can begin life together, makes Pancho Lopez
"Saint Pancho Lopez, the protector of ruined ranchers, and a
bandit."   All he asks for his reward is that one of the
"little ones is named after [him], Panchito or Panchita." He
then takes his gang and leaves, honoring the eleventh
commandment: "Thou shalt not be in another's way." Producers
had to provide censors notarized copies of Spanish language
translation of the script before the film could be approved
for exhibition.] **"The Bad Man"** [**El Hombre Malo**], **NYSAA**: Reel
eight, p4, 43 pages.

[1413] **HOT TAMALE**, Pathe: [This "neat cartoon" provided audiences with an enjoyable "burlesque on the romantic films" which featured serenading señors and swooning señoritas. It opened in a little Spanish town where Alphonse Mouse was singing to his sweetie and strumming his guitar beneath her balcony. Invited into the house, she performs a tango to show her appreciation, but the hero's rival intercedes. After a lot of action, Alphonse vanquishes his tough rival and wins his little mousita for ever.] **FD**:8.10.30.

[1414] **LA INCORREGIBLE** SV **MANSLAUGHTER**, P, Joinville: [Enriqueta Serrano took Claudette Colbert's role in this Spanish language version. She was the accused, carelessly responsible for the death of a motorcycle policeman, who was prosecuted by the dedicated D A that just happened to be in love with her. In prison she interacts with her former maid and after she does her time she returns home. With a new outlook on the social graces, many of her snobby habits have changed and she is ready for a new life with the man who put her behind the bars. Only in Hollywood, even in its Spanish versions.] **V**:7.30.30.

[1415] **IN GAY MADRID**, MGM: [Metro may well have been considering this film as a possible Spanish language production, for the local and overseas market both, with the still considerable weight of Roman Navarro's name as the attraction, but it settled for what proved to be just another talker using lots of singing Spaniards. It would seem that characteristic of young Spanish lads, Ricardo liked to dally with the señoritas and little else. Dad wanted the boy to be a serious student, and sends him to university in provincial Santiago. Once there, his studies continue, but the subjects remain the same. He is especially interested in a newly discovered, sweet and simple maiden, but his past catches up with him which causes many complications. The university scenes are unintentionally a scream, with young Spanish students saying things like, "and how" "real fun" and even "swell." It should be noted that one who would be so important in future more positive characterizations, by providing the world with most enjoyable music that is still with us today, received his screen credit as, Xavier Cugat in this film. The song he played was "Santiago."] **EHW**:10.4.30, **V**:**NYT**:6.8.30, **FD**:6.22.30]

[1416] **LADRON DE AMOR** aka **CUANDO EL AMOR RIE** SR **LOVE GAMBLER**, F: [The cast: Jose Mojica, Mona Maris, Luana Alcaniz, Carlos Villarias, Carmen Rodriguez, Rafael Valverde, Rosita Granada.]

[1417] **THE LAND OF MISSING MEN**, Tiffany: [This film is significant because it further indicates that Hollywood was still trying to find the balance between too much and too little Spanish 'spoke' in any given western production. The accepted stereotypes are continued, the murderous bandits are Mexicans. Emilio Fernandes makes his first appearance in a Hollywood production and receives praise for his "realistic appearance", but more important, when he speaks, he does so "with a Spanish accent that sounds real and no doubt so."

Attention was paid to detail to enhance the realism "particularly in the use of Spanish when one of the bandit group speaks to another." It was a problem that Hollywood and later television never decided completely how to handle, whatever the language. How much German should a Nazi speak to characterize him? Should all the Germans or the Spaniards speak only their native tongue and should what was said be translated? The answer for Spanish was simpler, broken English was by far, more well received by audiences throughout the nation. In the last reel of this film, Bob Steele and Fuzzy St John capture the murderers of at least five men, Anglos. Lopez, the bandit leader, was brought to justice, cursing in Spanish that required no translation.] **EHW:10.4.30**.

[1418] **THE LASH** aka **AMIGO**, FN: [This film adaptation of the novel, **Amigo**, by Lanier Virginia differs in some important ways from earlier versions of Masked Avengers righting the wrongs of Spanish California after its conquest by the United States in the Mexican War of 1845. There are no Spanish tyrants oppressing poor peons here, significantly, the villains are United States officials and others who now consider that all property in Spanish California belongs to the new conquerors. Land titles and quaint Mexican customs were a thing of the past and the sooner the "foreigners" living in their former homeland realized that, the better it would be for all concerned. One thing about this film is not very different, with characters named, Francisco and Dolores Delfina, Rosita Garcia, Lupe, Juan and Concha, not one is played by a Hispanic. Richard Barthelmess is the young Don returning from Mexico City to find his homeland overrun by ruthless North Americans. "The story doesn't place the Americans in a very favorable light" according to **Variety**, but it gave the Anglo lead a chance to be the hero, "El Puma" who stood up to the oppressors. The songs which grace this production are sung in Spanish, a practice that would continue unchanged until the arrival of the flood of singing cowboys. What may well have answered a question for a significant number of those who viewed the film was the explanation given by the sweet chiquita, Mary Astor, to her lover's quire about why Mexicans referred to North Americans as Gringo's. "By the way, why do the Spaniards call us Americans Gringos? [Dolores] "Why, my uncle told me it started at the time the American army was in Mexico. Your soldiers used to sing a song that went "The Green goes over the Hill." [Howard] "The Green goes? ..... Green goes... Oh, ha .. ha .. it's gringos." Submitted to censorship, these lines in the script, "Tie him up, the Son of a bitch, had the underscore removed, because it was considered to be "Indecent." For an other version on the origin of the terms see: ""Gringo" and "Greaser," **The Mexican Review**:11.16, p12.] **EHW**:11.22.30, **V**:12.17.30, **NYT**:1.1.31. Script: The Lash, Reel 7, p1, 26 pages.

[1419] **LAST OF THE DUANES**, F: [Some western film historians have considered this film itself, a good subject for the study of how Hollywood "creatively" adapted certain novels to the screen. This particular Zane Grey novel was filmed for the screen four times, in 1919, 1924, 1930, and 1941. In 1930,

David Howard produced a Spanish language version entitled, **El Ultimo De Los Vargas** [1459] in which the lovely, Luana Alcaniz played the female lead.] **FD**:9.14.30.

[1420] **LEATHERNECKING**, RKO: [This strictly musical comedy fluff has Louise Fazenda and Benny Rubin providing most of the laughs, but the action centers on a Marine private who falls for a rich society dame. She is really taken with him when he tells her that he is an officer, yet it all falls apart when she learns the truth. But this was Hollywood and all is well in the last real when he saves her party friends whose boat has sunk and left them helplessly stranded on some island. It is then discovered that he also had been decorated for bravery in the fight against Sandino in Nicaragua. For this the socialite really gives him a reward.] **FD**:9.14.30

[1421] **LETS GO NATIVE**, P: [Jeannette MacDonald and Jack Oakie hoke it up on a boat bound for Argentina which becomes ship wrecked somewhere on a unknown Caribbean island inhabited only by a lot of hip swinging hula girls. After Oakie makes himself king of the island, he orders all these ladies to attend him and teaches them how to speak Brooklyn English. All this fun prompts one of the other characters to sneak a racy line by the censors when he quips: "It was one of the Virgin Islands before he got there." Hot stuff for 1930, but understandable because of the tropical location.] **V**:9.3.30, **FD**:8.31.30.

[1422] **THE LIFE OF THE PARTY**, W: [Two New York girls lose their jobs in a music shop and decide to go to Havana where the big money was known to be, to try their luck at a little gold digging. One is nice, the other not so and as such must pay Hollywood's price, no matter how easy the pickings were among those wild Cubans. The other is rewarded with a nice rich North American husband who was vacationing there.]

[1423] **LOVE COMES ALONG**, RKO: [Bebe Daniels starred in this romantic melodrama set in Cuba, with a scenario based on Edward Knoblocks's **Conchita, a Romantic Play in Three Acts**, 1924. When Johnny Stark's tramp steamer stops over at Caparoja some where in the Caribbean, he is introduced to the local jefe, Colonel Sangredo, a tightfisted dictator, but also a fun loving fellow who welcomes him and tells him of the local pleasures. Quickly, Johnny and Happy meet Peggy, a stranded North American actress who sings for her supper at the local cantina. Sangredo at the same time notices that his lady, Carlotta has deserted him and so he employs Peggy to sing at his fiesta. By this time Johnny has succumbed to the romantic tropical surroundings and declares his love for the lady, but expresses his displeasure at her singing for the soldier. She loves him also, but rebukes him for trying to tell her what not to do. When she sings to her man at the fiesta, the Colonel has him arrested, but Peggy obtains his release on the promise of dinning with the lecherous dictator. In the final reel, the two friends rescue the singer from a fate worse than and sail off into the blue Caribbean together.] **V**:2.5.30, **NYT**:2.1.30.

[1424] **MANY MOONS**, P: [A nine minute Paramount short featuring a lot of beautiful Caribbean scenery and music. "It is the beauty of the tropical skies and moonlight that provides the principal pleasure" in this film.] **FD**:9.14.30.

[1425] **A MEDIA NOCHE** aka **Evidencia**, F: [The Hispanic cast included: Lia Tora, Juan Torena, Lucio Villegas and Alfredo del Diestro.]

[1426] **MEN WITHOUT LAW**, C: [One of the most respected and liked of western stars, Buck Jones found himself in Mexico with attractive company, Carmelita Geraghty as Junatia Del Rey, this time a daughter, but usually, one must assume, an actress who never tired of playing the loving chiquita sitting in the cantina waiting for her Anglo to pass by. Victor Sarno played the Señor Del Rey, owner of the large hacienda that Buck helps save for him.] **V**:12.3.30, **FD**:10.30.30, afic.

[1427] **MONSIEUR LE FOX** SV **MEN OF THE NORTH**, MGM: [This romance of the French Canadian North woods has Luis Alonso, soon to be Gilbert Roland playing, Louis Le Bey, a healthy "Canuck" who loved a lot of ladies and was the role model for all the men. More frequently than not in Hollywood characterizations, for the French to be lascivious was expected, so it was for Hispanics, but in their case, the aura was usually more sinister. In this version, his sexy Canadian señorita was Rosita Ballesteros. Also included in the cast were: Vincente Padula, Ralph Navarro, and Maria Calvo who tried to capture the lumber jacking Roland for herself.] **V**:12.17.30.

[1428] **OKLAHOMA CYCLONE**, Tiffany: [In this "lively western with [a] substantial plot" Bob Steele as cowboy Jim Smith travels to the border where he found "a barrel of lively action". There he showed his loyal following in the audience "some real smacking between" his hero self and the villain. The lady much of the fighting was about was Nita Rey, one of many lovely Mexicans señoritas, whose function was just that. Hector Sarno was the Hispanic heavy who gave the man of steel some trouble, but not enough to cause any real problems. It was always that way and necessary for Anglo audiences.] **FD**:9.14.30.

[1429] **ONE MAD KISS**, F: [This film was designed by Fox for the Central and Latin American markets, what it might make "within the jurisdiction of Mr. Hoover" would just be that much better. The entire cast was comprised of Latin American imports and featured, Don Jose Mojica, who Fox had attempted to promote as a major star, for that specific audience. Reviewers generally considered it a low budget production with a strictly formula scenario. A Spanish Robin Hood type, bandit, lovable outlaw, defends his unidentified Latin Republic against the evil designs and corruption of an evil dictator. "Mojica, a tall fellow with glistening teeth appears as Sevedra, the benignant outlaw, who not only outwits the combined army and navy of the country, but wins the girls from the scheming official." His specialty was of course, knife throwing. Mona Maris as Rosario the dancing girl,

Antonio Moreno as the dictator, Don Estrada and Tom Patricola completed the cast.] **V**:7.23.30, 7.19.30.

[1430] **ON THE BORDER**, W: [The famous Rin Tin Tin, "Rinty" to his friends, found his four little paws crossing the Rio Grande, in this tale of smuggling Chinese immigrants across the Mexican border. Don Jose may have provided a serious test for the famous K9's intelligence because of his difficulty speaking comprehensible English, but the pup star seemed to enjoy the Spanish ballads and his Hispanic friend's guitar strumming. Armida, as Pepita, provided the proper "paprika", a spice Hollywood seemed to prefer in its Latin stars. In this one she is the daughter of the Don who rules an empire of sheep that she enjoys singing to, until the undercover border patrolman, an Anglo, appears to change her tune [58, 381, 597].] **V**:2.5.30, **NYT**:2.3.30, **FD**:2.9.30, **afic**.

[1431] **ORIENTE Y OCCIDENTE** SV **EAST IS WEST**, [Lupe Velez played Ming Toy, the same sexy little Chinese vamp she portrayed to plaudits in the English version. See **East is West** [1398.].] **V**:11.5.30.

[1432] **PASSION FLOWER**, MGM: [The two cousins in this romantic melodrama set in Spain marry into two different social levels. Dulce weds Morado, a wealthy Spanish aristocrat, but Cassy ends up with the family chauffeur, Dan Wallace. A little Hollywood inversion there, Renaldo was usually found behind the wheel driving for the Anglo family. In this case, Dan wants to make it on his own and refuses the generous wedding gift/offer made by the Don of his own farm. After a few years he has fathered a family, but this has done little to improve his social standing. He still works on the docks as a stevedore, but his wife is loyal, honest and hardworking, a treasure in itself. When the Don makes the offer again, Dan accepts. It works for a while, but soon after Morado has died, Dan finds himself doing his widow. She plys him with all the comfort and ease he could want and even takes him to Paris, but he cannot forget his family and his loyal wife. In the final scene, he leaves the lady and heads back home to the farm where all are waiting [874].] **V**:12.2.30, **NYT**:12.24.30.

[1433] **THE PHANTOM OF THE WEST**, Mascot: {Serial 10 episodes} [Although there are Hispanic characters throughout the story line, there are none in the cast. The tale has Francisco Cortez escaping from prison, a lifer for a crime that he did not commit, assuming the role of the mysterious phantom, searching for the killers of his father. Mona Cortez, as the female lead, helped this early "fugitive" in his ten week quest to clear his name and establish his innocence.]

[1434] **EL PRECIO DE UN BESO** = **THE PRICE OF A KISS**, F: [Fox studio's striving to keep its lead in the Spanish language productions put together an excellent cast of Hispanic players for this Spanish musical romance, directed by an Anglo, Marcel Silver. Jose Mojica, whose popularity grew with every new film, sang the lead in this pleasant fluff without much substance. Mona Maris, Antonio Moreno and Tom Patricola provide solid support and everyone seemed to be having a good time trying to maintain what little story line there was. Boy meets girl, girl meets other boy, both do a lot of singing which help her choose between them. Even in Spanish productions, the second tortilla might get to kiss the señorita, but not for very long. Also included were: Enrique Acosta, Carlos Villarias, Juan Torena and Martin Garralaga. See: **One Mad Kiss** [1429]] **FD**:8.1.33.

[1435] **EL PRESIDIO** SV **THE BIG HOUSE**, MGM: [The English version was filled with "screws", "stool pigeons" and Wallace Beery as the big bully behind the bars. Chester Morris had the lead. In the Spanish talker those roles were played by Jose Crespo and Juan de Landa. The remainder of the Hispanic prisoners and their women were: Luana Alcaniz, Tito Davison, Giovanni Martino, Luis Llaneza, Juan de Homs, Romualso Tirado, Jose Soriano Visca, Cesar Vanon, Alma Real and Antonio Vidal.] **V**:7.2.30.

[1436] **EL PRINCIPE GONDOLERO** = **THE GONDOLIER PRINCE**, P: [This was one of Paramount's best Spanish language films in terms of production values and cast. Reviewers praised it as "Exceptionally fine" combining romance, comedy and musical numbers "against a colorful background." Having a studio right outside of Paris which allowed for foreign location shooting was a distinct advantage. Although they maintained a connection with French film makers for much longer, the studio in Joinville closed before the end of the decade. The cast consisted of: Roberto Rey, Rosita Moreno, Andres de Segurola, Manuel Arbo, Jose Pena "Pepet", Juan de Homs, Elena Landeros and Luis Llaneza. The songs and musical segments were directed by Eduardo D. Venturini.] **FD**:9.13.33.

[1437] **EL PROCESO DE MARY DUGAN** SV **THE TRIAL OF MARY DUGAN**, MGM: [In the English version of this courtroom drama and mystery, Norma Shearer played the beleaguered Mary. Maria F. Ladron de Guevara took her role in the Spanish remake. The Hispanic cast featured some of the best from south of the border: Jose Crespo, Ramon Pereda, Rafael Rivelles, Elvira Morla, Juan de Landa, Adrienne D'Ambricourt, Romualdo Tirado, Celia Montalvan, Julio Villarreal and Paco Moreno.] **V**:3.4.31.

[1438] **RANCHO OF THE DON**, [In another strictly formula production, Hector Sarno was warned to keep clear of the Don's pretty daughter, Nita Rey, who plays, Carmelita, the object of the young Hispanic's affection. Macho that he is, he ignores the advice and finds himself in a lot of trouble which requires the not so fragile heroine to save him by riding for help.]

[1439] **RIDN' LAW**, Biltmore: [The review for this Jack Perrin western, which included in its cast possibly the greatest of all Hollywood western stunt men, Yakima Canutt, is more significant as an indication of the growing discomfort some critics were experiencing with this type of production, and certain practices employed by the industry itself, than it was, as a criticism for this particular film. It also indicated that the reviewer must have been confident that his corruption of the word "Hispanic" would not offend his Anglo readers. "Inane western. Breaks all bonds of propriety for even a western, if such a thing is possible. Construction is terrible and appears to be put together more like a gang of high school kids would than a group of professionals. Useless anywhere. The little Mex heroine [of late all western heroines are Mex] forgets that she is supposed to put on a spick accent at times and resorts to perfect English." Enough.] **V**:7.9.30.

[1440] **ROGUE OF THE RIO GRANDE**, SonoArt: [Jose Bohr, a Spanish actor, who would later devote himself almost exclusively to acting in and directing made in Mexico films, played the role of "El Malo" in this one. As the badman, the fun loving Robin Hood/"Pancho Villa", type was aided in his adventures by a trusty Mexican sidekick named, Pedro. After he robs the across the river town bank of Sierra Blanca and "makes a clean get-a-way," he is annoyed to learn that the reward being offered for him is so little. His Hispanic honor and pride offended, he returns to show up the sheriff by enjoying himself in the local cantina with a beautiful and sleek chiquita, the young curvaceous, Myrna Loy, who just loved to sing and dance and be admired by all. From her he is astounded to learn that the town law enforcer was in reality, a crook. First things first. After capturing the lady's heart, he has the sheriff blamed for his own crime. Having accomplished his purpose and a little extra, the two head back across the Mexican border to happily ever after it in the land of song, sunshine and honor. The songs in this "musical western" included, "Argentine Moon," "Carmita" and the "Song of the Bandoleros."] **V**:12.17.30, **FD**:12.7.30, afic.

[1441] **ROMANCE OF THE WEST**, Capital Film Exchange: [This Jack Perrin western was considered strictly formula stuff, "from the old file", filled with all the hard riding, shooting and fighting required in such adventures. In this one the Anglo hero found himself in Mexico where he happened onto a girl in distress. She had been lured across the Rio Grande under false pretenses by a prize fighter and his manager. Unwilling to do their bidding, they left her stranded, but when Jack returned across the line, they kidnaped her. Forced to act the cowpoke showed the burley prize fighter just how the land punches and where. Although the little lady was most appreciative for being saved, and despite the fact that she wanted to get a lot closer to her hero, there was no chance. Western stars knew all too well as they rode off in to the sunset, alone, that that was the way it had to be. In these formula pieces, women were to be saved and used a bit, but it took a whole lot of stuff to get the heros to go to the altar. Pedestrian as this ride through the west might have been, it would be taken once again in the 1946 remake.] **FD**:8.10.30.

[1442] **ROUGH ROMANCE**, F: [Hollywood moved Antonio Moreno way north of the border into Canada for this exercise in applying his accent to the French Canadian villain he was scripted to live in for a while. There he was forced to fight George

O'Brien for the pretty little French canuck lady and lost. Of all of these attempts at ethnic characterizations, his may well have been the most successful in fulfilling the writers conception of how a Spaniard playing at being French spoke English in Canada.]

[1443] **SANTE FE TRAIL**, P: [The significance of this minor entry has little to do with its simple stock scenario. Sheeps and cows once more compete for the grazing rights, this time on the huge estate of Juan Castinado's Spanish Acres. There are indians and indian curses which are utilizes by the baddie cow men to steal the old Don's lands, but the hacienda is saved for him by a less superstitious Anglo good guy who falls for Maria Castinado. All of this is routine, but the fact that the Spanish characters speak their native tongue, without translation for the audience proved to be of some consequence. It was an artistic touch that for bilingual viewers was certainly an innovation, but considering that even today some states are still trying to pass legislation to make English or American the official language, this innovation for 1930 was too far ahead of its times. Audiences reacted negatively, and even laughed, at what they could not comprehend and producers were quick to realize that this was not a commercial idea. Very few subsequent westerns ever employed this technique again. From this point on, the only untranslated Spanish spoken in films was what was unnecessary for the audience to understand, and included only the most common and easily understood of expressions.] **EHW**:10.25.30, p42, **V**:10.29.30, **FD**:10.19.30, **NYT**:10.18.30, **MPG**.

[1444] **THE SEA BAT**, MGM: [For this **Film Daily** reviewer that was just one big ocean out there, filled with a lot of foreign stuff, once you left the friendly shores of the U. S. of A. It was explained that the author who had provided the material for this film's script had never been to either the South Seas or the Bahamas, [how different could the two places be anyway?] Despite that, the writer had set the action in one of those places and according to the critic, she had written a "corking" good story. Raquel Torres, as Nina, was the warm blooded, darkskinned lady that starred in this story of two Caribbean sponge divers who both wanted to bed down with the local beauty. One was not at all nice, John Miljan, which becomes obvious when he allows his friend Carl to die attempting to suck oxygen out of sea water while trying to avoid a giant devil bat manta ray. As the writer would have it, that was the one that Nina had actually loved. The difficulty she had dealing with his death then drives her to accept voodoo as her religion. The island was filled with it. She also puts out a contract on the sea bat and offers herself as the bait. Meanwhile, Charles Bickford, as the Reverend Sims, has managed to escape from Devil's Island (I'm not making this up either) and finds his way to the Bahamas. As attracted to the lovely Nina as he is and despite the depredation he had suffered in that horrid hell hole, he found him self to be more a man of the cloth than a possible suitor. Her subscription to Vodun revolted him. In time he has his way with her. She comes to realize that Christ was right and that that black god was not one that good folk, white or darkskinned listened to. While all this reconverting was taking place, Miljan discovers that Sims was really an escaped prisoner as well a preacher and threatens to turn him in. [Is this one heckofa story or not?] With all three of the principles in a motorboat the sea bat intercedes. Apparently holding no grudge because of the bounty, the bat kills the heavy which allows the other two to enjoy some of the most beautiful sandy beaches and azure blue/green waters anywhere in the world, that is, on the screen. Actually much of this film was shot along the attractive beaches of Mazatlan, Mexico, where the active surf is sometimes filled with sizable stones not found in the more tranquil waters of the Bahamas.] **FD**:8.10.30, **NYT**:3.2.30.

[1445] **EL SECRETO DEL DOCTOR** SV **THE DOCTORS'S SECRET**, P/Joinville: [This film was also made into a French version with an all French cast. The story was a familiar one long before 1930. An unhappy wife runs off with her lover and is forced to return because he has been killed by a bus or some other convenient scripters vehicle. In Joinville, Italians were frequently used as Hispanics as they were in this production. In this cast they included: Eugenia Zuffoli, Manuel Soto, and Jose Bodalo.] **V**:10.29.30.

[1446] **LA SEVILLANA** SV **CALL OF THE FLESH** aka **SEVILLA DE MIS AMORES**, MGM: [Concerned with the problems the talkers created for film with Hispanic characterizations, and with some hope of capitalizing on the reputation of their major Mexican asset, MGM gave Roman Navarro his opportunity to direct a production aimed specifically at the Spanish speaking audiences. Navarro not only directed this piece, he was also the star leading an all Hispanic cast which included: Conchita Montenegro, Rosita Ballesteros, Jose Sortiano Biosca, Martin Garralaga, and Maria Calvo.] **V**:9.17.30, 3.11.31.

[1447] **SI EL EMPERADOR LO SUPIERA** SV **HIS GLORIOUS NIGHT**, [The English version of this film proved to be a disaster for one of the great lovers of the silent screen, John Gilbert. When the ladies who had once swooned over his silent love making heard it in sound, they laughed. In the Spanish version, Jose Crespo, destined to have a significant influence in Hollywood, was a superior sound lover, well, he was Hispanic. The señorita lovelies who admired the smooth ways and tight uniforms of the star included, Maria Alba, Elivira Moria, Luis Llaneza, and Carmen Rodriques. Also included were: Juan Aristi Eulate and Juan de Homs.] **V**:10.9.29.

[1448] **SI, SI, SEÑOR**, Educational: [This fifteen minute short featured a new Hispanic discovery, Tom Patricola, showing off some of his dancing and strumming skills. Considered to be a "good comedy story", the actor also exhibited his comedic abilities. Tom and friend played a couple of desert tramps somewhere on the Mexican border who "swipe" the clothes of another couple of swimming señors, one of which was on his way to visit the daughter of the local hacienda to ask for her hand in marriage. Neither the father nor the daughter had ever seen the prospective suitor so it was possible for Tom to take his place, which he does by displaying his serenading ability, much to the delight of the señorita. To add a few problems right in the middle of one of his numbers, the writers reintroduced the very wet and very mad señors. After a little scuffling for the audience, and despite the fact that the frauds have been exposed, it proves too late for the two wet others. The lady "has taken a fancy to her musical American Caballero" and of course "he cops the prize."]

[1449] **SOLDIERS AND WOMEN**, C: [This rather sordid tale of female treachery takes place under the tropical sun in Haiti while Uncle Sam's boys, mainly Marines, were teaching the locals the true meaning of democracy. It was good duty for the men, especially the southerners that made up the majority of the occupation corps, a reminder of days of old, but for the officer's wives, it proved boring. One such lady becomes tired of her husband and has her commandant dad transfer an old flame to the island so that she might have a little diversion in her otherwise drab life .... it goes on from there and results in the death of the husband and her eventual suicide. As might be expected, none of the locals play anything but subservient parts, while doing a lot of obeying, bowing and work for the whites. Actually, the Haitian occupation was the harshest of all those in the Caribbean and resulted in the death of more that 2200 locals without any charges of murder being brought against the Marine troops.] **V**:5.14.30.

[1450] **SOMBRAS DE GLORIA** = **BLAZE OF GLORY**, Sono-Art: [This Spanish version of **Blaze of Glory**, evoked a review in **Variety** that is worth reproducing here almost in its entirety because of the clarity of its exposition in explaining the problems inherent in producing Spanish language versions of regular Hollywood issues. "Imitative of Dowling's own version, just as sobby and badly acted. Engendered with a conglomeration of dialect Spanish enunciation that ranges from the Greek manner to the Mexican. It is not likely that this film will reap in Spanish localities unless the novelty angle is strong enough to carry it. Regardless of the dialect a foreigner speaks, when he must listen to his mother tongue from the stage, screen or platform it's got to be the original and undefiled. It's as true of Spaniards as it is others. Even more precise with Spanish nationals. They limit their dialect to those within their borders, and with so many existent Spanish speaking countries it's doubly necessary to attain a fundamental speaking plane acceptable to all. There's only one plane, unadulterated Castilian. Any other rumples the national pride somewhere. The Argentinan [sic] won't go for the Mexican and the Mexican won,t go for the Yucatan. One other fault with trying to shoveover Spanish versions of American made pictures is lack of actors. In this version the cast is way below par. Using foreign casts leaves other loopholes, such as giving the picture American atmosphere. In one spot in the film the American hero who speaks in Spanish, is asked to sing an "American" song, and he sings it in "English."" The audience laughed. Although this critique is splashed with bits snobbish superiority, it is a solid, contemporary, evaluation of the problems these films created. Once the first talkers reached Spain, the dubbed versions caused serious problems. "The Spanish capital [was] all hot and bothered. The poor English and worse Spanish" was decried by the Royal Academy. Producers were caught in a lingual nightmare generated by insulted national pride on either side of the pond. See also: **Cascarrabias** [1387]] V:2.26.30, 2.12.30, FD: 2.16.30.

[1451] **SONG OF THE CABALLERO**, U: [Ken Maynard is the hero in this western "with songs" set in the days of the Dons on the beautiful California coast. Everyone is in Spanish costumes and most sing almost continuously, especially the gypsies. It was a happy place to be. The script has Ken at least not liked, by a neighbor rancho owner who drove his sister from the hacienda simply because he hated her lover. When she comes to him, Ken is gracious and helps her out. The brother is offended. The action requires the western star to be the typical Anglo type superhero. More familiar with firearms, Ken is still able to withstand the onslaught of ten or more swordsmen singlehandedly. In the end all are happy and reunited, the foe is vanquished. The laughs are provided by two Anglo 'sidekickistas,' who have more problems with the señoritas and the Spanish customs than any of the more serious adversities. After all, they had Ken on their side.] V:7.9.30, FD:7.13.30.

[1452] **SONG OF THE WEST**, W: [Eventually everyone who hung out at the ole Hollywood corral was at one time or other roped into riding out into a western. This "operetta" was Joe E. Brown's turn. With a wagon train that makes it fairly quickly to Spanish California in gold rush days, the large mouthed comedian was able to promote a significant number of laughs as he faced the worst of the west. Unintentionally humorous were the "tango orchestra" and the adagio dancers which gave the interior scenes of the saloon, "an 1880 nightclub look."] V:3.5.30, FD: 3.2.30.

[1453] **SOUTH SEAS**, Gifford Pinchot-Mrs. Gifford Pinchot: [This expedition sponsored by the National Museum in Washington, D. C. and the Philadelphia Academy of Natural Sciences had the Pinchot family traveling on their schooner, the **Mary Pinchot**, on what was truly a wondrous adventure, one that must have been the envy of every member of the audience. They sailed from New York south through the Panama Canal, across to the Galapagos Islands to the Marquesas and eventually returning to stop off at the San Blas island off the coast of Panama where they spent some time with the still somewhat primitive indians that inhabited that island paradise.] afic.

[1454] **THE STORM**, U: [This was Lupe Velez's, first film for Universal, in it she played the daughter of a Canadian smuggler who was shot by the Mountie she loved. Having moved three thousand miles from the border more familiar to her, she played this role "with an accent that is a cross between

Spanish and French, half the time doing a flashing Spanish
señorita, the other half a piquant you femme frog." Those
Variety reviewer's really had a way with words when expressing
their ethnic stereotypes.] **V**:8.27.30.

[1455] **EL TERRIBLE TOREADOR**, Disney: [One of the very first
exposures very young children have to stereotyping comes from
cartoons. This is even more true today because of
television's function as a babysitter for otherwise very busy
parents with little time to entertain their progeny. When the
peace treaty was signed between the two rivals, the movies and
television a most profitable commerce was finally made
possible. Films were now shown in the living rooms of middle
class North America, and Saturday morning was devoted to
cartoons. Speedy Gonzales was on his way, but in 1930 this
brief clip played in many theaters much to the delight of
every audience. The toreador was terrible, the bull was
better, especially, to use the macho words popularized by a
president, at "kicking but."] **NYT**:3.3.30.

[1456] **THE TEXAN**, P: [First made in 1920 and set in South
America, the film then caused a protest from the State
Department because it implied that one of its members was a
shady character. [**A Double Dyed Deceiver** [841]]. This version
of O'Henry's tale featured a handsome young Gary Cooper, as
the on the edge of the law personality, the Llano Kid, who
loved freedom and gambling. After having enjoyed some
excitement in a border town where he shot a card sharp in self
defense and evaded a bible thumping sheriff, he found himself
on a train with Thatcher, the con man. This smooth talking
crook soon involved the Kid in a plot to pass him off as the
long lost son of Señora Ibarra, heir to vast South American
lands. Convinced this might prove entertaining, he is
tattooed where the lost Enrique once was, and takes his
Spanish speaking ability to meet to old and now jubilantly
happy señora. Of course he is accepted, but he falls in love
with the sweet niece, Fay Wray and soon rejects the whole
project, in effect becoming the defender of the Hacienda
against Thatcher and his gang. The sheriff some how makes his
way to this south of the border location and is so impressed
with the wounded kid's change in character that he allows him
to stay, forever. One reviewer was not so much impressed with
the story as he was Fay's performance: "The most astonishing
thing about this, ... is the Spanish accent of Fay Wray. Cast
as a daughter of Latin America, she out-Lupes Lupe, out-
Armidas Armida with the E-sounding I's and melting diphthongs
and vowels. I thought it simply a phenomenal exhibition of a
true mimic power--unless of course, I am mistaken and Miss
Wray has lived among the Felipes and Juanitas all her life."
Had this film been made three years later, he might well have
added, possibly its not so surprising, if she can talk to big
black monkeys, she can certainly speak, Mexican.] **V**:5.21.30,
NYT:5.17.30, **FD**:4.27.30, **The Film Spectator**, 4.26.30, p20.

[1457] **TIGER ROSE**, W: [Lupe Velez in her first all dialogue
feature shared screen time with Monte Blue and the greatest of
the first four legged stars, Rin Tin Tin, all struggling to

make the audience believe that there was some reason they all should have been in Manitoba. The Canadian accent was a beauty.] **V**:1.1.30.

[1458] <u>TODA UNA VIDA</u> SV <u>SARAH AND SON</u>, P: Joinville: [This scenario provided good material for a Spanish language script. A selfless mother/wife puts up with the brutality of her drunken husband because of their child. He finally bolts with the baby and sells it to a rich family. The mother spends the rest of the film searching, until her dying husband revels the child's whereabouts. Spanish audiences loved this tearjearker. The cast included: Carlos Diaz de Mendoza, Isabel Barron, and Lusito Pena.] **V**:3.19.30.

[1459] <u>EL ULTIMO DE LOS VARGAS</u> SV <u>LAST OF THE DUANES</u>, F: [This was Zane Grey translated to the Hispanic screen. The Spanish cast included Luana Alcaniz, Vicente Padula, Martin Garralaga, Carmen Rodriguez, and Juan de Landa. See: [1419].]

[1460] <u>UNDER A TEXAS MOON</u>, W: [This was the first western totally in Technicolor and starred Frank Foy as the most amorous Don Carlos who could so easily be swayed from his purpose by lovely señoritas, that the writers were forced to fill the script with an endless supply of such beauties. In one scene, the critic noticed, possibly with some envy, "there were so many [beautiful señoritas] in a hacienda that it looked as thought the Don Juan had picked a spot for himself that called for the Mexican army." [He apparently knew little of the love making capabilities Hollywood scribes had imbued their Hispanic's with.] Aside from all of this, there were two Lolita's, one Dolores and one Raquella, both very interested in the healthy young swain, not to mention the lovelies in the general pool. One of the Lolita's wanted him to kill Pancho Gonzales who was causing her problems. She explains that he might himself be killed in performing the service, but promises that "she would flower his grave for all time," if that happened. Don Carlos could see little future in the venture, so he sets out after the rustlers for seven thousand in gold instead. When yet another lady stops him, "He regales this dark-eyed wench" with tall tales of his bull fighting ability. Enthralled, she listens expectantly to his having been in the corrida with six at once. Asked what happened, he laughs and answers, 'I ran like h--l." Everyone in this film speaks in the vogue vernacular of functional illiterates, Hollywood's new conception of 1860's Mexico. Myrna Loy, and Betty Boyd were the Anglo chiquitas, Armida and Mona Maris the Mexican imports.] **V**:4.9.30, **NYT**:4.4.30, **FD**:4.6.30, <u>Film Spectator</u>:4.26.30.

[1461] <u>UN HOMBRE DE SUERTE</u>, P, Joinville: [The Hispanic cast included: Roberto Rey, Maria Luz Callejo, Rosario Pino, Carlos San Martin, Amelia Munoz, Valentin Parera and Joaquin Carrasco.]

[1462] <u>EL VALIENTE</u> SV <u>THE VALIANT</u>, F: [Paul Muni brought life to this character on death row waiting to go to the chair, Juan Torena did the same in the Spanish version. He was supported by: Angelita Benitez, Ralph Navarro, Juan de Landa, Julio Villarreal, Carlos Villarias and Maria Calvo.] English review, V:5.15.29.

[1463] **LA VOLUNTAD DEL MUERTO** SV **THE CAT CREEPS**, U: [George Melford directed Antonio Moreno in this Spanish language version of John Willard's Broadway Play, **Cat and the Canary**, distributed throughout Latin America as **El Gato**. With Lupita Tovar and Manuel Granado in assistance, this English mystery translated well as an early talker. It proved a success in the domestic market as well as throughout the Americas.] V:11.12.30.

[1464] **WINGS OF ADVENTURE**, Tiffany: ["Another in the series of alleged life just across the Mexican border with villainous rebels, federal troops and the U. S. border patrol all mixed in for a wild and wooly jumble of plot." Characterized as an "unimportant western" to be used "in double feature bills," the briefly, very popular Armida, was the female lead and provided audiences with "quite a bit of Mex chatter." It meant "nothing at all to American audiences," but proved entertaining. The story involved a pair of North American flyers captured by Villa type revolutionaries. "These birds" who are forever shouting, ""Viva" something" and singing unintelligible songs, have a leader who wants the warm Armida. She wants to escape with the Anglo and with the help of the United States Cavalry, once more on the Mexican side of the border, all are saved. Hollywood would continue to use its own interpretation of international law, which justified the crossing of national boundaries to protect North American lives, from the very earliest times, to this present day. [**Delta Force II**, a recent example.] The affect of such acculturation on audiences cannot be dismissed, not that many would question such presidential action, seeing it on film certainly always proved that it was the right thing to do.] V:8.13.30, FD:8.10.30, afic.

[1465] **WU-LI-CHANG** SR **MR. WU**, MGM: [One of the first, but least successful of the great Chinese criminologist, who practiced their trade from the twenties to the fifties, Mr Wu, originally portrayed by an orientalized Lon Chaney, was in this version played by an orientalized Ernesto Viches, which seems fair considering how many time Sessue Hayakawa (**Jaguar's Claws** [757]) played Mexican characters. Included also in the cast were: Angelita Benitez, Jose Crespo, Marcela Mivon, Mrs Sojin, Martin Garralaga, and Jose Soriano Viosca.] V:4.20.27.

[1466] **ZAMPA**, UA: [This ten minute "Swell Musical" was "a high-grade presentation of the operatic story concerning an inhuman Don Juan, Zampa, a swaggering philanderer [who] takes a fancy to a young lady who is about to be married." He has her prospective husband sent off to military duty then kidnaps her from the church she was praying in. When her maid protests, appealing to her patron saint, Zampa has her carried away and the statue of the saint brought to the local cantina for laughs. Not all the Spanish aristocracy was tied to the church. Eventually the girl's lover returns to fight the lecherous and sacrilegious blaggard during which Zampa falls off a balcony onto the spear held by the statue. That was fair. This production was considered to be a "short of the better type."] FD:9.14.30.

1931

[1467] **ALOHA**, Tiffany: [Raquel Torres' lovely darkskinned body helped her land a leading role in this poor remake of **White Cargo**. Considered by some critics the kind of movie that even those addicted to double features would walk out on, the Mexican import was still ordered to the mouth of the volcano for purification when she discovered that she was not the white woman that she once thought she had been.] **V**:4.29.31.

[1468] **EL AMOR SOLFENADO = LOVE TO MUSIC**, Sp/Cineas-Renacimiento: [**Variety** thought this to be a potential money maker in Spanish territory, but indicated that it was "impossible to fathom Spanish likes and dislikes in pictures." Once more alluding to the varieties of Spanish spoken by various Hispanic nationalities on either side of the Atlantic: "So many different jargons of Spanish exist it is almost always safe to say most of the Spanish speaking peoples don't understand pictures in their own language, unless it's the particular Spanish of the community." This picture made in Spain should be good in that nation, but South Americans and Mexicans, they predicted, would not like it. They were correct, such nationalistic preferences were reserved to their own native film industries, still in their early stages of development. It will not be until the internalization of the industry in the sixties that sufficient blurring of individual national pride will allow the viewing of other national products without serious offense. This film was a significantly improved product which played well in the Spanish language market. A talker, it was a musical with a jealous husband who has a music teacher instruct both his wife and mistress. In the process, the teacher who knows nothing of music learns a lot about the ladies and starts his own school.] **V**:12.8.31.

[1469] **THE ARIZONA TERROR**, Tiffany: [For Ken Maynard fans, a popular entry in which he managed to foil the evil designs of a murdering cattle thief named Cole Porter that operated on this side of the border, but received assistance from his Hispanic henchman, Vasquez. The lovely Lina Basquette, was the female attraction for whom Ken performed all the heroics.] **MPH**: 10.17.31, **V**:9.29.31, **FD**:9.27.31.

[1470] **AVENGER**, C: [Some where between the showing of **In Arizona** in 1929 [1338] and the **Gay Caballero** in 1932 [1562], making the Mexican the hero, reached its popular peak, there certainly would be other Mexican good guys to follow, but never again so many in so brief a period. "Mex heros" had become the fad for the epicenter of such indulgences. Whereas at one time the "Mex in a western meant the villain," it was sound that helped change the characterization. "The Mex dialect" was popular with the neighborhood kids. They liked it and liked talking like the "Mex hero." Always aware that the industry required as much "coin" as possible to keep the flickers flickering throughout fantasy land, the producers sought every opportunity to find one more Mexican hero. This time the favorite of many, a good guy who would die tragically but heroically saving a friend in Boston's Coconut Grove holocaust, Buck Jones, was scripted into Mex hero duds. Never having played anything but what he was in real life, an honest cowpuncher, he was turned into the "Black Shadow," an avenger with a moustache, sideburns and heavy "Mex dialect--when he could remember it." Adults loved the novelty and the kids were even more "enthusiastic supporters."] **V**:4.22.31.

[1471] **BORDER LAW**, C: [In this solid little western Buck Jones was on the other side of the avenging border as an undercover Ranger infiltrating a gang of baddies across the Rio to bring them to justice. Jones insisted that his characterizations as a hero not be stretched to transcend credulity, he disliked the super hero nonsense and the fight staged in the Mexican cantina is a good example of this. He received almost as good as he gave, but triumphed only after the final blow, just ahead of the villain he was fighting. The amorous and sweetly seductive cantina girl was Lopita Tovar, a prize, well worth fighting for, on either side of the border.] **V**:9.15.31, **FD**: 9.13.31.

[1472] **CAMINO DEL INFIERNO** SV **THE MAN WHO CAME BACK**, F: [Raoul Walsh directed Janet Gaynor and Charles Farrell in the sentimentalized English version of the original gripping play which dealt with the problems of dope addiction and the road back to civility. In the Spanish version, Maria Alba and Juan Torena make the tortuous journey in a much more realistic fashion. They were well supported by:Carlos Villarias, Rafael Valverde, Ralph Navarro, Carmen Rodriguez and Lucio Villegas.]

[1473] **CAPTAIN THUNDER**, W: [Most film goers are probably unaware that there are a significant number of archives located throughout the United States which house volumes of material on productions remembered only by those interested in film and film history. For example, the bulk of Warner Brothers invaluable film related material is housed at the University of Southern California in the capable charge of Leith Adams. Such conscientious and incredibly knowledgeable individuals provide invaluable service as custodians of valuable archives for writer/researchers. They deserve more thanks than they receive. So, thanks, Leith! Almost all of Warner's productions have some file material available. In an era when print media was the primary means of conveying news and information, much of it, related to film, was saved for future historians to evaluate. Even a minor production such as this produced a significant body of material. The **Press Sheet** supplied to exhibitors to help promote a particular film was usually eight folio pages long and filled with advice on 'ballyhooing' a film like, **CAPTAIN THUNDER** ... "HOT TAMALE HEARTBREAKER," "the Glamorous Adventures of an Amorous Adventurer." Victor Varconi starred as "El Captain Thunder" in this "Hard Riding Romance of Old Mexico" where he broke "Mexican Heads and Hearts." Many pictures of a handsome, cigarette smoking, Captain Thunder and a very lovely Spanish looking señorita, Fay Wray, adorn the pages of this promotion. The Captain was promoted as the "grandest lover on the Rio Grande! Kid Casanova on horseback! He wrote the book of love ... a chapter every night ... one for every boudoir in Mexico!" Warners also published the **SCRIPT**, out of Beverly Hills, which provided a brief scenario of many of its productions, this one included. Despite all this noise, **Variety** was barely luke warm with its comments. An "unimportant burlesque ... purporting to detail the glamorous sincerity of a Mexican Robin Hood amid incongruous surroundings, unbelievable situations and characters." The Captain was an "unvarying villain" who always smiled, and kept his word, and granted any wish to a lovely señorita. Having promised the heavy that he would wed him to the lady of his choice, he discovers that the woman he has chosen loves another. To remedy the fault while still honoring his pledge, he makes the two get married at gun point and then shoots the groom immediately, freeing the lady for the man of her choice. "Carrida mia." But the critic was not convinced, no matter how "rumbatic the female." According to the trade, "there was nothing in contemporary Mexican History to give such a glamorous air to that unsettled territory." Although Hollywood had attempted to romanticize the Mexican bandit into an acceptable form, **Variety** was apparently not convinced.] **MPH**: 5.16.31, P36, **V**:5.13.31, **NYT**: 5.11.31, **Script**, 1.18.30, **Warner Brothers Press Sheet**, "Captain Thunder." UCS. Students interested in a good general list of archival sources might begin with: **Nancy Allen. Film Study Collections**: Ungar, 194 pages.

[1474] **CARNE DE CABARET SV TEN CENTS A DANCE**, C: [The Hispanic title was certainly more descriptive than the English one. Barbara Stanwyck and Ricardo Cortez were the stars in the English version, Lupita Tovar and Ramon Pereda in the other. The supporting cast included Rene Cardona, Carmen Guerrero, Soledad Jimenez and Maria Calvo.]

[1475] **LE CHANTEUR DE SEVILLE**, MGM: [Ramon Navarro directed this all French version of the **Call of the Flesh**.] **V**:3.18.31.]

[1476] **CHERI BIBI SV THE PHANTOM OF PARIS**, MGM: [John Gilbert played the starring role in the English version of this tale of murder in Paris, Ernesto Vilches in its Spanish counterpart. The other Hispanic players were: Maria F. Lardon de Guevara, Maria Tubau, Maria Luz Callejo, Eduardo Arozamena Jose Soriano Viosca, Manuel Arbo and Manuel Paris.] English review, **V**:11.17.31.

[1477] **THE CISCO KID**, F: ["A swashbuckler with a heart. A rogue who lived for romance. A villain only to men. A hero to women, ... rough-riding, quick-shooting, hard-living son-of-a-gun", all that was Fox's new edition of the Cisco Kid. This was the first of the new formatted Cisco adventures, from this time on saddled with a loyal, but frequently inept, except when essential, sidekick, in this case Gordito. Neither had learned to speak any better since the last time. Cisco to Carmencita: "Oh no no. My Spanish she is not so good. You see, my-my-my father she was born in San Luis Obispo and my mother he is come from Portugal, so I like much better the English to speak." And the good Cavalry captain was still looking for him. In this adventure, Warner Baxter continues as the Robin Hood of the border and there's a purdy widda woman with lots of kids he likes, who is about to be evicted by 'oil canacito Harry'. So the kid steals $5000 and gives it to the lady for the rent. She is very happy and so is Carmencita, Conchita Montenegro, a recent import, who really loves the Anglo, but that could never be scripted until the last sequel. Realizing, that in reality, the Mexican bandit has a truly good heart, Sergeant Dunn allows Cisco and friend to escape and all is well, save for the longing looks as the lovers leave for their respective sides of the border.] **MPH**:10.10.31, p46, [six page promotion], 10.24, 31, back cover, 12.5.31, p67, **V**:10.27.31, **FD**:10.25.31, 10.13.31, back page, **NYT**:10,24,31, **FD**:10.25.31, Script: **The Cisco Kid**, p9, [54 pages] NYSAA.

[1478] **CLEARING THE RANGE**, Allied: [Hoot Gibson returns home to find the murderer of his brother and experiences a series of misadventures. In one of them he is mistaken for that Spanish bandit that could be found almost anywhere in 1931. In the final reel George Mendoza is discovered to be the real culprit. Hoot is cleared, and the Mexican was duly punished.] **V**:5.27.31, **FD**:5.24.31.

[1479] **EL CODIGO PENAL** SV **THE CRIMINAL CODE**, C: [More prison stuff, with screws and stoolies and plans to break out. Walter Houston led the way out in the English version and Barry Norton in the Spanish remake. The Hispanic cast included: Carlos Villarias, Maria Alba, Manuel Arbo, Mario Calvo, Julio Villarreal, Alfredo del Diestro, and Ramon Peon. Several other Anglo's were also in on the break.] English review: **V**:1.7.31.

[1480] **EL COMEDIANTE**, MGM: [The cast included:Ernesto Vilches, Angelita Benitez, Maria Calvo, Manuel Arbo, Antonio Vidal and Jose Soriano Viosca.]

[1481] **LAS COMPANAS CAPISTRANO**, Sp/J. H. Hoffberg: [**Film Daily** was severely critical of this "All-Spanish production of old California". They considered it to be "amateurish" in all its aspects. Exhibiting an attitude not unfamiliar to **Variety**'s usual condescending appraisal of south of the border film goers, they ventured that "This one may prove okay for uncritical South American audiences, but it is way below the standard of other foreign films .... It rates a poor production in all departments, carelessly directed [by Leon de la Mothe], with a weak story [written by the same] loosely put together." Of course the same story had been lensed on this side of the pond many times, but with the aid of more advanced Hollywood technology. This was Spanish California days from a Spanish writer, and much the same, save that it was being "indifferently acted" by an entire Spanish cast. There was a typical tyrannical governor who found himself in the midst of a rebellion who sets out to bring in the ringleader. The señorita he assigns to the task falls in love with her prey and everybody does a great deal of singing for no apparent reason save that the Spanish are a gay, fun and music loving people. In the final analysis the critic considered it "too loose to rate serious attention." As one of the major trades, exhibitors paid attention to **Variety**'s evaluations, not so much for critical comment, but in terms of increasing their own potential profit.] **FD:11.29.31.**

[1482] **CONOCESA TU MUJER SV DON'T BET ON WOMEN**, F: [Something of a French farce has a bored sophisticate, Rafael Rivelles accepting a wager that he can kiss the wife of his best friend, Julio Pena. He does so on a lark without realizing that she truly loves him. He never discloses his true feelings. The lovely lady was Carmen Larrabeiti and the others in the cast: Ana Maria Custodio, Manuel Arbo, Miguel Ligero, Enriqueta Soler, and Rafael Calvo.]

[1483] **THE CONQUERING HORDE**, P: [The action for this film was set in Texas after the Civil war and was concerned mainly with settling the problems created by that bloody conflict. Almost invariably, Hollywood cast its sympathy with the those forces south of the Mason Dixon line and that was especially true for Texas. But still, the reestablishing of law and order, even if under Union supervision, was necessary. There were indians to deal with, railroads to build, civilization to advance and carpetbaggers to clear out. And for laughs there were the necessary Mexican characterizations for the second time, worth every bit of what he was called, a character named, Cinco Centavos was included in the cast.] **V:4.1.31.**

[1484] **CUANDO TE SUICIDAS?** P, Joinville: [The cast was comprised of: Imperio Argentina, Manuel Russell, Fernando Soler, Carmen Mavascues and Jose Isbert.]

[1485] **CUBAN LOVE SONG**, MGM: [Metropolitan opera star Laurence Tibbits and a vivacious, even voluptuous, Lupe Velez starred in this film taken from an alleged to be, Cuban folk song, the "Peanut Vendor". Velez was the pv and Tibbits the visiting Marine, buddy to the immortal Jimmy Durante. Marines do as marines will and immediately after one of them has done Lupe, he leaves for WWI. The sweet señorita waves as the company marches out of Havana to the strains of the "Cuban Love Song." Wounded in the war, he, Tibbits, who would have fared better in grand opera, is returned to his San Francisco sweetheart and nursed back to health by her tender loving care. Enjoying great success in business, the now married couple leave for New York to relocate. But there was always something missing. One night ten years later, in a night club, the strains of rhumba music reminded the former marine of warmer evenings in the tropics. Returning to Cuba, he finds Durante, who has been hanging around just waiting for him to do so. Joyfully reunited, their happiness ends quickly when they find that Lupe has died of a broken heart. But before heading for her reward, it would seem that she had provided her errant lover with the fruit of their passion which he returns home with to give to his apparently broad minded wife. (Well it will work for Gregory Peck and Jennifer Jones, some time later.} Lupe was wonderful as the Cuban peanut vendor who gave away a bit more than her heart. The title song became a national hit, a trans media promotion that would continue to be employed with increasing frequency.] **MPH**: 10.24.31, **V**:12.8.31, **FD**:12.6.31.

Lupe's career was soaring at this time. The **Saturday Evening Post** took advantage of that fact to help it along a little more with a laudatory article describing her hot Latin temperament, explaining that it was the result of her being born in San Luis Potosi, Mexico during a hurricane. In Hollywood she was referred to as the "Wildcat" or the "Stormy Petrel." The **Post** was lovingly sarcastic about her accent: "Miss Velez now speaks perfect English, if you make certain natural allowances for her youth, inexperience and the fact that she cannot speak English perfectly. She speaks it enthusiastically." As such, this quality would insure Lupe's success for the remainder of her career. Audiences loved it. January 2, 1932, pp26-7.

[1486] **LA DAMA ATREVIDA** SV **THE LADY WHO DARED**, FN: [Some critics felt that Luana Alcaniz's performance in this Spanish version was superior to that given by Billy Dove in the English production. The mainly Mexican cast included: Ramon Pereda, Martin Garralaga, Antonio Vidal, Ligia de Golconda, Alfredo del Diestro, and Delia Magana.] See: **The Lady Who Dared** [1514].

[1487] **DAYBREAK**, MGM: [In this film Roman Navarro played a young Viennese guardsman who fell so deeply into debt that he seriously contemplated suicide. He was saved from doing so by the love of a naughty lady who had also fallen from grace. Hollywood's solution for this socio-economic melodrama was deceptively simple. They married the unfortunates to one another so that they might live happily ever after.] **V**:6.2.31.

[1488] **DON JUAN DIPLOMATICO** SV **THE BOUDOIR DIPLOMAT**, U: [Uncharacteristically, **Variety** was quick to praise this Spanish language version made by Universal. They predicted a good box office and complemented the cast, especially the female entries, Lia Tora and Celia Montalvan, although the male lead, Miguel Faust Rocha, was considered a bit "wooden." It was felt that it would do well not only in the local "Span/Lang houses", but as a feature anywhere else throughout the Americas. It's opening in Argentina was well received and it played successfully throughout the Americas. Also in the cast were: Enrique Acosta, Juan Aristi Eulate, Eduardo Arozamena, Julio Villarreal and Rafael Navarro.] **V**:4.22.31. See also: **Alfonso Pinto**, "When Hollywood Spoke Spanish", **Americas**, October 1980, pp3-8, which features a good selection of photographs including some of the players in this film.

[1489] **DOS NOCHES** = **TWO NIGHTS**, Mex/ Fanchon Royer/MGM: [This Spanish version of **Revenge at Monte Carlo** used a Mexican cast to restore a deposed president, not of one of the Latin republics, but of a mythical European nation, a little lesson learned from Hollywood. Although this service was provided across the pond, this writer is unfamiliar with any Latin film scenario that involved the nationals of a South American republic coming north to save a troubled leader in the United States ala Richard Harding Davis. Now there's plot potential, it might even help reduce the deficit. Included in this cast were: Jose Crespo, Conchita Montenegro, Litas Santos, Carlos Villarias, Romualdo Tirado, Juan Martinez Pla, Antonio Cumellas and Martin Garralaga.] LCFL: Clippings. FD:5.10.33.

[1490] **DRACULA** SV **DRACULA**, U: [This was one of the more successful Spanish versions, it played very well throughout the North American circuit and even better, south of the border. Carlos Villarias played a sufficiently sinister lead, but Lopita Tovar, who would be used in secondary roles in other Hollywood features, was the real reason audiences flocked to see this one. The dream factory on that other coast, seriously underestimated the star potential of many Hispanic actors and actresses introduced to local audiences by these Spanish language films. Sadly for all, these fine performers were offered only limited access to Hollywood features. They were there only because producers thought they would increase profits by speaking Spanish. Yet the experience for most was still valuable in as much as many of those players acquired the skills necessary to provide the backbone of the Mexican film industry's dynamic growth in the late thirties and forties.]

[1491] **DREYFUS**, British International: [Playing the main character, Cedric Hardwicke left the British stage for this, his first role in films. His portrayal of the Jewish officer, wrongly convicted, because of his race, was lauded, but the film caused some minor rioting in France even thirty-five years after the original incident. This case which continued to reintroduce audiences to the tortures and isolation featured in the French penal colony at Devil's Island, would continue throughout film history, to be France's most frequent reason for protesting and even threatening to ban the importation of Hollywood product. More serious protests would be made in 1940, when a more graphic description of the prisons dehumanizing affect will be offered in **Devil's Island**.] MPH: 5.2.31, p44.

[1492] **DUGAN OF THE BAD LANDS,** Mono: [Monogram was the production company for this compact and effective western. Along with Republic studios these two elites of Hollywood's poverty row, would be responsible for perpetuating accepted western stereotypes from the mid thirties, throughout the forties and well into the fifties. Julian Rivero, as Pedro, a Mexican border smuggler, makes his first appearance in this tale of two friends helping out a sheriff who has a crooked deputy. Rivero would be many a western hero's loyal and humorous Hispanic sidekick. Always acceptably lecherous, but a devoted tonto to the end.] MPH:8.8.31, 8.17.31, V:9.15.31.

[1493] **DE FRENTE MARCHEN!** SV **DOUGHBOYS**, MGM: [In it's own lovable style, possibly the most important daily in the entertainment world expressed its feelings about Spanish language productions: "The good news of **"Variety"** that American producers are laying off remakes in foreign languages came a bit too late. Should have included this one in the basket. (Most of these films were produced in 1930-1931, very few there after, see: **Luces de Buenos Aires** [1522]) / Boring practically throughout, the few dozen words in Spanish spoken by Keaton are almost unintelligible. Conchita Montenegro is entirely so and the rest worst than third-raters./ **"De Frente Marchen!"** shows local audiences war shots of the most crazy nature possible. While 90% of the world was engaged, the other 10% is represented by Spanish-speaking population, so that dressing up Spaniards in American war kits adds the reverse angle of ridicule to what should be a funny picture./ If Metro had sent this one down in the original, with cut-in dialog, (it would have made a hit.) As it is, Palace and Grand Splendid audiences are wondering what it's all about. Metro doesn't tell 'em. / (This film) is quite bad enough to start another Spanish American War." **Variety**, more often than not, did not sympathize with Hollywood's attempt to satisfy the Hispanic audience's desire for Spanish speaking versions of successful English language productions. By 1936, the producers would stop trying. The cast also included: Buster Keaton, Romualdo Tirado, Juan de Landa, Victor Potel and Martin Garralaga.] **V:4.22.31.**

[1494] **EN CADA PUERTO UN AMOR** SV **WAY FOR A SAILOR**, MGM: [The English version of this film brought John Gilbert a lot closer to losing whatever was left of the appeal he had possessed in the silents. Jose Crespo did a superior job as the hard boiled sailor in the Spanish version. It would have been difficult not to with the enchanting Conchita Montenegro as his prize. Others in the cast included: Juan de Landa, Romualdo Tirado, Elena Landeros and Rosita Granada.] **V:12.17.30.**

[1495] **ESCLAVAS DE LA MODA** SV **ON YOUR BACK**, F: [Self sacrificing mother loves her boy and works her way up in business to provide him with a college education, but he squanders himself on a lady who loves only clothes and the other man who provides for her. This scenario was a natural for the Hispanic cast: Carmen Larrabeti, Julio Pena, Blanca de Castejon, Enriqueta Soler, and Felix de Pomes.]

[1496] **LA FIESTA DEL DIABLO** SV **THE DEVIL'S HOLIDAY**, P, Joinville: [A very busy lady at the Paris studio, Carmen Larrabeiti, was called upon this time to play the role in which Nancy Carroll had excelled in "persuasively" portraying the "icy-hearted, strictly business, vamping chiseler" who becomes the soul-miserable repentant, every broken hearted little boy's dream. The cast also included: Tony D'Algy, Felix de Pomes, Carlos Diaz de Mendoza, Miguel Ligerto, Amelia Munoz, Manuel Russel and Mercedes Servet.] **V:5.14.30.**

[1497] **THE FIGHTING SHERIFF**, C: [Another Buck Jones western very similar to all the other entries, but considered by western film historian, Buck Rainey, "one of his best." The señorita that he defended and liked from afar was Nina

Quartero who played, Tiana, as always in Buck's movies, a lovely Mexican lady.] **V:5.27.31**.

[1498] <u>**LA FRUTA AMARGA**</u> SV <u>**MIN AND BILL**</u>, [Marie Dressler and Wallace Beery starred in this classic. <u>**Variety**</u> praised the pair of troopers by claiming that no two other Hollywood players could have even have considered the roles. In the Spanish version, Virginia Fabregas, who came to be called the "Mexican" Marie Dressler," probably did so because of her star performance in this film. She was supported by Juan De Landa, Elvira Moria, Maria Luz Callejo, Julio Pena, Juan de Homs, Alma Real and Juan Duval.] English review, <u>**V**</u>:11.26.30.

[1499] <u>**GENTE ALEGRE**</u>, MGM: [The cast included: Roberto Rey, Rosita Moreno, Ramon Pereda, Delia Magana, Carmen Rodriguez, Vicente Padula, Maria Calvo and Luis Llaneza.]

[1500] <u>**GIPSY BLOOD**</u>, Indy/Arthur Dent: [This year's reinterpretation of the Merimee-Bizet combination provoked significant displeasure with some reviewers. Fooling around with one's accepted stereotypes, especially established classics, could drip a little sarcasm from the tip of a scribes acid pen. "Nobody will recognize" this "old and well-loved friend," masquerading "under a name which ill benefits" her. By comparison he thought that <u>**The Merchant of Venice**</u> might well be called, <u>**His Pound of Flesh**</u>, a film adaptation from the works of "Will Shaka-da-Spear." This more operatic version of the Spanish vamps destruction of several stalwart soldiers was sung by Marguerite Namara who was considered to be "seductive,! fascinating! pulsating with the passion of Spanish blood!!", at least those stereotypes were sacred. But, this film, although it might have satisfied "the unfortunates who [had] never heard <u>**Carmen**</u> on the operatic stage, or seen earlier productions, was considered to have failed. That long line of "Carmens, Don Joses and toreadors" who had engraved their image on generations, might well have lamented this production. Or so some felt.] <u>**NYT**</u>:11.22.31, VIII, p6.

[1501] <u>**GOD'S COUNTRY AND THE MAN**</u>, Syndicate: [Considered above the "routine blah" of many western hosopreys, this tight little production used Julian Rivero in what would become his most enduring part, the somewhat lecherous, but loyal, extra sidekick, George (to be) "Gabby" Hayes, occupying the first position. With these two friends, Rivero, having once been a "bad an", Tom Tyler patrolled the Mexican border. In this case they were keeping a close eye out on the operation of certain gun smugglers that threatened the security of one particular town. It seems the baddies were using it to run their contraband over the border, so the boys had to wait for them to leave, before they could act, so no innocent person would be harmed. They do and of course there's a lady that helps.] <u>**FD**</u>:6.7.31.

[1502] <u>**HARD HOMBRE**</u>, Allied Pictures Corp: [Hoot Gibson in one of his most liked films plays "Peaceful" Patton for many laughs instead of the usual hokey melodrama. He is really a wimp, but resembles a tough and as such commands authority and a lot of smiles until the real heavy returns. Lina Basquette helps out as the warm blooded señorita Peaceful does not know what to do with. Everyone enjoyed watching her trying to show him how to be a real macho man.] **V**:10.6.31, **FD**:9.20.31.

[1503] **HAY QUE CASAR AL PRINCIPE** SR **PAID TO LOVE**, F: [Conchita Montenegro took on Virginia Valli's role as the innocent apache dancer sent on a diplomatic mission to some Zenda like kingdom where she finds herself in the bedroom of the Prince. The very lucky aristocrat was Jose Moijica who tried to make the most of his good fortune, but was bested at every turn by the most attractive super heroine. Both were aided in their affair by Miguel Ligero, Manuel Arbo, and Pepe Alcantara in the supposedly somewhere in the Balkans swashbuckler.]

[1504] **HELL BOUND**, Tiffany: [At the end of a long career, of which he could be proud, having played almost a hundred character roles in support of various male leads, Leo Carillo could claim two distinct continental homelands. Many of the Latin nations south of the border could call him their own, but Italy had almost an equal right. In the thirties, he found himself most frequently a Hispanic, but also one of the sons of Italy where he could just as easily be at Wrigley field, with the rest of the gang, planning to knock off some rival member of the mob. He had a talent for what audiences considered the dialect spoken by typical Mexican bandits, or typical Chicago mobsters. In this film he was Nick Cotrelli gunned down by machine gun fire on old Broadway.] **NYT**:5.9.31.

[1505] **HOLLYWOOD, CIUDAD DE ENSUENO**, = **HOLLYWOOD, CITY OF ILLUSION**, Sono Art--World Wide. Hispano/Universal: [Universal offered the Spanish language market an insiders look at the internal working of the city of fantasy, illusion and delight with this film. Although produced in 1931, it did not reach the Teatro Variedades until some time later. Critics considered it less action filled than the 1933 Fox entry with a similar theme, **Ciudad de Catron** [1601] the plot has the hard boiled head of the studio, Lia Tora, discovering South American talent Jose Bohr and giving him his shot at the big time. In doing so she falls in love with him and has to deal with all of the complications the fame she afforded him helped create. Part of that problem was a little pretty, Nancy Drexel, who wanted to learn just enough Spanish "to make love." Enrique Acosta, Elena Landeros and Cesar Vanoni were also cast.] **NYT**:4.4.34, **FD**:4.10.34.

[1506] **HOMBRES EN SU VIDA** SV **THE MEN IN HER LIFE**, C: [Old stuff has a classy well to do and very sexy lady, Lupe Velez, falling for reformed diamond in the rough and no longer a bootlegger good guy. Luis Alonso, not yet Gilbert Roland, was the lucky guy who kept Lupe from jail. The others in the cast included: Ramon Pereda, Carlos Villaria, Luis Alberni.] English review, **V**:12.1.31.

[1507] **HORIZONTES NUEVOS** SV **THE BIG TRAIL**, F: [This two million dollar western in its English version scenically directed by Raoul Walsh, had early treckers led by John Wayne, making their way laboriously to Oregon. Some of the footage was used in the Spanish language version. George Lewis, a Hollywood Anglo in many western border films was starred. The Hispanic cast included Carmen Guerrero, Roberto Guzman, Allan Garcia, Martin Garralaga, Tito Davison, Carlos Villarias, Julio Villarreal, Lucio Villegas, and Renee Torres. See the **Big Trail**, 1930 [1377].]

[1508] **HOTTER THAN HAITI**, U: [Slim Summerville and Harry Gibbon, a solid comedy team especially in short featurettes, found themselves in Central America this time and had what was considered then, a little fun with the natives. In one scene Slim was trying to type a letter to a señorita on what he thought to be a local typewriter. Never very bright he was in reality using a detonator designed for explosive charges. This natural mistake was overlooked because his screen stupidity served the purpose. Audiences howled with laughter when they watched the local natives screaming at the top of their primitive lungs and running wildly in all directions when Slim accidently blew up their ramshackle huts. It was a different time, but not all that much.] **MPH:12.5.31.**

[1509] **HURRICANE HORSEMAN**, Willis Kent: [The Anglo hero here is a gunsmith who travels from the banks of the Pecos to the shores of the Sabine fixing shootnirns that need repair. As he approaches the border he comes across a band of outlaws that are holding a Spanish woman, Marie Quillan, prisoner. Sensing she must be saved, he devises a plan which involves repairing their guns. Having done so he sneaks off with the sleek señorita. When the gang tries to shoot them down, they realize that they have really overpaid the gunsmith, none of their weapons will fire a single shot, which allows the two to make an easy escape.] **V:11.17.31.**

[1510] **I LIKE YOUR NERVE**, FN: [The younger Douglas Fairbanks was given the starting assignment in this tale of a bookworm/weakling, (you can tell by the glasses) who is transformed into an Anglo hero like dad, when a gypsy lady tells him he needs a change of scenery. One reviewer could not figure out whether he had traveled to "South or Central America" for the action despite the fact that he had driven there by auto. Wherever he was, there was a young Loretta in trouble. Her father had been caught with his fingers in the till and the evil Minister of Finance of this imaginary Latin Republic was forcing her to wed against her wishes. The new Douglas, realizing the problem, manages to extort the $200,000 from the minister using a phoney kidnapping ruse. He then gives it to the little señorita for her delinquent dad. It wasn't great, but Doug Junior had to make it without much help from dad, and he certainly did. The incredible expansion cable television has experienced in recent times has given rise to at least three channels that feature many of the older black and whites. American Movie Classics, intelligently hosted by Bob Dorian and filled with informative background material on many of the older films, is a gold mine of entertainment for even the disinterested in historical background. Douglas Fairbanks Jr. is a frequent guest, plugging books and providing more than interesting information on many of these older classics. This film, along with hundreds of other classics listed in these pages have been shown in the past few years. Coupled with Turner broadcasting's TNT and TBS, films that might have been left to die, buried and forgotten in dusty archives forever are now frequently featured in the living rooms of more than a hundred million viewers on a daily basis.] **V**:9.15.31.

[1511] <u>EL IMPOSTOR</u> SV <u>SCOTLAND YARD</u>, F: [Edmund Lowe played the romantic high class thief in the English version of enjoyable mystery, Juan Torena in the Spanish language one. The object of infection was Blanca de Castejon, and Carlos Villarias did the chasing.]

[1512] <u>IN YOUR SOMBRERO</u>, Vitaphone: [This seven minute short had crammed into that brief time span just about every stereotypical situation Hollywood had created since its first days. Although the tone of the review was generally negative, audiences had become so comfortable with the characterizations that they continued unchanged throughout the decade. This attempt to spoof what so many thought might have been a real life situation apparently failed. "There is hardly a bright spot in this short of a newspaper reporter who is captured by Mexican bandits and who after much slapstick stuff and meaningless procedure escapes. The reporter is freed from his cell by a native girl, who puts him in a truck that has driven into the prison yard. The truck is filled with canned goods but in each can is some smuggled ammunition. They drive out of the prison confines and while escaping throw the cans at their pursuers causing many explosions, but little laughter."] **FD**:11.15.31.

[1513] <u>LA JAULA DE LOS LEONES</u> SV <u>THE LION'S JAWS</u>, Ci-Ti-Go Productions: [<u>Variety</u>, more often than not, cynical and condescending with regard to Hispanic productions and Hispanics in general, was in character with its criticism of this work: They considered it an "inferior picture." "Photography and sound are both bad and cast playing is of the meller [melodrama] type. But Spanish audiences are said to like this sort of thing." Our Hispanic hero has a little luck when on the same day he picks up a poor old blind lady with a nina and obtains a job as a lion trainer. It could happen! Within ten years, the dineros are rolling in. Two nurses attend the Señora and the little hija wants to marry the brave performer. Then tragedy, the old lady dies, and grief stricken, he allows his gros gatos to claw him to death. Made in Hollywood, all the actors spoke a different dialect of Spanish, "Pure Spanish, Cuban, Mexican, its all mixed up." No matter, the Latin houses loved it. The cast featured: Romualdo Tirado, Alicia Bell, Amelia Bell, Luis Mendoza Lopez, Jose Pena "Pepet", and Alfonso Pedrozo.] **V**:3.27.31, **FD**:3.8.31.

[1514] <u>THE LADY WHO DARED</u>, FN: [Critics panned this Billy Dove production as being lifeless, devoid of emotion and without action. She is married to he who is a consular officer in an unidentified South American post, They speak Spanish there, but they frequently did in Hollywood's Brazil. He is completely unaware of his lady's extra marital activities, possibly because "he was one of those screen husbands who has the wool pulled over his eyes, and likes it." She's hot for some mixture of moralist and diamond smuggler, so that goes nowhere. The only Hispanics one sees are for identifying location and atmosphere. As if to provide evidence that the censor's were having their way, one critic wrote: "this is strictly a talking picture. It seems to have been made along lines that might constitute a translation of the Hays Production Code."] **V**:6.9.31.

[1515] **LARIATS AND SIX SHOOTERS**, Cosmo: [Reviewed as: "AVERAGE WESTERN DEALING WITH SMUGGLING OVER THE MEXICAN BORDER", Jack Perrin played a deputy sheriff that tried real hard to stop that illegal traffic, and did, in the last reel but he had one heck of a time doing it.] **FD**:10.25.31.

[1516] **LASCAR OF THE RIO GRANDE**, U: [Based on the poem "Lascar," this tragic romance tells the story of a fiery Mexican girl, "a creature of impulse," who flirts with, hates, and finally sacrifices her life for a man she really loves. It was old in 1913, but with stars like Leo Carillo, Johnny Mack Brown and Slim Summerville, Dorothy Burges, as the sweet, selfsacrificing señorita had a lot of solid support and assistance dying for her hombre.] **MPW**:10.01.31, **FD**:12.13.31.

[1517] **LAW OF THE RIO GRANDE**, Indy: [If there was such a thing in this production it was difficult to discern. Producers merely tried to capitalize on the significant popularity that anything even closely related to the border or that river enjoyed in 1931.] **V**: 8.11.31, **FD**:8.9.31.

[1518] **LA LEY DEL HAREN** SV **FAZIL [THE LAW OF THE HAREM]**, F: [Fox was really reaching into the distant past with this touch of the **Sheik** to provide audiences with another Spanish language scenario. In this adaptation, for lack of a better word, the Sultan of the Sands became a romantic singing Arab Prince, because the Latin star had an excellent singing voice known throughout the Americas. Jose Mojica, who played the part as well as it was scripted, was made to meet Parisienne beauty, Carmen Larrabetti, and when she heard him singing, her heart palpitations beat the desert sands into a dust storm that only highlighted their passionate embraces. Here were Arab passions seeking to have European morals willingly submit to the seduction of a Mexican sheik. The onlookers and faithful retainers could only dream. Few of the reviewers were satisfied with the story, but they liked the vamping efforts of Maria Alba. Also included were, Julio Villarreal, Miguel Ligero, Rafael Calvo, and Ralph Navarro.] **FD**:6.20.33.

[1519] **LA LLAMA SAGRADA** SV **THE SACRED FLAME**, W: [Martin Garralaga took on Conrad Nagel's role in this Somerset Maugham play about a flyer who was crippled in an air crash on his wedding day and is forced to stay in a wheelchair until his merciful mother turns out his lights and grounds him for good.

Elvira Morta was the mom and Luana Alcaniz the unhappy wife. Also included were Joan de Homs, Carmen Rodriguez and Antonio Vidal.] English review:**V**:11.27.29

[1520] **MAMA**, F: [The cast included Catalina Barcena, Ravael Rivelles, Maria Lux Callejo, Julio Pena, Andres de Segurola, Felix de Pomes, Enriquita Soler, Jose Nieto and Rafael Calvo.]

[1521] **LO MEJOR ES RIER SV LAUGHTER**, P, Joinville: [First a Broadway play, this comedy drama was brought to the talking screen with Nancy Carroll as the star who chose to leave wealth for the poor composer she loves. In the Spanish version, Imperio Argentina, now recognized as a real talent, took on the role of the heroine. Her supporters included: Pepe Romeu, Manuel Russel, Miguel Ligero, Rosita Diaz Gimeno, Antonio Monjardin, and Antonia Arevalo.] English review, **V**:10.1.30.

[1522] **LUCES DE BUENOS AIRES** = **LIGHTS OF BUENOS AIRES**, P, Joinville: [One of the most innovative responses to the language problem created by the introduction of talking pictures was Paramount's attempt to set up a complete studio system in Joinville, France where foreign nationals could be employed to make films that would appeal to various nationalities, the Spanish, Latin American and French markets being of foremost concern. Carried to the extreme, one assumes that there would have had to be a Serbo/Croation division established in Soloniki to guarantee profits in the Kingdom of the South Slav's, another on the Bolivian Altiplano, with subdivisions for the Quecha, Ayarama and the Hispanics that ruled them. **Film Daily** reported that Paramount was making plans for "ninety versions" of "twenty scheduled" films in "13 languages", certainly a challenge for the casting department. Not to make light of this sincere attempt on Hollywood's part to tailor their productions to the various sensitivities of differing nationalities, it proved, in the long run, unnecessary: The world wanted and demanded the best films produced anywhere, Hollywood's. "Luces" was a good example of the effort to adapt to various nationalistic needs. Using an Argentine cast, "excellent tango music, snappy Spanish dialogue of the kind Argentines like" and some good comedy, this film was a success. The scenario was simple and familiar to North American audiences, the local merely shifted from New York to Buenos Aries. A big time producer goes to the outback and has his car breakdown. As it is being repaired he hears of a local lady who can really sing. In no time at all he has her convinced to come to the big city, where he makes her a star. Once there, he wants to be her only nightly attraction, but the rich young rancher who loves her follows and when he sees all, he scorns her. Yet, the rancher's faithful gauchos have also followed and they take action. First they seize the cash box, and then they lasso the lady right off the stage, tie her up and deliver her to her man. It was a "wow." Other products of the Joinville office were not and film making there would end after five years of effort. **Charles Ford** provides a brief survey of the operation with **"Paramount At Joinville"**, **Films in Review**,

November 1961, pp541-550.] "JOINVILLE MAKING 110 IN 12 LANGUAGES," FD: 8.26.30, "FRENCH-SPANISH VERSIONS FOR 20 PARIS PICTURES," FD:9.5.30, V:11.10.31.

[1523] **THE MALTESE FALCON**, W: [Vienna born of Spanish parents, Ricardo Cortez was the first Hollywood star to give life to the immortal character created by the fertile mind of Dashil Hammet. He was the silver screen's first Sam Spade.] NYT:5.29.31.

[1524] **THE MAN FROM DEATH VALLEY**, Mono: [When Tom Tyler decides to return to his home town to rekindle an old flame he discovers that a some local heat has been warming his former sweetheart's fires. Worse, or better, he also learns that the hot blooded lawman who has replaced him is crooked and involved with a bunch of Mexican bandits, led by Gino Corrado. The baddies had counted on robbing the town bank, but not on Tom's arrival. In short order the hero thwarts their plans, puts his rival in the cooler and "wins back his lady."] V:10.13.31.

[1525] **MOONLIGHT AND ROMANCE**, P: [Paramount used this entertaining seven minute short to display the talents of two of its most recent Hispanic imports. Former ballroom dancer, Rosita Moreno and Latin singing sensation, Nino Martini provided the song and dance, "south of the border" style.] FD:2.22.31.

[1526] **LA MUJER X** SV **MADAME X**, MGM: [As the ultimate screen portrait of feminine suffering and selfsacrifice this film would be remade numerous times. Maria F. Landron starred in the Spanish version. Jose Crespo was the husband and both were well supported by the following Hispanic players: Rafael Rivelles, Julio Pena, Juan Martinez Pla, Carmen Rodriquez, Luis Llaneza, Manuel Arbo, Henry Armetta, Fred Malatesta and Agostino Borgato.]

[1527] **99 WOUNDS**, Tiffany: [Tom Tyler was the Anglo lead in this western set on the border where there was a lot of trouble between warring indians who help up across the Rio Grande and attacked settlers on the other side, whenever they wanted to cause a little trouble. With the help of the lovely [none of these ladies were ever unattractive], Trilby Clark, as Carmencita Esteban, the cute cantina chiquita, he soon discovered that the real baddies were whites who dressed up in Indian gear to make the local native Americans, from either side of the river, look bad. With hands stretched across the border Tom and Carmencita recruited the real "redskins" to help resolve the problem. Rarely provided with the opportunity to vindicate themselves on the silver screen, the Indios willingly helped capture the renegade Anglos.] MPG.

[1528] **PAGAN LADY**, C: [When girls/women of the thirties indulged themselves with a little free love experimentation, it was a lot easier if such warm blooded exercises took place in the tropics. The tropical locale for this film was Havana, which from early times was considered the sin capital of the

Caribbean. In this one the lady belonged to a gangster, but was attracted by this sappy looking bible thumper who tried to show her the right path. That apparently led to a little island retreat where they spent the night, not necessarily praying. When it was time to repent, she could not, being the bad lady, keep the boy. As was usually the case for males sowing wild seeds, so to speak, he was allowed to return to the comfort of his chapters and verses, without having to help with the harvest. For the lady, screen pain was required. After sufficient suffering, she even attempts to reform her gangster friend by presenting him with a little pregnant present. All this was way too much for the Production Code, such sordid scenarios could not be allowed to have happy endings. Much of the action in this movie was filmed against the lush tropical beauty of the Cuban island and in a real waterfront Havana cafe. The latter was destroyed in a scene that could have been substituted without much notice as a continuation of the fight sequence in **Her Man** [1411], all except the tropical storm which hits the island, a little PCA punishment for such lewd behavior. But reviewers were impressed with its realistic staging.] **V**:9.22.31.

[1529] **PANAMA**, ["Torrid tale of tropical señoritas ...." With Fifi Dorsay as the number one temptress.] **MPH**:5.9.31. LCFL: **Pressbook.**

[1530] **EL PASADO ACUSA** SV **GOOD BAD GIRL**, C: [Good girl with bad reputation, Luana Alcaniz, fails to tell the boy she marries that she had once been a gangsters moll. Disaster follows when he learns the truth of her "checkered past," those rules were tough then. The other Hispanics in the cast included: Carlos Villarias, Maria Calvo and Julio Villarreal.] English review, **V**:5.20.31.

[1531] **PRIM** Sp: [Cast exclusively with Spanish actors, this faithful retelling of the life and death of General Prim, a 19th century progressive politician was applauded by the critics as a significant technical advance over prior productions. The story was told with historical accuracy and sensitivity, without "the usual histrionics" and melodrama, and was "made with special good taste." The epilogue presented a scene showing King Amadeo de Saboya paying homage to the assassinated soldier.] **V**:3.11.31.

[1532] **PUEBLO TERROR**, Cosmo: [Possibly Hollywood's greatest stuntman, Yakima Canutt received screen credits as an actor in this border indian tale, but all of the Hispanics included were merely incidental and were not mentioned.] **FD**:9.12.31.

[1533] **LOS QUE DANZAN** SV **THOSE WHO DANCE**, FN: [Antonio Moreno was given the lead in the Spanish language version of this film. It was basically cops and robbers stuff with Antonio, playing an undercover policeman who joins the mob to discover who had killed his baby brother. The denouement comes when the mobsters give a dance to entertain their molls, including the lovely Maria Alba, and the guilty gangster gets his. Other Hispanics included were: Pablo Alvarez Rubio, Teresa

Renner, Tito Davison, Alfredo de Diestro, Martin Garralaga and Jose Soriano Viosca.] English Review, **V**:7.9.30.

[1534] **RESURRECTION**, U: [In this talking version of the Tolstoy play, Lupe Velez took the role of Katerina Maslova which Dolores Del Rio had so well portrayed in the 1927 silent version [1244].] **V**:1.28.31.

[1535] **RESURRECCION SV RESURRECTION**, U: [This Spanish language version also featured Lupe Velez and included an all star cast of Hispanic actors, mostly Mexican: Luis Alonso, Gilbert Roland, Miguel Faust Rocha, Soledad Jimenez, Amelia Senisterra and Eduardo Arozamena.]

[1536] **RIDERS OF THE CACTUS**, Hooper-Connell: [Considering the number of border westerns produced at this time, **Riders** merely reinforced what had become firmly established in the minds of the audience and the general public. The Mexican border was the place to smuggle stuff like, drugs, arms, ammunition and illegal aliens. In the thirty's it was the Chinese, later the locals would become the contraband and almost always Mexican bandits would be responsible for these illicit actions.] **V**:7.21.31, **FD**:8.16.31.

[1537] **SALAGA DE LA COCINA SV HONEY**, P, Joinville: [This comedy filled with humorous complications had the owners of a large estate renting it out so that they could send their sick dad some dollars. Not able to leave their home, the brother and sister become the maid and butler. Fun follows. The Hispanic cast included: Roberto Rey, Amparo Miguel Angel, Miguel Ligero, Carmen Jimenez, Enriqueta Soler, and Luis Llorens Vidal.] **V**:4.2.30.

[1538] **SOMBRAS DEL CIRO SV HALF WAY TO HEAVEN**, P, Joinville: [Amelia Munoz took on Jean Arthur's role in this Spanish version. She knew that the jealous "catcher" had allowed the boy "flyer" she loved to fall to his death. The melodrama that then unfolded was worked out with the help of Feliz de Pomes, Tony D'Algy, Miguel Ligero, Alfredo Hutado, Antonia Areyalo and Rafel Calvo.] English review, **V**:12.11.29]

[1539] **SON OF INDIA**, MGM: [The problems of interracial love, forbidden by the Production Code, were complicated even further by having the Mexican Roman Navarro, in his first talker which did not require him to sing, play the son of an Indian jewel merchant. The dark skins were apparently considered to be a good match. Although the French director had the white lady's brother try to explain the impossibility of such a union to Roman and he accepted it in the first version, even feeling lucky, satisfied that the blanca really loved him, Louis B. Mayer later insisted that there be a happy ending, after all, Roman had become a very rich high caste Indian. In Hollywood money, a lot of of it, often washed everything white.] **V**:7.28.3, **FD**:7.26.31.

[1540] **LO STORMO ATLANTICO**, Trans-America Film: [This silent production could be considered a newsreel. It provided audiences with "the official photographic record of the famous flight of General Balbo's air squadron from Italy to South America." The dozens of planes stopped to refuel at Gibraltar, flew to Natal and then on to Rio. The air shots were considered to be superior and the film was thought to be a sure hit, especially for the Italian market.] FD:7.26.31.

[1541] SQUAW MAN, MGM: [The only difference there was in this Cecil B. DeMille remake of the earlier version was that the Indians talk in their own Hollywood gibberish, they no longer sell cattle, some of them were oil rich, and a few of them go to college. More significantly, Lupe Velez was, Naturich, the squaw woman, and as sexy a one as any strong brave could ever have wanted.] V:9.22.31, FD:9.20.31.

[1542] STRANGERS MAY KISS, MGM: [Although the subject matter in this film was considered at the time controversial, reviewers felt that the director had handled it with some delicacy. This was not a time when the heroine was allowed the same latitude scripters provided for the hero. Neither society nor the Production Code could condone non adherence to "the conventions" even if the lady loved a world traveling international newsman who's views on marriage prevented their permanent union. They could have fun in the tropics for a while and did so during the honeymoon time they experienced on a "trip to Mexico," but that could not be allowed to last. When the cad was suddenly "called to Rio de Janeiro" all knew he was not the marrying kind, and that he would leave the liberated lady in that land of love all by herself. For a while the still attractive Norma Shearer managed with a little help from friends like Henry Armetta, but in the end she was forced to pay price for violating the code's double standard.] FD:4.12.31.

[1543] SU NOCHE DE BODAS SV HER WEDDING NIGHT, P, Joinville: [Paramount used a rising, way south of the border star, to play Clara Bow's role in this smart, sophisticated comedy, Imperio Argentina. She was well supported by a cosmopolitan Hispanic cast which included: Pepe Romeu, Manuel Russel, Miguel Ligero, Rosita Diaz, Gimeno, Antonio Monjardin and Antonia Arevalo.] English review, V:10.1.30.

[1544] SU ULTIMA NOCHE SR THE GAY DECEIVER, MGM: [In this feature Ernesto Vilches plays an out of town actor separated from his family who becomes involved with the sensuous and devil may care, Conchita Montenegro. She is also married, but unconcerned that her husband knows about her activities. The English version was far more tame than this one in Spanish. The other Hispanics in the cast included the beautiful Maria Alba, Juan de Landa, Paul Ellis, and Romualdo Tirado.] English review, V:10.6.26.

[1545] TEXAS RANGER, C: [There was a lot of hard riding and fast shooting in this fan pleaser which had Buck Jones as an undercover Ranger at first suspecting that the "attractive" Carmelita Geraghty was a bad bad bandita. But as it turned out, this was not the year for Mexican malevolence. She had killed no one, just rustled cattle from those who had taken hers. After they began sortinitout all out together, the real culprits had no chance and soon wereaheadin for the whoscow.] V:5.6.31, FD:5.10.31.

[1546] **TRAIL OF THE GOLDEN WEST**, Cosmo: [You could never trust halfbreeds at any point in Hollywood's history, this time the mongrelized misfits with more than likely some Mexican and indian blood, threaten a wagon train. The mixing of bloods would have to wait forty years for Hollywood's approval.] V:2.18.31, FD:2.15.31.

[1547] **TRADER HORN**, Metro: [The scene is set in Africa, but Duncan Renaldo is Trader Horn's [Harry Carey] faithful sidekick, "Peru" with experience in his own native jungles. This movie is more a series of related scenes than a story, the wild animals might well have been the real stars for most audiences, but Peru does fall in love with the jungle princess, that was fair, both had dark skin. She returns the favor by saving the two adventurers from being the main entre at a super feast, for which she is banished from the tribe and consequently forced to flee to safety with them. This works out well, Peru's Latin charm had captured her heart. Renaldo, destined to be a future Cisco Kid, also managed to practice a little of his broken English on the natives. That worked too, Hollywood's primitives never spoke anything but gibberish from the first days of sound.] V:2.11.31.

[1548] **TRANSGRESSION**, Radio: [This slightly modernized remake of **The Next Corner**, 1924 [1061], had critics wondering if the males in the audience would really accept the "exceptional altruism of the husband" who forgave Kay Francis's naughty indiscretion with Ricardo Cortez. A not unfamiliar theme, the husband works too hard and provides the wife with everything that she wants, including too much free time. Ricardo comes along in Paris and smooth talks the lady with his warm Latin charm and all of a sudden, with the urging of several girl friends, she finds herself in his Spanish villa back home across the Pyrenees. There, to insure his hold over Kay, and before the fun starts, he has her write a note to her husband telling all and asking for a divorce. Just then, the father of another girl the slick Spanish seducer has sullied, steps between them and shoots the devilish debaucher. But, alas, the mail coach has left with the letter. The remainder may be deduced. In the final reel, the forgiving husband receives the bad news in the form of a letter, but refuses to read it. Some kind of a guy, not too many of them around, and certainly not in Hollywood's Hispanic countries. Possibly because Kay only placed herself within the "occasion of sin" without consummating her desires, the Production Code felt she had learned her lesson and would be a good wife ... at least so long as she avoided Latin gigolos.] V:6.16.31. **AMC**.

[1549] **TWO GUN CABALLERO**, Imperial: [Little else needs be said about this wonderfully stereotypical production with Consuelo Dawn as "Rosita": "You look, sad, señor. Come, Rosita will make you laugh. ... You are an Americano, Yes? ... Rosita likes very much the Americano. Does not the Americano likes Rosita?" BOB: "The señorita dances very charmingly." LOPEZ: "What are you doing Here? ... If you know who Lopez is, then you do not make flirt with his woman." ROSITA: "No No! The Americano does not flirt with me. I flirt with him. ... You do not come and I am so lonesome. I flirt with him. Why? Because he look just, almost like my Lopez. Of course he is not quite so handsome as my Lopez." This film did all right with the kids, and some time later, it would be immortalized in song: ["In a little cafe ... just the other side of the border ... she was giving him looks that made his eyes water" ... [but] she belonged to that man Jose ... and Jose sends the gringo on his way ...."] One can hear it weekly on any oldies station.] **FD**:12.13.31. Script: The Two Gun Caballero, p3, [13 pages] NYSAA.

[1550] **TWO GUN MAN**, Tiffany: [Strictly a formula western with Ken Maynard and his famous horse, Tarzan, chasing the cattle rustlers off the range, and into the jailhouse. Not always every little boys favorite part, but as was the case in so many of these Saturday afternoon favorites, it was required to have a Spanish señorita adding a little spice. In this one, Lucille Powers played Nita Martan, a pleasant mixture of both sides of the Rio Grande.] **FD**:6.7.31, **V**:6.16.31.

[1551] **UN CABALLERO DE FRANC** aka **UN HOMBRE DE FRANC** SV **EVENING CLOTHES**, P, Joinville: [In the early silent version of this French classic, Adolph Menjou played the nice, but often boorish, provincial land owner who marries out of convenience and is forced to go to the city to learn lessons in love and manners, which in the end makes his bride love him. In this Spanish talker the role belonged to Roberto Rey. Gloria Guzman was the sweet mademoiselle. The supporting cast included:Gabriel Algara, Rosita Diaz Gimeno, Antonia Colome, Luis Llaneza, Marita Angeles, Pedro Elviro "Pitouto".] English review, **V**:3.23.27.

[1552] **WELL OF FORTALEZA**, Pathe: [This travelogue designed for those who were not fortunate enough to venture much further than the neighborhood theater, took its viewers to beautiful Porto Rico for this nineteen minute short subject. Some in the audience may well have been pleased that they were seeing the island only on film in as much as there apparently was still danger to be found there despite the North American occupation and renovation of that island paradise. It would seem that some of the local wells were filled with deadly poison that unsuspecting visitors might chance to drink from.] **MPH**:2.21.31, p47.

[1553] **WOMAN HUNGRY**, FN: [Even though most of the studios were conscious that abjectly negative characterizations of Mexican nationals could hurt the industries growing trade with Mexico, some still considered it worth while to portray the Mexican as a lascivious lout lusting after white skinned women. This production prompted a serious note to Col. Jason Joy of the MPPDA expressing concern: "I notice that First National has another picture ... with Mexican villains in it. They are getting away with murder on their Mexican stuff down there, but they are going to get into trouble sooner or later, just as sure as there is a tomorrow. / They seem to insist upon using material of this sort ... **Woman Hungry** has Mexican types that are entirely unnecessary. They could have been just ordinary western low class type individuals. ... if there is any way that you can hammer this home, I wish you would try to do it. Someone in that studio is certainly "hip" on the Mexican problem. One of these days something is going to irritate the Mexican people ... and the company that stands in the way of a flag waving piece of propaganda is going to get badly burnt, and its very apt to be First National. The slightest spark touches these people off down there in the wrong way ... the whole industry [could] suffer as well as the individual company."] **Letter from Frederick Herron, Foreign Manager to Col. Jason Joy, 3.13.31,** **Viva Villa** file, [Production Code]

[1554] **WOMEN OF ALL NATIONS**, Fox: [The two boisterous rivals for every woman in the world, Marines Flagg and Quirk, beat themselves up from one silver screen duty port to another until they finally became part of the occupation troops in Nicaragua. There they spend more time chasing the señoritas, than they do Sandino. The latter was not mentioned by name, but referred to merely as the local bandit. The adventures these two began in **What Price Glory?** [1201] and continued in **A Girl in Every Port** [1289], had by now degenerated into a lot more womanizing than war making. The Central American scenes could have been filmed in any skid row saloon.] **V**:6.2.31.

[1555] **YANKEE DON**, Capital: [This western began out east where the Anglo hero was a tough in Manhattan's Bowery. Longing for the more open spaces, he drifts out west where he eventually encounters an aging Spanish Don who is having lots of trouble with local baddies. Opting to do good, he signs up for the duration, organizes the hacienda's vaqueros into a disciplined {Hell's Kitchen} fighting force and defeats the attacking desperados. Throughout all this, the luscious Lupita Tovar has been looking on with love in her eyes. She admired the Anglo-easterner's agility and manliness. He had done a bit of looking at the shapely señorita himself, but it was not meant to be. So, his work completed, the old Don secure, the lady willing, his heart heavy, he waved and cursing his screen writer, the hero rode off into the sunset.] **V**:5.20.31.

1932

[1556] **AGUILAS FRENTE AL SOL** = **EAGLES ACROSS THE SUN**, Mex: [This was Mexico's second all talking feature. Antonio Moreno as the director, included himself in the cast appearing in his one hundred and second feature film.]

[1557] **AMAZON HEAD HUNTERS**, PP: [Although typical Hollywood fiction was responsible for perpetuating some of the more severe Hispanic stereotypes, other negative images focused on South America itself were afforded the added legitimacy most audiences ascribed to the so called documentary. Highlighting the possible dangers that the Southern Hemisphere seemed to be filled with, this film instilled both conscious and unconscious imagery in audiences that remained with them throughout their lives. No other region of South America was more subject to this type of film making than the Brazilian Amazon. Filled with an incredible variety of flora and fauna much of which is still today unclassified, Hollywood scripters have forever embellished it with their own monstrous creations. More recently the **Cousteau Chronicles** which featured the Amazon, while pointing out its dangers, helped dispel some of the accepted mythology which emphasizes man eating fish and plants eating men, men eating men and the most dreaded of all, Jivaro head hunters. All of these fears have been properly exploited and perpetuated by more than a score of Hollywood fantasies. In this production audiences were told that they were about to witness the "exploits of the courageous explorer, the Marquis de Wavrin [who had travelled through] three thousand miles of torrential rivers and dense jungles ... to reach his goal, the Jivaro head hunters of Ecuador." Forsaking the comforts and pleasures of Paris, the Marquis had fearlessly invaded "the hazards of the Scalp Country in the depths of the Amazon jungle, a region of strange, inaccessib[ility] and filled with dangers." Later, audiences were treated with graphic evidence of this claim. There he had had the good fortune to witness one of the most secret of the Boro ceremonies, that which involved the Palm Tree maggots. A narrator described the scene for the audience: "-- Boros invoking the spirits of the maggots which live in the decayed trunk of fallen palms and are gathered and eaten as a great delicacy. / The mysterious rites now being ended, the women are allowed to return -- to call them back a tom tom is beaten -- two sorts of tom toms, one representing man, the other woman -- are used. / The costumes - or lack of them - must have made Wavrin homesick for his dear Paris -- and the Folies Bergere. / The prisoner's dance. This is a remnant of an ancient man eating custom when the Boro slew and ate their enemies like the true cannibals they were." The nudity in the production was accepted by the censors because the breast's and derrieres that were being exposed did not belong to white women. The same permission was granted the **National Geographic Magazine**. **Variety** claimed that the nudity in this film represented more exposed skin on the screen than had ever been seen before.] [See the discussion on darkskinned nudity in **The Forgotten Village** 1941 which was the subject of a New York Supreme Court decision.] **V**:11.15.32, **FD**:11.17.32, NYSAA, Script: **The Amazon Head Hunters**, p7, 15 pages.

[1558] **BARRANCO**, Fr: [Tramel a popular French comedian of the era, plays a Parisian tramp who is mistreated until it is discovered that he has inherited a valuable Mexican silver mine. Then all life changes. The shots of the mine and related scenes were probably taken somewhere in a Normandy rock quarry.] **V**:7.12.32.

[1559] **BEYOND THE ROCKIES**, RKO: [In the early thirties Tom Keene was one of Hollywood's successful cowboys, with the addition of Julian Rivero as a loyal and lady loving sidekick, he became even more popular. Rivero's role almost always involved his leering through a window at some, usually overweight cook or other domestic and offering to steal something that she might want. This comedy angle played well with audiences and enhanced the regular hard riding, roping and catching those bad guys, all knew would eventually happen. Rivero's character was said to have "robbed many banks", "killed many men", "loved many women, but [the former bandit] had never forgotten to be a gentleman." This early talker is another of the many sagebrush sagas which has been recovered and restored for exhibition on Saturday or Sunday morning cable channels which have successfully brought back the weekend western double and triple features [39].] **V**:9.20.32, **FD**:7.8.32. AMC.

[1560] **BIRD OF PARADISE**, RKO/Radio: [Dolores Del Rio was provided with her most provocative part in this production in which she gave a "truly fine performance ... as the savage princess Luana, a role made to order for this electric young Mexican, and one that will go down in the archives as among the best thing she has ever done." **Variety** was correct with this prediction and also with it's forecast that the advertising provided "spicy billing" possibilities. The ads which appeared in **Motion Picture Herald**, in light and dark shades leave no room for imagination about Dolores's bosoms. They appear to be completely nude and not unexcited. The Production Code could try to keep such scenes from the screen, but had little power over the ad copy. Soon to be a factor, the Catholic Legion of Decency would complain vehemently about the nudity employed in such ads with mixed results. For Del Rio though, the exercise was one of elation and her version of "South Seas calisthenics was the subject of much talk" and controversy, to say nothing of delightful stimulation. Although quite innocent, all of this lascivious behavior with a very young Joel MaCrea, had to be punished and in the last scene she finds herself falling into an erupting volcano, a fitting way for her to go. The other Hispanic considered an ideal type for this South Sea frolic was Sophie Ortego, who played an old native woman.] **MPH**: 5.16.31, **V**:9.13.32.

[1561] **BLONDE VENUS**, P: [In this fantasy Marlene Dietrich sang "Hot Voodoo" in a gorilla suit. It has to be seen to be truly appreciated and can be on TNT. The scene would not play well in down town Port of Prince.] **V**:9.27.32. **TNT**.

[1562] <u>BORDER DEVILS</u>, Artclass release: [The action in this western takes place on the Mexican border, where he who is responsible for all the trouble and evil deed doing is a never to be seen oriental who has significant control over the locals that do his bidding. The plot involves an Anglo hero who works at clearing his name after he had been forced to do bad time in an Arizona border prison.] **V**:5.17.32, **FD**:3.20.32, **NYSAA**, Script: <u>Border Devils</u>, 21 pages.

[1563] <u>BROKEN WING</u>, P: [In this variation of the <u>Dove</u> [1283], Leo Carrillo, joined the growing ranks of "good-natured Mexican killer[s]." As Captain Innocencio of El Suelo, Mexico, he was "a man not to scoff at," the chief of police, but also on record as the "the Mayor, the prosecuting attorney, the judge and the Lord High Executioner when it pleases him to snuff out a life." In Hollywood's Mexico that was possible. There appears to have been a conscious effort on the part of the producers to balance Carrillo's villainous traits, with likeable ones emphasized by "acts of goodness." The object of his affection was once more the vivacious Lupe Velez, a Hispanic Lolita, who, while accepting all the gifts her enterprising swain has stolen from others to give to her, is really in love with a North Americano flyer, Melvyn Douglas. When the latter's plane crashes on the outskirts of town, the gracious bandit takes care of him, not knowing who he really is. The gringo knows not either, the crash having induced a temporary amnesia to build a little tension. With a little loving Lolita helps him remember and when the jefe finds the two in a warm embrace, Douglas is forced to face a firing squad, despite all of the señorita's protestations. Of course, he is saved and the Captain knows that there are a lot of other señoritas in El Suelo he can steal for. Carrillo's accent kept audiences laughing throughout the film [966].] **V**:3.29.32, **NYT**:3.26.32.

[1564] <u>EL CABALLERO DE LA NOCHE</u> SR <u>DICK TURPIN</u>, [First filmed as a silent in 1925, this Spanish remake of the classic featured: Jose Mojica, Mona Maris, Romualdo Tirado, Manuel Paris and Andres de Segurola.]

[1565] <u>ERAN TRECE</u> SV <u>CHARLIE CHAN CARRIES ON</u>, F: [It might be surprising to discover how many consider Charlie, of all the screen detectives even including Sam Spade, to be that one who has the firmest grip on peculiar delight. Certainly several generations have enjoyed watching him sleuth out the baddies. Anyone who could so easily spout wisdom as sagacious as, "He who feeds chicken, deserves egg," in whatever language, even on a bad day, deserves first place in line. In later life three different Charlies will make five separate journey's south of the border, twice to Mexico, but in this film he was there speaking Spanish. Manuel Arbo would have the honor of portraying Honolulu's finest right at home in stereotypical style as the prolific father of thirteen little Chans. His supporting cast included: Juan Torena, Ana Maria Custodio,

Blanca de Castejon, Antonio Vidal, Jose Nieto, Rafel Calvo, Miguel Liggero, Amelia Sante, Luana Alcaniz, and Carmen Rodriguez. Two others were also included, the Mexican, Martin Garralaga and Brazilian, Raul Roulien. Although the former would find his way into many future Hollywood westerns, the latter would soon play the second lead, hired to lose the glamorous Del Rio to the Anglo, in the musical sensation **Flying Down to Rio** [1607].] Script: **UCLA Film Archive, Fox Collection**.

[1566] **ESPERAME**, P/Joinville: [This Hispanic musical entry featured the singing of Carlos Gardel, who possessed one of the best loved voices throughout Latin America, Carlos Gardel. A talented musician who also acted, wrote and sang all the songs for this Spanish Language fluff. His supporting cast included: Goyita Herrero, Lolita Benavente, Manuel Paris, Jaime Devesa, Manuel Bernardos, and Jose Arguelles.]

[1567] **THE GAY CABALLERO**, F: [When a former football hero decided to return to his ancestral estates back west, he was displeased to discover that much of his property had been acquired by the villainous, Paco Morales, a hidalgo with an insatiable appetite for increasing his own lands at the expense of the local Anglos. Paco was assisted in this land grabbing by Jito, a giant evil deed doer that all the natives feared. All, that is, save the trusty "El Coyote," one of Hollywood's many 1930's western Robin Hoods, who could aim his pistolas as accurately as Sherwood's stalwart swain could shoot his arrows. As the action unfolds the former grid star and the canine crusader discover that they had been childhood friends and so they agree to combine forces to combat the present danger. The necessary señorita in all of this was Conchita Montenegro, as lovely a cantina cutie as ever crossed her knees. The big highlight was the big fight in the small cantina between the big Coyote and the even bigger, Jito. But Victor McLaglen, former heavy weight contender for the heavyweight crown, although he had his hands full, managed to mangle the Mexican giant. Law, order and all lands were temporarily restored to the border. Two Hispanic newcomers were introduced as minor players, Martin Garralaga, who would appear in some fifty more Hollywood films and Juan Torena, who would not. It was good fun for adults and kids, the accents and characterizations remained unchanged.] **V**:3.29.32, **NYT**:3.26.32, **FD**:2.14.32.

[1568] **GIRL OF THE RIO**, aka **THE DOVE**, [In Great Britain] RKO: [The first version of this Belasco play was made in 1928 [1283] and the next would appear in 1939, as the, **The Girl and the Gambler**. Each enjoyed commercial success with basic characterizations remaining unchanged even in the first year of the world conflict. Don Jose Maria Lopez y Tostado never improved his accent nor learned much English in any of the remakes, he had to speak like audiences knew Mexican's did. He also had to continue to pursue the always adorable, señorita, in this case, Dolores Del Rio. She forever put him off, preferring the company of the handsome young Americano and in the final reel, he always acquiesced. "The bes caballero in all of Mejico," had a big heart, was rich and had several dozen other señoritas who provided him with a lot less trouble.] V:1.12.32, NYT:1.9.32, FD:1.10.32, AMC.

[1569] THE HALF-NAKED TRUTH, Radio: [Lee Tracy, would be a hunted man across the border in the following year for having insulted the Mexican government, [1712] but in this film he was the archetypical public relations man promoting the obvious finer points of a Coney Island cooch dancer played by a sexy Lupe Velez. She allows herself to be badgered and pushed until her fiery temperament subdued the very fast talking Tracy. It was a comedy that pleased most. Lupe's constant slips, and misuse of English words would become her most enduring characteristic in the roles that followed. It was the screen persona audiences loved when she began the Mexican Spitfire series.] V:1.3.33, FD:12.31.32, AMC.

[1570] HEY, HEY, WESTERNER, Vitaphone: [This eighteen minute all Technicolor musical short may well have been more worthwhile for highlighting the scenic landscape beauty of its southwest location, than for its stereotypical scenario. The action had Eddie Nugent portraying a Broadway playboy who was left a significant "wad of dough" on the condition that he would go to Mexico and stay there for a year. A scripter's punishment for having enjoyed too much of the good life. Once there he took full advantage of all the typical situations and characterizations that audiences had come to associate with life south of the border which the scribes felt should have provided the laughs. To add to his problems they have a couple of New York lawyers arrange for some fake Mexican bandits to hold him up, but by that time, being a North American, he has of course become the leader of all the locals who provide him with protection and drive the baddies away. As should be expected, the señoritas loved and treated him like the white god of the Anglos that was every Hollywood writer's fantasy. Tinsel Town's darkskinned women loved that white flesh.] FD:8.24.32.

[1571] HOMBRES EN MI VIDA SV MEN IN HER LIFE, C: [As a fairly active lady, Lupe Velez played Julia Clark and was involved with a very attractive cast of Mexican stars, Ramon Pereda, Luis Alonso (Gilbert Roland), Carlos Villarias, and Luis Alberni, all of which were willing to sell their souls for her favors.] V:12.1.31.

[1572] EL HOMBRE QUE ASESINO SV STAMBOUL, P/London: [This intriguing mystery featured Rosita Moreno, Ricardo Puga, Carlos San Martin, Helen D'Agly, Gabriel Algara, Luis Llaneza, and Antonio Martinez.]

[1573] HUDDLE, MGM: [Roman Navarro was given the lead in this Hollywood version of the "American" dream. As an Anglo stalwart, dissatisfied with being only a full bodied steel worker, he decided to go to Yale. It could happen! And it did, after the writers provided him with admission papers. Once there, he managed to excel in his academic pursuits, but more importantly, he discovered that he had been provided with an aptitude for football and without much trouble, made the team. This, as you should know, allowed him to score the winning points in the last seconds of the big game. Prior to this, some of the snobby Eli's had failed to accept him as one of their own, darkskinned laborer that he appeared to be, but when they discovered that he had actually almost died from a ruptured appendix winning that game for the big Blue, there was nothing they could do but adopt him as one of their own. Only on the silver screen could a poor little Mexican boy become an Anglo and find such happiness walking the streets of New Haven, even today.] V:6.21.32.

[1574] **THE KID FROM SPAIN**, G/UA: [As the nation moved deeper into the depression this very successful musical [the first run charged $2.00 a ticket, when ten dollars a week was good pay] brought some smiles to many faces. Eddie Cantor and Robert Young were starred in this production in which the majority of characterizations were Mexican. Despite this, the only Hispanic listed in the credits was Julian Rivero, who played a minor role as Dalmores. Cantor had been the Anglo roommate and "chum" of Ricardo Young, a fairly light skinned Mexican, before both were expelled from the ivy halls for being found in the women's quarters after hours. It was a simpler time then. After the two friends separated, Eddie became implicated in a bank robbery through no fault of his own. Forced to leave the country, he remembered Ricardo's invitation to come live in Mexico at the family's palatial hacienda. Trying to cross over at the border station proved to be a riot of laughs, with Eddie only being allowed in after convincing the guard that he was matador. The remainder of the film was played for laughs and was filled with romantic complications, confusions and every stereotype audiences had grown accustomed to seeing. Staged as a musical, it featured numerous songs and early Busby Berkeley dance routines. The Goldwyn girls of 1932, Betty Grable, Paulette Goddard, and Jane Wyman had minor roles as beautiful señoritas. The final scene staged in the corrida was like no bull fight ever staged before. The atmosphere was old Mexico and the laughs pure Hollywood musical comedy.] **V**:11.22,32, **FD**:11.19.32. **AMC**.

[1575] **KONGO**, MGM: [In this screen writer's nightmare Lupe Velez played the woman of a "deformed trader." She was a seductive animal of the tropical jungle who lived by primitive urges and primordial instincts which naturally forced her into the arms of another white man. This little tryst almost results in her decapitation and consumption by the locals, some of which have not forgotten their cannibalistic ways, when Walter Houston (who has gone completely native forgetting that he had once been white) decides to let them have their fun with her for betraying him.] **V**:11.22.32, **AMC**.

[1576] **MARIDO Y MUJER** SV **BAD GIRL**, F: [This story of a young boy and girl who happen to meet at a park and spend and unintentionally productive night together was more easily slipped by the censors in its Spanish version. His only punishment was being forced by the writers to temporarily give up his dream of being a business man so that he could do the right thing for his fertile young lover. The Hispanic cast included: Conchita Montenegro, Rosita Granada, Allan Garcia, Jose Nieto, Mimi Aguglia, and Paco Moreno.]

[1577] **MATA HARI**, MGM: [Still a box office draw, Roman the imperial Russian officer, Navarro was double-crossed in this classic story of betraying ones lover for ones country. Pure Hollywood the hapless fool is allowed to be blinded by both fate and an accident that takes his sight and still, he is not allowed to know that his lady has elected to face the firing squad without telling him that he was her only reason to live. Silver screen "Teutons" had duty to the fatherland instilled in their character early in Hollywood's history, but some managed a little romance.] **V**:1.5.32.

[1578] **MEN OF CHANCE**, RKO: [In this melodrama Latin lover, Ricardo Cortez played Johnny Silk, married to Mary Astor in Paris and one heckofa horse race handicapper. With this talent he provides for all his woman's needs. Problems develop, but they get solved.] **V**:1.5.32, FD:1.3.32.

[1579] **MI ULTIMO AMOR** = **HIS LAST LOVE**, F: [Also listed as **Su Ultimo Amor**, this established formula, starred Jose Mojica and Ana Maria Custodio. She had been forced by her poor family to marry a rich older man, but was still in love with the less prosperous fisherman whose beautiful voice could sing the fish right out of the water. As it happened, scripters being much the same the world over and these guys were working for Fox, Jose turns out to be even richer than the old gentleman. It takes little imagination to work out the rest, but the final scene, which featured a fiesta at the latter's mountain home, was a sensation with audiences north and south. It would be a tossup deciding which of the two stars Latin audiences liked better, Mojica or Carlos Gardel. Jose would make some movies for Hollywood until the war broke out and then surprises the film community by entering a monastery. Carlos would not see the decade end. The cast also included: Mimi Aguglia, Elvira Moria, Carmen Rodriguez, Andres de Segurola and Nancy Torres.] **NYT**:8.19.33.

[1580] **MYSTERY RANCH** aka **THE KILLER**, F: [**Variety**'s review indicated that sophisticated New York audiences, especially those at the famed Warner Brothers Winter Garden Theater, would always react to a western, as a western, no matter what Hollywood called it. There were always pseudo cheers and hoorays for the heros and loud boos and hisses for the villains. In this case the baddies were a band of Mexican Apaches led by a renegade Anglo who had captured the blonde beauty. This of course required the attention of the American cavalry.] **V**:7.5.32.

[1581] **NIGHT RIDER**, Supreme Features: [Harry Carey appeared to be a stranger in this town where a mysterious night rider was causing lots of problems for the town folk. They suspected that any new face might be the one behind the mask. As it turned out, he was really undercover law sent to catch the baddie. George, latter to be "Gabby", Hayes provided some of the comedy, the Mexican laughs were furnished by Julian Rivero.] **V**:7.19.32. **FD**:5.22.32.

[1582] **PANAMA FLO**, RKO/Pathe: [In this production, Charles Bickford plays a terrible tough named, McTeague who's alias was the "King of South America." As the scene shifts from New York to Panama, McTeague finds himself falling for Helen Twelvetrees, an Anglo beauty hiding out as a cantina girl in a dingy Canal Zone saloon. Without much trouble, he convinces her to accompany him to his Jungle palace, where keeping house for him provides more opportunity than keeping the sailors constantly away. For a while it works, but complications develop when her former lover shows up at the compound. She thinks he's looking to take her back to the big city, but what he really wants is the "King's" secret map. In the denouement she saves the treasure, Mcteague sends her back to New York, but with an assurance that he will join her there later. Panama was pictured as it usually was, a place where sailors went to do a lot of drinking, find easy women, and as real hide out, if one happened to be running from the law, where one could blend in with derelicts and the waste product of humanity. Two remakes would follow: **Panama Lady** in 1939 and **Panama Sal**, in 1957.] **V**:1.26.32, **NYT**:1.20.32, **FD**:1.24.32. Script: Panama Flo, 39 pages. NYSAA.

[1583] **THE PHANTOM OF CRESTWOOD**, Radio: [Ricardo Cortez starred in this spooky mystery of black mail, murder and Spanish pride. He happened to be the head of a bunch of fairly bad baddies, but not so bad that they would take advantage of those who could not afford it. Falsely accused of being the real villain, he and his boys invade the palatial home of the Andes family in Southern California. Calling upon his experience as the original Sam Spade, he eventually uncovers the real culprit among the gathered socialites. The grand señora of the casa had been responsible for all the bodies, her motive, Spanish pride. Old grandfather Santiago Andes had once owned all of Southern California and the old dame apparently thought that the thousand acres or more she had left was insufficient to maintain the high station the family once enjoyed. To protect the family name from the blackmailer she had killed him. The others she disposed of to throw the law off the scent. In the finally scene Cortez graciously allowed the old señora to jump off a cliff so that no further scandal would be attached to the survivors. If there was a moral for this semiSpanish tragedy might well have been, "pride commeth before the fall."] **V**:10.18.32. AMC.

[1584] **PRIMAVERA EN ONTONO** = **SPRINGTIME AND AUTUMN**, F: [In 1932 Hollywood was still searching for some solution to solve the problem of synthesizing multinational Spanish. Criticism came from both sides of the river and also from across the big pond. In this effort the producer located most of the action in "Andalucia, (which avoided) the necessity of having ... characters use the Castilian pronunciation in place of the more wide spread Hispano-American." Fox, as well as other production companies had also concluded that Latin audiences enjoyed "highly sentimental" films and so designed some of the scenarios during this period of competition for the Hispanic market. To balance the sadness, significant comedy relief was required. The **NYT** considered this effort "from a technical standpoint ... about one of the best in Spanish that ha[d] been shown in New York." Catalina Barcena was praised for her portrayal of the successful middle aged prima donna long separated from a faithful husband because of her career and then reunited with him because of a shared love for their daughter, the "charming Luana Alcaniz." Antonio Moreno played the sympathetic "caballero of Andalucia," supported gracefully by his best amigo, Raul Roulien. Audiences were pleased at Harlem's newly reopened Teatro Variedades. Also included were: Julio Pena, Luana Alcaniz, Mimi Aguglia, Hilda Moreno, Romualdo Tirado, Adrienne D'Ambricourt, Maria Calvo, Jose Pena "Pepet", and Agostino Borgato.] **NYT**:5.18.33.

[1585] **LA PURA VERDAD** SV **NOTHING BUT THE TRUTH**, P/Joinville: [Paramount Hispanic players in this Spanish version film were Manuel Russel, Maria Bru, and Jose Isbert.]

[1586] **RIDER OF THE WEST**, Trem Carr/Sono Art-World Wide: [One more of several thousand little westerns which required the necessary addition of a Mexican character to help create the proper atmosphere. This time it was Jose Dominguez's task to look and talk Mexican.] **V**:7.12.32.

[1587] **SANTA**, Compania Nacional Productora: [This film is significant for numerous reasons: Directed by Antonio Moreno it introduced New York audiences to Mexico's first sound production and signaled the rebirth of that nation's motion picture industry. Although Mexican film makers had been making films since the first of the century, revolutionary upheaval well into the 1920's and the ease of acquiring a superior product from the north, greatly inhibited the development of the native industry. **Santa** was received well by the Latin press in New York, but while Anglo critics marked it as a significant improvement over past works, they criticized its production values which they felt were significantly inferior in comparison to work done in Hollywood. The sound was barely audible and the camera work shaky.   Antonio Moreno received little praise for his directorial debut and Lopita Tovar, not her usual plaudits. Although "two generations of Mexicans" supposedly wept over this story of a blind "pock marked" piano player who provided the music for the action on the second floor bordello, the reaction was not quite the same in New York. Possibly a bit too downbeat for some of the Anglo critics, this story of self sacrifice had Santa in love with one of the working ladies who had sold herself into a life of shame when she was abandoned by a heartless Mexican officer.   It gets worse, when she becomes ill, near death, the unrequited lover pays for her operation with his last peso's, but its too late, she dies.
A decade before the conservative **Outlook** had written on what they thought to be Latin taste in film: "Strange creature is the South American ... What is considered a "sure fire" hit in the States does not work ... below the Great Belt. Happy endings leave the Audience dissatisfied.   The inevitable

embrace in the last reel is not seldom met with an open sneer ... No less than half a dozen murders ... can satisfy him. Suicides are even more in vogue. And if you want to please his heart thoroughly, kill the hero and make the heroine fade away mourning!" **Variety** felt that local audiences would "have to put up with a good deal for the sake of 100% Mexican" production and while there were some good scenes, it was considered to be far below North American standards. But before the end of the decade, they would join many other's in expressing concern about the Latin market competition from both Mexico and Argentina. In a second review some months later, the first indications of such possibility were there: "It's Mexico's first and has been cleaning up in the foreign market ... Latins seemingly like this sort of thing." Certainly the best history of the Mexican film industry, which includes a list of all of its product is: **Carl Mora, Mexican Cinema, Reflections of a Society 1896-1980**, University of California Press, 1982. The preface to this valuable edition includes a nostalgic remembrance of his childhood introduction to these films in New York's Spanish language circuit.] **V**:5.31.32, 9.13.32, **Maria Moravsky, "What the Public Wants Below the Equator," The OUtlook**:9.27.22, p129.

[1588] **SOUL OF MEXICO**, Mrs. Juliet Barrett Rublee: [It's always nice when people pay off by honoring commitments they are not required to, motivated by nothing more than a desire to do the right thing: In the midwinter of 1932 this film was premiered at the Roerich Museum in New York City. In attendance, aside from other prominent dignitaries, was Jose Manuel Puig Casauranc, Mexico's Ambassador to the United States and Mrs. Dwight W. Morrow, [Lindy's mother in law] and the wife of the former United States Ambassador to Mexico. Mrs. Rublee was herself, the wife of the ambassador's legal counsel, and not an unwealthy lady. Having spent some three years among the Mexican upper classes and a significant amount of time traveling throughout Mexico herself, she had decided to give North American audiences, filmed images of our southern neighbor far different than those projected by Hollywood. Present also by invitation were producers and distributors who viewed the production cut from more than 150,000 feet of exposed stock shot at the lady's own expense. It was her stated intention to employ this film in an effort to help change accepted views: "Many people still think of Mexico as a land of bandits and dry cactus .... It is really the wonderland of the South, ... such a beautiful and fascinating country ... our next door neighbor, it is a pity so few know anything about it." Certainly a crowd pleaser for the many Mexican dignitaries present, the distributors paid their respects but, questioned its marketability even as a travelogue. Accepted by some, it received limited distribution.] **NYT**:2.5.32.

[1589] **SOUTH OF RIO GRANDE**, C: [The critics felt that Buck Jones did a good "Warner Baxter in this one and got away with it nicely." In this Cisco Kid spin off Buck played an avenging Mexican Rurales officer, underplayed the dialect and emphasized characterization. The non stop action, not only righted wrongs, it was a great crowd pleaser. Mona Maris, as an adventuress herself and not the lead, received more plaudits and critical acclaim than the more frail Angleress who required all the protection. Profitable for the producers, it would be remade in 1942.] **V:5.20.32.**

[1590] **SOUTH OF SANTE FE**, Sono Art/World Wide: [At some point in the depression years, especially after the birth of Republic Studios in 1936, Saturday afternoons in major metropolitan areas and a myriad of smaller towns, came to belong to the double western feature and the adventure serial. In thousands of theaters filled with millions of popcorn and candy crunching children having the time of their lives, and for the most part, knowing it, a few good guys like Bob Steele taught lots of bad guys lessons they would not soon forget. Simple morality melodramas, the western would continue to dominate Saturday matinees throughout the forties and into the fifties. For most in the audience it was as sacred a ritual as the next day's more somber requirements. Films like this one with Bob Steele playing the hero were an essential quantity for the nostalgic equation. Although many of the baddies were no longer Hispanics, a significant number still continued to reside in Mexico. In this one Bob had to deal with Mexican renegades that were working both sides of the border.] **MPG.**

[1591] **TEX TAKES A HOLIDAY**, Argosy: [This Poverty Row, low budget, western featured a new Mulitcolor process, but neither the color nor the scenario, were well received by reviewers. For the critics it was just one more mysterious stranger speaking broken "Mex-English" assuming the role of avenger and righting all the wrongs that seemed to forever afflict those living on the border. By this date audiences expected the residents of the Rio Grande region to speak in a distinctive manner and both hero and heroine were given some credit for "sprinkling" their roles with "acceptable dialect."] **V:12.13.32.**

[1592] **TIGER SHARK**, FN: [Some time after the advent of sound **Variety** apparently appointed itself something of an expert on Hollywood's regional speaking disorders: "Edward G. Robinson does dialect again, this time Portuguese. As only a Portuguese could find technical flaws, others will have to take the actor's word and characterizations. He makes the part sit up and talk." Until Spencer Tracy became the quintessential "portguee" in **Captain's Courageous**, Robinson's portrayal of the sympathetic Latin sailor remained unchallenged. Never destined to be a Don Juan, in this film the accomplished actor's love life was further complicated when a shark chews off one of his hands. The hook he is given as a replacement proves handy for catching fish, but is of little assistance in helping hold the affection of the woman he loves. While fishing for tuna off the coast of Mexico, she falls for the more whole and handsome first mate. Captain Mascareno's Latin blood boils as he decides which of two he is going to feed to the sharks first, but he proves unable to harm either of his betrayers. Realizing that the woman cares only about his money, it proves too much for him to bear. In the final scene he speaks some pathetic final words in what broken English he can muster and then jumps into the sea.] **V**:9.27.32.

[1592a] **TRAPPED IN TIA JUANA**: [Cast included Duncan Renaldo.]

[1593] **LA VIA DE ORO** = **THE GOLD ROUTE**, Arg: [This was the first Argentine sound film that the **NYT** made reference to: "At last the young Argentine film industry has outgrown its swaddling clothes and demonstrated its ability to take its place with the "grown-ups" of the audible screen world." A simple story of smuggling silk across the Parana River, the reviewer still pointed to the numerous technical flaws in the films production. Despite this the effort was considered to be "the first Argentine talking picture on a technical level with the best foreign films," which of course placed it several levels below any Hollywood production. A nice little backhanded, paternalistic compliment.] **NYT**:1.3.32, VIII, p6.

[1594] **WHITE ZOMBIE**, UA: [Four truly classic horror films were produced in the early thirties, a quartet of little beauties which still have the power to terrorize audiences today. Three of the four are frequently featured on **AMC**, **TNT** and other cable channels, but the less well known has lately been rediscovered and revived. **Dracula**, **Frankenstein**, and **The Mummy**, never left the theaters for long, but **White Zombie**, more atmospheric and, for many, much more frightening, was rarely seen on television screens until recently it was showcased on some New York channels. News coverage of that most troubled of Caribbean islands, Haiti, may well have helped repopularize the Zombie theme. **The Serpent and the Rainbow** provided viewers with the latest and most lurid interpretation of the problems the living dead face in today's complex society. This farfetched fantasy actually attempted to pass itself off as an authentic scientific study conducted by a Harvard researcher who claimed conclusively that such undead creatures currently live in present day Haiti. In response to last winter's revolutionary turmoil one of the television tabloids, devoted more than fifteen minutes to showing "real Zombies" as "they exist today in Haiti," and claimed that the power structure used the undead to keep the masses in line. All of this inane activity aside, the story was much better in the original black and white. Bela Lugosi starred in that production of which the **New York Times** said: "The idea of the picture is that in Haiti there are individuals who dig up bodies, invest them with motive power but not with intelligence, and set them to work. They make good servants. They can carry off blondes without getting ideas in their heads, which helps in these mad days." Something of a racist's dream they also possessed the convenience of disposability for "when they have served their purpose ... they can be made to walk off high cliffs." This the critic felt, that that would also have been a good idea for the producers. While all four of these films have remained popular and have spawned numerous remakes, only the zombie acquired the aura of legitimacy. It would seem that not a few people in the United States really believe that reviving the black dead is possible, in Haiti, it is even more commonly accepted. This may well be because throughout that poverty stricken nation, beneath the Roman Catholic veneer, the religions belief of Vodun are still an everyday part of daily life. Papa Doc Duvalier allowed his people to think that he was the high priest of voodoo to instill fear and better control the population. In 1932 **Variety** tried to explain it all in terms of the Obi religion which was a "super development" of Voodoo. This film, an adaptation of W. B. Seabrook's 1929, **The Magic Island**, an another allegedly fact based novel and Broadway play, was responsible for popularizing the term "zombie" throughout the nation.] **V**:8.2.32, **NYT**:7.29.32.

1933

[1595] **ALMAS ENCONTRADAS** = **HAUNTED SOULS**, Mex: [This simple, sentimental Spanish romance was designed for Hispanic audiences in true Latin tear jerking style. Not only were the men in this one drunks, the women were "bad," one assumes, according to some standards. Yet, all find redemption in the true love they share for each other.] **FD**:7.7.33.

[1596] **BARBARIAN**, MGM: [Ramon Navarro still had some pulling power at the box office when the studio called upon him to do this variation on **The Sheik**. As such he played an Egyptian prince in desert guide disguise to win the halfbreed Myrna Loy away from her white mate. Pure Hollywood, it was the singing guide who won her, but the desert prince of royal blood that was allowed to keep the lady in his tent.] **V**:5.16.33.

[1597] **BREED OF THE BORDER**, Mono: [Bob Steele in a slight change of pace, was hired to protect a man that turns out to be a crook and takes him across the Mexican border. Of course Bob discovers the plot, especially after he has been clobbered by the culprit. Then, in combination with the little lady who poses as a cantina cutie in the border cafe the heavies use as an exchange spot for the smuggling activities, Bob captures the whole gang and in the process saves her from a life of crime. The film was advertised as: "Snappy Western of Mexican Border Bandits Has Modern Slant With Speed Car Chase."] **V**:5.16.33, 5.10.33.

[1598] **THE CALIFORNIA TRAIL**, C: [Buck Jones, usually a favorite with the critics even considering the genre which he served best, received little praise for his work in this Mexican western. Critics were dissatisfied with the production values, the action, the acting and especially the scenario in this case. Something of a one man Magnificent Seven, Butch came to the puebla just prior to the occupation of California territory by the United States. He soon discovered that the town was controlled by a nasty Mexican tyrant who, with his equally villainous brothers were fleecing the peon population. With just a bit of super Anglo effort, he manages to right all wrongs. The lovely señorita was still another "Dolores," by far the Hollywood's scripters favorite and most used name for their female Hispanic characterizations. Those who criticized the heroics failed to take into consideration that almost any Hollywood Anglo, especially one cut from the rawhide Buck Jones was scripted out of, was at least the equal of six, or seven Mexicans, and that was on a bad day.] **V**:8.1.33.

[1599] **LA CANCION DEL DIA** = **THE SONG OF THE DAY**, Spain/Trilla: [Spanish musical romance films were popular with production companies on both sides of the Atlantic in 1933. Those made in Barcelona had the advantage of foreign locations which added a look and flavor that Fox could not always capture in its domestic product. This work was something of a Horatio Alger story which chronicled the rise of a poor orphaned boy and his troop of musical performers from the streets of Madrid to ultimate stardom.] **FD**:8.28.33.

[1600] **CENTRAL AIRPORT**, FN: [Many of the early films which deal with the rise of commercial aviation have a Latin American content. After Lindy proved it was possible to fly over a lot of water without getting wet, he was asked by his government to begin mapping out possible air routes to the Caribbean and south of the border capitals. Havana was one of the first cities outside of the continental forty-eight to enjoy regular air service, first from Miami and then New York. In this film the typical love triangle eventually throws most of the cast into the warm waters of the Caribbean, just off the Cuba coast Big John Wayne has a minor role as a pilot, but had to be rescued himself. The survivors were brought to Havana where some of the film's action takes place. The location was identified by a sign and torrential rains.] **V**:5.9.33. AMC.

[1601] **CIUDAD DE CATRON = CARDBOARD CITY**, F: [Another of the Spanish dialogue films with a blend of Hispanic and Anglo celebrities, Catalina Barcena, Antonio Moreno, Jose Crespo, Lionel Barrymore, Roland Young and Janet Gaynor were the stars poking fun at Hollywood make believe and doing it in Spanish. Also included were: Andres Segurola, Julio Pena, Luis Alberni and Carlos Villarias.] **NYT**:2.28.34, **FD**:2.28.34.

[1602] **DUCK SOUP**, P: [Certainly one of the classics that brought a lot of smiles to depression weary audiences, **Variety**'s review for this film mentions only the essential ingredients, the zany antics of the Marx Brothers. With almost everyone in the cast playing straight for the boys, the sexy lady they cast as the female temptress to lead a very willing Groucho down the garden path, was the seductive Raquel Torres. She played the naughty Spanish bad lady who was assigned to detract the new prime minister from his duties. Needless to say, Groucho enjoyed every lusty second of her delegated duties.] **V**:11.28.33.

[1603] **EISENSTEIN IN MEXICO**, Sol Lesser: [In an effort to recoup some of the expenses incurred in producing **Thunder Over Mexico** [1640], and sooth a bit of the controversy the film had generated, new Eisenstein footage was released in what **Film Daily** characterized as a "travelogue on a grand scale," with nothing of a "political nature" that Upton Sinclair, the sponsor, claimed it showed. The scenes included were magnificently "lensed" but watching the marching styles of policeman, soldiers and fireman was considered "little reason for fuss." Other scenes included many close ups of native types, all very indian in character, fiestas, merry making and "somber religious ceremonies." The "amorous byplay" of Mexicans in canoes and the "sensuous rhumba" of the dancers were also shown. In effect the production might well have been filmed, although somewhat less expertly, by any tourist with a modern VCR. Although certainly sympathetic toward

Mexico, if the film expressed a political orientation, it was not apparent.] **FD**:11.2.33.

[1604] **EMPEROR JONES**, UA: [One of the most distinct historical differences between the Old World, Europe and the New, all the Americas, north and south after the revolutionary period which began in Concord in 1775 and ended with the battle of Ayacoucho in the Peruvian Andes in 1826, was the fact that monarchy was barred from both hemispheres. Republics ruled on this side of the pond and there was little room for Kings, Queens or Emperors. In time, all of the Americas wrote these rules into their respective constitutions, but as always, there proved some exceptions. Three present day hemispheric nations can claim to have had two emperors each: Brazil had two as did Mexico and Haiti. While all of the royalty will eventually make its way to film, this was the first to focus on Henri Christophe, the Emperor of Haiti. Fascinated by his rise to power and subsequent downfall, Eugene O'Neil used him as the prototype for the main character in his play and this film. Certainly, this was Paul Robeson's most memorable role and elevated him to immediate film stardom. His portrayal of Brutus Jones, railroad porter transformed to absolute dictator of Haiti, satisfied every racist's fear and fantasy of what would happen if a black man ever achieved power. Having killed a man over a woman, Jones escapes a chain gang and stokes his way into the Caribbean where he jumps ship and swims to Haiti. There he, with the help of some white slime, makes himself feared and eventually, by the use of his brutality, becomes the ruler of the "primitive natives." As such he abuses all his powers and terrorizes even those who have made him Emperor. [Some whites may well have shuddered.] The natives think he is immortal because of a staged ruse, and that only a silver bullet will kill him. In time his flagrant misuse of power provokes rebellion, which drives him into the jungle where his cowardice makes him cringe at every sound. A local Lone Ranger delivers the fatal bullet, reflecting a pattern long established in early Haitian history.] **V**:9.26.33, **NYT**:9.22.33, **FD**:9.16.33, **Newsweek**:9.23.33, p32, **Commonweal**:10.6.33, p532, **Nation**:10.11.33, p419, **Canadian Magazine**, 11/33, p35, **DAR**.

[1605] **END OF THE TRAIL**, C: [One of the first talkers in which Hollywood attempted to present a sympathetic portrayal of the redman, this was in effect, an interesting early experiment at providing a little screen justice for the indian, but it fell pretty flat, even later reviewers found fault with its orientation: "The film was stilted, larded with endless pontifications documenting the Anglos' despicable history of malfeasance toward the red men." No success at the box office, audiences with depression problems of their own had little sympathy for the plight of the indian. The lack of similar films indicates that Hollywood would wait for forty years before making any real effort at changing its indian image. Hispanics would fair somewhat better because of the Production Code's concern for the Latin Market. Not a lot of indians bought tickets to the theaters [341].] Brian Garfield's **Western Films** [A Complete Guide], New York: Rawson

Associates, 1982 is one of the many film histories with an extensive listing of annotated western features.

[1606] **FLAMING GUNS**, U: [Nearing the end of a most successful career, Tom Mix was not very selective about the films he appeared in, this was not one of his best. Somewhere in Texas the writers made him fall in love with the Banker's daughter. Then they turned the lady's entire well-to-do family against him, especially her father. This forced the two love birds to fly over the border where they planned to look for a padre and settle down to enjoy the Mexican sunset.] **MPG**.

[1607] **FLYING DOWN TO RIO**, RKO: [This first musical comedy set in Brazil captivated North American audiences immediately. The scenario reflected twenty years of accepted stereotyping blended with Hollywood's bizarre conception of upper class Brazilian cafe society life. It was a sensational musical which had the beautiful Dolores Del Rio pursued by two friends. One of the buddies was a North American band leader, Jean Raymond, the other a very rich Brazilian, Raoul Roublien. Although charming, rich, and handsome, the audience knew from the first, that that would not be enough to prevent the Anglo from winning the sultry, darkskinned lady's affection. As was almost always the case, Hollywood's Hispanic women chose Anglo men when the writers told them to do so. While all of this was going on, Fred Astaire and Ginger Rogers teamed up for the first time and danced the "Carioca." The routine electrified audiences everywhere and began the public's love affair with that most enduring of dance teams. It also added another entry to the list of South American rhythms already popular in the North. At this time the Production Code Administration was more concerned with the erotic nature of the dance performed by "the entire colored troop," than they were with the other ethnic stereotypes shown. They were especially worried that the Brazilian dancers created an "offensive sex suggestiveness" which apparently was not exhibited by the two fair skinned Anglos. Except for the very upper class rich, most of the other Brazilians portrayed, who were not black, were played as buffoons. In the final scene the gracious Brazilian accepted the role written for him. Realizing that his lady loved his Anglo friend and that only duty bound them together, he boarded the air liner they were both heading north in, gave the guy the gal and then exited by parachute as the Latin rhythms followed him down to his beloved Rio. It was a wow!] **V**:12.26.33, **NYT**:12.22.33, **FN**:12.20.33, **Newsweek**:12.30.33, p31, **Flying Down to Rio** file, Special Collections, AAMPAS. Script: 33 pages, NYSAA.

[1608] **HAVANA WIDOWS**, FN: [This little piece of gold digging fluff was received with mixed reviews. It starred Joan Blondell and Glenda Farrell as two out of work chorus girls who borrow money from a hood to go find sugar daddy's in a Havana night club, the legendary, Sloppy Joe's. Of course what they find has more to do with the heart than with dollars, but the last reel rewards the pair with a pleasant gold and silver lining. Although not anticipated the scene shift from New York to the Cuban capital created some problems in production. This information was uncovered at the Warner Archive at USC which has a file on almost all that production company's movies. All files vary and include from very little information to more than a casual student might want. Most provide a "synopsis" sheet which is just that, it lists the cast and outlines the story. Many files contain most of the correspondence generated during the films production, including inter-office memos, letters to and from the PCA and mail received from citizens concerned with the film, before and after its production. Frequently the **Hollywood Reporter's** "Critical Reviews" of the film as "they appeared in THE NEW YORK DAILIES" are included. The file for this film indicated that the production problems experience during location shooting in Havana resulted from the revolt against the bloody Machado dictatorship which erupted as the company began filming. Apparently there was also a problem involved in staging one of the dance numbers. Not having brought the cast from **Forty Second Street** with them, the local ladies proved to be unsuitable as chorus girls and so the director was forced to obtain them from Hollywood. Reviews from the **World-Telegram**, the **Times**, the **News**, the **American**, the **Post**, the **Mirror**, the **Herald-Tribune** and the **Journal**, were neatly packaged in the **Reporter**'s booklet. That is not always the case. If specific material is desired students and researchers interested in using this facility are advised to make an appointment. **V**:11.28.33, **FD**:11.25.33. DAR.

[1609] **HOT PEPPER**, F: [When Edmund Lowe and Victor Mclaglen were first teamed as the marines, Quirt and Flagg in the anti-war heroics of **What Price Glory**, they gave their various roles a most convincing depth of feeling. Two subsequent productions saw their parts degenerate into mere macho womanizing. In this film, the fourth teaming of the pair, they made the transition from sympathetic characters caught up in the throes of war, to two hungry hounds sniffing after women all over the world. They were little more than slapstick comedians competing for favors from the sensuous Lupe Velez. Spending much of her time in panties or skimpy silk outfits, she portrayed, according to one not displeased reviewer, a "believable ... bundle of South American hot stuff [that is] when not forgetting the dialect" she employed to identify her place of birth.] **V**:1.24.33.

[1610] **IT'S GREAT TO BE ALIVE**, F: [The Spanish language version of this film was a success with Latin audiences throughout South America and with the domestic Hispanic market, but it fared far less well with regular movie goers. It is possible that its bizarre script may have created some insecurities with the Anglo audiences that could not be accurately vocalized. The Brazilian tenor, Raoul Roulien, starred in this tongue in cheek tribute to male fantasy, as a well to do playboy who, after fighting with his lady takes off in his personal plane to cross the Pacific. Because of the protective atmosphere provided by his aircraft, he is saved from being affected by a world wide epidemic that kills off the entire male population. After crashing and being captured by the hungry females, he is auctioned off for the highest price to the randy group, but is saved from a fate worse than who can imagine by the authorities. A real romantic, he refuses all the offers, electing to return to his own lady's waiting arms. See: **El Ultimo Varon Sobre La Tierra**, 1642.] **V**:7.11.31.

[1611] **KING OF THE ARENA**, U: [In this western looking for an acceptable variation, Ken Manyard was personally recruited by the governor of Texas to find the culprit, the Masked Death, who has been responsible for shooting people with chemical bullets that left what remained of the victims in a black blob. Once on the case he made a connection between where the dead have been found and their proximity to a traveling wild west show. Luckily for all, he just happened to once have been a part of that outfit. After rejoining the attraction, he soon discovered who the lethal gunman was masquerading as and puts an end to his deadly act. Much of the action in the last reel took place in Mexico where the Masked Death was unmasked, and laid to final rest.] **V**:8.29.33.

[1612] **LADY FOR A DAY**, C: [This was the first filming of Damon Runyon's story of Apple Anny and her life long selfless devotion to her daughter. The girl had lived a life of comfort and ease while attending a European private school, and had not seen her mother since early childhood. Throughout that time, Anny has saved every penny for the girl's welfare. Possibly the first identifiable "bag lady", she worked the streets and lived in New York amid a cast of other eccentric street people who survived by their wits alone. The crisis comes when the girl wants to come home to show off the son of a Spanish Count that has asked her to be his wife. The Spanish vice consul in New York wants to make sure that the daughter is good enough to marry such an important aristocrat, a Spanish Grandee, and he plans a reception for the entire family. Almost dying of despair because she will be found out, all of the loveable characters help in the deception which even includes the big hearted Mayor of New York as well as the Governor. The proud Spanish father is completely fooled by some of New York's lowest and gladly consents to giving his son up for marriage. Remade as **A Pocketful of Miracles**.] **V**:9.12.33.

[1613] **LA LLORONA** = **THE CRYING WOMAN**, Mex/Eco Films: [This was the first real Mexican horror film and significantly, its character and scenario were pure Hispanic. A llorona, according to Mexican folk mythology, was a wailing maternal ghost which morns the loss of its dead child. The character will be featured in many subsequent Mexican horror films [1767], including, **La Herencia de la Llorona**, 1946, **El Grito de la Muerte**, 1958 and **La Maldicion de la Llorna**, 1961. This film was directed by the Cuban, Ramon Peon, and its male star, Fernando de Fuentes, will be responsible for the most popular of all Mexican fantasy films of this period: **EL FANTASMA DEL CONVENTO**, [1671].]

[1614] **LAND OF CHEWING GUM**, Principal Pictures: [A brief informative film trip from the first tapping of the sap trees in Mexico which produce the resin necessary to create chewing gum, to the slot machines where it was sold.] **DAR**.

[1615] **LAND OF THE FEATHERED SERPENT**, Principal Pictures: ["In this travelogue audiences traveled through the ruins of the ancient city of Giarranuato [do not look for it in an historical atlas] which hundreds of years ago was one the most prosperous cities of the American continent. Chicheutzas, [possibly, Chichen Itza] the sacred city of the Mayans and Merida the capital of Yucatan provided home bound movie goers with views of a modern city and very old pyramids." This was another of the four Principal Pictures short subjects which focused on Mexico in 1933.] **DAR**.

[1616] **LAUGHING AT LIFE**, indy: [Victor McLaglen, who had lived a life of adventure as a soldier of fortune in various parts of the world, had, because of this, paid little attention to his family, just time enough to create one and leave them on their own. As the film opened he found himself leading a successful revolution in a war torn South American republic, who didn't in those days? With victory at hand, he established himself as the country's dictator and ruled with a firm Anglo hand. In time, a young North American engineer, shows up to help with reconstruction, you guessed it, it turns out to be the new ruler's son. The only credited Hispanic in the cast was Conchita Montenegro who played the Latin love interest, all others cast were Anglos.] **V**:7.18.33.

[1617] **LAW AND LAWLESS**, Majestic Pictures: [Jack Hoxie, as popular with his fans as any western star, teamed up with Julian Rivero in this buddies beating up the bandits on the border to save the sweet señorita from sure death in the very opening scene of this very typical hosopry. She was properly obsequious and gratefully took the pair back to the family hacienda where the patron hired them to stop all that cow stealing which had been plaguing him and his local rancher friends. Jack had some trouble understanding his pal's pronunciations, but that did not prevent the two from bringing in the rustlers. Jose de la Cruz and Elviro Sanchez were the Hispanic members of that bunch.] **FD**:4.12.33.

[1618] **MAN FROM MONTEREY**, Schleslinger: [John Wayne was featured in this favorite and most easily reworked of formula scenarios, the Spanish land grant given to an aristocratic Don, long before the take over of the territory by the United States. The on rush of North Americans hungry for newly conquered land usually threatened such holdings, but there was always a defender, either a Zorro type or some sympathetic Anglo, who provided protection for the oppressed. In this one big John, not yet the "Duke", looked real purdy, if just a bit out of place, in Spanish avenger costume. He would be much more comfortable guarding Anglos or winning more territory for his home side of the Rio Grande. But in Monterey he had the always lovely Nina Quatero to help him improve his Hispanic sympathies.] **V**:8.22.33, **DAR**.

[1619] **MAN OF ACTION**, C: [Julian Rivero was Don Miguel, friend and pal of Ranger Tim McCoy in this formula border western. He was a good Mexican, loyal to his Anglo superior and spoke English as he always had in all of his prior appearances.]

[1620] **MANO IN MANO**, = **HAND IN HAND**, Mex/Nuevo: [Filmed in the rugged terrain of northern Mexico this, "amateurish in spots" production was filled with colorful action and western types. It was an early Mexican version of a Hollywood "B" western and contained numerous characterizations not unfamiliar to those north of the Rio Bravo. Carmen Guerrero played the active heroine in the Hispanic hosopry and provided valuable assistance to the "strapping, sympathetic" hacendado, Miguel A. Ferriz as he fought off the ravages inflicted on his rancho by the very villainous, Rene Cardona in what was probably his most sinister portrayal. Luis G. Barreiro was also included. This production, actually one of the first Mexican talkers, was revived and reshown to the patrons of the Teatro Hispano in 1938. For those who might have remembered, it provided a good indication of how much improvement in overall production values, the films from just across the river had achieved in those few years since 1933.] **FD**:2.23.33, **NYT**:2.20.33, 6.19.39.

[1621] **MATTO GROSSO**, Principle Adventure Pictures: [Filmed in Brazil's River of Doubt region, familiar to audiences because of the exploits of Theodore Roosevelt and an adventure there which almost cost him his life [783], these new views showed that little had changed, it was still mysterious and forbidding. Hollywood's Amazon jungle would continue to be as menacing as it had always been: "Nature in this strange region is revealed at her most fantastic in the gargoyle features and twisted bodies of the native fauna. Some of the animals must be seen to be believed. The company includes the tapir, half horse and half rhinoceros; the jabiru, a huge stork with a bright scarlet collar [a native legend told that a company of jabiru, approaching a Spanish encampment at night put the invaders to rout by their resemblance to uniformed soldiers] a hideous fish called the piranha, with a bull dog face and jaws that can bite a man's foot off, boot and all; a giant bat with vampirish tendencies and extraordinary [sic] repulsive features and tiny armadillos which becomes quite spheroid like baseballs at the approach of an enemy. The natives, an ugly and malformed race are the least interesting of the jungle sights." This requires little commentary. For the great majority of North Americans, until the destruction of rain forest became a primary issue of concern, this description was the Amazon. Especially those ugly little natives that the **National Graphic Society** so loved to photograph in all their primitive nakedness, with only a little selective male airbrushing.] **NYT**:1.14.33, **FD**:1.14.33.

[1622] **MELODIA DE ARRABAL** = **SUBURBAN MELODY**, P/Joinville: [Carlos Gardel, "the popular Argentine Tango singer, and composer" would star in this romantic love story, and continue to be one of the most popular Latin American actors through out the decade until his untimely death in 1940. His attractive co-star, Imperio Argentina, was cast as his music teacher. He had been a convict and was working on the outskirts of Buenos Aires. After a number of scripted problems, they fall in love and are provided with a happy ending. Despite the tendency toward sentimental productions, there usually were happier endings in Argentine productions. This was neither, but a Paramount product made in France. The remainder of the cast included: Vincente Padula, Jaime Devesa, Helene D'Algy, Filipe Sassone, Manuel Paris and Jose Arguelles.] **NYT**:8.5.33.

[1623] **[La] MELODIA PROHIBIDA** = **FORBIDDEN PARADISE**, F: [The variation in the exact translation of title for this Fox film was merely a promotional gimmick designed to attract more English speakers into the audience. The Fox regulars, with a few new additions, enjoyed making this modern fantasy of the garden of eden. Jose Mojica, as usual led the singing ensemble, but sans figleaf and in modern dress. He had been assigned the pleasant duty of courting Conchita Montenegro and Mona Maris as they lured him through the streets of Mexico's modern metropolis and into some of the lesser lighted areas which were more suited for love. Reviewers praised its solid production values, which was merely another way of saying that the budget was a bit above the usual, shadows did not show at night time and there were few anachronisms which audiences could pick out in the film. Tom Patricola was also included in the fun.] **FD**:3.28.34, 10.10.33.

[1624] **MEXICO TODAY**, Principal Pictures: [This Principal short subject focused on the "Life and customs" of the contemporary and "progressive Mexico City" which included "modern structures and broad streets." It provided a dramatic contrast to those views of the capital and the country side which had been popular just a decade before. For a comparison with 1918 see: [1624].] **DAR**.

[1625] **MR. BROADWAY**, Broadway Hollywood Production: [Someone thought it would be a good and inexpensive idea to simply turn the camera on a long list of Hollywood and Broadway personalities and let them be themselves. Lupe Velez was one of the many, and she pleased everyone with her own personal brand of English.] **V**:9.19.33.

[1626] **NIGHT FLIGHT**, MGM: [This very early saga of commercial flying could boast of a cast which included, two Barrymore's, Helen Hayes, Clark Gable, Robert Montgomery, and the multiethnic looking, Myrna Loy, who played a Brazilian pilot's wife. As it was written, the Hispanics in this cast were incidental helpers to the Anglo's who provided the backbone of the Trans-Andean European Mail service. This was important stuff, and only determined Anglo's could have sweated over the organization, fly the beat up crates through the worst of weather, over some of the highest mountains in the world at the continuous risk of their lives. The task for the natives was simple and important: They were required to watch with wonder and amazement. And besides, there was a little extra feature in this one for the locals, life saving serum had to be flown through impossible conditions to save a stricken city suffering from an epidemic of infantile paralysis. Everyone played their role to the hilt, the competition was tough and all were properly, that is, politely condescending to the natives.] V:10.10.33 FD:5.22.32.

[1627] **LA NOCHE DEL PECADO** = **THE NIGHT OF SIN**, C: [Colombia joined the Spanish language producers with this entry directed by the respected Mexican, Miguel Contreras Torres. It featured Ramon Pereda, Virginia Zuri, Juilo Villareal and Enrique Herrera in a "routine melodrama" "aided by musical touches" and good performances by the entire cast. The scenario combined romance with business and gambling with murder, apparently considered by some to be every day and night occurrences in the sinful life of some obviously very well to do Mexico City residents.] FD:12.29.33.

[1628] **NO DEJES LA PUERTA ABIERTA** SV **PLEASURE CRUISE**, F: [Fox's Spanish language version of this film starred Raul Roulien, Rosita Moreno and Tom Patricola. With but a few alterations, it followed the English dialogue closely. It also proved to be a lively comedy in both languages and an "encouraging commercial success." Others in the cast included: Romualdo Tirado, Mona Maris, George Lewis and Juan Torena.] FD:11.13.33.

[1629] **OUTLAW JUSTICE**, Majestic: [In Hollywood jargon, this was the "stencil" in which the hero, Jack Hoxie, allows himself to be branded as a baddie to catch the other real badmen. There was a lot of nervous popcorn crunching among the kids when this took place. The innocence in those audiences was always wanting to believe that the unjustly accused would be vindicated. What frequently eased the tension, was the comedy relief, which in this case was supplied by a new import from south of the border, Chris Pin Martin, who played a very polite, but terribly inept and bumbling Mexican bandit.] V:2.28.33, FD:2.23.33.

[1630] **PARAMOUNT PICTORIAL #6**, [This little short subject filler includes some scenes of "typical Mexican dancers."] DAR.

[1631] **QUANDO EL AMOR RIE** = **WHEN LOVE LAUGHS**, F: [Another of the Fox Spanish language films featuring Jose Mojica singing his heart out to Mona Maris in a romantic musical set in the days "when the descendants of the Conquistadors ruled California." Although there were some slight anachronisms in this production, "much of the montage [lent] a certain air of authenticity to the film." The script called for the young, dashing, hard-riding Don to boast in the cantina, that not only could he tame the high spirited mare that belonged to Don Alvarado, but that he could also break his equally fiery daughter. Dangerous words indeed for any but a real macho. It's all worked out in the last reel with the magic of music that soothes all savage beasties. The young rogue had been taught some enchanted tunes by a mysterious old indian, tunes that exercised the power of domination over all animals, especially the wilder ones, women in general. Having won his wager, all ended well in a chorus of song and dance. The supporting cast includes Carlos Villarias, Carmen Rodriguez, Rafael Valverda and Rosita Granada.] **NYT**:10.17.33, **FD**:10.18.33.

[1632] **EL REY DO LOS GITANOS** = **THE KING OF THE GYPSIES**, F: [Another of the Fox Spanish language productions with Rosita Moreno, who had come to be a favorite with the Hispanic audience and Anglo reviewers. She was supported by Jose Mojica and Julio Villareal, by this time, both super stars in Mexico. The sentimental plot involved the complications which develop in love triangles on either side of the Rio Grande. Others in the Hispanic cast were: Romualdo Tirado, Martin Garralaga, Antonio Vical and Paco Poreno.] **FD**:5.31.33.

[1633] **RIO THE MAGNIFICENT**, MGM: ["A James Fitzpatrick "Traveltalk" with the capital of Brazil as its subject. The good Daughters thought it exhibited "Beautiful photography and an excellent explanatory talk." An MGM short subject.] **DAR**.

[1634] **SAVAGE GOLD**, Harold Auten: [This film purported to be the account of Commander Dyott's expedition to the head hunting region of the Ecuadorian Amazon. Certainly still not an easy task for the times, it was more Hollywood than **Amazon Headhunters** [1557], with a magic camera that seemed to be in the thick of the chase when those hungry for heads to shrink, hunters were chasing the scared from out under their pit helmets, whites through the rain forest jungle. By this time it was accepted as old hat that you could lose your head in those regions of South America, and probably much more. The head shrinking was documented somewhat more clearly in this production, but the critics thought it less terrifying. Audiences had learned to expect the unknown and the dangerous from such places, and so long as they were safely in their seats, they were willing to join any expedition that would bring new thrills. South of the border was forever filled with them.] **V**:8.1.33.

[1635] **SECRETS**, UA: [Early pioneering days in California had Mary Pickford struggling with a philandering husband forced to save her sanity by remembering the good old days of childhood in flashbacks to New England. The beautiful Mona Maris played Señora Martinez to insure the audience that this soaper was taking place in Spanish territory. No other Hispanics were credited.] **V**:3.21.33.

[1636] **SENSATION HUNTERS**, Mono: [Because of the Panama Canal, which attracted all forms of rough and tough types along with a significant number of sailors to the several hundreds of bars the "Zone" was legendary for hosting, any number of local and imported beauties were required by Hollywood to service these, hungry for lots of things, patrons. Sometimes, usually more often than not, the scribes would send absolute innocents there to be preyed upon randy rouges. It was always tough duty for the ladies in Panama. **Panama Flo** [1582] had discovered this earlier, the **Panama Lady** would do so in 1939. This Monogram production received rave reviews for its seventy four minutes of steamy scenes. The formula for this film had long been established. The Zone's multiracial night life notoriety dated back to early construction times and was eventually translated from fiction to film. In this version there was a kindly keeper of the ladies who worked her cafe, one who felt bad for the innocent thrown into such unsavory employment. When one particular young thing's lover becomes seriously ill, and she has to go out on the street to support him, the owner, now a veteran, Juanita Hansen, provides her with other means of support. When the boy recovered, all were grateful that virtue had been preserved. Especially the PCA. The cast was comprised of varying degrees of tough type ladies, all had seen the back of the barn, but were pure of heart. Those who had been there more often, were necessarily Hispanic. The reviewers only criticism for this production concerned the singing, but he might have realized that writers did not send their players to Panama to listen to a Swedish song bird. It was suggested that exhibitors advertise the film with: "Hitting the High Spots in Panama's Hot Spot's." **Panama Hattie** would carry on the tradition in 1943, **Panama Sal** in 1952.] **V**:1.9.34.

[1637] **SOLDIERS OF THE STORM**, C: [Regis Toomey was the Anglo hero of this more modern border patrol story which had smugglers working back and forth across the Mexican line. The location placed the headquarters for the operation in Texas, but the hideout, which could only be reached by airplane, was in Mexico. To gain information Toomey first flirted with the "Spanish" waitress at the local cantina, it was fun, but unproductive. When he later saved the daughter of a politician from some desperados, he sadly discovered that her father was involved with the smugglers. Although he and the girl might have become an item, his duty came first. Stunt flying was used to provide some extra thrills and a little diversion. All of the actors were Anglo's.] **V**:5.23.32, **DAR**.

[1638] **SOMEWHERE IN SONORA**, W: ["Duke" Wayne as he was coming to be known, was just at the beginning of his long ride through the next forty years of motion picture history when writers rode him into Sonora. This one had worked before in silent days [1256] and was well received again because of the young stalwart's performance. It seems that as a Rodeo performer, Big John had been accused of fixing a stagecoach race, by some bads. Audiences knew better, but John had to hightail it across the border to Mexico where he fell in with some local bandidos. Pretending to join their ranks, he convinced his former boss's son, who had been "forced" into riding with the gang, that there was a better way to earn a few pesos. Now on the right side of the law, the two thwart the bandit plan to rob the silver mine. At this stage in his career, Wayne was usually reewarded with the girl. So, having accomplished his purpose, he headed for home with the pretty señorita, satisfied that he had done his duty. The Hispanic characters were included only for atmosphere.] **V**:6.27.33, **FD**:6.7.33, **DAR**.

[1639] **THE SON-DAUGHTER**, MGM: [Roman, this time the Oriental prince in disguise, Navarro, loved a young Helen Hays who unfortunately was not the son her oriental parents had wanted to give to the Chinese Revolution. But to please them she sacrificed her love for the big guy in order to marry Warner Orland, destined to be scripted as an oriental many times after this part. She marries him because of his wealth with which she could finance her share of the rebellion. That pleases her parents, but results eventually in having her husband become a poor man.] **V**:5.16.33.

[1640] **THUNDER OVER MEXICO**, Upton Sinclair/Principal Pictures: [**Thunder Over Mexico**, was the first film with Mexico as its basic theme to cause a nation wide controversy. Lasting over a year in its initial phase, the political flack continued throughout the decade involving film makers and politicians alike. Most recently, **Que Viva Mexico**, Eisenstein's original title for the work, was put together to be shown on public television and for sale to commercial stations. Few of the contemporary reviews discuss much of the films artistic merit; most involved themselves with the controversy that developed between the man who was paying the bills, Upton Sinclair, and the Russian film artist/director, Sergi Eisenstein, "a well known communist from Russia" as some called him. Socialists, capitalists, and fascists all expressed their views in no uncertain terms, not so much about the film, but about each other in what might be considered little more than name calling. Possibly the most objective brief paragraph describing the film appeared in an unlikely source, the Daughters of the American Revolution monthly film guide: "Beginning with the ruins of Aztec grandeur, and the interesting structures of the Mayans, we have here a historical drama, based on the brutal social injustice meted out to the peons of Mexico during the reign of Diaz. Breathtaking in its magnitude, grandeur, historical interest and beautifully flowing photography, this work ... is that of a master craftsman and will provide exceptional entertainment. Some gruesome scenes.... [for] Adults and young people." This may well be the longest flight into liberal territory that the good Daughters ever took, and represents a fair appraisal of the work. Cut from more than fifty four miles [280,000 feet] of film shot by the Russian master, the 7000 feet shown were not his final work but that of Sinclair, Don Hayes and Sol Lesser. The movie's graphic imagery included a thin story line involving a young man's lady being raped by the vicious hacendado's men. For protesting the poor peon was buried up to his neck and trampled by the patron's vaqueros. Although some censors had ordered this last scene cut, it remained in many prints as the most brutal scene in the film, one which of course provokes the rebellion of the masses and the promise of eternal happiness there after. Politicians of every color had more trouble with that ideological promise, than the lovely bare breasted, brown beauties tastefully spliced into this production.] **V**:9.26.33, **NYT**:9.25.33, 11.1.33, **DAR**, **NR**:7.5.33, [Correspondence], 10.4.33, pp213-14, **Nation**:7.19.33, pp83-4, 10.4.33, **LitDig**:10.7.33, **Living Age**: July 1932, pp462-3. **Vanity Fair**, October, 1933, "Que Viva

Mexico," The Complete Films of Eisenstein, Dutton, 1974. Thunder Over Mexico, file: NYSAA. The entire episode is outlined at great length in: The Making and UnMaking of QUE VIVA MEXICO!, Harry M. Geduld and Ronald Gottesman, editors, the correspondence relating to the controversy, 1970.

[1641] THROWING THE BULL, C: [A short subject showing the interesting variations in how bullfighting was practiced in Spain, Mexico and Japan.] DAR.

[1642] EL ULTIMO VARON SOBRE LA TIERRA SV IT'S GREAT TO BE ALIVE, F: [This Spanish language film was more of a success both north and south of the border than its English counterpart. First made in 1924 as a silent, Raoul Roulien starred in both versions. In this one he was surrounded by "an ample supply of good-looking Hollywood girls, speaking more or less Spanish." The "enchanting" Rosita Moreno led the cast of Hispanic regulars: Romulado Tirado, Carmen Rodriguez, Mimi Aguglia and Hilda Moreno. This version varies from the English one [1610] in the final scene. Instead of opting to go back to his lady, the choice was taken out of his hands. It was left to a formal and "solemn" session of the "League of Nations" to decide which country would enjoy having the services of the "recently discovered and captured last man on earth."] NYT:6.12.33.

[1643] UNA VIDA POR OTRA = ONE LIFE FOR ANOTHER, Mex/Inter American: [The New York Times provided reviews for the general public, Variety, as a trade journal, was concerned more with the business of film and with those involved in it's actual production and sale. Having read all of each's critical contributions, in relation to Hispanic films, it is postulated here that the former was far more generous in it's evaluations of foreign product, than the latter. The Times generally presented a more favorable assessment of the Spanish language product. Variety, more concerned with business, may well have felt the need to protect it's own and consciously or not, took a more competitive approach to criticizing the foreign productions, especially those from south of the border. They did so despite the fact that few doubted the superior product, in almost all cases, was being made on the California coast. The following provides a good example of what might be considered an unnecessarily superior approach to criticism: "This is one of the many Mexican films which have been coming here lately. If the Mexicans want to get into the Spanish market, they'll have to do better. Production as a whole is too amateurish. Actors, with the exception of Villareal all sound like kids in a first grade reading their lines." After having scanned the scenario, the trade journal finds serious fault with the filming of the action. Boy and girl walk arm in arm in park and carve their initials and kiss. They immediately fall in love after which the girl is arrested. To earn some dollars, she has agreed to take the rap for a good price for a rich lady surely heading to jail. The boy then disappears to resurface later and offer his help: "And still the Spanish film producers wonder why Spanish speaking countries prefer American talkers. Reason is that as they are used [sic] to American product, where actors do things naturally, Spanish talkies are overacted, which makes them ridiculous. Another big mistake is that producers engage actors of different nationalities with peculiar drawl or singsong." There was a bit of North American national pride, and possibly a little smackaroo of capitalism in that review. The NYT's considered the film "an interesting murder mystery" "well calculated to keep the audience in suspense until near the final reel." They made note of the "rather poor photography" but explained that despite that, "the actors, including the various unnamed supporters [did] "effective work." They also praised the authentic scenes included of the Mexican capital. Certainly a different point of view.] V:7.10.34, NYT:2.11.33.

[1644] UNA VIUDA ROMANTICA = THE ROMANTIC WIDOW, F: [Catalina Barcena led the all Hispanic cast in this romantic comedy, another of the Fox Spanish language entries. This one was fun and filled with humorous romantic complications. The scenario involved a still very attractive widow who took a job as the secretary of "the Mexican actor," Luis Alonso, (Gilbert Roland), a handsome young novelist. Although he was tempted to make advances, he remained throughout most of the film, a perfect "caballero". His lady was the Argentine beauty, Mona Maris, who played the successful, but very jealous actress that objected to what she considered to be too convenient a situation. All was resolved in the final reel when the widow won the first prize at a masquerade ball which apparently also included, the novelist. Juan Torena, Julio Pena, Maria Calvo, Romualdo Tirado and Julia Bejarano, were also included.] NYT:9.4.33.

[1645] UP BELOW THE EQUATOR, Principle Picture: [This Principle short traveled audiences to South America, where they were shown "Life in the high Andes of Peru." That included "lamas which served many purposes to their owners, glorious scenery and beautiful Lake Puma."] DAR.

[1646] VOODOO, Principle Adventure Pictures: [There is certainly room for a little research in this one. During the Marine occupation of Haiti in 1925, Sergeant Faustian Wirkus was posted to the off island of La Gonave, as the solitary white administrator over more than 10,000 natives. They soon crowned him king and he accepted the title for more than three years. In 1933 he returned to his island kingdom with a camera and shot a half hour plus of film which documented in travelogue form the native religious practices, including frenzied bathing in cold water streams, the symbolic sacrificing of chickens and goats and other "gruesome exhibitions of Voodoo practiced on the island of Haiti." Principle was shown the film and they provided for its distribution.] NYT:3.27.33, DAR.

[1647] WESTERN CODE, C: [Lots of "well sustained" western hoke with Tim McCoy as the Texas Ranger looking for that real badman who rode with a halfbreed Mexican type played at its very best by Emilio Fernandez, who liked to be considered the personification of "el Indio."] **V**:2.21.33.

[1648] **YO** ... **TU** ... **Y** ... **ELLA** = **I** ... **THOU** ... **AND** ... **SHE**, Fox: [Already having made a name for himself as more than merely a Mexican actor, Gilbert Roland no longer Luis Alonso, was given the lead in this Spanish language attempt to continue the Fox lead in the production of Spanish language films for the domestic Hispanic and Latin American markets. As the romantic Latin lover he was fortunate enough to be provided with two Hispanic beauties to chase about for a while, Mona Maris and Rosita Moreno. After having been naughty just long enough, he was welcomed back home by his faithful and forgiving wife, Catalina Barcena. That was allowed then. The PCA punished Anglo women for such offenses, but the men were usually allowed to go home with their tails between their legs for a little proper scolding. Although the film was simply one more of its genre, it helped the studio recognize the leading man capabilities of the handsome young Hispanic. Gilbert Roland would remain a macho attraction for the next forty years, (and with the same lady at home throughout that time.} The cast also included: Conchita Montenegro, Valentin Parera, Julio Pena, Jose Pena "Pepet".] **NYT**:12.5.33.

1934

[1649] **ADVENTURE GIRL**, indy: [The critics were a bit tough on this young adventuress, implying that her book, "Cradle of the Deep," was a "beautiful bit of prevarication," and that the film she put together to prove what she had written was as good a lie by any other name, as the "old Baron Munchausen ever told." Apparently acquiring a sloop from friends to begin her adventures, once at sea she encountered a fierce Atlantic storm whose violent force threw her into what audiences today would call the "Bermuda Triangle", somewhere on the outer southern edge of the Caribbean. Her mast split into the proverbial smithereens, she realized how fortunate she was to be alive. But more importantly, the storm had somehow blown her craft within reach of the Sargasso sea home of the **Isle of Lost Ships** [1340]. From one of the derelicts there she managed to replace her mast, on another she found a long lost map. Able to continue, the adventure now became a treasure hunt. What luck! The problem was that to acquire the prize she had to venture to the land of the forgotten past, Guatemala, where rumor had it that the stupid natives, primitives that they were, had no conception of gold's value. Once there the locals at first welcomed her, but hospitality soon turned to fear. Outnumbered several hundred to one, the indians still managed to capture the intrepid Anglo heroine and decided to take her up the Rio Dolce where they could offer her as a human sacrifice to their fire god. In just the nick of time, her male companion arrived and singlehandedly rescued the lady. Leaving the pyramids behind, having had the foresight to keep the sloop under full sail [there must have been a real big anchor] the two escaped to sea. The dumbfounded natives were left on shore waving their arms frantically and wondering just how many of them it would have taken to beat those white skinned devils. Well, maybe the critics weren't so tough after all.] **V**:8.14.34, **AMC**.

[1650] **EL AGUA EN EL SUELO** = **WATER ON THE GROUND**, CIFESA: [The scenario and production values of this Spanish import were praised and considered to be a "distinct improvement" over those of the recent past. It was a story about a beautiful young Spanish girl who was encouraged in her charitable works, by an equally handsome young priest. Although their relationship was completely innocent, the good works they performed working together attracted the attention of a local scandal sheet which printed a "double-entendre" poem which implied that the padre and the señorita were in love. The lie forced them to leave and travel different paths for years until they were rejoined and exonerated in the last reel. Some critics felt that this production had "approximate[d] Hollywood standards in technique."] **V**:5.1.34, **NYT**:2.4.35. **FD**:2.6.35.

[1651] **BOLERO**, P: [George Raft starred as the lead in this production built around the sexually intoxicating strains of that seductive rhythm created by the Frenchman, Joseph Maurice Ravel for his ballet by the same name. Certainly not expressed in those terms in 1934, but yet implied, especially in the promotion for this film, some countries had banned the music because of its felt affect on the untutored population. For that reason it may have been the favorite of Latin Quarter cabarets. George might have been a bit heavy for this part, but he certainly gave it his all before he started packing a rod for the mob. The title and music would be used in more sexually explicit situations, two of which would feature the lovely, Bo, of whom some say, "who cares if she's talented," Derek. Bo's **Bolero** was set in Spain, the other **10**, at a Mexican tourist resort. Both would involve the sexual act as the music played, the former in more graphic terms than the other.] **V**:2.20.34.

[1652] **BOLICHE**, Orphea/Sp: [Reviewed from Havana, the critic explained that the Spanish film industry, although flooding the Cuban market with entries, had met with little success until this production. Utilizing the well known Argentine singing trio of Irusta, Fugazot and Demare, the light musical comedy provided solid entertainment. Love interest and sight gags were all present, as was the introduction of five new tango's. Of all the Latin dance imports, none spanned the century with more popularity than the tango. No matter how **Forbidden** the **Dance**, it will never take the tango's place in the hearts of true romantics.] **V**:7.31.34, **NYT**:5.28.35, **FD**:5.31.35.

[1653] **THE BORDER MENACE:** [This little bit of border nonsense is included because there seems to be a general agreement among historian's of western films that this is by far, the worst "B" western ever made. Wild Bill Cody starred, but no identifiable Hispanics were known to have traveled through this unbelievably bad piece of fun.]

[1654] **LA BUENAVENTURA** = **THE FORTUNE TELLER**, W: [Warner's Spanish language entry employed a little extra to capture some of the established Fox audience, it featured Enrique Caruso Jr. who sang the lead this operetta which utilized an already popular Victor Hugo musical score. Well received, it was a hit at home and throughout the South American circuit. The Hispanic cast included: Anita Campillo, Luis Alberni, Rosa Rey, Antonio Vidal, Emilia Leovalli, Paul Ellis, Marcela Nivon, and Emilio Fernandez.] **FD**:3.8.34, 9.18.34.

[1655] **EL CANTANTE DE NAPOLES** = **SINGER OF NAPOLES**, W: [Warner's borrowed freely from Fox's pool of Hispanic players for this musical tribute to the city by the bay which all must see before they die. Enrico Caruso Jr. was surrounded with a grouping of all-star Hispanic players including: Mona Maris, Samuel Pedrazo, Francisco Moran, Enrique Acosta, Carmen Rios, Emilia Levovalli, Antonio Vidal, Maria Calvo and Martin Garralaga.] **FD**:2.26.35.

[1656] **UN CAPTAIN DE COSACOS**, F: [Jose Mojica wrote and sang most of his songs to Rosita Moreno in this Spanish language costumer. They were supported by the Fox family Hispanics: Mona Maris, Andres de Segurola, Julio Pena and Tito Coral.]

[1657] **CAT AND THE FIDDLE**, Metro: [Roman Navarro sang with no less than Jeannette MacDonald, in this film. They were lovers living in sin in Paris, and the lady was paying all the bills. It was fun for a while, but in time the Latin love bird found it necessary to assert himself and try his wings. In less time than it took to ruffle his true loves feathers, he was caged by another canary, more lovely and with even richer plumage. More kept than he had been before, the bill and cooing ends when her old buzzard catches them pecking at each other in his nest. After the feathers stopped flying, the feed bill was canceled forever. Navarro then returned to his old roost, where his first love was waiting. When she offered to save his failing musical production, he agreed to stay.] **V**:2.12.34.

[1658] **COME ON MARINES**, P: [Typical "gung ho" stuff from the boys who had to leave the salubrious and accommodating climes of San Diego for more dangerous, but adventurous possibilities in the Philippines. There an old "devil dog" rescues a stranded group of shipwrecked children and also apprehends a notorious bandit. Hollywood's Anglo savior tradition operated in all of the Hispanic lands which invariably required such service, it was so written.] **NYT**:3.24.34.

[1659] **EL COMPADRE MENDOZA** = **MY FRIEND MENDOZA**, Aguila/Mex: [Two of the Mexican Revolution's most important protagonists became the subject of separate film biographies in 1934. This one produced in Mexico, was the first to attempt a dramatization of Emiliano Zapata's "agrarian bands" and their struggle against the forces of the large hacendados who wanted to keep land from the peons that served them. Villa's life was produced by Warner Brothers [1712]. Audiences on both sides of the border knew from the beginning that "el compadre Mendoza," the rich latifundista, would not be able to maintain friendly relations with both the Federal officials and the Zapatista leader. Neither the fact that he was godfather to the Don's child nor that he secretly loved his friend's wife, could alter his allegiance to the revolutionary cause. Most knew that the tragic unfolding of historical events would make enemies of the former friends. The scenario was aptly direct, without histrionics or too much melodrama, a complaint too frequently used against Hispanic productions. The **New York Times** was so impressed with this film, it predicted that soon Mexican producers would "have nothing more to learn from Hollywood on the technical side." The cast included, Alfredo del Diestro, Carmen Guerrero, Antonia Frausto and Luis G. Garreiro] **NYT**:11.19.34.

[1660] **CORAZONES EN DERROTA** = **VANQUISHED HEARTS**, ALFA/Mex: [There were major differences in orientation between Mexican and Hollywood film makers in 1934, different views on life and society. North American critics accustomed to a steady diet of happily ever after endings, considered the Mexican product to be, too often too morbid, too unreal, and too unhappy. It may have never occurred to them that if film reflected national character, consciousness or society in general, that there might be good reason for the difference in each others individual output. When Mexico exposed the fatalistic side of its collective soul on the screen, audiences were not intending to see the light fluff of leggy 42nd street dancers. There is no intention here to justify either industry's philosophy of film making, both wanted to make dollars, but it should be pointed out that when the Mexican film makers set out to create a reflection of daily life, they frequently produced tragedy. It was easily done, there was a lot of it readily at hand. From the start of this film, audiences knew that the chances for a happy ending were slim. One sister was getting married [Señorita Zea], the other has spent her life in a wheel chair [Aurora Bermudez], and her malevolence increased with every passing day. The audience at the Teatro Campoamor, in New York's Spanish Harlem, knew that the bad sister was going to ruin the other's happiness, and she did before the second reel began. Before the film ended, both of them were dead, along with several other family members. In 1934, this was not necessarily a subject that a fighting the depression Hollywood might have chosen to film, they were promoting fantasy, that was their business and the audience paid a lot of coin to support it. It was simply a different approach. Included in this Mexican feature were flash backs to the beginning days of the Madero revolt against the Porfirato. For a generalized view of the make up of these audiences see: **William D. Allen, "Spanish-Language Films in the US. Their Audience is Wide but Humble,"** *Films in Review*, July-August 1950, pp1-4.] **NYT**:10.10.34, **FD**:10.11.34.

[1661] **COWBOY HOLIDAY**, Beacon: [A "so-so western" featuring Big Boy Williams who assists the not so bad, bad men and helps reestablish the honor of one particular notorious desperado. The latter appears to be at least part Anglo, but his loyal buddy, Julian Rivero, could not seem to remember if he were playing serious melodrama or comedy. As the trusty sidekick, he was this time portrayed as a bumbling Mexican at times mean, but more often funny.] **FD**:12.30.34.

[1662] **LA CRUZ Y LAS ESPADA** SV **THE CROSS AND THE SWORD**, F: [A musical romance in Spanish produced by Fox and set in the missionary days of the Spanish conquest of lower California when brave priests, the Franciscans, created a new and secure frontier among the hostile tribes they pacified, for God, but also for their King. There was a romantic interest, a fiesta with lots of dancing of the jota, daily life on the mission grounds, a wedding ceremony and celebration with colorful costumes. A lot of action and it all took place long before any Anglo ever set foot on either coast. Appropriately enough, the Spanish California historical tale featured an all Hispanic cast, one which North American audiences was becoming more familiar with. The very popular Mexican singing star, Jose Mojica led the way, with Anita Campillo as his co-star. Also included were: Lucio Villegas, Carmen Rodriquez, Paco Moreno and Martin Garralaga.] **NYT**:8.13.34, **FD**:2.6.34.

[1663] **CUESTA ABAHO** = **THE DOWNFALL**, aka **THE DOWNWARD PATH**, P: [This Paramount entry for the Spanish language market starred Mona Maris, Vincente Padula and Carlos Gardel, the Argentine singer. The latter's attendance at the opening of the new Spanish Language theater in Harlem, the Teatro Campoamor, increased the excitement of the large crowd significantly and reflected an appreciation for his art. In this film Mona Maris played a beautiful, slender, and not so really bad vamp, who competed with the equally lovely, but sweeter and much more wholesome [sound familiar], Anita Campillo, for the affection of the temporarily prodigal, Paduala. The opening scenes in an Buenos Aries cafe, shifted quickly to Paris and New York and then returned to the Argentine. There was lots of action and lots of love, which Latin audiences enjoyed every bit as much as more tragic fare. The Hispanic cast also included: Anita Campillo, Jaime Devesa, Suzanne Dullier, Carlos Spaventa and Manuel Peluffo.] **NYT**:8.14.34, **FD**:7.18.34.

[1664] **A DEMON FOR TROUBLE**, Steiner: [Bob Steele played a bit more of the lover in this western than he had heretofore been asked to in his other films. Having followed a little lady to her ranch, he was hired and employed there until he unknowingly beat up her brother, a not so nice guy. The hombre deserved it, but Bob was fired anyway. After this the brother sells the ranch, is killed for the money and Bob is of course accused of doing the foul deed. Knowing who the real killer is, he escapes and heads for the border where he is befriended by Don Alvarado, a notorious Mexican bandit. But whereas the times had somewhat transformed that character, the bandit turns out to be one of the nicer variety willing to take some time off his usual activities to help the Anglo clear his name. In time they manage to trick the baddies and expose the entire plot. Although the bandit, helped in the capture, his part was mainly played for the usual laughs. He spoke Mexicanized English and proved helpful, but it was all accomplished in a clown like manner.] **FD**:8.10.34.

[1665] **DOS MAS UNO DOS** = **TWO AND ONE, TWO**, F: [A creative Spanish language comedy in which the very attractive Rosita Moreno was featured playing a dual role as the feignedly demure niece of Lady Caroline [Carmen Rodriguez] and the more modern Peggy, "an imaginary" but strictly "up to date cousin." The two personalities were made to compete for the handsome young scientist [Valentine Parera] who did not like the new breed of señoritas. Both wooed the young swain, and captured his heart which created humorous complications. But all was cleared up in the final reel when he discovered that the lovely ladies were one and the same and as such he would not need not give one up to have the other. The cast also included Andres de Segurola and Carlos Montalban.] **NYT**:10.27.34, **FD**:10.30.34.

[1666] **DOS MUJERES Y UN DON JUAN** = **TWO WOMEN AND ONE DON JUAN**, J. Mier: [Identified as the first Spanish dialogue film made in Spain, it utilized "the Andalusian pronunciation" for conversations which seemed "more home like to Americans and Hispano-Americans than would have been the case if the action had been located in Madrid." Included in the cast was the Spanish version of a North American blond, Consuelo Cuevas, and the fiery brunette dancer, Mapy Cortes, who would make a brief, but entertaining splash, before moving from the movies to marriage. The action takes place in Sevilla which allowed the producers to introduce some "pleasing music and dancing ... with a real Spanish flavor."] **NYT**:1.4.34.

[1667] **DOS MONJES** = **TWO MONKS**, Mex/Proa: [Unconsciously helping to establish what would become a significant and important genre, Hispanic horror films, Director Bustillo Oro produced these two tales of the eternal triangle narrated by a creepy old monk in a spooky old Spanish monastery. Audiences were advised by the critics that "a fair knowledge of Spanish was necessary "for a full appreciation of this picture." The focus of the story was the fatal romance and death of a "rather attractive" heroine, Magda Haller. The girl loves two boys, one tries to shoot the other but kills her by mistake and himself dies a victim of hallucinations while madly playing the organ. What brought this about was the mortal enmity between two brothers, both monks. Told in flash backs, at first one is lead to believe that the other brother monk is guilty. The details are explained as the young monk seeks the absolution of the prior. When the other gets to tell his side as he recovers from an injury he received, a new version is presented for consideration, quite at variance with the first, which had the audience fairly convinced, but now wondering who was really at fault. Along with several other similar productions, these macabre Mexican films relied more on the monsters within the individual personality and the sexually repressive perversity of a contorted Catholicism, than did their North American counterparts which emphasized more tangible bogeyman. These films, enjoyed some vogue at the time, but with the bizarre productions that they evolved into in the fifties and sixties, they developed a cult following that along with the assistance of cable television, is still strong today.] **NYT**:7.21.35, **FD**:1.22.35.

[1668] **DRUMS O'VOODOO**, Indy: [The drums were beating somewhere in a Louisiana bayou in this one. There, both Christian and Voodoo practitioners were conducting a struggle against the forces of evil. They were employing all of the powers their various divinities could manifest to ward off the villainous doings of an individual who wanted to destroy a Christian preacher, but it was a tough fight. The cast was entirely negro and made up of unknowns. There were views of jungle worship right here on the North American mainland, even worse, the Christian minister had a virginal niece, but she was ready to give up that distinction. Morris McKinney, the only professional in the cast, was willing to help her. He wanted the beautiful maiden "as an attraction for his 'jook', a southern cabaret-brothel [and] just walk[ed] [into the church] drew his razor and announce[ed] he [was] going to take her." From the first, Hollywood scripters gave Hispanic's knives as the favored weapon. Razors were reserved for blacks, both still use them in today's films. As movies required their Hispanics to speak in dialect so were the blacks ordained. It was nightly fare on the **Amos and Andy Show**. In this production all spoke the dialect most comfortable to the white audience: "What you mean Ebenezer by coming here disturbing the ancient worship of the voodoo gods? ... Why is dat devilish imp of de devil troubling you?" It was like that throughout until good triumphed over evil.] **V**:5.15.34, **FD**:5.12.34. Script: **Drums O'Voodoo**: 40 pages. **NYSAA**.

[1669] **ENEMIGOS** = **THE ENEMIES**, Atlantida/Mex: [This was the second Mexican feature presented at the Teatro Campoamor and dealt with an imaginary incident alleged to have taken place during the revolution against Diaz involving the supporters of Zapata and the Federalista followers. Señor Delgado a Zapatista leader, devoted to the cause of the peasants, apparently fell prey to an aristocratic loyalist lady who was responsible for the death of many of his comrades. She offered him his life in return for his services, he refused. Mexican scripters enjoyed their little fantasies also, but the **NYT** was pleased with this production praising the import for "an air of authenticity lacking in films of this type made north of the Rio Grande."] **NYT**:8.18.34, **FD**:8.23.34.

[1670] **EL ESCANDALA** = **THE SCANDAL**, Mex/Rex: [This Mexican production was directed by Enrique del Campo and featured Julian Soler, Rosita Castro, and Carmen Guerrero, by now a talented and experienced cast. They were favorites of the Spanish Language audience. The script described the activities of a reformed libertine who after his rejuvenation put an end to his many scandalous affairs and married Rosita, but not before Carmen presented the reformee with a lot of pleasant grief.] **FD**:9.24.34.

[1671] **EL FANTASMA DEL CONVENTO** = **THE PHANTOM OF THE CONVENT**, Mex/Producciones Fesa: [The master of the Mexican grotesque cinema, De Fuentes, produced this first rate fantasy on location in the Teotzotlan monastery. It was considered to be both a "macabre and lyrical story" of a wife trying to seduce her husband's friends ... it includes a sinful monk, mummified corpses and books dripping with blood and was well received.]

[1672] **FIGHTING RANGER**, C: [One more of the sixty plus entries Buck Jones provided for the entertainment of all, but especially the kids of the Saturday matinee, this one was a remake of 1931's **Border Law** [1471]. Buck and loyal friend had to head across the border to avenge the death of his brother. After lots of hard riding and fast shooting, they did. Much of the action took place in Mexico with the pretty Tonita, an Anglress, providing the rather tame love interest.] **V**:4.17.34.

[1673] **FLAMING GOLD**, RKO: [Featuring Pat OBrien without his cassock and Bill Boyd, without a horse, the two friend were wildcatters in the Mexican oil fields, in this film. These appeared to belong only to Standard oil, but a few other independent Anglos were trying to get their share. Had they known, they might have worked a little faster, the Mexican expropriation of North American, British and Dutch oil interests were just around the corner. Although the two buddies were fighting the precursors of Pemex, the real enemy headquarters was back somewhere on Broadway, "Number 26" to be exact. Standard Oil of New York real address, from which the orders to put the two independents out of business allegedly came. Apparently, the one well the friends had been working into the Mexican subsoil was giving the big guys too much competition. Hollywood promoted individual Anglo enterprise in Mexico, but it could not allow big business to quash it, the company's plot failed. Standard's man back in Mexico was an idiot and after igniting one of the company's many drills in hopes of burning out the independents, the raging backfire threatened the entire oilfield. The manger then tried to recruit the two to help extinguish the conflagration. They refuse. After a bit of local love stuff with some imported Anglo ladies the entire scene shifted back to New York. The fire might well have burned down much of Mexico, but the problem was not mentioned again. Ironically, all of the local Mexican help was treated with the usual Anglo condescension in this film, and that was one of the real reasons along with very low wages that provoked the Cardenas government in 1938 to expropriate all foreign oil interests. Only the coming of WWII allowed for an acceptable settlement.] **V**:2.20.34, **AMC**.

[1674] **FOUND ALIVE**, Ideal Picture Corp: [Interesting because elements of such marital/social problems are still with us, this little cameo pivoted on the point that the father was awarded custody of the male child by the courts. The mother refusing to abide by such a decision, takes the child and heads south of the border where she looks through a few thousand feet of jungle film for a proper place to hide her son from the authorities. New York critics did not like the film and were beginning to use the snappy little sarcastic phrases to pan such productions as they felt inadequate: ""Found Alive" might better have been left undiscovered."] **NYT**:2.12.34.

[1675] **FOUR FRIGHTENED PEOPLE**, De Mille/P: [The action here took place in the Malayan jungle where Leo Carillo was called upon to be a half caste local, proud of his "demi-Caucasian" half and willing at every turn, even when faced with "pygmy cannibals," to give up his life for the heroine. She was there to teach the little guys birth control, what else? Such self sacrifice remained the scripted fate of all the unpure who resided in that uncertain limbo of the viewing public's accepted ethnic attitudes.] **V**:1.30.34.

[1676] **LAS FRONTERAS DEL AMOR** = **LOVE'S FRONTIERS**, F: [Fox scored another money making little piece of Spanish language fluff with this one. Jose Mojica, scripted as a very successful entertainer tired of performing and singing his heart out to so many anonymous audiences, decides to return back to the good life and sing to his sheep instead. But in 1934, even the back country of Hollywood's more or less primitive Mexico was not immune to the technological advances of the modern world, and one day, a lovely lady dropped out of the sky in an out of gas auto gyro. It could have happened! A real fire ball, Rosita Moreno, soon discovered there was no

Pemex station handy, so she decided to stay and help Jose count his sheep. It was a natural, audiences knew and hoped for what eventually happened. Fox sent a good camera crew to shoot location footage which reviewers praised as excellent. Also included were: Rafael Corio, Juan Martinez Pla, Carmen Rodriguez and Chito Alonso.] **NYT**:12.4.34, **FD**:12.5.34.

[1677] **FURY OF THE JUNGLE**, C: [One of the real beauties of 1934 this film's blatant racism, even considering the times, was pretty harsh. The writers placed some of the world's worst white scum, the refuse of mankind, along with a "South American native girl" in a village on the edge of a rain forest in this one. One of the few attractive locals in a slimy jungle filled with ugly indians, she was used by camp members at will. When the first white woman they had seen in years was finally written into their little community, she arrived with her dying brother. All were interested, in her and how quickly it would take for the brother to die. Hollywood's tropical jungles bred that kind of insensitivity. After he finally died, the white men "gone native", fought each other for the surviving sister. The native girl, apparently fond of having been misused for so many years, went crazy with jealousy, tried to kill her competition, but failed. Throughout the production and with varying degrees of success, the exiles attempted to use accents to identify their former homeland. Usually humorous or worth a few smiles, the white man's burden stuff usually exhibited in Hollywood productions was, in this South American jungle, at least, unfunny.] **V**:3.13.34.

[1678] **GRANDEROS DEL AMOR** = **GRENADIERS OF LOVE**, F: [Leading the way in Spanish language productions Fox used the popular Brazilian, Raul Roulien and the vivacious Conchita Montenegro as the feature attractions in this Viennese tale of the Tyrolean hills. It was all fluff and music, with Raul as a serious composer of modern stuff being challenged to write an old operetta. Searching for material up in the mountains, he discovered an old castle which housed an old count and his lovely young daughter. North American audiences were presented with Mexican actors playing non Mexican or Hispanic parts, actually portraying Europeans, not something they were accustomed to. It may well have generated at least a little conversation. The stars were supported by the regular Fox Hispanic players: Romualdo Tirado, Paco Moreno, Maria Calvo, Andres de Segurola, Valentin Parera, and Tito Davison.] **NYT**:9.4.34, **FD**:9.5.34.

[1679] **HOLLYWOOD PARTY**, MGM: [Simply another attempt to utilize almost everyone on the lot in a film without a plot for purely exploitation purposes. In this one Lupe Velez attended Jimmy Durante's party "wearing the most extreme decollete yet". It may not have been a hit with the critics, but it certainly was with the males in the audience, if their wives allowed them to look at the lovely lady that had captured Tarzan's heart.] **V**:5.29.34.

[1680] **LAUGHING BOY**, MGM: [Cast included Roman Navarro and Lupe Velez who played a young indian couple on a New Mexico reservation, but it was not that simple. Laughing Boy loved Slim Girl and she he for a while, but when she falls for a white man and becomes his lover, he makes her a whore. Laughing Boy then stops the smiling and plans to do the pale face in, but the Production Code made him kill Lupe instead. Bad ladies had to be publicly punished on the screen in the Hollywood of 1934, all of them got theirs in some way.] **V**:5.15.34.

[1681] **LAUGHING WITH MEDBURY IN SOUTH AMERICA**, C: [This eight minute Columbia short might have raised some question about Argentine agriculture. It is quite possible that there were such things, but one wonders just where in that nation rubber plantations might have been located. Traditional leader in rubber production throughout South America, Brazil was followed [far behind] by Bolivia, Colombia, Ecuador, Peru and Venezuela. Argentina according to this film, once the traditional shots of beautiful Buenos Aires were established, was also a producer. One was told that the "trip [was] made interesting" by the usual "Medbury chatter." That must have been interestingly inventive.] **FD**:3.8.34.

[1682] **LEARNED ABOUT SAILORS**, F: [The cast here was entirely Anglo. Action traveled from Shanghai to Los Angeles. There's a sailor who falls for the lady who sings the songs in the sleazy dive. There are also two con-men involved and all of them make it back to the coast where the hucksters convince sailor, Lew Ayres, and singer, Alice Faye, that a "pseudo-shotgun wedding would save the pair from complications with the authorities." Of course the obvious happens and they really do love each other. For no reason at all, the scribes added a little diversion to the plot by having Harry Green play an Argentine showman, Jose Lopez Rubenstein, who was "assigned a more than usually sympathetic chore and milk[ed] it." Around this time, as a result of significant pressure, especially, from the Catholic Legion of Decency, and fearing that a boycott lodged against it's films could really hurt profits, the MPPDA, began issuing their seals of cleanliness. Exhibitors would not show a film unless it had earned it's seal. This piece of harmless fluff received #5.] **V**:7.31.34.

[1683] **MADAME DU BARRY**, W: [The critics did not like Dolores Del Rio in this role, they felt that her characterization was "barely believable". But then, this was Busby Berkeley's first attempt at producing musical numbers for the French Emperor's court.] **V**:10.30.34.

[1684] **MARIE GALANTE**, F: [Certainly an interesting bit of foreign intrigue focusing on the activities of a villainous agent who desired to blow up the United States fleet as it passed through the Panama Canal thereby rendering the great waterway inoperative. Marie Galante, played by Kitti Gallian, a beautiful blond import from France in her first Hollywood film, became involved in a whirlwind of international plotting. How she was able to maintain her virtue and

naivety through to the last reel was a credit to the
Production Code censors. Considering that she had been
shanghaied from her innocent life in a French coastal village
by a lecherous sea captain and escaped only after putting into
port in the Yucatan, she must have been at least agile.
Eventually, she worked her way down through Central America
singing for her bread while trying to reach the Canal Zone
where she might find passage back to France. There, with her
virtue still in place, the real action began. Marie now became
the center of a conspiracy plotted by a teutonic type to
destroy a fair chunk of the North American navy. Neither the
Hun nor the oriental involved were identified as German or
Japanese. There were foreign markets involved and possible
complications with the respective governments to be
considered, but the accents made it obvious where the baddies
were from. Spencer Tracy, the North American agent, believed
the girl to be innocent and used her to foil the evil
intentions of the others. Other agents working independently
for the same purpose were also involved in this complicated
intrigue. In the last reel the Canal's integrity along with
that of the intrepid's lady was preserved.] **V**:11.27.34,
NYT:11.21.34.

[1685] **MURDER IN TRINIDAD**, F: [Not much mystery, but solid
entertainment for those supporters of Sherlock's most loyal
companion, Nigel Bruce. Alone, in this production set in one
of Her Majesty's Caribbean colonies, he was the super-sleuth
and the critics gave him credit for carrying the film. Had
this been a romance, the wondrous beauties of this tropical
paradise [Trinidad] might have been featured, but as a
mystery, it required a more menacing atmosphere. So, the
image makers transformed the island's natural pitch pits into
places of extreme danger. With a little improper lighting,
these became "a bad swamp", "so filled with quicksand that
only those who knew where to step" could cross it. But more
than this protected the hideout of the diamond thieves, the
"swamp was also filled with crocodiles" and hideous reptiles
like those present in all of Hollywood's South American
jungles. Scenes like this may well have encouraged those in
the audience who planned to travel to the tropics to obtain
their shots, and equip themselves appropriately. Accordingly,
a pit helmet would frequently have been required.] **V**:5.29.34,
NYT:5.16.34.

[1686] **NADA MAS QUE UNA MUJER** = **ONLY A WOMAN**, F: [Supposed to
be the Spanish language version of MGM's **Pursuit** [1791], it is
difficult to understand where the correlation between the two
scripts exists. This film, set in the Philippines concerns
the selfsacrificing love of an Argentine artist who is forced
to eke out a living by reciting poetry describing her native
Argentina. She does this to support her young Anglo lover
blinded by local "bravos". Berta Singerman, "an Argentine
diseuse" well known throughout the Americas, starred as the
femme lead. The cast included: Juan Torena, Luana Alcaniz,
Carmen Rodriguez, Alfredo de Diestro, Lucio Villegas and
Julian Rivero who had already appeared in several Hollywood

productions practicing his broken English.] **NYT**:11.26.34, **FD**:11.27.34.

[1687] **NEATH THE ARIZONA SKIES**, Mono: [Dominated by John Wayne's presence, this story about a young woman's problems with her oil rich land, included the usual señorita, but also served to introduce Artie Ortego as a minor Hispanic character who would remain much same in scores of other productions.] **MPG**.

[1688] **ORO Y PLATA** = **GOLD AND SILVER**, Hispano/Mexicana: [The "attractive" Carmen Guerrero starred as the innocent rural maiden in this Spanish dialogue. Adolfo Giron, played her father, portrayed as a rugged, but tender hearted man, who was confronted by Alfredo de Diestro, a selfish selfcentered city slicker. His hardboiled dad, was Julio Villareal. By now a familiar cast of characters to North American audiences, and critics, the production was well reviewed. Hispanic audiences really liked it. They were always pleased to see virtue triumph.] **FD**:7.26.34.

[1689] **PALOOKA**, UA: [Even with Jimmy Durante watching out for his ace fighter, Joe Palooka, and Joe's mom helping out, saving the pleasant pug from the little Spanish cooch dancer with the seductively swaying torso, proved to be a tough fight to the finish. She was finally KO'd in the last round by the nice little Anglo lady, who's virtue could not be questioned. As an extra Jimmy did his now famous, **Dinka-dinka-do** routine in between rounds.] **V**:3.6.34.

[1690] **PECADOS DE AMOR** = **SINS OF LOVE**, Aguila Films: [Heralded in the Mexican press as a "National Picture," critics North of the Rio wondered why so much was made of a scenario that had been "passe" ten years before. Part of the answer might have been found in the fact that a North American director was used for this Mexican made movie. Basically a story of infidelity, the nobel youth in this film managed to find the strength to forgive his lovely for her indiscretion with the rich banker. Always a favorite with the romantics in the audience, love triumphed in the last reel, but some of the machos watching might have had a bit of a problem with the hero's forgiving nature. If they did not, certainly, later screen writers on both sides of the border would have. One has but to see Anthony Quinn in **Revenge**, to understand how scripters north of the Rio Grande would have their cuckolded Hispanic husbands punish the unfaithful wives that strayed into other bed, for whatever reason.] **NYT**:8.29.34, **FD**:4.25.34.

[1691] **EL PRISIONERO 13** = **PRISONER NO.13**, Mex: [This tragic bit of old Mexico proved to be a powerful production. Its impact on an unsigned reviewer is worth reprinting and indicates a strong sympathy for the rebel cause in the Mexican Revolution probably influenced **Viva Villa** [1712]: "In presenting this Spanish language version of an outrage typical of the military despotism under which the people of the nation on the other side of the Rio Grande suffered for so many long years Señor Fuentes, the director, relentlessly and logically carries his argument to the bitter end. Made in Mexico, this indictment of the system that put unlimited powers of life and death into the hands of often brutal army officers and local "caciques" [formerly indian chieftains, by 1900 the term referred to local political bosses], has an air of absolute authenticity. ... Persons familiar with Mexican history know that it is not at all exaggerated. ... [The story] is calculated to grip the spectators to the dramatic finish and leave them filled with admiration for the unknown revolutionists who died like real "hombres.""] **NYT**:4.30.34, **FD**:3.30.34.

[1692] **THE PRIVATE LIFE OF DON JUAN**, Br: [For his last appearance in a feature film, Douglas Fairbanks was surrounded by beautiful ingenues, including Merle Oberon, to help him portray the last days of Sevilla's native son and Spain's greatest legendary lover. His reviews were mixed but his performance was still adequate enough to please some of critics and most of the ladies. Just a little portly for the role, Fairbanks enjoyed playing the most recognized of Spain's super-machos for whom "Susceptible Seville femmes, ... not loath to two-timing their señors, [threw] rope ladders down from their balconies to facilitate the ingress and exit of the trepidacious Don Juan." Much of the legendary Latin Lover mythology stems from the amorous activities ascribed to this once most active swordsman of Sevilla.] **V**:12.18.34, **NYT**:12.8.34, **Newsweek**:12.1.34, p22, **NR**:1.9.35, p246.

[1693] **PROFANACION**, Indo-America: [A Spanish language version of the **Mummy**, it will later be duplicated by Hollywood with only slight reshaping in the **Mask**. Returning once more across the river, **The Wrestling Women vs. The Aztec Mummy** will blend both films into an incredible mixture making the heroine's, well known wrestling stars and the heavy, an ancient Aztec, god. But back in 1934, the affects of having dug up that certain tomb tucked away on the Egyptian desert which was still claiming it's victims, according to the press, more than a decade after it had been violated by "non-believers", continued to intrigue movie makers on both sides of the Rio Grande. Quite naturally, considering the influence Hollywood exercised on film making throughout the world, it was only a matter of time before Mexico's own amazing archeological cites, began producing their own "maldiciones" [curses] to afflict any who would violate sacred ground. Possibly the most interesting part of this picture was the prelude which showed the burial of the Aztec chief, "the unearthing of whose body furnishes the excuse for the subsequent profanation."] **NYT**:7.31.34, **FD**:2.1.34

[1694] **QUIEN MATO A EVA** = **WHO KILLED EVA**, Mex/Duquesa Olga: [Two of the most popular regular Mexican stars of the Spanish language productions appear in this mystery, Jose Bohr and Julio Villarreal. One was the bored son of a rich father, the other a thief, so the two team up to break the monotony and make a few pesos. On their first caper, they chance on the dead body of a blond lady and shift their focus from committing to solving a crime. Successful in their efforts, they were, pleased that they had remained on the right side of the law.] V:12.22.34, FD:12.27.34.

[1695] **RIACUELO**, [River of life], Sono Film: [With this attraction for the Teatro Campoamor in Harlem, Argentina made its first bid to break into the North American film export market. Well received, the film described the various cross currents of Buenos Aries city life from a sympathetically portrayed pick pocket who is reformed by the love of an honest woman, to another young lad who falls in love with a poor cabaret singer. Over all it satisfied local critics who felt that this "initial Argentine import" gave audiences "intriguing views of the work and play of the people whose activities kept the big river pulsating with commerce."] NYT:12.8.34, FD:12.10.34.

[1696] **RIDING SPEED**, Superior: [A western star of many silent films, Buffalo Bill Jr. had lost significant riding speed by the time he acted in and directed this production which had him dealing with the ever present smugglers operating on the other side of the border. After he brought them to justice this time, he hung up his spurs.] **MPG**.

[1697] **ROMANCE TROPICAL**, Juan Viugie: [In an attempt to please the broad base of its audience by presenting films produced in any of the Hispanic areas, the Teatro Campoamor advertised this work as the "first 100 percent Puerto Rican motion picture." Although there were complaints about the Puerto Rican pronunciation "of the tongue of Cervantes", the scenario proved exciting. Much of the action allegedly took place on the off shore island of "Mu" which the producers claimed was inhabited by still "semibarbaric islanders." There legend had it, that one of the local ladies was something of a Puerto Rican Pocahontas, responsible for saving her man, an explorer friend, from her father's ax. It would seem that some Hispanic scripters also had certain fixed ideas about racial purity, because they allowed their pure blooded adventurer from the mainland to look and lust after his savage lady, but he was certainly not given the opportunity to love her forever. Complications like this never proved to be a problem for well read writers anywhere, there was a standard procedure to be followed. Audiences had learned to accept that such an interracial transgressor would be killed off by her own people while trying to escape with her man. This was necessary so that the lover could marry the "pura" or pure blooded lady that was always waiting for him, in this case, apparently only a few miles away in San Juan.] NYT:10.15.34, FD:10.16.34.

[1698] **SAGRARIO**, ASPA/Mex: [It is difficult to see where the shrine or holy place is in this "grim tragedy". Without a moments comic relief to ease the grating strain, the story outlines the problems experienced by a husband recently released from prison married to a "tolerably attractive wife" whose daughter is just coming into womanhood. As the much desired attraction of all the males in the vecindad, she provokes a trying series of events which may have made the father miss the solitude of prison. The beautiful young lady was played by Maria Luisa Zea, considered then a promising new prospect, she only made one brief appearance for Hollywood.] **NYT**:1.22.34, **FD**:1.24.34.

[1699] **LA SANGRE NANDA** = **THE CALL OF THE BLOOD**, Mex: [This Spanish language film introduced yet another new face, Elisa Robles, to the ever expanding members of the Mexican film family. The very "attractive" slender Miss Robles was the discovery of Argentine great, Jose Bohr, who chose her to play in this advertised as "a Socialist film". Apparently the socialism involved the rich son of a Argentine foundry/smelter owner who eventually felt some sympathy for the plight of the factory workers, to say nothing of the foreman's sister. In the inevitable disturbance required in the last reel, she took a bullet intended for her rich man, a little noblesse from the working classes who were apparently still licking the boots of their masters.] **NYT**:5.17.34, **FD**:5.16.34.

[1700] **SEÑORA CASADA NECESITA MARIDO** = **A MARRIED WOMAN NEEDS A HUSBAND**, F: [Fox tried a little humor with this Spanish language entry which featured the noted Catalina Barcena as the highly volatile central character in this farce. She was driving him, Antonio Moreno, crazy, but he had her well on the way there too. Both require a little jealous interest, provided by Jose Crespo and Valentin Parera, to bring them back to the same, saner path. Along the way Catalina displayed at least her versatility by doing a Mae West impersonation with appreciated gusto. Also included in the cast were Barbara Leonard, Romualdo Tirado, Mimi Aguglia, Tito Coral, Jose Pena "Pepet", Movita Castaneda and Carlos Villarias.] **NYT**:2.11.35, **FD** 2.12.35.

[1701] **SOBRE LAS OLAS** = **OVER THE WAVES**, Latino Films/Mex: [Most significant because this was the first Spanish language film to "carry a concession to Americans unfamiliar with the tongue of Cervantes in the shape of superimposed English titles." This was done to try to broaden the base of the Anglo viewing public, Hollywood had long employed the practice for their very first exports south. Aside from that, this was a tight little production which recounted how one of Mexico's most popular waltzes was written. It was solid if somewhat, sentimental entertainment, a theme not unfamiliar to the Anglos in the audience. There was a lot of sympathy cast for the young musician who was too poor to accept the affection of the wealthy girl that loved him. In return, he could only offer her his creation, a new waltz, for which she had provided the inspiration.] **NYT**:3.17.34, **FD**:3.21.34.

[1702] **LA SOMBRA DE PANCHO VILLA** = **THE SHADOW OF PANCHO VILLA**, Mex/C: [Considered by some "a notable contribution to the pictorial history of modern Mexico," this film describing the bloody events of Mexican Revolution, 1910-1914, was superior in many ways to **Viva Villa** [1712]. Although Villa hardly appeared in this Mexican production, the atmosphere, the conditions, the "types" shown on the screen seemed "almost too real," for some when compared with Hollywood's sentimental approach to the main character. Hollywood would try to soften its approach to Villa for North American audiences. Having been considered a bandit, not a revolutionary, by most people north of the Rio Grande for most of his life, it took some reshaping of character to make Villa a sympathetic hero with local audiences. The Mexican production did not have that problem, Villa himself, and what his men had done in breaking the oppression of the Diaz regime was recognized and appreciated. Villa was not considered to be a bandit in Mexico, he had achieved the status of a martyred hero, who died for the revolution even if it was some years after the fighting was over. This work focused on the decisive battle at Zacatecas, where Villa broke the back of the old regime. It continued the story through his defeat some years later by an old comrade, Obregon, at the battle of Celeyas. All of the revolutionary songs were sung and provided an excellent sound track for the dynamic action. Although the production values were not those Hollywood might have provided, this was and still is a superior film for seeing Villa through Mexican eyes.] **NYT**:1.8.34, **FD**:1.9.34.

[1703] **STRICTLY DYNAMITE**, RKO: [Jimmy Durante and Lupe Velez made this fast paced mayhem a pleasure throughout most of what was the Latin lady's desire to obtain a bigger part of the radio program they shared. Although her accent was not over-emphasized, her aggressive and warm temperament, could not be held in check. Using her feminine charms on all who required a little convincing, the seductive Latin lady, obtained all she desired.] **V**:7.10.34, **FD**:7.5.34. AMC.

[1704] **SU ULTIMA CANCION** = **HIS LAST SONG**, Cinematografia Mexicana: [Maria Luisa Zea was given a starring role in this addition to the growing number of Spanish language films shown on a regular basis in New York and other major metropolitan Hispanic markets in 1934. The scenario employed a familiar Hollywood heartbreaker. A one time big success in the music world had fallen lower than the drinks he regularly spilled off the table. Emptying the bottle had provided him with the only support he had known for some time, that is, until the beautiful young Maria came into the picture. Then like all but the most cynical of misogynist, he was moved by her love, moreover she inspired him to one last great moment. Sadly, that moment was hardly filled with sixty seconds before he discovered that she only cared for him as a father and the young swain was going to get all the goodies; the fall which this produced in the last reel was fatal. Life continued with the young. Many left the theaters with wet eyes.] **NYT**:5.9.34.

[1705] **EL TANGO EN BROADWAY**, P: [This Paramount Spanish language musical comedy starring Carlos Gardel, the popular Argentine singer and actor. The scenario itself described the activities of a rich South American uncle who comes to the United States to visit his nephew. The formula piece required the nephew to immediately dig up a fiancee which the old señor has come to meet hoping to be there for the wedding. The romantic complications that followed pleased Anglo as well as Latin audiences. The tango numbers were especially well produced and danced. Other members of the all Spanish speaking cast included: Blanca Vischer, Vincente Paudla, Trini Ramos, Jamie Devesa, and Manuel Peluffo. Lots of songs and dancing, all Hispanic style and all were very entertaining. See: **Don Juan Diplomatico** [1488] The Pinto article cited there makes reference to this film, and it includes a good picture of the lobby card used to advertise it.] **FD:1.3.35**.

[1706] **TIBURON** = **SHARK**, Cinematografia Mexicana: [The sharks referred to here were the same kind, called by the same name, that infest the lower regions of the underworld in almost all metropolitan areas, loan sharks, as much a problem in Mexico City as they were in Manhattan. The Mexican approach to the problem differed from that which was usually taken by Hollywood. In this version, there were no real good guys, those who were trying to take advantage, were not much worse than their victims. That orientation would not come north for years. Local audiences wanted their good guys, so did the Production Code Administration.] **NYT:4.18.34**.

[1707] **EL TIGRE DE YAUTEPEC** = **THE TIGER OF YAUTEPEC**, Mex/FESA: [For the reviewer this film was "further" evidence of advances the Mexican motion picture industry had made in recent times. It also served to introduce another "charming young actress in the person of Lupita Gallardo." In the film Lupita was the daughter of one of the best families in Yautepec. She fell for the good guy bandit, El Tigre, who simply held up stages for a living, but was as loveable as Frank Sinatra would be sometime later in the **Kissing Bandit**. Something of a nationalist, Lupita had made some noise about wanting to promote the Mexican film industry at the movie's premiere in Mexico City the year before. By way of praise some of the New York reviewers advised her that she had already done her part in doing so with her performance in this film.] **NYT:10.20.34**, **FD:10.22.34**.

[1708] **LA TRAVIESA MOLINERA** aka **IT HAPPENED IN SPAIN**, Sp/D'Arrast-Soriano/UA: [This was the first "Spanish pic" to get world-wide distribution and was considered "plenty Spanishy." "Slow in spots" the critics felt it had to be so or it "wouldn't be faithfully Spanish if [had it been] given speed a la Americana." They felt that the "Siesta action" aided the picture's exotic qualities and that is should be shown in the "class houses." The story involved a simple Spanish love quadrangle. The mayor and the millers's wife were having an affair so the miller "slapped back" with the Mayor's spouse. The interplay between the four sparked a lot of dramatic action. The picture's opening received a "tough break" in Spain because of the very early beginnings of revolutionary activity, a general strike closed down the country for a while dramatically affecting sales.] **V:11.6.34**.

[1709] **TRES AMORES** = **THREE LOVES**, [The **NYT** gave top "histrionic honors" to the only non Hispanic lady in this one, Mona Maris, the Argentine vamp was given good grades, as was Abuta Campillo, but Mimi Aguglia of Italy was considered "superior" playing the mother for a day of a well to do, but very insensitive youth, Carlos Villarias. Selected from a home of indigent females, she was paid to be maternal and played her role so convincingly that son and audience alike, wanted it become a full time occupation. Two Latin lovely's were competing for the lad. As the gold digger only interested in increasing her fortune, Mona lost out to the nicer lady. Anita, less interested in herself was more steady and took the selfish swain after she was convinced that he had reformed. Yes, this story line should sound familiar. The other Hispanic members were: Andres de Segurola, Soledad Jimenez, Enrique Acota and the very lovely, Movita Castaneda.] **NYT**:11.5.34, **FD**:11.7.34.

[1710] **TRUMPET BLOWS**, P: [If the Academy gave awards for originality in miscasting and sheer insanity in creating inane scenarios, certainly this film would win top honors, possibly for all time [although casting Bobby Benson as a Hispanic gang lord should be awarded honorable mention.] In this film Adolphe Menjou was given a dual role. He was in one guise Pancho Lopez, the rich hacendado, respected by all. In his other capacity, he played Pancho Gomez, a most feared bandit. In this character, it is difficult to understand why a casting director thought that anyone, anywhere, at any time, would be able to see his Hispanic qualities, even with the help of bandoleers, mustache and broad brimmed sombrero. As ludicrous, even discounting hindsight, was placing George Raft, [well, he had been in **Bolero** [1651]], in a brilliant suit of lights as a matador trying vainly to avoid being gored, dancing about the corrida, getting mad and shooting the bull with his gat, enough, it was simply a case of classic miscasting. Possibly it reflected an attitude that believed one had simply to use the outer trappings of Hispanic identifiers and a little broken English to create a proper Mexican character. Complicating all of this was an involved, completely unbelievable script which was supposed to reflect the problems of the south of the border rich. It must be remembered that this film was not played for laughs. Raft was Manuel Montez, who had been afforded the dubious benefits of a Northern education and was returning home as the story opened. Happy to be back on the hacienda, he was displeased that Señor Montez, alias Pancho Gomez, the retired bandit, wanted him to marry Carmela Ramirez, an aristocrat. Manuel faced a crisis. He preferred to cuddle with Chulita, and she he, but that property was supposed to belong to his brother who had been paying the all the bills during his absence. Unable to hurt him, Raft decided to go to Mexico City and become a matador, which he does. Chulita followed and they lived in sin, guilty but happy to be together. All this caused Pancho much pain. Finally realizing this, Manuel, loyal brother that he was, decided to end it. But not having had his fill of the señorita, in his weakness, he took to drink and kept the lady. The problem was that tequila in the matador in the corrida on a hot Sunday afternoon proved to be a deadly mixture. Manuel became sloppy with the bulls. Meanwhile, realizing that Manuel had decided to let the bulls settle the issue of who would snuggle with the señorita, she appealed to the bandit brother. Although he was still a hunted and wanted hombre, Pancho, at the very last moment found himself jumping into the rink to distract the bull and save his brother. In doing so he managed to attract the attention of entire corrida crowd, the federales, and the bull, but he did save his hermano, and forgave him for taking his woman before making good his escape. Lets see ya top that for a script! Moreover, in this entire script, filled with Mexicans, there was not one represented in the leading cast. Sidney Toler, destined for a very long run as the replacement oriental for Warner Oland, emulated the latter by also playing a Mexican in Anglo oriental style, Pepi Sancho. Truly a unique piece of film.] **V**:4.17.34, **NYT**:4.14.34.

[1711] **TU HIJO** = **THY SON**, Mex/indy: [A sad, highly sentimental production, in which an old childless couple get to take care of a young woman's child when she dies, leaving them something to live for.] **NYT**:12.17.34, **FD**:12.18.34.

[1712] **VIVA VILLA!** W: [So far as Hollywood was responsible for at least helping to establish the general viewing public's historical interpretation of Mexican history and specifically that of its revolutionary leaders, this film represents a major reinterpretation of what had been commonly cranked out of the various studio production companies. In the decade after Villa's death, his exploits had acquired a heroic quality, even for many North Americans. A semiofficial biography had glorified his career for much of the reading public. The Mexican film industry had realistically dramatized his life and exploits and that product had been well received in New York and Los Angles [1702]. The time was right for Hollywood to try its hand at reshaping accepted views of the only individual to have ever successfully invaded United States territory and lived to enjoy the fact thereafter. **Viva Villa**'s Production Code file details the early history and development of the project first proposed by Paramount. The correspondence therein clearly indicates that the studio was "willing to throw the sympathy "either toward or away from Villa" "whichever the censorship requirements" demanded. Moreover, they realized that it was absolutely essential to work closely with the Mexican government on the project or else the film would never be exhibited south of the border, at least in Mexico. The project passed from Paramount to RKO and was finally acquired by MGM. One thing is clear from the all the correspondence, the primary concern was making a marketable product that would also be acceptable to the Mexican government, what ever the historical reality might be.

The public's response to the film was positive, but the reviewers expressed mixed feelings, Villa was portrayed as a bandit, but a patriotic one. Critics emphasized the point: "The Villa of the photoplay is an ignorant, lecherous and homicidal peasant, cruel, stupid and childishly savage. But he also was, the narrator insisted, patriotic, filled with a hatred for the oppressor of his people, [and] intensely loyal to his chief, the martyred President Madero." Hollywood had created according to the Catholic **Commonweal**, "a fictional character ... an inconceivably childish person of deep loyalties and great disinterestedness who fought brutally because of ignorance and of the single-minded intensity of his devotion to a cause." But for the public, the film was "grand fare" "for the man who liked his steaks rare and drank his whisky straight." That Wallace Beery, considered by many a comedic type, was chosen for the role, offended some on both sides of the border, yet he gave one of the great performances of his life and the film was nominated by the Academy for Best Picture, something not one of the subsequent reenactments could claim. A new promotional feature was employed to market the opening of the film. Aside from all of the usual ballyhoo used for such things, the producers were able to secure a radio preview aired nationwide a few days before the actual opening. It provided for the radio audience a "thrilling radio dramatization of the great MGM attraction," and was described to would be exhibitors as the "greatest advance plug, with nation wide coverage for and picture in film history." It apparently worked.] **V**:4.17.34, **NYT**:4.11.34, 4.15.34, **FD**:3.6.34, [p12], 4.12.34, Literary Digest:4.28.34, **New Outlook**:5/34, p42, **Commonweal**:4.27.34, **Nation**:5.2.34, p516, Scholastic:9.22.34. Script, Viva Villa: NYSAA. Production Code Files.

[1713] **WEST OF THE PECOS**, RKO: [In this western Richard Dix as Pecos Smith rode the range and protected the border from incoming marauders. Maria Alba, the lovely señorita was the object of his affection, when he could find the time. There were included, but not credited other incidental Mexican characterizations.] **V**:1.1.35, **FD**:12.29.34.

[1714] **WONDER BAR**, WB/FN: [Al Jolson ran the wonder bar where the elite met to tap their feet, and look each other over. Dolores Del Rio was the object of the owner and Dick Powell, the singer's ardent desire. She had it for the villainous Ricardo Cortez, but all they did was dance as a team for the club. Her affections were not unnoticed, but he was required as a Latin lover to crave another man's wife. It went around like that a lot in this Paris nightery as the strains of "Tango Del Rio" and "Dark Eyes" tightened everyone's emotions. Although the Hispanic's stayed in character, the most memorable feature of this film was Jolson in painted black face, singing "I'm Going to Heaven on a Mule" where he meet a black faced Archangel Gabriel, Saint Peter, and others ... shades of dose Green Pastures.] **V**:3.6.34, **FD**:2.17.34, Literary Digest:3.17.34, p37, **Newsweek**:3.17.34, p37.

1935

[1715] **A LAS SOBRE EL CACHO**, U: [This was Universal's Spanish language version of **Storm Over the Andes** [1799] in which Antonio Moreno played repeated his role as the general whose wife becomes enamored with the Anglo lead. In the Spanish version the Anglo aviator was played by Jose Crespo and the lady by Lupita Tovar. Also included in this experienced cast of Hispanics were: Barry Norton, Romualdo Tirado, Julio Pena, Juan Torena, George Lewis, Lucio Villegas, Anita Camargo, Alma Real, and Paco Moreno.] **NYT**:3.28.39.

[1716] **ANGELITA** = **LITTLE ANGEL** aka **ANGELINA O EL HONOR DE UN BRIGADIER**, Fox: [Fox brought the "charming" Rosita Diaz Gimeon all the way from Spain to play the lead in this dialogue film because of her popularity with Latin audiences. Rosita played the convent-bred daughter of a "flirtatious mother and a stern Spanish officer" who has just returned from fighting the insurrectos in the Philippines in the 1880's. Quickly, she became involved in romantic intrigue. Her combination of coyness and coquetry attracted a young poet [Julio Pena], but also her mother's former lover [Jose Crespo], the little angel had wasted little time. After she eloped with mom's beau, dad found the pair and although the proverbial duel was played somewhat for laughs, it still resulted in death, and a little tarnishing of the angel's wings. The veteran Hispanic cast included: Enrique de Rosas, Julio Pena, Jose Crespo, Countess Rina de Liguoro, Andres de Segurola, Martin Garralaga, Jose Pena "Pepet".] **NYT**:9.11.35.

[1717] **AN OLD SPANISH ONION**, RKO: [Short Subject: Ruth Etting starred in this brief spoof of Spanish romance.] **DAR**.

[1718] **ARGENTINE ARGOSY**, F: [Short Subject: "Interesting travelogue of Buenos Aires. Excellent."] **DAR**.

[1719] **ASEGURE A SU MUJER** = **INSURE YOUR WIFE**, Fox: [A romantic comedy which extended the principle of insurance to marital infidelity. Argentine writer, Julio Escobar created this "sparkling comedy" for Fox which proved to be the first such script by a Latin writer for a North American film. Antonio Moreno and Conchita Montenegro were the couple that required help. Brazil's Raul Roulien was given the job of saving a floundering company called the Fidelity Insurance Company, he accomplished the task almost overnight by striking at the heart of the Latin ego. He simply changed the name of the failing concern to the "InFidelity Insurance Company." Supported by the attractive Mona Maria "as alluring as usual" in her customary role as the irresistible vamp, the romantic complications all this created were real audience pleasers. The cast also included: Luis Alberni, Barbara Leonard, and Carlos Villarias.] **NYT**:3.12.35, **FN**:3.13.35.

[1720] **BIG BROADCAST OF 1936**, P: [Jack Oakie and George Burns ran through this madcap adventure trying to save the radio station from default by utilizing a new kind of portable television that would pick up events anywhere, Gracie's grandfather had invented it. Oakie sang on the Radio as a romantic character called, Lochinvar, and as such captured the hearts of all the ladies. One of them, very rich and very Latin, Ysobel de Nargila, decided she wanted him for her own and took him to her island which was filled with stereotypical happy South American types. There, he soon learned that none of her conquests survived the marriage night, maybe because the señora was such hot stuff, and maybe because her henchmen, the sinister Gordonio, killed them off. After leaning this, the remainder of the film had Jack frantically trying to escape back to civilization.] **V**:9.18.35.

[1721] **BOHEMIOS** = **BOHEMIANS**, Mex/Cinomatografica Mexicana: [Considered a minor effort from south of the border, the film claimed to show the life styles of Mexico City's "impecunious" artist community. Audiences were treated to another new face, Amelia de Ilisa. In her first substantial role she played an attractive blond who managed to vamp away the young painter from his loyal lady and after some romance, cause his death.] **NYT**:9.16.35, **FD**:8.7.35.

[1722] **BORDER GUNS**, Indy: [Bill Cody rode the banks of the Rio Grande in this light hos opry, jus continuen inalong line of Anglo protectors of the sacred side.] **LCFL: Press book**.

[1723] **BORDERTOWN**, W: [Certainly the most important film produced in 1935 involving Mexican characterizations, and one which points specifically to the major role that the Production Code Administration had in curbing the more negative stereotypes that were commonly ascribed to Mexicans and Mexican-Americans. In the final script, there were at least four submitted to the PCA office, Paul Muni played Johnny Ramirez, a Mexican who was also an American who somehow "manage[d] to pass the bar exam" but was immediately disbarred, because he lost his hot Latin temper while trying his very first case. Disenchanted with the system he hitch hiked to a Mexican bordertown where he finds work in a gambling house. In no time at all he worked his way up from being the bouncer in the dive, to owning it. On the way up, Betty Davis, the former owner's wife, had helped. She liked him despite the fact that he was a "greaser", but he preferred another more classy lady. Rejected by the Mexican, Davis killed her husband and blamed Johnny, but cracked completely in court and he is freed. Meanwhile, the writers killed off the "white woman" to prevent the two from continuing their [interracial] illicit affair. All this reaching above his granted station drives Johnny back to the Catholic Church. He sells the place and endows school so other little brown children will not have to suffer the fate of a poor education. Unable to do anything about the color of his skin, he then goes back to "his people," which **Variety** does not identify.

Some of the lines that the PCA censored from the second and third copy of the script, would have been harsh even for a scenarist some twenty years before: "Gimme that ball chili." A policeman speaking: "On your way Greaser". "Tough little greaser." Davis in anger screaming, "greaser -greaser". To Johnny: "I guess you're not used to associating with white people". "You lazy greaser," "You greasers are all alike". And, Johnny admitting in disgust, "I'm a greasy little Mexican". There were fifty or so more uses of such terms, not one of which Joe Breen's office allowed into the final script. That script cast Muni as semisympathetic character, the victim of his race, circumstance, and fate.] **V**:1.29.35, **FD**:1.24.35, **New York American**:1.24.35, **Daily News**, 1.24.35, **Daily Mirror**, 1.24.35, DAR. **Bordertown**: file, USC. PCA. Script, **Bordertown** NYSAA. AMC.

[1724] **BULL FIGHT**, Educational: [A Terry-Toon cartoon with a "bull's eye view of the Arena."] DAR.

[1725] **EL CABALLO DEL PUEBLO**, Arg/Lumiton: [This well received Argentine feature which played at the Teatro Campoamor was a race horse yarn which combined crooked touts and ladies in love. The **NYT** reviewer for this film made the point expressed elsewhere in these pages about the difference between Argentine and Mexican productions. Part of the reason for this centers on the fact that the population of the most southern of American nations more closely parallels that of the United States, than Mexico's. Argentina had also opened its doors to European immigrants between 1870 and 1920. For example, more than a million Italians immigrated to both the United States and Argentina during that period. Further, Argentina was even more efficient in exterminating its indigenous population than was the United States. Neither nation considered what remained of their Indian population appropriate for intermarriage. Conversely Mexico's population after some four hundred and fifty years plus was much more homogeneous, the product of a multiplicity of various unions between Spaniards, and Indians and combinations there of, but essentially more traditionally Hispanic in character. Argentina attempted to emphasize its European outlook and connection. Mexico, after the revolution displayed pride in its Indian origins. Mestizos, the union of Spanish and Indian cultures, made up the bulk of the population. Commenting on the different orientations, the reviewer explained that: "Contrary to the majority of their Mexican confreres, the Argentine cinema producers favor happy endings a la Hollywood. Consequently when the first couple of reels show the handsome and honorable owner [Enrique Serrano] of the favorite for the big national race in love with the fairly attractive daughter [Irma Cordoba] of a formerly prosperous business man now in the clutches of a rich scoundrel [Señor Thorry], determined to marry the girl and win the race by hook or crook, the audience feels that the director will see justice done in at the finish." One wonders if that implies that the Mexican cinema people would have preferred injustice in the denouement.] **NYT**:12.15.35.

[1726] **CAPTAIN BLOOD**, W: [In this remake [1031] of the Douglas Fairbanks classic, Errol Flynn may be considered to have inherited the title of Hollywood's number one swashbuckler from the old master, no one else could have done it so well. The scenario used was much the same as the silent version, with Peter Blood sentenced to transportation to Jamaica for life servitude. While there, he was purchased by Olivia de Haviland's father, the cruel Col. Bishop, who liked to beat him as much as the lady secretly loved him. When the Spanish decided to attack Port Royal, Peter and other slaves managed to escape and captured the Hispanic ship in the harbor. Hunted men they did only what was left for them to do, they hoisted the Jolly Roger and "signed the articles" pledging themselves to brotherhood of the sea. From that time on these corsairs of the Caribbean led by Flynn, muscular and bare chested, took on companies of Spaniards whose thin mustaches and puffy sleeves, sinister and effeminate, were no match for the Anglo heros, no matter their number. All who had signed now enjoyed one adventure after another, sinking the ships of all nations, all, save those of mother England. They were spared despite the fact that nation had branded them all outlaws and ordered their hanging on "execution dock." Virgin Gorda, a Spanish possession, was used as general headquarters. Blood's chief nemesis aside from the Spanish and Col. Bishop was the evil and sadistic Basil Rathbone, Captain Levasseur. Partners for less time than it took to fill the sails, fighting over shares and Olivia ended their brief association. In the final scene, Captain Blood and crew were all repatriated having served England well, albeit unofficially, on the Spanish Main. For those of us as children who dreamed of sailing with the handsome Tasmanian, ready to follow him against any number of Spaniards, had we been afforded the opportunity, it was not difficult to identify the enemy. England represented all that was good and honorable, Spain, did not. Later, the **Sea Hawk** would leave no doubt as to who the good guys and bad guys were. That was clear enough in westerns, but these pirate films introduced audiences, although unknowingly, to la leyenda negra, the "Black Legend" which in its most simplistic form, is translated as just that, England was good and protestant and ruled by enlightened monarchy, Spain was bad, Catholic and despotic.] **V**:1.1.36, **FD**:12.19.35, **Canadian Magazine**:1/36, p33, **Commonweal**:1.3.36, p272 **Newsweek**:12.28.35, p24-5, **Scholastic**:1.25.36, p28, **Time**:12.30.35, p16, AMC.

[1727] **EL CAPITAN TORMENTA**, Metropolitan Pictures Corp. [One of the very last of the Spanish Language entries included two players that would make the transition to regular Hollywood films, Fortunio Bonanova and the lovely Lupita Tovar. Juan Torena was also included.]

[1728] **CHUCHO EL ROTO**, Cinematografica Mexicana: [This semi-historical romance of a Mexican Robin Hood was considered by critics a credit to the "rapidly growing screen industry on the other side of the Rio Grande." Jesus Arriaga was a legendary folk hero who, ignored by his wife, chose to become Mexico's Robin Hood during the early part of Porfirio Diaz's regime. He was eventually captured by the dictator's dreaded rurales and died in the famous fortress prison of San Juan de Ulua in Vera Cruz. All of these scenes were depicted in what was considered a very good Mexican product. To flavor the production, the director added a few extras scenes, one of which was an elaborate ball held in the home of the proud aristocratic lady, which allowed for use of many lovely period gowns typical of 1880 Mexico. Sympathy was cast for the rebel.] **NYT**:3.30.35. **FD**:12.5.34, 4.2.35.

[1729] **CLEMENCIA**, Mex/Nacional Productions: [Further proof of "improvements in technique" by the Mexican film industry were to be found in this story based upon Ignacio Altmirano's novel which focuses on the French intervention in Mexico of 1864. The film had everything, a semi-historical motion picture required, love, real and pretended, patriotism and treason, valor and cowardice. Further, the director refused to change the script to provide a Hollywood happy ending, Maximilian was still afforded the fate of all those who would be Emperor in the New World, he was shot in the last reel. Juarez's forces triumphed.] **FD**:8.22.35, **NYT**:8.20.35.

[1730] **COLORFUL GUATEMALA**, MGM: [Short Subject: "Fitzpatrick Travel Talk in exquisite color with good music and very interesting narrative."] **DAR**.

[1731] **CONTRA LA CORRIENTE** = **AGAINST THE CURRENT**, RNS: [By this time Roman Navarro's personal life encouraged him to shy away from the silver screen. When he took his place more in the shadows, he exercised his writing and directing talents. This was his first production as such reviewed by the Big Apple seers. The **New York Times** critic was at best curt and felt that the effort "signified [no] epoch-making changes". Apparently, an old familiar story to some, the blond Luana Alcaniz played an attractive heiress that fell for and married a poor boy. Because of this he was forced to "treat her rough" to prove to her that he was a "tough hombre." "Jose Caraballho [made] a fine towering figure" as the young Argentine swimmer who won the lady's heart, to say little of her fortune. Also included in the cast were: Jose Crespo, Alma Real, Carmen Samaniegos, and Ramon Guerrero. The film was released through RKO.] **NYT**:3.10.36, **FD**:3.12.36.

[1732] **CORAZON BANDOLERO** = **HEART OF A BANDIT**, Mex-Film: [This Mexican production certainly used a title that North American audiences could easily understand and a character they had grown fond of seeing. Apparently at least this Mexican director, Raphael Sevilla, thought it better to join the ranks of an already established stereotype. In what was considered a "good action drama" starring J. J. Martinez Casado and Victoria Blanco the scene for the drama was set back in the days of the Second Empire headed by Maximilian, with the two stars leading the opposition in support of Juarez and making a few pesos for themselves along the way. The bandit turned revolutionary remained one of the most enduring of Hollywood stereotypes throughout film history.] **FD**:3.6.35.

[1733] **CRUZ DIABLO** = **THE DEVIL'S CROSS**, Paul H, Bush: [This Spanish production was directed by Fernando de Fuentes. Colombia which had ended it's Spanish language experiment merely served as the distributor for the film. Much of the same cast responsible for previous entries were in this romantic Robin Hood like adventure. Set in 17th century Mexico, Ramon Pereda and Lupita Gallardo were starred as the defenders of the impoverished peasantry. The little extra twist this production provided its surprised audience was that the bandit aside from taking all the gold he could from his victims, also branded them on the forehead with a very warm cross. He was also thought to be in league with el diablo.] **FD**:4.10.35.

[1734] **CYCLONE RANGER**, Indy: [One of several thousand cattle rustling scenarios, this one had the rustler going straight after he had seen Nina Quartaro, the sweet young señorita. Bill Cody as the Anglo hero received a lot a help from his faithful, loyal and always pleasingly lecherous side kick, Pancho Gonzales, played by an Anglo. Nina was the only Hispanic in this tale of adventure on the border.] **V**:5.22.35, **FD**:3.20.35.

[1735] **EL DANCING**, Sono: [A Spanish dialogue import from Argentina featuring Armanda Ledesma. Filled with lots of attractive Argentine ladies, this little quickie chronicled a single night of fun out on the cuidad, Buenos Aries. It was life and love in an Argentine cabaret, and not much more. Carlos Gardel furnished the music and several comedians provided some indication of what was considered funny in the port city.] **NYT**:1.29.35. **FD**:1.30.35.

[1736] **DE LA SARTEN AL FUEGO**, Metropolitan Pictures Corp. [Although by 1935 the Spanish language experiment was pretty much over, a few independents were still willing to try their luck: The cast in this one was made up of five year veterans: Rosita Moreno, Juan Torena, Romualdo Tirado, Corzon Montes, Rudolph Ament, Martin Garralaga and Louis Hickus. The film was released through 20th Century-Fox.]

[1737] **DESERT TRAIL**, Mono: [John Wayne continued his long ride through the western genre with this film in which he and his side kick were accused of robing a bank. Not guilty they were forced to take time off from Rodeo riding and find the real baddies. Carmen LaRoux as Juanita provided the Mexican spice and Artie Ortega rode along with the Duke for the second time.] **V**:8.21.35, **FD**:8.20.35.

[1738] **DEVIL IS A WOMAN**, P: [In 1935, if you wanted a real hunk of Hispanic woman playing the ultimate vamp, and "flirtatious vixen," then apparently you had to look for her somewhere along the banks of the Rhine in the person of Marlene Dietrich. In this femme fatal scenario she was the irresistible Concha Perez, the "devil trollop," who, using her naturally warm personality, and other hot stuff, totally destroyed Lionel Atwill and had her way with Cesar Romero. Edward Everett Horton played a character called Don Paquito for the only laughs in this otherwise melodramatic tale set in Spain and briefly in Paris. Don Alvarado, having lost some of his box office draw, had a small part as Morenito.] **V**:5.8.35, **FD**:4.17.35.

[1739] **THE DEVIL ON HORSEBACK**, Grand National: [Lili Damita and Del Campo starred in this musical with an Argentine flavor. The hero was a bandit Robin Hood who roamed the Pampas until he found the lovely Lili, but she the personal property of a rich coffee heir. They were only visiting in that land of wheat, cattle, but very little coffee growing, (Brazil's coffee growing areas were apparently close enough to Argentina for these Hollywood writers) when confronted by the bandit. Most of the film's action revolved around Del Campo's attempt to win away the French señorita's heart. In the film the bandit was successful, but Errol Flynn really captured Damita and took her out of movies to make her his leading lady on a permanent basis, well, for a while anyway.] **MPG**.

[1740] **EL DIA QUE ME QUIERAS** = **THE DAY YOU LOVE ME**, P: [There was sadness attached to this dialogue film by Paramount, the beloved throughout South America, Carlos Gardel who had achieved the status of super star, had died before this film was released. Basically a musical with fine performances from all including Rosita Moreno at her most "simpatica" best, it also jabbed quite harshly at the business aristocracy of the Argentine capital. Scenes traveled from Buenos Aries via shipboard to Hollywood. The cast also included: Tito Luisardo, Manuel Peluffo, Jose Luis Tortosa, Fernando Adelantad and Suzanne Dullier.] **NYT**:8.27.35, **FD**:4.3.35. [The Sono production company of Argentina would produce **La Vida de Carlos Gardel** in June of 1940, a film biography/tribute to the popular performer's colorful and eventful career.]

[1741] **DONA FRANICISQUITA**, Iberica: [This gay bit of old Spain was a fairly routine romance "made acceptable" by some "passable singing" and pleasant music taken on location in various street cafes. Aside from that it also unintentionally forecasted troubled times ahead, for Spain, other European nations and the industry itself. The Germans knew the significant affect film could have on the population and they moved to control what they euphemistically called, unpatriotic [non-aryan] directors. Those who were fortunate enough, sought employment elsewhere. The **NYT** so indicated by stating: "The novelty of Hans Behrendt guiding a picture in Spain is probably explained by the Nazi ban on many of the ablest German directors." The Puerto Rican actor and well known performer to Harlem audiences, "in the flesh and as a shadow", Fernando Cortes, played the young man who had to be saved from the clutches of "the seductive music-hall artiste, Matilde Vasquez, through the genuine love of the rather attractive Raquel Rodrigo, the Dona of the title.] **NYT**:4.27.35. **FD**:4.29.35.

[1742] **DON QUINTIN EL AMARGAO** = **DON QUINTIN, THE BITTER**, Sp/Filmofono: [Ricardo Urgotti's first "Spanish tongue" reel was considered by **Variety** to be a sure box office success in the Latin American market. With solid performances from all, especially with Luita Esteso as the comedienne, this typical Hispanic "tearjerker" was produced for his Empresa Sagarra circuit of Spanish language film houses which usually featured the Fox product. The story was a sad one in which husband who suspected his wife of infidelity threw her out into the streets. Unknown to him, she was carrying his child and after the infant was born, she left the baby on his door step. He gave it away and twenty years of bitterness passed in a few hundred feet of film. Now a beautiful young señorita, the daughter was engaged to a man who her father had vowed to kill. Incredibly, and possibly with a little Hollywood influence, it all worked out in the last reel with everyone reunited.] **V**:10.30.35.

[1743] **DRAKE OF ENGLAND**, Associated British Picture Production: [The vast majority of North American movie goers by this time had been unconsciously conditioned by the Black Legend. The following review provides a good indication of how pervasive its influence had been. Without even being aware of it, the following review expressed well the unconscious acceptance of La Leyenda Negra: "This ambitious attempt to portray on the screen the exciting adventures, against all odds, of the glamorous piratical adventurer who founded Britain's sea fortunes, is worthwhile. The routing of the Spanish Armada by a handful of ships under the bold shabby Devon pioneer, the looting of the enemy's treasures by bravado and cunning makes for exciting entertainment", to say nothing of continuing established historical interpretations.] **V**:5.29.35, **Canadian Magazine**:8/35, p25.

[1744] **ELIZABETH OF ENGLAND**, Br./BIP/Alliance: [The above production [1743] was also reviewed under this title with slightly different credits. Although **Drake** makes the point clearly, the following is an even more sympathetic and historically framed justification for English foreign policy in the 17th century: "The story of Sir Francis Drake and his marine blows which shattered Spain's power is sympathetically and dramatically told in this picture .... It rings out with sincerity and moves at a rapid pace. Performances are generally good .... Although the yarn at times suffers from inadequate development, [why bother to add too much background for sending the Armada] the picture holds audience interest consistently. From a production standpoint, it is lavish and painstaking. In England's darkest days, Drake comes to the fore as a worthy adversary to confront Spain. Surrounded by treason [he] goes from one success to another, climaxing his career with the defeat of the Spanish Armada." The good guys and the bad guys were not too difficult to identify.] **FD**:9.8.35.

[1745] **ESCAPE FROM DEVILS ISLAND**, C: [One more of the many films which depicted the horrors of solitude and physical punishment which the prisoners of the French Penal colony off the coast of Guianas were forced to endure. There, the depressions of daily life were sparked only by thoughts of escape, which rarely occurred. In this version, Victory Jory as Dario, managed to do so, but he gets only as far as the boat that was to take he and his friend to Venezuela. There were no French protests over this one. That would come later, just before the war. See: **Devil's Island**, 1939.] **V**:11.27.35, **NYT**:11.25.35, **FD**:11.26.35, DAR.

[1746] **FANTASY OF THE MONASTERY**, Mex/FESA: [Director Fernando de Fuente's shift from semi-historical productions to mysteries was not so well received as his other works for the Spanish language audiences. As in his prior work in this genre, his scenario places three close individuals in an old Spanish monastery which is inhabited with the ghost of the past. The husband, best friend and wife apparently have gone there for counseling, after some fairly creepy happenings, which might be called spiritual counseling all is resolved in the last reel. It would seem that if you have a wife who is getting tired of your affections and your best friend is looking good to her, take the pair to an old monastery and let the ghost speak to them directly. It worked in this production.] **NYT**:4.22.35, **FD**:4.24.35.

[1747] **FIGHTING CABALLERO**, Superior: [Someone in production simply thought that "Caballero" would be a bigger draw than "cowboy." The action took place on the border, but there were no Hispanic characterizations.] **MPG**.

[1748] **FIGHTING MARINES**, Mascot: (Serial 12 Episodes) [Although President Roosevelt's Good Neighbor Policy had already been placed into effect in the Americas, it would not really be implemented in Hollywood until World War II presented the Germans and the Japanese as serious threats to the United States itself and its hegemony over the hemisphere. Then, waging their own war with film, Hollywood's Latin American characterizations changed significantly. And besides, there was also business to think about. But in this action packed weekly adventure the Marines were still below the border trying to establish a landing field on Halfway Island, located somewhere in the Caribbean and inhabited by the Tiger Shark and his men. The group of evil looking bandits were cast in appearance as Hispanic pirates serving a madman whose gravity gun destroyed Marine planes and whose activities were directed against the well meaning civilizing intentions of the United States. Although there are no direct references to the Marine campaign in Nicaragua, some could still make the association.]

[1749] **FLIRTING WITH DANGER**, Mono: [A comedy involving a pair of fun loving, devil-may-care types who the scripters at Monogram employed as "gun powder mixers" and experts. After this had been established, they were sent to work somewhere in a South American dynamite plant which produced apparently humorous, but explosive results. The incidental Hispanics were there only to be acted upon and provide additional ammunition for the laughs.] **V**:3.6.35.

[1750] **FRISCO KID**, W: [Jimmy Cagney was cast as an Al Capone on Frisco's Barbary Coast where he plays a monomaniacal and violent Irishman who wanted to be the only boss by the bay. Much of the story deals with the activities of the vigilantes and those few Hispanics portrayed were the remnants of the former population. Lili Damita as the seductive Bella Morra, was the beautiful object of his affection, but she was not the reason for his regeneration. A nice Anglo girl did that. The French Lili was there to add the Hispanic spice and provide the occasion of sin for the Frisco Kid.] **NYT**:11.25.35, **FD**:10.30.35.

[1751] **GOLD RUSH**, Vitaphone: [Short Subject: "See America First series. America from 1845-49 along the Santa Fe Trail. Exceptionally good in narrative and interesting photography."] **DAR**.

[1752] **EL HEROE DE NACOZARI**, Cia National: [Although the reviewer doubted the veracity of the claim that this story was based on a actual incident that had occurred some short time before, he considered the production a "good railroad drama" highlighted by an act of civic heroism which had taken place in Mexico. The derailment and crash had taken place in 1932 resulting in the loss of some twenty lives and must have provoked some heroic action on the part of the populous, but for the reviewer, that was assuming a lot for Mexicans.] **FD**:9.24.35.

[1753] **HI GAUCHO!** RKO: [If there were two words that immediately brought [Hollywood's] Hispanics to mind in the North American public of 1935, they were "tango" and "gaucho". The film industry had instilled both of those images in the minds of the viewing public. By this time this musical romance set in Argentina was quite familiar to audiences. As usual the Spanish señorita had refused to marry her parents choice of suitors, she preferred the more notorious bandit type to the approved thin blooded aristocrat. John Carroll provided the third side of the triangle in his debut playing Lucio, the loyal gaucho of the hacienda who saved the lady from both the bandit and the other she had scorned. The accents were heavy and the English broken, but some historical research had to have been done for this production. When Rod La Roque as Escurra, the robber, evaded arrest and the good Lucio was charged in his place, the formalities were performed in a classic old Spanish provincial style: "Lucio Valera, by order of the August Audiencias, administering the Province of Paredo, under the glorious favor of his Regal Excellency, the South American Viceroy of His Serene, Pious and Devoted Majesty, Ferdinand, by the Grace of God, King of Spain ... I arrest you."] **V**:4.29.36, **MPG**, **DAR**. **NYSAA**, Script: **Hi Gaucho!**, 26 **pages**.

[1754] **HISTORIC MEXICO CITY**, MGM: [Short Subject: "Beautiful music, color effects and good narrative comments make this an outstanding travelogue. Excellent entertainment."] **DAR**.

[1755] **UN HOMBRE PELIGROSO** = **A DANGEROUS MAN**, Produciones Latinas: [This was the first Spanish dialogue film "evidently American made" that was criticized as at best mediocre, a "would be romantic tragi-comedy" that was funny in all the wrong places. The "loud laughter" of the Spanish speaking audiences at what was intended to be serious drama indicated the failure of this production. The scene was a California picnic with gypsies, music, gangsters and a hero all looking for the favors of the "comely Anita Compillo." The fights over the young señorita and the dialogue employed provoked the laughter.] **NYT**:10.14.35, **FD**:10.17.35.

[1756] **EL HOMBRE QUE SE REIA DEL AMOR** = **THE MAN WHO LAUGHED AT LOVE**, Sp/Star Film: [A Spanish language version of the timeless tale involving the "Don Juan" whose laughing at love turns him into a gloomy, disillusioned individual in the last reel. Rosita Diaz was introduced to audiences in this film and received rave reviews as did the more established Maria Fernanda Ladron de Guevara who was the "center of this tragedy."] **NYT**:7.18.35.

[1757] **IDOLOS DE LA RADIO** = **IDOLS OF THE RADIO**, Arg/Rio de la Plata: [This Argentine dialogue production provided the film audience with a look at some of their favorite radio performers. In the early days of both these new forms of media communication, there was still much rivalry, but this film treated radio with respect and tried to show audiences what life behind the scenes at a popular radio station was like. The action concerned a contest between a new voice, belonging to the poor young outbacker and the old established pro headliner with just enough talent to get by. The results were fluff, with maybe just a little more sentimentality than would have been found just outside L.A.] **NYT**:1.1.35, **FD**:7.5.35.

[1758] **I LIVE FOR LOVE**, W: [Dolores Del Rio played, Donna Alvarez, "a temperamental South American stage import" in this production which **Variety** felt could not stand by itself with out double bill support. As the hot tempered lead she was eventually forced into the arms of the Anglo who had been the frequent cause of her outbursts. They credited the Latin super star with a "nice performance", but thought that the cameraman had favored her, his lens had "follow[ed] her everywhere." Don Alvarado was provided a small role as Rico Cesaro, a minor player.] **V**:10.23.35.

[1759] **INCA-CUZCO**, Inter-Continental: [In 1916 Yale's own Hiram Bingham astounded the world with the news that he had discovered the secret city of the Inca's, Machu Picchu. The pictures he brought back for the **National Geographic Society** indicated that he had done just that. He had found the last refuge that that once proud civilization had established while seeking to escape the Spanish. That discovery ensured that Hiram would certainly go on a lot more similar expeditions, well financed ones at that. This twenty-minutes of film footage was evidence of his return to the land of the Inca: "An interesting record of the recent Bingham Expedition to Cuzco, Peru, for the purposes of delving into the ancient Inca ruins." The journey took audiences high up into the Andes "over dizzy mountain peaks", "torrential rivers and through the ruins of huge structures built by the Incas [actually by the peoples the Inca's had themselves subjugated] centuries" before. Something of a showman, Bingham staged the filming to coincide with the visit of Prince George and the Prince of Wales, for whom the natives were staging special dances. Actually much of the footage was taken in the city itself and could have been filmed by any traveler with the opportunity and fortitude to visit that favorite capital of Inca Kings.] **FD**:1.15.35.

[1760] **IN CALIENTE**, FN/W: [Falcons made of gold, encrusted with precious jewels and painted black, so they can be sought through the ages, may well be the "stuff dreams are made of," but scripts like this production's were just as certainly pure Hollywood. The scribe speaks: "Well, there's this tough guy, newspaper man, a critic, who reviews this Mexican dancer's performance, lets call her Rita Gomez, no, Espanita, say he's too busy to see her do her stuff and he pans the show without having seen her dance. Her hot temper is really boiling over this. Meanwhile, his girl, some dumb blonde bombshell, wants to put the noose around his neck, he's stupid enough to let it happen, but then ... we need some comedy here, think? Say his friend, some one like Edward Everett Horton takes him to Caliente to avoid the blond. He could then meet the dancer and without knowing it's the one he bruised, fall for her, but she's so mad she wants her pound of fleshinski. She gives him a little trouble but quickly falls for him like a ton of bricks, he's Anglo and she's a Mex and there you go." That was the story line and it worked. Added to this were Busby Berkeley's dance routines all of which were very popular with the audience. With Spanish atmosphere, señorita's, songs and lines like "Muchacha at last i've gotcha where i wantcha muchacha," maybe a little south of the Equator, but it proved to be right in the middle of a lot a coins for the moguls coffers. Dolores Del Rio as the sultry and seductive dancer was at her best. Leo Carrillo as Jose Gomez was the comic foil whose English had not improved 'a beet' in years. The Del Marcos' dazzled audiences with their dance routines. "The Lady in Red" and "Muchacha" production numbers were spectacular. "Muchachas in Mexico were a lot livelier." The Mexican tourist industry should have picked up the cost for this production, most of characterizations continued accepted stereotypes, and the general tone indicated that there was a lot of fun to be had in Agua Caliente that could not be found back home.] **V**:7.3.35, **NYT**:1.27.35, DAR, **FN**:6.27.35.

[1761] **LA ISLA MALDITA** = **THE ACCURSED ISLAND**, Mex/Jose Hernandez: [This work was not considered as good as some of the other Mexican imports because the attempt at creating a terrifying situation apparently failed, at least in the reviewer's estimation. The scenario had five fugitives escaping from a Pacific penal colony only to discover that they had landed on an island where the natives killed and mummified their victims. Some things are universal on the screen. After a lot of arrows pierce everybody in the group save that of the hero and heroine, they learn from their rescuers that they actually did not have to escape at all.

Javier would have been cleared of the murder he had been accused of if only he had remained to serve out his time. The cast included: Luis G. Farreiro, Mario Tenorio and Carmen Torreblanca.] **NYT**:12.2.35.

[1762] **JUAREZ Y MAXIMILIANO**, C: [This was the first serious treatment of the life and times of Mexico's most revered president, Benito Juarez, whose struggle against the conservative forces of the church, large landowners and military, resulted in the war of La Reforma, an attempt to free the nation's millions of oppressed indians from the servitude they had endured for centuries. The **NYT** reviewer for this piece made reference to "certain elements in this country" (the reference was to the big oil companies whose proprieties had been expropriated by the Mexican government) who were calling on the United States government to intervene on their behalf. He apparently saw a parallel with the French intervention that establish Maximilian as Emperor of Mexico in 1864. The French had been seeking empire, the unidentified "elements" only wanted their oil fields back. This Spanish language production was somewhat a documentary with director, M. Contreras Torres presenting the Mexican interpretation of the facts. Maximilian was portrayed more sympathetically then he would be in Hollywood's 1939 version, but not as intelligent. The scene in which Carlotta confronted Napoleon III and realized that he would no longer support his puppet, her husband, was highly dramatized. This refusal sealed the unfortunate Maximiliano's fate, cost him his life and drove his beautiful young wife to madness. She was played by Medea de Novara, and was said to have actually resembled the tragic Empress. In 1939 Warner Brothers made the classic **Juarez**, with it's scenario constructed from a popular historical novel. During its production, Miguel Contreras Torres, sued the Brothers claiming that his new production **Juarez and Maximilian** aka **Maximilian and Carlota** [1939] had been plagiarized and that **Juarez** was a direct steal. Considering the existence of this earlier version, and having reviewed the files at the Warner collection at USC, it is difficult to understand why Warner's made an out of court settlement which in essence bought all rights to that production.] **NYT**:2.16.35, **FD**:2.20.35.

[1763] **JULIETA COMPRA UN HIJO** = **JULIETA BUYS A BABY**, F: [For a while this film was prevented from being shown because of its subject matter. Julieta, Catalina Barcena, left her man at the altar when she discovered something in his past that bothered her. She then traveled the world looking for a likely father for a child she would very much liked to have and was willing to pay for. The problem with the censors was that she wanted to pay for a "temporary" husband or only his services. One of the handsome possibilities was Luis Alonso (Gilbert Roland), and another Julio Pena. The authorities in Albany had a problem with such liberal views in 1935. It may well have been passed simply because it was a Spanish language film designed specifically for Hispanic audiences. The cast included: Luana Alcaniz, Soledad Jimenez, Barbara Leonard, Agostino Borgato and Rosa Rey.] **NYT**:3.25.35, **FD**: 3.27.35.

[1764] **JUNGLE ANTICS**, P: [Short Subject: "Friendly animals in South America jungle. Fine photography and narrative. Interesting for any audience."] **DAR**.

[1765] **LAWLESS BORDER**, Spectrum: [In this attempt to modernize the western, Bill Cody was cast as a government agent working with a representative of the Mexican government. The two undercover G-men then "work their way into the confidences of the revolutionary Mexican leader" who was smuggling materials across the border and actually became part of the "revolutionary outfit." Sensitive to possible Mexican complications, the producers of this conspiracy made one of the leaders a North American, the other a Mexicano. It may be that the Anglo conspirator was the real boss, but that was never made clear. One thing was sure, he had a pretty sister who became involved with the hero and she was apparently unaware that her brother had Napoleonic tendencies. Once the plot was hatched to capture the culprit and lead him back to this side of the border, his spies told him that the two were really undercover G-men. In the gunfight that followed, the Mexican was shot, but Cody escaped back to the ranch himself to be shot by the sister who wanted to keep her brother out of jail. In the end Wild Bill brought in his man and the girl accepted it. Aside from Hoppy's films, this is one of the few early entries that portrayed such close cooperation by the law enforcement agencies of the sister nations. The treatment of the Mexican law man was sympathetic. More important, he was not played like a second banana.] **FD**:12.11.35.

[1766] **LAWLESS FRONTIER**, Mono: [John Wayne cleared himself in this western after he had been falsely accused of running guns across the border. It turned out that the real "bad hombre" was Pandro Santi who had designs on a pretty señorita that the big John was protecting. For revenge the not so nice Mexican lied and had the Anglo accused of his own crimes. Worse he had his gang go after honest John, but as it was written, "gangs don't mean nothing to Wayne", he managed to trick the halfbreed and finally made "him bite the dust." It was in his contract. Artie Ortego received cast credit in one of the reviews, but not the other.] **V**:1.22.35, **FD**:1.3.35.

[1767] **LA LLORONA**, Mex/Eco Films: [An ancient legend allowed this film to blend happenings in very early Mexican history with those of more modern times. The legend claimed that Miriana, mistress of Cortez during the Conquest, was driven mad by the conquistador's cruelty in taking their baby son from her. [Historically, this is not accurate. But more to the point, after the Mexican Revolution, Cortez was not a really popular figure in a Mexico that wanted to emphasize it's Indian roots.] Because of this she cursed his descendants from that time on which "spelled death for at least one male child in every generation," who would die around the age of four. The death would be horrible and accompanied with great wailing, which gave its name to the curse and the title to the film. Having explained all this for the audience, the film moved to more modern times, where a Mexican father, who believed in the myth, attempted to protect his son from what he was sure would be death by having him wear a mysterious ring supposed to posses magical proprieties. The ancient Aztec ring had a special "sacred Aztec seal" designed for that purpose. After a lot of worrying and flash backs to the days of Cortez, there was a happy ending. The scenes of ancient Mexico, Cortez and of colonial times were well done and reflected a Mexican interpretation of those events. Today, there is not one statue of Cortez in Mexico City. Cortez is considered to be a despoiler, a destroyer of ancient cultures, not a hero, despite the fact that he was the most enlightened of all the Conquistadors [1613].] **NYT**:7.20.35.

[1768] **LUCKY BOOTS**, Beacon/Equity: [An assorted group of baddies knew that this now dead Mexican bandit had left a treasure buried in the ground somewhere on this ranch. One of the outlaws, Tom London wanted it real bad. After a lot of fighting which killed off most of the cast, the old bandits treasure remained undiscovered.]

[1769] **MADRE QUERIDA** = **BELOVED MOTHER**, Mex/Aspa: [Considered technically inferior to most of its predecessors from south of the border, this tearjerker from beginning to end concerned itself with lost love. Maria Morales was the beloved mother who had to say goodbye to her lover and not see him again for fourteen years. When she does, she dies in his arms with everybody crying including the son, who critics thought was the most convincing sobber of all.] **NYT**:12.23.35.

[1770] **MARCH OF TIME**, #9, RKO Radio: [Sometimes a superior documentary of current world conditions, this episode included a presently familiar sequence: "The second subject shows the U. S. Secret Service, the coast guard and the narcotics division cooperation to trap the large dope-smuggling ring which last spring flooded the south with heroin. The smashing of the ring, very interestingly re-enacted, also broke up a band which was fomenting a revolution in Honduras." One is very tempted to say: Le plus ca change, le plus ces la meme choise. It's good to know that the present DEA is hard at work keeping up the long tradition of solid service, but having very little effect. One might think that sixty years of plugging the holes might have accomplished something. Or that someone might have realized that if there were no market, the suppliers would die out. Who's selling spats these day's?] **FD**:12.11.35.

[1771] **THE MARINES ARE COMING**, Mascot: [This little gem had some bizarre moments. The scenario was strictly formula, two Marines and one girl, one was nice and the other something of a smartaleck and a cheat. The lady could not make up her mind until a "little Mexican spitfire in the person of Armida" joined the action. She steals this picture set in the jungles of Central America from the three who received top billing. The bad boy Marine went for Armida, which apparently left the goodie for the good girl. Meanwhile the jungle was filled with so called bandits, Hollywood's conception of Sandino's freedom fighters who were portrayed as less than brave. When Haines, the less nice jarhead, decided to reup and continue with the Corps, he singlehandedly defeated, "the whole army of equatorial banditi." Some of these "Central American characters" had Russian accents, which the reviewer found hard to take. Shades of things to come. The Mexican Armida, sang "My Brazilian Baby" somewhere in Central America to make it all complete.] **V**:2.27.35.

[1772] **MARTIN GARATUZA**, Mex/Aguila: [The producers of this film dug deep into the archives for this script which resulted in a "happy combination of old-fashioned melodrama and comedy." There was much action in what was essentially a period piece set three hundred years in the past during the Spanish Colonial period when the Viceroy was the most powerful official in the colonies. He was essentially the alter ego of the king of Spain. In this story there was a plot against the Viceroy, two young lovers separated and rejoined, the death bed acknowledgement of an illegitimate daughter and good sword fighting, all set in the 17th century America.] **NYT**:9.30.35, **FD**:10.1.35.

[1773] **MERCEDES**, Sp/Barcelona: [A pleasant comedy starring Carmelita Aubert and Hector Morel filled with singing, dancing and romance, "blended in [a] fairly entertaining story of a girl whose father turns her out because she chose a poor singer for a husband." It was the same all over Hollywood's Hispanicdom, daughters were required to listen, or else.] **FD**:5.16.35.

[1774] **MEXICAN IDYLL**, Audio Production: [Short Subject: One of the "Musical mood" series photographed by Robert Bruce. Symphony orchestra under the direction of Rosario Bourdon. Beautiful music was interpreted through exquisite scenes in the new three color process. In this short subject "Cielito Lindo" and "La Golondrina" were illustrated by pastoral Mexican scenes. Considered by the lady previewer to be "unusually worthwhile".] **DAR**.

[1775] **MIXING IN MEXICO**, Screen Attraction Co: [Short Subject: Musical cartoon of Mutt and Jeff in Bull arena. "Inferior animation. Novel in color." [1133]] **DAR**.

[1776] **MORALS OF MARCUS**, Br/Real Art Gaumont: [This was real live Hollywood from across the pond. The luscious Lupe Velez managed to escape from the Harem of a fat and toothless Syrian somehow or other and found herself in the cabin of an English lord. It could have happened! Pleased, he took his little darkskinned prize back to the ancestral estates to show the family. Not surprisingly there were complications. Lupe ran to Paris because she thought he only wanted to marry her out of pity. He finally finds her in the last reel singing her sorry little broken heart out with a meexed Spanish/French accent that had all in the audience ready to do whatever she wanted. Even less surprising, she wanted the Anglo lord.] **V**:4.10.35, 1.15.36.

[1777] **LOS MUERTOS HABLAN** = **THE DEAD SPEAK**, Mex/Luis Bueno: [Considered a good drama, this Mexican product was based on the theory "that the eye retains an image of the last thing seen by a person before death." A plausible conception which was handled "with ingenuity from a suspense angle" by the director who received solid help from his cast, Julian Soler and Amelia de Llisa. It was shown to appreciative audiences at the Teatro Campoamor.] **FD:11.26.35**.

[1778] **MURDER IN THE FLEET**, MGM: [Starring a young Robert Taylor, almost all of the action in this naval mystery took place on a new battle cruiser loaned out by the navy in hopes of swapping it for a little free advertising. The connection here involves the fact that foreign agent was trying to steal this ship's most secret and revolutionary fire equipment. It was the last word in ultra modern and the agent were trying to take it across the border to Mexico where his foreign power bosses were waiting. This baddie had to be stopped at all costs, so no one was let off the ship until he was uncovered. In the thirties Mexico, Macao, Shanghai and Constantinople were the best places to find foreign agents, those in Mexico were usually conspiring against the United States.] **V:6.5.35**. **AMC**.

[1779] **MUTINY ON THE BOUNTY**, MGM: [Part of the bounty that mutiny was all about had to do with remembrances of nights spent beneath the palms with lovelies like Movita, the beautiful Mexican import, who played the south sea attraction called, Tehani in the award winning production.] **AMC**.

[1780] **MYSTERY WOMAN**, Fox: [Gilbert Roland was the male lead in this story of a falsely accused husband doing time for spying against his country, France. Roland played a goodhearted crook who liked the poor guys wife, but was honorable throughout and simply helped her nab the real spy responsible for having her husband arrested. It was purely a business arrangement for that slim Latin lover with the thin mustache that would find his way into more than eighty feature films.] **FD:1.8.35**.

[1781] **THE NIGHT IS YOUNG**, MGM: [Once more Ramon Navarro played a Viennese aristocrat, an archduke who fell in love with a commoner, but one with talent, a very beautiful ballerina.] **V:1.5.35**.

[1782] **NOCHES DE BUENOS AIRES** = **BUENOS AIRES NIGHTS**, Lumiton: [This Argentine production shown at the Teatro Campoamor featured Fernando Ochoa, and Tita Merello, "et al." It may have been assumed that the others were so familiar that they needed no introduction, or they simply were not worth listing. It was considered "satisfactory entertainment", a back stage romance of "familiar type, but generally interesting."] **FD:12.11.35**.

[1783] **NO MATARAS** = **THOU SHALL NOT KILL**, Hispano International Film Corp of Hollywood: [Directed by Miguel C. Torres, it starred Ramon Pereda and Adriana Lamar. In Mexican films, it was a real good idea to follow such helpful hints, the price for not listening was usually more severe than the consequences were up north.] **FD**:11.12.35.

[1784] **PARADISE CANYON**, Mono: [In this last film for the production company that launched his career, John Wayne plays a "government sleuth," in "cowboy regalia" assigned to uncover the counterfeiters operating on the Mexican border. The minor characters include Mexicans merely to set the scene, die and be captured.] **V**:9.18.35, **FD**: 5.14.35.

[1785] **PATHE TOPICS No 4**, RKO: [Short Subject: "Christophe Citadel in Haiti." Actually the largest fortress structure in the Americas, it was built at the expense of at least 20,000 lives as a retreat in case Napoleon wanted to waste another 20,000 of France's best troops in a futile effort to regain the lost colony.] **DAR**.

[1786] **PAYASADAS DE LA VIDA** = **TRICKS OF LIFE**, Mex/Latino: [This Spanish dialogue picture introduced Gloria Morel to New York audiences in a formula tragedy which worked out for most of the cast in the last reel. When the son of a wealthy Mexican aristocrat fell in love not only with the circus, but more so, with the circus owner's daughter, the father objected and did all he could to prevent the union. Then in a flashback, he recognized the other parent. Both he and the girl's father had loved the same lady back in 1914, he had lost his only chance at true love. He could not deny that chance to his son. Circus and cabaret scenes added a little color to this otherwise somber production which ended more happily than most Mexican productions.] **NYT**: 3.18.35, **FD**:3.19.35.

[1787] **PIERNAS DE SEDA** SV **SILK LEGS**, 20th/F: [By this date, Rosita Moreno and Raul Roulien were a familiar and well liked team, they headed the Hispanic cast for this film. Also included: Enrique de Rosas.]

[1788] **POWDERSMOKE RANGE**, RKO Radio: [Three buddies, two of them old friends from the silents, Hoot Gibson, and Harry Carey and the new kid, Ginin Williams found themselves in this western buying a hacienda from a friendly Don in a town called Quatros that had been part of a huge Spanish land grant. That was nice but, the head heavy, the boss of the Tres Pero's outfit wanted to own the entire territory and so he made a lot of trouble for the trio and the old Señor. Old Don Manuel was killed because he would not sell his property, actually, he had refused to part with the "Documento" that the United States government had given him which confirmed his grant. The atmosphere was entirely old deep southwest with properly obsequious Mexican servants in every part of the hacienda. In the last reel the three Anglo amigos disposed of the baddies and settled in to enjoy a long life on their own little piece of what had once been the Spanish kings private domain.] **V**:3.11.36. **AMC**.

[1789] **PUBLIC HERO NO. 1**, MGM: [Although Joseph Calleia was born on the island of Malta, he was so enmeshed in the Mexican genre that audiences accepted him as a sinister, mysterious Hispanic without question. In his first major supporting role he was characterized by critics as a "sad-eyed Latin Killer, filled with melancholy bitterness." He continued to play, much the same character in supporting roles for the next three decades, usually as some type of Hispanic menace. He did so for the last time in 1962's **Johnny Cool**.] **FD**:5.16.35, **NYT**:6.8.35.

[1790] **EL PULPO HUMANO** = **THE HUMAN OCTOPUS**, Mex/Cuauhtemoc: [This old fashioned mystery melodrama set in more modern Mexico focused on the avaricious character of a heartless money lender played by Arturo Campoamour. The audience knew he would get his in the end, but waited to see just how it would be done. His flirtatious wife, Margot Erbeya, was due for a little punishment herself. The scenes of modern Mexico City and those of hacienda life provided interesting views, but were considered inferior to what had come to be expected from the growing Mexican film industry.] **V**:5.6.35, **FD**:5.9.35.

[1791] **PURSUIT**, MGM: [This solid seventy-five minutes of chase scenes utilized an airplane first, then in rapid succession, a truck, flivver, and lastly the broken down wagon of a old preacher, all in an attempt to return the kidnapped child of a Mexican mother back home to her for the $20,000 reward. All through the action, the baddies were trying to recapture the child for themselves, but Chester Morris managed to evade there every move and reunite mother and child. A Mexican film in the following year, **Que Hago con La Criatura**, told the same story, but with the action taking place south of the border, it did so at a slower pace.] **V**:10.9.35.

[1792] **EL RAYO**, Mex/Atlas: [Hispanic audiences were once more presented with a semi-legendary Mexican Robin Hood galloping across the screen of the Teatro Campoamour, robbing the Mexican rich and giving the proceeds to the peon poor. El Rayo, lightening or the flash, had been sent to Sinaloa prison unjustly and when he escaped, he took up his avenger role with a purpose. Antonio R. Frausto was the properly dashing hero who dressed in traditional black to scourge the unjust. His señorita was the sweet, Amparo Arozamena, who waited patiently for him to work it out of his system, which he did, but only after he captured the villainous, Martinez Casado. The latter's negative characterizations were not unlike those Hollywood painted of such individuals. Despite the fast paced action, critics considered the pictorial representations of old Mexico to be "decidedly inferior."] **NYT**:10.19.35, **FD**:5.9.35.

[1793] **EL RELICARIO** = **THE RELIQUARY**, Sp: [This pre civil war Spanish production provided audiences with some of the best bull fighting sequences that had ever been filmed. When the camera moved out of the corrida it filmed the love story of a young señorita and her bull fighting man who had been mauled very badly but recovered because of the power of prayer and the skill of the surgeon. Nieves Aliaga was the lovely whose beauty was more the cause of tragedy than joy for the young matador, Jose Alcazaba. The brilliant bull fighting sequences were all taken in the giant corrida in Sevilla.] **NYT**:12.31.35.

[1794] **REMEMBER THE ALAMO**, Vitaphone: [Short Subject: "Places of historical interest based upon events of 1819-1845 prove interesting. We visit West Point and Annapolis ... and localities in Texas."] **DAR**.

[1795] **ROSA DE FRANCIA**, F: [A good example of Hispanic history according to Hollywood, this time produced for Spanish language audiences. This episode in the troubled reign of Philip V, "founder of the Bourbon dynasty in Spain" required some research and was made with considerable "elegance." It was a costumer of grand style, with elaborate sets representing court life in both Spain and France. The costumes were carefully reconstructed period pieces. Antonio Moreno was a convincing monarch who abdicated the Spanish throne in 1724 to become the king of France, but experienced significant trouble with his second and most interfering wife, played by Elizabeth Farness. The cast featured some of the best from both sides of the border: Consuelo Frank, Enrique de Rosas, Don Alvarado, Maria Calvo, Rosa Rey, Jose Pena "Pepet", Tito Davison, Carlos Montalban, Martin Garralaga, Manuel Paris, Lucio Villegas, Darcy Corrigan and Miss America material, Jinx Falkenburg.] **NYT**:10.28.35, **FD**:10.29.35.

[1796] **RUMBA**, P: [By now it should be evident to those who have made their way through these pages, that spin-off's were nothing new even in 1912. By 1914 most of the basic scenarios had been established. The search for variations continued from then till now. In 1935 **Rumba** was more or less **Bolero** [1651] with some extra hip movements and a different rhythm. Next to the tango, this Cuban import was more popular with North Americans than any other Latin dance, reaching the peak of its popularity during the WWII years. Although the scenario in this film was complicated, the film was more than twenty-five percent George Raft rumbaing with three different partners, two of which were Margo and Carol Lombard. The Mexican beauty had taught him the dance in the "Cuban jungles" and the latter made him bring it north to New York. Problem was that there were baddies there waiting to bump off the toughguy. Once they arrived, Margo could not perform, but Carol could, and she really could move that tight little torso to those sensual sounds. The Cuban location shots were good and recognizable by any one who had ever traveled there, but the only Hispanic to receive cast credit was Margo. All of the others used were incidental and merely helped create some Cuban atmosphere.] **V**:2.27.35, **NYT**:2.25.35, **FD**:2.23.35, DAR.

[1797] **RHUMBA ORCHESTRA**, Vitaphone: [Short Subject: This lively production filled with the sensuous rhythms of a lively Cuban band, and some attractive dancing ladies was one of the few shorts that the good Daughters did not think suitable for viewing. Not surprisingly, they considered it filled with "suggestive dancing" and a "waste of time." The Good Neighbor Policy was not one of their favorite numbers either.] DAR.

[1798] **SE HA FUGADO UN PRESO** = **A PRISONER HAS ESCAPED**, Orphea Film: [Director Benito Perojo blended a classic chase theme, an escaped prisoner, all the problems that he faced, and turned out this humorous burlesque for his Spanish language audiences. Juan de Landa played the burly fugitive who fumbled his way to freedom with the full support of all his viewers.] **NYT**:5.20.35.

[1799] **STORM OVER THE ANDES**, U: [From 1928 through 1935 Bolivia and Paraguay fought a bitter and bloody conflict over who would control most of the Gran Chaco, a "green jungle hell" thought to be oil rich. Hollywood finally became involved in the conflict with this production. There are letters in the PCA files for this work which indicate how sensitive the various foreign departments of each of the combatants were to the making of the film. They were also concerned that sympathy might be cast in the enemies' direction. For Hollywood it was just another pair of buddies, far from home, soldiers of fortune who were trying to straighten out some more of South America's problems. Jack Holt left the western range for more powerful ponies in the sky and sold his services to one of the combatants, where his aerial mastery of the high sky above proved to be of great service. He was not so smooth when falling for the General's señorita during a local fiesta, but managed to struggle through the romance by saving his officer's [Antonio Moreno] life in the skies over the jungle. Stock shots of the area indicated that it was infested with "crocodiles or alligators [or whatever those things are that Tarzan manages so well,"] all of which might have been a real surprise to the locals. Mona Barrie was Antonio's lady, but Juanita Garfias was given more latitude to fun and frolic as Pepita. The Spanish language version was entitled **A Las Sabre el Cacho** [1715], Moreno once again played the General and the two other leads were Jose Crespo and Lupita Tovar.] **V**:10.2.35, **FD**:9.25.35, **Hollywood Reporter**, 10.25.35, **Canadian Magazine**:10/35, p42, **Catholic News**, 1.25.36, **Christian Century**, 10.23.35, **DAR, Time**:9.23.35, p46. Script: **Storm Over The Andes**, NYSAA. PCA.

[1800] **SUNDAY SPORTS IN MEXICO**, F: ["Sunday in Mexico City. Good Narrative."] DAR.

[1801] **SUSANA TIENE UN SECRETO** = **SUSANA HAS A SECRET**, Orpheafilm: [This "amusing comedy" starring Rosita Diaz and Ricardo Nunez told the story of a "sleep-walking bride" who wandered into a stranger's bedroom, try that one on your spouse if you're in desperate need, then run. She does all this moving about the night before the wedding, but no one knows but her and the lucky fellow. At least she thinks he was lucky, that was the plot, she cannot remember, but becomes more worried as she tries not to think about it.] **FD**:6.7.35.

[1802] **TANGO BAR**, P: [**Variety**'s opening comments reviewing this film provide a good indication of how they felt about the Spanish language experiment after four years of industry effort and their attitude toward the Latin American market as a whole. "This is the last picture made by Carlos Gardel,

South American star, who was killed in an air crash a few weeks ago. It is by no means a good picture, according to American standards, but is a pleasant little musical which would do good business in Latin American territory under normal circumstances." At best a mediocre product they felt it would still make money south of the border, but considering that the star has been killed, and assuming that all Latin movie goers were sentimental, it was going to be a smash. With added condescension they continued their critical review for Anglo readers: "Carlos ... was tops in his own field and songs by him or films with him, have always been good in South America, Spain and other Latin territories. It is a bit hard for the average not-Latin to figure out just why. He was under average in height and not too romantic appearing according to U. S. standards. Also he was well in his 40's and showed it." Certainly not among the credits to be read at his wake, the reviewer continued his dilemma but pointing out that Paramount had invested a mere $25,000 in one of its productions made in the Paris studio which grossed over $400,000. At best nationalistic faint praise for the dead Hispanic star. It was apparently impossible for this reviewer to understand that the Latin's concept of "macho" did not have to include tall good looks, but was more concerned with inner essence, individual behavior and defying fate. The film itself was thin in plot, but utilized Gardel's talents and included lots of singing and dancing which eventually brought the señorita [Rosita Moreno] and señor together in the last reel. Packed houses at the Campoamor were a better tribute to the memory of "one of their great favorites." The cast also included: Enrique de Rosas, Tito Lusiardo, Jose Luis Tortosa, Collette, d'Arville, Manuel Peluffo, Carmen Rodriguez, Susanne Dullier, Jose Nieto and William Gordon.] **V**:7.17.35, **NYT**:7.6.35, **FD**: 7.9.35.

[1803] **TE QUIERO CON LOCURA** = **I'M CRAZY ABOUT YOU**, F: [Not so faint traces of **King of Hearts** can be found in the Fox dialogue presentation which teamed two favorites of the Latin American market, Rosita Moreno and Raul Roulien, in a delightful comedy with a bit of a message. Since the earliest days of the silents any well scripted Hispanic señorita knew that she would not be required to marry the señor her parents had chosen to be her master for life. In this film to avoid doing just that, Rita feigned insanity and found herself on the other side of the wall with Raul. Inside the asylum the almost continual singing and dancing made it so pleasant that the crazies appeared better off than the people on the outside. With something of a heavy hand, the Anglo director tried to emphasize the point by showing scenes of war, pestilence, and senseless accidents. The cast included: Rosita Moreno, Raul Roulien, Enrique de Rosas, Carlos Villarias, Lucio Villegas and Nanette Noriega.] **NYT**:11.4.35, **FD**:11.5.35.

[1804] **TIERRA, AMOR Y DOLOR** = **LAND, LOVE AND SUFFERING**, Mex/Atlas: [If someone was fighting a bull on the screen in 1935 or any other time for that matter, those who were watching were more than likely doing so in Mexico. That was the case in this film which also offered "attractive views old and new which" "so fascinate[d] the tourist" from the north. All this provided the background for a familiar tale of the hard working, "husky country bred" young, Domingo Soler, who had to somehow find a way to over come the love he had for his pretty but selfish, "flirtatious and worthless wife," Consuelo Frank. Romantic hearts in the Spanish speaking audience could only wish him luck.] **NYT:8.10.35, FD:8.14.35.**

[1805] **LOS TRES BERRETINES** = **THE THREE AMATEURS**, Arg/Lumiton: [This Argentine comedy produced a good share of laughs at the Teatro Campoamor in Harlem. Luis Sandrini was a young man who moved out of his parent's home into a very lively neighborhood where the action was even faster than he thought it would be. There, Luisa Vehil, an attractive young señorita, proved to be more woman than he could handle.] **FD:1.8.35.**

[1806] **TRIBU**, Mex/Miguel Contreras Torres: [Contreras, one of the then leading, new breed of Mexican directors, turned back the pages of history four hundred years for this Spanish language film about the Tribu, allegedly one of the last of the Aztec tribes to be conquered by Conquistadors. For historians, the young director's conception of how the tribe was induced to pay tribute to the King of Spain, must simply be considered an interesting reflection of his own historical interpretation of the Conquest. Neither Spaniard nor Indio were treated as villains, the only one so scripted was the high priest who was angered at losing his prestigious position within the Tribu community. An added touch of realism was his use of the Zapotec dialect still understood and even spoken in the more remote regions of highland Oaxaca.] **NYT:1.10.35.**

[1807] **UNA SEMANA DE FELICIDAD** = **ONE WEEK OF HAPPINESS**, Iberica: [Even for someone very familiar with films, who likes them as much as he does sharing a coffee ice cream with the warm wet lips that love him, it's still amazing that screen writers everywhere could reuse the same script so many times, if just that little variation could be found. This dialogue film for the foreign and domestic market, included an Argentinean this time, who was not pleased that his father wanted him to make good on the pledge that the patron made to his friend some twenty years past. That pledge had joined their two lovely children to be wed when they were older. After this the friend had moved to Spain. Many years later the boy was sent there to meet his lady and be married.
While waiting for father to join him, during his last week of freedom, the young man determined to make it a good one and you know the rest. It was much the same anywhere Hollywood exercised some influence over the local industry and they certainly did that in Mexico, Spain and Argentina. Luckily for all, the boy in this Spanish production just happens to fall in love with the very lady he had been promised to.] **FD:1.19.35, NYT:1.15.36.**

[1808] **UNCONQUERED BANDIT**, Steiner: [Tom Tyler was cast as "half English and half Spanish" in this western melodrama with "better story material than usually [was] found in this type of picture." The scenario involved having the half and half's father killed by the Clayton gang which forced his Hispanic parts to "swear vengeance." Sinister as that half was, when he finally met Clayton's niece, he decided to "decoy her thus striking [his enemy] with a subtle weapon." Apparently he planned to kill her with a broken heart, but while "making false affection to her", surprise of surprises, "Tom actually [fell] in love", which forces his foolish half to confess his deception. But Hollywood forgave such offenses when love was at work even in westerns, and so the did lady. The problem was that the "Night Hawk" Tom had teamed up with then tried to get him hanged and almost succeeded. But the hero escaped and found the proof necessary to have his former partner punished. The lady was his reward, which pleased both half's of his make up. Halfbreeds did not usually fair so well on the screen, but part of him was Anglo. Although there was not as much action in this Tyler adventure as in others, reviewer's thought that keeping the "kids in suspense" to the end was an even better idea. That may have been so, but most of those kids liked it only up to the part where instead of kissing his horse, the hero kissed that darn girl. Nice simple times those were.] **FD**:1.8.35.

[1809] **UNDER THE PAMPAS MOON**, F: [The critics spanned a broad spectrum in this, South American adventure film where the Cisco Kid traveled to the Pampas plains still unable to speak English. The **NYT** thought it so bad that it was good camp, before that was fashionable. "Antique humor" from the early days of the talkers, apparently six years was an eternity for that daily. In reality Warner Baxter simply was wearing a wider belt and using knives and bolas instead of his trusty pistola when he led his boys into action. The script had a passenger plane touching down on the rancho where Cesar Campo was a gaucho. The passengers were rich and beautiful people, jet setters, in the days of prop planes, who elected to stay for the big race in which Cesar's horse won all. Seeing this one of the rich Portenos wanted the horse for the races in Buenos Aries, but Baxter would not sell. The remainder of the action involved recovering the valuable animal taken from the gaucho. Six years after the talkers Hollywood still had not resolved the problem of conveying foreign speech. Should all speak the same? Should the Spaniards speak Spanish with subtitles? Almost always, as with many of the other problem languages and especially Spanish, because they could be played for laughs, the broken English routine was employed. In this one the entire cast spoke some variation of 'I theenk' gibberish, which one must admit had it's comic moments, but which also served to reaffirm accepted views of inferiority, simply because of the inability to speakadaenglis. It's what makes many North American's surprised that foreigners speak a foreign language even in their own countries, a felt cultural imperialism that causes significant embarrassment. In this film the dance numbers were staged by Veloz and Youlanda the, most frequently employed hoofers when Hollywood needed Latin lookers to express Latin rhythms. There was also a lovely new face and shape in this one that would eventually change her name from Rita Cansino to Rita Hayworth.] **V**:5.31.35, **FD**:6.1.35, DAR.

Feature Film List 1935   521

[1810] **VIDAS ROTAS** = **BROKEN LIVES**, Sp/Inca: [Lupita Tovar, Maruchi Fresno, and Enrique Zabala were featured in this "well acted drama" about a handsome violinist who strayed from his wife and had an affair "with an innocent maid." He liked the way she did his ties, but his wife introduced him to other uses for the iron. The attractive outdoor scenes were taken in Spain's beautiful countryside not too long before the bombs began rearranging it during the bloody civil war.] **FD**:8.6.35.

[1811] **LA VIOLETERA** = **THE FLOWER GIRL**, Sp/Fr: [This combined effort used both French and Hispanic players: Raquel Meller, who had starred in the silent version and Suzanne Blanchetti. Emile Drain was the male lead in this tale of recounting some selected parts of Seville's gypsy singer who is chosen to become the official singer in the French court and proves to be the favorite of all the ladies.] **FD**:1.15.35.

[1812] **EL VUELO DE LA MUERTE** = **DEATH FLIGHT**, Sp/Producciones Pereda: [The ill fated flight of the Spanish aviators, Barberan and Collar who were killed on the last leg of their goodwill mission flying from Sevilla to Mexico City provided the inspiration for this adventure story. Ramon Pereda used the death flight idea in this production which detailed the tragic events that followed when his main character discovered that the love of his life was enamored with a musician. As a member of the Mexican Aviation Corps he was informed that the Spaniards had crashed to their death. This combined with the fear that his lady would not love him forever apparently takes away his reason for life. In despair he rushes to the then Valbuena field, mounts his craft, and heads out in the fierce storm to be in the company of his missing compatriots. Romantics liked it, he chose his own time to die.] **NYT**:4.16.35.

[1813] **WEST INDIES CRUISE**, F: [Short Subject: Magic Carpet Series. "Life and customs of [the] West Indies with glimpses of ruins dating from rule of black emperor Christophe of Haiti."] **DAR**.

[1814] **WONDERLAND OF MEXICO**: [This feature film was one of a planned ten part series of "Saturday morning presentations on travel and adventure", shown in the fall of 1935 at the Carnegie Hall by Harold R. Peat and Company. This particular segment boasted of footage taken by not less than Amelia Earhart during some of her record making flights over unchartered Mexican territory.] **FD**:8.22.35.

Indexes

Feature Film Titles Index

[A]

Across the Border, 1914 [421]
Across the Border, 1922 [890]
Across the Isthmus, 1909 [38]
Across the Isthmus 1912 aka Panama Canal Across the Isthmus in 1912 1912 [225]
Across the Mexican Border, 1911 [116]
Across the Mexican Line, 1911 [117]
Across the Pacific, 1926 [1159]
Across the Rio Grande, 1913 [321]
Across the Rio Grande, 1916 [630]
Across To Singapore, 1928 [1263]
Adam and Eva, 1923 [961]
Adventure Girl, 1934 [1649]
The Adventurer, 1927 [1264]
Adventures in Diplomacy, 1914 [422]
The Adventures of American Joe, 1912 [226]
The Adventures of Captain Kettle, 1922 [891]
Aflame In the Sky, 1927 [1205]
Afraid To Love, 1927 [1206]
After Big Game, 1915 [537]
After Many Years, 1930 [1367]
El Agua En El Suelo = Water On the Ground, 1934 [1650]
Aguilas Frente Al Sol = Eagles Across the Sun, 1932 [1556]
Ah Sing and the Greaser, 1910 [74]
The Air Hawk, 1924 [1017]
The Air Mail, 1925 [1090]
A Las Sobre El Cacho, 1935 [1715]
The Alcade's Conspiracy, 1912 [227]
All the Winners, 1920 [838]
Alma De Gaucho aka Alma Gaucha 1930 [1368]
Almas Encontradas = Haunted Souls, 1933 [1595]
Aloha, 1931 [1467]
Aloma of the South Seas, 1926 [1160]
Along the Border, 1916 [631]
Along the Rio Grande, 1917 [729]
The Altar of the Aztecs, 1913 [323]
Amazon Head Hunters, 1932 [1557]
The American Consul, 1917 [730]
The American Girl, 1917 (Serial) The Tyrant of Chiracahua, [731]
The American Girl, 1917 (Serial) The Fate of Juan Garcia, [732]
The American Insurrecto, 1911 [118]
The American Toreador, 1922 [892]
The Americano, 1915 [538]
The Americano, 1916 [632]
Amor Audaz SV Slightly Scarlet, 1929 [1369]
El Amor Solfenado = Love To Music, 1931 [1468]
An Adventure of the Mexican Border, 1913 [322]
An American Invasion, 1912 [228]
An Arizona Escapade, 1912 [229]
An Arizona Wooing, 1915 [539]
An Old Silver Mine in Peru, 1910 [76]
An Old Spanish Onion, 1935 [1717]
Andy Goes A-Pirating, 1914 [423]
Angelita = Little Angel aka Angelina O El Honor De Un Brigadier, 1935 [1716]
Anne of Little Smoky, 1921 [850]
Another Man's Wife, 1924 [1018]
Antigua, 1918 [773]
The Apache Kind, 1913 [324]
Apache Love, 1913 [325]
Apache Raider, 1928 [1265]
The Arab, 1924 [1019]

Argentine Argosy, [1718]
Argentine Love, 1924 [1020]
The Argonauts, 1911 [119]
Arizona, 1913 [326]
Arizona, 1918 [774]
The Arizona Cat Claw, 1919 [822]
The Arizona Kid, 1930 [1370]
The Arizona Terror, 1931 [1469]
Arizona Whirlwind, 1927 [1207]
Arizona Wildcat, 1928 [1266]
The Armadillo, 1913 [327]
Arms and the Gringo, 1914 [424]
Army Maneuvers in Cuba, 1911 [120]
Artful Kate, 1911 [121]
Asegure A Su Mujer = Insure Your Wife, 1935 [1719]
Asi Es La Vida SV What a Man, 1929 [1371]
At Dawn, 1914 [425]
At Mexico's Mercy, 1914 [426]
At the Break of Dawn, 1911 [122]
At the Gringo Mine, 1911 [123]
At the Stroke of the Angelus, 1915 [540]
At the Trail's End, 1911 [124]
Avenger, 1931 [1470]
The Avenging Arrow, 1921 (Serial) [851]
The Aztec Treasure, 1914 [427]

[B]

Bachelor Daddy, 1922 [893]
The Bad Man, 1923 [962]
The Bad Man, 1930 [1372]
Bad-Man Mason, 1914 [428]
The Bad One, 1930 [1373]
The Bag of Gold, 1912 [230]
The Bandit's Mask, 1912 [231]
The Bandit's Spur, 1912 [232]
The Bandit's Waterloo, 1908 [22]
Bandolero, 1924 [1021]
Barbarian, 1933 [1596]
Barbarous Mexico, 1913 [328]
The Bargain, 1914 [429]
Barranco, 1932 [1558]
Basque Wedding, 1914 [430]
The Battle of Ambrose and Walrus, 1915 [541]
The Battle of San Juan Hill, 1913 [329]

Battle of Torreon and Career of Gen. Villa, 1914 [431]

The Battle of Vera Cruz, 1914 [432]
Battles of Falkland Island, 1928 [1267]
The Bearcat, 1922 [894]
Beau Bandit, 1930 [1375]
Beauty and the Bad Man, 1925 [1091]
Beauty in Chains, 1918 [775]
The Bedroom Window, 1924 [1022]
Behind the Lines, [633]
The Bells of San Juan, 1922 [895]
Below the Equator, 1927 [1208]
Below the Rio, 1923 [963]
Ben Hur, 1925 [1092]
Bess of the Forest, 1911 [125]
Betrayed, 1917 [733]
Betty's Bandit, 1912 [233]
Beyond the Border, 1925 [1093]
Beyond the Rio Grande, 1930 [1376]
Beyond the Rockies, 1909 [39]
Beyond the Rockies, 1932 [1559]
Big Broadcast of 1936, 1935 [1720]
Big Stakes, 1922 [896]
The Big Trail, 1930 [1377]
Bill Brennan's Claim, 1917 [734]
Billy and His Pal, 1911 [126]
Billy the Kid, 1930 [1378]
Bird of Paradise, 1932 [1560]
The Bird of Prey, 1918 [776]
The Black Box, 1915 [542]
The Black Butterfly, [634]
The Black Mantilla, 1917 [735]
The Black Pirate, 1926 [1161]
Black Sheep, 1912 [234]
Black Sheep, 1921 [852]
The Blighted Spaniard, 1914 [433]
Blind Alleys, 1927 [1209]
The Blind Gypsy, 1913 [330]
Blinky, 1923 [964]
Blockade, 1928 [1268]
Blonde Venus, 1932 [1561]
Blood and Sand, 1922 [897]
The Blood of the Arena, 1917 [736]

Bluebeard's Seven Wives, 1926 [1162]
The Blue Streak, 1926 [1163]
Bohemios = Bohemians, 1935 [1721]
Bolero, 1934 [1651]
Bolibar, 1928 [1269]
Boliche, 1934 [1652]
Bombs and Bandits, 1917 [737]
Bonita of El Cajon, 1911 [126]
Border Blackbirds, 1927 [1210]
Border Cavalier, 1927 [1211]
The Border Detective, 1912 [235]
Border Devils, 1932 [1562]
The Border Fury 1919 (Serial) The Adventures of Ruth [839]
Border Guns, 1935 [1722]
Border Intrigue, 1925 [1094]
Border Justice, 1926 [1164]
Border Law, 1931 [1471]
The Border Legion, 1918 [777]
The Border Legion, 1924 [1023]
The Border Legion, 1930 [1379]
The Border Maid, 1924 [1024]
The Border Menace, 1934 [1653]
Border Patrol, 1928 [1270]
Border Patrol, 1929 [1319]
Border Raiders, 1918 [778]
The Border Raiders, 1921 [853]
The Border Ranger, 1911 [128]
The Border Rider, 1924 [1025]
Border Romance, 1930 [1380]
The Border Runner, 1915 [543]
The Border Scouts, 1922 [898]
Border Sheriff, 1926 [1165]
"A Border Tale", 1910 [75]
Border Town, 1922 [899]
Bordertown, 1935 [1723]
Border Vengence, 1925 [1095]
Border Whirlwind, 1926 [1166]
Border WildCat, 1929 [1320]
The Border Wireless, 1918 [779]
Border Women, 1924 [1026]
Borrowed Husbands, 1924 [1027]
The Bowl-Bearer, 1915 [544]
Braga's Double, 1915 [545]
Branded Man, 1928 [1271]
Branded Sombrero 1927 [1272]
Brand of Cowardice, 1916 [635]
Brand of Cowardice, 1925 [1096]
The Brand of Lopez, 1920 [840]
The Brazilian Ring, 1909 [40]

Breed of the Border, 1925 [1097]
Breed of the Border, 1933 [1597]
Breed of the Sunset, 1928 [1273]
The Bride of Guadeloupe, 1915 [546]
Bride of Hate, 1916 [636]
The Bridge of Fancy, 1917 [738]
The Bridge of San Luis Rey, 1929 [1321]
Bright Lights, 1930 [1381]
The Bright Shawl, 1923 [965]
Broadway, 1929 [1322]
The Broken Mask, 1927 [1274]
The Broken Trail, 1911 [129]
The Broken Wing, 1923 [966]
Broken Wing, 1932 [1563]
Broncho Billy--Outlaw, 1914 [434]
Broncho Billy and the Greaser, 1914 [435]
Broncho Billy's Brother aka Bronco Billy's Cowardly Brother, 1915 [547]
Broncho Billy's Greaser Deputy, 1915 [548]
Broncho Billy's Mexican Wife, 1912 [236]
Broncho Billy's Mexican Wife, 1915 [549]
Broncho Billy's Redemption, 1910 [77]
Broncho Billy's Strategy, 1913 [331]
Broncho Billy's Way, 1913 [332]
Broncho Twisted, 1927 [1212]
A Brother in Arms, 1911 [130]
The Buccaneers, 1913 [333]
Bucking the West, 1924 [1028]
Bud Nevins--Bad Man, 1911 [131]
La Buenaventura = The Fortune Teller, 1934 [1654]
Buenos Aires, 1917 [739]
The Bull Fight, 1924 [1029]
Bull Fight, 1935 [1724]
The Bull Fighter, 1927 [1214]
A Bull Fight in Mexico, 1910 [78]
The Burial of the Maine, 1912 [237]
Buried Treasure, 1921 [854]

The Buried Treasure of Corbe, 1916 [637]
Butterflies in the Rain, 1926 [1167]

[C]

The Caballero, 1930 [1382]
El Caballero De La Noche SR Dick Turpin, 1932 [1564]
The Caballero's Way, 1914 [436]
El Caballo del Pueblo, 1935 [1725]
Cactus Crandal, 1918 [780]
Cadiz, Spain, 1917 [740]
California, 1927 [1214]
California in 49, 1924 [1030]
California in 49, 1927 [1215]
The California Revolution of 1846, 1911 [132]
A California Romance, 1922 [900]
The California Trail, 1933 [1598]
The Call of Home, 1922 [901]
The Call of the Angelus, 1913 [334]
Call of the Flesh, 1930 [1383]
Camille, 1927 [1216]
Camino Del Infierno SV The Man Who Came Back, 1931 [1472]
Camoens, the Portuguese Shakespeare, 1911 [133]
Las Campanas de Capistrano, 1930 [1384]
La Cancion Del Dia = The Song of the Day, 1933 [1599]
El Cantante De Napoles = Singers of Napoles, 1934 [1655]
Canyon of Adventure, 1928 [1275]
Canyon of Fools, 1923 [967]
The Canyon of Light, 1926 [1168]
The Canyon of Missing Men, 1930 [1385]
El Capitan and the Land Grabbers, 1913 [335]
El Capitan Tormenta, 1935 [1727]
Captain Alvarez, 1914 [437]
Captain Blood, 1924 [1031]
Captain Blood, 1935 [1726]
Captain Careless, 1928 [1276]
Captain Courtesy, 1915 [550]
Un Captain De Cosacos, 1934 [1656]
Captain Fly-By-Night, 1922 [902]
Captain Macklin, 1915 [551]
Captain Rivera's Reward, 1912 [238]
Captain Thunder, 1931 [1473]
The Captive God, 1916 [638]
Captured by Mexicans, 1914 [438]
The Capture of Aguinaldo, 1913 [336]
The Capture of Trenches at Canaba, 1899 [8]
Careers, 1929 [1323]
Carlos and Elizabeth, 1924 [1032]
Carmelita's Revenge, 1914 [439]
Carmen, 1910 [79]
Carmen, 1913 [337]
Carmen, (Essanay), 1915 [552]
Carmen, (Fox), 1915 [553]
Carmen, (Lasky-Paramount), 1915 [554]
Carmen, 1917 [741]
Carmen, 1928 [1277]
Carmenita the Faithful, 1911 [134]
Carne De Cabaret SV Ten Cents A Dance, 1931 [1474]
La Carta SV the Letter, 1930 [1386]
Cascarrabias = Grumpy, 1930 [1387]
Casey's Border Raid, 1917 [742]
Cat and the Fiddle, 1934 [1657]
The Cattle King of Arizona, 1911 [135]
The Cavalier, 1928 [1278]
Cavanaugh of Rangers, 1918 [781]
Celebrations on the Ranch, 1912 [239]
Central Airport, 1933 [1600]
A Central American Romance, 1910 [80]
A Certain Young Man, 1928 [1279]
The Changing Woman, 1918 [782]
Le Chanteur De Seville, 1931 [1475]
Charge of Gauchos, 1928 [1280]
The Charmer, 1925 [1098]

Charros, Gauchos y Manolas, 1930 [1388]
Chasing the Moon, 1922 [903]
The Cheat, 1923 [968]
Cheri Bibi SV The Phantom of Paris, 1931 [1476]
Chicago After Midnight, 1928 [1281]
A Child of the Rancho, 1911 [136]
Children of Jazz, 1923 [969]
Chiquita, the Dancer, 1912 [240]
Christopher Columbus, 1910 [81]
The Chronicles of America, 1924 [1033]
Chucho El Roto, 1935 [1728]
The Chuncho Indians, 1910 [82]
Cintra, a Picturesque Town of Portugal, 1911 [137]
Cipher Key, 1915 [555]
Circus Mary, 1915 [556]
The Cisco Kid, 1931 [1477]
City of Mexico, 1913 [338]
Ciudad De Catron = Cardboard City, 1933 [1601]
Class Mates, 1914 [440]
Class Mates, 1924 [1034]
Clearing The Range, 1931 [1478]
Clemencia, 1935 [1729]
The Climbers, 1927 [1217]
The Clod, 1913 [339]
Clothes Makes the Pirates, 1925 [1099]
Clouds in Sunshine Valley, 1916 [639]
Coals of Fire, 1911 [138]
Cocaine, 1922 [904]
Cocaine Traffic aka The Drug Terror, 1914 [441]
Cocoa Industry, Trinidad, British West Indies, 1908 [23]
The Cocoanuts, 1929 [1323a]
Cock o' the Walk, 1930 [1389]
Code of Marcia Gray, 1916 [640]
Code of the Cow Country, 1927 [1218]
El Codigo Penal SV The Criminal Code, 1931 [1479]
Col. E.D. Baker, 1st California, 1911 [139]
Col. Heeza Liar in Mexico, 1914 [442]
Colonel Heeza Liar and the Bandits, 1916 [642]
Colonel Heeza Liar Captures Villa, 1916 [641]
Colorful Guatemala, 1935 [1730]
Col. Theodore Roosevelt's Expedition in the Wild, 1918 [783]
Columbus, 1923 [970]
El Comediante, 1931 [1480]
Come On Marines, 1934 [1658]
The Coming of Amos, 1925 [1100]
The Coming of Columbus, 1912 [241]
The Coming of the Padres, 1914 [443]
Common Law, 1916 [643]
The Common Law, 1923 [971]
El Compade Mendoza = Ny Friend Mendoza, 1934 [1659]
Las Companas Capistrano, 1931 [1481]
Conchita, the Spanish Belle, 1909 [41]
Condemned, 1929 [1324]
Conocesa Tu Mujer SV Don't Bet On Women, 1931 [1482]
The Conquering Horde, 1931 [1483]
The Conquering Power, 1921 [855]
The Conspirators, 1909 [42]
Contra La Corriente = Against the Current, 1935 [1731]
Corazon Bandolero = Heart of a Bandit, 1935 [1732]
Corazones En Derrota = Vanquised Hearts, 1934 [1660]
The Cost of Hatred, 1917 [743]
A Cowboy and a Lord, 1911 [140]
Cowboy Holiday, 1934 [1661]
The Cowboy Pastime, 1915 [557]
The Cowboy's Baby, 1908 [24]
A Cowboy's Generosity, 1910 [83]
The Cowboy's Innocence, 1911 [141]
The Coward, 1912 [242]
The Crackerjack, 1925 [1101]
Cradle Snatchers, 1927 [1219]
Crashin' Thru, 1923 [972]
Crazy To Marry, 1921 [856]

The Crimson Dove, 1917 [744]
Crooked Trails, 1916 [644]
Crossroads, 1922 [905]
'Cross the Mexican Line, 1914 [444]
The Crow's Nest, 1922 [906]
The Crucial Test, 1911 [142]
The Cruise To Vera Cruz, 1921 [857]
Cruz Diablo = The Devil's Cross, 1935 [1733]
La Cruz y Las Espada SV The Cross and the Sword, 1934 [1662]
Cuando Te Suicidas? 1931 [1484]
Cuba Steps Out, 1925 [1102]
Cuban Love Song, 1931 [1485]
The Cuckoos, 1930 [1390]
El Cuerpo Del Delito SV The Benson Murder Case, 1930 [1391]
Cuesta Abaho = The Downfall aka The Downward Path, 1934 [1663]
A Cup of Cold Water, 1911 [143]
Cyclone Cavalier, 1925 [1103]
Cyclone of the Range, 1927 [1220]
Cyclone Ranger, 1935 [1734]
Cytherea, 1924 [1035]

[D]

La Dama Atrevida SV Lady Who Dared, 1931 [1486]
Dancer of Barcelona, 1929 [1325]
Dancer of Paris, 1926 [1169]
The Dancers, 1925 [1104]
El Dancing, 1935 [1735]
The Dancing Cheat, 1924 [1036]
Dangerous Coward, 1924 [1037]
The Dangerous Flirt, 1924 [1038]
Dangerous Paradise, 1930 [1392]
The Daughter of the Don, 1917 [745]
A Daughter of the South, 1918 [784]
The Daughters of Senor Lopez, 1912 [243]
Daughters of the Don, 1922 [907]
Daybreak, 1931 [1487]

The Dead Line, 1914 [445]
The Death Dice, 1915 [558]
De Frente Machen! SV Doughboys, 1931 [1493]
De La Sarten Al Fuego, 1935 [1736]
Delightful Rogue, 1929 [1326]
Del Mismo Barro SV The Common Clay, 1930 [1393]
A Demon For Trouble, 1934 [1664]
Derelict, 1930 [1394]
The Desert Flower, 1925 [1105]
Desert Gold, 1919 [823]
Desert Gold, 1926 [1170]
Desert Rider, 1929 [1327]
Desert Trail, 1935 [1737]
Desert's Toll aka The Devil's Toll, 1926 [1171]
The Desperado of Panama, 1914 [446]
Devil is a Woman, 1935 [1738]
The Devil May Care, 1929 [1328]
The Devil On Horseback, 1935 [1739]
A Devil With Women, 1930 [1395]
The Devil's Bowl, 1923 [973]
The Devil's Cargo, 1925 [1106]
Devil's Island, 1926 [1172]
Dewey, 1911 [144]
El Diablo, 1916 [645]
The Diamond Bandit, 1924 [1039]
Diamond Carlise, 1922 [908]
The Diamond Smugglers, 1911 [145]
Diamonds Adrift, 1921 [858]
El Dia Que Me Quieras = The Day You Love Me, 1935 [1740]
The Dictator, 1915 [559]
The Dictator, 1922 [909]
El Dios Del Mar SV The Sea God, 1930 [1396]
The Dismissal of Silver Phil, 1918 [785]
The Divine Solution, 1912 [244]
A Divorce of Convenience, 1921 [859]
Do and Dare, 1922 [910]
Dolly's Deliverance, 1914 [447]
Dolores De Aranda aka The Lady of Sorrow, 1914 [448]

Dona Franicisquita, 1935 [1741]
Dona Mentrias SV The Lady Lies, 1930 [1397]
Don Caesar De Bazan, 1912 [245]
Don Carlos, 1910 [84]
Don Dare Devil, 1925 [1107]
Don Desperado, 1927 [1221]
Don Juan, 1926 [1173]
Don Juan and Charles V, 1912 [246]
Don Juan Diplomatico SV The Boudoir Diplomat, 1931 [1488]
Don Juan of the West, 1928 [1282]
Don Juan: or a War Drama of the 18th Century, 1909 [43]
Don Mike, 1927 [1222]
Don Q, Son of Zorro, 1925 [1108]
Don Quickshot of the Rio Grande, 1923 [974]
Don Quintin El Amargao = Don Quintin, the Bitter, 1935 [1742]
Don Quixote, 1909 [44]
Don Quixote, 1916 [646]
Don Quixote, 1923 [975]
Don X, 1925 [1109]
Dope, 1914 [449]
Dos Mas Uno Dos = Two and One, Two, 1934 [1665]
Dos Monjes = Two Monks, 1934 [1667]
Dos Mujeres y Un Don Juan = Two Women and One Don Juan 1934 [1666]
Dos Noches = Two Nights, 1931 [1489]
A Double Dyed Deceiver, 1920 [841]
The Double O, 1922 [911]
The Dove, 1928 [1283]
The Dove and the Serpent, 1912 [247]
Down by the Rio Grande, 1924 [1040]
Down in Mexico, 1910 [85]
Down on the Rio Grande, 1913 [340]
Dracula SV Dracula, 1931 [1490]
Drake of England, 1935 [1743]
Drama in a Spanish Inn, 1907 [15]

The Dream of Loco Juan, 1914 [450]
Dreyfus, 1931 [1491]
The Dreyfus Affair, 1908 [25]
The Drifter, 1929 [1329]
Driftin' Sands, 1928 [1284]
The Drug Traffic, 1923 [976]
Drums of Love, 1928 [1285]
Drums O'VooDoo, 1934 [1668]
Duck Soup, 1933 [1602]
The Dumb Girl of Portici, 1916 [647]
Dugan of the Bad Lands, 1931 [1492]
Durand of the Bad Lands, 1925 [1110]
Dust of Desire, 1919 [824]

[E]

Eagle Dance, Pueblo Indians, 1898 [1]
Eagle of the Sea, 1926 [1174]
The Easterner, 1907 [16]
East is West, 1930 [1398]
The Eavesdropper, 1909 [45]
The Ebony Shrine, 1930 [1399]
Eisenstein In Mexico, 1933 [1603]
Elizabeth of England, 1935 [1744]
Elusive Isabel, 1916 [648]
Emperor Jones, 1933 [1604]
En Cada Puerto Un Amor SV Way For A Sailor, 1931 [1494]
The End of the Game, 1919 [825]
The End of the Trail, 1913 [341]
End of the Trail, 1933 [1605]
The Enemies of Women, 1923 [977]
Enemigos = The Enemies, 1934 [1669]
En La Tierra Del Sol = In the Land of the Sun, 1926 [1175]
En Nombre de la Amistad SV Friendship, 1930 [1400]
Episode of Cloudy Canyon, 1913 [342]
Episode of the Cuban, 1909 [46]
Eran Trece Sv Charlie Chan Carries On, 1932 [1565]
El Escandala = The Scandal, 1934 [1670]

Escape From Devils Island, 1935 [1745]
Esclavas De La Moda SV On Your Back, 1931 [1495]
Esperame, 1932 [1566]
Estrellados SV Free and Easy, 1930 [1401]
The Eternal Duel, 1914 [451]
The Eternal Three, 1923 [978]
The Eternal Woman, 1929 [1330]
Evangeline, 1929 [1331]
The Evil Eye, 1913 [343]
The Evil Eye, 1916 [649]
The Evil One, 1913 [344]
Exile, 1917 [746]
The Exciters, 1923 [979]

[F]

A Fair Exchange, 1911 [146]
Fantasca, the Gypsy, 1912 [248]
El Fantasma Del Convento = The Phantom of the Convent, 1934 [1671]
Fantasy of the Monastery, 1935 [1746]
Fascination, 1922 [912]
Fast and Fearless, 1924 [1041]
The Fear Within, 1915 [560]
Female Bandit, 1910 [86]
La Fiesta Del Diablo SV The Devil's Holiday, 1931 [1496]
The Fight for Freedom: A Story of the Southwest, 1908 [26]
Fighting American, 1924 [1042]
Fighting Bob, 1909 [47]
Fighting Bob, 1915 [561]
Fighting Boob, 1926 [1176]
Fighting Caballero, 1935 [1747]
Fighting Coward, 1924 [1043]
Fighting Demon, 1925 [1111]
Fighting Edge, 1926 [1177]
Fighting For Gold, 1919 [826]
Fighting Fury, 1924 [1044]
The Fighting Gringo, 1917 [747]
The Fighting Hombre, 1927 [1223]
Fighting Legion, 1930 [1402]
The Fighting Lieutenant, 1913 [345]
Fighting Mad, 1921 [860]
Fighting Marines, 1935 [1748]

Fighting Ranger, 1934 [1672]
The Fighting Sheriff, 1931 [1497]
The Filibusters, 1912 [249]
A Filipino Cock Fight, 1902 [9]
Filipino Scouts, 1904 [11]
Filipinos Retreat From Trenches, 1899 [7]
Fine Feathers, 1917 [748]
The Fire Cat, 1921 [861]
A Five Foot Ruler, 1917 [749]
The Flag of Two Wars, 1913 [346]
Flame of Passion, 1915 [562]
Flame of the Argentine, 1926 [1178]
Flaming Arrow, 1913 [347]
Flaming Gold, 1934 [1673]
Flaming Guns, 1933 [1606]
Flesh and the Devil, 1926 [1179]
Flight, 1929 [1332]
Flirting With Danger, 1935 [1749]
The Flower Girl of Las Palmas, 1911 [147]
Flower of the Night, 1925 [1112]
Flying Down To Rio, 1933 [1607]
The Flying Fleet, 1929 [1333]
The Flying U Ranch, 1927 [1224]
Following the Flag, 1916 [650]
Following the Flag in Mexico, 1916 [651]
Following Villa in Mexico, 1916 [652]
Fool's Gold, 1915 [563]
Fools Paradise, 1921 [862]
Footsteps of Aztecs, 1926 [1180]
Forbidden Cargo, 1925 [1113]
Forbidden Hours, 1928 [1286]
Forked Trails, 1915 [564]
For the Flag, 1913 [348]
For the Love of a Toreador, 1913 [349]
For the Soul of Rafael, 1920 [842]
Fortune's Mask, 1922 [913]
Found Alive 1934 [1674]
Four Frightened People, 1934 [1675]

Four Horsemen of the
  Apocalypse, 1921
  [863]
Four Horsemen of the
  Apocalypse, 1926
  [1181]
The Fourth In Salvador, 1917
  [750]
Framed 1927 [1225]
Frisco Kid, 1935 [1750]
From Headquarters, 1929 [1334]
From the Artic to the Tropics,
  1910 [87]
Las Fronteras Del Amor =
  Love's Frontiers, 1934
  [1676]
La Fruta Amarga SV Min And
  Bill, 1931 [1498]
La Fuerza Del Querer SV The
  Big Fight, 1930 [1403]
The Fugitive, 1925 [1114]
Fury of the Jungle, 1934
  [1677]

[G]

Galas De La Paramount SV
Paramount On Paramount, 1930
  [1404]
The Game Chicken, 1922 [914]
A Game of Wits, 1914 [452]
Gas Oil and Water, 1922 [915]
The Gateway of the Moon, 1928
  [1287]
The Gaucho, 1927 [1226]
The Gay Caballero, 1932 [1567]
The Gay Defender, 1927 [1227]
General Crack, 1929 [1335]
General John Regan, 1921 [864]
Gente Alegre, 1931 [1499]
The Gentlemen From America,
  1923 [980]
Geronimo's Last Raid, 1912
  [250]
Ghost Breaker, 1922 [916]
The Ghost of Old Morro, 1917
  [751]
The Ghost of the Hacienda,
  1913 [350]
The Ghost of the Rancho, 1918
  [786]
The Ghost Wagon, 1915 [565]
Gipsy Blood, 1931 [1500]
The Girl and the Greaser, 1913
  [351]

Girl From Frisco: 1916
  (Serial) Border Wolves
  [653]
Girl From Havana, 1929 [1336]
The Girl From Rio, 1927 [1228]
Girl From the West, 1923 [981]
The Girl He Didn't Buy 1928
  [1288]
A Girl In Every Port, 1928
  [1289]
Girl of the Golden West, 1915
  [566]
Girl of the Golden West, 1923
  [982]
Girl of the Golden West, 1930
  [1405]
Girl of the Rio, 1932 [1568]
Girl of the West, 1911 [148]
Girl on the Stairs, 1925
  [1115]
A Girl Spy in Mexico, 1913
  [352]
The Girls of Pine Tree Ranch,
  1912 [251]
God's Country And The Man,
  1931 [1501]
Gold Diggers, 1923 [983]
Gold Dust, 1916 [654]
Gold Grabbers, 1922 [919]
Gold Rush, 1935 [1751]
Golden Dreams, 1922 [917]
The Golden Gift, 1922 [918]
The Good Bad Man, 1916 [655]
Good Men and Bad, 1922 [984]
The Grandee's Ring, 1915 [567]
Granderos Del Amor =
  Grenadiers of Love, 1934
  [1678]
The Grand Old Flag, 1913 [353]
The Greaser, 1915 [568]
The Greaser and the Weakling,
  1912 [252]
The Greaser's Gauntlet, 1908
  [27]
The Greaser's Revenge, 1914
  [453]
Great Bull Fight, 1902 [10]
The Great Divide, 1924 [1045]
The Great Divide, 1930 [1406]
The Greater Love, 1913 [354]
Greater Love Hath No Man, 1911
  [149]
The Great Nitrate of Soda
  Industry in Chile, 1911
  [150]
The Gringo, 1914 [454]

The Grip of the Past, 1914 [455]
Growing and Gathering Cacao Beans, 1913 [355]
The Grudge, 1915 [569]
The Gun Fighter, 1917 [752]
The Gunfighter, 1916 [656]
The Gun Runner, 1928 [1290]
The Gun Smugglers, 1912 [253]
Guns and Greasers, 1918 [787]
Gypsy Blood, 1921 [865]
Gypsy Code, 1930 [1407]
A Gypsy Duel, 1904 [13]
The Gypsy Flirt, 1912 [254]
The Gypsy Gambler, 1914 [456]
Gypsy Love, 1913 [356]
Gypsy Passion, 1922 [920]
A Gypsy Romance, 1914 [457]
The Gypsy Trail, 1915 [570]
The Gypsy Wife, 1912 [256]
A Gypsy's Love, 1912 [255]
Gypsy's Revenge (Lubin), 1907 [17]
Gypsy's Revenge (Vitagraph), 1907 [18]
A Gypsy's Revenge, 1908 [28]
Gypsy's Warning, 1908 [29]
The Gypsy's Warning, 1913 [357]

[H]

Haitian Night Tales, 1919 [827]
The Half-Breed, 1916 [657]
The Half-Breed, 1922 [921]
The Half-Breed's Foster Sister, 1912 [257]
The Half-Breed's Sacrifice, 1912 [258]
The Half-Breed's Treachery, 1912 [259]
The Half-Naked Truth, 1932 [1569]
Hands Across the Border, 1926 [1182]
The Hands of the United States, 1910 [88]
Happiness Ahead, 1928 [1291]
The Happy Warrior, 1925 [1116]
Hard Hombre, 1931 [1502]
Havana, Its Streets, Buildings and Fortresses, 1912 [260]
Havana Widows, 1933 [1608]
Hay Que Casar Al Principe SR Paid To Love, 1931 [1503]
The Headhunters, 1913 [358]
Heading South, 1918 [788]
Heads Up, 1925 [1117]
The Heart Bandit, 1924 [1046]
The Heart of a Bandit, 1915 [571]
The Heart of Bonita, 1916. [658]
The Heart of Juanita, 1919 [828]
The Heart of Paula, 1916 [659]
Heart of a Siren, 1925 [1118]
Heart of the Sunset, 1918 [789]
The Heart of Texas Ryan, 1917 [753]
Hell Bound, 1931 [1504]
Hell Harbor, 1930 [1408]
Hell's Heroes, 1930 [1409]
Hell's Hinges, 1916 [660]
Hell's Hole, 1923 [985]
Hell's Island, 1930 [1410]
Her Chum's Brother, 1911 [151]
Her Fathers's Gold, 1916 [661]
Her Husbands Trademark, 1922 [922]
Her Last Resort, 1912 [261]
Her Man, 1930 [1411]
Her Maternal Right, 1916 [662]
Her Own Country, 1912 [262]
Her Own Way, 1915 [572]
Her Reputation, 1923 [986]
Her Sacrifice, 1911 [152]
Her Spanish Cousins, 1914 [458]
El Heroe de Nacozari, 1935 [1752]
The Heroine of San Juan, 1916 [663]
He Waits Forever, 1914, [459]
He Who Gets Slapped, 1924 [1047]
Hey Hey Westerner, 1932 [1570]
Hi Gaucho! 1935 [1753]
High Steppers, 1926 [1183]
Hills of Missing Men, 1922 [923]
His Mexican Bride, 1909 [48]
His Mexican Sweetheart, 1912 [263]
His Majesty the Outlaw, 1924 [1048]
His Military Figure, 1917 [754]
His Own Law, 1924 [1049]
His Pajama Girl, 1920 [843]

His Spanish Wife, 1910 [89]
His Supreme Moment, 1925 [1119]
Historic Mexico City, 1935 [1754]
Hold Them Yale, 1928 [1292]
Hollywood, Ciudad De Ensueno, = Hollywood, City of Illusion, 1931 [1505]
Hollywood Party, 1934 [1679]
El Hombre Malo SV The Bad Man, 1930 [1412]
Un Hombre Peligroso, = A Dangerous Man, 1935 [1755]
El Hombre Que Asesino SV Stamboul, 1932 [1572]
El Hombre Que Se Reia Del Amor = The Man Who Laughed At Love, 1935 [1756]
Hombres En Mi Vida SV Men In Her Life, 1932 [1571]
Hombres En Su Vida SV The Men In Her Life, 1931 [1506]
Home of the Seal, 1911 [153]
The Honor of the Flag, 1911 [154]
The Honor System, 1916 [664]
Horizontes Nuevos SV The Big Trail, 1931 [1507]
Hot Heels, 1928 [1293]
Hot Pepper, 1933 [1609]
Hot Tamale, 1920 [844]
Hot Tamale, 1930 [1413]
Hotter Than Haiti, 1931 [1508]
House of Hate, 1918 (Serial) [790]
Huddle, 1929 [1337]
Huddle, 1932 [1573]
Hurricane Hal, 1925 [1120]
Hurricane Horseman, 1931 [1509]
Hutch of the USA, 1924 [1050]
Hysterical History Comedies: When Columbus Discovered America, 1924 [1051]

[I]

I Can Explain, 1922 [924]
I Like Your Nerve, 1931 [1510]
I Live For Love, 1935 [1758]
I Want To Forget, 1918, [792]
Idolos De La Radio = Idols of the Radio, 1935 [1757]
The Immortal Alamo, 1911 [155]
Importing Cattle from Mexico into the United States, 1913 [359]
El Imposter SV Scotland Yard, 1931 [1511]
In Barcelona, 1921 [866]
In Blossom Time, 1911 [156]
In Caliente, 1935 [1760]
In Gay Madrid, 1930 [1415]
In Golden Days, 1908 [30]
In Mexico, 1916 [665]
In Monkey Land, 1917 [755]
In Old Arizona, 1909 [49]
In Old Arizona, 1929 [1338]
In Old California, 1910 [91]
In Old California, 1929 [1339]
In Old Florida, 1911 [158]
In Old Madrid, 1911 [159]
In Old Mexico, 1915 [575]
In Old Panama, 1913 [361]
In Sage Brush Country, 1915 [576]
In the Amazon Jungle, 1915 [573]
In the Days of Gold, 1911 [160]
In the Days of the Padres, 1914 [460]
In the Heart of Peggy, 1911 [161]
In the Land of the Cactus, 1913 [360]
In the Land of the Tortilla, 1916 [666]
In the Latin Quarter, 1914 [461]
In the Latin Quarter, 1915 [574]
In the Name of Love, 1925 [1121]
In the Nick of Time, 1911 [162]
In the Palace of the King, 1923 [987]
In Your Sombrero, 1931 [1512]
Inca-Cuzco, 1935 [1759]
La Incorregible SV Manslaughter, 1930 [1414]
The Indian Maid's Sacrifice, 1911 [157]
Inez De Castro, 1910 [90]
Inez From Hollywood, 1924 [1052]
The Infamous Don Miguel, 1913 [362]
The Insurrection, 1915 [577]

La Isla Maldita = The Accursed Island, 1935 [1761]
The Island of Cuba, 1918 [791]
The Isle of Hope, 1925 [1122]
Isle of Lost Ships, 1923 [988]
Isle of Lost Ships, 1929 [1340]
The Isle of Strife--Cuba, 1912 [264]
It's Great To Be Alive, 1933 [1610]

[J]

Jack and Jill, 1917 [756]
The Jaguar's Claws, 1917 [757]
The Jaguar Trap, 1915 [578]
La Jaula De Los Leones SV The Lion's Jaws, 1931 [1513]
The Jealousy of Miguel and Isabella, 1913 [363]
Jeanne of the Woods, 1915 [579]
Jerry in Mexico, 1916 [667]
The Jest of Jealousy, 1915 [580]
Jewels of Desire, 1927 [1229]
Joanna, 1925 [1123]
Juan and Juanita, 1912 [265]
Juarez After th Seige, 1911 [163]
Juarez y Maximillano, 1935 [1762]
Juggling with Fate, 1913 [364]
Julieta Compra Un Hijo = Julieta Buys a Baby, 1935 [1763]
A Jumble in the Jungle, 1924 [1053]
Jungle Antics, 1935 [1764]
The Jungle Child, 1916 [668]
A Jungle Revenge, 1915 [581]
Just Tony, 1922 [925]

[K]

The Kaiser, 1918 [793]
Keith of the Border, 1918 [794]
Kennedy Square, 1916 [669]
Kernal Nutt In Mexico, 1916 [670]
The Key to Yesterday, 1914 [462]
The Kick-Back, 1922 [926]
The Kid, 1916 [671]

The Kid From Spain, 1932 [1574]
The Kid Is Cleaver, 1918 [795]
The Killer, 1921 [867]
King of the Arena, 1933 [1611]
The Kingfisher's Roost, 1922 [927]
Kinkaid, Gambler, 1916 [672]
The Kinship of Courage, 1915 [582]
The Kiss, 1921 [868]
A Kiss in the Dark, 1925 [1124]
Knickerbocker Buckaroo, 1919 [829]
Kongo, 1932 [1575]

[L]

Ladron De Amor aka Cuando El Amor Rie SR Love Gambler, 1930 [1416]
Lady For A Day, 1933 [1612]
Lady of the Pavements, 1929 [1341]
Lady Robin Hood, 1925 [1125]
The Lady Who Dared, 1931 [1514]
Land Baron of San Tee, 1912 [266]
The Land of Adventure, 1915 [583]
Land of Chewing Gum, 1933 [1614]
Land of the Feathered Serpent, 1933 [1615]
The Land of Missing Men, 1930 [1417]
Lariats And Six Shooters, 1931 [1515]
Lasca, 1919 [830]
Lascar of The Rio Grande, 1931 [1516]
The Lash aka Amigo, 1930 [1418]
The Last Dance, 1914 [463]
Last of the Duanes, 1930 [1419]
The Last Rites of the Maine and the Burial of It's Dead, 1912 [267]
Last Trail, 1921 [869]
Laughing At Life, 1933 [1616]
Laughing Boy, 1934 [1680]
Laughing With Medbury In South America, 1934 [1681]

Launching of the Battleship Rivadavia, 1911 [164]
Law and Lawless, 1933 [1617]
Law of the Rio Grande, 1931 [1517]
Lawless Border, 1935 [1765]
Lawless Frontier, 1935 [1766]
The Lawless Legion, 1929 [1342]
La Ley Del Haren SV Fazil [The Law of the Harem], 1931 [1518]
Learned About Sailors, 1934 [1682]
Leathernecking, 1930 [1420]
Legion of the Condemned, 1928 [1294]
Less Than Kin, 1918 [796]
Lets Go Native, 1930 [1421]
Liberty, 1916 [673]
Lieut. Danny, USA, 1916 [674]
Life, 1928 [1295]
The Life of an American Cowboy, 1906 [14]
The Life of General Villa, 1914 [464]
The Life of the Party, 1930 [1422]
The Light of Western Stars, 1918 [797]
The Light of Western Stars, 1925 [1126]
The Lighthouse by the Sea, 1915 [584]
The Lightning Rider, 1924 [1054]
Lisbon Before and After the Revolution, 1910 [92]
Lisbon, Portugal, 1917 [758]
The Little Gypsy, 1915 [585]
The Little Senorita, 1914 [465]
The Living Book of Nature, 1917 [759]
La Llama Sagrada SV The Sacred Flame, 1931 [1519]
La LLorna = The Crying Woman 1933 [1613]
La Llorna, 1935 [1767]
The Loaded Door, 1922 [928]
Lo Mejor Es Rier, 1931 [1521]
The Lone Wagon, 1924 [1055]
The Long Arm of the Law, 1911 [165]
The Long Arm of Law and Order, 1916 [675]

Looking For Trouble, 1926 [1184]
The Loser's End, 1924 [1056]
Lost and Found, 1923 [989]
The Lost City, 1920 [845]
The Lost Ledge, 1915 [586]
Lost Mine, 1907 [19]
The Lost World, 1925 [1127]
A Lot of Bull, 1922 [929]
The Lotus Woman, 1916 [676]
Love and War in Mexico, 1913 [367]
Love Comes Along, 1930 [1423]
Love in Madrid, 1911 [166]
Love in Mexico, 1910 [93]
Love Life and Liberty, 1913 [366]
Love Mart, 1927 [1230]
The Love of Conchita, 1913 [365]
Love of Paquita, 1927 [1231]
Love of Sunya, 1927 [1233]
Love on the Rio Grande, 1925 [1129]
Love Parade, 1929 [1343]
Love Pirate, 1928 [1296]
Love Sacrifice, 1914 [466]
The Love Thief, 1916 [677]
'A Love Tragedy in Spain', 1908 [31]
Love Under Spanish Skies, 1909, [50]
Loves of Carmen, 1927 [1232]
Love's Redemption, 1921 [870]
Love's Savage Hate, 1915 [587]
Love's Wilderness, 1924 [1057]
The Lovely Senorita, 1914 [467]
A Lover's Oath, 1925 [1128]
Lovers?, 1927 [1234]
The Loyalty of Don Luis Verugo, 1911 [167]
Luces De Buenos Aires = Lights of Buenos Aires, 1931 [1522]
Luck of Roaring Camp, 1910 [94]
Lucky Boots, 1935 [1768]
The Lucky Horseshoe, 1925 [1130]
Lure of Gold, 1922 [930]

[M]

Madame Du Barry, 1934 [1683]
Madeira, Portugal, 1911 [168]

Mademoiselle Midnight, 1924 [1058]
Madero Murdered, 1913 [368]
Madre Querida = Beloved Mother, 1935 [1769]
The Maiden of the Pie-Faced Indians, 1911 [169]
The Maltese Falcon, 1931 [1523]
Mama, 1931 [1520]
The Man Above the Law, 1918 [798]
The Man From Argentina, 1915 [588]
The Man From Death Valley, 1931 [1524]
Man From God's Country, 1924 [1059]
The Man From Mexico, 1914 [468]
The Man From Mexico, 1918 [799]
Man From Monterey, 1933 [1618]
The Man From the West, 1914 [469]
The Man in the Sombrero, 1916 [678]
Man of Action, 1933 [1619]
Man of Courage, 1922 [931]
The Man Who Waited, 1923 [991]
The Man Who Was Afraid, 1917 [760]
The Man Without A Country, 1917 [761]
The Man Without A Country, 1925 [1131]
Man's Lust for Gold, 1912 [268]
Man's Man, 1918 [800]
A Man's Man, 1923 [990]
Mano In Mano = Hand In Hand, 1933 [1620]
Manresa, a Spanish Town, 1911 [170]
Many Moons, 1930, [1424]
Mare Nostrum, 1926 [1185]
March of Time, #9, 1935 [1770]
Margarita and the Mission Funds, 1913 [369]
Maria Rosa, 1916 [679]
Marido Y Mujer SV Bad Girl, 1932 [1576]
Marie Galante, 1934 [1684]
Marimba Land, 1920 [846]
The Marines Are Coming, 1935 [1771]
Mark of Zorro, 1920 [847]

The Marshal's Capture, 1913 [370]
Martin Garatuza, 1935 [1772]
Martinique, West Indies, 1917 [762]
The Martyrs of the Alamo, 1915 [589]
The Mask of Lopez, 1923 [992]
The Mask of Lopez, 1927 [1235]
The Masked Dancer, 1914 [470]
The Massacre of the Santa Fe Trail, 1912 [269]
The Master Key, 1915 [590]
Masters of Men, 1923 [993]
Mata Hari, 1932 [1577]
Matto Grosso, 1933 [1621]
A Media Noche aka Evidencia, 1930 [1425]
Melita's Ruse, 1912 [270]
Melita's Sacrifice, 1913 [371]
Melodia de Arrabal = Suburban Melody, 1933 [1622]
La Melodia Prohibida = Forbidden Paradise, 1933 [1623]
Men of Chance, 1932 [1578]
The Men She Married, 1916 [680]
Men Without Law, 1930 [1426]
Mercedes, 1935 [1773]
A Message To Gracia, 1916 [681]
Mexicana, 1929, [1344]
Mexicali Rose, 1929, [1345]
The Mexican (American), 1911 [171]
The Mexican (Lubin), 1911 [172]
The Mexican, 1914 [471]
Mexican As It Is Spoken, 1911 [173]
Mexican Bill, 1909 [51]
The Mexican Chickens, 1915 [591]
Mexican Conspiracy Out-Generaled, 1913 [372]
A Mexican Courtship, 1912 [271]
A Mexican Defeat, 1913 [373]
Mexican Domain, 1910 [95]
A Mexican Drama, 1909 [52]
Mexican Elopement, 1912 [272]
Mexican Filibusters, 1911 [174]
Mexican Fishing Scene, 1898 [3]

The Mexican Gambler, 1913 [374]
The Mexican Hatred, 1914 [472]
Mexican Idyll, 1935 [1774]
Mexican Insurrection, 1913 [375]
The Mexican Joan of Arc, 1911 [175]
A Mexican Legend, 1910 [96]
A Mexican Love Story, 1908 [32]
A Mexican Mine Fraud, 1914 [473]
A Mexican Mix-Up, 1912 [273]
The Mexican Rebellion, 1914 [474]
The Mexican Revolutionist, 1912 [274]
A Mexican Romance, 1911 [176]
A Mexican Romance, 1912 [275]
A Mexican Rose Garden, 1911 [177]
Mexican Rurales Charge, 1898 [4]
The Mexican Sleep Producer, 1913 [376]
Mexican Sniper's Revenge, 1914 [475]
The Mexican Spy, 1913 [377]
A Mexican Spy in America, 1914 [476]
Mexican Sweethearts, 1909 [56]
A Mexican Tragedy, 1913 [378]
The Mexican Tumblers, 1910 [100]
A Mexican Warrior, 1914 [477]
Mexican's Crime, 1909 [53]
The Mexican's Faith, 1911 [97]
A Mexican's Gratitude, 1909 [54]
The Mexican's Gratitude, 1914 [478]
The Mexican's Jealousy, 1910 [98]
The Mexican's Last Raid, 1914 [479]
The Mexican's Revenge, 1909 [55]
A Mexican's Ward, 1910 [99]
Mexico, 1914 [480]
Mexico Street Scene, 1898 [5]
Mexico To-Day, 1918 [801]
Mexico Today, 1933 [1624]
Midnight, 1922 [932]
The Midshipman, 1925 [1132]
Mike and Jake in Mexico, 1913 [379]

The Millionaire, 1927 [1236]
The Millionaire Cowboy, 1924 [1060]
The Mill by Zuyder Zee, 1915 [592]
The Miner's Peril, 1914 [481]
The Mission Father, 1911 [178]
The Mission in the Desert, 1911 [179]
Mi Ultimo Amor = His Last Love, 1932 [1579]
Mixed Blood, 1916 [682]
Mixing in Mexico, 1925 [1133]
Mixing in Mexico, 1935 [1775]
M'Liss, 1918 [802]
The Mojave Kid, 1927 [1237]
The Moment of Victory, 1918 [803]
The Money Maniac, 1921 [871]
Money to Burn, 1926 [1186]
Monsieur Le Fox SV Men of the North, 1930 [1427]
Moonlight And Romance, 1931 [1525]
The Moorish Bride, 1912 [276]
Morals of Marcus, 1935 [1776]
Moran of the Lady Letty, 1922 [933]
Moran of the Marines, 1928 [1297]
Motoring Thru Spain, 1929 [1346]
Mr Barnes of New York, 1922 [924]
Mr. Billings Spends His Dime, 1923 [994]
Mr. Broadway, 1933 [1625]
Los Muertos Hablan = The Dead Speak 1935 [1777]
La Mujer X SV Madam X, 1931 [1526]
Murder In the Fleet, 1935 [1778]
Murder In Trinidad, 1934 [1685]
Musical Drill, 1904 [12]
Mutiny On the Bounty, 1935 [1779]
My American Wife, 1922 [935]
My Son, 1925 [1134]
Mysteries of Yucatan, 1923 [995]
Mysterious Island, 1929 [1347]
"The Mystery of the Maine", 1911 [180]
Mystery Ranch aka The Killer, 1932 [1580]

Mystery Woman, 1935 [1780]

[N]

Nada Mas Que Una Mujer = Only A Woman, 1934 [1686]
Native Life in the Philippines, 1914 [482]
Neath The Arizona Skies, 1934 [1687]
Nedra, 1915 [593]
Ne'er Do Well, 1915 [594]
The Ne'er-Do-Well, 1923 [996]
Nell of the Pampas, 1912 [277]
Neptune's Daughter, 1914 [483]
Never Too Late To Mend, 1911 [181]
The New Ranch Foreman, 1912 [278]
The News Parade, 1929 [1298]
The Next Corner, 1924 [1061]
Night Cry, 1926 [1187]
Night Flight, 1933 [1626]
The Night Hawk, 1924 [1062]
A Night in Old Spain, 1915 [595]
The Night is Young, 1935 [1781]
The Night of Love, 1927 [1238]
Night Rider, 1932 [1581]
The Night Ship, 1925 [1135]
99 Wounds, 1931 [1527]
Nipped, 1914 [484]
La Noche Del Pecado = The Night of Sin, 1933 [1627]
Noches De Buneos Aires = Buenos Aires Nights, 1935 [1782]
No Dejes La Puerta Abierta SV Pleasure Cruise, 1933 [1628]
No Mataras = Thou Shall Not Kill, 1935 [1783]
No Other Woman, 1928 [1299]
North of the Rio Grande, 1922 [936]
North of 36, 1924 [1063]
The Nut Cracker, 1926 [1188]
Nutty Delivers the Message to Garcia, 1914 [485]

[O]

The Oath of Conchita, 1913 [380]
The Obstinate Sheriff, 1915 [596]
The Octoroon, 1909 [57]
Odds Against Her, 1919 [831]
Oklahoma Cyclone, 1930 [1428]
Old California, 1914 [486]
The Old Fool, 1923 [997]
Old San Francisco, 1927 [1239]
Old Spain, 1922 [937]
Old Spanish Customers, 1926 [1189]
On El Monte Ranch, 1912 [279]
On the Border, 1909 [58]
On the Border, 1913 [381]
On the Border, 1915 [597]
On the Border, 1930 [1430]
On the Brink of War, 1916 [683]
On the Cactus Trail, 1912 [280]
On the High Card, 1921 [872]
On the Mexican Border, 1910 [101]
One Mad Kiss, 1930 [1429]
One Million in Jewels, 1923 [998]
One Week of Love, 1922 [938]
Only Road, 1918 [804]
The Opening of the Panama Canal, 1914 [487]
Oro y Plata = Gold and Silver, 1934 [1688]
Oriente y Occidente SV East Is West, 1930 [1431]
Our Banana Supply, 1909 [59]
Outlaw Justice, 1933 [1629]
The Outlaw's Revenge, 1915 [598]
The Outlaw's Sacrifice, 1912 [281]
The Outside Woman, 1921 [873]

[P]

The Padre's Strategy, 1913 [382]
The Pagan, 1929 [1348]
Pagan Lady, 1931 [1528]
The Palace of Pleasure, 1926 [1190]
Palooka, 1934 [1689]
Pals First, 1926 [1191]
Pals of the Prairie, 1929 [1349]
Panama, 1931 [1529]
Panama Canal, 1907 [20]
The Panama Canal, 1912 [282]
The Panama Canal, 1913 [383]
Panama Canal, 1915 [599]

The Panama Canal in 1911 1911 [182]
The Panama Canal Today, 1913 [384]
Panama Flo, 1932 [1582]
Panama, The Earth Divided, The World Divided, 1912 [283]
Panama Hat Industry, 1913 [385]
Panama-Pacific Exposition, 1914 [488]
Papinta, 1910 [102]
Papita's Destiny, 1913 [386]
Paradise Canyon, 1935 [1784]
Paramount Pictorial #6, 1933 [1630]
El Pasado Acusa SV Good Bad Girl, 1931 [1530]
The Passion Flower, 1921 [874]
Passion Flower, 1930 [1432]
Passion's Pathway, 1924 [1064]
Pastime in Chili, 1911 [183]
PATHE EXCHANGE, INC: 1916
  #30 Somewhere in Mexico [684]
  #30 Mexico at a Glance [685]
  #30 Guantanamo Bay, Cuba [686]
  #31 Mexican Crisis [687]
  #31 Columbus, New Mexico [688]
  #31 San Diego, California, [689]
  #31 Columbus, New Mexico, [690]
  #32 El Paso, Texas, [691]
  #41 Somewhere in Mexico, [692]
  #41 Marathon, Texas [693]
  #55 El Paso, Texas [694]
  #55 Galveston, Texas [695]
  #56 El Paso, Texas, [696]
  #57 Fort Sam Houston, [697]
  #57 El Paso, Texas, [698]
PATHE NEWS REELS, 1912
  #13 El Paso, Texas [284]
  #22 Del Rio, Texas [285]
PATHE NEWS REELS, 1914
  #6 Neuevo Laredo [489]
  #7 Colon Panama [490]
  #24 Mexico City [491]
  #27 Mexico City [492]
  #28 Mexico City [493]
  #32 In the Gulf of Mexico [494]
  #32 Washington D.C. (John Lind) [495]
  #33 Mexico City [496]
  #33 Vera Cruz [497]
  #35 Havana, Cuba [498]
  #35 Chihuahua, Mexico [499]
PATHE NEWS REELS, 1915
  #66 Juarez, Mexico [600]
PATHE REVIEW, 1922
  #185 Pyrenees, Spain [939]
PATHE REVIEW, #15 1927 [1240]
PATHE TOPICS, #4 (Haiti) [1785]
PATHE'S WEEKLY, 1911
  #47 Rio, Brazil [184]
  #51 Lisbon, Portugal [185]
PATHE'S WEEKLY, 1913
  #31 Mexico City [387]
  #50 San Juan, Mexico [388]
  #76 Hermosillo, Mexico [389]
Paths To Paradise, 1925 [1136]
Patria, 1916 [699]
The Patriot, 1916 [700]
Pawns of Fate, 1915 [601]
Payasadas de la Vida = Tricks of Life, 1935 [1786]
The Pearl of the Antilles, 1915 [602]
Pearl of the Army, 1917 (Serial) International Diplomacy [763]
Pecados De Amor = Sins of Love, 1934 [1690]
Pedro's Revenge, 1913 [390]
Pedro's Treachery, 1913 [391]
Peg of the Pirates, 1918 [805]
The Penalty of Jealousy, 1913 [392]
The Penitents, 1915 [603]
The Penniless Prince, 1911 [186]
Pepita's Escapades, 1912 [286]
Percy, 1925 [1137]
A Perfect Gentleman, 1928 [1300]
Perilous Leap, 1917 [764]
Perils of the Secret Service, 1917 (Serial) Man In the Trunk [765]
Peru, 1918 [806]
Peter the Pirate, 1927 [1241]
The Phantom Buster, 1927 [1242]
The Phantom Flyer, 1928 [1301]
The Phantom of Crestwood, 1932 [1583]
The Phantom of the West, 1930 [1433]

Picturesque Havana, 1916 [701]
Picturesque Waterfalls of Northern Spain, 1911 [187]
Piernas de Seda SV Silk Legs, 1935 [1787]
The Pilgrim, 1923 [999]
The Planter, 1917 [766]
Playthings of Destiny, 1921 [875]
The Poisoned Flume, 1911 [188]
The Pony Express, 1907 [21]
The Pony Express, [1138]
Portugal Today, 1927 [1243]
The Portuguese Centaurs, 1911 [189]
Portuguese Joe, 1911 [190]
Portuguese Joe, 1912 [287]
The Power of the Angelus, 1914 [500]
Powdersmoke Range, 1935 [1788]
Prairie Pirate, 1925 [1139]
The Prayers of Manuelo, 1912 [288]
El Precio De Un Beso = The Price of a Kiss, 1930 [1434]
President Taft's Tour of the Panama Canal, 1913 [393]
El Presido SV The Big House 1930 [1435]
The Pretty Sister of Jose, 1915 [604]
Pride of Jennico, 1914 [501]
Pride of Palomar, 1922 [940]
Prim, 1931 [1531]
Primavera En Ontono = Springtime and Autumn, 1932 [1584]
El Principe Gondolero = The Gondolier Prince, 1930 [1436]
The Prisoner, 1923 [1000]
A Prisoner of Cabanas, 1913 [394]
A Prisoner of Mexico, 1911 [191]
The Prisoner of Zenda, 1922 [941]
El Prisionero 13 = Prisoner No. 13, 1934 [1691]
The Private Life of Don Juan, 1934 [1692]
El Proceso De Mary Dugan SV The Trial of Mary Dugan, 1930 [1437]
Profanacion, 1934 [1693]

Pro Patria, 1915 [605]
A Proposal from the Spanish Don, 1913 [395]
Proud Flesh, 1925 [1140]
Prowlers of the Sea, 1928 [1302]
Public Hero No. 1, 1935 [1789]
Pueblo Indians, Albuquerque, N.M. 1912 [289]
A Pueblo Legend, 1916 [702]
Pueblo Terror, 1931 [1532]
Pueblos of Southwestern United States, 1917 [767]
El Pulpo Humano = The Human Octopus, 1935 [1790]
La Pura Verdad SV Nothing But The Truth, 1932 [1585]
Pure Grit, 1924 [1065]
Pursuit, 1935 [1791]

[Q]

Quando El Amor Rie = When Love Laughs, 1933 [1631]
The Quarter Breed, 1916 [704]
Los Que Danzan SV Those Who Dance, 1931 [1533]
Queen Elizabeth, 1912 [290]
Quemado, 1924 [1066]
Quicker'n Lightnin', 1925 [1141]
The Quicksands, 1914 [502]
Quicksands, 1923 [1001]
Quien Mato A Eva = Who Killed Eva, 1934 [1694]
The Quitter, 1916 [704]

[R]

Race Prejudice, 1908 [33]
Raiders of the Mexican Border, 1912 [291]
Rainbow Ranger, 1924 [1067]
Ramona, 1910 [103]
Ramona, 1916 [705]
Ramona, 1928 [1928]
Ramona's Father, 1911 [192]
The Ranch Man's Daughter, 1911 [193]
The Ranchman's Vengeance, 1911 [194]
Rancho of the Don, 1930 [1438]
The Ranch Woman, 1912 [292]
The Ranger, 1919 [832]
The Rangers Reward, 1912 [293]
El Rayo, 1935 [1792]
Reckless Sex, 1925 [1142]
Recoil, 1924 [1068]

The Red Dance, 1928 [1304]
The Red Girl, 1908 [34]
Red Hot Romance, 1922 [942]
The Red Lily, 1924 [1069]
Red Majesty, 1929 [1350]
The Red Mark, 1928 [1305]
Refuge, 1915 [606]
Rejuvenated Mexico, 1922 [943]
El Relicario = The Reliquary, 1935 [1793]
Remember The Alamo, 1935 [1794]
The Renegade Brother, 1911 [195]
The Renegades Vengeance, 1914 [503]
Resurrection, 1927 [1244]
Resurrection, 1931 [1534]
Resurreccion SV Resurrection, 1931 [1535]
The Return, 1914 [504]
Revelation, 1918 [807]
Revenge, 1928 [1306]
The Revenue Officer's Deputy, 1914 [505]
Revolution In Mexico, 1912 [294]
The Revolutionist, 1912 [295]
Rex Beach On the Spanish Main, 1917 [768]
El Rey Do Los Gitanos = The King of the Gypsies, 1933 [1632]
Riacuelo, [River of Life], 1934 [1695]
Rider of the West, 1932 [1586]
Riders of the Cactus, 1931 [1536]
Riders of the Range, 1923 [1002]
Riders of the Rio Grande, 1929 [1351]
Riding Speed, 1934 [1696]
Ridn' Law, 1930 [1439]
The Right to Happiness, 1915 [607]
Rimrock Jones, 1918 [808]
The Ring of a Spanish Grandee, 1912 [296]
Rio Grande, 1920 [848]
Rio Rita, 1929 [1352]
Rio the Magnificent, 1933 [1633]
River of Romance, 1929 [1353]
The Road Agents, 1909 [60]
The Road To Romnce, 1927 [1245]
Roarin Broncs, 1927 [1246]
Rogue of the Rio Grande, 1930 [1440]
Rogues and Romance, 1921 [876]
Rolling Down to Rio, 1922 [944]
A Romance in Old Madrid, 1909 [61]
Romance in Old Mexico, 1909 [62]
Romance in the Andes, 1909 [63]
A Romance of Mexico, 1915 [608]
A Romance of Old California, 1915 [609]
A Romance of the Border, 1912 [297]
A Romance of the Rio Grande, 1911 [196]
Romance of the Rio Grande, 1929 [1354]
Romance of the West, 1930 [1441]
Romance Ranch, 1924 [1070]
Romance Tropical, 1934 [1697]
Rosa De Francia, 1935 [1795]
The Rose of California, 1912 [298]
The Rose of Old St. Augustine, 1911 [197]
The Rose of San Juan, 1913 [396]
Rose of the Golden West, 1927 [1247]
Rose of the Philippines, 1910 [104]
Rose of the Ranch, 1910 [105]
Rose of the Rancho, 1914 [506]
Rosita, 1923 [1003]
Rough Diamond, 1921 [877]
The Rough Neck, 1916 [706]
The Rough Riders, 1927 [1248]
Rough Romance, 1930 [1442]
The Royal American 1927 [1249]
The Rubber Industry of the Amazon, 1911 [198]
Rubber Tires, 1927 [1250]
Rumba, 1935 [1796]
Rumba Orchestra, 1935 [1797]
The Rum Runners, 1923 [1004]

[S]

The Sacred Bracelet, 1915 [610]
Saddle Hawk, 1925 [1143]
Sagrario, 1934 [1698]
Sailors Beware, 1927 [1251]
The Sainted Devil, 1924 [1071]
Salaga De La Cocina SV Honey, 1931 [1537]
La Sangre Nanda = The Call of the Blood, 1934 [1699]
Santa, 1932 [1587]
Sante Fe Trail, 1930 [1443]
Saragossa, 1913 [397]
Savage Gold, 1933 [1634]
Saved by the Flag, 1911 [199]
Scaramouche, 1923 [1005]
Scarlet Days, 1919 [833]
The Scarlet Honeymoon, 1925 [1144]
Scarlet West, 1925 [1145]
Scenes in Manila, 1913 [398]
The Sea Bat, 1930 [1445]
The Sea Hawk, 1924 [1072]
Sea Horse, 1926 [1192]
Sea Tiger, 1927 [1252]
The Secret of Lost River, 1915 [611]
The Secret of Padre Antonio, 1913 [399]
The Secret of the Dead, 1915 [612]
The Secret of the Palm, 1911 [200]
The Secret Treasure, 1913 [400]
The Secret Treaty, 1914 [507]
Secrets, 1933 [1635]
El Secreto Del Doctor SV The Doctor's Secret, 1930 [1445]
Se Ha Fugado Un Preso = A Prisoner Has Escaped, 1935 [1798]
SELIG-TRIBUNE: 1916
 #27 Saltillo, Mexico [707]
 #27 Columbus, New Mexico [708]
 #28 Near Guerrero, Mexico [709]
Senor Americano, 1929 [1355]
Senor Daredevil, 1926 [1193]
Senora Casada Necesita Marido = A Married Woman Needs A Husband, 1934 [1700]
The Senorita, 1909 [64]
Senorita, 1927 [1253]
The Senorita's Butterfly, 1912 [299]
The Senorita's Conquest, 1911 [201]
The Senorita's Remorse, 1912 [300]
The Senorita's Sacrifice, 1911 [202]
The Senor's Silver Buckle, 1915 [613]
Sensation Hunters, 1933 [1636]
Serenade, 1921 [878]
La Sevillana SV Call of the Flesh, aka Sevilla De Mis Amores, 1930 [1446]
Shady Lady, 1929 [1356]
Shame, 1918 [809]
Shaved in Mexico, 1915 [614]
The She Devil, 1918 [810]
She's A Sheik, 1927 [1254]
The Sheriff, 1918 [811]
The Sheriff's Blunder, 1916 [710]
The Sheriff's Decision, 1911 [203]
The Sheriff's Punishment, 1911 [204]
The Shooting of Dan McGrew, 1924 [1073]
Shorty Lays A Jungle Ghost, 1917 [769]
Shorty's Trip to Mexico, 1914 [508]
The Showdown, 1928 [1307]
The Show of Shows, 1929 [1357]
Si El Emperador Lo Supiera SV His Glorous Night, 1930 [1447]
Si, Si, Senor, 1930 [1448]
The Silent Command, 1923 [1006]
The Silver Lining [879]
Silver Spurs, 1922 [945]
The Singing Fool, 1929 [1358]
Siren of Seville, 1924 [1074]
Siren of the Tropics, 1928 [1308]
The Sisal Industry in the Bahamas, 1910 [106]
A Sister of Six, 1916 [711]
A Sister to Carmen, 1913 [401]
Sky High, 1922 [946]
The Sky Ranger 1928 [1309]
The Slave Market, 1917 [770]
Slightly Used, 1927 [1255]
A Small Town Idol, 1921 [880]

Small Trades in Havana, 1912 [301]
The Smuggler's Daughter, 1912 [302]
Snatched from a Burning Death, 1915 [615]
Sobre Las Olas = Over the Waves, 1934 [1701]
Soldier of Fortune, 1914 [509]
Soldier of Fortune, 1919 [834]
Soldiers and Women, 1930 [1449]
Soldiers of the Storm, 1933 [1637]
La Sombra de Pancho Villa = The Shadow of Pancho Villa, 1934 [1702]
Sombras De Gloria = Blaze of Glory 1930 [1450]
Sombras Del Ciro SV Half Way To Heaven, 1931 [1538]
Something's Rotten in Havana, 1913 [402]
Somewhere In Grenada, 1916 [712]
Somewhere In Mexico, 1916 [713]
Somewhere In Sonora, 1927 [1256]
Somewhere In Sonora, 1933 [1638]
The Son-Daughter, 1933 [1639]
Son of His Father, 1925 [1146]
Son of India, 1931 [1539]
Song of the Caballero, 1930 [1451]
Song of the West, 1930 [1452]
Soul of Mexico, 1932 [1588]
South American Indians, 1909 [65]
South of the Equator, 1924 [1075]
South of Panama, 1928 [1310]
South of Rio Grande, 1932 [1589]
South of Sante Fe, 1932 [1590]
South Sea Love, 1924 [1076]
South Seas, 1930 [1453]
The Spaniard, 1925 [1147]
Spanish Army, 1909 [66]
A Spanish Cavalier, 1912 [303]
Spanish Costumes and Dances, 1916 [715]
The Spanish Dancer, 1923 [1007]
A Spanish Dilemma, 1912 [304]
Spanish Frontier, 1910 [107]

The Spanish Girl (Phoenix Film), 1909 [67]
The Spanish Girl (Essanay), 1909 [68]
The Spanish Gypsy, 1911 [205]
The Spanish Jade, 1915 [616]
The Spanish Jade, 1922 [947]
A Spanish Love Song, 1911 [206]
Spanish Loyalty, 1910 [108]
Spanish Marriage, 1909 [69]
The Spanish Omelet, 1914 [510]
The Spanish Parrot-Girl, 1913 [403]
The Spanish Revolt of 1836, 1912 [305]
A Spanish Romance, 1908 [35]
A Species of Mexican Man, 1915 [617]
The Spider and the Rose, 1923 [1008]
The Spirit of the Flag, 1913 [404]
The Spitfire of Seville, 1919 [835]
The Sponge Industry in Cuba, 1913 [405]
Spook Ranch, 1925 [1148]
The Squall, 1929 [1359]
Squaw Man, 1931 [1541]
The Stage Robbers of San Juan, 1911 [207]
The Stampede, 1911 [208]
Stand and Deliver, 1928 [1311]
Stark Mad, 1929 [1360]
Stars and Stripes in Mexico, 1916 [715]
Stock Farming in South America, 1915 [618]
Stolen Moments, 1921 [881]
A Stop-Off in New Mexico, 1915 [619]
The Storm, 1930 [1454]
Lo Stormo Atlantico, 1931 [1540]
Storm Over The Andes, 1935 [1799]
Stormy Seas, 1923 [1009]
The Story of the Mexican Border, 1913 [406]
Strangers May Kiss, 1931 [1542]
Strictly Dynamite, 1934 [1703]
The Stronger Will, 1928 [1312]
The Student Prince, 1927 [1257]

The Struggle for Life, 1911 [209]
The Substitute, 1911 [210]
Such A Little Pirate, 1918 [812]
Sugar Making in Cuba, 1913 [407]
Sunday Sports in Mexico, 1935, [1800]
Sundown, 1924 [1077]
A Sun Kissed Isle, 1918 [813]
Sunny Spain, 1923 [1010]
Su Noche De Bodas SV Her Wedding Night, 1931 [1543]
Susana Tiene Un Secreto = Susana Has A Secret, 1935 [1801]
Su Ultima Cancion = His Last Song, 1934 [1704]
Su Ultima Noche SR The Gay Deceiver, 1931 [1544]
Suzanna, 1923 [1011]
Sword of Valor, 1924 [1078]

[T]

The Taint of Fear, 1916 [716]
A Tale of Texas, 1909 [70]
THE TAMPICO INCIDENT - PATHE NEWS REELS, 1914
  Tampico Incident, 4.23 [511]
  Tampico Incident, 5.27 [512]
  Tampico Incident, 5.20 [513]
Tangled Tangoist, 1914 [514]
Tango Bar, 1935 [1802]
Tango Cavalier, 1923 [1012]
The Tango Craze, 1914 [515]
El Tango En Broadway, 1934 [1705]
The Tango Flat, 1914 [516]
The Tango in Tuckerville, 1914 [520]
A Tango Spree, 1914 [517]
A Tango Tangle, 1913 [408]
A Tango Tragedy, 1914 [518]
Tango Troubles, 1914 [519]
The Tarantula, 1913 [409]
The Tarantula, 1916 [717]
Tell It To the Marines, 1926 [1194]
The Temptress, 1926 [1195]
Te Quiero Con Locura = I'm Crazy About You, 1935 [1803]
The Terms of the Will, 1911 [211]
The Terrible One, 1915 [620]

El Terrible Torreador, 1930 [1455]
A Terror of the Plains, 1910 [109]
The Test of Love, 1911 [212]
The Test of Manhood, 1914 [521]
The Texan, 1930 [1456]
The Texas Ranger, 1931 [1545]
Tex Takes a Holiday, 1932 [1591]
That Devil Quemado, 1925 [1149]
Thieves Gold, 1918 [814]
Those Who Dare, 1925 [1151]
Thorns and Orange Blossoms, 1922 [948]
The Thread of Destiny, 1910 [110]
3 Bad Men, 1926 [1196]
Three Miles Out, 1924 [1079]
Throwing the Bull, 1933 [1641]
Thunder Island, 1921 [882]
Thunder Over Mexico, 1933 [1640]
Thundering Hoofs, 1924 [1080]
A Thwarted Vengeance, 1911 [213]
Thy Name is Woman, 1924 [1081]
Tiburon = Shark, 1934 [1706]
Tides That Meet, 1915 [621]
Tierra, Amor y Dolor = Land, Love and Suffering, 1935 [1804]
Tiger Love, 1924 [1082]
Tiger Rose, 1930 [1457]
Tiger Shark, 1932 [1592]
El Tigre de Yautepec = The Tiger of Yautepec, 1934 [1707]
The Tigress, 1927 [1258]
Till We Meet Again, 1922 [949]
Tin Gods, 1926 [1197]
Tis the Bull, 1922 [950]
The Tobacco Culture in Cuba, 1913 [410]
Toda Una Vida SV Sarah and Son, 1930 [1458]
The Toll of Fear, 1913 [411]
Tommy Becomes a Toreador, 1912 [306]
Tony the Greaser, 1911 [214]
Tony the Greaser, 1914 [522]
Too Many Kisses, 1925 [1151]
The Toreador's Oath, 1914 [523]
Toreador's Romance, 1914 [524]

The Torrent aka Ibanez's Torrent, 1926 [1198]
To the Brave Belong the Fair, 1913 [412]
Tracked, 1911 [215]
Trader Horn, 1931 [1548]
A Tragedy in Panama, 1915 [622]
The Tragic Wedding, 1911 [216]

The Trail of Gold, 1912 [307]
Trail of the Golden West, 1931 [1546]
Trail of '98, 1928 [1313]
The Trail of the Serpent, 1915 [623]
Train Hour in Durango Mexico, 1898 [6]
Training Fighting Cocks in Cuba, 1912 [308]
A Traitor to his Country, 1914 [525]
Transgression, 1931 [1547]
The Trap, 1914 [526]
Trapped in Tiajuana, 1932 [1592a]
La Traviesa Molinera aka It Happened in Spain, 1934 [1708]
A Treacherous Shot, 1912 [309]
Tres Amores = Three Loves, 1934 [1709]
Los Tres Berretines = The Three Amateurs, 1935 [1805]
Tribu, 1935 [1806]
Trifling Women, 1922 [951]
Triple Action, 1925 [1152]
A Trip Through Mexico, 1911 [217]
A Trip to the Argentine, 1915 [624]
Tropical Love, 1921 [883]
The Troubadour, 1915 [625]
The Troubadour of the Rancho, 1913 [413]
Trumpet Blows, 1934 [1710]
Tu Hijo = Thy Son, 1934 [1711]
12-10, 1919 [836]
The Two Brothers, 1913 [414]
Two Daughters of Havana, 1911 [218]
Two Gun Caballero, 1931 [1549]
Two Gun Man, 1931 [1550]
Two Lovers, 1928 [1314]
The Two Sides, 1911 [219]
Typical Mexican Aspect, 1919 [837]

[U]

El Ultimo De Los Vargas SV Last of the Duanes, 1930 [1459]
El Ultimo Varon Sobre La Tier SV It's Great To Be Alive, 1933 [1642]

Un Caballero De Franc aka Un Hombre De Franc SV Evening Clothes, 1931 [1551]
Un Hombre De Suerte, 1930 [1461]
Una Semana De Felicidad = One Week of Happiness, 1935 [1807]
Una Vida Por Otra = One Life For Another, 1933 [1643]
Una Viuda Romantica = The Romantic Widow, 1933 [1644]
Uncle Sam In Mexico, 1914 [527]
Uncle Sam Watching the Mexican Border, 1911 [220]
Uncle Sam's Boys on the Mexican Border, 1912 [310]
Uncle Sam's Defenders, 1916 [718]
Uncle Sam's Tribute to the Heros of the Maine, 1912 [311]
Unconquered Bandit, 1935 [1808]
The Unconquered Woman, 1922 [952]
Under A Texas Moon, 1930 [1460]
Under Fire in Mexico, 1914 [528]
Under Mexican Skies, 1912 [312]
Under the Black Flag, 1913 [415]
Under the Pampas Moon, 1935 [1809]
Under the Tropical Sun, 1911 [221]
Under the Yoke, 1918 [815]
The Unexpected, 1916 [719]
Untamed, 1918 [816]
Untamed, 1929 [1361]
Up Below The Equator, 1933 [1645]
Up San Juan Hill, 1909 [71]
Uriel Acosta, 1914 [529]

U.S. Marines Under Fire in Haiti, 1916 [720]

[V]

A Vacation in Havana, 1910 [111]
Valencia, 1926 [1199]
El Valiente SV The Valiant, 1930 [1462]
The Valley of Hunted Men, 1928 [1315]
Vampire, 1916, [721]
The Vanishing American, 1925 [1153]
The Vaquero's Vow, 1908 [36]
Vengeance is Mine, 1913 [416]
The Vengeance of Najerra, 1914 [530]
The Vengeance of the Vaquero, 1914 [531]
La Via De Oro = The Gold Route, 1932 [1593]
Vidas Rotas = Broken Lives, 1935 [1810]
Views of Peru and Bolivia, 1920 [849]
Villa-Dead Or Alive, 1916 [722]
Villa of the Movies, 1917 [771]
La Violetera = The Flower Girl, 1935 [1811]
The Violin Maker, 1915 [626]
The Virgin, 1924 [1083]
Virgin Lips, 1928 [1316]
Virtuous Liars, 1924 [1084]
Viva Villa! 1934 [1712]
Volcano, 1926 [1200]
La Voluntad Del Muerto SV The Cat Creeps, 1930 [1463]
Voodoo, 1933 [1646]
The Vow of Ysobel, 1912 [313]
El Vuelo De La Muerte = Death Flight, 1935 [1812]

[W]

Wand Dance, Pueblo Indians, 1898 [2]
The War Extra, 1914 [532]
War in Mexico, 1914 [533]
War-Ridden Mexico, 1916 [723]
War with Huerta, 1914 [534]
A Wartime Wooing, 1911 [222]
Was It Bigamy? 1925 [1154]
Watchful Waiting, 1916 [724]

The Wayfarer, 1912 [314]
Web of the Law, 1923 [1013]
The Wedding Guest, 1916 [725]
Well of Fortaleza, 1931 [1552]
A Western Child's Heroism, 1912 [315]
Western Code, 1933 [1647]
A Western Episode, 1912 [316]
A Western Heroine, 1911 [223]
Western Justice, 1910 [112]
Western Wallop, 1924 [1085]
West Indies Cruise, 1935 [1813]
West of the Pecos, 1934 [1713]
West of the Rio Grande, 1921 [884]
West of the Rockies, 1929 [1362]
Wet Gold, 1921 [885]
What Great Bear Learned, 1910 [113]
What Happened to Rosa? 1921 [886]
What Price Glory, 1926 [1201]
What Women Did For Me, 1927 [1259]
When A Man Rides Alone, 1918 [817]
When California Was Won, 1911 [224]
When California Was Young, 1912 [317]
When Danger Smiles, 1922 [953]
When Dawn Came, 1921 [887]
When Hearts are Trumps, 1912 [318]
When Luck Changes, 1913 [417]
Where East is East, 1929 [1363]
Whip Woman, 1928 [1317]
White Gold, 1927 [1260]
White Mice, 1926 [1202]
White Shadow, 1928 [1318]
The White Vaquero, 1913 [418]
White Zombie, 1932 [1594]
The Whole Town's Talking, 1926 [1203]
Why Worry, 1923 [1014]
A Wife's Romance, 1923 [1015]
The Winding Trail, 1918 [818]
Winds of the Pampas, 1927 [1261]
Wings of Adventure, 1930 [1464]
The Winner, 1914 [535]
Winners of the West, 1921 [888]

Winter Bathing in the West Indies, 1910 [114]
A Wise Fool, 1921 [889]
The Witching Eye, 1929 [1364]
With Car and Camera Around the World, 1929 [1365]
With Davy Crockett at the Fall of the Alamo, 1922 [954]
With Taft in Panama, 1909 [72]
With This Ring, 1925 [1156]
With Wings Outspread, 1922 [955]
Within an Inch of His Life, 1914 [536]
Within the Cup, 1918 [819]
Without Mercy, 1925 [1155]
Wolf Song, 1929 [1366]
Wolf's Trail, 1927 [1262]
Wolves of the Border, 1918 [820]
Woman and the Law, 1918 [821]
The Woman God Forgot, 1917 [772]
Woman Hungry, 1931 [1553]
The Woman in Chains, 1923 [1016]
The Woman in the Box, 1915 [627]
Woman of all Nations, 1931 [1554]
Woman Who Fooled Herself, 1922 [956]
A Woman's Secret, 1924 [1086]
Women and Gold, 1925 [1157]
Wonder Bar, 1934 [1714]
The Wonderful Adventure, 1915 [628]
Wonderland of Mexico, 1935 [1814]
Wonders of the Sea, 1922 [957]
Wonders of the Wild, 1925 [1158]
Wu-Li Chang SR Mr. Wu, 1930 [1465]

[Y]

Yankee Consul, 1924 [1087]
Yankee Don, 1931 [1555]
Yankee Doodle Jr., 1922 [958]
The Yankee Girl, 1915 [629]
A Yankee in Mexico, 1913 [419]
Yankee Madness, 1924 [1088]
A Yankee Man O'Warsman Fights for Love, 1908 [37]
Yankee Senor, 1926 [1204]
Yankee Speed, 1924 [1089]

The Yaqui, 1916 [726]
The Yaqui Cur, 1913 [420]
The Yaqui Cur, 1916 [727]
The Yaqui Girl, 1910 [115]
The Yellow Jacket Mine, 1909 [73]
Yellow Men and Gold, 1922 [959]
Yo ... Tu ... Y ... Ella = Thou ... And ...She, 1933 [1648]
You Never Know, 1922 [960]
Young Wild West Cornered by Apaches, 1912 [319]
Young Wild West on the Border, 1912 [320]

[Z]

Zampa, 1930 [1466]
Zoo Arrivals From South America, 1916, [728]

Actors and Actresses Index

[A]

Acosta, Enrique: 1371, 1401, 1434, 1488, 1505, 1655, 1709.
Adelantad, Fernado: 1740.
Aguglia, Mimi: 1576, 1579, 1584, 1642, 1700, 1709.
Alba, Maria: 1388, 1391, 1403, 1409, 1447, 1472, 1479, 1518, 1533, 1544, 1713.
Alberni, Luis: 1506, 1571, 1601, 1654.
Alcaniz, Luana: 1393, 1395, 1400, 1416, 1419, 1435, 1459, 1486, 1519, 1530, 1565, 1584, 1686, 1731, 1763.
Alcantara, Pepe: 1503.
Alcazaba, Jose: 1793.
Algara, Garbriel: 1551.
Aliaga, Nieves: 1793.
Alonso, Chito: 1676.
Alonso, Luis: See, Gilbert Roland.
Alvarado, Don: 1187, 1220, 1233, 1299, 1321, 1373, 1401, 1576, 1664, 1738, 1758, 1795.
Alvarez, Rubio Pablo: 1533.
Ament, Rudolph: 1736.
Amerise, Franciso: 1368.
Anderson, G. M.: 302.
Angel, Amparo Miguel: 1537.
Angeles, Marita: 1551.
Arbo, Manuel: 1396, 1436, 1476, 1479, 1480, 1482, 1503, 1526, 1565.
Arbuckle, "Fatty": 811, 856.
Arevalo, Antonia: 1512, 1543.
La Argentina, (Imperio Argentina): 1404, 1484, 1521, 1543, 1622.
Areyalo, Antonia: 1538.
Arguelles, Jose: 1566, 1622.
Aristi Eulate, Juan: 1374, 1448.
Armetta, Hentry: 1526, 1542.
Armida: 1335, 1380, 1430, 1456, 1460, 1464, 1771.
Arozamena, Eduardo: 1476, 1488, 1535.
Arozamena, Amparo: 1792.

Astor, Mary: 1052, 1418, 1578.
Atwill, Lionel: 1738.
Aubert, Carmelita: 1773.
Ault, Marie: 1295.
Ayres, Lew: 1682.

[B]

Ballesteros, Richard: 1427.
Ballesteros, Rosita: 1446.
Banky, Vilma: 1238, 1314.
Bara, Theda: 553, 810, 815.
Barbe, Carlos: 1403.
Barcena, Catalina: 1520, 1584, 1601, 1644, 1648, 1700, 1763.
Barreiro, Luis, G.: 1620.
Barrie, Moana: 1799.
Barrymore, John: 468, 799, 1173, 1335.
Barrymore, Lionel: 635, 1096, 1401, 1601.
Barthelmess, Richard: 965, 1418.
Basquette, Lina: 1502.
Baxter, Warner: 1146, 1338, 1354, 1477, 1589.
Beach, Rex: 768, 789, 996, 1068.
Beery, Noah: 1008, 1100, 1126, 1147, 1283, 1340, 1357.
Beery, Wallace: 869, 1045, 1138, 1200, 1372, 1435, 1498, 1712.
Behrendt, Hans: 1741.
Bejarano, Julia: 1644.
Bell, Alicia: 1513.
Bell, Amelia: 1513.
Bell, Jr., Ricardo: 1384.
Benavente, Lolita: 1566.
Benitez, Angelita: 1462, 1480.
Benson, Bobby: 1710.
Berkely, Busby: 1683, 1761.
Bermudez, Aurora: 1660.
Bernardos, Manuel: 1566.
Bickford, Charles: 1582.
Biosca, Jose Sortiano: 1446.
Blanco, Victoria: 1732.
Blanchette, Suzanne: 1811.
Blondell, Joan: 1608.
Blue, Monte: 802, 1058, 1159, 1162, 1334, 1357, 1457.
Bodaio, Jose: 1445.
Bogart, Humphrey: 1395.

Bohr, Jose: 1371, 1440, 1505. 1694, 1699.
Bonavi, Humberto: 1368.
Borgato, Agostino: 1526, 1584, 1763.
Bow, Clara: 1543.
Boyd, Bill: 1673.
Boyd, Betty: 1460.
Brown, Jose: 1452.
Brown, Johnny Mack: 1378, 1516.
Bruce, Nigel: 1685.
Bruce, Robert: 1774.
Buffalo Bill, Jr: 1246.
Burns, George: 1720.
Burns, Vinnie: 532.
Bushman, Francis, X.: 1280.
Byington, Spring: 624.

[C]

Cagney, Jimmy: 1750.
Calleia, Joseph: 1789.
Callejo, Maria Luz: 1461, 1476, 1520.
Calvo, Maria: 1391, 1395, 1401, 1427, 1446, 1462, 1474, 1479, 1480, 1530, 1584, 1644, 1655, 1678, 1795.
Calvo, Rafael: 1482, 1518, 1520, 1538, 1565.
Cambel, Colin: [Producer] 594.
Campillo, Anita: 1654, 1662, 1663, 1715.
Campo, Enrique del: 1670.
Cansino, Rita: See, Rita Hayworth.
Cantor, Eddie: 1574.
Canutt, Yakima: 1439, 1532.
Capra, Frank: 1332.
Caraballho, Jose: 1731.
Cardona, Rene: 1393, 1474, 1620.
Carey, Harry: 633, 747, 814, 926, 972, 1054, 1062, 1093, 1270, 1313, 1548, 1581, 1788.
Carillo, Leo: 1504, 1516, 1675, 1761.
Carroll, Nancy: 1521.
Carrosco, Joaquin: 1461.
Cassinelli, Dolores: 850.
Castaneda, Movita: 1700, 1709.
Castejon, Blanca de: 1495, 1511, 1565.
Castle, Mrs. Vernon: 684.
Castro, Rosita: 1670.
Chaney, Lon: 1047, 1363, 1463.
Chaplin, Charlie: 554, 999.

Chautard, Emile: 1401.
Chevalier, Maurice: 1343.
Clark, Marguerite, 604.
Cody, (Wild) Bill: 1164, 1207, 1653, 1722, 1734.
Cohn, Harry: [Producer] 1332.
Coleman, Ronald: 1238, 1314, 1324.
Colome, Antonia: 1551.
Compillo, Anita: 1755.
Conesa, Manuel: 1403.
Contreras Torres, Miguel: 1627, 1762, 1783, 1806.
Cooper, Gary: 1294, 1366, 1456.
Cooper, George: 470.
Coral, Tito: 1656.
Cordoba, Pedro: 552, 679, 784, 977, 1021.
Corrado, Gino: 1382, 1524.
Corrigan, Darcy: 1795.
Cortes, Mapy: 1666.
Cortez, Fernando: 1741.
Cortez, Ricardo: 969, 1022, 1022, 1061, 1138, 1147, 1198, 1200, 1290, 1302, 1333, 1380, 1399, 1411, 1433, 1474, 1523, 1546, 1578, 1583, 1714.
Crawford, Joan: 1361.
Crespo, Jose: 1435, 1437, 1447, 1465, 1494, 1489, 1526, 1601, 1700, 1715, 1716, 1731, 1799.
de la Cruz, Jose: 1395, 1617.
Cuevas, Consuelo: 1666.
Cugart, Xavier: 1415.
Custer, Bob: 1166, 1176, 1351.
Custodio, Ana Maria: 1482, 1565, 1579.

[D]

D'Ambricourt, Adrienne: 1437.
Damita, Lily: 1325, 1739.
D'Algy, Helen: 1572, 1622.
D'Algy, Tony: 1496, 1538.
D'Ambricurt, Adrienne: 1584.
Dana, Viola: 818.
Daniels, Bebe: 914, 936, 979, 1020, 1200, 1253, 1254, 1352, 1423.
D'Arcy, Roy: 1407:
D'Arville, Collette: 1802.
Davies, Marion: 854.
Davis, Betty: 1723.
Davison, Tito: 1403, 1435, 1507, 1533, 1678, 1795.

Daw, Marjorie: 774, 829.
Dawn, Conswelo: 1549.
Del Campo: 1739.
Del Diestro, Alfredo: 1425, 1479, 1486, 1533, 1659.
DeMille, Cecil B: (Director) 506, 772, 1401, 1541.
Del Rio, Dolores: 1123, 1163, 1183, 1191, 1201, 1203, 1226, 1232, 1244, 1287, 1299, 1303, 1304, 1306, 1313, 1331, 1337, 1241, 1373, 1534, 1568, 1560, 1607, 1683, 1714, 1758, 1760.
Desmond, William: 860.
Devessa, Jamie: 1566, 1622, 1663, 1705.
Dexter, Eliot: 971.
Diaz de Mendoza, Carlos: 1386, 1496.
Diaz Gimeno, Rosita: 1521, 1543, 1551.
Diaz, Rosita: 1756, 1801.
Dietrich, Marlene: 1561, 1738.
Dix, Richard: 959, 1001, 1150, 1227, 1297, 1713.
Dominquez, Beatrice: 470.
Doro, Maria: 836.
Dorsay, Fifi: 1529.
Douglas, Melvyn: 1563.
Dove, Billie: 1230, 1486, 1514.
Drain, Emile: 1811.
Drexel, Nancy: 1505.
Duan, Dorothy: 1168.
Dullier, Suzanne: 1663, 1740, 1802.
Durante, Jimmy: 1485, 1679, 1689, 1703.
Duval, Juan: 1387.

[E]

Ellis, Paul: 1388, 1544, 1654.
Elviro, Pedro, "Pitouto": 1551.
Erbeya, Margot: 1790.
Escobar, Julio: 1719.
Estrada, Don: 1429.
Esteso, Luita: 1742.

[F]

Fairbanks, Douglas: 632, 655, 657, 774, 788, 790, 829, 847, 1075, 1090, 1108, 1161, 1163, 1226, 1253, 1311, 1357, 1510, 1692.

Fair, Elinor: 896.
Falkenburg, Jinx: 1795.
Farrar, Geraldine: 552, 679.
Farreiro, Luis, G.: 1761.
Farrell, Charles: 1472.
Farrell, Glenda: 1608.
Faye, Alice: 1682.
Fazenda, Louise: 1420.
Fernanda, Maria: 1756.
Fernandes, Emilo: 1417, 1647, 1654.
Fernandes, Nellie: 1374.
Ferriz, Miguel: 1620.
Flynn, Errol: 1726, 1739.
Ford, Harrison: 1140.
Francis, Kay: 1547.
Frank, Consuelo: 1795.
Fresno, Maruchi: 1810.
Frausto, Antonia: 1659.
Frausto, Antonio, R: 1792.
Friganza, Trixe: 1098, 1401.
Fuentes, Fernando de: 1613, 1691, 1733, 1746.

[G]

Gable, Clark: 1626.
Gallardo, Lupita: 1707.
Gallian, Ketti: 1684.
Garbo, Greta: 1179, 1195.
Garcia, Allan: 1507.
Garcia, Carmelita P: 1397.
Gardel, Carlos: 1566, 1579, 1622, 1663, 1705, 1735, 1740, 1802.
Garfias, Junita: 1799.
Garralaga, Martin: 1388, 1434, 1446, 1465, 1486, 1489, 1493, 1507, 1519, 1533, 1565, 1567, 1632, 1655, 1662, 1716, 1736, 1795.
Garreiro, Luis: 1659.
Gaynor, Janet: 1472, 1601.
Geraghty, Carmelita, [Carmencita]: 1168, 1310, 1426, 1545.
Gibson, Hoot: 894, 899, 928, 980, 1143, 1148, 1478, 1502, 1788.
Gilbert, John: 900, 1070, 1447, 1476, 1494.
Gish, Dorothy: 424, 965.
Godowsky, Dagmar: 1084.
Golconda, Ligia, de: 1486.
Gomez, Carlos: 1388.
Gonzales, Myrtle: 470, 658.
Gordon, William: 1802.

Granada, Rosita: 1494, 1631.
Grandado, Manuel: 1463.
Green, Harry: 1682.
Guerrero, Carmen: 1369, 1387, 1474, 1507, 1620, 1659, 1670, 1688.
Guerrero, Ramon: 1731.
Guevara, Elias: 1384.
de Guevera, Maria F. Lardon: 1437, 1756.
Guzman, Roberto: 1393, 1507.
Guzman, Gloria: 1551.

[H]

Hall, Franklin: 386.
Haller, Magda: 1667.
Hansen, Juanita: 981, 1636.
Harding, Ann: 1405.
Hardwicke, Sir Cedric: 1491.
Hart, Neal: 927, 930, 973.
Hart, William, S: 429, 569, 638, 660, 742, 779.
deHaviland, Olivia: 1726.
Hayakawa, Sessue: 840, 1463.
Hayes, George, "Gabby": 1501, 1581.
Hayes, Helen: 1002, 1639.
Hayworth, Rita: 1809.
Hersholt, Jean: 1408.
Herrera, Enrique: 1627.
Herrero, Goyita: 1566.
Hickus, Louis: 1736.
Hoffman, Ruby: 559.
Holt, Jack: 1126, 1332, 1799.
de Homs, Juan: 1401, 1435, 1436, 1447, 1519.
Horton, Edward Everett: 1188, 1738, 1760.
Houston, Walter: 1372, 1479.
Hoxie, Jack: 911, 974, 1044, 1085, 1107, 1165, 1184, 1617, 1629.
Hutado, Alfredo: 1538.

[I]

de Ibarguren, Luis: 1384.
Ilisa, Amelia, de: 1721
Isbert, Jose: 1484.

[J]

Jimenez, Carmen: 1537.
Jiminez, Soledad: 1395, 1474, 1535, 1709, 1763.
Johnson, Orrin: 561.

Jolson, Al: 1714.
Jones, Buck: 1110, 1272, 1273, 1426, 1470, 1471, 1497, 1545, 1589, 1598, 1672.

[K]

Karlof, Boris: 1113.
Keaton, Buster: 1019, 1401, 1493.
Keene, Tom: 1559.
King, Carla: 1119.
Kirkham, Kathleen: 774.

[L]

Lamar, Adriana: 1783.
de Landa, Juan: 1435, 1437, 1459, 1462, 1493, 1494, 1544, 1798.
Landeros, Elena: 1436, 1494, 1505.
Lane, Lola: 1336.
Lardon de Guevara, Maria: 1476, 1526.
LaRoux, Carmen: 1384, 1737.
LaRoque, Rod: 1100, 1244, 1292, 1375.
Larrabeiti, Carmen: 1386, 1397, 1482, 1495, 1496, 1518.
Laurel and Hardy: 1251.
Ledesma, Armanda: 1735.
LeGrey, Sheila: 1385.
Leonard, Barbara: 1700, 1763.
Leonard, Marion: 337.
Levovalli, Emilia: 1655.
Lewis, George: 1507, 1627.
Ligero, Miguel: 1482, 1496, 1503, 1518, 1521, 1537, 1538, 1543, 1565.
Llaneza, Luis: 1435, 1436, 1447, 1551, 1572.
Llisa, Amelia, de: 1777.
Lombard, Carol: 1370, 1796.
Long, Walter: 1088.
Lopez, Pancho: 1372.
Lowe, Edmund: 1511, 1608.
Loy, Myrna: 1159, 1359, 1389, 1406, 1460, 1596, 1626.
Lubitsch, Ernst: 865.
Lusiardo, Tito: 1802.
Lyon, Ben: 1162.

[M]

Actors and Actresses Index

McCoy. Tim: 1214, 1264, 1327, 1619.
MaCrea, Joel: 1560.
MacDonald, Jennette: 1343, 1404, 1421, 1657.
McLaglen, Victor: 1201, 1233, 1395, 1567, 1607, 1609, 1616.
MacQuarrie, Albert: 829.
Magana, Delia: 1371, 1387, 1388, 1486.
Malatesta, Fred: 1526.
Manyard, Ken: 1550, 1610.
Margo: 1796.
Maris, Mona: 1354, 1370, 1393, 1395, 1416, 1434, 1429, 1460, 1564, 1589, 1623, 1628, 1631, 1635, 1648, 1655, 1656, 1663, 1709.
LaMarr, Barbara: 1081, 1118.
Martan, Nita: 1550.
Martin, Carlos San: 1572
Martin, Cris Pin: 1378, 1629.
Martinez, Antonio: 1572.
Martinez, Casado: 1732, 1792.
Martinez Pla, Juan: 1676.
Martini, Nino: 1525.
Martino, Giovanni, 1435.
Marx, Harpo: 1151.
Mattison, Matty: 1055.
Mavascues, Carmen: 1484.
Maynard, Ken: 1193, 1256, 1275, 1342, 1355, 1402, 1451, 1469, 1550, 1611.
Meller, Raquel: 1811.
Mendoza Luis: 1513.
Menjou, Adolphe: 1124, 1369, 1551.
Milano, Adita: 878.
Miller, Ruth: 913.
Mivon, Marcela: 1465.
Mix, Tom: 471, 631, 644, 710, 753, 826, 877, 903, 910, 925, 946, 1130, 1168, 1193, 1204, 1212, 1253, 1266, 1329, 1606.
Mojica, Jose: 1429, 1416, 1434, 1503, 1518, 1564, 1579, 1623, 1632, 1656, 1662, 1676.
Moliana, Tula: 859.
Monjardin, Antonio: 1521, 1543.
Montalban, Carlos: 1665, 1795.
Montalvan, Celia: 1437, 1488.
Montenegro, Conchita: 1382, 1446, 1477, 1489, 1493, 1494, 1503, 1544, 1567, 1576, 1616, 1623, 1648, 1678, 1719.
Montes, Cora: 1384.
Montes, Corzon: 1736.
Montez, Lola: 1190.
Montt, Christina: 1368.
Moran, Francisco: 1655.
Morel, Gloria: 1786.
Morel, Hector: 1773.
Moreno, Antonio: 669, 717, 790, 935, 979, 989, 1007, 1023, 1082, 1175, 1185, 1195, 1317, 1323, 1354, 1391, 1429, 1434, 1442, 1463, 1533, 1584, 1587, 1556, 1601, 1700, 1715, 1719, 1795, 1799.
Moreno, Paco: 1437, 1576, 1662, 1678, 1715.
Moreno, Rosita: 1369, 1396, 1404, 1499, 1436, 1525, 1572, 1628, 1632, 1642, 1648, 1656, 1662, 1665, 1676, 1678, 1736, 1740, 1787, 1802, 1803.
Moreno, Hilda: 1584, 1642.
de Morgan, Estrella: 856.
Moria, Elvira: 1437, 1447.
Morra, Bella: 1750.
Morris, Chester: 1791.
Morta, Elvira: 1519, 1579.
de la Mothe, Leon: 1481.
de la Motte, Marguerite: 774, 847, 1151.
Movita, [Castaneda]: 1396, 1779.
Muni, Paul: 1462, 1723,
Munoz, Amelia: 1461, 1496, 1538.
Murry, Mae: 912.
Mutt and Jeff: 1775.

[N]

Namara, Marguerite: 1500.
Nargila, Ysobel de: 1720.
Navarro, Ralph: 1400, 1427, 1462, 1472, 1488, 1518, 1538.
Navarro, Roman (Roman Samaniegos): 880, 934, 941, 951, 1005, 1019, 1069, 1081, 1092, 1129, 1132, 1234, 1245, 1257, 1263, 1279, 1286, 1299, 1328, 1333, 1337, 1344, 1348, 1383, 1415, 1446, 1472, 1475, 1487, 1539, 1573, 1577,

1596, 1639, 1657, 1680,
1731, 1781.
Nazimova: 1134.
Negri, Pola: 865, 968, 1003,
1007, 1098, 1112.
Nelson, J. Arthur: [Director]
528.
Niblo, Fred: 1401
Nieto, Jose: 1520, 1565, 1802.
Nivon, Marcela: 1371, 1654.
Noriega, Nanette: 1803.
Norman, Mable: 886, 1011.
Norton, Barry (Alfredo Biraben):
1387, 1391, 1404, 1479,
1715.
Nova, Hedda: 835.
Novara, Medea: 1762.
Nugent, Eddie: 1570.
Nunez, Ricardo: 1801.

[O]

Oakie, Jack: 1421, 1720.
Oberon, Merle: 1692.
O'Brien, Pat: 1673.
Oland, Warner: 684, 1239, 1710.
Oro, Bustillo: 1667.
Ortega, Art: 566, 1176.
Ortego, Sophie: 1560.

[P]

Padula, Rosita: 1427.
Padula, Vicente: 1369, 1388,
1391, 1393, 1403, 1427,
1459, 1499, 1622, 1663.
Parada, Miguel: 1381.
Parera, Valentin: 1461, 1648,
1678, 1700.
Paris, Manuel: 1374, 1400, 1476,
1564, 1566, 1622, 1795.
Patchouli, Poll: 860.
Patriocla, Tom: 1429, 1434,
1448, 1623, 1628.
Pedrozo, Alfonso: 1513.
Pedrazo, Samuel: 1655.
Peluffo, Manuel: 1663, 1705,
1740, 1802.
Pena, Luis: 1386, 1458.
Pena (Pepet), Jose: 1396, 1436,
1513, 1584, 1648, 1700,
1716, 1795.
Pena, Julio: 1397, 1482, 1495,
1498, 1520, 1526, 1584,
1601, 1644, 1648, 1656,
1715, 1716, 1763.
Peon, Ramon: 1479.

Pereda, Ramon: 1369, 1391, 1396,
1404, 1437, 1474, 1486,
1506, 1571, 1627, 1783,
1812.
Perojo, Benito: 1798.
Perrin, Jack: 1095, 1439, 1441,
1515.
Pickford, Mary: 702, 1003, 1226,
1635.
Pidgeon, Walter: 1128, 1287.
Pino, Rosario: 1461.
Pla, Juan Martinez: 1526.
Pomes, Felix de: 1495, 1496,
1520, 1538.
Potel, Victor: 1493.
Powell, William: 1202.
Power, Tyrone, Sr: 766, 1182.
Pulido, Juan: 1404.

[Q]

Quartaro, Nina: 1305, 1330,
1497, 1618, 1734.
Quinn, Anthony: 1690.

[R]

Raft, George: 1651, 1710, 1796.
Ramos, Trini: 1705.
Ramirez, Rosita: 1185.
Raquello, Edouardo: 1310.
Rathbone, Basil: 1726.
Real, Alma: 1435, 1715, 1731.
Reid, Wallace: 444, 796, 916.
Renaldo, Duncan: 1321. 1349,
1548.
Renner, Teresa: 1533.
Revier, Dorothy: 1083.
Rey, Nita: 1428, 1438.
Rey, Roberto: 1537.
Rey, Rosa: 1654, 1763, 1795.
Rico, Mona: 1368, 1395.
Riggs, George: 1368.
Rina de Liquoro, Countess: 1716.
Ring, Blanch: 629.
Rin Tin Tin: 1430, 1457.
Rios, Carmen: 1655.
Rivero, Julian: 1166, 1371,
1492, 1501, 1559, 1574,
1581, 1617, 1619, 1661,
1688.
Rivelles, Rafael: 1437, 1482,
1520, 1526.
Robles, Elisa: 1699.
Rocha, Faust: 1535.
Rodrigo, Raquel: 1741.

Actors and Actresses Index

Rodriquez, [also:Rodriques, and Rodriguez,] Carmen: 1416, 1447, 1459, 1472, 1519, 1526, 1565, 1579, 1631, 1642, 1662, 1665, 1676, 1802.
Rodriques de la Vega, Cecilio: 1386.
Roland, Gilbert {Luis Alonso}: 1132, 1216, 1230, 1247, 1283, 1333, 1427, 1506, 1535, 1571, 1601, 1644, 1648, 1763, 1780.
Roland, Ruth: 851.
Romero, Cesar: 1738.
Romeu, Pepe: 1521, 1543.
Roosevelt, Buddy: 1242.
Rosas, Enrique, de: 1716, 1778, 1795, 1802, 1803.
Roulien, Raul: 1565, 1607, 1610, 1628, 1678, 1787, 1803.
Rubin, Benny: 1382, 1420.
Ruiz Morgas: Carmen: 1397.
Russell, Manuel: 1484, 1496, 1521, 1543.

[S]

Samaniegos, Carmen: 1731.
Sanchez, Antone: 1362.
Sanchez, Elviro: 1617.
San Martin, Carlos: 1461.
Sante, Amelia: 1565.
Sarno, Hector: 1428, 1438.
Sarno, Victor: 1426.
Schenck, Joseph, M: [Producer] 1342, 1358.
Segurola, Andres, de: 1233, 1335, 1436, 1387, 1391, 1400, 1403, 1436, 1564, 1520, 1579, 1601, 1656, 1665, 1678, 1709, 1716.
Senisterra, Amelia: 1535.
Sennett, Mack: 1213.
Serrano, Enriqueta: 1414.
Servet, Mercedes: 1496.
Serrano, Enrique: 1725.
Sevilla, Raphel: 1732.
Shearer, Norma: 1437.
Silva, Roberto Sao: 1384.
Silver, Marcel: 1434.
Solano, Maragarita: 1229.
Soler, Domingo: 1804.
Soler, Enriqueta: 1482, 1495, 1520, 1537.
Soler, Fernando: 1484.
Soler, Julian: 1670, 1777.

Soto, Manuel: 1445.
Sotomayor, Ignacio: 1384.
Stanwyck, Barbara: 1345, 1474.
St. John, Fuzzy: 1417.
Steele, Bob: 1237, 1273, 1276, 1284, 1417, 1428, 1590, 1598, 1664.
Summerville, Slim: 1516.
Swanson, Gloria: 922, 935, 1232.

[T]

Talmadge, Norma: 1283.
Talmadge, Richard: 1163.
Tarzan: 1193, 1342.
Taylor, Robert: 1778.
Tenorio, Mario: 1761.
Thebe, Rosemary: 848, 860.
Thompson, Fred: 1066.
Tirado, Romualdo: 1435, 1437, 1489, 1493, 1494, 1513, 1544, 1564, 1584, 1627, 1632, 1642, 1644, 1678, 1700, 1715, 1736.
Toler, Sidney: 1710.
Toomey, Regis: 1637.
Tora, Lia: 1425, 1488.
Torena, Juan: 1393, 1425, 1434, 1462, 1472, 1511, 1565, 1567, 1628, 1644, 1686, 1715, 1727,1736.
Torreblanca, Carmen: 1761.
Torres, Miguel: 1783.
Torres, Nancy: 1579.
Torres, Raquel: 1318, 1321, 1327, 1401, 1444, 1467, 1602.
Torres, Renee: 1507.
Tortosa, Jose Luis: 1740, 1802.
Tovar, Lupita: 1463, 1471, 1474, 1490, 1555, 1587, 1715, 1727, 1799, 1810.
Tracy, Lee: 1569.
Tracy, Spencer: 940.
Tubau, Maria: 1476.
Twelvetrees, Helen: 1411, 1582.
Tyler, Tom: 1224, 1501, 1524, 1527, 1810.

[U]

Ulrich, Lenore: 659.
Urgotti, Ricardo: 1742.

[V]

Valli, Virginia: 1503.

Valverde, Rafael: 1403, 1416, 1472.
Valentino, Rudolf: 574, 863, 897, 933, 1019, 1020, 1071.
Vanon, Cesar: 1371, 1435, 1505.
Vehil, Luisa: 1805.
Velasco, Consuela: 858.
Velez, Lupe: 1226, 1244, 1251, 1259, 1311, 1335, 1341, 1354, 1363, 1366, 1398, 1408, 1431, 1454, 1457, 1485, 1506, 1534, 1535, 1541, 1563, 1569, 1571, 1575, 1609, 1625, 1679, 1680, 1703, 1776.
Vendrell, Lolita: 1371.
Vidal, Antonio: 1435. 1480, 1486, 1519, 1565, 1654, 1655.
Vidal, Luis Llorens: 1537.
Vilches, Ernesto: 1387, 1404, 1463,1476, 1480, 1544.
Villarias, Carlos: 1369, 1391, 1393, 1401, 1416, 1434, 1462, 1472, 1479, 1489, 1490, 1506, 1507, 1511, 1530, 1571, 1601, 1631, 1700, 1709, 1803.
Villarreal, Julio: 1396, 1437, 1462, 1479, 1488, 1507, 1518, 1530, 1627, 1694.
Villasenor, Salvador: 1384.
Villegas, Lucio: 1425, 1472, 1507, 1663, 1686, 1715, 1795, 1803.
Viosca, Jose Soriano: 1435, 1463, 1476, 1480, 1533.
Vischer, Blanca: 1705.

[W]

Walsh, Raoul: 375, 553, 664, 878, 989, 1147, 1201, 1233, 1304, 1338, 1472, 1507.
Warner, J. B: 896.
Warwick, Virginia: 892.
Wayne, John: 1197, 1377, 1507, 1600, 1618, 1638, 1687, 1737, 1766, 1784.
White, Pearl: 790.
Whitman, Gayne: 1187.
Williams, "Big Boy": 890, 1661, 1788.
Williams, Clara: 386.
Wong, Anna May: 1171.
Wray, Fay: 1294, 1379, 1456, 1473.

[Y]

Young, Robert: 1574.

[Z]

Zabala, Enrique: 1810.
Zambrano, Ernesto, 1384.
Zea, Maria Luisa: 1698, 1704.
Zea, Senorita: 1660.
Zuffoli, Eugenia: 1445.
Zuri, Virginia: 1627.

Countries and Place Names Index

[A]

Amazon: 87, 198, 573, 668, 783, 1225, 1276, 1298, 1334, 1557, 1621, 1635, 1350.
Antigua: 773.
Argentina: 65, 164, 277, 437, 545, 555, 618, 760, 863, 984, 1020, 1071, 1104, 1144, 1155, 1178, 1195, 1234, 1259, 1264, 1267, 1274, 1280, 1291, 1291, 1322, 1330, 1343, 1367, 1421, 1488, 1587, 1593, 1622, 1663, 1681, 1682, 1686, 1695, 1699, 1719, 1725, 1731, 1735, 1739, 1740, 1752, 1757, 1782, 1805, 1807, 1809.
Arizona: 48, 135, 229, 326, 364, 411, 507, 744, 822, 829, 853, 867, 1017, 1048, 1207, 1212, 1260, 1266, 1338, 1354, 1370, 1469, 1470, 1562, 1687.

[B]

Bahamas: 593, 537, 1347.
Barbados: 1031.
Bolivia: 849, 864, 1287, 1681, 1715, 1799.
Brazil: 40, 184, 669, 754, 755, 759, 795, 944, 966, 1228, 1350, 1514, 1540, 1565, 1604, 1607, 1621, 1626, 1631, 1678, 1681, 1719.
Buenos Aires: 1622, 1681, 1718, 1735, 1740.

[C]

California: 10, 30, 94, 103, 119, 167, 132, 192, 224 228, 230, 367, 396, 546, 566, 699, 711, 777, 825, 842, 843, 888, 892, 900, 907, 923, 982, 1008, 1030, 1063, 1106, 1108, 1112, 1139, 1214, 1215, 1222, 1226, 1227, 1239, 1273, 1275, 1278, 1303, 1339, 1355, 1418, 1751.

California: Spanish/Mexican Territory: 43, 60, 91, 103, 129, 132, 139, 143, 167, 178, 192, 195, 226, 228, 230, 234, 238, 298, 305, 317, 335, 367, 369, 396, 443, 486, 506, 550, 566, 609, 657, 705, 716, 745, 842, 847, 851, 868, 871, 882, 888, 900, 902, 907, 940, 923, 1008, 1030, 1063, 1108, 1125, 1138, 1247, 1339, 1481, 1452, 1481, 1598, 1631, 1635, 1662.
Canada: 889, 908.
Caribbean: 23, 88, 106, 264, 415, 624, 773, 791, 855, 883, 914, 950, 957, 969, 988, 1122, 1200, 1217, 1248, 1276, 1308, 1340, 1365, 1408, 1421, 1423, 1528, 1594, 1600, 1604, 1649.
Cayenne: 1172.
Central America: 730, 750, 800, 956, 958, 960, 988, 1009, 1101, 1154, 1316, 1332, 1360, 1394, 1395, 1508, 1510, 1554, 1684, 1771.
Chile: 150, 183.
China: 1430.
Colombia: 1239, 1681.
Columbus, New Mexico: 652, 677, 688, 690, 708, 723.
Costa Rica: 59, 739, 768.
Cuba: 46, 111, 120, 121, 151, 186, 200, 215, 218, 221, 222, 264, 301, 308, 346, 353, 362, 366, 501, 508, 559, 602, 663, 681, 686, 717, 752, 791, 793, 803, 809, 914, 955, 965, 993, 998, 1021, 1084, 1102, 1124, 1248, 1298, 1302, 1336, 1365, 1411, 1485, 1528, 1600, 1608, 1613, 1652, 1796.
Cuzco: 1759.

[D]

Dutch Republic: 605, 1314.

[E]

Ecuador: 1632, 1681.
El Salvador: 750.

Countries and Place Names Index

[F]

Falkland Island: 1267.
Florida: 156, 161, 296.

[G]

Germany: 792, 794, 831, 832, 863, 1241, 1267.
Guatemala: 846, 1399, 1649, 1730.

[H]

Haiti: 425, 637, 720, 827, 950, 1364, 1449, 1508, 1561, 1594, 1604, 1688, 1785, 1813.
Havana: 111, 180, 185, 218, 260, 264, 301, 311, 402, 498, 509, 701, 791, 793, 857, 879, 955, 969, 998, 1102, 1288, 1293, 1336, 1356, 1394, 1411, 1422, 1485, 1528, 1600, 1608, 1652.
Honduras: 768, 1770.

[J]

Jamaica: 415, 563, 875.
Japan: 684, 841, 940.

[L]

Lisbon: 92, 185.

[M]

Madrid: 61, 159, 162, 166, 212, 604, 876, 912, 987, 1415, 1599, 1666.
Martinique: 762, 1200.
Mexico: 3, 4, 5, 6, 19, 21, 24, 28, 32, 34, 36, 39, 47, 48, 49, 51, 52, 53, 54, 55, 56, 62, 63, 64, 70, 73, 77, 78, 93, 95, 96, 97, 98, 99, 100, 101, 109, 110, 113, 115, 118, 125, 126, 127, 130, 131, 135, 136, 140, 141, 143, 146, 148, 149, 154, 155, 162, 163, 165, 171, 172, 173, 174, 175, 176, 177, 178, 181, 188, 191, 193, 194, 196, 199, 201, 202, 203, 204, 216, 217, 219, 220, 223, 229, 231, 232, 233, 235, 236, 239, 240, 242, 244, 251, 252, 253, 257, 258, 258, 259, 261, 263, 265, 266, 268, 267, 268, 269, 271, 272, 273, 274, 275, 281, 284, 285, 288, 289, 291, 293, 294, 295, 297, 302, 307, 310, 312, 313, 314, 315, 316, 317, 318, 320, 321, 322, 323, 328, 331, 332, 338, 339, 340, 342, 343, 345, 347, 351, 352, 354, 359, 360, 363, 364, 365, 367, 370, 372, 373, 374, 375, 376, 377, 378, 379, 380, 381, 382, 387, 388, 389, 391, 392, 400, 406, 409, 411, 412, 413, 416, 417, 418, 419, 420, 421, 424, 426, 427, 428, 431, 432, 433, 434, 435, 436, 438, 442, 443, 444, 445, 447, 448, 450, 451, 452, 453, 554, 458, 464, 468, 469, 471, 472, 473, 474, 475, 476, 477, 480, 481, 491, 492, 493, 494, 495, 496, 497, 498, 499, 500, 503, 504, 505, 506, 507, 511, 512, 513, 521, 522, 523, 527, 528, 532, 533, 534, 567, 568, 569, 571, 575, 576, 580, 582, 586, 589, 590, 591, 596, 597, 598, 600, 601, 602, 603, 607, 608, 611, 612, 613, 614, 617, 620, 621, 627, 629, 630, 631, 632, 633, 635, 638, 639, 641, 642, 644, 645, 649, 650, 651, 653, 654, 658, 659, 660, 661, 664, 665, 666, 667, 679, 682, 683, 684, 685, 687, 688, 689, 690, 691, 692, 693, 694, 695, 696, 697, 698, 699, 700, 704, 707, 708, 709, 710, 712, 713, 715, 716, 718, 719, 722, 723, 724, 726, 727, 731, 732, 733, 734, 735, 737, 742, 743, 748, 756, 757, 760, 764, 765, 766, 767, 771, 772, 774, 776, 778, 779, 780, 781, 785, 786, 787, 789, 792, 795, 797, 798, 801, 802, 811, 814, 816, 817, 823, 824, 825, 828, 830, 832, 833, 837, 839, 840, 843, 844, 845, 848, 853, 858, 860, 862, 867, 872, 878, 884, 890, 892, 893, 896, 902, 905, 911, 918, 922, 925, 926, 927, 929, 938, 940, 943, 950, 953, 954, 962, 963, 966, 972, 973, 978, 991, 995, 999, 1001, 1004, 1018, 1023, 1026, 1028,

Countries and Place Names Index

1041, 1045, 1048, 1053, 1054,
1056, 1058, 1059, 1060, 1064,
1067, 1070, 1077, 1080, 1089,
1091, 1094, 1096, 1097, 1110,
1120, 1126, 1133, 1136, 1139,
1145, 1146, 1152, 1153, 1158,
1163, 1164, 1166, 1177, 1180,
1182, 1187, 1193, 1204, 1207,
1214, 1223, 1237, 1242, 1250,
1256, 1262, 1283, 1307, 1309,
1312, 1315, 1338, 1342, 1345,
1349, 1358, 1370, 1372, 1375,
1376, 1379, 1380, 1399, 1405,
1421, 1450, 1472, 1485 1542,
1553, 1556, 1563, 1565, 1570,
1574, 1586, 1587, 1588, 1597,
1603, 1604, 1611, 1613, 1614,
1615, 1620, 1623, 1627, 1632,
1637, 1638, 1640, 1646, 1659,
1660, 1667, 1669, 1670, 1672,
1673, 1676, 1680, 1691, 1693,
1701, 1702, 1706, 1707, 1710,
1712, 1721, 1725, 1728, 1729,
1732, 1733, 1753, 1756, 1761,
1762, 1763, 1764, 1767, 1775,
1778, 1790, 1792, 1800, 1804,
1807, 1810, 1814.

[N]

Nassau: 1268.
Nicaragua: 762, 768, 1297, 1332, 1420, 1554, 1748.

[P]

Panama: 225, 283, 313, 361, 385, 446, 488, 622, 650, 739, 747, 762, 763, 996, 1289, 1310, 1332, 1334, 1453, 1529, 1582.
Panama Canal: 20, 38, 71, 72, 182, 225, 282, 283, 361, 383, 384, 385, 393, 446, 487, 490, 594, 599, 763, 996, 1006, 1336, 1053, 1453, 1636, 1684.
Panama Canal Zone: 20, 1582, 1636, 1684.
Paraguay: 1799.
Peru: 76, 82, 153, 806, 849, 1321, 1645, 1681, 1759.
Philippines: 7, 11, 104, 144, 336, 348, 358, 398, 404, 425, 482, 502, 522, 572, 610, 770, 815, 1159, 1194, 1276, 1658, 1686, 1716.
Portugal: 137, 168, 185, 189, 190, 287, 529, 584, 746, 758, 970, 1134, 1156, 1190, 1243, 1338, 1365, 1381, 1477, 1592.
Puerto Rico: 813, 883, 956, 1160, 1217, 1552, 1697, 1741.

[R]

Rio De Janero: 573, 576, 795, 969, 1208, 1227, 1289, 1542, 1607, 1633.

[S]

Sargasso Sea: 988, 1340, 1649.
Spain: 15, 22, 31, 46, 50, 61, 66, 84, 90, 107, 142, 155, 187, 202, 212, 238, 241, 245, 290, 303, 329, 348, 366, 397, 415, 422, 430, 458, 482, 486, 500, 529, 595, 605, 637, 647, 714, 721, 736, 740, 775, 770, 810, 838, 840, 847, 866, 871, 876, 892, 902, 903, 912, 916, 937, 939, 947, 948, 953, 959, 965, 970, 980, 987, 993, 1003, 1010, 1021, 1033, 1055, 1061, 1072, 1074, 1081, 1082, 1086, 1130, 1140, 1150, 1162, 1167, 1185, 1217, 1222, 1227, 1239, 1245, 1248, 1269, 1275, 1277, 1285, 1295, 1302, 1325, 1326, 1346, 1349, 1365, 1387, 1399, 1415, 1432, 1447, 1450, 1468, 1531, 1547, 1605, 1651, 1666, 1692, 1708, 1716, 1726, 1738, 1741, 1743, 1744, 1752, 1753, 1770, 1793, 1795, 1802, 1806, 1807.
South America: 824, 881, 890, 901, 910, 932, 968, 961, 989, 1016, 1068, 1073, 1115, 1119, 1186, 1188, 1205, 1228, 1249, 1253, 1361, 1395, 1468, 1481, 1505, 1510, 1514, 1557, 1582, 1600, 1607, 1609, 1610, 1616, 1634, 1645, 1654, 1677, 1681, 1705, 1740, 1749, 1752, 1758, 1764, 1799, 1802, 1809.

[T]

Texas: 70, 155, 201, 284, 285, 310, 421, 504, 532, 545, 573, 589, 618, 630, 653, 658, 691, 693, 694, 695, 698, 699, 753, 761, 764, 780, 794, 801, 817,

926, 954, 1026, 1063, 1065,
1067, 1164, 1226, 1242, 1262,
1270, 1271, 1284, 1352, 1402,
1460, 1483, 1545, 1611, 1637,
1647, 1794.
Trinidad: 23, 1685.

[V]

Venezuela: 422, 1360, 1681.
Virgin Islands: 1423.

[Y]

Yucatan: 1614, 1684, 1707.

Subject Index

[A]

Adams, Leith: 1473.
Aquinaldo: 336, 675, 1159.
Air planes/Aviation: 955, 1017, 1090, 1205, 1294, 1301, 1329, 1332, 1333, 1464, 1519, 1538, 1600, 1626, 1637, 1715, 1799, 1809, 1812.
Alamo: 155, 589, 954, 1794.
All American Canal: 20.
AMC/American Movie Chanel: 1510, 1559.
Anderson, G. M. {Broncho Billy}: 54, 77, 97, 236, 302, 321, 322, 342, 434, 435, 547, 548, 549.
Andes: 62, 782, 861, 1119, 1626, 1645.
Angelus: 334, 500, 540.
Anglo Female [Angleress] Heroine: 136, 673, 712, 763, 776, 790, 839, 851, 1253.
Anglo Heavy: 85, 110, 194, 290, 265, 340, 347, 365, 392, 421, 425, 660, 734, 869, 1059.
Anglo Loves Senorita: 55, 239, 391, 612, 839, 984.
Anglo problems with Spanish/Mexican: 719.
Anglo Savior/Hero: 35, 54, 80, 83, 126, 160, 226, 273, 437, 590, 583, 649, 751, 756, 834, 872, 877, 896, 947, 990, 1050, 1107, 1111, 1178, 1202, 1273, 1276, 1284, 1334, 1386, 1418, 1423, 1426, 1441, 1443, 1470, 1471, 1509, 1555, 1590, 1626, 1649, 1658, 1766, 1771, 1799.
Anglo Savior Syndrome: 160.
Anglo Super Hero: 14, 21, 82, 109, 130, 135, 191, 348, 358, 395, 419, 436, 454, 481, 508, 550, 551, 632, 656, 676, 710, 734, 786, 817, 834, 851, 909, 984, 412, 442, 474, 479, 559, 637, 641, 642, 648, 674, 742, 747, 749, 763, 774, 800, 910, 945, 953, 990, 1041, 1080, 1088, 1097, 1103, 1117, 1149, 1176, 1212, 1220, 1225, 1266, 1316, 1330, 1332, 1376, 1380, 1451.

Anglo Wins Senorita: 15, 46, 64, 313, 392, 395, 403, 436, 444, 453, 474, 614, 984, 1059, 1097, 1150, 1568.
Animals, Dangerous on land: 783, 1127, 1584, 1620, 1764, in sea: 957.
Anti-Imperialist League: 525.
Apaches: 48, 129, 250, 319, 324, 324, 325, 347, 690, 807, 1265, 1580.
Archeologist: 542, 1027.
Argentina/Mexican Production Compared: 1725.
Argentina: Paralles with United States: 1725.
Armadillo: 327.
Arriaga, Jesus: 1728.
ASPCA: 914.
Aztec: 323, 427, 586, 638, 801, 1028, 1153, 1180, 1237, 1639, 1693, 1767, 1806.

[B]

Banana Republic, Hollywood Stereotype: 1395.
Bandit equated with Revolutionary: 426, 438, 635, 679.
Barbarous Mexico: 328, 726.
Belasco, David: 982, 1568.
Belgrano, Juan: 1280.
Bingham, Hiram: 1759.
Blasco-Ibanez, Vicente: 736, 863, 897, 1185, 1195, 1198, 1405.
Black Hero: 1236.
Black Legend {La Leyenda Negra}: 290, 303, 610, 647, 987, 1033, 1072, 1726, 1743.
Bond, James: 422.
Beach, Rex: 768.
Border, The: 16, 22, 27, 39, 52, 55, 58, 64, 75, 85, 101, 116, 117, 128, 130, 135, 173, 174, 181, 199, 201, 206, 220, 235, 240, 263, 269, 280, 291, 293, 297, 302, 310, 319, 320, 321, 322, 326, 340, 343, 345, 350, 352, 359, 372, 373, 381, 392, 406, 412, 420, 421, 424, 426,

429, 431, 439, 445, 448, 477, 526, 532, 543, 554, 557, 563, 567, 582, 597, 611, 612, 631, 673, 712, 752, 777, 778, 780, 792, 817, 823, 853, 860, 867, 884, 896, 898, 905, 946, 950, 964, 999, 1013, 1017, 1023, 1024, 1025, 1026, 1048, 1049, 1094, 1095, 1110, 1136, 1137, 1170, 1182, 1210, 1211, 1270, 1338, 1345, 1352, 1353, 1354, 1402, 1405, 1406, 1430, 1440, 1471, 1477, 1492, 1501, 1527, 1532, 1536, 1562, 1597, 1617, 1619, 1637, 1653, 1696, 1722, 1747, 1766, 1784.
Border, Affects of: 58, 116, 201, 442, 480.
Border Smuggling see Smuggling on the Border.
Border Mobilization: 635, 670, 677.
Border Patrol/Texas Rangers: 24, 127, 128, 196, 293, 421, 504, 630, 757, 780, 794, 817, 926, 1026, 1065, 1067, 1152, 1164, 1165, 1242, 1262, 1270, 1301, 1319, 1320, 1352, 1402, 1430, 1464, 1545, 1619, 1647.
Border Patrol, Air: 1309.
Border, Rejuvenation: 377, 504, 630, 716, 742, 760.
Border Tension: 291.
Border, U.S. Troops on see U.S. Troops on the Border.
Bowie, Jim: 589.
Breen, Joe: 1723.
Broken English: See, Dialect.
Broncho Billy: 54, 77, 236, 331, 332, 434, 547, 548, 549.
Bullfighting: 10, 28, 41, 62, 78, 183, 271, 306, 349, 467, 510, 523, 524, 736, 840, 897, 950, 1010, 1011, 1021, 1029, 1074, 1080, 1147, 1189, 1213, 1232, 1382, 1455, 1500, 1574, 1641, 1709, 1724, 1775, 1792, 1804.
Burr, Aaron: 1131.

[C]

Cabel TV: 847, 1510.
California: 1214, 1273, 1278, 1303.
California, Gold Rush Days: 10, 30, 94, 119, 566, 777, 825, 982, 1030, 1063, 1106, 1239, 1751.
California, Independence: 132, 224, 711, 888, 900, 907, 1030, 1214, 1215, 1222, 1227, 1275, 1355, 1418.
California, Spanish/Mexican: 43, 60, 91, 103, 129, 139, 143, 167, 178, 192, 195, 226, 228, 230, 234, 238, 298, 305, 317, 335, 367, 369, 396, 443, 454, 486, 503, 506, 546, 550, 566, 609, 657, 705, 745, 842, 847, 851, 868, 882, 900, 902, 923, 940, 1008, 1030, 1063, 1108, 1112, 1125, 1138, 1247, 1339, 1452, 1481, 1598, 1631, 1635, 1662.
Camarena, Victor: 597.
Camoens: 133.
Cannibals: 1557.
Cannibals, pygmy: 1675.
Cannibalism: 358, 1276.
Cantina Girl: 62, 152, 247, 275, 381, 382, 470, 595, 667, 780, 804, 818, 828, 833, 859, 862, 869, 918, 967, 996, 1114, 1137, 1260, 1307, 1409, 1423, 1426, 1440, 1471, 1527, 1567, 1582, 1597, 1636.
Carioca: 1607.
Cartoons: 442, 485, 541, 591, 641, 642, 670, 675, 713, 724, 1133, 1413, 1455, 1724, 1775.
Carmen/Carmen type: 28, 31, 44, 79, 134, 166, 212, 337, 349, 401, 439, 450, 463, 510, 552, 553, 554, 608, 679, 741, 815, 865, 924, 959, 983, 1059, 1168, 1189, 1201, 1232, 1232, 1277, 1295, 1299, 1471, 1477, 1497, 1500, 1527.
Carranza: 538, 652, 723, 837.
Carrizal: 694, 696.
Caruso, Enrique: 1654, 1655.
Celeyas, Battle of: 1702.
Censorship: 78, 112, 297, 429, 838, 859, 1149, 1161, 1169, 1214, 1269, 1277, 1310, 1355, 1412, 1418, 1421, 1514, 1542, 1557, 1560, 1576, 1639, 1683, 1712, 1723.
Cervantes: 44, 974.
Chaco War: 1715, 1799.
Charly Chan: 1565.
Chewing Gum: 1614.
Chichen Itza: 1615.

Chinese: 24, 28, 74, 764, 1148.
Christopher Columbus: 81, 241, 970, 1051.
Christophe, Henri: 1604, 1813.
Cisco Kid: 418, 436, 1370, 1477, 1548, 1589, 1809.
Cocoa Industry: 23.
Cock Fighting: 9, 308, 751, 914.
Congressional Hearings, Patria see Patria, Congressional Hearings:
Conquistadores: 767, 772, 998, 1767.
Cortez, Hernando: 772, 1153, 1399, 1767.
Continental Morality: 1199, 1228, 1389.
Cousteau, Chronicles: 1557.
Crothers, George: 600.
"La Cucaracha": 490, 1058, 1355.
Cugat, Xavier: 1388, 1415.

[D]

Darkie: 892, 1088.
Darkskinned Lady/Senorita: 35, 64, 75, 98, 118, 127, 188, 199, 231, 279, 322, 348, 475, 482, 544, 549, 581, 719, 826, 868, 874, 896, 936, 959, 966, 989, 1042, 1091, 1129, 1305, 1308, 1348, (Dirty skinned: 1359) 1444, 1570, 1607, 1776.
Davis, Richard Harding: 747, 834, 877, 909, 1075, 1103, 1117, 1202, 1264.
Devil's Island: 25, 1057, 1172, 1324, 1373, 1404, 1410, 1444, 1491. 1745.
Dewey: 144.
Diaz, Porfiario: 163, 175, 191, 464, 587, 1670, 1702, 1728.
Dialect English: 1406, 1459, 1504, 1548, 1563, 1567, 1568, 1569, 1589, 1591, 1592.
Dollar Diplomacy: 913.
Don Juan: 45, 1130, 1173, 1460, 1666, 1692, 1755.
Don Quixote: 44, 646, 975.
Dorian, Bob: 1510.
Doyale, Arthur Conan: 1127.
Drake, Sir Francis: 1743.
Dreyfus: 1491.
Drugs/Narcotics: 441, 449, 543, 628, 764, 904, 976, 1367.
Drugs on the Border/Smuggling: 235, 597, 778, 843, 887, 928, 1001, 1056, 1165, 1329, 1342, 1770.
Dubbing: 1412.
Durland, Addison: 1338.
Dutch Republic: 592, 605, 1314.
Dueling: 32, 158, 218, 286, 324, 456, 510, 602, 669, 853, 1078, 1238. Duel, Bullwhip: 1195.
Duty Transcends Love: 501.
Dyott, Comander: 1634.

[E]

Earhart, Amelia: 1814.
Eisenstein, Sergio: 1602, 1641.

[F]

Falkland Islands: 1267.
Federalista's. Federal officer and soldiers: 253, 274, 285, 352, 367, 372, 379, 433, 437, 438, 474, 475, 476, 451, 464, 477, 480, 493,534, 575, 591, 598, 1120.
Fielding, Rommaine: 322, 360, 391, 411.
Fiesta-Siesta Land: 55, 95, 328, 365, 459, 619, 851, 966, 1083, 1088, 1107, 1339, 1380, 1406, 1579, 1603, 1662, 1708, 1799.
First:
 Argentine Sound Film Shown in New York: 1593.
 Female Private-eye in Cuba: 1336.
 Fox Talker with Hispanics: 1338.
 Mention of Drugs in South America: 1367.
 Mexican Film For USA Export: 1587.
 Musical Western: 1352.
 Paramount Musical Romance with Hispanic theme: 1366.
 Talker in Argentina: 1343.
 Talker Set in Cuba: 1356.
 Talker with Dialect Dialogue: 1326.
 Talker with Good Badman theme: 1326.
 Talker with Spanish: 1322.
 Talker with Spoken Spanish: 1345.
 Talker with Spanish Theme Song: 1339.
 Technicolor Western: 1460.

Use of critical reviews and author credits: 175.
Use of Subtitles: 1701.
Verbal discription of Panama Canal in talker: 1336.
Flag: See Old Glory.
Freemont, General: 888, 1222.
French Intervention in Mexico: 1058, 1729, 1762.

[G]

Gavin, John: 22.
General Balbo: 1540.
Geronimo: 250.
Germany: 1241, 1267.
Germans in Mexico: 831, 832.
Gil, Portes: 1358.
Going Native: 425.
Goldwyn Girls: 1574.
Good Badman: 77, 418, 655, 657, 788, 962, 1139, 1149, 1278, 1283, 1326, 1338, 1372, 1412, 1429, 1563.
Good Badman, Hollywood Formula: 1326.
Good Neighbor Policy: 1748.
"Greaseball": 892.
Greaser: 19, 21, 24, 27, 34, 39, 54, 74, 97, 110, 116, 125, 194, 214, 252, 288, 331, 340, 345, 351, 434, 435, 447, 453, 470, 521, 522, 547, 548, 563, 568, 731, 753, 781, 787, 798, 820, 862, 867, 892, 911, 1045, 1089, 1204, 1723.
"Green Hell": 1799.
Grey, Zane: 823, 1126, 1170, 1379, 1419, 1459.
Griffith, D. W.: 103, 589, 702, 705, 833.
Gringo: 116, 123, 313, 381, 396, 424, 454, 472, 526, 532, 613, 747, 751, 801, 848, 861, 923, 1089, 1112, (Origin of term: 1418).
Guerillas: 677, 1255.
Guerilla Cruelty: 528.
Gun Running: 421, 508, 677, 706, 997, 1142, 1356, 1395.
Gypsy: 13, 17, 18, 29, 30, 31, 33, 37, 62, 205, 216, 248, 254, 255, 256, 330, 356, 357, 455, 456, 457, 570, 585, 587, 736, 850, 865, 885, 920, 1007, 1078, 1086, 1238, 1258, 1277, 1306, 1335, 1359, 1407, 1451, 1500, 1510, 1623, 1755.

[H]

Halfbreed: 34, 98, 157, 175, 194, 251, 257, 258, 259, 277, 312, 324, 341, 342, 347, 370, 380, 435, 535, 565, 571, 573, 611, 644, 653, 657, 704, 715, 764, 744, 798, 861, 906, 921, 1023, 1177, 1200, 1303, 1315, 1546, 1596, 1646, 1766.
Hammet, Dashil: 1523.
Harte, Bret: 94.
Hayakawa, Sessue: 840.
Hays Papers: 1214.
Hays, Will: 893, 950, 1035, 1367, 1557. See also, Censorship.
Headhunters, 336, 358, 1557, 1634.
Hearst, William Randolf: 484, 699, 854, 940.
Hispanic as Incidental Location Identifyers: 16.
Hispanic Avenger: 847, 1008, 1082, 1108, 1278, 1418, 1429, 1440, 1470, 1481, 1567, 1589, 1618, 1728, 1733, 1739, 1792, 1809.
Hispanic Bad Lady: 41, 676, 859, 1118.
Hispanic Cruelty: 366, 391, 726, 994, 1003, 1039.
Hispanic Hero/Heroine: 86, 450, 1055, 1125.
Hispanic Female, Faithless: 67, 69, 215.
Hispanic Hot Blood/Passion: 17, 62, 206, 218, 358, 362, 439, 725, 818, 874, 881, 912, 948, 968, 982, 1084, 1195, 1201, 1219, 1223, 1252, 1285, 1295, 1331, 1444, 1500, 1502, 1529, 1569, 1609, 1760.
Hispanic Lust: 22, 643, 874, 952, 1003, 1091, 1423.
Hispanic Play Anglo: 1333.
Hispanic Sexual Superiority Mythology: 206, 874, 1460.
Hispanic Pride: 612, 851, 818, 1285, 1440.
Hispanic, Sinister: 824, 881.
Hispanic Showcase for Latins: 1357.

Hispanic Portrayals,
  Sympathetic: 26, 40, 45, 214, 219, 288, 617, 1044.
Hollwood Hispanic Historical Interpretation: 81, 240, 589, 970, 1051, 1795.
Hollywood's Horses: 772.
Homogenous Hispanics: 313, 448.
Horses, Spanish, [Influence in North America]: 772.
HUAC: 263.
Huerta: 432, 442, 491, 496, 511, 534, 538, 641.
Human Sacrifice: 638, 1141.

[I]

Ibanez, Vincente Blasco: (see: Blasco-Ibanez, Vincente.)
Incas: 861, 1027, 1237.
Imperialism: 348, 482, 637, 1248.
Incas: 1759.
Indians, Various: 62, 65, 76, 82, 96, 103, 358, 611, 612, 1350, 1453. See also **Aztecs, Mayans, Incas, Apache, Yaqui.**
Inquisition: 303.
"Insulted": 112.
Insurectos: 88, 92, 118, 163, 174, 175, 191, 249, 253, 348, 352, 353, 358, 366, 427, 459, 467, 522, 525, 577, 583, 620, 673, 681, 706, 749, 815, 876, 965, 1332, 1716.
Irish/Hispanics/Mexicans: 682, 826, 848, 864, 1193.

[J]

Jackson, Helen Hunt: 103, 705.
Jaguar: 573, 575 578, 581, 728, 757, 783.
Japonese: 484, 699, 757, 940.
Joinville: 1522.
Jungle: 40, 440, 542, 573, 578, 581, 622, 668, 766, 769, 783, 861, 901, 1034, 1053, 1057, 1225, 1237, 1255, 1287, 1316, 1324, 1332, 1334, 1350, 1360, 1361, 1548, 1557, 1575, 1582, 1604, 1621, 1634, 1668, 1674, 1675, 1677, 1685, 1689, 1764, 1771, 1796, 1799.
Juarez Benito: 1058.
Juarez, Mexico: 480, 561, 600, 1729, 1732, 1762.

[K]

Knives, Stilletos, daggers: 19, 49, 56, 60, 70, 125, 179, 213, 233, 236, 254, 276, 293, 309, 349, 354, 380, 378, 409, 439, 453, 456, 467, 542, 556, 558, 608, 670, 676, 828, 862, 974, 1081, 1150, 1157, 1222, 1227, 1306, 1314, 1330, 1411, 1429, 1668, 1809. See also **Stabbing.**

[L]

Latin Love Making: 874.
Latin Lover: 43, 790, 935, 1071, 1162, 1219, 1279, 1299, 1326, 1415, 1472, 1692.
Latin American Market: 1322, 1355, 1382, 1429.
Latin Market: 826, 1180, 1468, 1481, 1490, 1505, 1522, 1552, 1587, 1610, 1643, 1654, 1663, 1704, 1712, 1725, 1742, 1802, 1803.
Latin Quarter: 459, 574, 807, 819.
La Leyenda Negra/ The Black Legend: 290, 303, 610, 647, 987, 1033, 1072, 1726, 1743.
La Llorna: 1767.
Ley Fuga: 620.
Legion of Decency: 1052, 1560, 1682.
Lesser, Sol: 1602.
Lissauer, Herman: 81.
London, Jack: 1302.
Lynching: 1221.

[M]

Machu Picchu: 1759.
Madero: 220, 274, 368, 653, 1660, 1712.
"Maine": 46, 111, 237, 267, 312, 681, 1248.
Marines: 88, 353, 432, 442, 533, 720, 834, 857, 944, 1194, 1201, 1212, 1297, 1332, 1334, 1420, 1449, 1485,1554, 1646, 1658, 1748, 1771.
Maugham, Somerset: 1519.
Maxmilian and Carlota: 1058, 1729, 1732, 1762.
Mayan: 995, 1360, 1399, 1615, 1640, 1649.

Mayer, Lous, B.: 1539.
McKinley, William: 71.
Melville, Wilbert: 271.
Message to Garcia: 71, 681.
Mexican Aversion to Work: 413.
Mexican as Oriental: 1398, 1565.
Mexican, Bad: 19, 24, 34, 53, 70, 83, 101, 109, 113, 134, 172, 208, 292, 314, 315, 347, 374, 419, 438, 448, 472, 481, 503, 538, 619, 704, 725, 732, 733, 774, 786, 802, 905, 925, 991, 1146 Villain: 1567, 1611, 1640.
Mexican, Bad Lady: 34, 37, 52.
Mexican Bandit: 86, 95, 127, 140, 743, 146, 165, 201, 203, 210, 216, 223, 232, 281, 307, 350, 361, 363, 365, 382, 412, 418, 426, 436, 444, 464, 472, 474, 473, 526, 546, 540, 566, 567, 569, 571, 576, 580, 596, 598, 621, 635, 641, 645, 667, 673, 682, 700, 710, 716, 719, 737, 742, 776, 780, 788, 789, 795, 797, 818, 822, 829, 833, 834, 838, 851, 853, 878, 890, 893, 899, 902, 911, 926, 930, 931, 972, 982, 999, 1046, 1060, 1089, 1096, 1120, 1126, 1152, 1165, 1204, 1207, 1227, 1250, 1256, 1327, 1323, 1338, 1342, 1350, 1352, 1357, 1417, 1477, 1512, 1524, 1545, 1559, 1570, 1588, 1597, 1617, 1620, 1629, 1638, 1664, 1702, 1712, 1732, 1733, 1739, 1768.
Mexican Bandit, Lovable: 1472, 1477.
Mexican Bests Anglo: 85, 265.
Mexican Braceros: 261, 390.
Mexican Constitution: 538. 211.
Mexican Dialect:/Broken English: 1338, 1370, 1372, 1375, 1406, 1450, 1456, 1468, 1470, 1485, 1504, 1513, 1522, 1563, 1589, 1591, 1609, 1665, 1668, 1710, 1776, 1806.
Mexican Equated with Indian: 96, 192, 289, 380, 767, 921, 1145.
Mexican Equated with Spainard: 416, 433, 448, 500, 613, 953.
Mexican Film Industry: 1652, 1695, 1706, 1707, 1729, 1790.
Mexican Not Punished for Killing Anglo: 1105.
Mexican, Good: 97, 471.
Mexican Hero: 1470.

Mexican Historical Interpretation: 1702, 1712.
Mexican Horror Films: 1613, 1667, 1671, 1693, 1746, 1767, 1777.
Mexican Kills Anglo without Punishment: 417.
Mexican Lazy: 106.
Mexican, Lecherous: 125, 275, 396, 612, 867, 1045, 1466, 1559, 1734.
Mexican Love Triangle: 105, 147, 366.
Mexican Lusts for Anglo Woman: 21, 112, 162, 188, 193, 214, 316, 522, 568, 757, 785, 789, 825, 922.
Mexican Male Weds Anglo: 110.
Mexican Marie Dressler: 1498.
Mexican Meanacing: 14, 112, 113, 802, 1392.
Mexican Oil Expropriation: 1673.
Mexican Passion: 101, 381, 605, 818.
Mexican Protest anti-Mexican Films: 368, 893, 962, 999, 1214, 1283, 1357. See also Spanish Protest.
Mexican Revolution: 117, 118, 163, 191, 274, 284, 285, 294, 328, 338, 339, 352, 365, 372, 373, 375, 376, 378, 379, 387, 388, 389, 426, 438, 442, 451, 459, 464, 467, 472, 473, 474, 477, 480, 489, 527, 528, 532, 533, 534, 538, 541, 560, 587, 591, 600, 620, 621, 641, 653, 673, 731, 789, 814, 837, 848, 1640, 1659, 1670, 1702, 1712.
Mexican Revolution, Rebel Sympathy: 191, 339, 451 459, 464, 474, 480, 538, 620.
Mexican Revolution, Unsympathetic: 587.
Mexican Robin Hood: 1728, 1733, 1739.
Mexican, Savage Renegades: 39, 51, 589.
Mexican Saves Anglo: 536.
Mexican Sheriff: 1054.
Mexican Spy, female: 117, 352, 377, 452, 476, 507, 732, 779, 902.
Mexican, Superstitious: 343, 350, 558, 649, 786, 1767.
Mexican, Sympathetic portrayals, Early: 26, 110. Later: 1044.

Mexican, Treacherous: 34, 77, 99, 109, 115, 148, 251, 279, 391, 480, 539, 605, 652, 674, 679, 712, 753, 816, 1349.
Mexican Vengence, Male and Female: 73, 101, 169, 209, 213, 380, 381, 390, 395, 454, 471, 544, 547, 558, 568, 575, 608, 676, 677, 743, 751, 804, 817, 818, 851, 861, 947, 1018, 1044, 1294, 1306, 1330.
Mexicans, Early use in Cast: 506.
Mexicans Salute the Flag: 154, 353, 432.
Mexico Invades USA: 699.
Mexico, Positive Views: 810, 837.
Miscegenation: 1539.
Miriana: [Cortez's Mistress] 1767.
Monarchy in the Americas: 1604.
Monogram Studio: 1492.
Monroe Doctrine: 720, 1058, 1247, 1267.
Montezuma: 1153.
Moors: 276, 937.
Morgan, Sir Henry: 415.
Morrow, Dwight, W.: 1588.
MPPDA: 893, 969, 1682.
Mt. Pele: 762, 1200.
Mu: 1697.
Muculley, Johnson: 846.
Murietta, Joaquin: 833, 1227.
Mutual Film Company: 464.
Mythical Central and South American Republics: 551, 577, 583, 629, 637, 800, 877, 932, 942, 958, 994, 1050, 1075, 1103, 1107, 1117, 1290, 1421, 1423, 1429, 1510, 1514, 1720.

[N]

Napoleon III: 1058, 1762.
National Gerographic Society: 283, 1350, 1399, 1557, 1619, 1759.
National Guard: 633, 650, 652, 716, 718, 748, 760.
Neutrality Act: 1249.
Newsreel Men: 1298.
New York State Board of Review: 1169.
Nigger: 733.
Norris, Little Chucky: 109, 130, 1212.

Nudity: 1557.

[O]

Octoroon: 57, 1043.
O'Henry: 751, 782, 803, 841, 913, 1338, 1456.
O'Neil, Eugene: 1604.
Oil Fields: 538, 862, 871, 922, 1117, 1307, 1316.
Old Glory: 88, 154, 181, 199, 214, 320, 345, 346, 353, 373, 404, 432, 472, 650, 674, 699, 715, 722, 1248, 1554. See also: Mexicans salute flag.

[P]

Padres, Spanish Missions: 110, 143, 157, 178, 270, 298, 318, 369, 380, 382, 396, 399, 415, 433, 443, 454, 461, 588, 595, 611, 789, 797, 815, 887, 1039.
Panama Canal: 20, 38, 72, 182, 225, 282, 283, 361, 383, 384, 385, 393, 446, 487, 490, 594, 599, 763, 996, 1006, 1453.
Panama Canal Zone: 20.
Panama Pacific Exposition: 488, 599.
Pani, Alberto J: 924.
PCA = Production Code Administration: 1113, 1229, 1345, 1514, 1528, 1538, 1542, 1553, 1560, 1605, 1607, 1636, 1680, 1706, 1712, 1723, 1799.
Patria, Congressionaial Hearings: 699.
Pershing, Black Jack: 631, 641, 642, 650, 801.
Philippines/Insurrection/Occupation: 7, 8, 11, 12, 104, 144, 336, 348, 358, 404, 425, 482, 502, 525, 572, 610, 769, 815, 159, 1276.
Peabody Museum: 637.
Philip II/Spanish Court: 84, 245, 246, 987, 1795.
Pirates: 333, 423, 805, 812, 854, 933, 1031, 1072, 1122, 1161, 1241, 1726, 1748.
Piranha: 1557, 1619.
Pope Pius X: 241.
"Portguee": 1592.
Port Royal: 1726.

Pre Arranged Marriage: 299, 318, 365, 371, 460, 718, 868, 917, 1011, 1082, 1179.
Preparedness: 722.
Prescott, W. H.: 638.
Prim, General: 1531.
Propaganda, Films as: 792.
Protest: 155, 242, 368, 793, 841, 1214, 1338, 1357, 1412, 1456, 1491, 1745.
Protest, French: 1491.
Pugi Casauranc, Jose Manuel: 1588.

[Q]

Quintana Roo: 115.

[R]

Race Hatred: 171, 425, 477, 565, 703.
Race Prejudice: 309, 313, 455, 36, 699, 733, 906, 940, 950, 1115, 1145.
Race Riot: 683.
Racism: 1697, 1714, 1741.
Republic Film Studios: 1492.
Revolution/revolutionaries,
  General: 26, 46, 88, 89, 92, 117, 118, 132, 174, 175, 191, 253, 274, 284, 285, 294, 295, 308, 328, 339, 348, 366, 375, 376, 378, 389, 426, 427, 432, 438, 442, 451, 459, 462, 464, 467, 472, 474, 475, 477, 480, 500, 538, 541, 551, 560, 561, 577, 583, 587, 589, 620, 621, 630, 641, 653, 658, 659, 664, 673, 676, 706, 726, 730, 731, 732, 747, 750, 795, 800, 801, 814, 834, 837, 848, 876, 882, 909, 910, 913, 935, 942, 958, 960, 962, 965, 969, 978, 985, 990, 994, 1005, 1075, 1088, 1099, 1101, 1103, 1117, 1149, 1190, 1202, 1249, 1290, 1300, 1302, 1304, 1310, 1320, 1332, 1356, 1368, 1374, 1389, 1395, 1464, 1587, 1604, 1615, 1639, 1640, 1659, 1670, 1691, 1702, 1708, 1712, 1764, 1765, 1770, 1778.
Revolution, Portugal: 1190, 1395.
Revolution, South American: 42, 88, 89, 462, 632, 730, 747, 751, 795, 834, 882, 909, 910, 913, 942, 960, 965, 969, 985, 994, 1014, 1050, 1075, 1088, 1101, 1616.
Revolution, Spain: 92, 305, 876, 1135.
Revolutionaries: 800, 958, 1103, 1290, 1300, 1310.
Rhumba: 1485, 1603, 1796, 1797.
River of Doubt: 1621.
Robeson, Paul: 1604.
Roman Catholic Church: 1594.
Roosevelt, Teddy: 641, 783.
Rublee, Juliet Barrett: 1588.
Runyon, Damon: 1613.
Rurales: 4, 345, 557, 612, 1041, 1589, 1728.

[S]

Sandino: 1255, 1332, 1420, 1554, 1771.
San Juan Hill: 71, 329.
San Juan de Ulua: 1728.
Santiago, Battle of: 142.
Saragassa: 397.
Sargasso Sea: 988, 1340, 1649.
Saturday Evening Post: 1036, 1045, 1051, 1485.
Seabrook, W. B.: 1594.
Senorita Betrays Her Country for Anglo: 46, 55, 98, 222, 745.
Senortia Choses Mexican Over Anglo: 322, 896.
Senortia Loves Anglo: 35, 47, 49, 83, 139, 192, 209, 239, 116, 122, 297, 298, 360, 526, 544, 572, 745, 815, 842, 858, 882, 945, 1050, 1078, 1112, 1163, 1284, 1287, 1448, 1563, 1568, 1760, 1765, 1607.
Senorita Saves Anglo: 36, 75, 80, 128, 141, 201, 231, 394, 419, 504, 631, 797, 860, 862, 868, 905, 1290, 1405, 1512.
Senorita, Self Sacrificing: 45, 49, 127, 152, 206, 240, 354, 404, 502, 658, 823, 830, 8933, 1195, 1308.
Senorita Vamp/Seductrous/Flirt: 29, 56, 68, 79, 121, 358, 401, 510, 552, 553, 554, 588, 604, 629, 659, 801, 840, 856, 865, 893, 912, 936, 983, 1002, 1118, 1169, 1223, 1295, 1313, 1549, 1663, 1689, 1709, 1716, 1720,

1738, 1790, 1804. Deadly: 232, 409, 751.
Serials: 542, 653, 673, 699, 712, 719, 731, 732, 763, 765, 790, 839, 1433.
Sinclair, Upton: 1602, 1604.
Sisal: 106, 115.
Smuggling: 31, 128, 145, 174, 302, 421, 505, 554, 597, 751, 771, 764, 778, 814, 853,,915, 928, 1001, 1024, 1079, 1081, 1164, 1165 1177, 1242, 1246, 1290, 1302, 1310, 1315, 1329, 1381, 1454, 1492, 1515, 1536, 1636, 1696, 1778.
Smuggling, Aliens: 946, 1309.
Smuggling, Arms: 174, 253, 424, 504, 508, 814, 997, 1146, 1249, 1302, 1501, 1512, 1765, 1766.
Smuggling, Rum: 914, 915, 1004, 1018, 1113, 1268, 1315.
Smuggling, Jewels: 145, 579, 998, 1430.
Soldier of Fortune: 80, 372, 437, 474, 509, 676, 800, 891, 942, 969, 990, 1042, 1204, 1299, 1334.
Songs: 1339, 1344, 1352, 1414, 1440, 1485, 1760, 1771, 1774.
Sound, Problems Created by: 1278, 1358.
Spanish American War: 71, 142, 249, 329, 346, 362, 366, 394, 663, 700, 809, 965, 993, 1248, 1302.
South America Invades USA: 648.
Spanish Armada: 1745.
Spanish Army: 66.
Spanish Bandit: 22, 202, 369, 560, 595, 625, 629, 721, 795, 810, 924, 955, 980, 1015, 1021, 1082, 1107, 1253, 1298, 1316, 1332, 1334, 1478, 1752, 1771.
Spanish, Castillian Spoken: 1387.
Spanish Colonial Period: 603, 647, 1321, 1752, 1771.
Spanish Conquest: 1662
Spanish Cruelty: 1003.
Spanish Dancer: 53, 210, 239, 463, 754, 878, 1325, 1380.
Spanish Film Industry: 1650, 1652, 1708.
Spanish Florida: 156, 158, 197, 296.
Spanish Horses: 772.
Spanish Land Grants: 1040, 1239, 1618, 1788.
Spanish Language Films: 1335, 1368, 1373, 1382, 1384, 1387, 1415, 1419, 1425, 1434, 1436, 1438, 1450, 1468, 1490, 1503, 1505, 1587, 1611, 1618, 1627, 1631, 1631, 1632, 1644, 1648, 1654, 1655, 1656, 1663, 1669, 1670, 1671, 1679, 1686, 1691, 1693, 1700, 1701, 1704, 1706, 1727, 1729, 1733, 1736, 1742, 1746, 1755, 1756, 1763, 1788, 1798, 1799, 1802, 1810, 1811, 1812.
Spanish Language Films, Problems Created By: 1358, 1412, 1417, 1451, 1468, 1522, 1584, 1644, 1666, 1701, 1809.
Spanish Pride: 1583.
Spanish Main: 415, 768, 812, 854,1031, 1072, 1099, 1726.
Spanish Taste/preference in Films: 1584, 1587, 1663
Spanish Temptress: 1602, See also: Carmen.
Spanish Treachery: 15, 84, 300, 611, 1314.
Spanish Vengeance: 35, 67, 68. See, Vengeance.
Spanish Versions: 1369, 1371, 1386, 1391, 1393, 1396, 1397, 1400, 1401, 1403, 1404, 1412, 1414, 1427, 1431, 14371, 1445, 1446, 1447, 1458, 1459, 1462, 1463, 1465, 1472, 1474, 1476, 1479, 1482, 1486, 1489, 1490, 1493, 1494, 1495, 1506, 1511, 1513, 1518, 1526, 1530, 1533, 1537, 1538, 1543, 1544, 1565, 1571, 1572, 1576, 1585, 1614, 1628, 1642, 1686.
SPCA: 78.
Squaw Saves Anglo: 14.
Stabbing: 31, 53, 298, 300, 353, 414, 549, 659, 731, 754, 757, 828, 1285.
Stars and Bars: 346.
Stereotyping: 19, 79, 328, 473, 506, 705, 844, 854, 865, 912, 982, 1108, 1118, 1307, 1389, 1492, 1500, 1512, 1549, 1559, 1568, 1574, 1607, 1710.
Subtitles: 1701.
Sutter, Captain John: 1030, 1215.

[T]

Taft, William Howard: 72, 163, 393.
Tampico Incident: 511, 512, 513, 857.
Tango: 408, 514, 515, 516, 517, 518, 519, 520, 933, 1012, 1140, 1147, 1274, 1413, 1453, 1522, 1622, 1652, 1705, 1753, 1796, 1802.
Teatro Campoamour: 1659, 1662, 1669, 1695, 1697.
Teatro Hispano: 1619, 1620.
Teatro Variedades: 1505, 1584.
Teotzotlan Monastery: 1671
Texas Rangers: See, Border Patrol.
Three Police Forces: 1196.
Tikal: 1237, 1399.
Toreador: 61, 271, 306, 349, 523, 524, 841, 897, 1011, 1232, 1344, 1455, 1500.
Torreon: 431, 493.
Torture: 34, 117, 128, 303, 379, 394, 539, 597, 737, 743, 765, 817, 993, 1100.
Trade Follows Film: 969.
Travelogues: 23, 59, 76, 87, 107, 108, 114, 137, 153, 168, 170, 183, 184, 185, 187, 189, 198, 217, 260, 264, 301, 327, 338, 355, 361, 397, 398, 405, 407, 410, 430, 618, 624, 729, 739, 740, 791, 806, 846, 849, 866, 943, 1053, 1158, 1208, 1240, 1424, 1552, 1588, 1603, 1614, 1615, 1624, 1630, 1641, 1730, 1751, 1754, 1794, 1800.
Treasure: 1649, 1768.
Tropical Love: 151, 562, 766, 883, 855, 1122, 1035, 1036, 1408, 1423, 1449, 1485, 1528, 1529, 1697.
Tropical Customs: 768.
Tropical Rain Forest: 1034.
Tropical Storm: 875, 1394.
Tropics, General, Paradise: 215, 221, 483, 622, 858, 956, 965, 1016, 1034, 1036, 1124, 1200, 1288, 1307, 1326, 1395, 1424, 1684.
Tropics, Influence of: 425, 909, 922, 1036, 1124, 1167, 1269, 1308, 1361, 1408, 1423, 1449, 1485 1528, 1542, 1575.

[U]

United States Border Mobilization: 635, 670, 677.
United States Cavalry: 664.
United States Cavalry crosses the Border: 426, 444, 677, 742.
United States Cavalry Comes to the Rescue: 47, 49, 149, 162, 167, 172, 210, 347, 715, 815, 922, 1182, 1186, 1247, 1464, 1580.
Unites States Navy: 494, 497, 686, 944.
United States Intervention: 80, 88, 220, 432, 472, 532, 533, 561, 633, 650, 651, 720, 827, 1179, 1255.
United States Occupations: 105, 336, 358, 425, 482, 502, 525, 572, 663, 720, 739, 791, 815, 827, 857, 950, 1159, 1449, 1508. 1552, 1646.
United States Secret Service: 1770.
United States Soldiers on the Border: 130, 220, 340, 345, 476, 477, 512, 534, 621, 674, 685, 693, 694, 697, 698, 950.
United States State Department, Protest: 841, 940.
United States Troops in Mexico: 527, 528, 532, 533, 534, 633, 635, 641, 650, 675, 691, 692, 715.
United States Troops Come to Rescue: 117, 154, 322, 353, 358.

[V]

Vengeance, General: 17, 28, 33, 35, 57, 67, 73, 115, 131, 144, 157, 162, 175, 178, 194, 199, 205, 206, 209, 213, 222, 229, 349, 373, 380, 381, 416, 419, 454, 503, 531, 544, 587, 608, 644, 677, 743, 776, 804, 818, 861, 896, 1018, 1021, 1095, 1155, 1161, 1278, 1281, 1330, 1808.
Vera Cruz: 154, 432, 442, 527, 695, 724, 857, 1728.
Verne, Jules: 1347.
Villa: 375, 431, 464, 480, 561, 598, 635, 641, 650, 651, 652, 666, 674, 684, 685, 692, 699,

707, 709, 722, 760, 771, 1659, 1702, 1712.
Villa, Invasion/Columbus, New Mexico: 650, 651, 652, 684, 686, 688, 690, 708, 715, 722, 723.
Virgin Gorda: 1726.
Virgin Queen: 290.
Volstead Act: 914, 1113.
Voodoo: 1151, 1364, 1444, 1561, 1646, 1668, [**Nightly news on Haitian Voodoo:** 1594. **Haitian Occupation:** 1449.

[W]

Walsh, Raoul: 375, 664, 878, 989, 1338.
Warner Brothers Archives: 1472, 1608.
de Wavrin, Marquis: 1557.
Watchful Waiting: 442, 675, 724.
Weyler, "Butcher": 353, 362, 366.
White Man's Burden: 568, 1677.
Wilder, Thorton: 1321.
Woodrow, Wilson: 442, 716, 720, 722, 724.

[Y]

Yale: 970, 1149. 1292, 1332, 1337, 1573, 1759.
Yankee Insurrectionist: 427.
Yaqui: 115, 420, 630, 726, 727, 823, 905, 1158, 1170.
Yucatan: 995.

[Z]

Zapata: 174, 191, 464, 538, 561, 1659, 1669.
Zapotec: 1806.
Zimmerman Telegram: 699, 780.
Zombie: 1594.
Zorro: 646, 847, 1108, 1125, 1618.

About the Author

ALFRED CHARLES RICHARD, JR., is Professor of Latin American History at Central Connecticut State University. He is the author of *The Panama Canal in American National Consciousness* (1990) and "Postum, Post-Toasties and Patriotism" in *Advertising and Popular Culture* (1992).

On Reference Shelf - Does Not Circulate